# An Economic Analysis of Crime and Justice

THEORY, METHODS, AND APPLICATIONS

## QUANTITATIVE STUDIES IN SOCIAL RELATIONS

*Consulting Editor: Peter H. Rossi*

UNIVERSITY OF MASSACHUSETTS
AMHERST, MASSACHUSETTS

### *In Preparation*

*Nancy Brandon Tuma and Michael T. Hannan,* **SOCIAL DYNAMICS: *Models and Methods***

*Michael D. Maltz,* **RECIDIVISM**

### *Published*

*Peter Schmidt and Ann D. Witte,* **AN ECONOMIC ANALYSIS OF CRIME AND JUSTICE: *Theory, Methods, and Applications***

*A. Basilevsky and Derek Hum,* **EXPERIMENTAL SOCIAL PROGRAMS AND ANALYTIC METHODS: *An Evaluation of the U. S. Income Maintenance Projects***

*Walter R. Gove and Michael Hughes, with contributions by Omer R. Galle,* **OVERCROWDING IN THE HOUSEHOLD: *An Analysis of Determinants and Effects***

*Ronald S. Burt,* **CORPORATE PROFITS AND COOPTATION: *Networks of Market Constraints and Directorate Ties in the American Economy***

*Peter H. Rossi, James D. Wright, and Andy B. Anderson (Eds.),* **HANDBOOK OF SURVEY RESEARCH**

*Joan Huber and Glenna Spitze,* **SEX STRATIFICATION: *Children, Housework, and Jobs***

*Toby L. Parcel and Charles W. Mueller,* **ASCRIPTION AND LABOR MARKETS: *Race and Sex Differences in Earnings***

*Paul G. Schervish,* **THE STRUCTURAL DETERMINANTS OF UNEMPLOYMENT: *Vulnerability and Power in Market Relations***

*Irving Tallman, Ramona Marotz-Baden, and Pablo Pindas,* **ADOLESCENT SOCIALIZATION IN CROSS-CULTURAL PERSPECTIVE: *Planning for Social Change***

*Robert F. Boruch and Joe S. Cecil (Eds.),* **SOLUTIONS TO ETHICAL AND LEGAL PROBLEMS IN SOCIAL RESEARCH**

*J. Ronald Milavsky, Ronald C. Kessler, Horst H. Stipp, and William S. Rubens,* **TELEVISION AND AGGRESSION: *A Panel Study***

*Ronald S. Burt,* **TOWARD A STRUCTURAL THEORY OF ACTION: *Network Models of Social Structure, Perception, and Action***

The list of titles in this series continues on the last page of this volume

# An Economic Analysis of Crime and Justice

THEORY, METHODS, AND APPLICATIONS

PETER SCHMIDT

Department of Economics
Michigan State University
East Lansing, Michigan

ANN D. WITTE

Department of Economics
University of North Carolina at Chapel Hill
Chapel Hill, North Carolina

1984

ACADEMIC PRESS, INC.

*(Harcourt Brace Jovanovich, Publishers)*

Orlando San Diego San Francisco New York London
Toronto Montreal Sydney Tokyo São Paulo

ACADEMIC PRESS, INC.
Orlando, Florida 32887

*United Kingdom Edition published by*
ACADEMIC PRESS, INC. (LONDON) LTD.
24/28 Oval Road, London NW1 7DX

Library of Congress Cataloging in Publication Data

Schmidt, Peter.
An economic analysis of crime and justice.

(Quantitative studies in social relations)
Includes bibliographical references and index.
1. Crime and criminals--Economic aspects--United States. 2. Recidivism--United States--Statistical methods. 3. Criminal justice, Administration of--Simulation methods. 4. Prisons--United States--Costs. I. Witte, Anne D., Date . II. Title. III. Series.
HV6791.W57 1983 364'.072 83-3863
ISBN 0-12-627180-1

PRINTED IN THE UNITED STATES OF AMERICA

84 85 86 87 9 8 7 6 5 4 3 2 1

# Contents

## II. Testing the Economic Model of Crime

## III. The Use of Production and Cost Theory in Criminal Justice Research

# Preface

In this book, we apply economic theory and econometric methods to various problems in criminology. It should not be surprising that economists would approach such problems differently than would psychologists, sociologists, or criminal justice professionals, both because economic theory imposes a particular view of the world and because economists tend to use somewhat different statistical techniques than do other social scientists. We hope to convince the reader of the potential usefulness of the economists' approach to criminology.

There are three separate parts to the book. Part I contains statistical analyses of various measures of criminal recidivism. This work was part of several research projects that we carried out, beginning in 1973. As our work progressed, it struck us that many of the models and methods of analysis that we were developing had potential application in areas other than those in which we were working. Furthermore, we could find no single source that described the methods we were using. (Indeed, many of them have been developed only quite recently.) Therefore, we provide (in Chapters 2, 4, and 6) surveys of statistical methods for analyzing qualitative and limited dependent variables of various kinds. These chapters should be of interest to a fairly wide audience, including economists as well as noneconomists. The applications (in Chapters 3, 5, 7, and 8) of these methods to the analysis of criminal recidivism should be of interest both because they illustrate the use of these statistical techniques and because the substantive results are valuable.

The impetus for Part II and Part III was somewhat different. We felt that recent developments in economic theory provided useful guidance for researchers studying crime and the operation of the criminal justice system. However, much of this research could be comprehended easily only by those with considerable background in economics. Further, this research appeared in widely scattered places, and its application to the study of criminal justice issues was often far from obvious. We have structured these two parts so that they begin with an introduction to the particular economic theory that will be utilized. Thus Part II, which provides empirical estimates and tests of the economic model of crime, begins (in Chapter 9) with a survey of economic models of crime. This survey should be useful to anyone wishing to know what sort of assumptions go into economic models of crime and what sorts of conclusions result. Similarly, we begin Part III, which estimates long- and short-run cost functions for large-scale prisons, with a survey (Chapter 13) of the economic theory of cost and production and its application to public organizations. This survey will be of limited interest to readers with much economic training, but it should be useful for noneconomists. The empirical chapters in Parts II and III should be of substantial interest to anyone interested in the workings of the criminal justice system.

We hope that the book will be useful for students and scholars in economics, political science, planning, psychology, and sociology and for applied researchers in both the public and private sectors. Economists may find it useful to see how their ideas and techniques are applied. Noneconomists may find our surveys of economic ideas and econometric methods useful. Finally, our empirical work yields substantive conclusions of some importance, which should be useful for anyone interested in criminology.

This book was jointly written, and both authors share the credit or blame for all of it. The order of authors' names is alphabetical and is of no other significance. However, it is accurate to report that the first author was primarily responsible for Part I, whereas the second author was primarily responsible for Parts II and III of this book.

# Acknowledgments

Full acknowledgment of all individuals who aided us in the course of the work reported in this book would consume extensive space and make for tedious reading. Thus, we shall try to make our acknowledgments comprehensive but often not specific.

Collection of the 1969 and 1971 North Carolina data set required the cooperation of many released inmates. The individuals in this sample were usually very cooperative and helpful in providing detailed information about their postrelease experiences. The data set that resulted from their help is unique and is a source of strength for many of our analyses. We express our sincere appreciation for their help in our work.

Most of the work reported in this book was both expensive and time consuming to complete. Without funding, little or none of it would have been done. Original funding for the collection of the 1969 and 1971 data was provided by the National Institute of Law Enforcement and Criminal Justice, U.S. Department of Justice. As so often happens, money ran out before the project was completed. Fortunately, the University of North Carolina Research Council provided additional funding that allowed us to finish the project. Funding for the analyses reported in Part I was provided by the North Carolina Department of Correction. Funding for our review of economic models of crime (Chapter 9) was provided by the National Institute of Mental Health as a part of a much larger project designed to analyze family violence.

Finally, our estimation of cost functions for prisons was sponsored by the National Institute of Law Enforcement and Criminal Justice, U.S. Department of Justice. Many individuals who worked for these funding agencies provided guidance and support for our efforts. We would particularly like to thank George Silberman, who helped us guide the prison cost function project through many difficult and trying times.

Although funding was a necessary condition for most of our work, it was by no means the only necessity. The work required two other important elements: the cooperation of many individuals in federal, state, and local government and an able staff. We were truly blessed in both regards. Personnel of the North Carolina Department of Correction provided invaluable aid in collecting the 1969 and 1971 data set and provided us with all data for the 1975 release cohort. We would particularly like to thank Jerry Allen, Lena Basemore, Adrian Brancatto, Kip Kautzky, Ken Parker, Martha Upchurch, and Jeff Williams. Personnel of the Federal Bureau of Prisons and the California Department of Corrections provided us with data and guidance for our work on prison cost functions. Data collection in both the federal and California systems required the time and knowledge of people in many areas of the California Department of Corrections and the U.S. Department of Justice. We would like to especially thank Jim Parks and Vida Ryan of the California Department of Corrections and Howard Kitchener, Harriet Lebowitz, and Jerry Prather of the Federal Bureau of Prisons.

During the course of our research we often had truly exceptional persons working with us. The following individuals provided a level of knowledge and dedication far in excess of that required by their jobs: James Bachman, Pamela Reid, Carl Rizzo, and Von Underwood.

Turning from the research reported to the actual preparation of this manuscript, Betsy Pierce provided exceptionally able and thorough typing for Parts II and III of this book, and Kelli Sweet provided the same for Part I.

Finally, we would like to thank our families for their tolerance and support of our efforts. At many times we were thinking of our research when we should have been listening to them.

# Chapter 1

## Overview

This book is composed of three parts. These parts are more or less independent of each other, though they are connected by the statistical methodology and data that are used.

The first part of the book, consisting of Chapters 2–8, discusses models of criminal recidivism. This is of course a common topic in criminology, but there is little here that would be familiar to most economists. Indeed, the relatively sophisticated statistical methodology employed is intended to be the distinguishing feature of Part I. Most measures of recidivism have peculiar features that make standard statistical techniques (e.g., use of the linear regression model) inappropriate. Therefore, we attempt to introduce the reader to more appropriate techniques and to convince him or her through the application of these techniques that they are worth the extra work involved. These statistical techniques have broad potential application for researchers in criminal and civil justice but have seldom been used in these fields to date. We describe a number of potential applications in the introduction to Part I.

Chapter 2 provides a survey of the statistical analysis of qualitative outcomes. The fact of recidivism or nonrecidivism is a qualitative outcome, and the models of Chapter 2 are therefore potentially useful for analyzing, among other things, the determinants of this measure of recidivism. In Chapter 3 we use one of the models presented in Chapter 2, the logit model, to analyze two measures of recidivism, either of which is more informative than the common yes/no measure. One analysis is of the level of seriousness of the most serious recidivist conviction; felony, misdemeanor, or no conviction are the three possible outcomes. A second analysis is similar but has slightly different outcomes defined: conviction for a crime against a person, a crime against property, or another (miscellaneous) crime; or no conviction. This analysis gives insights concerning the way in which criminals' careers develop, particularly as regards crime switching.

Chapter 4 surveys the statistical analysis of censored and truncated outcomes. We pay particular attention to the Tobit model, which is designed for the analysis of outcomes that are censored at zero, that is, outcomes that cannot be negative and are often zero. Length of sentence is such an outcome, and in Chapter 5 we use the Tobit model to analyze the total length of recidivist prison sentences that an individual receives. Another interesting feature of the analysis is that we validate our models by using them to predict outcomes for a sample of individuals (the "validation sample") who were not included in the sample used in estimating the models (the "estimation sample").

Chapter 6 surveys the statistical analysis of survival time; that is, of the time until an event occurs. The particular application addressed in Chapter 7 is length of time from release until recidivism. Two major points are made. First, as is by now well known, it is necessary to recognize that the survival time is censored by the length of the follow-up period. (We cannot observe a length of time greater than the length of the follow-up period, and some individuals will not have become recidivists by the end of the follow-up.) Second, it is important to use individual characteristics (if they are available) as explanatory variables. This point seems to be little appreciated in the criminological literature; most analyses of time until recidivism still assume individuals to be identical. As in Chapter 5, our models are validated by prediction outside the sample. The models are very accurate: They predict numbers of recidivists within a few percentages of the actual numbers, and they also accurately predict the timing of recidivism.

Finally, Chapter 8 uses the models of Chapters 5 and 7 to evaluate a correctional program. The method used compares the actual outcomes of program participants with those predicted by our models. Although we encounter many of the usual problems in such nonexperimental evaluations, our results seem quite reasonable.

The second part of the book, consisting of Chapters 9–12, discusses the economic model of crime. This model is surveyed from a theoretical point of view in Chapter 9. Because the model basically postulates that individuals make rational comparisons of the returns to legal and illegal activities, it is intuitively clear that crime should be deterred either by increased opportunity to conduct lawful activities or by increased sanctions for criminal offenses. The real question addressed in Chapter 9 is what assumptions are necessary for unambiguous results to hold. As is shown, these assumptions are really quite stringent.

In Chapter 10 we attempt to test the economic model of crime by analyzing two measures of criminal activity: the arrest rate (arrests per month at risk) and the conviction rate. Because these outcomes are censored at zero, the Tobit model is used once again. The results give weak support to the model. There is some evidence that increased sanctions deter crime, but very weak results are obtained for the effects of legitimate opportunities.

In Chapter 11 we investigate the nature of the labor market for prison releasees. Although the single word "dismal" might suffice, we analyze the determinants of two measures of labor market success: wage and stability of employment. The explanatory variables most favored by "human capital" theorists, age and education, do not appear to be very important. Finally, in Chapter 12 we allow the wage and arrest rate to be simultaneously determined. This alters some, but not most, of the comparable results of Chapters 10 and 11.

The third part of the book, consisting of Chapters 13–16, estimates cost functions for prisons. Cost functions give costs (either total or average) for a unit of production as a function of its level of output and the prices of its inputs. In Chapters 13 and 14 we survey the economic theory of cost and production, and we discuss the problem of suitably defining the inputs and output of a prison. In Chapter 15 we estimate short-run cost functions for federal and California prisons, and in Chapter 16 we estimate a long-run cost function for a group of Federal Correctional Institutions. (The distinction between "long-run" and "short-run" is that the capital stock is assumed to be fixed in the short run but variable in the long run.) In both cases we arrive at interesting results, chief of which is the optimal size (in the sense of minimum average cost) for such prisons. It appears quite clear that bigger prisons are cheaper (per confined person-day) than smaller prisons.

Following our conclusions in Chapter 17, there are three appendixes describing the data sets used in our analyses. It is impossible to do good empirical work with bad data, and we are pleased with the accuracy and detail in our data sets. Appendix A describes our data on a sample of 641 men who were in prison in North Carolina in 1969 or 1971. This data set is not an especially representative sample of the North Carolina (or national) prison population, but it contains very detailed information about the individuals in it, and the information on postrelease activities is unusually accurate and complete. Appendix B describes our data on all 4881 individuals released from prison in North Carolina in the first 6 months of 1975. As such it is very clear what population the data represent. The level of detail and accuracy is good, though not as good as for the previous data set. Appendix C describes our data on 27 federal prisons, monthly from November 1975 through June 1978, and on 10 California prisons, quarterly from July 1968 through June 1978. Although the federal data set is stronger than the California set, both are good; the information about characteristics of inmates is especially notable.

Overall, the book represents the end product of an enormous investment in the collection of original data and in the use of sophisticated models in its analysis. We hope that the result justifies this investment and that others will be encouraged to use similar techniques.

# PART I

## Statistical Analyses of Recidivism

In this part of the book, our primary aim is to present and illustrate the use of a number of statistical techniques that allow the modeling of commonly used measures of criminal activity in a careful and correct manner. The most frequently used measures of criminality tend to be either qualitative (i.e., a series of discrete categories), limited (i.e., the range of values observed is restricted in some way), or not normally distributed (e.g., skewed). Variables with any of these characteristics cannot be correctly analyzed using traditional multivariate statistical techniques (such as ordinary and generalized least squares) that assume that dependent variables have continuous, unrestricted normal distributions.

The first chapter of this part contains our discussion of proper methods of analyzing qualitative (categorical) dependent variables. Such variables occur in many studies of criminality and in studies of both the criminal and civil justice systems. For example, studies of police, court, and correctional decisions frequently analyze categorical variables, such as whether a particular subject is arrested [e.g., see Hepburn (1978)], whether or not a defendant released on bail shows up for court, or the type of sentence that a defendant receives [e.g., see Clarke, Freeman, and Koch (1976) or Clarke and Koch (1976)]. Correctional research is frequently concerned with such things as whether or not an individual is paroled or whether after release he or she returns to crime [e.g., see Gottfredson, Wilkins, and Hoffman (1978), Cook (1975), or Palmer and Carlson (1976)]. In Chapter 2 we discuss and compare a number of techniques designed to analyze such dependent variables. This discussion should prove to be of use to researchers analyzing any of the above topics or a number of other similar topics of interest to students of deviant behavior and our legal system.

To make our discussion more concrete, in Chapter 3 we analyze two different categorical dependent variables. We begin by analyzing a measure of recidivism that incorporates a crude concept of seriousness, as well as analyzing the traditional zero–one measure of whether an individual is convicted of an offense after release. Specifically, the variable we analyze falls into three possible categories, depending on the individual's most serious conviction during the follow-up period: (1) no conviction, (2) conviction for a misdemeanor, and (3) conviction for a felony. We analyze this variable using the logit model, which allows us to study the effects of a variety of individual characteristics on the probability of each of the three possible outcomes.

This type of analysis is of potential use to correctional researchers in a number of ways. First, it can be used to evaluate correctional programs when random assignment is not possible. (For a discussion of such use in another context, see Chapter 8.) Even when random assignment is possible, statistical modeling of the outcome variable is useful in that it improves the efficiency, in a statistical sense, of the measurement of programmatic effects. [For a discussion, see Cain (1975).] Such improvement can be of great importance because most correctional programs have only small effects on postrelease behavior. Second, it can be used as part of population projection models to predict future prison populations.

Our second analysis in Chapter 3 also uses the logit model but differs from the first analysis in a number of ways. In this analysis, we consider the type of crime that an individual commits. The dependent variable is the nature of the most serious crime for which an individual is convicted during a follow-up period. It falls into one of four possible categories: (1) no conviction, (2) conviction for a property offense (such as larceny or robbery), (3) conviction for an offense against a person (such as rape or assault), and (4) conviction for another type of offense (such as drug use or carrying a concealed weapon). This analysis is designed to provide insights concerning the factors that lead to criminal specialization and crime switching. Most previous work in this area has used simpler methods, such as Markov chains. [Petersilia, Greenwood, and Lavin (1977) provide a review of this literature.] We believe that our models provide valuable new insights as to the factors associated with particular offense patterns. This type of research can also lead to the development of better techniques for developing criminal typologies.

In Chapters 4 and 5 of this part, we turn our attention to the proper methods of analyzing censored or truncated dependent variables. Such variables are quite frequently used in justice research. For example, many authors analyze the seriousness of criminal activity when seriousness is measured by time sentenced or by a continuous "seriousness index" such as the one developed by Sellin and Wolfgang (1964). [See Wolfgang, Figlio, and Sellin (1972) or Schmidt, Sickles, and Witte (1979).] At other times, researchers analyze the number of offenses per unit time "at risk." [See Peterson and Braiker (1980), Witte (1980), or Greenwood (1981), for an example.] Researchers of court proceedings are frequently interested in the determinants of the length of sentence imposed [e.g., see Dawson (1969), Diamond and Zeisel (1976), and Sutton (1978)], and correctional researchers are interested in the determinants of time spent in prison [e.g., see Myers (1982)]. In Chapter 4 we discuss and compare a number of techniques for analyzing such variables. This discussion should prove of interest to justice researchers analyzing any of the variables just discussed or a number of other similar ones.

To make our discussion more complete, in Chapter 5 we analyze the total time sentenced during a follow-up period for two different groups of individuals released from the North Carolina Department of Correction. In both cases, we analyze this dependent variable using the Tobit (censored normal regression) model. This model assumes that the underlying but unobservable variable of interest, in this case criminality, follows a normal distribution. However, if criminality is below some threshold level, we observe no prison sentence and the value of the dependent variable in this analysis is zero. The Tobit model assumes that the probability of observing no time sentenced is simply the cumulative density of the normal distribution up to the point of censoring (zero). The actual time sentenced for those receiving sentences is assumed to follow the normal density function above the point of censoring.

A major advantage of using this technique is that it allows us to use observations both for individuals who receive no prison sentence and for those who do. This improves both the generalizability and the efficiency of the estimates we obtain. Note that this dependent variable includes a traditional measure of recidivism (i.e., whether a releasee returns to prison) but contains additional information as well, namely, the length of the prison sentences received.

The results of such an analysis are of potential use to justice researchers in a number of ways. First, they can be used to evaluate rehabilitative programs when random assignment is not possible. (We illustrate this use of our models in Chapter 8.) Second, they can be used to predict the sentence lengths of returning inmates. This information can be quite useful to correctional planners. Finally, they can be used to predict future behavior of prison releasees.

In Chapters 6 and 7 of this part, we discuss and use techniques designed to analyze the timing of an event such as return to prison. This type of analysis is generally referred to as survival analysis or failure time analysis, and although it has been used for some time in the biostatistics literature, it has been adopted by justice researchers only recently. We believe that survival analysis has wide-ranging uses in both civil and criminal justice research and that it will see increasing use in the future. For example, survival analysis could be used to analyze the factors affecting the length of time that it takes to "clear" police cases, that it takes to process court cases, or that a once-convicted civil or criminal offender remains free of further violations.

In Chapter 7 we analyze the length of time a prison releasee will remain free of crime. This analysis reveals an important advantage of survival analysis over more traditional analyses that consider only whether or not an event occurred during the period of observation (e.g., the follow-up period). Such traditional analyses consider only the overall level of failure or success during the period of observation, whereas survival analysis considers the timing of failure or success as well. Consideration of the timing of the event of interest is important for a number of reasons. First, if information on the timing of the event of interest is available, it is statistically inefficient not to use it. Second, survival analysis allows us to predict the rate at which the event of interest occurs for any desired period of time, rather than just for the actual length of observation. To illustrate this last point, suppose that we had data that contained information on individuals for the first 24 months after release from prison. A traditional analysis of this data would consider only whether an individual failed during the period—a variable that would assume a value of one (failure) or zero (no failure during the follow-up period). A survival analysis would consider the timing of failure for those who fail as well as the fact that successful individuals did not fail during the follow-up period. The traditional analysis would allow us to predict the probability that an individual would fail within 24 months after release, whereas the survival analysis would allow us to predict the probability of failure for each of the 24 months of the follow-up period.

In Chapter 6 we discuss a number of techniques that have been used to estimate survival time. In Chapter 7 we illustrate the use of survival analysis, assuming that (1) survival time follows a censored lognormal distribution and (2) individual characteristics affect the time that an individual survives.

The final chapter of this part, Chapter 8, illustrates one possible use of the empirical models of recidivism that we develop in Chapters 5 and 7. Specifically, we use the models of time sentenced during a follow-up period (developed in Chapter 5) and of time until recidivism (developed in Chapter 7) to evaluate an innovative vocational training program for youthful offenders. The technique we use, which we call the "predicted-versus-actual" technique, uses our models to predict total time sentenced during the follow-up period and the recidivism rate for each month of the follow-up period. We compare these predicted values with the observed values for the group of youthful offenders who participated in the program. We find that the program significantly reduces recidivism during the first 6 months after release but has no significant effects after the early release period.

# Chapter 2

## Statistical Analysis of Qualitative Outcomes

### 2.1. Introduction

Qualitative variables are those for which no meaningful numerical value is available. Typically they represent the occurrence or nonoccurrence of some event. For example, an individual may be married or single. An individual released from prison may commit a specified offense within a specified period of time or may not. A particular house may be set on fire or may not. A defendent may be convicted or acquitted. The police either file formal charges in a case or do not. As noted in the introduction to Part I, students of deviant behavior and the legal system very frequently encounter such variables.

In some cases qualitative variables may in principle represent a well-defined numerical value. For example, for a particular house the variable "loss due to fire, in dollars" is an alternative to the qualitative variable representing simply whether or not there was a fire. But the qualitative variable may still be the appropriate one to analyze if information is lacking on the underlying variable (e.g., there are data on occurrence of fires but not on losses) or if the information on the underlying variable is unreliable (e.g., data on the occurrence of fires are probably more reliable than data on losses due to fire, even when the latter are available).

Qualitative variables are usually represented numerically by so-called dummy variables, which take on the value one when the event in question occurs and zero when it does not. For example, in one of the data sets we shall use, a dummy variable representing marital status equalled 1 for the 257 individuals who were married and 0 for the 384 individuals who were not married. The use of the values 0 and 1, rather than others like $\sqrt{2\pi}$ and 10, is completely arbitrary, and therefore it is vital that the methods used to analyze such data yield the same results regardless of which values are chosen for the dummy variables. This will be so for all of the methods we consider.

## 2.2. Least Squares with Dummy Variables

We shall now briefly discuss the linear regression model, its least-squares estimation, and the problems with its application to cases in which the dependent variable is qualitative. We begin by assuming that we have a sample of $N$ observations (each of which will typically represent an individual), which we shall index by $i = 1, 2, \ldots, N$; the order of the observations being arbitrary. Then a linear regression model specifies that

$$y_i = \beta_1 X_{i1} + \beta_2 X_{i2} + \cdots + \beta_K X_{iK} + \varepsilon_i. \tag{2.2.1}$$

Here $y_i$ is the value for individual $i$ of the "dependent variable" $y$, that is, of the variable we are attempting to analyze. The $X_{i1}, X_{i2}, \ldots, X_{iK}$ are the values, again for individual $i$, of the $K$ "explanatory variables" (or "independent variables") that we believe affect $y$. The "disturbance term" (or "error term") $\varepsilon_i$ represents random influences on $y$ that we are unable to capture in the model. Finally, the "regression coefficients" $\beta_1, \ldots, \beta_K$ are parameters that we hope to estimate and that tell us the amount by which a change in an explanatory variable will affect the dependent variable.

It is useful to rewrite the above model using matrix algebra. Define

$$X_i = \begin{bmatrix} X_{i1} \\ X_{i2} \\ \vdots \\ X_{iK} \end{bmatrix}, \qquad \beta = \begin{bmatrix} \beta_1 \\ \beta_2 \\ \vdots \\ \beta_K \end{bmatrix} \tag{2.2.2}$$

so that $X_i$ is the vector of explanatory variables for individual $i$ and $\beta$ the vector of regression coefficients. Then we have

$$X_i'\beta = \beta_1 X_{i1} + \beta_2 X_{i2} + \cdots + \beta_K X_{iK} \tag{2.2.3}$$

by the definition of the multiplication of vectors, and the model (2.2.1) can be rewritten as

$$y_i = X_i'\beta + \varepsilon_i, \qquad i = 1, 2, \ldots, N. \tag{2.2.4}$$

How $\beta$ should be estimated depends on what one is willing to assume about the variables in (2.2.4). One strong but common set of assumptions, which we shall call "ideal conditions," is that the $\varepsilon_i$, $i = 1, 2, \ldots, N$, are independently and identically distributed with mean zero and variance $\sigma^2$ and that the explanatory variables $X$'s are either nonrandom or else are independent of the errors $\varepsilon$'s. This implies that $E(y_i) = X_i'\beta$, where $E$ means expected value, that the variance of $y_i$ is $\sigma^2$ for all $i$, and that different $y_i$ are independent of each other.

The most common estimator of $\beta$ is the least-squares estimator $\hat{\beta}$, defined as

$$\hat{\beta} = \left(\sum_{i=1}^{N} X_i X_i'\right)^{-1} \sum_{i=1}^{N} X_i y_i. \tag{2.2.5}$$

Its name derives from the fact that it minimizes the sum of squared errors

$$\sum_{i=1}^{N} (y_i - X_i'\hat{\beta})^2 \tag{2.2.6}$$

with respect to possible choices of $\hat{\beta}$. One reason for its popularity is that the least-squares estimator $\hat{\beta}$ has a number of desirable properties when the ideal conditions just listed hold. In particular, the Gauss–Markov theorem assures us that, under ideal conditions, $\hat{\beta}$ is *unbiased* $[E(\hat{\beta}) = \beta]$, and, furthermore, that $\hat{\beta}$ is *efficient* in the sense that it has a smaller variance than any other linear unbiased estimator of $\beta$. If one makes the additional assumption that the $\varepsilon_i$ in Eq. (2.2.4) follow a normal distribution, then tests of hypotheses concerning $\beta$ (e.g., that certain elements of $\beta$ equal zero) are easily carried out using the $t$ and/or $F$ distributions. These tests are valid even without the assumption of normality of the $\varepsilon$'s if $N$ is large.

Having briefly reviewed the linear regression model, it is time to relate it to the topic of qualitative variables. Here it is essential to distinguish between qualitative explanatory variables $X$'s on the one hand and a qualitative dependent variable $y$ on the other.

Qualitative explanatory variables cause no problems whatever. In the previous discussion, nothing was assumed about the $X$'s except that they must be nonrandom or, if random, independent of the error terms. This simply reflects the implicit assumption that the $X$'s affect $y$ but that $y$ does not affect the $X$'s (i.e., there is no "feedback" from the dependent variable to the explanatory variables); whether the $X$'s are qualitative or continuous is immaterial. It is perfectly legitimate to run regressions with qualitative explanatory variables. Indeed, all analyses of variance and of covariance amount to doing exactly that.

Qualitative dependent variables are another matter. There are severe problems with using the linear regression model to analyze a qualitative dependent variable. To see these, we begin by noting that if $y_i$ equals one with probability $P_i$ and zero with probability $1 - P_i$, then $E(y_i) = P_i$. But if $y_i = X_i'\beta + \varepsilon_i$, then the assumption that $E(\varepsilon_i) = 0$ implies that $E(y_i) = X_i'\beta$ and thus that $X_i'\beta = P_i = P(y_i = 1)$. This is immediately troublesome because probabilities must of necessity be no smaller than zero and no larger than one, whereas $X_i'\beta$ is unbounded. Thus there is the possibility of the model implying probabilities outside the [0, 1] range. This is especially true if we are dealing with events where the true probabilities are close to zero or to one; for example, if we are analyzing a rare event. This difficulty is intrinsic to the use of a linear function, which is unbounded, to represent a probability, which is restricted to the interval [0, 1]. The only solution is to use a different functional form that is restricted to [0, 1]; this will be done in the next section.

There is one further point, of a more technical nature, that is often discussed in this context. If $y_i = X_i'\beta + \varepsilon_i$ and $y_i$ can take on only the values zero and one, then $\varepsilon_i$ can take on only the values $-X_i'\beta$ (when $y_i = 0$) and $1 - X_i'\beta$ (when $y_i = 1$). Given that the probabilities of these events are, respectively, $1 - X_i'\beta$ and $X_i'\beta$, a simple calculation reveals that the variance of $\varepsilon_i$ equals $X_i'\beta(1 - X_i'\beta)$. This is not a constant; it depends on $X_i$, which varies over the sample. The problem of nonconstant variance of the error term in a regression model is referred to as "heteroscedasticity;" it is a violation of the assumptions (referred to previously as the ideal conditions) that justify least-squares estimation. Heteroscedasticity causes the least-squares estimator of $\beta$ to be inefficient (though it remains unbiased), and it invalidates the usual simple $t$- and $F$-tests of hypotheses about $\beta$, even in large samples.

The heteroscedasticity problem can be solved by using a weighted least-squares procedure. Suppose we define $\sigma_i^2 = X_i'\beta(1 - X_i'\beta)$, the variance of $\varepsilon_i$. If we divide observation $i$ on the original model (2.2.4) by $\sigma_i$, we obtain

$$(y_i/\sigma_i) = (X_i'/\sigma_i)\beta + (\varepsilon_i/\sigma_i), \qquad i = 1, 2, \ldots, N, \tag{2.2.7}$$

and we note that the variance of $\varepsilon_i/\sigma_i$ is a constant (equal to one). Thus, weighting the observations by $1/\sigma_i$ eliminates the heteroscedasticity problem. Of course, $\sigma_i$ is not observable. Thus, in practice, we must use the following two-step procedure. First, estimate the original equation by least squares and use the resulting estimate $\hat{\beta}$ to form $\hat{\sigma}_i^2 = (X_i'\hat{\beta})(1 - X_i'\hat{\beta})$, $i = 1, 2, \ldots, N$. Second, weight by $1/\hat{\sigma}_i$; that is, regress $y_i/\hat{\sigma}_i$ on $X_i/\hat{\sigma}_i$ to obtain the estimator

$$\tilde{\beta} = \left(\sum_{i=1}^{N} \frac{1}{\hat{\sigma}_i^2} X_i X_i'\right)^{-1} \sum_{i=1}^{N} \frac{1}{\hat{\sigma}_i^2} X_i y_i \tag{2.2.8}$$

For large $N$, this weighted least-squares estimator is unbiased, is more efficient than the least-squares estimator $\hat{\beta}$, and leads to valid $t$- and $F$-tests of the usual kind.

The problem of heteroscedasticity can also be avoided by estimating the model by maximum likelihood methods rather than by a least-squares procedure. This option is unattractive because the main motivation for a linear model is to allow use of least-squares methods, which are much simpler computationally than maximum likelihood methods. However, it is worth mentioning here to reinforce the point that the heteroscedasticity problem is a technical one and can be solved without undue difficulty. The real problem with a linear model for a qualitative dependent variable, as previously argued, is that a linear functional form may be inconsistent with the requirement that a probability be in the interval [0, 1]. This can only be solved by choosing a different functional form, that is, by abandoning the linear model.

## 2.3. The Logit Model

As in the last section, suppose that $y_i$ equals one with probability $P_i$ and zero with probability $1 - P_i$. We wish to relate $P_i$ to a vector $X_i$ of explanatory variables in some reasonable way. The logit model does so by assuming that

$$\ln[P_i/(1 - P_i)] = X_i'\beta, \qquad i = 1, 2, \ldots, N. \tag{2.3.1}$$

(Here "ln" denotes natural logarithm.)

Although $P_i$ must be in the range [0, 1], the left-hand side of (2.3.1) is unbounded. It approaches infinity as $P_i$ approaches one and minus infinity as $P_i$ approaches zero. In other words, $P_i$ approaches one as $X_i'\beta$ approaches infinity and zero as $X_i'\beta$ approaches minus infinity.

This is also obvious if we solve Eq. (2.3.1) for $P_i$. The solution is

$$P_i = \exp(X_i'\beta)/[1 + \exp(X_i'\beta)] = 1/[1 + \exp(-X_i'\beta)]. \tag{2.3.2}$$

This is restricted to the range [0, 1] for any value of $X_i'\beta$.

The name "logit" derives from the fact that the right-hand side of (2.3.2) is of the form of the cumulative distribution function of the logistic distribution. That is, (2.3.2) says that $P_i = F(X_i'\beta)$, where $F$ is the logistic cumulative distribution function, namely,

$$F(s) = 1/(1 + e^{-s}). \tag{2.3.3}$$

The logit model is nonlinear and is not as easy to estimate as a linear model. The usual method of estimation is maximum likelihood. The form of the likelihood function is fairly simple. It is the product of $N$ probabilities, one for each observation, where for each observation we use the probability of the observed value of $y$. Thus, if $y_i = 1$, we use $P_i$ as before; if $y_i = 0$, we use $1 - P_i$. The likelihood function can therefore be written as

$$L = \prod_{i=1}^{N} [F(X_i'\beta)]^{y_i}[1 - F(X_i'\beta)]^{1-y_i}. \tag{2.3.4}$$

Here the $\prod$ represents multiplication, and $F$ is as defined in (2.3.3). Also note that because either $y_i$ or $1 - y_i$ equals zero for each $i$, only one term on the right-hand side of (2.3.4) contributes to $L$ for each $i$. The logarithm of the likelihood function is just

$$\ln L = \sum_{i=1}^{N} \{y_i \ln[F(X_i'\beta)] + (1 - y_i) \ln[1 - F(X_i'\beta)]\}. \tag{2.3.5}$$

There is no closed-form expression for the maximum likelihood estimator. Rather, the estimates are typically obtained by maximizing (2.3.5) numerically with respect to $\beta$. This involves the use of an iterative algorithm, starting from some set of initial guesses for $\beta$. Fortunately, it is known that the logarithmic likelihood function (2.3.5) is globally concave. This implies that it has no local maximum other than its global maximum and that this maximum will be reached from any set of starting values by any reasonable algorithm.

For large $N$, the maximum likelihood estimators of $\beta$ are unbiased and efficient and are normally distributed. Their variance–covariance matrix is given by the inverse of Fisher's "information matrix," which will be presented in the next section.

Finally, a word is in order concerning the interpretation of $\beta$. In a linear regression model, recall that the regression coefficients are the partial derivatives of the dependent variable with respect to the corresponding explanatory variables. Thus, in the linear probability model, the $j$th element of $\beta$ $(j = 1, \ldots, K)$ is the derivative of $P(y_i = 1)$ with respect to the $j$th variable in $X_i$. In the logit model this is not so, but a similar statement is true. Specifically,

$$dP(y_i = 1)/dX_{ij} = \beta_j P(y_i = 1)P(y_i = 0) \tag{2.3.6}$$

when probabilities follow the logit model. Thus, the $j$th element of $\beta$ is proportional to the derivative of $P(y_i = 1)$ with respect to the $j$th variable in $X_i$. The factor of proportionality is $P(y_i = 1)P(y_i = 0)$ and is positive and less than one. (Indeed, it is no greater than 0.25.) Thus the sign of $\beta_j$ has the usual interpretation (e.g., positive $\beta_j$ means that an increase in $X_{ij}$ increases $P_i$), but the size of $\beta$ requires some care. In particular, the elements of $\beta$ are much (at least four times) larger than the corresponding derivatives of $P_i$ with respect to $X_i$. One implication of this is that we should expect the coefficients in a logit analysis to be larger (in absolute value) than the coefficients obtained by least squares, simply because the coefficients have different meanings in these two cases.

## 2.4. The Polytomous Logit Model

In the previous section we discussed the logit model for the case in which the dependent variable is binary, that is, in which there are only two values, representing occurrence or nonoccurrence of some event. Such variables occur frequently in research on the legal system. For example, many legal decisions are analyzed in such a way that there are only two options: arrest or no arrest, jury trial or nonjury trial, prison sentence or no sentence, parole or no parole, and so on. Further, the most common measure of recidivism is whether or not an individual is rearrested (or reconvicted) during a follow-up period, which is also binary. However, legal researchers are increasingly interested in analyzing a richer set of outcomes. For example, in sentencing, judges' choices include a suspended sentence, fine or restitution, and imprisonment. The possible decisions fall into categories, but the number of categories is greater than two.[1] Similarly, in the analysis of deviant behavior, researchers often wish to consider more than just whether or not an offense occurs. They may also wish to consider the frequency with which offenses occur and the seriousness of offenses that occur.[2] Many measures of these aspects of deviancy are categorical but not binary. For example, the number of arrests (or convictions) during a follow-up period is a commonly used measure of the frequency or extent of criminal activity, and conviction for a felony rather than conviction for a misdemeanor or no conviction is a possible measure of seriousness. (See Chapter 3 for an analysis of the latter variable.) To analyze such variables we require a technique that allows for categorical but "polytomous" (multicategory) dependent variables.

The logit model of the last section is easily generalized to cover such cases. Suppose that there are $M$ possible outcomes and that we arbitrarily assign these the numerical values $1, 2, \ldots, M$. Then the logit specification is that

$$\ln[P(y_i = j)/P(y_i = k)] = X_i'(\beta_j - \beta_k), \qquad j, k = 1, 2, \ldots, M. \quad (2.4.1)$$

(As before, $i$ indexes observations from 1 to $N$.) Thus, by analogy to the specification of Eq. (2.3.1), the logarithm of the ratio of probabilities of events is a linear function of the explanatory variables.

Given Eq. (2.4.1) and the requirement that the probabilities of the events must sum to one, we can solve explicitly for the probabilities. The solution is

$$P(y_i = j) = \exp(X_i'\beta_j) \Big/ \sum_{k=1}^{M} \exp(X_i'\beta_k), \qquad j = 1, 2, \ldots, M. \quad (2.4.2)$$

However, as things stand in Eq. (2.4.2), not all of the $\beta$'s are estimable. Technically, the problem is that if any $K \times 1$ vector, say $\xi$, is added to each of the $\beta$'s, the term $\exp(X_i'\xi)$ will cancel out of the numerator and denominator of Eq. (2.4.2), and the probabilities of the various values of $y$ will remain unchanged. Thus, the data cannot distinguish between the set of $\beta$'s $(\beta_1, \beta_2, \ldots, \beta_M)$ and the set $(\beta_1 + \xi, \beta_2 + \xi, \ldots, \beta_M + \xi)$, and this indeterminacy must be removed before we estimate the model. Intuitively, one can only uniquely define $M - 1$ $\beta$'s, just as in the binary case ($M = 2$) where only one $\beta$ was defined.

In most of the early work with polytomous logit models, the convention (or "normalization") was adopted that

$$\beta_1 = 0. \tag{2.4.3}$$

We shall call this the "Theil normalization," after Theil (1969). This agrees with the practice followed previously in the binary case. In this case Eq. (2.4.1) can be written simply as

$$\ln[P(y_i = j)/P(y_i = 1)] = X_i'\beta_j, \qquad j = 2, 3, \ldots, M. \tag{2.4.4}$$

Thus, the parameters $\beta_j$ tell us how the explanatory variables affect the probability of occurrence $j$ relative to the probability of occurrence 1. If we wish to see how the explanatory variables affect the probability of occurrence $j$ relative to some other occurrence $k \neq 1$, then Eq. (2.4.1) tells us that the relevant parameters are $\beta_j - \beta_k$.

With the normalization $\beta_1 = 0$, the probabilities in Eq. (2.4.2) become

$$P(y_i = j) = \begin{cases} 1\Big/\left[1 + \sum_{k=2}^{M} \exp(X_i'\beta_k)\right] & \text{for } j = 1, \\ \exp(X_i'\beta_j)\Big/\left[1 + \sum_{k=2}^{M} \exp(X_i'\beta_k)\right] & \text{for } j = 2, \ldots, M. \end{cases} \tag{2.4.5}$$

The likelihood function is formed as the product of such probabilities, where for each observation we enter the probability for the value of $y$ that is actually observed. Thus, the likelihood function can be written as

$$L = \prod_{i \in I_1} P(y_i = 1) \prod_{i \in I_2} P(y_i = 2) \cdots \prod_{i \in I_M} P(y_i = M), \tag{2.4.6}$$

where $I_j$, $j = 1, \ldots, M$, is defined as the set of values of $i$ such that $y_i = j$. This just says that in Eq. (2.4.6), $P(y_i = 1)$ is entered for all $i$ such that $y_i = 1$; $P(y_i = 2)$ is entered for all $i$ such that $y_i = 2$; and so forth.

The maximum likelihood estimates are the values of $\beta_2, \beta_3, \ldots, \beta_M$ that maximize Eq. (2.4.6). As in the binary case, the maximization must be performed numerically, using an iterative procedure. Because the likelihood function is globally concave, this is not too difficult, at least if there are not too many parameters. However, it should be noted that the number of parameters climbs quickly with the number of explanatory variables and the number of outcomes. For example, with 5 values of $y$ and 10 right-hand-side variables, one would have $(5 - 1) \times 10 = 40$ parameters, and the numerical maximization of a function of 40 variables is very difficult and expensive.

For large sample sizes (large $N$), the maximum likelihood estimates are unbiased and efficient and are also normally distributed with the variance–covariance matrix given by the inverse of the information matrix. With the parameters arranged in the obvious order

$$\beta \equiv \begin{bmatrix} \beta_2 \\ \beta_3 \\ \vdots \\ \beta_M \end{bmatrix}, \tag{2.4.7}$$

the information matrix has the form

$$\mathscr{I} = \begin{bmatrix} \mathscr{I}_{22} & \mathscr{I}_{23} & \cdots & \mathscr{I}_{2M} \\ \mathscr{I}_{32} & \mathscr{I}_{33} & \cdots & \mathscr{I}_{3M} \\ \vdots & \vdots & & \vdots \\ \mathscr{I}_{M2} & \mathscr{I}_{M3} & \cdots & \mathscr{I}_{MM} \end{bmatrix}, \tag{2.4.8}$$

where

$$\begin{aligned} \mathscr{I}_{jj} &= \sum_{i=1}^{N} P(y_i = j)[1 - P(y_i = j)]X_i X_i', \qquad j = 2, 3, \ldots, M; \\ \mathscr{I}_{jk} &= -\sum_{i=1}^{N} P(y_i = j)P(y_i = k)X_i X_i', \qquad j, k = 2, 3, \ldots, M; \quad j \neq k. \end{aligned} \tag{2.4.9}$$

That is, if $\hat{\beta}$ is the maximum likelihood estimate of $\beta$ as defined in Eq. (2.4.7), then for large $N$, $\hat{\beta}$ is distributed as multivariate normal with mean $\beta$ and variance–covariance matrix $\mathscr{I}^{-1}$. This can be used to make inferences concerning $\beta$; for example, to test the hypothesis that an element of $\beta$ equals zero.

An alternative to the normalization that $\beta_1 = 0$ is the normalization that

$$\sum_{j=1}^{M} \beta_j = 0. \tag{2.4.10}$$

This is similar to the type of normalization used in analysis of variance, so we shall call it the ANOVA normalization [see Nerlove and Press (1973)]. In this case the probabilities of the various outcomes remain in the symmetric form of Eq. (2.4.2), and the likelihood function is still of the form of Eq. (2.4.6). The constraint is imposed simply by substituting $\beta_1 = -\sum_{j=2}^{M} \beta_j$

into the expressions in Eq. (2.4.2) before they are inserted into Eq. (2.4.6); the likelihood function is then maximized with respect to $\beta_2, \ldots, \beta_M$.

There is no substantive difference between the Theil and ANOVA normalizations. Indeed, the maximum likelihood estimates obtained with one normalization can easily be converted into the maximum likelihood estimates that would have been obtained with the other normalization. If

$$\hat{\beta}^* = \begin{bmatrix} \hat{\beta}_1^* \\ \hat{\beta}_2^* \\ \vdots \\ \hat{\beta}_M^* \end{bmatrix}$$

is the maximum likelihood estimator of the parameters with the ANOVA normalization and

$$\hat{\beta} = \begin{bmatrix} \hat{\beta}_2 \\ \hat{\beta}_3 \\ \vdots \\ \hat{\beta}_M \end{bmatrix}$$

the maximum likelihood estimator of the parameters with the Theil normalization, then $\hat{\beta}^*$ and $\hat{\beta}$ can easily be expressed in terms of each other. Specifically,

$$\hat{\beta}_j = \hat{\beta}_j^* - \hat{\beta}_1^*, \qquad j = 2, 3, \ldots, M, \tag{2.4.11}$$

and, conversely,

$$\hat{\beta}_j^* = \begin{cases} -\dfrac{1}{M} \sum_{k=2}^{M} \hat{\beta}_k & \text{for} \quad j = 1, \\ \hat{\beta}_j + \hat{\beta}_1^* & \text{for} \quad j = 2, 3, \ldots, M. \end{cases} \tag{2.4.12}$$

Furthermore, the same probabilities of all occurrences are implied regardless of which normalization is used, making the choice of normalization a question of which coefficients are easier to interpret. If the $\beta$'s are normalized in the ANOVA fashion, then the equivalent of (2.3.6) is

$$dP(y_i = j)/dX_{ik} = P(y_i = j)[1 - P(y_i = j)](k\text{th element of } \beta_j) \tag{2.4.13}$$

for $j = 1, 2, M$; $k = 1, 2, \ldots, K$. Here the elements of $\beta_j$ basically measure the effect of their corresponding explanatory variables on $P(y_i = j)$. If, on the other hand, the Theil normalization is used, the $\beta_j$'s measure effects of explanatory variables on the relative odds of occurrence $j$ and occurrence 1. Thus the ANOVA normalization may often be preferred on the grounds of ease of interpretation of the results.

## 2.5. Logit Models with Only Qualitative Regressors

In the discussion of the logit model presented in the preceding sections, no restrictions were placed on the form of the explanatory variables. These could have been continuous (cardinal) variables or qualitative variables, or we could have had some of each type of explanatory variable.

It is worth pointing out, however, that if *all* of the explanatory variables are qualitative, it is possible to avoid the computational burden of calculating the maximum likelihood estimates by a numerical search of the likelihood surface. This is so because the maximum likelihood estimates can be calculated in a simpler way and also because simpler methods of estimation exist in this case.

A thorough discussion of these methods is beyond the scope of this section; Bishop, Feinberg, and Holland (1975) give a comprehensive survey. It is easy to state the basic idea behind these methods, however. When all of the explanatory variables are qualitative, the sample can be split into "cells," within which all individuals have the same values of the explanatory variables. For example, if there are two explanatory variables, one with two values and one with four values, there would be eight such cells. (This amounts to creating the contingency table for the explanatory variables.)

For each cell, the logit model implies a probability for each possible value of the dependent variable. Thus if there are $M$ values of the dependent variable and there are $K$ cells, the logit model implies (population) probabilities $P_{jk}, j = 1, \ldots, M; k = 1, \ldots, K$. We can estimate these probabilities by the sample frequencies, say $f_{jk}$, where $f_{jk}$ is the number of observations in cell $k$ with value $j$ for the dependent variable divided by the total number of observations in cell $k$. Various methods of estimation then exploit the relationship between the $f_{jk}$ and $P_{jk}$.

For example, Theil (1970) uses the model in the form of Eq. (2.4.4). For cell $k$ ($k = 1, 2, \ldots, K$), the left-hand side of Eq. (2.4.4) is just $\ln(P_{jk}/P_{1k})$ and the right-hand side contains the dummy variables representing cell membership. Theil replaces the so-called "true logit" $\ln(P_{jk}/P_{1k})$ by the estimated logit $\ln(f_{jk}/f_{1k})$ and then regresses the estimated logits on the right-hand-side dummy variables. This regression consists of $K(M - 1)$ observations ($k = 1, 2, \ldots, K; j = 2, \ldots, M$). The observations must be weighted becuase the sampling variances of the estimated logits are not equal; they depend on the true logits and on the number of individuals in the cell. However, the weights are easily constructed. Thus Theil's method just calls for a linear regression and is computationally very simple.

Maximum likelihood estimates are obtained by the method of "iterative proportional fitting," described in detail by Bishop *et al.* (1975, Ch. 3). This is much simpler computationally than the maximum likelihood procedure described in the last section, but it is more difficult than Theil's method. Another possibility that they discuss is the "minimum $\chi^2$" estimator, which minimizes the conventional goodness-of-fit statistic

$$\sum_{j=1}^{M} \sum_{k=1}^{K} (f_{jk} - P_{jk})^2 / P_{jk}. \tag{2.5.1}$$

This statistic can then be used to test the adequacy of the model.

Models in which *all* of the explanatory variables are qualitative are likely to be rare. Therefore, the applicability of the methods mentioned in this section may be somewhat limited. Of course, a cardinal variable can always be made qualitative. For example, "age" might be replaced by the categories "young," "middle-aged," and "elderly." Clearly this entails a considerable loss of information, and it is not a practice we would recommend unless the computational burden of the maximum likelihood procedure of the last section is prohibitive. These techniques are still frequently used in legal research but have often been found to be poor predictors of future behavior.[3]

## 2.6. Probit Models

In the case of a dichotomous dependent variable, the probit model is similar to the logit model. It specifies that

$$y_i^* = X_i'\beta + \varepsilon_i, \qquad i = 1, 2, \ldots, N, \tag{2.6.1}$$

where $y_i^*$ is unobservable and the $\varepsilon_i$ are independently and identically distributed on $N(0, 1)$. It is assumed that the observable dummy variable $y_i$ is related to $y_i^*$ as

$$y_i = \begin{cases} 1 & \text{if } y_i^* > 0, \\ 0 & \text{if } y_i^* \leq 0. \end{cases} \tag{2.6.2}$$

Because $y_i = 1$ if $X_i'\beta + \varepsilon_i > 0$, and this occurs if $-\varepsilon_i < X_i'\beta$, we have

$$P_i = P(y_i = 1) = F(X_i'\beta), \tag{2.6.3}$$

where $F$ represents the cumulative distribution function of the $N(0, 1)$ distribution. That is,

$$F(s) = \int_{-\infty}^{s} (1/\sqrt{2\pi}) \exp(-\tfrac{1}{2}t^2)\, dt. \tag{2.6.4}$$

The only statistical difference between the probit and logit models in the dichotomous case is that the probit model uses the cumulative distribution function of the $N(0, 1)$ distribution [see (2.6.4)], whereas the logit model uses that of the logistic distribution [see (2.3.3)]. However, these functions are barely different except in the tails of the distribution. Therefore, unless one is analyzing a rare event, the results of logit and probit analyses should be almost the same.

When the dependent variable is *polytomous* (has more than two values), however, there are major differences between the logit and probit models. Indeed, in this case there are several different models to which the name "probit" is attached. We shall discuss two of these.

One polytomous probit model, discussed by Amemiya (1975), McKelvey and Zavoina (1975), and Akin, Guilkey, and Sickles (1979), assumes an *ordered* response. That is, although the cardinal values of the dependent variable are not available, it is assumed that the categories can be put in increasing (or decreasing) order. An example might be a case in which the dependent variable is an individual's income $y$, but data on income exist only by income class ($y \leq \$5000$, $\$5000 < y \leq \$10{,}000$, etc.). Let us number the categories 1, 2, ..., $M$ (as in the logit case) but with the understanding that the order is not arbitrary (as it was in the logit case).

The ordered probit model postulates an unobservable $y^*$, which is related to explanatory variables by Eq. (2.6.1). However, its relationship to the observed categories [the equivalent of (2.6.2)] becomes

$$y_i = \begin{cases} 1 & \text{if} \quad y_i^* < 0, \\ 2 & \text{if} \quad 0 \leq y_i^* < C_1, \\ 3 & \text{if} \quad C_1 \leq y_i^* < C_2, \\ \vdots & \\ M & \text{if} \quad C_{M-2} \leq y_i^*. \end{cases} \tag{2.6.5}$$

These imply the following probabilities for the various categories:

$$\begin{aligned} P(y_i = 1) &= F(-X_i'\beta), \\ P(y_i = 2) &= F(C_1 - X_i'\beta) - F(-X_i'\beta), \\ P(y_i = 3) &= F(C_2 - X_i'\beta) - F(C_1 - X_i'\beta), \\ &\vdots \\ P(y_i = M) &= 1 - F(C_{M-2} - X_i'\beta). \end{aligned} \tag{2.6.6}$$

Here $F$ is again the standard normal cumulative distribution function.

Note that this ordered probit approach is potentially quite useful in legal research. For example, in research on sentencing, the unobservable construct might be the culpability of the defendent and the observed variable might be the sentence decided on by the judge (e.g., suspended sentence, fine, or imprisonment).

Maximum likelihood estimates are obtained by maximizing the likelihood function, of the form of Eq. (2.4.6), with respect to the parameters $\beta$, $C_1$, $C_2, \ldots, C_{M-2}$. Note that the number of parameters is $K + M - 2$, where $K$ is the number of explanatory variables. For $M > 2$ this is less than the $K(M - 1)$ parameters of the logit model; for large $M$ it may be considerably less. This is advantageous both on statistical grounds and from the standpoint of computational expense.

A different probit model is the model of Hausman and Wise (1978). Their model is unordered and thus is similar in spirit to the logit model. With $M$ categories for the dependent variable, their probabilities are generated from an $(M - 1)$-dimensional multivariate normal distribution. This is analogous to the use of the (univariate) standard normal distribution for the dichotomous case $M = 2$. Unfortunately, the model is very difficult and expensive to estimate, especially for $M > 3$.

## 2.7. Discriminant Analysis versus Logit Analysis

Discriminant analysis is a familiar topic in multivariate analysis. It is designed to classify observations into populations. Thus, in a typical application, it may be assumed that automobile tires are "defective" or "not defective," and the tire manufacturer may try to decide to which group a tire belongs, based on measured characteristics of the tire.

Such an application is (or should be, in our opinion) different from a typical application of logit analysis, such as finding the determinants of the type of criminal activity. Essentially, the distinction is one of the nature of causation. The examples of McFadden (1976) are instructive in this regard. His first example is the problem of predicting the sex of a chick, based on characteristics such as its size and the frequency of its peep. This is a case where there are distinct groups (male and female), and these differ in their characteristics. Clearly, the causation is from sex to the various characteristics, not vice versa, and a discriminant analysis would be appropriate. The second example is an investigation of the way in which germination of seeds is influenced by light, temperature, moisture of the soil, etc. Here the causation is clearly from conditions of planting to germination. (It would be ridiculous to assert that there are populations of "good" and "bad" seeds, which differ in the moisture of the soil in which they are planted!) This is a case in which a logit analysis would be appropriate.

An argument for logit models can also be based on the sensitivity of a discriminant analysis to its distributional assumptions. Standard discriminant analyses are based on the assumption that the vector of characteristics has a multivariate normal distribution for each group and, furthermore, that the covariance matrices are identical (though the mean vectors are not).

Under these conditions it is well known that there is an implied logit model between the characteristics and group membership and that the parameters of the logit model are more efficiently estimated by discriminant analysis than by a maximum likelihood logit analysis. Efron (1975) gives some examples of this efficiency difference, which can be substantial. But a counterargument is that most sets of explanatory variables are very nonnormal; for example, they contain dummy variables, variables with skewed distributions, and so forth. In this case a discriminant analysis based on normality will give poor estimates of the logit parameters. This and related arguments are presented convincingly by Press and Wilson (1978), along with some numerical examples.

## 2.8. Summary

In this chapter, we gave an overview of some methods of analysis of models with qualitative dependent variables. Such methods are of great potential usefulness in criminological research because many variables of interest, or at least their observable proxies, are categorical in nature.

The choice of which technique to use for a particular analysis depends on a number of factors, the most important of which is the nature of the dependent variable. If the dependent variable is binary (two values), the logit and probit models are obvious possibilities, and it probably makes little difference which is used. If the dependent variable is polytomous (more than two values), however, the logit and probit models are quite different. The logit model does not assume any ordering of the various possible responses; it essentially treats them symmetrically. On the other hand, the ordered probit model assumes an ordinal ranking of the responses. This is most reasonable and useful where there is a meaningful but unobservable variable that can be thought of as generating the responses. Unordered versions of the polytomous probit model exist but are prohibitively expensive to use.

The nature of the explanatory variables is also relevant to the choice of statistical technique. If most or all of the explanatory variables are qualitative, categorical data analysis (as described in Section 2.5) may be an inexpensive alternative to a maximum likelihood logit analysis. On the other hand, if the explanatory variables are approximately normally distributed (a rare but possible case), discriminant analysis may be a reasonable choice of technique. However, it should be stressed that a considerable advantage of maximum likelihood analyses using the probit or logit models is that such assumptions about the explanatory variables are not necessary.

In the next chapter, we illustrate the use of the logit model by conducting two analyses of postrelease criminal activity.

## Notes to Chapter 2

1. For a recent review of sentencing research, see Panel on Sentencing Research (1982).

2. For a discussion of this in the context of measuring the outcome of rehabilitative programs, see Sechrest, White, and Brown (1979).

3. For recent examples of the use of this technique, see Solomon (1976) and Van Alstyne and Gottfredson (1978). The latter study finds that the categorical analysis technique results in poor predictions.

# Chapter 3

## Logit Analysis of the Nature of Criminal Activity

### 3.1. Introduction

In this chapter we apply the polytomous logit model to analyze the nature of recidivist criminal activity. The motivation for this is to be able to say something both about the determinants of recidivism and about the determinants of the nature of the recidivist offense.

Our first analysis, presented in Sections 3.3–3.4, is of the seriousness of recidivist offenses. Seriousness is measured by the distinction between misdemeanors and felonies; thus, the dependent variable that we analyze has three possible values—no conviction, conviction for a misdemeanor, or conviction for a felony—during a follow-up period after release from prison. Other possible indices of seriousness exist, such as the indices of Sellin and Wolfgang (1964), or Rossi, Waite, Bose, and Berk (1974), or the Center for Studies in Criminology and Criminal Law (1980), or time sentenced (which we shall analyze in Chapter 5). Nevertheless, the misdemeanor–felony distinction is an important legal distinction and provides a widely accepted measure of relative seriousness.

Our second analysis, presented in Sections 3.5–3.6, is of the type of recidivist offense. Type of crime is represented by three categories: crime against a person, crime against property, and other (miscellaneous, e.g., drug) offense. This categorization is often used in criminological research because the factors affecting commission of crimes in these different categories appear to be quite distinct. Some recent research results can be found in Peterson and Braiker (1980). Our dependent variable thus has four possible values, corresponding to these three categories plus the possibility of no conviction during the follow-up period.

The models will be fit to data on a group of individuals released from North Carolina prisons, as described briefly in the next section and in detail in Appendix A. The explanatory variables will be characteristics of the individual, including past criminal history. We shall be particularly interested in the effect of the nature of past offenses on the nature of subsequent offenses, in light of studies of criminal careers and crime switching in which the existence of such effects has been found. See, for example, Blumstein and Larsen (1972), Wolfgang, Figlio, and Sellin (1972), Petersilia, Greenwood, and Lavin (1977), Peterson and Braiker (1980), and Greenwood (1981). Hood and Sparks (1970), McCall (1975), and Petersilia (1980) provide surveys. Recent work on criminal careers indicates that there is extensive crime switching for most offenders. For example, see Wolfgang *et al.* (1972), Petersilia *et al.* (1977), Peterson and Braiker (1980), and Greenwood (1981). As far as we are aware, no one has previously attempted to analyze formally the factors associated with the switching phenomenon. One advantage of our approach over most previous work is that we can easily control for individual characteristics while examining the effects of past criminal history (and vice versa).

## 3.2. Data

The data used in this chapter are described in detail in Appendix A, so only a brief description will be given here. The data consist of information on the postrelease activities of two random samples, taken in 1969 and 1971, of 641 men who were in prison in North Carolina in either or both of those years. The activities of these men were followed for an average period of 37 months after their release from incarceration. Although the sample was drawn from a single administrative area, the population from which it was drawn is quite representative of the population in medium- and minimum-custody prison units throughout North Carolina.[1] The data are unusually complete in three senses. First, they contain detailed information on postrelease activities, because 71% of the sample of inmates was interviewed, at an average of 37 months after their release. Second, the criminal records are unusually complete. They were obtained by contacting officials in all areas where there was any indication that an individual lived after release or where self-report, FBI check, or the records of the North Carolina Department of Correction indicated that an individual had contact with criminal justice authorities. Finally, it should be emphasized that this data set is essentially a random sample of *all* releasees. Unlike many other data sets, it is not limited to individuals on parole.

### 3.3. Analysis of the Seriousness of Criminal Activity

In this section we shall analyze the seriousness of criminal activity during a follow-up period after release from prison. Specifically, the dependent variable is a measure of the most serious crime[2] for which the individual is convicted during the follow-up period. Three possible outcomes are considered:

(1) NONE, indicating that the individual was not convicted of any crime during the follow-up period;
(2) MIS, indicating that the most serious conviction was for a misdemeanor; and
(3) FEL, indicating that the most serious conviction was for a felony.[3]

This dependent variable is qualitative and has three possible values (NONE, MIS, FEL). An appropriate model for this case, which we shall use here, is the polytomous logit model of Section 2.4. A case could also be made for the ordered probit model of Section 2.6, but in this case the logit model is probably easier to interpret and explain. The reason is that, in the ordered probit model, the estimated coefficients would give the effects of the explanatory variables on the underlying unobservable (presumably, "seriousness") and would be hard to interpret, because seriousness has no obvious cardinal measure. In the logit model, on the other hand, the coefficients yield easily interpretable inferences about the effects of the explanatory variables on the probabilities of the three possible outcomes. Such inferences are interesting to the extent that the probabilities of the possible outcomes are interesting, which we feel is true in this case. If the possible outcomes were of interest *only* as observable indicators of seriousness, the ordered probit model would probably be preferable.

Because little theoretical or empirical work has been done on the determinants of the seriousness of criminal activity, the explanatory variables that we use are essentially those variables that have been found to be associated with individual criminal activity in previous studies.[4] Specifically the explanatory variables used are as follows:

(1) *CNST*, a constant term;
(2) *RACE*, a dummy variable equal to one for whites and zero for nonwhites;

(3) *CONVBS*, the number of convictions prior to the one leading to the sample sentence;
(4) *MF*, a dummy variable equal to one if the sample sentence was for a felony and zero if for a misdemeanor;
(5) *ALKY*, a dummy variable equal to one if the individual's record indicates a serious problem with alcohol or use of hard drugs;
(6) *AFA*, the age (in hundreds of months) at the time of the individual's first arrest;
(7) *SUPER*, a dummy variable equal to one if the individual's release from the sample sentence was supervised (e.g., parole) and zero otherwise;
(8) *AAR*, the individual's age (in hundreds of months) at the time of release from the sample sentence;
(9) *LENG*, the length (in tens of months) of the individual's follow-up period;
(10) *PERSON*, a dummy variable equal to one if the sample sentence was for a crime against a person and zero otherwise;
(11) *PROPTY*, a dummy variable equal to one if the sample sentence was for a crime against property and zero otherwise;
(12) *RULE*, the number of prison rule violations during the sample sentence;
(13) *MS*, a dummy variable equal to one if the individual was married when released from the sample sentence and zero otherwise;
(14) *SG*, the number of years of schooling completed;
(15) *WR*, a dummy variable equal to one if the individual participated in the North Carolina prisoner work release program and zero if he did not.

Appendix A contains more detail about these variables. The sample contained 596 individuals (out of the original 641) on whom this information was available.

The maximum likelihood estimates of the parameters of the logit model are given in Tables 3.1 and 3.2. Table 3.1 gives the results for the Theil normalization. Thus, for example, the numbers in the column headed "MIS/NONE" are the coefficients of the explanatory variables in an equation whose dependent variable is the logarithm of the ratio of the probability that the most serious conviction is a misdemeanor (MIS) to the probability of no conviction (NONE); the positive coefficient of *RACE* indicates that the probability of MIS increases relative to the probability of NONE if an individual is white. Table 3.2 gives the results for the ANOVA normalization. Thus the numbers in the column headed "NONE" are the coefficients representing the effects of the explanatory variables on the probability of

**TABLE 3.1.** Results of Logit Analysis of the Seriousness of Criminal Activity—Large Specification, Theil Normalization[a]

| Variable | MIS/NONE | FEL/NONE | FEL/MIS | $\chi^2$ |
|---|---|---|---|---|
| *CNST* | .59607 | .58473 | −.011342 | |
| | (0.75) | (0.71) | (−0.02) | |
| *RACE* | .51513 | .42313 | −.091998 | 5.73 |
| | (2.39) | (1.21) | (−0.29) | |
| *WR* | .31417 | −.43965 | −.75382 | 6.10 |
| | (1.49) | (−1.20) | (−2.21) | |
| *ALKY* | .87052 | .75775 | −.11277 | 15.04 |
| | (3.86) | (2.12) | (−0.35) | |
| *SUPER* | .15621 | −.59185 | −.74806 | 3.64 |
| | (0.60) | (−1.41) | (−1.90) | |
| *CONVBS* | .09104 | .07366 | −.017388 | 5.26 |
| | (2.28) | (1.44) | (−0.48) | |
| *RULE* | .28800 | .08003 | −.20797 | 12.69 |
| | (3.27) | (0.66) | (−2.03) | |
| *AAR* | −.50911 | −.39151 | .11840 | 13.15 |
| | (−3.62) | (−1.69) | (0.55) | |
| *AFA* | .21556 | −.75452 | −.97001 | 9.37 |
| | (1.41) | (−2.15) | (−2.88) | |
| *LENG* | .35557 | .28229 | −.073282 | 20.34 |
| | (4.50) | (2.37) | (−0.68) | |
| *MF* | −.89607 | .29429 | 1.1903 | 12.14 |
| | (−2.78) | (0.60) | (2.66) | |
| *MS* | .13685 | −.11897 | −.25581 | 0.71 |
| | (0.61) | (−0.31) | (−0.70) | |
| *SG* | −.061812 | .025620 | .087431 | 3.11 |
| | (−1.46) | (0.33) | (1.21) | |
| *PERSON* | −.36852 | −.61722 | −.24870 | 1.91 |
| | (−1.22) | (−1.02) | (−0.43) | |
| *PROPTY* | −.057209 | .09092 | .14813 | 0.13 |
| | (−0.19) | (0.19) | (0.34) | |

[a] Values in parentheses under coefficients are asymptotic *t* ratios.

no conviction; the negative coefficient of RACE, for example, indicating that the probability of NONE decreases if an individual is white. Both tables give the asymptotic "*t* ratios" of the coefficient—that is, the ratio of the coefficient to its asymptotic standard error, where the latter is obtained as the square root of the appropriate element of the information matrix.[5] These *t* ratios are asymptotically distributed as $N(0, 1)$ under the null hypothesis that the associated coefficient equals zero. (Thus, a *t* ratio in excess of 1.96 in absolute value indicates statistical significance at the 5% level, for a two-tailed test, etc.) Also in both tables the numbers in the column labeled "$\chi^2$" are the chi-squared test statistics used to test the joint significance of

**TABLE 3.2.** Results of Logit Analysis of Seriousness of Criminal Activity—Large Specification, ANOVA Normalization[a]

| Variable | NONE | MIS | FEL | $\chi^2$ |
|---|---|---|---|---|
| *CNST* | −.39360 | .20247 | .19113 | |
| | (−0.78) | (0.55) | (0.49) | |
| *RACE* | −.31275 | .20238 | .11038 | 5.73 |
| | (−1.93) | (1.46) | (0.52) | |
| *WR* | .04183 | .35600 | −.39782 | 6.10 |
| | (0.26) | (2.47) | (−1.77) | |
| *ALKY* | −.54276 | .32776 | .21499 | 15.04 |
| | (−3.23) | (2.31) | (1.00) | |
| *SUPER* | .14521 | .30142 | −.44664 | 3.64 |
| | (0.76) | (1.74) | (−1.74) | |
| *CONVBS* | −.05490 | .03614 | .01876 | 5.26 |
| | (−1.95) | (1.92) | (0.71) | |
| *RULE* | −.12268 | .16532 | −.04265 | 12.69 |
| | (−1.98) | (3.36) | (−0.62) | |
| *AAR* | .30021 | −.20890 | −.09130 | 13.15 |
| | (2.84) | (−2.24) | (−0.65) | |
| *AFA* | .17965 | .39521 | −.57487 | 9.37 |
| | (1.27) | (3.06) | (−2.57) | |
| *LENG* | −.21262 | .14295 | .06967 | 20.34 |
| | (−3.73) | (2.92) | (0.98) | |
| *MF* | .20059 | −.69548 | .49488 | 12.14 |
| | (0.86) | (−3.44) | (1.68) | |
| *MS* | −.005960 | .13089 | −.12493 | 0.71 |
| | (−0.03) | (0.83) | (−0.152) | |
| *SG* | .01206 | −.04975 | .03768 | 3.11 |
| | (0.35) | (−1.67) | (0.79) | |
| *PERSON* | .32858 | −.03994 | −.28864 | 1.91 |
| | (1.29) | (−0.17) | (−0.76) | |
| *PROPTY* | −.01124 | −.06845 | .07968 | 0.13 |
| | (−0.05) | (−0.36) | (0.27) | |

[a] Values in parentheses under coefficients are asymptotic *t* ratios.

the coefficients of a particular variable. These are asymptotically distributed as $\chi_2^2$ under the null hypothesis that the particular variable has no effect on any of the probabilities. (Note that, unlike the *t* ratios, they do not depend on the normalization.)

The 5% critical point of $\chi_2^2$ is 5.99, and the 10% critical point is 4.61. Thus we see in Tables 3.1 and 3.2 that not all of the explanatory variables have coefficients significantly different from zero at usual confidence levels; this is not surprising, given the large number of explanatory variables with which we started. In particular, the variables *MS*, *SG*, *PERSON*, and *PROPTY* all have $\chi^2$ statistics well below the 10% critical point, and all of their *t* ratios are also below the 10% critical point with a single exception, the coefficient of *SG* on MIS in the ANOVA normalization. Even this coefficient is only very marginally significant (a $t$ ratio of $-1.67$ versus a critical point of $\pm 1.64$). A likelihood ratio test of the joint significance of all four variables yielded a test statistic of 6.57, which is insignificant against the usual critical points of the $\chi_8^2$ distribution. These four variables were therefore dropped from further analysis. It may be noted that the least significant of the variables that were retained is *SUPER*, but it has a somewhat higher $\chi^2$ statistic than the variables that were dropped and one $t$ ratio that was near significance at the 5% level ($-1.90$ in the FEL/MIS equation, Theil normalization).

The results for our reduced specification, consisting of the original list of explanatory variables minus *MS*, *SG*, *PERSON*, and *PROPTY*, are given in Tables 3.3 and 3.4. The format of these tables is the same as for Tables 3.1 and 3.2, as described previously.

In discussing these results, it is convenient to separate the variables roughly into those that mainly affect the probability of some future conviction and

**TABLE 3.3.** Results of Logit Analysis of the Seriousness of Criminal Activity—Reduced Specification, Theil Normalization[a]

| Variable | MIS/NONE | FEL/NONE | FEL/MIS | $\chi^2$ |
|---|---|---|---|---|
| *CNST* | −.10143 | .83607 | .93745 | |
| | (−0.25) | (0.92) | (1.06) | |
| *RACE* | .55595 | .45439 | −.10156 | 6.93 |
| | (2.63) | (1.33) | (−0.33) | |
| *WR* | .30503 | −.48086 | −.78589 | 6.50 |
| | (1.46) | (−1.32) | (2.32) | |
| *ALKY* | .88674 | .76646 | −.12027 | 15.78 |
| | (3.95) | (2.15) | (−0.37) | |
| *SUPER* | .098358 | −.67029 | −.76864 | 3.92 |
| | (0.39) | (−1.62) | (−1.98) | |
| *CONVBS* | .094241 | .07950 | −.014736 | 5.57 |
| | (2.35) | (1.56) | (−0.42) | |
| *RULE* | .27512 | .083882 | −.19124 | 11.82 |
| | (3.19) | (0.70) | (−1.88) | |
| *AAR* | −.46633 | −.46539 | .000942 | 17.31 |
| | (−3.53) | (−2.16) | (0.00) | |
| *AFA* | .21158 | −.69666 | −.90824 | 8.55 |
| | (1.39) | (−1.99) | (−2.72) | |
| *LENG* | .34561 | .27653 | −.069081 | 19.69 |
| | (4.43) | (2.31) | (−0.64) | |
| *MF* | −.90199 | .30702 | 1.2722 | 13.86 |
| | (−3.27) | (0.90) | (3.34) | |

[a] Values in parentheses under coefficients are asymptotic $t$ ratios.

those that mainly affect the seriousness of the future conviction should one occur. Specifically, the variables *RACE*, *ALKY*, *CONVBS*, *AAR*, and *LENG* all affect the probability of NONE but have only insignificant effects on the relative probabilities of FEL and MIS; the variables *WR*, *SUPER*, *AFA*, and *MF* have only insignificant effects on the probability of NONE but do affect the relative probabilities of MIS and FEL. The variable *RULE* does not fit either pattern.

We begin with those variables that primarily affect the probability of a conviction. Consider first the variable *LENG*. From Table 3.4 we see that *LENG* has a negative effect on NONE and a positive effect on MIS and FEL (with the latter statistically insignificant). This is very reasonable, because in a longer follow-up there is necessarily more chance to be convicted of both felonies and misdemeanors. From Table 3.3 we see that *LENG* has only a small and insignificant effect on the relative probability of FEL versus MIS. Thus, even though the effect of *LENG* on MIS in Table 3.4 is significant and the effect on FEL is not, the *difference* between these

**TABLE 3.4.** Results of Logit Analysis of Seriousness of Criminal Activity—Reduced Specification, ANOVA Normalization[a]

| Variable | NONE | MIS | FEL | $\chi^2$ |
|---|---|---|---|---|
| *CNST* | −.24488 | −.34631 | .59119 | |
| | (−0.67) | (−1.01) | (1.02) | |
| *RACE* | −.33678 | .21917 | .11761 | 6.93 |
| | (−2.12) | (1.63) | (0.57) | |
| *WR* | .05861 | .36364 | −.42225 | 6.50 |
| | (0.36) | (2.54) | (−1.89) | |
| *ALKY* | −.55107 | .33567 | .21539 | 15.78 |
| | (−3.31) | (2.34) | (1.00) | |
| *SUPER* | .19064 | .28900 | −.47964 | 3.92 |
| | (1.01) | (1.71) | (−1.89) | |
| *CONVBS* | −.05791 | .03632 | .02159 | 5.57 |
| | (−2.05) | (1.96) | (0.83) | |
| *RULE* | −.11967 | .15545 | −.03579 | 11.82 |
| | (−1.97) | (3.20) | (−0.52) | |
| *AAR* | .31057 | −.15482 | −.15576 | 17.31 |
| | (3.71) | (−1.36) | (−1.03) | |
| *AFA* | .16169 | .37327 | −.53497 | 8.55 |
| | (1.14) | (2.92) | (−2.41) | |
| *LENG* | −.20738 | .13823 | .06915 | 19.69 |
| | (−3.64) | (2.85) | (0.96) | |
| *MF* | .19832 | −.70367 | .50534 | 13.86 |
| | (1.21) | (−3.70) | (2.27) | |

[a] Values in parentheses under coefficients are asymptotic *t* ratios.

two coefficients is insignificant, and we have no basis for concluding that the length of the follow-up period affects the probability of convictions for misdemeanors and felonies differently.

The effects of *ALKY* are very similar to those of *LENG*. To be an alcoholic or drug addict (*ALKY* = 1) decreases the probability of NONE but does not change the relative probability of FEL versus MIS. On the other hand, the effects of *AAR* are very similar but opposite in sign; to be older at release increases the probability of NONE without affecting the relative probabilities of FEL versus MIS. Finally, the effects of *RACE* and *CONVBS* are very similar to those of *ALKY* and *LENG*. To be white (*RACE* = 1) or to have more prior convictions decreases the probability of NONE but has no significant effect on the relative probability of FEL versus MIS.

These results can be summarized by noting that an individual is most likely to have no conviction during his follow-up period if he is comparatively old at release, is nonwhite, is not an alcoholic or drug addict, has had few previous convictions, and has had a short follow-up period. Conversely, the type of individual most likely to have been convicted during his follow-up period is a young, white alcoholic (or drug addict) with many previous convictions and a long follow-up period. None of these individual characteristics appears to affect the seriousness of the conviction (misdemeanor versus felony) if convicted.

We now turn to those variables that primarily affect the seriousness of the conviction rather than the probability of some conviction (namely, *AFA*, *MF*, *WR*, and *SUPER*). In Table 3.4 each of these has a positive effect on the probability on NONE, but one that is statistically insignificant at usual levels. However, each variable has effects on the probabilities of MIS and FEL that are significant (at least at the 10% level) *and* opposite in sign, and correspondingly has a strongly significant effect on the relative probability of FEL/MIS in Table 3.3.

The variable *MF* is negatively related to MIS and positively related to FEL. Thus, if the previous conviction was for a felony (*MF* = 1) rather than a misdemeanor (*MF* = 0), this increases the probability of a subsequent felony conviction and decreases the probability that the most serious re-conviction is for a misdemeanor. This is hardly surprising and is similar to the finding of Williams (1979), though it is perhaps a bit surprising that the nature of the previous conviction has no significant effect on the probability of no conviction.

The variables *AFA*, *WR*, and *SUPER* are all positively related to MIS and negatively related to FEL. Thus increased age at first arrest or release after participation in the work release program or under supervision increases the probability of MIS and decreases the probability of FEL. (The effect of *SUPER* may be at least partly because we classified parole violations as a misdemeanor.)

These results can be summarized by noting that the probability that the most serious reconviction is a misdemeanor is highest and that it is a felony is lowest for an individual who was old at time of first arrest, whose last previous conviction was a misdemeanor, and who was released on work release or under supervision. Conversely, the type of individual who is most likely to be convicted of a felony and least likely to have a misdemeanor as his most serious conviction is a prior felon who was young at his first arrest and had an unsupervised release.

Last, the variable *RULE* does not fit either of the patterns just discussed. To have more rule violations during the last imprisonment decreases the probability of NONE and increases the probability of MIS. Its effect on the probability of FEL is not statistically significant.

## 3.4. Further Results on Seriousness of Criminal Activity

To illustrate our results further, we used the fitted logit model to predict the probabilities that an individual's most serious conviction will be for a felony or a misdemeanor or that he will have no reconviction. This has been done in Table 3.5 for three hypothetical individuals with disparate personal characteristics, for various periods of time after release. We have given these hypothetical individuals very different characteristics to illustrate the importance of personal characteristics in determining the seriousness of postrelease criminal activity. These hypothetical individuals do not necessarily resemble any of the individuals in our sample.

The first section of Table 3.5 gives predicted probabilities for the "average individual," defined as an individual whose values for the explanatory variables equal the sample mean.[6] For various lengths of time (*LENG*), the table gives the values of *P*(NONE), *P*(MIS), and *P*(FEL) implies by the fitted model.

As would be expected, the probability of no conviction falls as the length of the follow-up period increases. It is approximately 43% after 1 year, 33% after 2 years, 25% after 3 years, and 9% after 6 years. The probability that the most serious conviction is for a misdemeanor rises with the length of time, which is also expected. After 1 year this probability is 51%; after 2, 60%; after 3, 69%; and after 6, 85%. Somewhat surprisingly, the probability of being convicted for a felony remains relatively stable as length of time changes. This probability hovers around 6% for all follow-up periods. For periods less than 8 months it is around 5%; it rises to a peak of 6.5% after approximately 4 years; and then again declines to approximately 6% for

**TABLE 3.5.** Predicted Probabilities of Various Outcomes during Postrelease Period

| Postrelease period (months) | "Average" case | | | "Best" case | | | "Worst" case | | |
|---|---|---|---|---|---|---|---|---|---|
| | *P*(NONE) | *P*(MIS) | *P*(FEL) | *P*(NONE) | *P*(MIS) | *P*(FEL) | *P*(NONE) | *P*(MIS) | *P*(FEL) |
| 1 | .522 | .426 | .051 | .808 | .190 | .001 | .139 | .499 | .362 |
| 2 | .514 | .434 | .052 | .803 | .196 | .001 | .136 | .502 | .362 |
| 3 | .506 | .442 | .052 | .797 | .201 | .001 | .132 | .505 | .362 |
| 4 | .497 | .450 | .053 | .792 | .207 | .001 | .128 | .509 | .362 |
| 5 | .488 | .458 | .053 | .786 | .213 | .001 | .125 | .513 | .362 |
| 6 | .480 | .466 | .054 | .780 | .218 | .001 | .122 | .516 | .362 |
| 7 | .472 | .474 | .054 | .774 | .224 | .001 | .118 | .520 | .362 |
| 8 | .463 | .482 | .055 | .768 | .230 | .002 | .115 | .523 | .362 |
| 9 | .455 | .489 | .055 | .762 | .237 | .002 | .112 | .527 | .362 |
| 10 | .447 | .497 | .056 | .756 | .243 | .002 | .109 | .530 | .361 |
| 11 | .438 | .505 | .056 | .749 | .249 | .002 | .106 | .533 | .361 |
| 12 | .430 | .513 | .057 | .743 | .256 | .002 | .103 | .536 | .361 |
| 14 | .413 | .529 | .058 | .729 | .269 | .002 | .096 | .543 | .360 |
| 16 | .397 | .544 | .059 | .715 | .283 | .002 | .091 | .549 | .359 |
| 18 | .381 | .559 | .060 | .701 | .297 | .002 | .086 | .555 | .358 |
| 20 | .365 | .575 | .060 | .686 | .312 | .002 | .081 | .561 | .357 |
| 22 | .350 | .589 | .061 | .671 | .327 | .002 | .077 | .567 | .356 |
| 24 | .334 | .604 | .062 | .656 | .342 | .002 | .072 | .573 | .355 |
| 26 | .319 | .618 | .062 | .640 | .358 | .002 | .068 | .579 | .353 |
| 28 | .305 | .632 | .063 | .624 | .374 | .002 | .064 | .584 | .352 |
| 30 | .291 | .646 | .063 | .608 | .390 | .002 | .061 | .589 | .350 |
| 32 | .277 | .659 | .064 | .591 | .407 | .002 | .057 | .595 | .348 |
| 34 | .263 | .672 | .064 | .574 | .423 | .002 | .054 | .600 | .346 |
| 36 | .250 | .685 | .064 | .557 | .440 | .002 | .050 | .605 | .345 |
| 42 | .214 | .721 | .065 | .506 | .492 | .003 | .042 | .619 | .339 |
| 48 | .182 | .753 | .065 | .454 | .543 | .003 | .035 | .633 | .332 |
| 60 | .129 | .807 | .064 | .355 | .642 | .003 | .024 | .658 | .318 |
| 72 | .089 | .845 | .062 | .267 | .730 | .003 | .016 | .684 | .303 |

long follow-up periods. (This last decline must be, of course, a statistical artifact, but it is too small to be worrisome.)

The second section of the table gives the predicted probabilities for a very favorable case. This would be an individual who is old ($AAR = 600$ months, or 50 years), nonwhite, not an alcoholic or hard dug user, had a supervised release from prison, had no previous convictions prior to his sample crime, committed no rule violations while in prison, was first arrested at an advanced age ($AFA = 4.8$ hundred months, or 40 years), had a sample sentence for a misdemeanor, and participated in the prisoner work release program when serving this sentence.

Such an individual is much more likely to receive no conviction and less likely to receive a misdemeanor than is our "average individual." However, the most dramatic feature of our "best case" is the decreased probability of a felony for the individual with favorable characteristics compared with the "average" individual.

Finally, the last section of Table 3.5 gives the predicted probabilities for a very unfavorable case. This would be an individual who is young ($AAR = 260$ months, or about 22 years), white, an alcoholic or hard drug user, had an unsupervised release from imprisonment, had four previous convictions and four rule violations during his sample sentence, was very young when first arrested ($AFA = 156$ months, or 13 years), had a sample sentence for a felony, and did not participate in the prisoner work release program when serving that sentence.

Comparing these probabilities with those for our "average" individual, the most dramatic change is the large increase in the probability of conviction for a felony, particularly in the period immediately after release from incarceration. The probability that such an individual will be convicted of a misdemeanor is not terribly different from that of the "average" individual, and the probability of no conviction is much lower than that of the "average" individual.

Because there were no individuals in our sample whose total characteristics were actually as favorable or unfavorable as those on which our "best" and "worst" cases are based, these results should be considered illustrative only. They are meant to demonstrate the type of predictions given by our model and the strong influence of personal characteristics on the probabilities of various types of crimes. Such predictions could be of considerable practical importance: for example, in prediction of future prison populations.

## 3.5. Analysis of Type of Criminal Activity

In this section we analyze the type of criminal activity during a follow-up period after release from prison. The dependent variable is the type of the most serious crime for which the individual is convicted during the follow-up period, and it has four values:

(1) NONE, indicating that the individual was not convicted of any crime during the follow-up period;
(2) PROP, indicating that the most serious conviction was for a crime against property;[7]
(3) PERS, indicating that the most serious conviction was for a crime against a person;[8] and
(4) OTHER, indicating that the most serious conviction was for a crime other than a crime against property or against a person.[9]

Once again we shall use the polytomous logit model of Section 2.4 for our analysis. In this case, the ordered probit model does not provide a reasonable alternative method of analysis, because there is no unambiguous ordinal ranking of these categories.

Our original specification contains the same explanatory variables as the original specification for the misdemeanor–felony analysis of Section 3.3. The results of the logit analysis for this original specification are given in Tables 3.6 (Theil normalization) and 3.7 (ANOVA normalization). The format parallels that of the earlier tables (e.g., Tables 3.1 and 3.2).

Not all of the variables in this original specification have coefficients significantly different from zero at usual critical levels. The 5% critical point of the $\chi_3^2$ distribution is 7.81, and the 10% critical point is 6.25. Thus for each of five variables (*MF*, *CONVBS*, *MS*, *SG*, and *WR*) we cannot reject the hypothesis that its associated coefficients are (jointly) zero. The $t$ ratios of these variables vary widely. The variables *SG* and *WR* have coefficients with low $t$ ratios (as well as insignificant $\chi^2$ statistics) and were dropped from the specification, whereas the variables *MF*, *CONVBS*, and *MS* were retained on the basis of some significant $t$ ratios. Incidentally, the $\chi^2$ statistic for the significance of the coefficients of *SG* and *WR* jointly was 6.47, which is insignificant in the $\chi_6^2$ distribution; this is further evidence that *SG* and *WR* are not very important.

The results for our reduced specification, consisting of the original list of variables minus *SG* and *WR*, are given in Tables 3.8 and 3.9. Once again, it is convenient to distinguish the variables primarily affecting the probability of a conviction from the variables primarily affecting the nature of the conviction. Six variables clearly affect the probability of a conviction but do not appear to have much effect on its type. These variables are *ALKY*, *AAR*, *CONVBS*, *LENG*, *RULE*, and *MF*. In Table 3.9 each of these variables has a significant effect on the probability of NONE. The results indicate that the probability of no conviction (NONE) for an individual is decreased and

**TABLE 3.6.** Results of Logit Analysis of Type of Criminal Activity—Large Specification, Theil Normalization[a]

| Variable | PERS/ NONE | PROP/ NONE | OTHER/ NONE | PERS/ PROP | PERS/ OTHER | PROP/ OTHER | $\chi^2$ |
|---|---|---|---|---|---|---|---|
| *CNST* | −.50319 | .87381 | −.16762 | −1.3770 | −.33559 | 1.0414 | |
| | (−0.46) | (0.85) | (−0.21) | (−1.46) | (−0.36) | (1.21) | |
| *RACE* | .25228 | .36795 | .61026 | −.11567 | −.35798 | −.24231 | 7.66 |
| | (0.71) | (1.30) | (2.72) | (−.32) | (−1.09) | (−0.96) | |
| *MF* | −.56841 | −.82009 | −.61353 | .25168 | .04513 | −.20656 | 4.86 |
| | (−1.17) | (−2.00) | (−1.81) | (0.51) | (0.10) | (−0.55) | |
| *ALKY* | 1.2374 | .79014 | .79467 | .44726 | .44272 | −.00454 | 16.29 |
| | (3.46) | (2.65) | (3.38) | (1.23) | (1.34) | (−0.02) | |
| *AFA* | −.24148 | −.18451 | .25403 | −.05696 | −.49551 | −.43855 | 6.28 |
| | (−0.79) | (−0.77) | (1.62) | (−0.17) | (−1.71) | (−2.02) | |
| *SUPER* | −.62679 | −.38794 | .31071 | −.23884 | −.93749 | −.69865 | 8.12 |
| | (−1.44) | (−1.09) | (1.15) | (−0.51) | (−2.28) | (−2.14) | |
| *AAR* | −.73733 | −.56926 | −.42814 | −.16806 | −.30919 | −.14111 | 14.64 |
| | (−3.10) | (−2.92) | (−2.95) | (−0.67) | (−1.40) | (−0.82) | |
| *CONVBS* | .10936 | .10068 | .08576 | .00868 | .02360 | .01492 | 5.85 |
| | (2.24) | (2.28) | (2.11) | (0.26) | (0.74) | (0.63) | |
| *LENG* | .44181 | .34459 | .33172 | .09723 | .11009 | .01287 | 21.00 |
| | (3.60) | (3.41) | (4.02) | (0.79) | (0.98) | (0.15) | |
| *PERSON* | 1.1374 | −.85891 | −.62289 | 1.9963 | 1.7603 | −.23603 | 18.94 |
| | (2.35) | (−1.72) | (−1.95) | (3.44) | (3.88) | (−0.49) | |
| *PROPTY* | .62719 | .35791 | .31133 | .26928 | .93852 | .66924 | 6.99 |
| | (1.30) | (0.98) | (−0.99) | (0.57) | (2.11) | (2.10) | |
| *RULE* | .20786 | .23384 | .27395 | −.02598 | −.06609 | −.04011 | 9.02 |
| | (1.66) | (2.33) | (2.98) | (−0.23) | (−0.61) | (−0.53) | |
| *MS* | .21291 | −.36561 | .24064 | .57852 | −.02773 | −.60626 | 5.08 |
| | (0.58) | (−1.16) | (1.03) | (1.47) | (−0.08) | (−2.14) | |
| *SG* | −.01724 | −.04562 | −.05705 | .02838 | .03981 | .01143 | 1.81 |
| | (−0.24) | (−0.77) | (−1.30) | (0.36) | (0.58) | (0.21) | |
| *WR* | −.07818 | −.02278 | .37258 | −.05540 | −.45076 | −.39535 | 4.73 |
| | (−0.22) | (−0.08) | (1.70) | (−0.15) | (−1.36) | (−1.53) | |

[a] From Witte and Schmidt (1979). Values in parentheses under coefficients are asymptotic *t* ratios.

thus that the probability of PERS, PROP, or OTHER is increased, the younger he is at release (low *AAR*), the more previous convictions he has (high *CONVBS*), the more rule violations he committed during the sample sentence (high *RULE*), the longer his follow-up period (large *LENG*), if he was an alcoholic or user of hard drugs ($ALKY = 1$), and if the previous incarceration was for a misdemeanor ($MF = 0$). These results seem reasonable and agree with the findings of our analysis of Section 3.3, except for the variable *MF*, which did not affect the probability of a conviction there. As

**TABLE 3.7.** Results of Logit Analysis of Type of Criminal Activity—Large Specification, ANOVA Normalization[a]

| Variable | NONE | PERS | PROP | OTHER | $\chi^2$ |
|---|---|---|---|---|---|
| *CNST* | −.05075 | −.55394 | .82306 | −.21837 | |
| | (−0.08) | (−0.87) | (1.42) | (−0.46) | |
| *RACE* | −.30762 | −.05543 | .06033 | .30264 | 7.66 |
| | (−1.80) | (−0.23) | (0.33) | (2.11) | |
| *MF* | .50051 | −.06790 | −.31958 | −.11302 | 4.86 |
| | (2.03) | (−0.21) | (−1.22) | (−0.53) | |
| *ALKY* | −.70555 | .53185 | .08459 | .08918 | 16.29 |
| | (−3.90) | (2.23) | (0.47) | (0.65) | |
| *AFA* | .04299 | −.19849 | −.14152 | .29702 | 6.28 |
| | (0.32) | (−0.92) | (−0.85) | (2.63) | |
| *SUPER* | .17600 | −.45079 | −.21193 | .48672 | 8.12 |
| | (0.86) | (−1.51) | (−0.88) | (2.72) | |
| *AAR* | .43368 | −.30365 | −.13558 | .00554 | 14.64 |
| | (3.83) | (−1.88) | (−1.05) | (0.06) | |
| *CONVBS* | −.07395 | .03541 | .02673 | .01181 | 5.85 |
| | (−2.39) | (1.46) | (1.40) | (0.73) | |
| *LENG* | −.27953 | .16228 | .06506 | .05219 | 21.00 |
| | (−4.52) | (2.01) | (1.03) | (1.04) | |
| *PERSON* | .08610 | 1.2235 | −.77281 | −.53679 | 18.94 |
| | (0.35) | (3.70) | (−2.24) | (−2.40) | |
| *PROPTY* | −.16844 | .45875 | .18947 | −.47977 | 6.99 |
| | (−0.72) | (1.44) | (0.82) | (−2.47) | |
| *RULE* | −.17891 | .02895 | .05493 | .09504 | 9.02 |
| | (−2.66) | (0.37) | (0.98) | (1.92) | |
| *MS* | −.02199 | .19093 | −.38760 | .21866 | 5.08 |
| | (−0.12) | (0.77) | (−1.86) | (1.43) | |
| *SG* | .02998 | .01274 | −.01564 | −.02707 | 1.81 |
| | (0.90) | (0.26) | (−0.39) | (−0.92) | |
| *WR* | −.06791 | −.14609 | −.09069 | .30468 | 4.73 |
| | (−0.40) | (−0.61) | (−0.48) | (2.12) | |

[a] Values in parentheses under coefficients are asymptotic *t* ratios.

far as the type of conviction is concerned, we see that none of the coefficients of these variables in the third, fourth, or fifth columns of Table 3.8 is significant at even the 10% level. As a result it is fair to conclude that these variables affect the probability of a conviction but do not influence the type of crime for which conviction occurs.[10]

The variables *PERSON* and *PROPTY*, which indicate the nature of the last previous offense, clearly influence the type of subsequent offense rather than the probability of a conviction. If the previous sentence was for a crime against a person (*PERSON* = 1), this drastically increases the probability of a subsequent conviction for a crime against a person (PERS),

**TABLE 3.8.** Results of Logit Analysis of Type of Criminal Activity—Small Specification, Theil Normalization[a]

| Variable | PERS/ NONE | PROP/ NONE | OTHER/ NONE | PERS/ PROP | PERS/ OTHER | PROP/ OTHER | $\chi^2$ |
|---|---|---|---|---|---|---|---|
| *CNST* | −.60435 | .46203 | −.59219 | −1.0664 | −.01216 | 1.0542 | |
| | (−0.57) | (0.60) | (−0.84) | (−1.10) | (−0.01) | (1.09) | |
| *RACE* | .24415 | .36557 | .61037 | −.12140 | −.36622 | −.24481 | 7.80 |
| | (0.69) | (1.30) | (2.74) | (0.34) | (−1.12) | (−0.97) | |
| *MF* | −.49234 | −.74395 | −.55260 | .25161 | .06026 | −.19135 | 4.87 |
| | (−1.02) | (−2.03) | (−1.65) | (0.51) | (0.13) | (−0.51) | |
| *ALKY* | 1.2182 | .78375 | .86076 | .43446 | .35746 | −.07701 | 18.26 |
| | (3.48) | (2.67) | (3.73) | (1.21) | (1.11) | (−0.29) | |
| *AFA* | −.25839 | −.18598 | .26007 | −.07241 | −.51846 | −.44605 | 7.44 |
| | (−0.84) | (−0.77) | (1.66) | (−0.22) | (−1.78) | (−2.05) | |
| *SUPER* | −.66646 | −.43133 | .29172 | −.23513 | −.95818 | −.72305 | 8.54 |
| | (−1.54) | (−1.22) | (1.10) | (−0.51) | (−2.34) | (−2.23) | |
| *AAR* | −.73996 | −.56445 | −.40981 | −.17551 | −.33016 | −.15465 | 14.36 |
| | (−3.10) | (−2.90) | (−2.86) | (−0.70) | (−1.49) | (−0.90) | |
| *CONVBS* | .11338 | .10609 | .09043 | .00729 | .02294 | .01566 | 6.22 |
| | (2.31) | (2.36) | (2.18) | (0.22) | (0.72) | (0.66) | |
| *LENG* | .44321 | .34102 | .31665 | .10219 | .12656 | .02437 | 20.56 |
| | (3.63) | (3.39) | (3.87) | (0.83) | (1.13) | (0.28) | |
| *PERSON* | 1.0976 | −.88421 | −.60191 | 1.9818 | 1.6995 | −.28231 | 18.40 |
| | (2.29) | (−1.77) | (−1.90) | (3.43) | (3.80) | (−0.59) | |
| *PROPTY* | .56658 | .30063 | −.36597 | .26595 | .93255 | .66660 | 7.04 |
| | (1.18) | (0.82) | (−1.17) | (0.56) | (2.10) | (2.09) | |
| *RULE* | .20142 | .22758 | .26281 | −.02616 | −.06139 | −.03524 | 8.54 |
| | (1.62) | (2.28) | (2.89) | (−0.23) | (−0.58) | (−0.46) | |
| *MS* | .19638 | −.37260 | .30278 | .56897 | −.10640 | −.67538 | 6.54 |
| | (0.54) | (−1.20) | (1.31) | (1.47) | (−0.31) | (−2.42) | |

[a] From Witte and Schmidt (1979). Values in parentheses under coefficients are asymptotic *t* ratios.

whereas it decreases the probability that the most serious subsequent conviction is for another type of crime (PROP or OTHER) and does not significantly affect the probability of no subsequent conviction (NONE). (From Table 3.8 we see that it also does not affect the relative odds of PROP versus OTHER). Thus a person with a history of offenses against persons is more likely to commit similar offenses and less likely to commit property or other offenses than is an individual with a history of other offenses. This finding confirms the common psychological and psychiatric belief in the uniqueness of the offender against persons and is consistent with recent research that indicates that offenders can be classified in terms of the maximum degree of violence that they are willing to use. [See Peterson and Braiker (1980) and Greenwood (1981).] However, our results contrast with some other studies

**TABLE 3.9.** Results of Logit Analysis of Type of Criminal Activity—Small Specification, ANOVA Normalization[a]

| Variable | NONE | PERS | PROP | OTHER | $\chi^2$ |
|---|---|---|---|---|---|
| *CNST* | .18363 | −.42072 | .64566 | −.40856 | |
| | (0.41) | (−0.57) | (1.24) | (−0.66) | |
| *RACE* | −.30503 | −.06087 | .06055 | .30535 | 7.80 |
| | (−1.79) | (−0.26) | (0.33) | (2.13) | |
| *MF* | .44722 | −.04512 | −.29673 | −.10538 | 4.87 |
| | (1.95) | (−0.13) | (−1.19) | (−0.47) | |
| *ALKY* | −.71568 | .50252 | .06807 | .14508 | 18.26 |
| | (−4.12) | (2.17) | (0.36) | (0.99) | |
| *AFA* | .04607 | −.21232 | −.13988 | .30614 | 7.44 |
| | (0.34) | (−0.99) | (−0.85) | (2.68) | |
| *SUPER* | .20152 | −.46494 | −.22981 | .49324 | 8.54 |
| | (0.99) | (−1.57) | (−0.97) | (2.78) | |
| *AAR* | .42856 | −.31141 | −.13590 | .01875 | 14.36 |
| | (3.79) | (−1.92) | (−1.06) | (0.20) | |
| *CONVBS* | −.07748 | .03591 | .02861 | .01295 | 6.22 |
| | (−2.47) | (1.49) | (1.49) | (0.78) | |
| *LENG* | −.27522 | .16799 | .06580 | .04143 | 20.56 |
| | (−4.50) | (2.09) | (1.04) | (0.83) | |
| *PERSON* | .09713 | 1.1947 | −.78708 | −.50478 | 18.40 |
| | (0.39) | (3.65) | (−2.28) | (−2.29) | |
| *PROPTY* | −.12531 | .44127 | .17532 | −.49128 | 7.04 |
| | (−0.54) | (1.38) | (0.76) | (−2.34) | |
| *RULE* | −.17295 | .02847 | .05463 | .08986 | 8.54 |
| | (−2.60) | (0.37) | (0.96) | (1.85) | |
| *MS* | −.03164 | .16474 | −.40424 | .27114 | 6.54 |
| | (−0.18) | (0.67) | (−1.98) | (1.79) | |

[a] Values in parentheses under coefficients are asymptotic *t* ratios.

[see Blumstein and Cohen (1978) and Williams (1979)], which use arrest histories and indicate that there is very little simple correlation between offense types in prior and subsequent arrests. An advantage of the present work is that it controls for other factors affecting crime type. When this is done, crime commission persistence appears for the violent offender.

On the other hand, if the sample sentence was for a property offense (*PROPTY* = 1), the main effect is to decrease the probability of a subsequent conviction in the OTHER category. This apparently is accompanied by increases in the probabilities of PERS and PROP rather than NONE; compare the third, fifth, and sixth columns of Table 3.8. Although the effect of *PROPTY* on the relative probability of property crime is not surprising, the increased relative probability of offenses against persons is, and this may indicate a progression of criminal careers from property offenses to those against persons. This provides at least weak confirmation of the extensive crime switching of property offenders found in previous studies [see Einstadter (1966), Petersilia *et al.* (1977), Peterson and Braiker (1980), and Greenwood (1981)]. Both the results for *PERSON* and *PROPTY* also support previous findings that past type of criminal behavior is a good predictor of future criminal behavior [see Morris (1974) and Wolfgang *et al.* (1972)].

The variable *RACE* affects both NONE and OTHER but not PERS or PROP; to be white (RACE = 1) decreases the probability of no conviction and increases the probability of a conviction in the OTHER category. The variable *MS* does not affect NONE or PERS, but affects the relative probability of PROP and OTHER; to be married (*MS* = 1) decreases the probability of property offenses but increases the probability of OTHER offenses. (This may reflect the fact that in North Carolina nonsupport statutes were rather stringently enforced.) Finally, the variables *SUPER* and *AFA* also primarily affect the probability of an offense in the OTHER category but have no other significant effects; to be older at time of first arrest (large *AFA*) or to have a supervised release from last imprisonment (*SUPER* = 1) increases the probability of OTHER offenses. (This effect of *SUPER* may be because technical parole violations belong to the OTHER category.)

## 3.6. Further Results on Type of Criminal Activity

To illustrate these results further, we have used the fitted logit model to predict the probabilities that an individual's most serious conviction will be for the various types of crimes considered. This has been done for three hypothetical individuals with different personal characteristics and for various periods of time after release. Basically, this is the same type of analysis as was presented in Section 3.4 for our misdemeanor–felony model.

First, we have predicted the probabilities of the four outcomes (NONE, PERS, PROP, and OTHER) for the "average individual"—that is, an individual whose explanatory variables equal the sample means.[11] As would be expected, the probability of no conviction falls as the length of the follow-up period increases: It is approximately 45% after 1 year, 35% after 2 years, 27% after 3 years, and 10% after 6 years. The probabilities of all three types of convictions rise with length of time, which is also as expected. After 1 year, the probabilities of PERS, PROP, and OTHER are 4% 12%, and 39%, respectively; after 3 years they have risen to 7%, 16%, and 50%; and after 6 years they are 13%, 20%, and 57%. Note that the probability of conviction for a property offense rises rapidly for the first 3 years after release but then tapers off. In contrast, the probability of conviction for an offense against a person continues to rise at about the same rate for as long as 6 years.

Second, we predicted the probabilities of various outcomes for an individual with very favorable (noncriminal) characteristics for various follow-up periods. This would be an old ($AAR = 600$ months, or 50 years), nonwhite, married person who is not an alcoholic or a user of hard drugs, whose release from imprisonment was supervised, whose sample sentence was for a crime in the "other" category, who had no previous convictions (before his sample crime), who committed no rule violations while in prison, and who was first arrested at an advanced age ($AFA = 480$ months, or 40 years).

Comparing this person with our "average" offender, the most striking difference is the drastically reduced probability of crimes against persons or property. The probability of conviction of an offense against persons within 3 years is less than 1% for our "favorable" individual, and the probability of conviction for a property crime is less than 2%. The probability of conviction in the "other" category is not affected as much; it is somewhat lower for short to medium follow-up periods, and somewhat higher for longer follow-up periods. The probability of no conviction is uniformly higher than it was for the "average" individual: 69% after 1 year and 51% after 3 years.

Finally, we predicted probabilities for a very unfavorable case. This would be a young ($AAR = 260$ months, or about 22 years), white, unmarried person who is an alcoholic or user of hard drugs, whose release from imprisonment was unsupervised, whose sample sentence was for a crime against a person, who has four previous convictions and four rule violations during his sample sentence, and who was very young when first arrested ($AFA = 156$ months, or 13 years). Comparing these probabilities with those for our "average" person, the most dramatic contrast is in the large increase in the probability of conviction for a crime against a person (41% after 1 year and 51% after 3 years) and the decrease in the probability of no conviction (12% after 1 year and only 5% after 3 years). The probability that the most serious conviction is for a property or other crime is actually lower for the "unfavorable" than for the "average" individual (except for very short follow-up periods), 14% after both 1 year and 3 years for property crime; this reinforces our previous conclusion about the uniqueness of the offender against persons.

Because there were no persons in our sample whose characteristics were all as favorable or unfavorable as the last two hypothetical individuals, these results should be considered as illustrative only. They demonstrate the strong influence of personal characteristics on the probabilities of various types of crimes and may provide insights for the development of criminal typologies.

### 3.7. Summary and Conclusions

In this chapter we performed two analyses of the nature of criminal activity following release from prison. In each case we sought to analyze not just the probability of recidivism but also the nature of the recidivist offense. The first analysis (Sections 3.3–3.4) dealt with the degree of seriousness of the most serious offense for which an individual is reconvicted; the three possibilities considered were no conviction, conviction for a misdemeanor, and conviction for a felony. Our second analysis dealt with the type of the most serious offense; the four possibilities considered were no conviction, conviction for a crime against a person, conviction for a crime against property, and conviction for any other type of crime. In both cases the polytomous logit model was applied to a sample of men released from the North Carolina prison system.

Although the results of the two analyses were naturally different in some ways, they also showed some strong similarities. In both analyses the most highly significant variables were the length of the follow-up period, age at release, addiction or nonaddiction to alcohol or hard drugs, and the nature of the previous offense. The first three of these influenced the probability, but not the nature, of a conviction in both analyses. (The number of previous convictions had the same effect in both analyses but far less significantly so.) These results indicate that an individual is more likely to be convicted of a crime during his follow-up period

(i) the longer his follow-up period;
(ii) the lower his age at release;
(iii) if he is an alcoholic or user of hard drugs.

We could also add:

(iv) the larger the number of previous convictions,

bearing in mind that this effect is not as strong as the other three. None of these variables appears to be useful in predicting the nature of the offense, either as to seriousness (misdemeanor versus felony) or type (crime against a person, versus crime against property, versus other crime).

The nature of the previous offense, on the other hand, was found to affect the nature of the subsequent conviction but not the overall probability of a conviction. In the analysis of seriousness of conviction (misdemeanor versus felony), the seriousness of the previous offense did not affect the probability of no subsequent conviction, but it did affect the seriousness of subsequent convictions considerably. An individual whose previous conviction was for a felony is more likely to be convicted of a felony and less likely to be convicted of a misdemeanor than an otherwise identical individual whose previous conviction was for a misdemeanor. This is a plausible and important finding, because it suggests that a concentration of the resources of the criminal justice system on the more serious offender may be appropriate. Such a concentration has also been suggested by researchers at Rand

Corporation, based on their research on criminal careers, to incapacitate the habitual criminals who are responsible for a disproportionate share of crimes.

Similarly, in the analysis of type of conviction (crime against person, versus crime against property, versus other crime), the type of previous conviction did not affect the probability of no conviction, but it did affect the type of subsequent convictions. An individual whose last previous offense was for a crime against a person is more likely to be convicted for another crime against a person and less likely to be convicted for a property or other crime than is an individual whose last conviction was for any other kind of crime. However, if the previous imprisonment was for a property crime, this seems to increase the probability of conviction for both property and for personal crimes but to decrease the probability of convictions for other crimes. Basically, individuals tend to commit again the same type of crimes that they have previously committed, though there is some evidence of property offenders switching to crimes against persons.

In each analysis there were additional explanatory variables that were found to affect the nature of the subsequent conviction, but not the overall probability of a subsequent conviction. This is valuable information that could not be obtained if the dependent variable were just a measure of recidivism (subsequent conviction or not).

We also provided predicted probabilities of various types of convictions for individuals with specified characteristics. These can be useful in checking the adequacy of the model and could also be used in a variety of policy-making applications, such as program evaluation (the subject of Chapter 8) or simulations of future trends in type of criminal activity.

## Notes to Chapter 3

1. However, owing to the original purpose for which the data were collected (an evaluation of the North Carolina prisoner work release program), it excludes men convicted of sex offenses, serious drug offenses, or as public drunks.

2. The most serious crime is defined as the one for which the longest prison sentence was received. If no prison sentence was imposed, seriousness is measured by the amount of the fine imposed. A suspended or probationary sentence is considered less serious than an active sentence but more serious than a fine.

Note that in North Carolina, felony versus misdemeanor is *defined* by length of sentence, so one cannot have a longer sentence for a misdemeanor than for a felony. The only way in which a misdemeanor should be counted as more serious than a felony, by our definition, is if the felony conviction resulted in a suspended sentence.

3. The felony–misdemeanor distinction in North Carolina is quite similar to most other states. A misdemeanor generally carries a prison sentence of 2 years or less. See Institute of Government (1970) for the details of this distinction.

4. Wolfgang *et al.* (1972) use multiple regression to analyze the determinants of the seriousness of criminal activities for juveniles. Their analysis is only partially comparable to the present analysis for three reasons. First, they are studying juveniles rather than adults. Second, they use a different measure of seriousness. Third, they use an inappropriate statistical technique, ordinary least-squares regression. However, we have taken direction from their findings where this seemed reasonable. Also, see Service (1972), Monohan (1981), and Witte (1980) for reviews of studies in this area.

5. Note that our "*t* ratios" are analogous and very similar to, but not identical to, "*t* ratios" as the term is used in statistics.

6. The sample means are as follows: $RACE = .503$, $WR = .462$, $ALKY = .481$, $SUPER = .316$, $CONVBS = 2.735$, $RULE = .672$, $AAR = 3.801$, $AFA = 2.803$, $MF = .308$. (The variable *LENG* takes on values from 1 to 72.)

7. Property crimes include such things as burglary, breaking and entering, and larceny and are defined in detail in Witte (1975, app. G). For the purpose of this analysis and in contrast to the other work, robbery is included in the property category. This change was made because we believe that, in general, robbery is carried out primarily for monetary gain.

8. Crimes against persons include murder, manslaughter, assault, rape, and kidnapping. Again, Witte (1975, app. G) provides an extended list of crimes in this category.

9. Crimes in this category include narcotic law violation, drunk and disorderly conduct, libel, gambling, vagrancy, and adultery. See Witte (1975, app. G) for an extended list of these crimes.

10. Note that this is a reasonable conclusion even though some of the coefficients of these variables in Table 3.9 are statistically significant, besides those affecting NONE. For example, *ALKY* has a significant positive effect on PERS as well as a significant negative effect on NONE. This is not really informative—we know already, if *ALKY* affects NONE, that of necessity it must affect at least one of PERS, PROP or OTHER. If we ask whether *ALKY* affects type of conviction, the question is not whether its coefficient for PERS is significantly different from 0 but rather whether it is significantly different from its coefficients for PROP and OTHER. From Table 3.8 (columns four and five), it is not.

11. The "average individual" is defined as a person whose values for the explanatory variables equal the sample mean. The sample means are as follows: $RACE = .503$, $MF = .308$, $ALKY = .473$, $AFA = 2.796$, $SUPER = .327$, $AAR = 3.789$, $CONVBS = 2.628$, $PERSON = .171$, $PROPTY = .421$, $RULE = .666$, $MS = .401$.

# Chapter 4

## Statistical Analysis of Censored or Truncated Outcomes

### 4.1. Introduction

A censored or truncated variable is one that is observed over only part of its range. The classic statistical example (Kendall and Stuart, 1973, p. 541) concerns the distribution of bullet holes in a target at a shooting range. Let $y$ be the distance from the center of the target for a particular shot. Clearly $y \geq 0$, so that $y$ has some one-sided distribution (e.g., lognormal or exponential). If the target is sufficiently wide that every shot will hit the target, estimation of the parameters of the distribution of $y$, given a sample of shots, is straightforward. However, suppose that the target has a radius $R$, with $R$ small enough that there is a nonnegligible probability that a shot may miss the target. In this case, we do not observe the variable $y$ for shots that miss the target; we only observe $y$ such that $y \leq R$. A sample of bullet holes in the target (i.e., a sample of $y$'s such that $y \leq R$) will be called a truncated sample; the only information it contains is the sample of values in the observable range. If, in addition, one has information on the number of shots that missed the target (though not by how much they missed), the sample will be called censored. Clearly a censored sample contains more information than the corresponding truncated sample.

As noted in the introduction to Part I, truncated and censored variables occur frequently in criminal justice research. For example, in analyzing the sentencing behavior of judges, one might have a sample of prison sentences meted out but no information on cases that did not result in a prison sentence; this would be a truncated sample. Alternatively, if one also had information on the number and nature of cases that did not result in a prison sentence, this would be a censored sample.

The cases in which we are interested here correspond to truncation or censoring on the dependent variable in a linear regression model. That is, we suppose that there is an underlying regression model

$$y_i = X_i'\beta + \varepsilon_i, \qquad i = 1, 2, \ldots, N, \tag{4.1.1}$$

of exactly the same form as in (2.2.4), satisfying the ideal conditions of Section 2.2. If $y_i$ were observed for every $i$, the model would be estimated by least squares, as given by (2.2.5). However, suppose that we observe $y_i$ only if it falls in a certain range. For example, suppose that we observe $y_i$ if $y_i \leq B$, where $B$ is a known point; this could arise if $y_i$ were individual income, the $X_i$ were determinants of the individual's income, and the sample were limited to low-income individuals.

If we observe $y_i$ and $X_i$ only for individuals $i$ such that $y_i \leq B$, the sample is truncated. If we observe such $y_i$ and $X_i$ but also observe $X_i$ (but not $y_i$) for $i$ such that $y_i > B$, the sample is censored. In either case, however, an important implication is that least squares is no longer an appropriate estimator for the parameters of the model. To see this, note that $y_i \leq B$ is equivalent to $\varepsilon_i \leq B - X_i'\beta$. Although one of the ideal conditions is that $E(\varepsilon_i) = 0$, the *conditional expectation* $E(\varepsilon_i|y_i \leq B) = E(\varepsilon_i|\varepsilon_i \leq B - X_i'\beta)$ does not equal zero and, in fact, depends on $X_i$. (We shall give an explicit expression for it in the next section, under the assumption that the $\varepsilon_i$ are normal.) Thus over the sample such that $y_i \leq B$, $E(\varepsilon_i) \neq 0$, and this implies that least squares over this truncated sample will give a biased and inconsistent estimator of $\beta$.

The rest of this chapter will be devoted to methods of obtaining consistent estimates of $\beta$, under the assumption that the $\varepsilon_i$ are normally distributed. In the case of complete samples, the normality of the errors is often assumed, but it is not essential, because the least-squares estimator remains unbiased and consistent under departures from normality. Unfortunatrly this is not the case in censored and truncated samples; consistency hinges on the truth of the assumption (here, normality) about the distribution of the errors. A more detailed discussion of this point can be found in Arabmazar and Schmidt (1982).

## 4.2. The Truncated Normal Model

Before proceeding to the regression model in which we are interested, we begin with a few facts about the truncated normal distribution. Thus suppose that the $y_i$, $i = 1, 2, \ldots, N$, are a random sample from $N(\mu, \sigma^2)$ but that we observe $y_i$ if and only if $A \leq y_i \leq B$, where $A$ and $B$ are known. We observe $n$ such observations, indexed $i = 1, 2, \ldots, n$, and the "original" number of observations $N$ is assumed not to be known. The density function of an observation from this truncated distribution is of the form

$$g(y) = \frac{(1/\sqrt{2\pi}\sigma)\exp[-(1/2\sigma^2)(y-\mu)^2]}{P(A \leq y \leq B)}. \tag{4.2.1}$$

The numerator is the usual density function of a variable distributed as $N(\mu, \sigma^2)$, and the denomination is the correct scale factor to ensure that the integral of $g(y)$ from $A$ to $B$ equals one. Now define $f$ to be the density of the standard normal distribution; that is,

$$f(y) = (1/\sqrt{2\pi})\exp(-\tfrac{1}{2}y^2). \tag{4.2.2}$$

Also define $F$ to be the cumulative distribution function (cdf) of the standard normal distribution; that is,

$$F(y) = \int_{-\infty}^{y} f(t)\,dt. \tag{4.2.3}$$

Note that

$$\begin{aligned} P(A \leq y \leq B) &= P\left[\frac{(A-\mu)}{\sigma} \leq \frac{(y-\mu)}{\sigma} \leq \frac{(B-\mu)}{\sigma}\right] \\ &= F(B^*) - F(A^*), \end{aligned} \tag{4.2.4}$$

where

$$A^* = (A-\mu)/\sigma \quad \text{and} \quad B^* = (B-\mu)/\sigma. \tag{4.2.5}$$

With these definitions we can write the density in (4.2.1) as

$$g(y) = \frac{1}{\sigma}\frac{f[(y-\mu)/\sigma]}{F(B^*) - F(A^*)}, \tag{4.2.6}$$

and the likelihood function for the sample of $n$ observations is just the product of terms like these; that is,

$$L = \prod_{i=1}^{n} g(y_i) \tag{4.2.7}$$

Johnson and Kotz (1970, pp. 81–82) give the mean and variance of the truncated normal distribution, respectively, as

$$E(y|A \le y \le B) = \mu + \frac{f(A^*) - f(B^*)}{F(B^*) - F(A^*)}, \tag{4.2.8}$$

$$\operatorname{Var}(y|A \le y \le B) = \sigma^2 \left\{ 1 + \left[ \frac{A^* f(A^*) - B^* f(B^*)}{F(B^*) - F(A^*)} \right] - \left[ \frac{f(A^*) - f(B^*)}{F(B^*) - F(A^*)} \right]^2 \right\}. \tag{4.2.9}$$

Note that if there is a single truncation of the form $y \le B$, this amounts to taking $A = -\infty$, and it is only necessary to set $f(A^*) = F(A^*) = A^* f(A^*) = 0$ in Eqs. (4.2.8) and (4.2.9). Similarly, if there is a single truncation of the form $y \ge A$, this amounts to taking $B = \infty$, and it is only necessary to set $f(B^*) = B^* f(B^*) = 0$ and $F(B^*) = 1$ in Eqs. (4.2.8) and (4.2.9).

With $A$ and $B$ assumed known, the maximum likelihood estimates of $\mu$ and $\sigma^2$ can be found by setting the expressions in Eqs. (4.2.8) and (4.2.9) equal to the sample mean and sample variance and then solving for $\mu$ and $\sigma^2$. Because $A^*$ and $B^*$ depend on $\mu$ and $\sigma^2$, this involves the solution of two highly nonlinear equations.

We now put the preceding discussion into a regression setting by dropping the assumption that the mean of the $y_i$ is a constant. If we assume that the original (not yet truncated) $y_i$ are independently but not identically normally distributed, with variance $\sigma^2$ but $E(y_i) = X_i'\beta$, then we have the regression model of Eq. (4.1.1). However, we still suppose as before that $y_i$ is observed if and only if $A \le y_i \le B$. The mean and variance of the truncated distribution of $y_i$ now vary over observations, because $X_i'\beta$ varies over observations. The mean and variance are still given by Eqs. (4.2.8) and (4.2.9) if $X_i'\beta$ replaces $\mu$ in Eq. (4.2.8) and in the definition of $A^*$ and $B^*$ in (4.2.5).

The computation of the maximum likelihood estimates is also more complicated in the regression case than in the constant mean case. The likelihood function is still of the form of (4.2.7), but with $X_i'\beta$ replacing $\mu$. Explicitly, it is given by

$$L = \prod_{i=1}^{n} \frac{1}{\sqrt{2\pi}\sigma} \frac{\exp[-(1/2\sigma^2)(y_i - X_i'\beta)^2]}{F(B_i^*) - F(A_i^*)}, \tag{4.2.10}$$

where $B_i^* = (B - X_i'\beta)/\sigma$ and $A_i^* = (A - X_i'\beta)/\sigma$. However, in this case there is no alternative to the direct maximization of the likelihood function by numerical (iterative) methods. This is potentially difficult because there is no guarantee that the likelihood function is globally concave, or even that it does not have multiple local maxima.

An example of the application of this model can be found in Hausman and Wise (1977). Their problem is the estimation of a regression function with income as the dependent variable, based on a sample of low-income individuals. This corresponds to a single (upper) truncation, because no data are available for individuals whose incomes exceed a certain limit.

In certain cases there may be estimates that are consistent and simpler computationally, although less efficient, than maximum likelihood. We shall discuss one such estimator, derived by Amemiya (1973), for the case of a lower truncation at zero ($A = 0$, $B = \infty$). Thus the model considered has $y_i = X_i'\beta + \varepsilon_i$, with $y_i$ observed if $y_i \geq 0$, and we are assumed to have $n$ such observations.

For this case, Eqs. (4.2.8) and (4.2.9) simplify considerably and imply

$$E(y_i|y_i \geq 0) = X_i'\beta + \sigma f_i^*/(1 - F_i^*), \tag{4.2.11}$$

$$E(y_i^2|y_i \geq 0) = (X_i'\beta)^2 + \sigma X_i'\beta f_i^*/(1 - F_i^*) + \sigma^2, \tag{4.2.12}$$

where $f_i^*$ and $F_i^*$ are shorthand for $f$ and $F$ (standard normal density and cdf) evaluated at $-X_i'\beta/\sigma$. Thus

$$E(y_i^2|y_i \geq 0) = (X_i'\beta)E(y_i|y_i \geq 0) + \sigma^2, \tag{4.2.13}$$

and we can write

$$y_i^2 = (y_i X_i)'\beta + \sigma^2 + \eta_i \tag{4.2.14}$$

where

$$\eta_i = (X_i'\beta)[E(y_i|y_i \geq 0) - y_i] + [y_i^2 - E(y_i^2|y_i \geq 0)].$$

Because $E(\eta_i|y_i \geq 0) = 0$, this can be regarded as a reasonable regression equation for the truncated sample ($y_i \geq 0$).

Because $\eta_i$ is correlated with the regressors $y_i X_i$, the regression (4.2.14) cannot be estimated consistently by least squares. Instead, Amemiya suggests the following two-step instrumental variables estimator:

(i) Regress $y_i$ on $X_i$, $i = 1, 2, \ldots, n$, and denote the fitted values of the $y_i$ by $\hat{y}_i$.

(ii) Estimate $\beta$ and $\sigma^2$ in (4.2.14) by

$$\begin{bmatrix} \hat{\beta} \\ \hat{\sigma}^2 \end{bmatrix} = \left[\sum_{i=1}^{n} \begin{pmatrix} X_i \hat{y}_i \\ 1 \end{pmatrix} (X_i' y_i, 1)\right]^{-1} \sum_{i=1}^{n} \begin{pmatrix} X_i \hat{y}_i \\ 1 \end{pmatrix} y_i^2. \tag{4.2.15}$$

Although it is not as efficient as maximum likelihood, this estimator is consistent, and it is simple computationally. Its main use is to provide good starting values for the iterative procedures used to calculate the maximum likelihood estimates.

## 4.3. The Censored Normal (Tobit) Model

The Tobit model is a particular censored normal regression model. Before we discuss it, we shall give a few general facts about censored normal distributions. These are closely related to the corresponding properties of truncated normal distributions, as discussed in the last section.

Suppose that we begin with a hypothetical random sample $y_i$, $i = 1, 2, \ldots, N$, from $N(\mu, \sigma^2)$. However, we observe $y_i$ if and only if $A \leq y_i \leq B$; otherwise we observe the events $y_i < A$ or $y_i > B$. The censoring points $A$ and $B$ are known.

The probability that $A \leq y \leq B$ is of the form $F(B^*) - F(A^*)$, exactly as in Eqs. (4.2.4) and (4.2.5) of the last section. Also $P(y < A) = F(A^*)$ and $P(y > B) = 1 - F(B^*)$ in the same notation. The likelihood function for the sample is the product of $N$ terms, of the following three types:

(i) For $i$ such that $y_i < A$, enter $P(y_i < A) = F(A^*)$;
(ii) For $i$ such that $y_i > B$, enter $P(y_i > B) = 1 - F(B^*)$;
(iii) For $i$ such that $A \leq y_i \leq B$, and hence $y_i$ is observed, enter the usual $N(\mu, \sigma^2)$ density

$$g(y_i) = (1/\sqrt{2\pi}\sigma) \exp[-(1/2\sigma^2)(y_i - \mu)^2]. \tag{4.3.1}$$

Finally, the moments of $y$ over its observed range are given by Eqs. (4.2.8) and (4.2.9), as before. The moments of $y$ over its whole range depend on what numerical value one assigns to the events $y_i < A$ and $y_i > B$.

The Tobit model corresponds to the censored normal case with the following modifications: (i) Instead of a constant mean $\mu$ for the underlying variable, we assume a mean $X_i'\beta$ that depends on explanatory variables $X_i$; (ii) There is only a lower truncation, at zero (i.e., $A = 0$, $B = \infty$, in the above notation); and (iii) The $y_i < 0$ are observed as $y_i = 0$.

Thus, the Tobit model can be expressed as follows. Let $z_i$, $i = 1, 2, \ldots, N$, follow a regression model of the usual type:

$$z_i = X_i'\beta + \varepsilon_i. \tag{4.3.2}$$

The $\varepsilon_i$ are independently and identically distributed as $N(0, \sigma^2)$. However, $z_i$ is unobserved, and instead we observe

$$y_i = \begin{cases} z_i & \text{if} \quad z_i > 0 \\ 0 & \text{if} \quad z_i \leq 0. \end{cases} \tag{4.3.3}$$

[That is, $y_i = \max(0, z_i)$.] It is assumed that observations on the explanatory variables ($X_i$) are available for all observations, whether $y_i = 0$ or $y_i > 0$. If the explanatory variables are available only for observations such that $y_i > 0$, we are back in the truncated case of the last section, and the rest of this section does not apply.

The Tobit model is often used to analyze nonnegative dependent variables for which zero is a common value in the sample. The classic example in economics is the amount that an individual spends for a new car in a given year. As another example, Clotfelter (1981) analyzes the factors affecting the underreporting of taxable income, where a value of zero is assigned to all individuals who report exactly or overreport. In both of these examples, zero is a common value for the dependent variable, as it also is in our application of the model in the next chapter, in which we analyze the total length of all prison sentences received by an individual in a given time period. Note that the extent to which one can identify an "underlying variable" (such as $z$ in the preceding equations) as a meaningful entity varies. In the "amount spent on a car" example, there is no clear interpretation for the underlying variable. In our "total length of sentences" example, on the other hand, we can perhaps view the underlying variable as an index of seriousness of criminal activity, which is unobserved, but for which time sentenced is an observable measure. It is therefore important to stress that the existence of a meaningful underlying variable is not necessary for the Tobit model to be an appropriate method of analysis.

With $y_i$ as defined in (4.3.3), we have

$$E(y_i) = (1 - F_i^*)X_i'\beta + \sigma f_i^*, \tag{4.3.4}$$

where $f_i^*$ and $F_i^*$ are again shorthand for $f$ and $F$ evaluated at $-X_i'\beta/\sigma$. This is the expectation of $y$ over the complete sample. The conditional expectation of $y_i$, $E(y_i|y_i > 0)$, given a positive observation, is still given by Eq. (4.2.11) and equals $E(y_i)/(1 - F_i^*)$.

Two things are noteworthy about these expressions. First, neither $E(y_i)$ nor $E(y_i|y_i > 0)$ is equal to $X_i'\beta$. This implies that the least-squares regression of $y$'s on $X$'s will give a biased and inconsistent estimate of $\beta$ and that this is so whether the limit observations (zeros) are included or discarded. Second, we must be careful about the interpretation of $\beta$. In a standard regression model it is the case that an element of $\beta$ is interpreted as the derivative of $E(y_i)$ with respect to an element of $X_i$, and thus it tells how much (on average) $y_i$ will change if $X_i$ changes. This is not true here, though a similar statement is true. Specifically, from Eq. (4.3.4) it follows that

$$\partial E(y_i)/\partial X_{ij} = (1 - F_i^*)\beta_j. \tag{4.3.5}$$

(Here $i$ indexes observations and $j$ indexes elements of $\beta$ and $X_i$.) Because

$0 < 1 - F_i^* < 1$, the sign of $\beta_j$ tells the direction of influence of the $j$th regressor on $E(y)$, as in a regression. However, the numerical value of this influence is smaller (in absolute value) than the coefficient $\beta_j$ would indicate, by an amount that varies over the sample. For example, in one of our analyses of total length of sentences, a dummy variable for alcoholism has a coefficient of approximately 45 (months). This should *not* be interpreted as saying that alcoholics accumulate sentences 45 months longer, on average, than non-alcoholics. Rather, the correct differential is 45 months times $1 - F_i^*$. Now $1 - F_i^*$ is the probability of a nonzero observation, and in our sample its average value would be .33 (because about one-third of our sample had nonzero time sentenced). Thus the correct differential would be approximately 15 months, not 45; the exact differential could, of course, be calculated from Eq. (4.3.5) for each individual.

The preferred method of estimation of the Tobit model is maximum likelihood. The likelihood function is made up of two parts, corresponding to the positive observations and to the observations equal to zero. For simplicity, suppose that the first $n$ observations are positive ($y_i > 0$), and the last $N - n$ observations have $y_i = 0$. Then the likelihood function is

$$L = \prod_{i=1}^{n} \frac{1}{\sqrt{2\pi\sigma}} \exp\left[ -\frac{1}{2\sigma^2}(y_i - X_i'\beta)^2 \right] \prod_{i=n+1}^{N} \left[ 1 - F\left( \frac{-X_i'\beta}{\sigma} \right) \right], \qquad (4.3.6)$$

the symbol $F$ representing, as usual, the standard normal cdf. The likelihood function, or more typically its logarithm, must then be maximized numerically by an iterative technique to find the maximum likelihood estimates. For large $N$, the variances of the MLEs can be gotten from the information matrix; see Amemiya (1973, pp. 1006–1007) for its form.

The computation of the maximum likelihood estimates is simplified by the knowledge that the likelihood function has a single local maximum; see Olsen (1978). Thus having found a local maximum from one set of starting values, we do not have to try other starting values. In fact, if we write the likelihood function in terms of the parameters $\sigma^* = 1/\sigma$, $\beta^* = \beta/\sigma$, it is globally concave, which assures that any reasonable algorithm will find the maximum. Having found the values $\hat{\sigma}^*$, $\hat{\beta}^*$ that yield the maximum, we can simply convert back ($\hat{\sigma} = 1/\hat{\sigma}^*$, $\hat{\beta} = \hat{\beta}^*\hat{\sigma}$) to the original parameters.

Several possible sets of starting values are available. The least-squares estimates are sometimes used despite their inconsistency; these should at least be scaled upward as indicated in the discussion following (4.3.5). Another possibility is the consistent estimator (4.2.15), based on the positive observations only. Given the convenient properties of the likelihood function, however, the choice of starting values should affect only one's computational cost, not the reliability of the results.

## 4.4. A Two-Part Tobit Model

In this section we discuss a model, developed by Cragg (1971), which is a generalization of the Tobit model in the sense that it is a more general model that includes the Tobit model as a testable special case. It is based on the observation that, in the Tobit model (4.3.2)–(4.3.3), a single set of parameters determines both the probability that $y = 0$ and the distribution of $y$ given that $y$ is positive. Thus any factor that decreases the probability that $y = 0$ must also increase the average value of the positive $y$'s. In terms of the analysis of the next chapter, for example, this means that we assume that the factors affecting the length of the prison sentence received are exactly the same as the factors affecting the probability of those events that lead us to observe no time sentenced (e.g., no criminal activity, dismissal of charges, or suspended sentences). This may or may not be a reasonable assumption.

There is a related difficulty that arises from the use of a single set of parameters in the Tobit model; namely, that it creates a connection between the probability of a zero observation and the shape of the distribution of the positive observations that may not always be reasonable. Consider Figure 4.1, which displays a graph of the density of $z_i$, where $z$ has mean $X_i'\beta$ and variance $\sigma^2$. The shaded area under the density function to the left of zero represents $P(z_i \leq 0) = P(y_i = 0)$. The remainder of the density gives the frequency of $y_i$ for positive values of $y_i$. Now, as illustrated in Fig. 4.1, when the probability of zero is less than $\frac{1}{2}$, $(X_i'\beta > 0)$, the density of the positive observations must have a single positive mode. By way of contrast, in Fig. 4.2 we see that when the probability of a zero is larger than $\frac{1}{2}$, $(X_i'\beta < 0)$, the distribution of positive observations must decline monotonically from zero. Thus the Tobit model cannot accurately represent cases where, for example, most observations are zero but the most frequent range of positive observations is not around zero.

One solution to this problem is to have one set of parameters determine the probability that $y = 0$ and another set determine the density of $y$ given that $y > 0$. Thus we suppose that the probability that $y_i = 0$ is determined by a probit model with parameters $\beta_1$ (see Section 2.6), so that

$$P(y_i = 0) = F(-X_i'\beta_1). \tag{4.4.1}$$

Next we suppose that the distribution of $y_i$, given $y_i > 0$, is $N(X_i'\beta_2, \sigma^2)$,

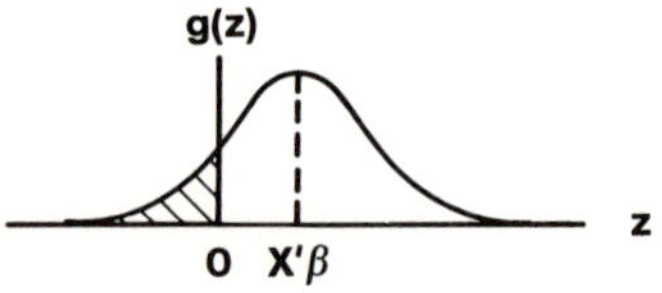


**Fig. 4.1.** Density of $z$, where $z$ is normally distributed with mean $X'\beta > 0$. The shaded area is the probability of a value of $z$ of less than zero.

truncated at zero as discussed in Section 4.2. For a sample of size $N$ with the first $n$ observations positive, we then have a likelihood function of the form

$$L = \prod_{i=1}^{n} P(y_i > 0)g(y_i|y_i > 0) \prod_{i=n+1}^{N} P(y_i = 0). \tag{4.4.2}$$

Given the assumptions just made, this becomes

$$L = \prod_{i=1}^{n} F(X_i'\beta_1) \frac{1}{\sqrt{2\pi}\sigma} \exp\left[ -\frac{1}{2\sigma^2}(y_i - X_i'\beta_2)^2 \right] \Big/ F(X_i'\beta_2/\sigma)$$
$$\times \prod_{i=n+1}^{N} F(-X_i'\beta_1). \tag{4.4.3}$$

This model contains the Tobit model as the special case corresponding to $\beta_1 = \beta_2/\sigma$. This is testable; in fact, this would be a useful test to apply in general to Tobit models, except that Eq. (4.4.3) is much harder to maximize than the Tobit likelihood function both because it contains more parameters and because it is not guaranteed to be concave.

Although it is hard to say exactly when this generalization of the Tobit model might be worth pursuing, we can at least repeat the following two points. First, this generalized model is likely to be useful if one is not sure that the factors decreasing the probability of a zero value and the factors increasing the average of the positive values are the same. For example, if one set of factors determines participation in criminal activity and a different set of factors affects judges' sentencing behavior, the Tobit model will not be suitable to analyze total length of sentences. Second, the generalized model may be useful if the fraction of zero observations implies an unreasonable distribution of positive values. This would be the case if the sample is mostly zeros but the mode of the positive observations is far from zero or if the sample is mostly positive but the mode is essentially zero. For example, in the analysis of the next section we observe total length of sentences equal to zero for about 70% of the sample, so the Tobit model would be considered questionable unless the most frequent positive values of total length of sentences are small.

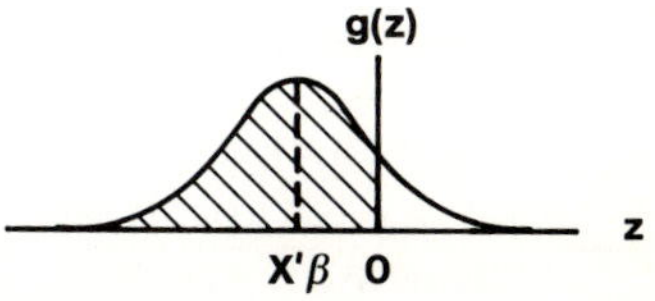


**Fig. 4.2.** Density of $z$, where $z$ is normally distributed with mean $X'\beta < 0$. The shaded area is the probability of a value of $z$ of less than zero.

### 4.5. A Sample Selection Model

In the Tobit model of Section 4.3 and in the truncated normal model of Section 4.2, the dependent variable $y$ is observed over only part of its range. An important implication is that the least-squares estimator, based on those observations for which $y$ is observed, is biased. This is an example of sample selection bias, a more general phenomenon that can occur whenever the rule for selection of the sample observations affects the distribution of the selected observations. Formally, if we consider the regression model $y_i = X_i'\beta + \varepsilon_i$, with a rule for selection of observations, we have

$$E(y_i|\text{selection rule}) = X_i'\beta + E(\varepsilon_i|\text{selection rule}). \tag{4.5.1}$$

In general, we can expect bias whenever $E(\varepsilon_i|\text{selection rule}) \neq 0$. If selection is purely random (random sampling) or if sample selection is based on explanatory variables (elements of $X_i$) that are by assumption independent of the error terms, then $E(\varepsilon_i|\text{selection rule}) = 0$ and there is no problem. On the other hand, if selection for the sample is based on the value of $y_i$, as in the preceding sections, sample selection bias is a problem.

However, sample selection need not be based on the value of the dependent variable itself for sample selection bias to occur. We may also wish to consider cases in which selection to the sample is based on a second variable, which is correlated with the dependent variable, in a sense to be made precise shortly. A general model for such cases (Heckman, 1979) is presented as follows. Consider the two-equation model

$$y_{i1} = X_i'\beta_1 + \varepsilon_{i1}, \qquad y_{i2} = X_i'\beta_2 + \varepsilon_{i2}; \qquad i = 1, 2, \ldots, N, \tag{4.5.2}$$

where the pairs of disturbances $(\varepsilon_{i1}, \varepsilon_{i2})$ are independently and identically distributed as bivariate normal with mean equal to zero and covariance matrix

$$\Sigma = \begin{bmatrix} \sigma_{11} & \sigma_{12} \\ \sigma_{12} & \sigma_{22} \end{bmatrix}. \tag{4.5.3}$$

Finally, we assume that $X_i$ and $y_{i2}$ are available for all $N$ observations but that $y_{i1}$ is measured only for the $n$ observations for which $y_{i2} > 0$.

A wide range of situations may fit this model. The classic example in economics concerns the explanation of wage rates for women. Here the second part of Eq. (4.5.2) is a probit equation explaining whether a woman works ($y_{i2} > 0$) or does not ($y_{i2} \leq 0$). The dependent variable $y_{i1}$ of the first equation is the woman's wage rate, and this is available only if she works. The problem is to estimate $\beta_1$, which gives the effects of explanatory variables on the (potential) wage rate, without incurring bias due to the exclusion of nonworkers.

Note that the variable $y_1$ is assumed to be meaningful for all observations (e.g., there is some potential wage rate that nonworkers would receive if they chose to work) but is observed only for some observations. This is rather different from the Tobit case, in which some value is observed for all observations, though it may be zero for some observations. For example, in the analysis of total length of sentences, we could use the two-equation sample selection model, letting $y_{i2}$ represent whether a prison sentence is given ($y_{i2} > 0$) or not ($y_{i2} \leq 0$) and letting $y_{i1}$ represent the length of the sentence to be given, if a sentence is indeed given. The problem with this usage is that it is not at all clear that it is meaningful to talk about $y_{i1}$ (the "potential sentence") existing with a nonzero value for observations such that $y_{i2} \leq 0$ (no sentence given). Thus the parameters $\beta_1$ would be very hard to interpret. In such a case either the Tobit model or its extended version of the last section would seem to be preferable.

We have assumed that $y_{i1}$ is observed if $y_{i2} > 0$; this is the sample selection rule. Now $y_{i2} > 0$ is equivalent to $\varepsilon_{i2} > -X_i'\beta_2$; thus the equivalent of Eq. (4.5.1) is

$$E(y_{i1}|y_{i1} \text{ observed}) = X_i'\beta_1 + E(\varepsilon_{i1}|\varepsilon_{i2} > -X_i'\beta_2). \tag{4.5.4}$$

The last term in Eq. (4.5.4) follows from the properties of the bivariate normal distribution and is

$$E(\varepsilon_{i1}|\varepsilon_{i2} > -X_i'\beta_2) = \frac{\sigma_{12}}{\sqrt{\sigma_{22}}}\left(\frac{f_i^*}{1 - F_i^*}\right), \tag{4.5.5}$$

where $f_i^*$ and $F_i^*$ are shorthand for the standard normal density and cdf, respectively, evaluated at $-X_i'\beta_2/\sqrt{\sigma_{22}}$. If we let $\lambda_i = f_i^*/(1 - F_i^*)$ and $\xi = \sigma_{12}/\sqrt{\sigma_{22}}$, inserting Eq. (4.5.5) into Eq. (4.5.4) gives

$$E(y_{i1}|y_{i1} \text{ observed}) = X_i'\beta + \xi\lambda_i. \tag{4.5.6}$$

From this perspective, least squares of $y_{i1}$ on $X_i$, using observations such that $y_{i1}$ is observed, is biased, because it omits the "regressor" $\lambda_i$. [Incidentally, the regressor $\lambda_i$ has a straightforward interpretation: $\sqrt{\sigma_{22}}\lambda_i = E(\varepsilon_{i2}|\varepsilon_{i2} > 0)$.] The exception, of course, is if $\xi = 0$, which is to say if $\sigma_{12} = 0$; this makes sense, because there should be no bias if the sample selection rule is uncorrelated with the error term in the equation of interest.

It is fairly easy to test for sample selection bias by testing whether $\xi = 0$ in Eq. (4.5.6). A two-step procedure is commonly used to do this. The first step is the estimation of the $y_{i2}$ part of Eq. (4.5.2), based on the complete sample. From this we can form an estimate $\hat{\lambda}_i$ of $\lambda_i$. The second step is the estimation of the $y_{i1}$ equation by regressing $y_{i1}$ on $X_i$ and $\hat{\lambda}_i$; the hypothesis $\xi = 0$ can be tested using a simple $t$-test. If we conclude that $\xi = 0$, the variable $\hat{\lambda}_i$ can be dropped. If not, it may pay to estimate (4.5.2) by maximum likelihood, though this is actually seldom done because of the computational expense involved.

## 4.6. The Simultaneous Tobit Model

We return now to the basic Tobit model of (4.3.2) and (4.3.3). A basic assumption that it shares with the usual regression model is that the explanatory variables $X_i$ can be treated as fixed. Statistically, it is assumed that the $X_i$ are either fixed (nonrandom) or independent of the error term $\varepsilon_i$. This amounts to the assumption of one-way causality between the $X_i$ and the dependent variable $y_i$; the $X_i$ affect $y_i$, as the model indicates, but the $y_i$ does not affect $X_i$.

Failure of this assumption leads to consideration of systems of simultaneous equations, a staple topic in econometrics. A treatment of this topic beyond the intuitive level is beyond the scope of this discussion. Briefly, if $y_i$ does affect one of the $X_i$, we need to enlarge our model by adding an equation showing this effect and estimate this enlarged system. Failure to do so (that is, treating $X_i$ as fixed when in fact it is affected by $y_i$) causes biased and inconsistent estimates, a problem usually called *simultaneous equations bias*.

The version of the simultaneous Tobit model that we present here was developed by Sickles and Schmidt (1979):

$$z_i = X_i'\beta_1 + \gamma_1 y_{i2} + \varepsilon_{i1}, \tag{4.6.1}$$

$$y_{i2} = X_i'\beta_2 + \gamma_2 y_{i1} + \varepsilon_{i2}, \tag{4.6.2}$$

$$\begin{aligned} y_{i1} &= \begin{cases} z_i & \text{if } z_i > 0 \\ 0 & \text{if } z_i \le 0 \end{cases} \\ &= \max(0, z_i). \end{aligned} \tag{4.6.3}$$

Here $y_{i1}$ is the Tobit variable that depends in Eqs. (4.6.1) and (4.6.3) on fixed explanatory variables $X_i$ and on $y_{i2}$; $y_{i2}$ is a standard dependent variable observed for all $i$, and depends in Eq. (4.6.2) on $X_i$ and $y_{i1}$. It is assumed that the error terms $\varepsilon_{i1}$, $\varepsilon_{i2}$ are independently and identically distributed as $N(0, \Sigma)$, with $\Sigma$ as given in Eq. (4.5.3).

Equations (4.6.1) and (4.6.3) constitute a Tobit model for $y_1$. However, Eq. (4.6.2) indicates that $y_1$ affects $y_2$ and thus that it is incorrect to treat $y_2$ as fixed in Eq. (4.6.1). Using standard Tobit analysis on Eq. (4.6.1) and (4.6.3) while treating $y_2$ as fixed would lead to inconsistent estimates.

This model may be estimated consistently by maximum likelihood. The likelihood function is unfortunately messy and therefore difficult and expensive to maximize. Let $g(\varepsilon_1, \varepsilon_2)$ be the density of the $N(0, \Sigma)$ distribution, and let the first $n$ observations be those for which $y_{i1} > 0$, so that the last $N - n$ $y_{i1}$ equal zero. Then the likelihood function is

$$L = \prod_{i=1}^{n} (1 - \gamma_1\gamma_2) g(y_{i1} - \gamma_1 y_{i2} - X_i'\beta_1, y_{i2} - \gamma_2 y_{i1} - X_i'\beta_2)$$

$$\times \prod_{i=n+1}^{N} \int_{-\infty}^{c_i} g(\varepsilon_1, y_{i2} - X_i'\beta_2)\, d\varepsilon_1, \tag{4.6.4}$$

where $c_i = -\gamma_1 y_{i2} - X_i'\beta_1$. (The difficult part of maximizing this is the need to calculate the integrals in the second part.) Alternatively, it is possible to use a computationally simpler procedure based on only the positive $y_{i1}$, analogous to Eq. (4.2.15) for the truncated normal case, to obtain estimates that are consistent but inefficient. The details can be found in Sickles and Schmidt (1979, p. 13). These estimates are useful mainly as starting values for the iterative calculation of the maximum likelihood estimates.

## 4.7. Summary

In this chapter we discussed methods of analysis of dependent variables that are censored or truncated. Such methods are of great potential interest in criminal justice research because many variables of interest, or at least their observable proxies, are either truncated or censored. Although at least some of the categorical variable techniques discussed in Chapter 2 are now quite extensively known and are used with increasing frequency in criminal justice research, techniques for the proper analysis of variables that are truncated or censored are much less well known and have seen very limited use. Indeed, one of the major criticisms of sentencing research discussed by the National Academy of Sciences' Panel on Sentencing Research (see Panel on Sentencing Research, 1982) was the failure of this research to deal with the sample selection problem that we discussed in Section 4.5.

The Tobit model of Section 4.3 is the best known and most widely used of the models that we discussed in this chapter. It is potentially appropriate when the dependent variable in a regression is nonnegative and when zero is a common value. However, it rests on rather strong assumptions and is restrictive in that it allows one set of parameters to determine both the probability that an observation be zero and the distribution of the positive observations.

In Section 4.4 we introduced a model, developed by Cragg (1971), that allows different factors (and parameters) to determine the probability that the dependent variable is zero, and its distribution given that it is positive.

This model contains the Tobit model as a special case and thus, when estimated, can be used to test for the appropriateness of Tobit analysis. Unfortunately, this model is much more difficult and costly to estimate than the Tobit model.

In Section 4.5 we discussed the sample selection problem. This problem has received considerable attention in labor economics (e.g., in connection with the estimation of wage equations for women) and has recently received some attention in criminal justice research. [See Rossi, Berk, and Lenihan (1980) or Panel on Sentencing Research (1982).] The sample selection problem arises whenever the rule for selection of the sample observations affects the distribution of the selected observations. This is certainly the case in censored or truncated samples. However, sample selection need not be based on the value of the dependent variable for sample selection bias to occur. It may be based on a second variable, which is correlated with the dependent variable. In this situation it is necessary to estimate a two-equation model that includes an equation for the probability of observing a nonzero value for the dependent variable as well as an equation for the value of the dependent variable when it is observed. When estimating such a model it is possible to test for the presence of sample selection bias.

In Section 4.6 we discussed the simultaneous Tobit model, which is a variant of the Tobit model but allows for feedback from the (censored) dependent variable to one of the explanatory variables. This model will be applied in Chapter 12 to analyze the interaction between criminality and success in the legal labor market.

# Chapter 5

## Tobit Analysis of the Total Length of Time Sentenced for Recidivist Offenses

### 5.1. Introduction

In this chapter we apply the Tobit model to analyze the total length of all prison sentences received by an individual during a specific follow-up time after his release from prison. The finding of a positive value for this variable corresponds to the usual definition of recidivism. However, compared with the usual binary (yes–no) measure of recidivism, this variable obviously contains additional information—the length of time sentenced for those individuals who do receive prison sentences.

It should be noted that, in this definition, parole revocations were not counted as prison sentences. The only prison sentences counted were for convictions for new criminal offenses. However, because less than 30% of our sample was on parole at the time of release, this distinction is less important than it would be if our sample were made up entirely of parolees.

This information on total length of sentences is potentially useful for at least two reasons. First, it is of interest because of the high cost of imprisonment. With such costs in mind, an understanding of the factors that determine the length of time an individual is sentenced should be of more than academic interest. (See Chapters 13–16 for a detailed analysis of the costs of operating large-scale prisons.) Second, the information on total length of sentences is of interest because it may be considered a measure of the seriousness of postrelease criminal activity. Although there is a good deal of controversy concerning an appropriate measure of the seriousness of criminal activity,[1] total length of sentences may be a useful measure of seriousness for a number of reasons. First, it correlates highly with other measures of seriousness.[2] Also, it avoids the statistical and conceptual problems associated with the analysis of ordinal, or noncontinuous, scales. Finally, total length of sentences has the advantage that it reflects the judge's perception of seriousness, which may be influenced by extenuating circumstances, the results of presentencing investigations, and knowledge of the presence or absence of plea bargaining.

In Section 5.2 we analyze total length of sentences for basically the same sample (of 641 men who were in prison in North Carolina in 1969, 1971, or in both years) used in Chapter 3. In Sections 5.3 and 5.4 we perform a similar but more complete analysis of a larger and more representative sample consisting of all individuals released from prison in North Carolina in the first half of 1975. Finally, we present our conclusions in Section 5.5. The models estimated here will also be used in Chapter 8 in a program evaluation.

## 5.2. Analysis of the 1969 and 1971 Data

The data used in this section are described briefly in Section 3.2 and in detail in Appendix A. Therefore we shall note here only that they consist of information on 641 men who were in prison in North Carolina in either 1969 or 1971 (or both years). However, because some information was missing for some observations, the number of observations actually analyzed was 582. (This is a few less than the 596 observations analyzed in Chapter 3, because a slightly different set of variables is used.)

The dependent variable that we analyze is the total length (in months) of all prison sentences received by an individual during his follow-up period and is denoted *TTSENT*. The follow-up period during which such sentences are compiled is the period from the individual's release from prison until the end of the period in which the data were gathered. The length of the follow-up period varied from 3 to 71 months, with an average of 37 months.

Approximately 68% of the individuals in the sample received no prison sentence during their follow-up period and therefore had a *TTSENT* value of zero. The remaining individuals had *TTSENT* values ranging from 1 to 480 months, with a mean value of 45 months.

From a statistical point of view, the salient features of *TTSENT* are that it is nonnegative and that zero is a common value. In the terminology of Chapter 4, it is censored (from below) at zero. Thus a potentially appropriate statistical technique to analyze *TTSENT* would be the Tobit model of Section 4.3, or its generalization described in Section 4.4. We do not choose to use the two-equation sample selection model of Section 4.5 because a zero value of *TTSENT* is numerically meaningful; it is not just an indication of nonobservability of the total length of time sentenced. (Also, it does not seem meaningful to impute a well-defined, though unobserved, "potential" value of total length of sentences to those who did not receive such a sentence.)

We have chosen to use the Tobit model to analyze *TTSENT* rather than the more general model of Section 4.4, mainly because of the extra difficulty and computational expense that the latter would entail. In using the Tobit model we are asserting that the factors influencing the probability of no prison sentence are the same as the factors influencing the distribution of positive sentences. This does not strike us as unreasonable in the present context. Furthermore, because only about 30% of our sample receives a positive sentence, the Tobit model should be expected to imply a small (nearly zero) mode for the positive values of *TTSENT*. In our sample the mode was at about 6 months, which is indeed small enough that we have no cause to question the specification seriously.

The explanatory variables that were used are essentially the same as those used in the analyses of Chapter 3. Specifically, the list of explanatory variables used is as follows: *CNST*, *RACE*, *CONPBS*, *WR*, *ALCHY*, *JUNKY*, *MS*, *AFA*, *AAR*, *PROPTY*, *PERSON*, *SG*, *RULE*, *MF*, *LENG*, and squared *LENG*. These variables are defined in Section 3.3, with the following three exceptions: (1) *CONPBS* is the number of convictions resulting in imprisonment, prior to the sample sentence; it differs from *CONVBS* of Section 3.3 in that it does not count prior convictions that did not result in imprisonment; (2) *ALCHY* is a dummy variable equal to one if the individual's record indicates a serious problem with alcohol and zero otherwise; and (3) *JUNKY* is a dummy variable that equals one if the individual's record indicates use of hard drugs. In Chapter 3 we used the single dummy variable *ALKY*, equal to one if either *ALCHY* or *JUNKY* equaled one.

The maximum likelihood estimates of the Tobit model with these explanatory variables and the dependent variable *TTSENT* are given in Table 5.1. The coefficients are as defined in Section 4.3. As discussed there, it is important to note that the size of a coefficient does *not* indicate the size of the effect of the associated variable on total length of sentences without some adjustment. The effect of a one-unit change in an explanatory variable on the dependent variable is given by the associated coefficient *multiplied by*

**TABLE 5.1.** Results Using 1969 and 1971 Data of Tobit Analysis of Length of Time Sentenced Large Specification

| Variable | Coefficient | $t$ Ratio |
|---|---|---|
| *CNST* | −31.4520 | −0.68 |
| *RACE* | 28.0709 | 2.55 |
| *CONPBS* | 2.6856 | 2.49 |
| *WR* | −27.0524 | −2.48 |
| *ALCHY* | 47.4526 | 4.06 |
| *JUNKY* | 37.8549 | 1.17 |
| *MS* | −28.1526 | −2.38 |
| *AFA* | −0.1425 | −1.77 |
| *AAR* | −0.1411 | −2.22 |
| *PROPTY* | 25.0125 | 1.97 |
| *PERSON* | 22.6309 | 1.36 |
| *SG* | 2.1931 | 1.01 |
| *RULE* | 3.0358 | 0.87 |
| *MF* | −10.1536 | −0.78 |
| *LENG* | 0.2050 | 0.11 |
| $LENG^2$ | 0.1216 | 0.05 |

the probability that the dependent variable be nonzero. This probability varies over individuals but, on average, would be roughly equal to the sample proportion of recidivists, which is about 0.32. Thus a *RACE* coefficient of about 28 does not indicate that a white individual ($RACE = 1$) will, on average, receive 28 months more in sentences than a nonwhite one ($RACE = 0$). Rather, the correct differential is about 28 times 0.32, or about 9 months.

The $t$ ratios are used to test the hypothesis that the associated coefficients are zero. In large samples a $t$ ratio is distributed as $N(0, 1)$ under the null hypothesis that its coefficient is zero.

Overall the results seem reasonable. The coefficients of the variables *CONPBS*, *WR*, *ALCHY*, *MS*, *AFA*, and *AAR* all have signs that do not appear unreasonable, and all are significant at the 5% level (for a two-tailed test), except *AFA*, which is significant at the 10% level. These results indicate that an individual will tend to have a smaller value of *TTSENT* the fewer previous convictions he has, if he participated in the work release program, if he did not have a serious alcohol problem, if he was married, and if he was relatively old both at time of first arrest and at release. These findings are quite similar to the findings of previous studies of recidivism. For a recent survey, see Monohan (1981). Greenwood (1981) reports similar results for individuals incarcerated in California, Michigan, and Texas.

The crime-type dummies *PROPTY* and *PERSON* are both positive, which seems reasonable; *PROPTY* is statistically significant at the 5% level. The variables *SG*, *RULE*, and *MF* all have coefficients that are insignificantly different from zero at the 5% level; none seems unreasonable in sign or magnitude. What is surprising, though, is that the length of the follow-up period *LENG* and its squared value $LENG^2$ do not have significant coefficients. Even when we dropped $LENG^2$, the coefficient of *LENG* remained insignificant; its $t$ ratio increased only to 0.74. Because *TTSENT* is the total length of time sentenced *during the follow-up period*, we would have expected it to be larger for individuals who were followed for longer periods. This is consistent with *LENG*'s positive coefficient. However, as just noted, the relationship we actually found was not statistically significant. This is probably because most individuals who return to criminal activity do so quickly. For the current sample, of those who were reconvicted, 69% were reconvicted during their first year after release and 90% within 2 years of release. Wilkins (1970) has noted this same rapidity of return as well as the fact that those who returned earlier also returned with more serious offenses. Waldo and Griswald (1979) also note that recidivism patterns are generally firmly set during the first 12 months after release.

The large and very significant positive effect of *RACE* is striking in light of the somewhat inconclusive previous work on the effect of race on recidivism. It is consistent with the earlier findings of Guze (1965), Schnur (1949), and Peterson and Braiker (1980), as well as with our results in Chapter 3 but is contrary to those of Mannering (1958), Cook (1975), Palmer and Carlson (1976), and Myers (1982). The unique feature of the current finding is its high degree of statistical significance, because previous studies have generally found, at most, marginally significant effects of race.

Because seven variables (*PERSON*, *SG*, *RULE*, *MF*, *LENG*, $LENG^2$, and *JUNKY*) each had coefficients that were insignificantly different from zero at the usual confidence levels, we redid the analysis without these variables. However, because the coefficient of *JUNKY* was insignificantly different from the coefficient of *ALCHY* (as well as insignificantly different from zero), rather than discard *JUNKY* we combined the variables *ALCHY* and *JUNKY* into the single dummy variable *ALKY*, equal to one for individuals with either a serious drug problem or a record of use of hard drugs. Because only one individual in the sample had both *ALCHY* and *JUNKY* equal to one, *ALKY* is virtually equal to $ALCHY + JUNKY$, and this combination of variables into a single variable follows from our inability to reject the hypothesis that their coefficients are equal.

For the variables still in the specification, the results were very similar to those just described, except that the coefficient of *PROPTY* fell to 16.64 and its $t$ ratio fell to 1.49. We therefore also dropped this variable from the specification and reran the model on the final set of remaining variables—*CNST*, *RACE*, *CONPBS*, *WR*, *ALKY*, *MS*, *AFA*, and *AAR*. These results are given in Table 5.2 and are still similar to those just discussed.

We can also test the joint significance of the variables we dropped using a likelihood ratio test. (This is analogous to the *F*-test of joint significance in a linear regression.) When we test the hypothesis that the coefficients of the variables dropped are all equal to zero and that the coefficients of *ALCHY* and *JUNKY* are equal, the likelihood ratio test statistic is 5.18. The relevant distribution is chi-squared with eight degrees of freedom, and 5.18 is easily seen to be far from significant at the usual levels. By way of contrast, if we test the hypothesis that the seven nonconstant variables in the specification (*RACE*, *CONPBS*, *WR*, *ALKY*, *MS*, *AFA*, *AAR*) all have coefficients equal to zero, the likelihood ratio test statistic is 60.76. This is significant at any reasonable level.

The results just presented indicate positive and significant effects on *TTSENT* of *RACE*, *CONPBS*, and *ALKY* and negative and significant effects on *TTSENT* of *WR*, *MS*, *AFA*, and *AAR*. The type of individual most likely to have a large value of *TTSENT* is a young, white, unmarried alcoholic (or hard drug user), who was first arrested at an early age, was young at the time of release, was not on the work release program, and had many previous prison convictions. Conversely, an old, black, married non-addict, who was relatively old when first arrested and when released, had not had many previous convictions, and was on the work release program is least likely to have a large value of *TTSENT*.

To see more precisely what this means, we have plotted in Fig. 5.1 the frequencies of *TTSENT* implied by our results for these two types of individuals, as well as for the "average" individual (i.e., characteristics equal to the mean values of the explanatory variables in our sample). The figure shows the probability that *TTSENT* is greater than *N* months. Note that

**TABLE 5.2.** Results Using 1969 and 1971 Data of Tobit Analysis of Length of Time Sentenced—Small Specification

| Variable | Coefficient | *t* Ratio |
|---|---|---|
| *CNST* | 28.3967 | 1.49 |
| *RACE* | 27.2002 | 2.50 |
| *CONPBS* | 2.6524 | 2.49 |
| *WR* | −27.0353 | −2.51 |
| *ALKY* | 44.9298 | 3.99 |
| *MS* | −30.2686 | −2.60 |
| *AFA* | −0.1669 | −2.15 |
| *AAR* | −0.1621 | −2.62 |

$P(TTSENT > 0)$ is the probability of at least one prison sentence and corresponds to a common definition of recidivism. It might also be worth pointing out that, as indicated earlier, our results do not indicate that these probabilities are very sensitive to the length of the follow-up period. Because the average length of the follow-up period was approximately 3 years, we can roughly interpret these as projected frequencies of *TTSENT* for various types of individuals during a follow-up period of approximately 3 years.

The solid line gives these probabilities for a hypothetical "average" individual, defined as one whose values of the explanatory variables equal the sample means; i.e., $RACE = 0.503$, $CONPBS = 2.19$, $WR = 0.462$, $ALKY = 0.481$, $MS = 0.311$, $AFA = 280.3$, and $AAR = 380.1$. This case corresponds to an "average" frequency for *TTSENT*. According to the figure, such an individual has a probability of receiving some sentence—that is, a probability of recidivism—of 27%. (This corresponds reasonably closely to the actual proportion of recidivists in our sample, 0.33.) The probability that such an individual will be sentenced to more than 2 years is 19%, and for 4 years the probability is 14%. Our "average" individual is relatively unlikely to receive a sentence of more than 8 years and very unlikely to receive a sentence of more than 20 years.

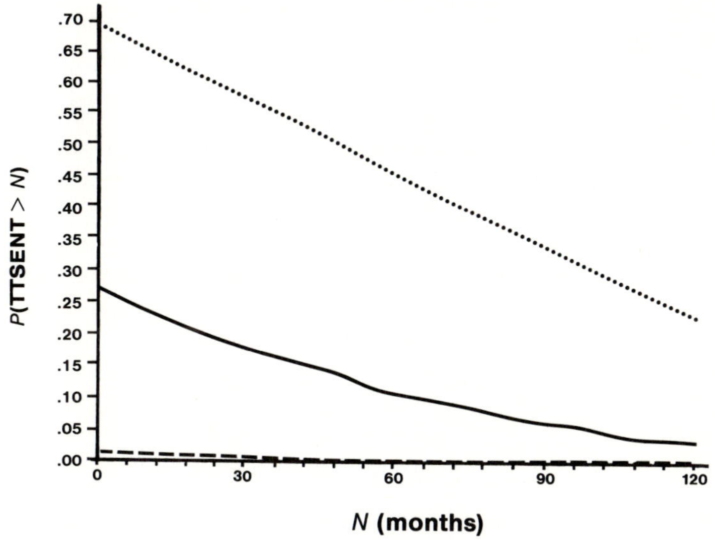


**Fig. 5.1.** Probabilities of various times sentenced for individuals with certain characteristics. Solid line indicates an "average" individual, dashed line indicates an individual with very favorable characteristics, and dotted line indicates an individual with very unfavorable characteristics.

The dashed line gives probabilities for an individual with very favorable characteristics; i.e., an old ($AAR = 600$), nonwhite individual who is married, is not an alcoholic or user of hard drugs, was fairly old when first arrested ($AFA = 480$), was on work release, and did not have any previous convictions. Such an individual's probability of some time sentenced is only 2%, which is strikingly less than the value of 27% for an "average" individual. The other probabilities are also much lower than for the "average" individual.

The dotted line gives probabilities for an individual with very unfavorable characteristics; that is, a young ($AAR = 216$) white who is not married, is an alcoholic or drug addict, was very young when first arrested ($AFA = 156$), was not on work release, and had four previous convictions. For such an individual there is a probability of recidivism of almost 70%. Such an individual is quite likely (probability = 24%) to receive a sentence of 10 years or more.

Because there were no individuals in our sample whose characteristics were all as favorable or unfavorable as those of the two hypothetical individuals just discussed, these results should be considered illustrative. They indicate the strong influence of personal characteristics on severity of recidivist crime that our model has found.

## 5.3. Analysis of the 1975 Data

The data used in this section and in Section 5.4 are described in detail in Appendix B, so only a brief description will be given here. Our original sample consisted of all individuals released from the North Carolina Department of Correction during the first 6 months of 1975. Information on the personal characteristics of these individuals was taken from the computerized inmate histories of the department. The postrelease record of the individuals was determined by a search of the department's records in February 1977. Thus, the follow-up period ranged from 25 to 31 months.

There were 4881 individuals released from the Department of Correction during the first 6 months of 1975. However, only 2216 (45%) of these individuals' records contained information on all the variables that we needed for our analysis of length of sentence. The most frequently missing item was information on drug or alcohol abuse, which was missing in 42% of the records.[3] Furthermore, this variable (*ALKY*) was the most highly significant variable in our analysis of the 1969 and 1971 data, so we felt that we should not proceed without it. We have therefore restricted our attention to the subsample of 2216 observations with complete observations.

Unfortunately, there are some significant differences between the subsample of 2216 observations for which all information is available and the rest of the original sample. In general, more information was available for individuals who had been in prison for shorter periods of time prior to their 1975 release, reflecting a steady increase in the quality and completeness of the department's inmate records. Differences in postrelease criminal activity were fairly small, though individuals with complete information tended to return earlier and with longer sentences.

Although the subsample with complete information is not completely representative of the population of 1975 releases, we decided that it was sufficiently representative to be worth analyzing. This was thought to be preferable to an analysis of a representative population with the omission of important variables. Some further evidence on the representativity of the sample will be presented at the end of Section 5.4.

Of these 2216 observations with complete data, 600 were randomly selected to be used to validate our model; this will be referred to as the *validation sample*. The remaining 1616 observations constitute the *estimation sample*. The proportions of individuals with positive length of sentence ($TTSENT > 0$) were essentially the same in the two subsamples: 200 of 1616 (12.4%) versus 74 of 600 (12.3%).

Based on the 1616 observations in the estimation sample, we performed a Tobit analysis of the dependent variable *TTSENT*, defined (as in the last section) as the total length of all prison sentences received during the follow-up period. The explanatory variables tried were essentially the same as in the last section, as well; *CNST*, *RACE*, *ALCHY*, *JUNKY*, *SUPER*, *CONVS*, *SEX*, *AAR*, *PROPTY*, *PERSON*, *MF*, *MS*, *WR*, *RULE*, and *SG*. These are defined in Section 3.3, except for *ALCHY* and *JUNKY*, which are defined in the previous section, and for the following two variables. First, *SEX* is a dummy variable equal to one for males and zero for females; it did not arise before because the 1969 and 1971 data set contained only males. Second, the variable *RACE* here is a dummy variable equal to zero for blacks and one for nonblacks. This differs slightly from the definition for the 1969 and 1971 data, in which *RACE* was equal to one for whites and zero for nonwhites. The difference is that Native Americans are grouped with whites here but were grouped with blacks in the previous data set. This was done because, in our examination of this data set, Native Americans appeared more similar in their actions to whites than to blacks. (There are 48 Native Americans among the 1616 observations in the estimation sample, so this is a minor but not trivial point.) Finally, two variables used in the last section are not used here: *AFA*, because it was too often missing and not worth the reduction in sample size it would have caused; and *LENG*, because it did not vary much in the current sample and was not important in the previous analysis.

The results for our Tobit analysis with the full set of explanatory variables are given in Table 5.3. (The format is the same as for Tables 5.1 and 5.2.) Six variables—*JUNKY*, *PERSON*, *MF*, *MS*, *WR*, and *RULE*—had coefficients that were not even close to being statistically significant at usual levels, having $t$ ratios less than 0.5 in absolute value. The $\chi^2$ statistic for the joint significance of these six variables was only 0.54, which is further evidence of their insignificance. These variables were therefore dropped from the model.[4] This raised the $t$ ratio of *PROPTY* to 1.70 but increased the absolute value of the $t$ ratio of *SG* to only 1.38; all other variables remained unambiguously significant. The variable *SG* was therefore dropped, but *PROPTY* was retained on the basis of significance at the 10% level. This yields our final specification, the results of which are given in Table 5.4. It may be noted that the likelihood ratio test statistic for the seven variables that were dropped in going from the original specification to the final one is 2.44, which is not close to the usual critical points of $\chi^2_7$. Also it may be noted that, for the variables in the final specification, the results in Tables 5.3 and 5.4 are not very different.

The results of Table 5.4 indicate that the type of individual who is most likely to have a large value of *TTSENT* is a young, black, male alcoholic with a lot of previous convictions, whose release was unsupervised, and whose sample crime was against property. Conversely, the type of individual who will tend to have a small (probably zero) value of *TTSENT* is an

**TABLE 5.3.** Results Using 1975 Data of Tobit Analysis of Length of Time Sentenced—Large Specification

| Variable | Coefficient | $t$ Ratio |
|---|---|---|
| *CNST* | −114.3451 | −2.35 |
| *RACE* | −28.8246 | −2.50 |
| *ALCHY* | 35.6414 | 2.85 |
| *JUNKY* | 3.2329 | 0.20 |
| *SUPER* | −47.8980 | −3.93 |
| *CONVBS* | 4.5061 | 3.65 |
| *SEX* | 75.3010 | 2.26 |
| *AAR* | −0.2609 | −4.02 |
| *PROPTY* | 20.9998 | 1.64 |
| *PERSON* | 4.7266 | 0.23 |
| *MF* | −4.3318 | −0.35 |
| *MS* | −3.5495 | −0.28 |
| *WR* | −4.5968 | −0.31 |
| *RULE* | 2.2805 | 0.42 |
| *SG* | −3.1714 | −1.31 |

old, nonblack, female nonalcoholic who had no previous convictions, whose release was supervised, and whose sample crime was not against property.

There are some strong similarities between these results for the 1975 data and the results of the last section for the 1969 and 1971 data. The coefficient of age at release *AAR* is significant and negative in both samples. Previous convictions (measured slightly differently, as *CONPBS* for 1969 and 1971 and as *CONVBS* for 1975) have a significant positive effect in both samples. Alcohol abuse (measured by *ALKY* for 1969 and 1971 and by ALCHY for 1975) has a significant positive effect in both samples. The effect of a previous property offense *PROPTY* was marginally significantly positive in both samples.

There are also some minor differences between the two sets of results. The work release dummy *WR* had a negative effect in both cases but was significant only for 1969 and 1971. The same is true for the marital status dummy *MS*. The variables *SUPER* and *SEX* had significant effects in the 1975 sample but were not used for the analysis of the 1969 and 1971 sample, whereas the opposite is true of the variable AFA.

The only major difference between the two sets of results is in the coefficient of the variable *RACE*. Our finding for the 1975 data, that blacks are likely to have higher values of *TTSENT*, is exactly the opposite of the finding previously reported for the 1969 and 1971 data. The definition of *RACE* in both analyses was checked carefully to make sure this difference was not due to inconsistency in coding the *RACE* dummy. We also checked to make sure that it was not due to the differing treatment of Native Americans discussed previously. The only remaining explanations are that (i) things changed significantly between the 1969–1971 period, when the previous samples' individuals were released, and 1975[5], or that (ii) either the previous finding or the present one is an artifact, owing to the nonrepresentative

**TABLE 5.4.** Results Using 1975 Data of Tobit Analysis of Length of Time Sentenced—Small Specification

| Variable | Coefficient | *t* Ratio |
|---|---|---|
| *CNST* | −147.0493 | −3.70 |
| *RACE* | −28.5621 | −2.52 |
| *ALCHY* | 36.4506 | 2.92 |
| *SUPER* | −50.9524 | −4.38 |
| *CONVBS* | 4.5643 | 3.71 |
| *SEX* | 75.6914 | 2.23 |
| *AAR* | −0.2554 | −4.16 |
| *PROPTY* | 21.2130 | 1.77 |

nature of the data used. This is especially possible considering that our usable data set for this analysis of 2216 individuals represents only 45% of the individuals released in the first half of 1975. In Chapter 7 we shall report some further results that hint that this might indeed be the cause of this phenomenon.

The estimated model presented in Table 5.4 was checked by using it to predict the values of *TTSENT* for the 600 observations in the validation sample. For each individual in the validation sample, the predicted *TTSENT* was the expected value of *TTSENT* for that individual, as given by formula (4.3.4). The average predicted value of *TTSENT* in the validation sample was 7.135, whereas the actual average *TTSENT* was 5.502. Thus the model overpredicts *TTSENT* in the validation sample by about 30%. Clearly, this is not very satisfactory. However, it should be noted that this prediction error, while large, is not statistically significant. The standard error of this difference, under the hypothesis of an adequate (correctly specified) model, is

$$\left(\frac{1}{600}\sum_{i=1}^{600} V_i\right)^{1/2}, \tag{5.3.1}$$

where $V_i$ is the variance of *TTSENT* for individual $i$. To calculate $V_i$, let $E_i$ be the expected value of *TTSENT* as given by Eq. (4.3.4), let $S_i$ be the expected value of $TTSENT^2$ conditional on $TTSENT > 0$ as given by Eq. (4.2.12), and let $1 - F_i^*$ be as used in either expression. Then the expected value of $TTSENT^2$ (*not* conditional on $TTSENT > 0$) is $(1 - F_i^*)S_i$, and it follows that the variance of *TTSENT* is

$$V_i = (1 - F_i^*)S_i - E_i^2. \tag{5.3.2}$$

We can therefore form a test statistic whose numerator is the difference between average predicted and average actual *TTSENT* and whose denominator is Eq. (5.3.1). Under the null hypothesis of correct specification of the model, this test statistic would be distributed as $N(0, 1)$ in large samples. In the present case, the test statistic is 1.43, which is not statistically significant at usual levels.

Of course, a 30% overprediction, even if it is statistically insignificant, is not satisfactory. What the preceding calculation tells us is just that *TTSENT* is hard to predict; even a correctly specified model will predict *TTSENT* only with a large variance. Although we shall try to refine the model in the next section to improve its predictive ability, we should realize at the outset that this will not be an easy task.

## 5.4. Analysis of Subsamples of the 1975 Data

In the last section we estimated our model on a sample of 1616 individuals and validated the model on a further sample of 600 individuals. These samples included all individuals for whom the necessary data were available. We shall now attempt to improve on those results by estimating *separate* models for various race, sex, and age groupings. The idea, of course, is that the effects of race, sex, and age may be more complex than those that can be captured by merely including *RACE*, *SEX*, and *AAR* variables in the specification. We are looking for interactions of *RACE*, *SEX*, and *AAR* with each other or with the other explanatory variables and allowing the error variance to be different across race, sex, and age subsamples.

In splitting our data into subsamples, we are faced with two conflicting considerations. First, we would like the individuals in each group to be as homogeneous as possible. This argues for a large number of finely defined groups. Second, we want a fairly large number of observations (say, a few hundred) in each group, to ensure good estimates. This means that we must limit the number of groups used, because we have only 1616 individuals in our estimation sample.

Our original plan was to separate the sample into the following six groups; (1) white male adults ($AAR \geq 252$); (2) black male adults; (3) white male youths ($AAR < 252$); (4) black male youths; (5) other males (mainly Native Americans); and (6) females. The smallest of these groups is Group (5), which contains only 48 observations in the estimation sample. It consists of males whose race classification is neither white nor black (e.g., Native American or Oriental). Because most of these individuals (44 of 48) are Native Americans, we shall simply refer to this as our sample of male Native Americans.

Because it was not clear that we could hope to fit a satisfactory model to only 48 observations, the subsample of male Native Americans was the first that we tried. It proved computationally impossible to obtain results with the full list of explanatory variables tried in Section 5.3 (except, of course, *RACE* and *SEX*, which do not vary in this subsample). However, we were able to obtain results for this subsample for the specification finally arrived at in the last section as reported in Table 5.4, except that, as noted previously, *RACE* and *SEX* have been necessarily deleted from this specification. These results were rather bizarre. The only variable whose coefficient even approached statistical significance was *SUPER*. Furthermore, *ALCHY* and *CONVBS* had the "wrong" sign (a sign different from that found for the entire sample of 1616). It appears that even this small a model cannot be satisfactorily estimated from only 48 observations.

There is one other point worth considering in this regard. In the overall analysis of the last section, Native Americans were treated implicitly as whites. This is so because our *RACE* variable was defined as zero for blacks and one for all nonblacks, including both whites and Indians. The reasons for this were that (i) in our preliminary analysis, a separate Native American dummy variable was always very insignificant and (ii) the relevant characteristics of the Native Americans more closely resembled those of whites than of blacks. One reasonable check on this classification is to validate the overall model on the 57 male Native Americans in our total sample of 2216 observations, treating them in turn as whites ($RACE = 1$) and blacks ($RACE = 0$). Treating them as whites was clearly better; the average predicted *TTSENT* of 7.424 was much closer to the actual average value of *TTSENT*, 6.667, than was the average predicted value of 10.092 that resulted from treating them as blacks.

The conclusion is that we were not able to arrive at a reasonable model for this subsample (male Native Americans) alone. Furthermore, it appears that there is little loss in treating the Native Americans as whites. As a result, we combined our subsample of male Native Americans with our two subsamples of white males. This gives us the following five subsamples to be used in the remainder of this section: (1) nonblack male adults; (2) black male adults; (3) nonblack male youths; (4) black male youths; and (5) females. A breakdown of the sample into these groups is given in Table 5.5.

We turn next to our subsample of females. We note at the outset that there are only 92 females in the estimation sample; this small sample size can be expected to cause some problems in obtaining a satisfactory model, and it does.

We first attempted to run the model containing all of the explanatory variables (except *SEX*) used in the overall analysis of Section 5.3. This proved

**TABLE 5.5.** Final Breakdown of 1975 Sample into Subsamples

| | Estimation sample | | Validation sample | |
|---|---|---|---|---|
| Category | Total observations | Observations $TTSENT > 0$ | Total observations | Observations $TTSENT > 0$ |
| Nonblack male adults | 612 | 74 | 231 | 24 |
| Black male adults | 474 | 59 | 178 | 24 |
| Nonblack male youths | 295 | 25 | 98 | 12 |
| Black male youths | 143 | 38 | 54 | 10 |
| Females | 92 | 4 | 39 | 4 |
| Total sample | 1616 | 200 | 600 | 74 |

computationally impossible, owing to apparent multicollinearity. (The algorithm would not converge.) Furthermore, the coefficients of *ALCHY*, *JUNKY*, *MS*, *WR*, *RULE*, *PROP*, and *PERS* were all very small (less than $10^{-14}$ in absolute value) and did not change across iterations of the algorithm.

We next ran the final specification (except *SEX*) of the overall model (see Table 5.4) on our subsample of females. The only variables that were statistically significant were *CNST* ($t = -12.30$) and *ALCHY* ($t = 10.94$). The reason *ALCHY* was so significant is that all four females with *TTSENT* > 0 have *ALCHY* = 1.

We next tried using all explanatory variables except those (listed previously) whose coefficients were very small in our first run; however, *ALKY* was included because of the result just mentioned. This run proved to be computationally feasible. *CONVBS* was very insignificant ($t = -0.46$), so it was dropped. This led to our final specification for females, the results of which are in Table 5.6.

Having arrived at a model for females, we next tested its predictions against those given by the overall model of Table 5.4. As was the case with our subsample of male Native Americans, this comparison was made difficult by the small number of individuals in the validation sample. There were only 39 females in the validation sample. Furthermore, these 39 individuals have different characteristics from the 92 individuals in the estimation sample; the mean value of *TTSENT* in the validation sample is 5.385, versus 0.848 in the estimation sample. As a result, it was decided to validate the models on all 131 females, recognizing that this gives an advantage to the model estimated only on the 92 females because in large part it is validated on the same sample on which it was estimated.

Nevertheless, the overall model did far better than did the females-only model reported in Table 5.6. For all 131 females, the average of *TTSENT* was 2.198. For the overall model, the average predicted value was 2.183, generating a test statistic of only 0.01. On the other hand, for the model for females the average predicted value was 1.337, yielding a test statistic of 2.05.

What this means is that we were unable to find a model for females only that generates better predictions for females than the overall model does. Indeed, the model we were able to generate predicted much more poorly than the overall model. What we tried next was to at least allow for interactions between *SEX* and some of the other explanatory variables in the overall model. Natural candidates for these interactions were those variables that were highly significant in the female model—*ALCHY*, *MF*, *SUPER*, *SG*. Unfortunately it proved impossible to include all of these interactions and the *SEX* variable itself, owing to multicollinearity between *CNST*, *SEX* and the *SEX–ALCHY* interaction. We tried dropping the *SEX–ALCHY*

**TABLE 5.6.** Results of Tobit Analysis of Length of Time Sentenced on Five Subsamples[a]

| | Females | | Nonblack male adults | | Black male adults | | Nonblack male youths | | Black male youths | |
|---|---|---|---|---|---|---|---|---|---|---|
| Variable | Coefficient | *t* Ratio | Coefficient | *t* Ratio | Coefficient | *t* Ratio | Coefficient | *t* Ratio | Coefficient | *t* Ratio |
| *CNST* | −473.9815 | −75.64 | −7.1261 | −0.23 | −104.7207 | −1.54 | 13.0822 | 0.22 | 370.5994 | 3.10 |
| *SUPER* | −73.4680 | −3.35 | −29.2442 | −2.72 | −45.2648 | −1.37 | −34.8355 | −1.64 | −30.0676 | −2.08 |
| *AAR* | 0.1122 | 1.89 | −0.2081 | −3.72 | −0.4571 | −2.50 | — | — | −1.8555 | −3.38 |
| *ALCHY* | 294.0501 | 46.92 | 41.6310 | 3.62 | — | — | — | — | 50.8109 | 2.54 |
| *CONVBS* | — | — | 2.4635 | 2.79 | 8.1359 | 2.42 | — | — | 18.2189 | 2.37 |
| *SG* | 10.7594 | 4.62 | −3.2593 | −1.65 | — | — | −11.5269 | −1.84 | — | — |
| *MF* | 53.3717 | 2.88 | — | — | — | — | −30.4911 | −1.34 | — | — |
| *RACE* | 26.7366 | 1.37 | — | — | — | — | — | — | — | — |
| *PROPTY* | — | — | 18.9777 | 1.69 | — | — | — | — | — | — |

[a] *N* values for subsamples are: females, 92; nonblack male adults, 612; black male adults, 474; nonblack male youths, 295; black male youths, 143.

interaction, but then the other three interactions were statistically insignificant, and we were led back to the original overall model. Therefore we simply concluded that the sample of females is too small to permit fitting a separate model for females.

Next we turn to our subsample of nonblack male adults. This constituted our largest subsample, 612 individuals. With this size sample, most of the problems we faced with male Native Americans and females did not occur.

We first ran the model with all explanatory variables (except race and sex). Certain variables were statistically insignificant: namely (with *t* ratios), *JUNKY* (0.27), *MF* (−0.18), *MS* (−0.94), *WR* (0.71), *RULE* (−0.77), and *PERSON* (0.66). Dropping these variables led to the specification and results given in Table 5.6.

Most of the results for this subsample were quite similar to those for the overall model of Table 5.4. The same explanatory variables were significant, except that *SG* is significant here but not in the overall model (and *RACE* and *SEX* do not appear here, of course). Most of the coefficients are even fairly similar in the two models—all are of the same sign, for example.

There were 231 nonblack male adults in the validation sample, which was enough to provide a good test of the predictive power of the model. The average value of *TTSENT* in the validation sample was 3.610 (which, incidentally, is fairly close to the average value for the estimation sample, 4.075). For the nonblack male adult model, the average predicted value of *TTSENT* was 4.432, yielding a test statistic of −0.75. This is better than the average predicted value of 5.541 and test statistic of −1.21 for the overall model applied to this group. Therefore, we conclude that the model for nonblack male adults, as given in Table 5.6, better accounts for the values of *TTSENT* of nonblack male adults than the overall model does.

Our subsample of black male adults contains 474 individuals. Nevertheless, almost all explanatory variables were insignificantly related to *TTSENT*. In this subsample our final specification for black male adults is given in Table 5.6 and contains only *CNST*, *SUPER*, *CONVBS*, and *AAR*. We left *SUPER* in the specification despite its low *t* ratio (1.37) to keep the specification from being ridiculously sparse. The other explanatory variables that were tried all had *t* ratios less than one in absolute value, as follow: *ALCHY* (0.55), *JUNKY* (0.84), *MF* (−0.29), *MS* (−0.17), *WR* (−0.93), *RULE* (−0.44), *SG* (−0.14), *PROPTY* (0.92), and *PERSON* (0.21). Furthermore, they were jointly insignificant, with the likelihood-ratio test statistic of only 5.15 being far less than the significance points of $\chi_9^2$.

We would not expect this simple a model to predict well, and it does not. The average value of *TTSENT* for the 178 black male adults in the validation sample was 6.775 (which was fairly close to the average in the estimation subsample of 6.320). The average predicted value of *TTSENT* for the model for black male adults was 10.429, yielding a test statistic of −1.15. On the other hand, the average predicted value of *TTSENT* from the overall model was 8.645, with a test statistic of −0.81. Incidentally, we also tried predictions based on the model for black male adults without *SUPER* included; its predictions were even worse than with *SUPER* included. We therefore concluded that we could not fit a reasonable model to the subsample of black male adults separately.

Our sample of nonblack male youths contains 295 individuals. As in the last analysis, most explanatory variables turned out to be insignificantly related to *TTSENT*. Our final specification is given in Table 5.6 and contains only *CNST*, *SUPER*, *SG*, and *MF*. We left in *MF* despite its low $t$ ratio (−1.34) to keep the specification from being too simple. The other explanatory variables were insignificant, as indicated by their low $t$ ratios: *ALCHY* (−0.84), *JUNKY* (0.96), *MS* (0.20), *WR* (0.37), *RULE* (0.38), *CONVBS* (0.05), *AAR* (−0.92), *PROPTY* (−0.12), and *PERSON* (0.99). The $\chi^2$ statistic, 6.45, was also insignificant.

In checking the predictions of the model, we again have a problem with the small size of the validation sample. There are 98 nonblack male youths in the validation sample. This is not a terribly small number, but it is nevertheless the case that the average value of *TTSENT* for these 98 individuals, 6.224, is considerably different than the average value for the 295 white male youths in the estimation sample, 3.648. We therefore decided to validate the model on the total of 393 white male youths.

For these 393 individuals, the average value of *TTSENT* was 4.290. For the overall model, the average predicted value was 7.415, with a test statistic of −2.47. For the subsample model, the average predicted value was 3.883, with a test statistic of 0.48, which is a clear improvement. Incidentally, we also made predictions with *MF* dropped from the nonblack male youth model; these were not as good as with *MF* included. Despite the simplicity of the model for nonblack male youths, as shown in Table 5.9, we therefore conclude that it is a better model for nonblack youths than the overall model is.

Our final subsample, black male youths, contains only 143 individuals. Nevertheless, we found more variables significantly related to *TTSENT* in this subsample than in the previous two subsamples. Our final specification is given in Table 5.6 and contains *CNST*, *ALCHY*, *SUPER*, *CONVBS*, and *AAR*. All of the coefficients look reasonable, though it is perhaps a bit surprising to find *AAR* significant in a sample of only youths. The other variables tried, with their $t$ ratios, were as follows: *JUNKY* (−1.38), *MF* (0.41), *MS* (0.79), *WR* (−0.01), *RULE* (1.37), *SG* (−0.20), *PROPTY* (1.46), and *PERSON* (−0.77). The $\chi^2$ statistic was 7.66.

The validation sample contained only 54 black male youths and had an average value of *TTSENT* of 8.167, which was different from the estimation sample average of 10.077. We therefore validated the model on the total sample of 197 black male youths. For these 197 individuals, the average value of *TTSENT* was 9.553. The overall model gave an average predicted value of 12.487 and a test statistic of −1.10. On the other hand, the model for black male youths gave an average predicted value of 10.656 and a test statistic of −0.66. We therefore conclude that, for the subsample of black male youths, the model for black male youths is superior to the overall model.

Our results for subsamples of the 1975 data are hard to summarize. Clearly, we have found differences in the models for the various race, sex, and age groups considered. For the most part, these are differences in which variables are significant or differences in the size of the coefficients. Only the model for females had "wrong" signs.

For the subsamples of nonblack male adults, nonblack male youths, and black male youths, the subsample models predicted better than the overall model, whereas for the subsamples of females and black male adults the opposite was true. The question of what model to recommend for the latter two groups is troublesome. There is no apparent basis for combining females with black male adults and estimating a model for these two groups jointly. The overall model can be used to make statements about these groups, but this is not very satisfactory because, if the subgroups really are fundamentally different, as it appears, the overall model is misspecified. Nevertheless, for lack of a better alternative, we shall use the overall model for these two groups.

The reader may recall that it was reported in Section 5.3 that the average value of *TTSENT* for the 600 individuals in the validation sample was 5.502. The average predicted value, using the overall model, was 7.135, and the statistic used to test the significance of this difference was equal to −1.43. We now attempt to see how much these predictions can be improved by using for each individual the "best" model for the subsample to which the individual belongs. That is, we separate individuals into the five groups described previously. Selecting the models that provide the best predictions, for females and black male adults, we use the overall model of Table 5.4. For nonblack male adults, nonblack male youths, and black male youths, we use the appropriate respective models of Table 5.6.

When this was done for the 600 individuals in the validation sample, the average predicted value of *TTSENT* was 6.090 (compared with the actual average value of 5.503 and the average predicted value from the overall model of 7.135), with a test statistic of −0.64 (compared with −1.43 for the overall model). We still overpredict *TTSENT*, but now only by 10.7%, compared with 29.7% for the overall model. This is a fairly impressive improvement and evidence that it is worth considering the subgroups of the data separately, as we have done.

Before closing this section, one other point needs to be made. The reader will recall that the models of the last two sections were based on a nonrandom data set. The 2216 individuals on whom all information was available constitute only 45% of the individuals released from North Carolina prisons in the first half of 1975. As noted previously, there are important differences in the group included and the group not included in this 45% sample. As such, our results may be misleading if applied to the entire prison population. However, we can get some evidence on the importance of the nonrandomness of our data by seeing how well the models predict for the 2665 individuals excluded from our estimation and validation samples because of missing values for *ALCHY* and/or *CONVBS*. This was done by assigning to those individuals with *ALCHY* missing the value $ALCHY = 0.424$ (the mean value for those individuals with *ALCHY* observed) and assigning to those individuals with *CONVBS* missing the value $CONVBS = 1.93$ (the mean value for those individuals with *CONVBS* observed). The predictions thus generated, using the best model for each subgroup (as previously), were quite satisfactory. The average predicted value of *TTSENT* was 7.256, compared with the true average value of *TTSENT* of 7.386. The test statistic for this difference was 0.27, which is quite insignificant. This suggests that the nonrepresentative nature of the data used to estimate our models may not be too much of a problem.

## 5.5. Summary and Conclusions

In this chapter we analyzed the total time to which an individual is sentenced (sum of all prison sentences received) during a follow-up period after release from prison. This variable is of interest both in its own right and because it is a measure of the seriousness of criminal activity. This analysis was done in Section 5.2 for a sample, taken in 1969 and 1971, of individuals who were in prison in North Carolina in either or both of those years, and in Sections 5.3 and 5.4 for a sample of individuals released from prison in North Carolina in the first half of 1975.

The results of our analysis of the 1969 and 1971 data indicate that the total length of sentences is longest for a young, white, unmarried alcoholic or drug addict, who was first arrested at an early age, was not on the work release program, was young at the time of his release from imprisonment, and had many previous prison sentences. On the other hand, our results for the 1975 data indicate that the type of individual most likely to have a large value of total length of sentences is a young, black, male alcoholic with many previous convictions, whose release from prison was unsupervised and whose sample crime was a crime against property. Although there are some differences in these results, chief of which is conflicting evidence on the effect of race, there are also some obvious similarities.

The results of our analyses are also somewhat encouraging because some of the variables that affect total length of sentences are subject to policy control. The total length of time sentenced was reduced significantly by participation in the North Carolina work release program in the 1969 and 1971 analysis and by a supervised release in the 1975 analysis. Time sentenced is also reduced significantly by increased age at release. Even if one is not willing to subscribe to a philosophy of "lock them up and throw away the key," this is encouraging because, given the gradual aging of the post-World War II baby boom generation and the present low levels of birth rates, the current crime problem may decrease naturally with time as the age distribution becomes less bottom-heavy. Finally, an important determinant of time sentenced after release is whether or not an individual has a serious alcohol problem. This would seem to indicate that effective programs to treat alcohol problems would be highly beneficial. The key word here is "effective." To date, most such programs have had marginal, if any, effects.

One of the most important aspects of the work reported in this chapter is that we were able to develop models of the total time sentenced after release that were able to predict accurately the average post release sentencing experience of individuals outside of the sample used to estimate the models. This is encouraging (and perhaps surprising), given the previous failure of most models of recidivism to predict well. However, it is consistent with more recent work [for an example, see Greenwood (1981), and for a survey, see Monohan (1981)] that has yielded better predictions than had previously been obtained. We believe that our ability to predict reliably stems from at least three factors; (1) the careful and thorough use of good data, which contains extensive individual information and detailed information on post-release recidivism; (2) the careful selection and use of appropriate statistical techniques; and (3) the estimation of group-specific recidivism models.

## Notes to Chapter 5

1. See Rossi, Waite, Bose, and Berk (1974) for a review and Center for Studies in Criminology and Criminal Law (1980) for a recently developed scale of seriousness.

2. Sellin and Wolfgang (1964) find that two measures of seriousness have high correlation (.875 and .938) with statutory sentence. Further, a study by Shaw (1976) finds that the Wolfgang–Sellin index of seriousness has a simple correlation of .68 with the actual length of sentence of men in the North Carolina prison system.

3. The only other variables for which information was at times missing were previous convictions (20%), years of schooling (0.04%), and marital status (2%). Most records that lacked

these variables also lacked *ALKY*, so that insisting on these variables in addition to *ALKY* removed only a further 3% of the original sample.

4. Note that *JUNKY* was dropped rather than combined with *ALCHY* as in the last section because its coefficient was insignificantly different from zero but significantly different from the coefficient of *ALCHY*.

5. One possible change explaining this reversal is that the habitual white misdemeanant, who was well represented in the previous sample, was by 1975 diverted from the prison system, either to probation or the county jails.

# Chapter 6

## Statistical Analysis of Survival Times

### 6.1. Introduction

In this chapter we are concerned with the statistical problems involved in analyzing the length of time until some specified event occurs. The particular application in which we are ultimately interested is the length of time from an individual's release from prison until his or her recidivism. However, the statistical problems in this application are basically the same as those involved in a variety of other applications involving survival times, such as analyses of survival times of medical patients, length of time until failure of equipment, and so forth. We shall therefore use the simple phrase "survival time" to describe the type of variable of interest.

Survival times are almost always censored or truncated. For example, suppose that a group of individuals is released from prison, and we observe their time until recidivism (return to prison). At the end of the follow-up period for these individuals, not everyone will have returned to prison. Thus we shall have observed the survival time only for individuals whose survival times are less than the length of the follow-up period, whereas for the other individuals all we know is that their survival times exceed the length of the follow-up period. In this case survival time is censored in exactly the sense described in Section 4.1. This must be taken into account in estimation, because it is not legitimate either to drop the observations with unobserved survival times (the nonrecidivists) or to set survival times for these observations equal to the length of the follow-up period. We can also consider the case in which we do not observe any individuals at release but only when they return to prison. In this case survival time is truncated rather than censored, because there is no information about nonrecidivists. Again, the term "truncated" is used here in exactly the same sense as in Section 4.1.

A further obvious feature of survival times is that they are nonnegative. The distributions assumed for survival times are therefore nonnegative and typically defined for all nonnegative times (i.e., from zero to infinity); examples of such distributions are exponential, Weibull, and lognormal.

To consider the problem of estimation in a general setting, suppose that the survival time $t$ is assumed to follow some particular distribution, characterized by a cumulative distribution function $F(t, \theta)$; here $\theta$ is the set of parameters to be estimated (e.g., the decay parameter in the exponential case). Let $f(t, \theta)$ be the corresponding density function. Both $F$ and $f$ are assumed to be defined for all $t > 0$.

First we consider the censored case. (This corresponds to the usual case of following a cohort of releasees for some time and observing which ones recidivate.) Here we assume a sample of $N$ individuals, with follow-up periods $T_1, T_2, \ldots, T_N$ (all of which may be equal, but need not be). Let $n$ be the number of recidivists, and let these observations be numbered 1, $2, \ldots, n$; observations $n + 1, \ldots, N$ are the nonrecidivists in the sample. For the recidivists, we observe survival times $t_i \leq T_i$, $i = 1, 2, \ldots, n$, whereas for the nonrecidivists we do not observe $t_i$, and we know only that $t_i > T_i$, $i = n + 1, \ldots, N$. Assuming that the individual outcomes are independent of each other, the likelihood function for the sample is of the form

$$\mathscr{L} = \prod_{i=1}^{n} f(t_i, \theta) \prod_{i=n+1}^{N} [1 - F(T_i, \theta)]. \tag{6.1.1}$$

Here the terms $f(t_i, \theta)$ for the recidivists are the appropriate densities for the survival times; they could also be written in the equivalent form $P(t_i \leq T_i) f(t_i | t_i \leq T_i)$, because

$$f(t_i, \theta | t_i \leq T_i) = f(t_i, \theta)/P(t_i \leq T_i). \tag{6.1.2}$$

The terms $1 - F(T_i, \theta)$ for the nonrecidivists are the appropriate probabilities of nonrecidivism given a follow-up of length $T_i$, because

$$1 - F(T_i, \theta) = P(t_i > T_i). \tag{6.1.3}$$

Maximization of Eq. (6.1.1) or its logarithm with respect to $\theta$ gives the maximum likelihood estimator.

Several points about this approach are worth noting. First, we are using the survival times for individuals for whom they are observed. This is valuable information, which should be used if it is available. Occasionally analyses are performed using only the information on whether individuals have recidivated by the end of their follow-up period, ignoring the timing of the observed returns. In this case we would maximize the likelihood function

$$\mathscr{L} = \prod_{i=1}^{n} F(T_i, \theta) \prod_{i=n+1}^{N} [1 - F(T_i, \theta)]. \tag{6.1.4}$$

This is a legitimate procedure in the sense that it does not cause bias or inconsistency, but it gives estimates that are inefficient relative to the MLEs from Eq. (6.1.1). If information on timing of return is available, it should be used [See Stollmack and Harris (1974)].

Second, characteristics of the individuals may or may not be used. A surprising number of analyses proceed on the assumption that the distribution of survival time is the same for all individuals. Sometimes there may be no data on individual characteristics, so such an assumption would be necessary. But if information on individual characteristics is available, it is likely to be useful; common sense and empirical evidence suggest that some individuals are more prone to recidivism than others. Such information can be incorporated by letting the parameters $\theta$ depend on these characteristics and a new set of parameters. For example, we shall discuss a lognormal model whose mean $\mu$ depends on individual characteristics as in a linear regression: $\mu_i = X_i'\beta$, where $X_i$ is a vector of these characteristics for individual $i$ and $\beta$ a vector of parameters.

We now turn to the truncated case. This is the case in which we have a sample of recidivists only. This would arise if we took a sample of individuals at their return to prison and not at their release. Suppose that our sample contains $n$ recidivists, with survival times $t_1, t_2, \ldots, t_n$. We now wish to construct the likelihood function, which will contain for each individual the density of $t$ conditional on the rule that determined representation in the sample.

For reasons that are not clear, the case most considered in the statistical literature is the case in which one starts with a cohort of $N$ releasees, but $N$ is unknown, and the only observations available are the survival times $t_i$ for the $n$ individuals who recidivate before the end of the follow-up period. These $n$ individuals appear in the sample because $t_i \leq T_i$, and the appropriate density is therefore $f(t_i, \theta | t_i \leq T_i)$, as given in (6.1.2). This yields the likelihood function

$$\mathscr{L} = \prod_{i=1}^{n} f(t_i, \theta | t_i \leq T_i) = \prod_{i=1}^{n} f(t_i, \theta)/F(T_i, \theta), \tag{6.1.5}$$

which can be maximized to obtain MLEs. Incidentally, it should be pointed out that this formulation proceeds conditionally on $n$. An alternative is to treat $n$ as random, in which case the size $N$ of the original cohort can also be estimated. Blumenthal and Marcus (1975) give some details of the latter procedure for the exponential case.

Unfortunately, the case just discussed does not seem to us to be relevant to most truncated samples. Suppose instead that the sample consists of all individuals (or a random sample thereof) who recidivated during some well-defined time period, such as calendar year 1981. Suppose that the $i$th individual in the sample ended his previous imprisonment on January 1, 1980. Then the condition for his representation in the sample is $12 \leq t_i < 24$, with $t_i$ measured in months, because this is the range of survival times that could yield his recidivism during calendar 1981. Thus, the appropriate density for this first observation would be

$$f(t_i, \theta | 12 \leq t_i < 24) = \frac{f(t_i, \theta)}{P(12 \leq t_i < 24)} = \frac{f(t_i, \theta)}{F(24, \theta) - F(12, \theta)}. \quad (6.1.6)$$

The likelihood function would be made up of $n$ terms of this form. In general, for observation $i$ let $U_i$ be the length of time from the individual's previous release until the end of the period in which the sample was drawn (in this case, 24), and let $L_i$ be the length of time from release to the beginning of the period in which the sample was drawn (in this case, 12). Then the appropriate likelihood function to maximize is

$$\mathscr{L} = \prod_{i=1}^{n} f(t_i, \theta)/[F(U_i, \theta) - F(L_i, \theta)]. \quad (6.1.7)$$

Censored samples are likely to be more frequent than truncated ones, because the most common type of data set used to study recidivism is a set of observations on a cohort of releasees. We shall therefore concentrate on the censored case in the remainder of this chapter.

The plan of this chapter is as follows. In Section 6.2 we discuss estimation of the model that assumes an exponential distribution for length of time. In Section 6.3 we discuss estimation under the assumption of a log-normal distribution. In Section 6.4 we discuss so-called "split models," which allow the ultimate failure rate (as follow-up time becomes very large) to be less than one. In Section 6.5 we discuss the concept of the hazard rate and some models built around this concept. In Section 6.6 we compare two possible explanations for decreasing hazard rates. In Section 6.7 we deal with the "proportional hazards model" of Cox, which attempts to minimize the effect of distributional assumptions. Finally, Section 6.8 contains our summary and conclusions.

## 6.2. The Exponential Case

In this section we suppose that the length of time until recidivism follows a one-parameter exponential distribution. This distribution has density

$$f(t) = \theta e^{-\theta t} \tag{6.2.1}$$

and cumulative distribution function

$$F(t) = 1 - e^{-\theta t}, \tag{6.2.2}$$

both defined for $t \geq 0$ and requiring $\theta > 0$. Its mean is $1/\theta$ and its variance is $1/\theta^2$. Its median (the "half life" in radioactive decay terminology) is its mean, multiplied by $\ln 2 = .693$.

This distribution has a constant hazard rate. This is discussed more fully in Section 6.5; briefly, it implies that the probability of recidivism in the next unit of time does not depend on how long the individual has already been out of prison. Although this feature of the exponential distribution is reasonable for some applications, such as radioactive decay, it may be unreasonable for application to recidivism. Nevertheless, the exponential case is worth considering, if only because it is widely considered in the literature.

We shall first discuss the censored case without using individual characteristics. This case has been analyzed extensively by Stollmack and Harris (1974), and earlier by others dating back at least to Deemer and Votaw (1955). As in Section 6.1, let there be $n$ recidivists, with times until recidivism $t_1, \ldots, t_n$, and let there be $N - n$ nonrecidivists, with follow-up times $T_{n+1}, \ldots, T_N$. The likelihood function (6.1.1) becomes

$$\mathscr{L} = \prod_{i=1}^{n} \theta \exp(-\theta t_i) \prod_{i=n+1}^{N} \exp(-\theta T_i). \tag{6.2.3}$$

This is maximized by the MLE

$$\hat{\theta} = n \bigg/ \left( \sum_{i=1}^{n} t_i + \sum_{i=n+1}^{N} T_i \right). \tag{6.2.4}$$

For large samples, $\hat{\theta}$ is normal with mean $\theta$ and variance

$$\theta^2 \bigg/ \sum_{i=1}^{N} [1 - \exp(-\theta T_i)],$$

which for large $N$ is adequately approximated by $\theta^2/n$, so that tests about $\theta$ are possible in large samples. The small sample distribution of $\hat{\theta}$ is discussed by Bartholomew (1963).

Now suppose that we wish to let the mean survival time depend on individual characteristics. One obvious possibility is to let the mean survival time $1/\theta$ be a linear function of individual characteristics:

$$1/\theta = X_i'\beta, \tag{6.2.5}$$

with $X_i$ the vector of characteristics of individual $i$. In this case the likelihood becomes

$$\mathscr{L} = \prod_{i=1}^{n} \frac{1}{X_i'\beta} \exp\left(\frac{-t_i}{X_i'\beta}\right) \prod_{i=n+1}^{N} \exp\left(\frac{-T_i}{X_i'\beta}\right). \tag{6.2.6}$$

This likelihood function would be maximized numerically with respect to $\beta$ to obtain the MLE of $\beta$; an analytic solution does not appear to be possible. It should also be noted that in this maximization we must constrain $X_i'\beta > 0$ for all $i$, which is a set of potentially bothersome restrictions to impose. This last difficulty could be avoided by relating $X_i'\beta$ to $\theta$ in a different way; for example, we could let $1/\theta = \exp(X_i'\beta)$ so that $X_i'\beta$ need not be restricted in sign. However, the advantage of the specification in Eq. (6.2.5) is that $\beta$ has a clear interpretation in terms of the effect of a change in $X_i$ on the expected survival time:

$$\beta_j = \partial E(\text{survival time})/\partial X_{ij}. \tag{6.2.7}$$

Also, if $X_i$ contains a constant term as well as characteristics that vary over individuals, we can test the hypothesis that individual characteristics matter by testing the hypothesis that the elements of $\beta$ (other than the coefficient of the constant term) equal zero.

## 6.3. The Lognormal Case

In this section we consider the case in which the survival time follows a lognormal distribution. We begin with some basic facts about that distribution. If $z$ is distributed as $N(\mu, \sigma^2)$, then $y = e^z$ has a lognormal distribution with mean

$$\xi = \exp(\mu + \tfrac{1}{2}\sigma^2) \tag{6.3.1}$$

and variance

$$\tau^2 = \exp(2\mu + \sigma^2)[\exp(\sigma^2) - 1] = \xi^2\eta^2, \tag{6.3.2}$$

where

$$\eta^2 = \exp(\sigma^2) - 1. \tag{6.3.3}$$

Clearly the density of $z = \ln y$ is the density of $N(\mu, \sigma^2)$:

$$f(\ln y) = (1/\sqrt{2\pi}\sigma) \exp[-(1/2\sigma^2)(\ln y - \mu)^2]. \tag{6.3.4}$$

There is generally no advantage to working with the density of $y$ itself, rather than of $\ln y$; they differ only in the Jacobian of the transformation $(y^{-1})$.

If individual characteristics are not used, the likelihood function (in terms of the parameters $\mu$ and $\sigma^2$) is

$$\mathscr{L} = -\frac{n}{2}\ln(2\pi) - \frac{n}{2}\ln(\sigma^2) - \frac{1}{2\sigma^2}\sum_{i=1}^{n}(\ln t_i - \mu)^2 + \sum_{i=n+1}^{N}\ln F\left(\frac{\mu - \ln T_i}{\sigma}\right), \tag{6.3.5}$$

where, as previously, for the $n$ recidivists $t_i$ is the survival time and for the $N - n$ nonrecidivists $T_i$ is the length of the follow-up period, and where $F$ is the cumulative distribution function for the $N(0, 1)$ distribution. No analytical solution exists for the maximization of (6.3.5), though a simple recursive formula can be derived if all $T_i$ are equal.

If individual characteristics are used, then there is a decision to be made about which parameters depend on these explanatory variables. One reasonable possibility is to let the mean survival time depend linearly on individual characteristics:

$$\xi_i = X_i'\beta, \qquad i = 1, 2, \ldots, N, \tag{6.3.6}$$

and then to assume $\eta^2$ (or, equivalently, $\sigma^2$) constant. Note that this implies that the variance of the survival time distribution is $\tau_i^2 = \eta^2\xi_i^2 = \eta^2(X_i'\beta)^2$. This model has been proposed by Amemiya and Boskin (1974) and applied to the timing of recidivism by Schmidt and Witte (1977, 1980). Noting that $\ln t_i$ is distributed as normal with mean $\ln(X_i'\beta) - \frac{1}{2}\sigma^2$ and variance $\sigma^2 = \ln(1 + \eta^2)$, we can form the likelihood function analogous to (6.3.5):

$$\mathscr{L} = -\frac{n}{2}\ln(2\pi) - \frac{n}{2}\ln\sigma^2 - \frac{1}{2\sigma^2}\sum_{i=1}^{n}[\ln t_i - \ln(X_i'\beta) + \tfrac{1}{2}\sigma^2]^2 + \sum_{i=n+1}^{N}\ln F\left[\frac{\ln(X_i'\beta) - \frac{1}{2}\sigma^2 - \ln T_i}{\sigma}\right]. \tag{6.3.7}$$

This is maximized numerically with respect to $\beta$ and $\sigma^2$ to obtain the MLEs. Their asymptotic variances are obtained from the information matrix, which can be found in Amemiya and Boskin (1974). It should be noted that it is necessary to constrain $\beta$ so as to make $X_i'\beta$ positive for all $i$, which complicates the computations.

An alternative lognormal model follows if we assume that $\mu$ (rather than $\xi$) is a linear function of the $X_i$. This amounts to taking logarithms of $t_i$ ($i = 1, \ldots, n$) and $T_i$ ($i = n + 1, \ldots, N$) and then applying the censored normal model with explanatory variables. This is the Tobit model of Section 4.3, but with censoring on the right at $T_i$ rather than on the left at zero. This is probably easier computationally than the model of Amemiya and Boskin but loses the easy interpretation of $\beta$ as the effect of $X_i$ on mean survival time.

## 6.4. Split Population Models

All of the models considered so far have assumed some cumulative distribution function $F(t)$ for the survival time. Note that $F(t)$ gives the probability of a failure (recidivism) up to and including time $t$. Also, being a cumulative distribution function, $F(t)$ necessarily approaches one as $t$ approaches infinity. This implies that every individual would eventually fail, which is sometimes argued to be unreasonable.

If one wants to model survival times when not all individuals would eventually fail, then one must find an alternative to simply specifying a cumulative distribution function. Maltz and McCleary (1977) have specified such a model for the exponential case, based on two assumptions. First, assume that there is a probability $\gamma$ that an individual would ultimately fail (given an infinite lifetime). Second, assume that the distribution of survival times, conditional on ultimate failure, is exponential.

This can be expressed mathematically as follows. Let $F$ be an unobservable variable with two values: one, implying ultimate failure, and zero, implying perpetual success. Then the first assumption is that

$$P(F = 1) = \gamma, \qquad P(F = 0) = 1 - \gamma. \tag{6.4.1}$$

Now let $g(t|F = 1)$ be the density of survival times for the ultimate failures, and $G(t|F = 1)$ be the corresponding cumulative distribution function. The second assumption is that

$$g(t|F = 1) = \theta e^{-\theta t}, \qquad G(t|F = 1) = 1 - e^{-\theta t}. \tag{6.4.2}$$

Note specifically that $g(t|F = 0)$ and $G(t|F = 0)$ *are not defined*.

Now let $T$ be the length of the follow-up period, and let $R$ be the (observable) variable equal to one if there is failure by time $T$ and zero if there is not. For the nonrecidivists in the sample, we observe only the event $R = 0$, the probability of which is

$$\begin{aligned} P(R = 0) &= P(F = 0) + P(F = 1)P(t > T|F = 1) \\ &= 1 - \gamma + \gamma e^{-\theta T}. \end{aligned} \tag{6.4.3}$$

On the other hand, for the recidivists, we observe the survival time $t$, and we know necessarily that $F = 1$, so the appropriate density is

$$\begin{aligned} P(F = 1)P(t < T|F = 1)g(t|t < T, F = 1) &= P(F = 1)g(t|F = 1) \\ &= \gamma\theta e^{-\theta t}. \end{aligned} \tag{6.4.4}$$

The likelihood function is made up of terms (6.4.4) for recidivists and (6.4.3) for nonrecidivists. Thus suppose as before that there are $N$ individuals: $n$ recidivists with survival times $t_i$, $i = 1, 2, \ldots, n$, and $N - n$ nonrecidivists with follow-up times $T_i$, $i = n + 1, n + 2, \ldots, N$. This yields the likelihood function

$$\mathcal{L} = \prod_{i=1}^{n} \gamma\theta \exp(-\theta t_i) \prod_{i=n+1}^{N} [1 - \gamma + \gamma \exp(-\theta T_i)]. \tag{6.4.5}$$

Maximum likelihood estimates can be obtained by maximizing Eq. (6.4.5). There is no analytical solution, though there are some simplifications if all follow-ups are identical; see Maltz and McCleary (1977)[1] or Anscombe (1961).

This model has been criticized, unjustly, on the basis of being "defective" in a technical statistical sense. [See, e.g., Harris *et al.* (1981).] Note that by the same argument that led to Eq. (6.4.3), the probability of an observed survival time less than or equal to $t$ is just $\gamma(1 - e^{-\theta t})$. If this were regarded as a cumulative distribution function for $t$, it would indeed be defective in the sense that it does not approach one as $t$ approaches infinity. However, this is irrelevant because this quantity is *not* the cumulative distribution function for $t$. Indeed, the survival time has a cumulative distribution function *only* conditional on $F = 1$; when $F = 0$, the survival time is not even defined. What is relevant from a statistical point of view is that Eq. (6.4.3) plus the integral of Eq. (6.4.4) from zero to $T$, must equal one, and this holds. This is an important statistical issue because the usual hypothesis testing procedures for the MLEs would be invalid if the criticism just related were valid.

This split model can be viewed as a model of two separate subpopulations, one with a failure rate of $\theta$ and the other with a failure rate of zero. A closely related model, considered by Harris *et al.* (1981), assumes subpopulations with failure rates $\theta_1$ and $\theta_2$, but with neither $\theta_1$ nor $\theta_2$ necessarily equal to zero (or, more than two subpopulations could be considered). This model has also been treated earlier by Mendenhall and Hader (1958).

These so-called split models are an important first step in recognizing that the population of releasees is heterogeneous. They help to avoid the long-term overprediction of recidivism that a one-parameter exponential model (or any other one-parameter model) probably implies. (For example, the Stollmack and Harris estimate of $\theta = .029$ implies 99% recidivism after 13 years, which seems clearly out of line.) However, in our opinion, a superior alternative, when the data allow, is to introduce individual characteristics into the analysis (e.g., as described in Section 6.2). Then each individual has his own individual failure rate. Not only will this generally fit the data better than will a model with constant failure rates across individuals, but it also permits drawing interesting and useful conclusions about the effects of individual characteristics on the failure rate. Furthermore, when individual failure rates are allowed, the implication that every individual would ultimately fail given an infinite lifetime does not strike us as bothersome, because some individuals with low failure rates can and will have very low probabilities of failure over their lifetimes.

## 6.5. The Hazard Rate

For a distribution of survival times with density $f(t)$ and cumulative distribution function $F(t)$, the *hazard rate* is defined as

$$h(t) = f(t)/[1 - F(t)]. \tag{6.5.1}$$

It represents the density of a failure at time $t$, conditional on no failure prior to time $t$. That is, it basically tells us the probability of a failure in the next unit of time, given that no failure has yet occurred.

The exponential distribution is the only distribution with a constant hazard rate. Certain physical processes do appear to have constant hazard rates and are therefore well fit by exponential models. Radioactive decay is the leading example; the probability that a particular radioactive particle will decay in the near future does not depend on the age of the particle. However, a constant hazard rate may not be reasonable in models of recidivism. It contradicts the obvious intuition that an individual who has gone 10 years without recidivism is less likely to recidivate next month than is a more recent releasee. If it is correct that an individual's probability of recidivism in the next time period decreases as his (successful) time since release increases, then the survival time distribution should have a decreasing hazard rate.

If one is unhappy with the constant-hazard-rate feature of the exponential distribution, one possibility is to look for another common distribution with a more reasonable hazard rate. For example, the half-normal distribution (the distribution of the absolute value of a normal with zero mean) has a decreasing hazard rate. The lognormal distribution has a hazard rate that first increases and then decreases. The Weibull distribution with parameter $\theta$ has an increasing hazard rate if $\theta > 1$ and a decreasing hazard rate if $\theta < 1$. (A variable $X$ has a Weibull distribution if $X^\theta$ has an exponential distribution.)

An alternative strategy is to start with a reasonable hazard rate and from it deduce the form of the distribution. If $h(t)$ is the hazard rate (for $t \geq 0$), then the cumulative distribution function $F(t)$ is given by

$$F(t) = 1 - \exp\left[ - \int_0^t h(x)\, dx \right]. \tag{6.5.2}$$

Thus this is a feasible approach as long as the hazard rate can be integrated. For example, if the hazard rate is linear in $t$, the distribution is the so-called linear failure rate distribution, discussed by Johnson and Kotz (1970, pp. 268, 283). Another example of this approach is given by Bloom (1979), who assumes the hazard rate $be^{-ct}$ and discusses estimation of the resulting model.

It should be noted that the requirement that $F(t)$ be a cumulative distribution function puts some restrictions on the form of the hazard rate. In particular, in order that $F(t)$ approach one as $t$ approaches infinity, it is necessary that

$$\int_0^t h(x)\,dx \to \infty \tag{6.5.3}$$

as $t$ approaches infinity. This condition is *not* satisfied in Bloom's case, because the integral in (6.5.3) approaches $b/c$ as $t$ goes to infinity; as a result the implied $F(t)$ approaches $1 - e^{-b/c}$, rather than one, as $t$ approaches infinity.

One way to resolve this difficulty with Bloom's model is to view it as a split model, as treated in the last section. Letting $F = 1$ for eventual recidivists, we can define

$$\gamma = P(F = 1) = 1 - \exp(-b/c). \tag{6.5.4}$$

Now note that

$$\text{“}f(t)\text{”} = b \exp(-b/c) \exp[-ct + (b/c) \exp(-ct)] \tag{6.5.5}$$

and

$$\text{“}F(t)\text{”} = 1 - \exp(-b/c) \exp[(b/c) \exp(-ct)] \tag{6.5.6}$$

are, respectively, the "density" and "distribution function" associated with Bloom's "hazard rate" of $be^{-ct}$. Now define

$$g(t|F = 1) = \text{“}f(t)\text{”}/\gamma, \qquad G(t|F = 1) = \text{“}F(t)\text{”}/\gamma \tag{6.5.7}$$

and note that $G(t|F = 1)$ is legitimate in the sense of approaching one as $t$ goes to infinity. For the recidivists in the sample the appropriate term in the likelihood function is

$$P(F = 1)g(t|F = 1) = \gamma\text{“}f(t)\text{”}/\gamma = \text{“}f(t)\text{”}, \tag{6.5.8}$$

and for a nonrecidivist with follow-up $T$ the appropriate term is

$$\begin{aligned} P(F = 0) + P(F = 1)P(t > T|F = 1) &= (1 - \gamma) + \gamma\left[1 - \frac{\text{“}F(T)\text{”}}{\gamma}\right] \\ &= 1 - \text{“}F(T)\text{”}. \end{aligned} \tag{6.5.9}$$

Thus the likelihood function that Bloom suggests, simply using "$f(t)$" and "$F(t)$", is consistent with this interpretation. However, in this split model the hazard rate (conditional on $F = 1$) is

$$h(t|F = 1) = \frac{\text{“}f(t)\text{”}}{\gamma}\bigg/\left[1 - \frac{\text{“}F(t)\text{”}}{\gamma}\right] = \frac{\text{“}f(t)\text{”}}{\gamma - \text{“}F(t)\text{”}} \tag{6.5.10}$$

and does *not* equal the "hazard rate" $be^{-ct}$ with which the model started. In fact,

$$h(t|F = 1) = b\exp(-ct)\{1 - \exp[-(b/c)\exp(-ct)]\}^{-1}, \tag{6.5.11}$$

which decreases *faster* than $e^{-ct}$. Thus Bloom's model is a split model of perhaps reasonable form, but it does not have the hazard rate that is claimed. What this illustrates is the danger in postulating a "hazard rate" that can not be a hazard rate. It would be better to start with an explicit split model and postulate a legitimate hazard rate.

## 6.6. Heterogeneity versus State Dependence

In many analyses of survival times, in the study of recidivism and elsewhere, hazard rates are found to be decreasing. For examples in the context of recidivism, see Wilkins (1970), Kitchener *et al.* (1977), Waldo and Griswold (1979), and Hoffman and Stone-Meierhoefer (1979). It is important to realize that there are two distinct reasons why this might be so.

The first possible reason for a group of individuals exhibiting a decreasing hazard rate is an obvious one; namely, that the indivuduals in the group may actually have decreasing hazard rates. Following the terminology used in labor economics, we shall call this *state dependence*.[2] In the present context, this occurs if the probability of recidivism for a given individual actually decreases with successful time since release. Time spent in the nonrecidivist state may increase one's ability at avoiding police or increase the attractiveness of one's legitimate alternatives; the point is simply that state dependence refers to an actual change in behavior over time, at the individual level, for whatever reason.

The second possible reason for a group exhibiting a decreasing hazard rate is *heterogeneity*. Suppose that hazard rates differ across individuals; in other words, some individuals are more prone to failure than others. Naturally, individuals with higher hazard rates will tend to fail earlier, on average, than individuals with lower hazard rates. As a result the average hazard rate of the surviving group will decrease with length of time since release, simply because the most failure-prone individuals have been selectively removed. This is true even if there is no state dependence. For example, if each individual has a constant hazard rate (i.e., survival time is exponential, at the individual level), but this hazard rate varies across individuals, Proschan (1963) proves that a group of such individuals will exhibit a decreasing hazard rate.

Methods exist for distinguishing between these two phenomena. We shall not discuss these here [a good reference is Heckman (1978)], other than to note that, if one believes in heterogeneity, then one should use individual characteristics in the model. Careful use of individual characteristics should substantially reduce the unobservable component of heterogeneity, and for this reason the arguments in favor of decreasing hazard rates may be less compelling if individual characteristics are used. However, use of individual characteristics will not remove a decreasing hazard rate if it is a result of state dependence.

A related point, and also an important one, is that when there is heterogeneity, we need to distinguish the unconditional distribution of failure times from the distribution conditional on individual characteristics. In trying to decide what kind of model (e.g., exponential, lognormal, Weibull) to fit, it is common practice to plot the frequencies of failure times and to use a distribution that looks qualitatively like this plot. In doing so, one has plotted the *unconditional* distribution of failure times. This is relevant if one is going to fit a model without individual characteristics as explanatory variables. However, if one believes in heterogeneity and intends to use individual characteristics as explanatory variables, what is relevant is the distribution of failure times *conditional* on these individual characteristics. The unconditional plot of failure time frequencies may be very misleading if it is used as evidence about the shape of the conditional distribution. For example, as we saw before, the conditional distribution may be exponential, yet the unconditional distribution would reveal a decreasing hazard rate.

## 6.7. The Proportional Hazards Model

The proportional hazards model, developed by Cox (1972), allows one to estimate the effects of individual characteristics on survival time without having to assume a particular form for the distribution function or hazard rate. This is potentially useful because, as argued at the end of the preceding section, the form of the distribution of survival time (conditional on individual characteristics) is not easy to discover. We shall return to this problem later in this section.

For an individual with a vector of characteristics $X$, the proportional hazards model assumes a hazard rate of the form

$$h(t|X) = h_0(t)e^{X'\beta}, \tag{6.7.1}$$

where $h_0(t)$ is a completely arbitrary and unspecified baseline hazard function. Thus it assumes that the hazard functions of all individuals differ only by a factor of proportionality, but it puts no further restriction on these hazard functions. The point is that $\beta$ can be estimated without specifying $h_0(t)$. Also, $h_0(t)$ can itself be estimated.

To consider estimation of $\beta$, we suppose (as before) that we have a sample of $N$ individuals, $n$ of whom fail before the end of their follow-up period. Let us order the observations so that individual 1 has the shortest observed time until recidivism, individual 2 has the second shortest time, and so forth. Thus for individual $i$, $i = 1, 2, \ldots, n$, we observe failure time $t_i$, with

$$t_1 < t_2 < \cdots < t_n. \tag{6.7.2}$$

We observe a vector of individual characteristics $X_i$ for each individual $i = 1, 2, \ldots, N$ (that is, for both recidivists and nonrecidivists). Finally, for each of the observed failure times $t_i$, $i = 1, \ldots, n$, we define $R(t_i)$ as the set of all $j = 1, \ldots, N$ such that individual $j$ was still at risk just prior to time $t_i$. Thus $R(t_i)$ includes ultimate recidivists who have not yet failed just prior to $t_i$ (namely $i, i + 1, \ldots, n$), as well as those nonrecidivists whose follow-up is at least of length $t_i$.

With these definitions, we can now define the "partial likelihood" function proposed by Cox (1975). For any failure time $t_i$ (any $i = 1, 2, \ldots, n$), the probability that it is individual $i$ who fails, given that exactly one individual from the set $R(t_i)$ fails, is

$$h(t_i|X_i)\bigg/\sum_{j\in R(t_i)} h(t_i|X_j) = \exp(X_i'\beta)\bigg/\sum_{j\in R(t_i)} \exp(X_j'\beta). \tag{6.7.3}$$

(Note that $h_0(t_i)$ has cancelled in going from the left-hand side of (6.7.3) to the right-hand side.) The partial likelihood function is formed by multiplying (6.7.3) over all $n$ failure times:

$$L = \prod_{i=1}^{n} \exp(X_i'\beta)\bigg/\sum_{j\in R(t_i)} \exp(X_j'\beta). \tag{6.7.4}$$

The estimate of $\beta$ found by maximizing Eq. (6.7.4) numerically with respect to $\beta$ is the partial maximum likelihood estimate. It is consistent and asymptotically normal, with asymptotic covariance matrix given by the inverse of the information matrix.

Incidentally, the word "partial" in partial likelihood refers to the fact that, with $h_0(t)$ unspecified, not all available information is useful in estimating $\beta$. For example, Eq. (6.7.4) depends only on knowing which individuals were still at risk when each observed failure occurred; the numerical values of the failure times $t_i$ or of the censoring times for the nonrecidivists are not used.

There are some complications if there are ties in the data—that is, if more than one individual fails at the same time. A good reference is Kalbfleisch and Prentice (1980, Ch. 4).

Once $\beta$ is estimated, say by $\hat{\beta}$, we can estimate the distribution function $F_0(t)$, which corresponds to $h_0(t)$ in Eq. (6.7.1). For $i = 1, 2, \ldots, n$, define

$$\hat{\alpha}_i = \left\{1 - \left[\exp(X_i'\hat{\beta}) \Big/ \sum_{j \in R(t_i)} \exp(X_j'\hat{\beta})\right]\right\}^{\exp(-X_i'\hat{\beta})} \tag{6.7.5}$$

Then the estimate of $F_0(t)$ that follows from $\hat{\beta}$ is

$$\hat{F}_0(t) = 1 - \prod_{i \ni t_i < t} \hat{\alpha}_i . \tag{6.7.6}$$

This is a step function: $\hat{F}_0(t) = 0$ for $t \le t_1$; $\hat{F}_0(t) = 1 - \hat{\alpha}_1$ for $t_1 < t \le t_2$; $\hat{F}_0(t) = 1 - \hat{\alpha}_1\hat{\alpha}_2$ for $t_2 < t \le t_3$; and so forth.

The estimated distribution function $\hat{F}_0(t)$ may be hard to interpret. Nevertheless, it may give some indication as to a reasonable distribution, and the effects of heterogeneity have been removed in arriving at it.

## 6.8. Summary and Conclusions

In this chapter we discussed the statistical analysis of survival time, defined as the time until some event (such as recidivism) occurs. Survival times are nonnegative and can be represented by a variety of distributions (e.g., exponential, Weibull, lognormal). Survival times are generally censored because not everyone in a cohort of releasees will have failed by the end of the follow-up period, and this must be taken into account in estimation. The cost of doing so is that we must generally resort to numerical maximization of a likelihood function to obtain estimates.

In recent years, a number of researchers have used statistical models of survival time to analyze recidivism. For examples of how these models have developed, see Stollmack and Harris (1974), Maltz and McCleary (1977), Witte and Schmidt (1977), Bloom (1979), Schmidt and Witte (1980), and Harris *et al.* (1981). We believe that this is a noteworthy and beneficial trend because analyses of survival times during a follow-up period are more informative and make more effective use of the data than analyses that consider only whether or not an individual failed (without regard to timing) during a follow-up period. Early work [for example, Stollmack and Harris (1974)] assumed that survival time followed an exponential distribution that was the same for all individuals. Although the exponential distribution is convenient to work with, its implicit assumption of a constant hazard rate is probably unreasonable. Most existing data [see Hoffman and Stone-Meierhoefer (1979), Kitchener *et al.* (1977), Waldo and Griswald (1979), and Wilkins (1970)] exhibit a decreasing hazard rate.

More recent work on the timing of recidivism has used distributions that allow for a decreasing hazard rate and has relaxed the assumption that all individuals have the same survival time distribution. Harris *et al.* (1981) and Maltz and McCleary (1977) have introduced "split population models" (see Section 6.4), which allow different failure rates for different groups and imply an overall decreasing hazard rate. This was an important step in the right direction. However, it seems preferable to us to allow each individual to have a different failure rate, by letting the failure rate (or whatever parameters are in the model) depend on individual characteristics, as done, for example, by Witte and Schmidt (1977).

This still leaves the problem of choosing an appropriate distribution for survival time. As argued in Section 6.6, this is an especially difficult problem when individual characteristics are used as explanatory variables, because what needs to be chosen is the distribution conditional on such characteristics, whereas a plot of the survival times reveals instead the unconditional distribution. One possible solution to this problem is to use the "proportional hazards model" of Cox (1972), which we described in Section 6.7. This model is well known in the biostatistics literature but apparently not so well known in the criminological literature. It allows estimation of the effects of individual characteristics on the hazard rate without having to assume a particular functional form for the hazard rate or distribution function. Furthermore, it allows one to estimate the distribution function of survival time, having taken the effects of individual characteristics into account. Thus the proportional hazards model can profitably be used to determine an appropriate distribution and an appropriate set of individual characteristics for use in further analysis.

## Notes to Chapter 6

1. In their equation (2), $e^{a\tau}$ should be $e^{-a\tau}$.

2. Sometimes in labor economics it is referred to as "true" state dependence, or as "duration dependence."

# Chapter 7

## Analysis of the Length of Time until Recidivism

### 7.1. Introduction

In this chapter we analyze the length of time from an individual's release from prison until his or her recidivism. It is widely recognized that length of time until recidivism is a much more informative variable than is the common binary (yes/no) measure of recidivism. For example, see Harris, Kayland, and Maltz (1981) or Stollmack and Harris (1974) for arguments to this effect. Here we note two good reasons for considering the timing of recidivism. First, from a statistical point of view, the information contained in the timing of recidivism should not be ignored. Second, estimation of the distribution of length of time allows one to predict rates of recidivism for any desired period after release, whereas analysis of the common binary measure of recidivism only allows one to predict the rate of recidivism for the particular follow-up period in the data used to estimate the model.

In Section 7.2 we present the results for our analysis of the data set (641 individuals who were in prison in North Carolina in 1969 or 1971) that was previously considered in Chapter 3 and in Section 5.2. In Sections 7.3 and 7.4 we analyze the data set (all individuals released from prison in the first half of 1975) previously considered in Sections 5.3 and 5.4. Our conclusions are presented in Section 5.5. These models will also be used in Chapter 8 in a program evaluation.

## 7.2. Analysis of the 1969 and 1971 Data

The data used in this section are described in detail in Appendix A, and briefly in Section 3.2. Therefore we shall simply remind the reader that the data consist of information on 641 men who were in prison in North Carolina in 1969 or 1971 (or both of those years). However, owing to missing information for some observations, the number of observations actually analyzed was 582.

The dependent variable analyzed is the length of time (in months) from release until the first arrest that resulted in a conviction, which we shall denote *LTFC*. (Thus we are defining recidivism, for purposes of this analysis, as reconviction, not reimprisonment; the conviction need not entail a prison sentence.) Statistically, this is a survival time problem, as discussed in the last chapter. Furthermore, the sample is censored because we can observe *LTFC* only up to the end of the individual's follow-up period. Thus the sample consists of some individuals (425) who were reconvicted during their follow-up period and for whom *LTFC* was therefore observed, and other individuals (157) who were not reconvicted during their follow-up period and for whom *LTFC* was not observed.

The statistical model applied was the censored lognormal model described in Section 6.3. That is, it is assumed that *LTFC* has a lognormal distribution, with mean a (linear) function of individual characteristics. Because not all individuals are convicted during their follow-up period, we need to recognize the censoring of the sample. Thus estimates are obtained by maximizing the likelihood function of Eq. (6.3.7).

The following explanatory variables were used in the analysis: *CNST*, *CONVBS*, *AAR*, *RACE*, *ALCHY*, *JUNKY*, *SUPER*, *SG*, *MS*, *MF*, *AFA*, *WR*, *PROPTY*, *PERSON*, *RULE*, and *TSERVD*. These variables are defined in Section 3.3, except for *ALCHY* and *JUNKY*, defined in Section 5.2, and *TSERVD*, defined as the length in months of the previous imprisonment.

The results for this specification are given in Table 7.1. The coefficients give the effect of the variables on the expected value of *LTFC* and the $t$ ratios are distributed (in large samples) as $N(0, 1)$ under the null hypothesis that the associated coefficient is zero.

The last nine variables listed in Table 7.1 have coefficients that are insignificantly different from zero at conventional levels. Furthermore, the coefficients of *ALCHY* and *JUNKY* are insignificantly different from each other. We have therefore reduced the size of our specification by combining

**TABLE 7.1.** Results of Analysis of Length of Time until Reconviction—Large Specification[a]

| Variable | Coefficient | "t Ratio" |
|---|---|---|
| *CNST* | 30.5968 | 1.93 |
| *RULE* | −1.8500 | −1.86 |
| *CONVBS* | −0.4208 | −2.02 |
| *AAR* | 0.05016 | 2.74 |
| *RACE* | −13.8990 | −3.22 |
| *ALCHY* | −19.9663 | −4.19 |
| *JUNKY* | −16.8197 | −2.01 |
| *SUPER* | 28.9001 | 0.59 |
| *SG* | 0.07630 | 0.09 |
| *MS* | 1.6820 | 0.44 |
| *MF* | 5.5513 | 0.89 |
| *AFA* | 0.01182 | 0.33 |
| *WR* | −2.0499 | −0.58 |
| *PROPTY* | −0.2552 | −0.06 |
| *PERSON* | 6.0431 | 0.88 |
| *TSERVD* | −0.00998 | −0.06 |

[a] From Witte and Schmidt (1977). $\sigma^2 = 1.9710$.

*ALCHY* and *JUNKY* into a single dummy variable *ALKY* (as described in Section 5.2) and by dropping the last nine variables listed. The $\chi^2$ statistic (likelihood ratio test statistic) used to test the validity of these ten restrictions was 7.218, which is very insignificant. This is reasonably good evidence in favor of imposing these restrictions.

The results for this reduced specification are given in Table 7.2. All the variables have highly significant coefficients. The results indicate that an individual is likely to go longer without a conviction the fewer previous

**TABLE 7.2.** Results of Analysis of Length of Time until Reconviction—Small Specification[a]

| Variable | Coefficient | "t Ratio" |
|---|---|---|
| *CNST* | 33.4346 | 5.38 |
| *RULE* | −1.1487 | −2.34 |
| *CONVBS* | −0.4918 | −3.70 |
| *AAR* | 0.0512 | 3.22 |
| *RACE* | −14.3138 | −3.41 |
| *ALKY* | −16.6306 | −5.47 |

[a] From Witte and Schmidt (1977). $\sigma^2 = 1.9225$.

convictions he has, the fewer rule violations he committed while last in prison, the older he is at release, if he is not an alcoholic or a user of hard drugs, and if he is black. These results are very consistent with those of our earlier analyses (in Chapter 3 and Section 5.2) of this data, the only real difference being the higher level of significance of *RULE* here than in the previous analyses.

It should be noted that the coefficients in Table 7.2 give the effects of the variables on the mean of *LTFC*. Thus, for example, the coefficient of *ALKY* of $-16.6$ indicates that an alcoholic or user of hard drugs will have a mean value of *LTFC* that is 16.6 months less than an individual who is a nonalcoholic and a nonuser of hard drugs. However, because the lognormal distribution is highly skewed, its mean may not be a good measure of what one intuitively thinks of as the "average" value of the distribution. In particular, the median of the distribution may be a better measure. The median of a lognormal distribution is the mean multiplied by $\exp(-\sigma^2/2)$. In our analysis of Table 7.2, $\hat{\sigma}^2 = 1.9225$, so the median is approximately 0.38 of the mean. Thus the effect of *ALKY* on median *LTFC* is only $(16.6)(0.38) = 6.3$ months. If one wanted to make a statement such as, "An alcoholic will, on the average, be convicted _____ months sooner than a nonalcoholic of otherwise identical characteristics," it may be more meaningful to fill in the blank with 6.3 (the partial effect of *ALKY* on the median of *LTFC*) rather than 16.6 (the partial effect of *ALKY* on the mean of *LTFC*).

As noted before, our results indicate that the type of individual most likely to be reconvicted soon is a young white addict with lots of rule violations and previous convictions. The type of individual least likely to be reconvicted is an old black nonaddict with no rule violations or previous convictions. It is perhaps informative, as a way of seeing more precisely what this means, actually to plot or list the lognormal distribution implied by our estimates for various values of the explanatory variables. This is done in Table 7.3, based on the parameter estimates given in the last three rows of Table 7.2. Also given are the mean, median, and mode of the implied distributions.

There are five cases considered. The first case represents the "average" case in that it takes all explanatory variables at their sample means: $RULE = 0.672$, $CVBS = 2.735$, $AAR = 380.107$, $ALKY = 0.483$, and $RACE = 0.503$. The mean predicted length of time until conviction for this case is 35.572 months and the median value is 13.556. Approximately 46% of these hypothetical "average" individuals are predicted to be reconvicted in 1 year and 66% within 2 years.

The other four cases considered are for a white addict, white nonaddict, black addict, and black nonaddict, respectively. In each of these four cases,

**TABLE 7.3.** *P(LTFC > n)* for Various Types of Individuals[a]

| $n$ | Average | White *ALKY* | White non-*ALKY* | Black *ALKY* | Black non-*ALKY* |
|---|---|---|---|---|---|
| 1 | 0.970 | 0.939 | 0.970 | 0.967 | 0.982 |
| 2 | 0.916 | 0.853 | 0.916 | 0.910 | 0.946 |
| 3 | 0.861 | 0.776 | 0.861 | 0.853 | 0.906 |
| 4 | 0.810 | 0.709 | 0.810 | 0.800 | 0.866 |
| 5 | 0.764 | 0.652 | 0.764 | 0.752 | 0.829 |
| 6 | 0.721 | 0.602 | 0.721 | 0.708 | 0.793 |
| 7 | 0.683 | 0.559 | 0.683 | 0.669 | 0.766 |
| 8 | 0.648 | 0.521 | 0.648 | 0.634 | 0.729 |
| 9 | 0.616 | 0.487 | 0.616 | 0.601 | 0.700 |
| 10 | 0.587 | 0.457 | 0.587 | 0.572 | 0.674 |
| 11 | 0.560 | 0.430 | 0.560 | 0.545 | 0.648 |
| 12 | 0.535 | 0.405 | 0.535 | 0.520 | 0.625 |
| 14 | 0.491 | 0.363 | 0.491 | 0.476 | 0.582 |
| 16 | 0.453 | 0.328 | 0.453 | 0.437 | 0.544 |
| 18 | 0.419 | 0.298 | 0.419 | 0.404 | 0.511 |
| 20 | 0.390 | 0.272 | 0.390 | 0.375 | 0.480 |
| 22 | 0.364 | 0.250 | 0.364 | 0.349 | 0.453 |
| 24 | 0.340 | 0.230 | 0.340 | 0.327 | 0.428 |
| 26 | 0.320 | 0.213 | 0.320 | 0.306 | 0.406 |
| 28 | 0.301 | 0.198 | 0.301 | 0.288 | 0.385 |
| 30 | 0.284 | 0.184 | 0.284 | 0.271 | 0.367 |
| 32 | 0.268 | 0.172 | 0.268 | 0.256 | 0.349 |
| 34 | 0.254 | 0.161 | 0.254 | 0.242 | 0.333 |
| 36 | 0.241 | 0.151 | 0.241 | 0.229 | 0.318 |
| 40 | 0.218 | 0.134 | 0.218 | 0.207 | 0.292 |
| 44 | 0.198 | 0.120 | 0.198 | 0.188 | 0.269 |
| 48 | 0.181 | 0.108 | 0.181 | 0.171 | 0.248 |
| 52 | 0.167 | 0.098 | 0.167 | 0.157 | 0.231 |
| 56 | 0.154 | 0.089 | 0.154 | 0.145 | 0.215 |
| 60 | 0.142 | 0.081 | 0.142 | 0.134 | 0.200 |
| 64 | 0.132 | 0.074 | 0.132 | 0.124 | 0.188 |
| 68 | 0.123 | 0.068 | 0.123 | 0.115 | 0.176 |
| 72 | 0.115 | 0.063 | 0.115 | 0.107 | 0.166 |
| Mean | 35.572 | 22.572 | 35.601 | 33.734 | 49.018 |
| Median | 13.556 | 8.602 | 13.567 | 12.855 | 18.680 |
| Mode | 1.969 | 1.249 | 1.970 | 1.867 | 2.713 |

[a] From Witte and Schmidt (1977).

the values of *RULE*, *CVBS*, and *AAR* were taken as the mean values for the appropriate subgroup of the data. The least favorable case is that of a white addict. The "average" white addict has a predicted mean value of *LTFC* of only 22.572 months and a median value of 8.602. Almost 66% of such individuals are predicted to be reconvicted within 1 year and 77% within 2 years. On the other hand, the most favorable case is that of a black nonaddict. The "average" black nonaddict has a predicted mean value of *LTFC* of 49.018 months and a median of 18.680. About 38% of such individuals are predicted to be reconvicted within 1 year and 57% within 2 years.

As another rough way of seeing how well the lognormal distribution fits the data, we can compare the predicted distributions as just given with the actual frequencies observed in the data. This is done in Table 7.4.

The main problem in making these comparisons is that we do not observe *LTFC* for all individuals, whereas the predicted frequencies for *LTFC* are the frequencies we should expect if we observed each individual long enough for him to be reconvicted. We have tried to minimize this by considering groupings of *LTFC* only through 24 months; the entire time period over 24 months is grouped as "25 and over." Any individual who was not reconvicted during his follow-up period was placed in the "25 and over" category. For the most part this grouping is correct, because, of the 159 individuals who were not reconvicted, 121 had follow-up periods in excess of 24 months and therefore would unambiguously have a value of *LTFC* of 25 or over. This still leaves 38 individuals who were not reconvicted and who were placed in the "25 and over" category even though their follow-up period was less than 25 months. Some of these individuals would no doubt have been convicted before 24 months had elapsed, if their cases had been followed for that long; this would mainly have been in the period 13–24 months, because only 7 individuals who were not reconvicted had follow-up periods of 12 months or less. As a result, our actual frequencies will somewhat overstate the number in the "25 and over" group and somewhat understate the number in the "13–24" group, relative to what we would probably have observed if all follow-up periods had been at least 24 months long.

With this in mind, the predicted frequencies for the average case match the observed frequencies for all individuals well. The biggest discrepancies are in the "13–24" and "25 and over" groups, and these discrepancies are in the direction expected, based on the argument of the previous paragraph. The comparisons of predicted and actual for the various race–addiction subgroups are not quite as favorable. In particular, we appear to underpredict *LTFC* substantially for black nonaddicts. Nevertheless, the results in Table 7.4 are good enough not to cast serious doubt on the adequacy of the model.

Another interesting question to investigate is the adequacy of the assumption that the underlying distribution of *LTFC* is lognormal. The lognormal distribution was chosen originally because it is relatively simple to use (though not as simple as an exponential distribution) and because its shape seemed reasonable. In particular, the fact that its hazard rate first increases and then decreases made it seem intuitively correct for recidivism data. Other studies of the pattern of recidivism find either continually decreasing

**TABLE 7.4.** Comparison of Actual and Predicted Frequencies of Reconviction[a]

| *LTFC* (months) | Frequency | |
|---|---|---|
| | Predicted | Actual |
| All individuals (582 cases) | | |
| 0–2 | 0.139 | 0.127 |
| 3–6 | 0.178 | 0.175 |
| 7–12 | 0.171 | 0.187 |
| 13–24 | 0.182 | 0.158 |
| 25 and over | 0.330 | 0.352 |
| White *ALKY* (172 cases) | | |
| 0–2 | 0.224 | 0.227 |
| 3–6 | 0.217 | 0.215 |
| 7–12 | 0.176 | 0.128 |
| 13–24 | 0.162 | 0.174 |
| 25 and over | 0.221 | 0.256 |
| White non-*ALKY* (121 cases) | | |
| 0–2 | 0.139 | 0.132 |
| 3–6 | 0.178 | 0.182 |
| 7–12 | 0.171 | 0.207 |
| 13–24 | 0.182 | 0.157 |
| 25 and over | 0.330 | 0.322 |
| Black *ALKY* (106 cases) | | |
| 0–2 | 0.147 | 0.104 |
| 3–6 | 0.184 | 0.217 |
| 7–12 | 0.172 | 0.255 |
| 13–24 | 0.181 | 0.170 |
| 25 and over | 0.316 | 0.255 |
| Black non-*ALKY* (183 cases) | | |
| 0–2 | 0.094 | 0.044 |
| 3–6 | 0.146 | 0.109 |
| 7–12 | 0.157 | 0.191 |
| 13–24 | 0.175 | 0.137 |
| 25 and over | 0.417 | 0.519 |

[a] From Witte and Schmidt (1977).

probabilities of recidivism [e.g., Hoffman and Stone-Meierhoefer (1979)] or probabilities that first increase and then decline [e.g., Kitchener *et al.* (1977)].[1] Unfortunately, the frequencies of recidivism reported in these studies, like the ones in Table 7.4, confound the effects of "true state dependence" with the effects of "heterogeneity," as discussed in Section 6.6.

The first set of results in Table 7.4 provides support for the lognormal assumption. Nevertheless, it would be prudent either to use a more robust model, such as the proportionate hazards model (see Section 6.7), or to try other distributional assumptions and see how well they fit the data. We choose the latter course, and therefore we estimated our final specification of the model in three additional ways: (1) by using the censored exponential model with explanatory variables, whose likelihood function is given by Eq. (6.2.6); or (2) by using the censored normal (Tobit) model of Section 4.3, with censoring by the length of the follow-up period; (3) by ordinary least squares, ignoring the censoring—that is, taking *LTFC* equal to length of follow-up for those not convicted. These results are given in Table 7.5.

Of particular interest in Table 7.5 is the maximized value of the likelihood function, which is a natural measure of which distribution best fits the data. It is marginally higher for the censored lognormal distribution than for the censored exponential and is much higher for either of these two distributions than for either the censored or uncensored normal. This clearly supports our choice of the lognormal distribution.

However, it is interesting to note that the signs of all coefficients are the same by all techniques and their levels of significance are roughly comparable. If our purpose were only to make statements about the direction of effect of the explanatory variables, the choice of distribution would not be important.

A final comparison between the various distributions is given in Table 7.6, which compares actual and predicted frequencies for the same groupings of *LTFC* as in Table 7.4 and for the "average" case. The predicted frequencies are again based on the sample mean values of the explanatory variables. Clearly the censored normal and least-squares analyses do not lead to very satisfactory predicted frequencies. It also appears that the fit of the lognormal distribution is better than that of the exponential; this is consistent with the likelihood values given previously.

Given the increasing prominence of prediction in the literature [e.g., Chaiken and Chaiken (1981); Greenwood (1981); Monohan (1981)], the improvement in predictive accuracy that we find by using distributions other than the normal should be of considerable interest. Our results indicate that the use of simple and generally available techniques such as ordinary least squares is likely to lead to poor and misleading predictions.

**TABLE 7.5.** Analysis of *LTFC* by Alternative Methods[a]

| Variable | Censored lognormal | | Censored exponential | | Censored normal | | Least squares | |
|---|---|---|---|---|---|---|---|---|
| | Coefficient | $t$ Ratio | Coefficient | $t$ Ratio | Coefficient | $t$ Ratio | Coefficient | $t$ Ratio |
| *CNST* | 33.4346 | 5.38 | 20.211 | 8.13 | 19.870 | 7.42 | 17.482 | — |
| *RULE* | −1.1487 | −2.34 | −1.3356 | −5.41 | −1.7158 | −3.36 | −1.5957 | −4.10 |
| *CVBS* | −0.4918 | −3.70 | −0.2642 | −4.56 | −0.3457 | −2.63 | −0.2677 | −2.64 |
| *AAR* | 0.05120 | 3.22 | 0.03249 | 4.94 | 0.0246 | 3.63 | 0.01671 | 3.33 |
| *RACE* | −14.3138 | −3.41 | −5.9078 | −4.00 | −5.9674 | −3.72 | −4.5015 | −3.70 |
| *ALKY* | −16.6306 | −5.47 | −10.258 | −6.83 | −8.1290 | −5.01 | −5.4944 | −4.81 |
| Log $L$ | −1695.508 | | −1717.933 | | −1964.300 | | −2365.134 | |

[a] From Witte and Schmidt (1977).

**TABLE 7.6.**[a] Comparison of Actual and Predicted Frequencies, for Various Distributions

| | Frequencies | | | | |
|---|---|---|---|---|---|
| | | Predicted | | | |
| *LTFC* (months) | Actual | Lognormal | Exponential | Normal | Least squares |
| 0–2 | 0.127 | 0.139 | 0.122 | 0.133 | 0.159 |
| 3–6 | 0.175 | 0.178 | 0.140 | 0.065 | 0.077 |
| 7–12 | 0.187 | 0.171 | 0.169 | 0.118 | 0.150 |
| 13–24 | 0.158 | 0.182 | 0.231 | 0.309 | 0.326 |
| 25 and over | 0.352 | 0.330 | 0.338 | 0.375 | 0.288 |

[a] From Witte and Schmidt (1977).

## 7.3. Analysis of the 1975 Data

The results of Section 7.2 give considerable support to the contention that the techniques of statistical survivor analysis can be useful in criminal justice research. In this section, we more or less repeat the analysis using a different data set which is more representative of the prison population. Also, because this data set is larger than the previous one, we are able to check the predictive accuracy of our model outside of the sample used to estimate it.

The data used here are described in detail in Appendix B and were also described in Section 5.3. Therefore we shall note only that the original sample consists of 4881 individuals who were released from prison in North Carolina in the first half of 1975. Of this sample, there were 2216 observations which contained all of the information needed for our analysis. This subsample of 2216 observations was further split into a validation sample of 600 and an estimation sample of 1616. It is with this estimation sample (1616 observations, with complete records) that we begin our analysis.

The dependent variable analyzed is the length of time (in months) from release until reimprisonment in North Carolina, which we will denote *LTFPC*. This is not the same as the dependent variable *LTFC* analyzed in the last section, the difference being essentially that in this section we consider only return to prison in North Carolina, whereas in the last section we considered any conviction (in North Carolina or elsewhere), whether it resulted in imprisonment or not. The present definition is required because in this data set we do not observe recidivist convictions not resulting in imprisonment in North Carolina.

To this data we fit the censored lognormal model described in Section 6.5 (and applied in the last section). It should be noted that the sample is heavily censored because only 200 of the 1616 individuals returned to prison in

North Carolina before the end of the follow-up. Thus it is important to use a statistical technique that takes this into account. The lognormal distribution was selected because of its successful application in the last section.

Our first specification included the explanatory variables *CNST*, *RACE*, *RULE*, *WR*, *CONVBS*, *AAR*, *SUPER*, *SG*, *MF*, *SEX*, *PROPTY*, *PERSON*, *MS*, *ALCHY*, and *JUNKY*. (All of these are as previously defined in Sections 3.3 or 5.2.) However, the last four variables were found to be insignificantly related to *LTFPC* at conventional levels. Their $t$ ratios are as follows: *JUNKY* (0.61), *MS* (−1.04), *PERSON* (0.71), *ALCHY* (−0.83). A likelihood ratio test of their joint significance yielded a test statistic of 3.40, which does not exceed the usual significance points of the $\chi_4^2$ distribution. We therefore considered a reduced specification obtained by dropping these four variables. The results are given in Table 7.7. We can seen that all the variables in this specification have coefficients that are significantly different from zero (as indicated by their $t$ ratios) at the 10% level, except for *SEX*. However, *SEX* was retained because dropping it yielded a significant likelihood ratio test statistic.

The results in Table 7.7 indicate that the type of individual who is likely to return to prison soonest is a young black male with a lot of previous convictions and rule violations and little formal education, whose sample crime was a felony that was not against property, whose release was unsupervised, and who participated in the work release program. For the most part these results seem reasonable (with the possible exception of the effect of the work release program). They are also mostly consistent with the results of our analysis of time sentenced using this data set (see Section 5.3), in the sense

**TABLE 7.7.** Results of Analysis of Length of Time until Reincarceration—Final Specification, Original Data Set[a]

| Variable | Coefficient | $t$ Ratio |
|---|---|---|
| *CNST* | 78.4427 | 0.78 |
| *RACE* | 41.0837 | 1.71 |
| *RULE* | −14.3200 | −3.22 |
| *WR* | −44.9062 | −1.70 |
| *CONVBS* | −5.2594 | −4.12 |
| *AAR* | 0.6567 | 2.90 |
| *SUPER* | 52.2803 | 2.20 |
| *SG* | 10.0841 | 2.58 |
| *MF* | −57.1570 | −2.12 |
| *SEX* | −104.7234 | −1.47 |
| *PROPTY* | −51.4826 | −1.84 |

[a] $\sigma^2 = 2.1752$.

that most of the variables that increase length of sentence also reduce length of time until recidivism, and conversely. Every variable that appears in both Tables 7.7 and 5.4 fits this pattern. However, some variables (*RULE*, *WR*, *SG*, *MF*) significantly affect *LTFPC* but not *TTSENT*, whereas *ALCHY* significantly affects *TTSENT* but not *LTFPC*.

Also, many of these results are consistent with the results of the analysis of *LTFC* using the 1969 and 1971 data, as reported in the last section (and Table 7.2). However, there are two major differences. The first is that the effect of *RACE* is precisely the opposite of what was found using the 1969–1971 data. This was found in Chapter 5 as well. The possible reasons for this were discussed there and will be discussed again later in this section. The second difference is that *ALCHY* and *JUNKY* are both insignificant in this analysis, whereas in the previous analysis alcohol and drug addiction were major explanatory variables. As with *RACE*, it is not clear whether this is an artifact owing to one or the other of the data sets or a reflection of actual change from the early to the mid 1970s. At least for *ALCHY*, we suspect that it is an artifact caused by the fact that many alcohol-related offenses (e.g., public drunkenness) do not result in a prison sentence.

At this point it is worthwhile to recall that, of the 4881 individuals who are potential members of our sample, information on all the variables used was available for only 2216. However, there was information on an additional 1632 individuals for all the variables used except *ALCHY* or *JUNKY*. Because *ALCHY* and *JUNKY* have now been dropped from the analysis, we can expand our usable sample from 2216 to 3848 individuals. This amounts to 70% of the individuals released from prison during the first 6 months of 1975. This is an important improvement, because our expanded data set is far more representative of the population of all releasees than the original data set was. In fact, individuals excluded from this expanded data set tend to be short-term (mean value of length of sample sentence served was only 5 months), misdemeanant offenders, who would not normally participate in correctional programs. Thus the expanded data set should be quite representative of those releasees who are potential participants in the correctional programs that our models will be used (in the next chapter) to evaluate.

The 3848 individuals in this enlarge sample were randomly split into an estimation sample of 2848 individuals and a validation sample of 1000 individuals. This is completely analogous to the split of the earlier sample (of 2216 individuals) into estimation (1616) and validation (600) samples. To estimate our basic model we randomly selected 1000 individuals from the estimation sample. This was done because a sample of 1000 is adequate to obtain reliable estimates and because estimation using 2848 data points would have exhausted our computer budget.

Using this data set, we estimated the model containing all the explanatory variables used previously, except *ALCHY* and *JUNKY*.[2] When this was done, the variables *RACE*, *SUPER*, *MF*, *WR*, *PROPTY*, and *SEX* turned out to be insignificantly related to *LTFPCV*. None of these variables had an asymptotic $t$ ratio over one in absolute value, and the likelihood ratio test statistic for their joint significance was only 2.10, which is far less than the usual critical points of the $\chi_6^2$ distribution. Therefore, these variables were dropped from the analysis.

The variables remaining in our specification are *CNST*, *RULE*, *CONVBS*, *AAR*, *SG*, *MS*, and *PERSON*. The results for this specification are given in Table 7.8. They indicate that the type of individual who is likely to return to prison soonest is young, single, and uneducated, has many previous convictions and rule violations, and committed a sample crime that was not against a person.

As is obvious at a glance, the results in Table 7.8 are considerably different from those in Table 7.7. Only four variables (not including *CNST*) were significantly related to *LTFPC* in both cases: *RULE*, *CONVBS*, *AAR*, and *SG*. (Each of these four variables had the same sign coefficient in both cases, as well.) However, six variables were significantly related to *LTFPC* in Table 7.7 but not in Table 7.8: *RACE*, *SEX*, *SUPER*, *WR*, *MF*, and *PROPTY*. Another two variables, *MS* and *PERSON*, were significantly related to *LTFPC* in Table 7.8 but not in Table 7.7.

Of course, the results in Table 7.8 should be more representative of the entire prison population than those in Table 7.7 because they were based on a more complete data set. However, the purpose of drawing these comparisons is to point out how important these differences are; in other words,

**TABLE 7.8.** Results of Analysis of Length of Time until Reincarceration— Final Specification, Expanded Data Set[a]

| Variable | Coefficient | $t$ Ratio |
|---|---|---|
| *CNST* | −179.1967 | −1.58 |
| *RULE* | −10.4744 | −2.31 |
| *CONVBS* | −12.0640 | −2.09 |
| *AAR* | 0.8102 | 1.95 |
| *SG* | 25.8254 | 2.74 |
| *MS* | 131.0160 | 1.94 |
| *PERSON* | 291.4832 | 1.62 |

[a]From Schmidt and Witte (1980). Reprinted from *Evaluation Reviews* **4** (5), p. 591 by permission of the publisher, Sage Publications, Inc. $\sigma^2 =$ 2.6471.

how easy it is to draw inappropriate conclusions by analyzing a nonrepresentative sample. These comparisons point out clearly that all of the results of Sections 5.3–5.4 must be viewed with some caution because they were based on the same nonrepresentative sample as the results of Table 7.7. We think that it is a considerable advantage of the present analysis that it was based on a sample that is fairly representative of the types of samples one encounters in program evaluation. As noted previously, the type of individual who was systematically excluded from the present sample is the short-term misdemeanant, who is also unlikely to participate in a rehabilitative program.

Incidentally, it is of some interest that *RACE* is one of the variables that was significantly related to *LTFPC* in the previous analysis (Table 7.7) but not in the present analysis (Table 7.8). In the previous analysis and in the Tobit analysis of Section 5.3, we noted that the coefficient of *RACE* had changed sign from the analyses of the 1969 and 1971 data. That *RACE* now becomes insignificantly related to *LTFPC* when the data set is made more representative tends to indicate that this sign reversal may well have been just an artifact (owing to the nonrepresentative nature of one or both of the previous data sets) rather than an indication of some actual change in behavior over time.

The estimated model, as given in Table 7.8, was checked by using it to predict probabilities of recidivism for the 1000 individuals in the new validation sample. Let $P_i$ be the probability implied by the model that individual $i$ will return to prison before the end of his follow-up period. Then, with a total of $N$ individuals in the validation sample (here $N = 1000$), the total number of recidivists predicted is $\sum_{i=1}^{N} P_i$. In the present case, our predicted number of recidivists, using this formula, is 178.66. The actual number of recidivists in the validation sample was 169. Thus we overpredict the rate of recidivism in the validation sample by 7.5%. This is a reasonably small error. Furthermore, this prediction error is statistically insignificant, in the following sense. Let $R$ be the actual number of recidivists and the $P_i$ be the predicted probabilities of recidivism, as before. Under the null hypothesis that our model is adequate, the test statistic

$$\left(R - \sum_{i=1}^{N} P_i\right) \Bigg/ \left[\sum_{i=1}^{N} P_i(1 - P_i)\right]^{1/2} \tag{7.3.1}$$

is distributed as $N(0, 1)$, for large $N$. In the present case the test statistic equals $-0.82$, which is not close to the usual critical points of $N(0, 1)$. Thus we conclude that our model does a good job of predicting the recidivism of the individuals in the validation sample. This is encouraging because accuracy of prediction outside the sample used for estimation is considered a good test of a model.[3] It is also encouraging because our models must predict accurately if they are to be useful for program evaluation.

## 7.4. Analysis of Subsamples of the 1975 Data

In the last section we estimated our model on a sample of 1000 individuals drawn at random from our estimation sample of 2848 individuals and validated the model on our validation sample of another 1000 individuals. The results were good; nevertheless, we shall now attempt to improve on them by estimating *separate* models for various race, sex, and age groupings. This procedure is precisely analogous to what was done in our Tobit analysis of *TTSENT*, as reported in Section 5.4.

It should be noted at the outset that *RACE* and *SEX* were insignificantly related to *LTFPC* in our analysis just reported. As a result there may not be as much to gain by looking at separate race, sex, and age groups as there was, say, in our analysis of *TTSENT*, where *RACE* and *SEX* were both important explanatory variables. However, there still may be interactions of *RACE*, *SEX*, and *AAR* with each other, or with other explanatory variables, that would not show up in our overall specification and that may be worth discovering.

As in the Tobit analysis of Chapter 5, we first planned a separation of the sample into six groups: (1) white male adults, (2) black male adults, (3) white male youths, (4) black male youths, (5) male Native Americans, and (6) females. These groups are as defined in Section 5.4.

Of these groups, we first tried analyzing the subsample of male Native Americans. This subsample consisted of the 77 male Native Americans in the 2848-individual estimation sample. However, we were unable to estimate a reasonable model for this group. Virtually no coefficients had statistically significant coefficients, and several had unexpected signs. Furthermore, the model for male Native Americans did not predict well, either in the estimation sample or in the validation sample. Therefore, as in Section 5.4, we combined our male Native Americans subsample with the two white male subsamples. This leaves us with five subsamples, to be used in the rest of this section: (1) females, (2) nonblack male adults, (3) black male adults, (4) nonblack male youths, and (5) black male youths. A breakdown of the sample into these groups is given in Table 7.9.

We turn next to our subsample of females. This subsample contains only 133 observations. We first ran the model using all explanatory variables originally tried for the overall model, except *SEX*. When this was done, each of the variables had a coefficient insignificantly different from zero. In

**TABLE 7.9.** Final Breakdown of Sample into Subsamples

| Category | Estimation sample: Total observations | Estimation sample: Number returning | Validation sample: Total observations | Validation sample: Number returning |
|---|---|---|---|---|
| Females | 133 | 10 | 54 | 5 |
| Nonblack male adults | 1110 | 180 | 365 | 50 |
| Black male adults | 961 | 147 | 357 | 58 |
| Nonblack male youths | 409 | 86 | 140 | 34 |
| Black male youths | 235 | 67 | 84 | 22 |
| Total | 2848 | 490 | 1000 | 169 |

fact, none of the *t* ratios was over one in absolute value. Under these circumstances it did not seem possible to choose among the explanatory variables on the basis of their statistical significance. We therefore simply chose the same final specification as for the overall model reported in Table 7.8. The results for this specification applied to the 133 females are given in Table 7.10.

As in the larger specification, none of the variables has a *t* ratio over one. Nevertheless, the results are not unreasonable; for example, the signs of the coefficients of all variables except *PERSON* agree with their counterparts in the overall model of Table 7.8.

We next tested this model's predictions agains those given by the overall model. Although there are only 54 females in the validation sample, their recidivism rate of 9.3% (5 of 54) is reasonably close to the recidivism rate of 7.5% (10 of 133) for the females in the estimation sample. As a result, we validated our models only on the 54 females in the validation sample. As just mentioned, the actual number of recidivist females was 5. The predicted number using the female subsample model was 4.115, yielding a test statistic of 0.46. On the other hand, the predicted number using the overall model was 9.041, yielding a test statistic of $-1.49$. We therefore conclude that the female subsample model of Table 7.10 better accounts for the recidivism of females than the overall model does. (Incidentally, we would reach the same conclusion if we validated both models on all 187 females.)

We next turn to our subsample of nonblack male adults. This subsample of the estimation sample contained 1110 observations. It was our biggest subsample and also the one for which we obtained the most satisfactory results.

The variables that we found to be significantly related to *LTFPC* were *CNST*, *CONVBS*, *SG*, *MS*, and *PROPTY*. The results for this specification are given in Table 7.10. As is clear from their *t* ratios, all of which exceed two in absolute value, all of these variables have coefficients that are signifi-

**TABLE 7.10.** Results of Analysis of Length of Time until Reincarceration on Five Subsamples

| Variable | Females[a] | | Nonblack male adults[b] | | Black male adults[c] | | Nonblack male youths[d] | | Black male youths[e] | |
|---|---|---|---|---|---|---|---|---|---|---|
| | Coefficient | *t* Ratio | Coefficient | *t* Ratio | Coefficient | *t* Ratio | Coefficient | *t* Ratio | Coefficient | *t* Ratio |
| *CNST* | 161.3525 | 0.06 | 408.1079 | 3.00 | 100.0704 | 0.96 | −62.2772 | −0.36 | −121.1007 | −0.85 |
| *RULE* | −101.2221 | −0.44 | — | — | −5.6854 | −2.78 | −10.6426 | −3.80 | −4.7360 | −1.92 |
| *CONVBS* | −35.7320 | −0.29 | −6.3796 | −3.58 | −5.9652 | −2.94 | — | — | — | — |
| *AAR* | 0.8359 | 0.11 | — | — | 0.5581 | 2.04 | 0.6822 | 0.99 | 0.8930 | 1.47 |
| *SG* | 7.8496 | 0.04 | 16.4592 | 2.01 | — | — | 8.4925 | 2.18 | — | — |
| *MS* | 16.7140 | 0.05 | 131.3447 | 2.25 | 99.6721 | 1.92 | — | — | — | — |
| *PERSON* | −31.4640 | −0.12 | — | — | — | — | 126.1094 | 1.07 | 99.5681 | 1.15 |
| *PROPTY* | — | — | −275.5290 | −2.97 | — | — | — | — | — | — |
| *MF* | — | — | — | — | −98.7898 | −1.58 | 41.6531 | 2.82 | −30.5736 | −1.50 |
| *SUPER* | — | — | — | — | 128.5761 | 1.97 | −73.2653 | −1.56 | 27.6289 | 1.38 |
| *WR* | — | — | — | — | — | — | −47.4701 | −2.48 | — | — |

[a] $N = 133$, $\sigma^2 = 2.0191$.
[b] $N = 1110$, $\sigma^2 = 2.8445$.
[c] $N = 961$, $\sigma^2 = 2.3599$.
[d] $N = 409$, $\sigma^2 = 1.4723$.
[e] $N = 235$, $\sigma^2 = 1.4399$.

cantly different from zero. These results, which indicate that a nonblack male adult is likely to return to prison sooner the more previous convictions he has, the less education he has, if he is single, and if his sample sentence was for a crime against property, are consistent with the results of the overall model.

Six other variables were insignificantly related to *LTFPCV*. Listed with their *t* ratios, they are: *AAR* (1.13), *SUPER* (1.17), *MF* (−0.01), *WR* (−0.87), *RULE* (−1.33), and *PERSON* (0.80). The likelihood ratio test statistic of the joint significance of these six variables was 8.78, which is insignificant when compared with the usual significance points of the $\chi^2_6$ distribution.

There were 365 nonblack male adults in the validation sample, which we judged to be more than enough to provide a good test of the model. The number of recidivists was 50. The predicted number using the nonblack male adult subgroup model of Table 7.10 was 58.9207, yielding a test statistic of −1.28. On the other hand, the predicted number using the overall model of Table 7.8 was 59.4163, yielding a test statistic of −1.36. As a result, we conclude that the nonblack male adult model better accounts for the recidivism of nonblack male adults than the overall model does.

Our subsample of black male adults contained 961 individuals. This is certainly a sufficiently large sample size for us to obtain good estimates.

Our final specification for this subsample is also given in Table 7.10. It contains the variables *CNST*, *CONVBS*, *AAR*, *SUPER*, *MF*, *RULE*, and *MS*. All of these variables had coefficients that were significantly different from zero at the 10% level, as judged by their *t* ratios, except for *MF*; it was included because its coefficient was significantly different from zero at the 10% level, using the likelihood ratio test. (The test statistic was 3.27, which exceeds the 10% critical point of $\chi^2_1$.) Our results indicate that a black male adult is likely to return to prison sooner the younger he is, the more rule violations or previous convictions he has, if his release was unsupervised, if he was a felon, and if he is single. With the exception of the effect of *MF*, these directions of effect are in agreement with those for the whole sample.

Four variables were insignificantly related to *LTFPC* in this subsample. With their *t* ratios, they are: *SG* (0.67), *WR* (0.89), *PROPTY* (−0.25), and *PERSON* (0.39). The likelihood ratio test statistic used to test their joint significance was also very insignificant.

Although this model seemed entirely reasonable, it did not predict as well as the overall model did. There were 357 black male adults in the validation sample. (This is certainly enough to test the models fairly.) Of these, 58 returned to prison during the follow-up. Using the black male adult subsample model of Table 7.10, the predicted number of recidivists was 54.9498, yielding a test statistic of 0.45. On the other hand, using the overall model of

Table 7.8, the predicted number was 55.9859, yielding a test statistic is 0.29. This indicates that the overall model better accounted for the recidivism rate of black male adults than the model for black male adults did.

Our subsample of nonblack male youths contained 409 individuals. Although this is a reasonably large number, the data suffered from a considerable multicollinearity problem, which made it very difficult to find a satisfactory specification.

The first indication of this problem was that it proved computationally impossible to perform any run on a specification that included both *PROPTY* and *PERSON*. When each of these variables was run separately in turn, together with all other explanatory variables except *RACE* and *SEX*, the run containing *PERSON* attained a higher value of the likelihood function than the run containing *PROPTY*. As a result, *PROPTY* was deleted from the list of explanatory variables to be tried further.

We next dropped the variables *CONVBS* and *MS* from the specification because their coefficients were insignificantly different from zero at the 10% level when judged either by their $t$ ratios or their likelihood ratio test statistic. Their $t$ ratios were, respectively, $-0.51$ and $-1.45$; the likelihood ratio test statistic for their joint significance was 2.66, which is not even close to the usual significance points of $\chi^2_2$.

With these variables deleted, we arrived at the final specification given in Table 7.10. Note that several of the variables listed there, especially *PERSON* and *AAR*, have coefficients that are insignificantly different from zero, as judged by their $t$ ratios. Nevertheless, their coefficients are significantly different from zero when judged by the likelihood ratio test.

The results given in Table 7.10 indicate that a nonblack male youth is likely to return to prison sooner the younger he is, the more rule violations he has, the less educated he is, if his release was supervised, if he was on work release, and if his sample sentence was for a misdemeanor that was not against a person. With the exception of the effect of *SUPER*, these results are in accord with our previous results.

There were 140 nonblack male youths in the validation sample. Of these, 34 were recidivists. The predicted number of recidivists using the nonblack male youth model of Table 7.10 was 30.4930, yielding a test statistic of 0.74. On the other hand, the predicted number using the overall model of Table 7.8 was 35.6242, yielding a test statistic of $-0.35$. This indicates that the best model to use for nonblack male youths is the overall model.

Finally, our subsample of black male youths contained 235 individuals. This is not an overly large number for this type of model, and we had some difficulty in finding variables that were strongly related to *LTFPC*.

Our final specification for this subgroup is given in the last section of Table 7.10. Only one of the variables, *RULE*, had a coefficient significantly different from zero at the 10% level, as judged by its *t* ratio. However, to have dropped the other variables would not have left much of a specification. There were five variables that were tried but not kept in the final specification. With their *t* ratios, they are: *CONVBS* (−0.24), *SG* (0.19), *WR* (0.97), *MS* (0.67), and *PROPTY* (0.13). The likelihood ratio test statistic for their joint significance was 6.00, which is far from significant.

The results of Table 7.10 indicate that a black male youth will tend to return to prison sooner the younger he is, the more rule violations he had, if his release was unsupervised, and if his sample crime was a felony that was not against a person. With the exception of the effect of *MF*, these results are in agreement with most of our other results.

There were 84 black male youths in the validation sample, of whom 22 were recidivists. Using the black male youth model of Table 7.10, the predicted number of recidivists was 26.423, yielding a test statistic of −1.08. Using the overall model of Table 7.8, the predicted number was 18.590, yielding a test statistic of 0.91. This leads us to conclude that, for the subsample of black male youths, we should use the overall model.

Having estimated separate models for our subgroups of the data, we now ask whether the use of these models allows us to make better predictions about the validation sample as a whole. Recall that in the last section, we reported the results of the validation of the overall model of Table 7.8. We overpredicted the number of recidivists in our validation sample by 5.7% (predicting 178.658, as opposed to the actual number of 169). This difference was not statistically significant; the test statistic was −0.82.

We now investigate the alternative of generating predictions by using, for each individual, the best model for the subgroup to which the individual belongs. We separate individuals into the same five groups previously described. In this section we have reached conclusions about which model provides the best predictions for each of these groups. Specifically, for females and nonblack male adults, we use the appropriate models given in Table 7.10. On the other hand, for the other three groups, we use the overall model of Table 7.8. That the overall model is the best model for three of these subgroups is just a reflection of the weak influence of race and sex on *LTFPC*, as discussed at the beginning of this section.

Nevertheless, use of the best model for each subgroup improves our predictions noticeably. The predicted number of recidivists in the validation sample, using the best model for each subgroup, is 173.236, which is considerably closer to the actual number of 169 than is the previous predicted number of 178.658. We now overpredict the recidivism rate by only 2.5%, as opposed to 5.7% formerly. The test statistic for the accuracy of the predictions is naturally smaller now (in absolute value), −0.36 versus −0.82.

Thus it appears that it was worth considering subgroups separately, even if only two of the subgroup models are actually used.

In performing all of the validations reported in this section, we have followed exactly the procedure detailed at the end of Section 7.3. That is, in calculating the probability $P_i$ of the $i$th individual's recidivism, we have always used for each individual the length of his or her own follow-up period. These probabilities are then added together to obtain the predicted number of recidivists, which is compared with the actual number of recidivists.

However, this procedure could also be applied over arbitrary time periods not exceeding the actual follow-up period. By doing this sequentially for various lengths of time, we can see whether the actual pattern of recidivism over time differs from the predicted pattern.

To be more explicit, let us change slightly the notation used in Section 7.3. In a group of $N$ individuals, let $R_m$ be the number who return to prison within $m$ months after release, where $m$ is an arbitrary number that need not equal the full length of the follow-up. Similarly, let $P_{im}$ represent the predicted probability of the $i$th individual returning to prison within $m$ months of his release. Then the predicted number of recidivists within $m$ months is $\sum_{i=1}^{N} P_{im}$, and the test statistic used to test the difference between the actual and predicted number is identical to (7.3.1), but with $R_m$ replacing $R$ and $P_{im}$ replacing $P_i$. The point is that this test can be carried out in turn for $m = 1, 2, 3, 4, \ldots,$ length of follow-up. In doing so, we can obtain a clearer picture of how actual and predicted rates of recidivism compare over time.

One point worth mentioning is that in this case not every individual had a follow-up period as long as 25 months. The follow-up times actually ranged from 20 to 25 months. If we are comparing actual to predicted recidivism for, say, $m = 23$ months, it is clear that the actual number of recidivists will likely be smaller than it would be if everyone had had a follow-up period that long. As a result, we must make sure that our predicted number of recidivists also reflects the fact that some individuals have follow-up periods less than 23 months. The correct way to do this is to enter into the test statistic for the $i$th individual with a follow-up period of, say, only 21 months, $P_{i,21}$ rather than $P_{i,23}$. More formally, for a given value of $m$, for individual $i$ we should use the probability $P_{im*}$, where for the $i$th individual $m*$ is the minimum of $m$ or of the length of his follow-up period. (Clearly, this complication would not arise if all individuals had follow-up periods of the same length.)

We have given the results of such an analysis in Table 7.11. Predictions were made here for the 1000 individuals in the validation sample and were based on the best model for each subgroup. We have made predictions by month for the period 2–25 months after release. Results for 1 month after

**TABLE 7.11.** Sequential Predictions on Validation Sample

| Number of months after release | Number of recidivists: Predicted | Number of recidivists: Actual | Test statistic |
|---|---|---|---|
| 2 | 10.323 | 10 | −0.11 |
| 3 | 18.090 | 17 | −0.27 |
| 4 | 26.536 | 25 | −0.31 |
| 5 | 35.305 | 39 | 0.65 |
| 6 | 44.203 | 44 | −0.03 |
| 7 | 53.117 | 54 | 0.13 |
| 8 | 61.977 | 62 | 0.00 |
| 9 | 70.740 | 74 | 0.41 |
| 10 | 79.380 | 84 | 0.55 |
| 11 | 87.879 | 95 | 0.81 |
| 12 | 96.227 | 104 | 0.85 |
| 13 | 104.420 | 113 | 0.90 |
| 14 | 112.455 | 116 | 0.36 |
| 15 | 120.331 | 131 | 1.06 |
| 16 | 128.050 | 141 | 1.25 |
| 17 | 135.614 | 148 | 1.17 |
| 18 | 143.025 | 151 | 0.73 |
| 19 | 150.288 | 154 | 0.33 |
| 20 | 157.406 | 161 | 0.32 |
| 21 | 163.132 | 164 | 0.08 |
| 22 | 167.437 | 165 | −0.21 |
| 23 | 170.430 | 167 | −0.29 |
| 24 | 172.290 | 169 | −0.28 |
| 25 | 173.236 | 169 | −0.36 |

release could also be generated, but 1 month seemed too short a period to be interesting. Similarly, 25 months represents the maximum follow-up period for our sample. As is clear from Table 7.11, we overpredicted recidivism for short and long follow-up times, and we underpredicted it for lengths of time in the middle of the 2–25-month range. At no point was the difference between the actual and predicted rate significantly different from zero at reasonable confidence levels. This is indeed strong support for the usefulness of our models for predictive purposes.

## 7.5. Summary and Conclusions

In this chapter we investigated the determinants of the length of time until recidivism. This was done using two data sets and two different definitions of recidivism. In both cases we fit a censored lognormal distribution, making use of individual characteristics as explanatory variables, as desdribed in Section 6.3.

Our first analysis, presented in Section 7.2, was of our 1969 and 1971 data set, and the definition of recidivism was reconviction. Our results indicate that an individual will return to criminal activity less rapidly if he is a relatively old, black, nonaddict who had no prior convictions and violated no rules during his sample sentence. We also performed some detailed checks on the adequacy of the lognormal model, including fitting of other distributions. The lognormal model fit noticably better than the alternative models considered. The main conclusions of our analysis would not have been reversed by use of a different distribution or by the use of a simpler technique such as ordinary least squares, but the resulting predictions would have been very unreliable.

Our second analysis, presented in Sections 7.3 and 7.4, was of our 1975 data set. Here the definition of recidivism was return to prison. The model was first estimated on a random sample of those individuals for whom complete data were available. However, because the alcohol and drug variables turned out to be insignificant, we were able (by dropping them) to enlarge our usable sample, thereby making it much more representative of the population of releasees.

The enlarged sample was randomly split into an estimation sample and a validation sample. The model was then estimated on a sample of 1000 individuals taken randomly from the estimation sample. We found that the type of individual who is likely to return to prison soonest is young, single, and uneducated, had many previous convictions and rule violations, and had a sample crime that was not against a person. This model was checked by making predictions for the 1000 individuals in the validation sample and comparing these to the actual number of recidivists in the validation sample. Our model overpredicted the recidivism rate by 5.7%; this difference was not statistically significant at usual confidence levels.

We next estimated separate models for females, nonblack male adults, black male adults, nonblack male youths, and black male youths. For each of these groups, a "best" model was chosen, the criterion of goodness being predictive accuracy. For females and nonblack male adults, the best model was a model estimated using data for that group only, whereas for the other three groups the best model was just the overall model. Predictions were again generated for the 1000 individuals in the validation sample, using for each individual the best model for his group. These predictions were better than those made using the overall model for everyone; we now overpredicted the recidivism rate by only 2.5%. In fact, we were now able to predict the number of recidivists for all lengths of time from 2 to 25 months after release, with predictive errors that were statistically insignificant. This result was unexpectedly good and is impressive evidence for the adequacy of our models for predictive purposes.

Most of the results of our two analyses are consistent with one another (and with the results of our analyses of Chapters 3 and 5). Where differences exist they are almost always one of significance (a variable being significant in one analysis, but not in another); the direction of effect is seldom ambiguous.

## Notes to Chapter 7

1. Actually, Kitchener *et al.* (1977) did not calculate probabilities of recidivism. However, such probabilities were calculated from their data by Hoffman and Stone-Meierhoefer (1979).

2. Note that the variables *MS* and *PERSON* were reentered into the specification to see if the expansion of the data set might make them significant. Indeed, it did. This points out the difference made by using the expanded data set and the importance of using the most representative data set possible. It is even quite possible that if we had values of *ALCHY* and *JUNKY* for all the individuals in our expanded data set, these variables too would be significantly related to LTFPC. Unfortunately, there is no way to check this possibility.

3. Many models fit well inside their estimation sample but predict poorly outside it. In other words, there are many historians but few prophets.

# Chapter 8

## Use of Models of Recidivism for Program Evaluation

### 8.1. Introduction

Evaluations of correctional programs, as well as many other types of social programs, have been greatly hindered because classical experimental designs are often either impossible for institutional reasons or simply too costly. In most correctional settings, random assignment of individuals to programs is not feasible owing to moral, legal, and administrative considerations. In addition, in the rare situations in which random assignment has been possible, the costs of following up both a control and an experimental group have often proven substantial.

To combat the first difficulty, researchers in the correctional field have often resorted to quasi-experimental techniques, particularly the use of comparison groups.[1] Although such techniques are extremely valuable, they generally do not reduce the cost of evaluating correctional programs. (Indeed, they often increase it.) In addition, the use of comparison groups makes it difficult to attribute any changes observed to program participation, because the group of participants in the correctional program usually differs significantly from the comparison group of nonparticipants in a number of important ways other than program participation. With such designs, it is necessary to control for these other differences which may lead to changed behavior before one can attribute an observed change to program participation. This requires a model that indicates the factors likely to affect the outcome of interest, and a statistical technique that will allow control for the factors identified.

In this chapter, we illustrate the use of statistical models in program evaluation. Specifically, we use the models estimated in Chapters 5 and 7 to evaluate a rehabilitative program for youthful offenders in North Carolina. The general principles involved are described in Section 8.2. Section 8.3 describes the program to be evaluated and the data used to evaluate it, and Sections 8.4 and 8.5 give the results of the evaluation. Our conclusions are presented in Section 8.6.

## 8.2. Techniques for Program Evaluation

If assignment of individuals to a program was purely random, program evaluation would involve no notable statistical difficulties. One would simply follow program participants and a control group of nonparticipants for a reasonable period of time and test for a significant difference in whatever outcome measure (e.g., rate of recidivism, time sentenced) is thought to reflect "success." Unfortunately, random assignment is usually not feasible in a correctional setting.

When assignment to the program is not purely random, we need to know something about the way in which assignment was performed to do a reasonable evaluation. Essentially, we need to distinguish between exogenous and endogenous assignment. Furthermore, both to understand this distinction and to perform the evaluation, a model of the outcome measure is required.

As an example, suppose that the outcome to be measured is length of time from release until recidivism and that the model of Section 7.3 (using the censored lognormal model, with individual characteristics) is taken to represent its determination accurately, at least in the absence of the program. We define *exogenous assignment* as the case in which the assignment rule is uncorrelated with the error term (disturbance) in the model. This will be the case if assignment is purely random, of course, but may also be the case if assignment depends on the explanatory variables in the model. To continue our example, age at release significantly affects the outcome under consideration. If the program assignment were based on age, a naive evaluation might attribute to the program effects that are a result of age. However, assuming that the model adequately captures the effects of age, we can use the model to separate the effects of age from the effects of the program.

On the other hand, we define *endogenous assignment* as the case in which the assignment rule for the program is correlated with the error term in the model. This is basically the case discussed in Section 4.5 under the heading of "sample selection bias." It can be expected to arise whenever assignment to the program depends on things that affect the outcome but are not adequately captured in the model. For example, participation in many correctional programs is voluntary. If the individuals who volunteer have a higher motivation for self-rehabilitation than those who do not volunteer, the program will appear more effective than it really is. This will be so even if we control for observable characteristics such as age or number of previous offenses; as long as motivation cannot be predicted perfectly by such variables (as seems clear), motivation will be present both in the model's error term and in the assignment rule, causing them to be correlated. Or, as another example, if the correctional staff assign individuals to a program and if they do not assign "dangerous" individuals to the program, the program will show a spurious effectiveness if "dangerous" individuals are in fact more prone to recidivism.

Endogenous assignment is a general problem, and it is a serious one because it biases program evaluations. To correct for it requires modeling the assignment process, as is clear in Section 4.5. However, in the case of the program that we shall evaluate in this chapter, we can argue that assignment was exogenous, so that no such sample selection bias arises.

That being the case, our method of program evaluation is very straightforward. We use the model that has been estimated on a random sample of releasees (this sample implicitly being our control group) to predict the outcome of interest for program participants. We then test whether the predicted outcomes differ significantly from the actual (observed) outcomes of these individuals. Under the null hypothesis that the program has no effect, we would not expect a statistically significant difference. A significant difference (e.g., an actual rate of recidivism significantly less than was predicted) is evidence for the effectiveness of the program. As a result we shall refer to this method of comparison as the predicted-versus-actual technique.

An alternative (and perhaps more conventional) technique is to estimate the model separately on the sample of program participants and on the control group and to test the hypothesis that the coefficients are equal for the two samples. (No difference corresponds to the null hypothesis of no effects of the program.) Or, one might pool the two samples, introduce a "dummy variable" equal to one for program participants and zero for nonparticipants, use this as an explanatory variable, and test whether its coefficient is zero, as it should be if the program has no effect.[2]

A substantial advantage of the predicted-versus-actual technique, and the reason it was used in the evaluation reported here, is that it does not require reestimation of the model. For complicated models, such as the censored lognormal model, it is much easier and cheaper to make predictions from the estimated model than it is to estimate the model. Substantial time, effort, and cost were involved in the analyses of Chapters 5 and 7 that led to the final models. On the other hand, the predictions used in our evaluation were very straightforward and cheap to obtain. Also, and perhaps more importantly, their generation does not require the same degree of statistical or computational expertise as estimation of the model did. The present technique seemed ideal, given our goal of providing the North Carolina Department of Correction with a method of evaluation that could be performed reliably without adding to their staff or computing capability.

## 8.3. The Program and the Data

The program evaluated in this chapter began in January 1975 at Sandhills Youth Center, a unit of the North Carolina Division of Prisons that houses approximately 160 minimum-custody, honor-grade inmates who are 16–18 years of age. The program has been conducted by the staff of Sandhills Community College under grants from the U.S. Department of Labor.

Inmates are transferred to Sandhills Youth Center during the later stages of their incarceration to prepare for release. The North Carolina Division of Prisons has two such prerelease centers for youthful offenders, Sandhills and Burke, and inmates are assigned to the two centers on the basis of their expected county of release. Inmates expected to be released in the eastern part of the state (i.e., Charlotte and east of Charlotte) are generally assigned to Sandhills, and those expected to be released in the western part of the state are generally assigned to Burke. Since February 1975, all inmates assigned to Sandhills Youth Center with 60 days or more remaining to be served have participated in the Sandhills Vocational Evaluation and Job/Educational Development program.

The program consists of three phases. During the first phase the inmate goes through a 3-week period of evaluation. The first week of this phase begins with an orientation to the program's purpose, facilities, personnel, and objectives. Next, the individual is given a number of tests (academic, personality, dexterity, interest surveys, etc.) designed to determine his level of academic achievement, vocational interest, and personal development. In addition, basic client data are collected.

Week 2 of this evaluation phase is composed of counseling, interviews, and work sample endeavors. The work samples are a vital and unique portion of the program. They allow the program participant to sample a typical vocational situation. For example, in the auto mechanics work sample, an inmate is provided an auto engine, mechanic's tools, and an illustrated manual. He is asked to perform various tasks with the engine, for example, removing and gapping the spark plugs. The individual is observed to determine his ability and asked about his interest after completion of the work sample. Work samples in machine shop work, drafting, electronics assembly, welding, carpentry, electrical work, auto mechanics, and drawing were available under the Sandhills program.

The third week of the evaluation phase consists of intensive interviews and counseling designed to develop a plan of action to remedy academic deficiencies, solve personality problems, and prepare the individual for an appropriate vocation. By the end of the third week the vocational evaluator and the individual agree on an appropriate plan and a formal evaluation meeting is held. In addition to the individual and his evaluator, the youth center's psychologist, a local vocational rehabilitation counselor, and a job developer from the program are present. These latter individuals will be responsible for aiding the individual in carrying out his plan.

Phase 2 consists of implementation of the agreed plan and preparation for release. During this phase the individual works closely with the program's job developer to obtain an appropriate job or school placement on release. In addition to developing a job and/or school plan, the job developer checks to see that the individual makes satisfactory progress in completing his adjustment plan. The continual coordination and follow-up by the job developer is probably the reason that most recommended services are received by program participants. At the end of this phase the individual is released.

The final phase of the program consists of a follow-up, which lasts for 90 days after release. During this phase the individual or a close associate is contacted once a month to determine if the program participant is adjusting properly. Unfortunately, the follow-up phase usually consists of nothing more than monthly phone contact.

The data set used to evaluate the program just described consists of information on 489 individuals who participated in the Sandhills Vocational Evaluation and Job/Educational Development Program and who were released between February 21, 1975, and February 21, 1977. We were unable to obtain information on an additional 25 individuals who participated in the program and were released during this period, either because computer data could not be found or because the Department of Correction's alphanumeric identifier could not be determined. We have no reason to believe that the omitted individuals differ systematically from those for whom we were able to obtain information.

Information on the personal characteristics of the 489 individuals was obtained from the computerized inmate histories of the North Carolina Department of Correction. The postrelease criminal activity of these individuals was determined by a search of North Carolina Department of Correction's records in June, 1977.

## 8.4. Evaluation Based on Time Sentenced

In this section we evaluate the Sandhills program described in the last section, based on our models of total time sentenced (*TTSENT*) developed in Chapter 5. The specific models used to generate predictions of *TTSENT* are given in Table 5.9 (for nonblack male youths) and Table 5.10 (for black male youths). These were the models that were found in Section 5.4 to provide the best predictions for these two groups.

The method of generating predictions and testing the significance of the difference between predicted and actual values is as described at the end of Section 5.3. To recapitulate briefly, the expected value of *TTSENT* is generated for each individual according to (4.3.4). The standard error of the difference between the average predicted and average actual *TTSENT* is then calculated according to (5.3.1) and (5.3.2). The ratio of the difference to its standard error is distributed as $N(0, 1)$, in large samples (which we have), under the null hypothesis of no program effects.

It should be noted at the outset that the variance of *TTSENT* [given by (5.3.2)] tends to be high. Therefore, differences between actual and predicted *TTSENT* will have to be very large indeed to be statistically significant. In other words, only an *extremely* successful program will be revealed as successful. This is important to realize at the outset, given the pessimism that often prevails in the wake of evaluations that report "no significant effect." [See Lipton *et al.* (1975), Martinson (1974), and Seechrest *et al.* (1979).]

It should also be noted that our models of *TTSENT* were based on a fairly nonrandom sample, containing only 45% of the individuals released from North Carolina prisons in the first half of 1975. However, this may be less serious than might appear, based on the following two observations. First, our models of *TTSENT* predicted relatively well for individuals for whom we had incomplete information, as reported at the end of Section 5.4. Second, the main reason for exclusion from the estimation sample was lack of a social history. Youthful offenders were less likely to lack a social history than older offenders. For example, 67% of the Sandhills sample had a social history; whereas, as noted previously, only 45% of the entire 1975 release cohort had such histories. In addition, as noted in Appendix **B**, individuals with social histories released during the first 6 months of 1975 were significantly younger than those without such histories, and we are making predictions here for youthful offenders.

The models of *TTSENT* on which our predictions are based were estimated using a sample in which follow-up times varied from 20 to 25 months. Therefore we begin by considering only those program participants with follow-up periods in this range. There were 113 such individuals out of the total of 489 program participants. Of these 113 individuals, we had information on all variables in our model for only 87.

For this group of 87 individuals we predicted *TTSENT* using our "best" models from Section 5.4; namely, the models of Table 5.6 estimated specifically for youthful offenders. Using these models, we predict a total value of *TTSENT* of 738.865 months. This is insignificantly different from the actual total of sentences received by this group during the follow-up period, 479 months. (The value of the test statistic for the difference between predicted and actual *TTSENT* is $-1.29$, which is insignificant at normal levels of statistical significance.) However, it should be stressed that the predicted value exceeds the actual by some 54%, a rather considerable difference in the direction that would indicate the program to be effective. This underscores the point made previously, that because of the high variability of *TTSENT*, differences will have to be very large to be statistically significant.

Noting the phased nature of the Sandhills program, we felt it would also be instructive to compare the predicted and actual time sentenced for only those individuals who completed the entire program. If program effects are present, particularly later phase effects, those individuals should have more favorable postrelease outcomes than all program participants. For the group of 70 individuals who completed the program, had follow-up periods between 20 and 25 months, and had no missing information, we predict a value of *TTSENT* of 610.740 months, which is insignificantly different from the total sentences those individuals received during the follow-up, 311 months. The value of the test statistic for the difference between predicted and actual is $-1.64$. This value is higher than that for all program participants and is very close to being statistically significant at the 10% level for a two-tailed test. In addition, the predicted total time sentenced is almost double (96.4% higher than) the actual value. Indeed, it should be emphasized that statistical tests are designed to be conservative, in the sense that one puts a severe limit (e.g., 5% or 10%) on the probability of a type 1 error (in this context, calling a program effective if it is not). The cost of this is that we may be very likely to make a type 2 error (failing to call a program effective even though it is). The fact that predicted and actual *TTSENT* are not significantly different at the 10% level does not mean that this program is ineffective. Indeed, the substantial difference between predicted and actual *TTSENT* is fairly strong evidence that it is effective. The evidence is just not quite strong enough for us to be 90% sure that it is effective.

A major problem with using only individuals who complete the program is that program completion may be endogenous. We are comfortable with the assumption that participation in the program is exogenous, since assignment to Sandhills is determined by place of residence (eastern vs. western part of North Carolina), and program participation (given assignment to Sandhills) was for the most part not voluntary. However, program completion was voluntary, and for the reasons discussed in Section 8.2, there may well be sample selection bias in our results for the sample of those who completed the program. To pursue this possibility does not seem worthwhile, in this case, given the weak nature of the results obtained.

Finally, we explored the importance of the length of the follow-up period by using our model to predict *TTSENT* for individuals with follow-ups of

**TABLE 8.1.** Actual and Predicted Total Length of Time Sentenced in North Carolina for Sandhills Program Completions with Full Information, Various Follow-up Periods

| Months after release $M$ | Number of individuals with follow-up > $M$ | Total length of sentences (months) | | Test statistic |
|---|---|---|---|---|
| | | Predicted | Actual | |
| 4 | 252 | 1876.877 | 647 | −3.79 |
| 5 | 248 | 1827.739 | 647 | −3.69 |
| 6 | 238 | 1774.520 | 647 | −3.57 |
| 7 | 216 | 1558.398 | 647 | −3.09 |
| 8 | 200 | 1461.481 | 647 | −2.85 |
| 9 | 194 | 1427.512 | 647 | −2.76 |
| 10 | 182 | 1365.080 | 635 | −2.64 |
| 11 | 174 | 1302.369 | 515 | −2.91 |
| 12 | 155 | 1113.521 | 467 | −2.59 |
| 13 | 139 | 1018.109 | 431 | −2.46 |
| 14 | 128 | 942.488 | 383 | −2.43 |
| 15 | 116 | 880.712 | 383 | −2.25 |
| 16 | 110 | 834.251 | 383 | −2.09 |
| 17 | 105 | 814.512 | 383 | −2.02 |
| 18 | 99 | 786.845 | 383 | −1.93 |
| 19 | 81 | 695.494 | 359 | −1.72 |
| 20 | 73 | 654.891 | 359 | −1.56 |
| 21 | 59 | 573.265 | 359 | −1.21 |
| 22 | 35 | 366.034 | 249 | −0.82 |
| 23 | 20 | 210.794 | 201 | −0.90 |
| 24 | 15 | 181.097 | 201 | 0.20 |
| 25 | 6 | 70.611 | 60 | −0.16 |
| 26 | 3 | 44.151 | 48 | 0.08 |
| 27 | 1 | 35.770 | 48 | 0.17 |

various lengths. Table 8.1 reports these results for the 252 individuals who completed the Sandhills program and for whom all information necessary to estimate our models was available. As can be seen in this table, use of our models of *TTSENT* for individuals with short follow-up periods will tend to make programs appear more effective. (Use of the models of *TTSENT* for individuals with overly long follow-up periods would, of course, have the opposite effect.) For example, if individuals with follow-up periods of less than 19 months are included, the Sandhills program would have been judged successful, based on a two-tailed test at the 10% level. This illustrates the importance of being careful about the length of the follow-up period in our analysis.

We can summarize the results of this section as follows. We have found some evidence that the Sandhills program (or some other feature of Sandhills) is effective in reducing *TTSENT*. However, this evidence is not very strong; the differences we found could arise by chance with a probability of about 10%.

## 8.5. Evaluation Based on Time until Recidivism

In this section we evaluate the same program as was evaluated in the last section, but now based on our model of length of time from release until recidivism (*LTFPC*) that was estimated in Section 7.3. Note that this model was found in Section 7.4 to give better predictions for both black youths and nonblack youths than were models estimated separately for those groups.

The method of generating predictions and testing the significance of the difference between predicted and actual values is as described at the end of Section 7.4. This is done for lengths of time between 2 and 27 months, the latter being the maximal follow-up period in the program sample.

The sample used in Section 7.3 to estimate our model of *LTFPC* was much more representative of the population of North Carolina releasees than was the sample used for our models of *TTSENT*. This is a good reason to have more faith in this evaluation than in the evaluation of the last section. Because exclusion from the estimation sample was primarily based on a missing value for number of previous convictions (*CONVBS*), the primary factor to consider is the degree to which information on *CONVBS* would have been missing during the first six months of 1975 for people who participated in the program to be evaluated. As noted in Section 7.3, this variable was missing primarily for short-term misdemeanant offenders. Also, younger individuals were significantly more likely to have information on *CONVBS* than were older individuals. Because only youthful offenders participated in the Sandhills program, our models of *LTFPC* should be appropriate for

Sandhills program participants. Indeed, only 13 of the 489 Sandhills participants for whom we had other necessary information lacked information on *CONVBS*.

Table 8.2 reports the actual and predicted number of individuals returning to prison in North Carolina at various times after release. As can be seen in this table, participants in the vocational evaluation program had significantly lower (10% level, two-tailed test) recidivism rates than predicted by our models for months 2, 3, 5 and 6. On the other hand, there are no significant differences between actual and predicted numbers of returnees beyond six months. Indeed, what difference does exist is in the direction of more

**TABLE 8.2.** Actual and Predicted Number of Recidivists for All Sandhills Program Participants with Full Information[a]

| Months after release | Number of recidivists | | Test statistic |
|---|---|---|---|
| | Predicted | Actual | |
| 2 | 9.741 | 3 | −2.18 |
| 3 | 17.188 | 8 | −2.26 |
| 4 | 24.902 | 17 | −1.63 |
| 5 | 32.372 | 20 | −2.26 |
| 6 | 39.418 | 25 | −2.40 |
| 7 | 45.634 | 36 | −1.50 |
| 8 | 51.200 | 49 | −0.32 |
| 9 | 56.400 | 61 | 0.65 |
| 10 | 61.140 | 69 | 1.08 |
| 11 | 65.486 | 72 | 0.87 |
| 12 | 69.252 | 76 | 0.89 |
| 13 | 72.533 | 81 | 1.09 |
| 14 | 75.386 | 84 | 1.09 |
| 15 | 77.854 | 89 | 1.40 |
| 16 | 80.040 | 90 | 1.24 |
| 17 | 82.023 | 93 | 1.35 |
| 18 | 83.716 | 96 | 1.51 |
| 19 | 85.080 | 96 | 1.33 |
| 20 | 86.229 | 99 | 1.55 |
| 21 | 87.110 | 99 | 1.44 |
| 22 | 87.683 | 99 | 1.37 |
| 23 | 88.055 | 99 | 1.32 |
| 24 | 88.314 | 100 | 1.41 |
| 25 | 88.471 | 100 | 1.38 |
| 26 | 88.538 | 100 | 1.38 |
| 27 | 88.556 | 100 | 1.38 |

[a] From Schmidt and Witte (1980). Reprinted from *Evaluation Review* **4** (5) p. 595 by permission of the publisher, Sage Publications, Inc. Sample includes individuals who did not complete the program; $N = 476$.

returnees than predicted, which, if significant, would indicate deleterious long-term effects of the program.

One question that remains is the extent to which the favorable outcome for the first six months should be attributed to program participation or to some other unique feature of the Sandhills Youth Center. To explore this question we compared Sandhills Youth Center to the other N.C. Division of Prisons Youth Center, Burke. This exploration appears adequate because, as noted previously, sample selection bias should not exist as inmates were assigned to Sandhills or Burke only on the basis of expected county of release; so far as we are aware, there is no reason to suspect that "easterners" are systematically different from "westerners." There do appear to be significant differences in atmosphere and programs between Sandhills Youth Center and Burke Youth Center other than the program under consideration. First, Burke is a small unit, housing approximately 60 residents, whereas, as noted previously, Sandhills is larger, housing approximately 160 residents. Burke's main program thrust is through offsite placement at Western Carolina Center's Sheltered Workshop and a local community college. Both Sandhills and Burke have full-time academic schools, and Sandhills has vocational courses on site as well. Approximately 75% of Burke's inmates are involved in offsite programs. Burke houses its inmates in 2 open dormitories, whereas Sandhills houses inmates in a single building with 4 inmates per room. Burke has no gymnasium, whereas Sandhills does. Sandhills has a lower inmate–staff ratio (2.34 vs. 4.38), and staff racial composition more nearly approximates inmate racial composition at Sandhills than at Burke. Overcrowding is present and of a similar degree at both units.

Given these differences between Sandhills and Burke, it is impossible to attribute unambiguously the favorable results for the early postrelease period to program participation. One can only say that something in the Sandhills experience significantly lowers the probability of recidivism immediately after release. Indeed, this points up a weakness in the present technique when applied to a prison unit or group-specific program. If either the prison unit or group differs significantly from the system norm in a way not controlled for by our models, unambiguous attribution of effects is not possible. However, favorable results obtained using our models are useful even in such situations as they may, as in the present case, indicate the possible length of program effect and point up programs for which more costly experimental designs may be merited. In the present case, for example, our results would at least point to the need to compare Sandhills program participants and Sandhills nonparticipants.

The results obtained seem reasonable. Considering the relatively perfunctory nature of the follow-up effort and its termination after 90 days, one would expect the maximum program effects to occur in the period immediately after release. Later atrophy of favorable effects could either be because of failure to find jobs in the releasees' fields of training or failure to keep jobs that are obtained.

We also performed a similar analysis of only those individuals who completed the entire Sandhills program. If differential effects of the later phase of the program are present, individuals who complete the program should have more favorable postrelease outcomes than the group of all program participants. Table 8.3 reports the actual and predicted number of individuals who completed all phases of the Sandhills program returning at

**TABLE 8.3.** Actual and Predicted Number of Recidivists for Sandhills Program Completions with Full Information[a]

| Months after release | Number of recidivists: Predicted | Number of recidivists: Actual | Test statistic |
|---|---|---|---|
| 2 | 7.460 | 1 | −2.39 |
| 3 | 13.183 | 5 | −2.30 |
| 4 | 19.118 | 12 | −1.68 |
| 5 | 24.949 | 15 | −2.07 |
| 6 | 30.436 | 17 | −2.55 |
| 7 | 35.260 | 25 | −1.82 |
| 8 | 39.542 | 33 | −1.11 |
| 9 | 43.567 | 41 | −0.42 |
| 10 | 47.228 | 47 | −0.04 |
| 11 | 50.595 | 49 | −0.24 |
| 12 | 53.475 | 52 | −0.22 |
| 13 | 56.008 | 54 | −0.29 |
| 14 | 58.260 | 57 | −0.18 |
| 15 | 60.251 | 60 | −0.04 |
| 16 | 62.009 | 62 | −0.01 |
| 17 | 63.621 | 64 | 0.05 |
| 18 | 65.019 | 67 | 0.28 |
| 19 | 66.131 | 67 | 0.12 |
| 20 | 67.076 | 68 | 0.13 |
| 21 | 67.811 | 68 | 0.03 |
| 22 | 68.261 | 68 | −0.04 |
| 23 | 68.544 | 68 | −0.07 |
| 24 | 68.743 | 69 | 0.04 |
| 25 | 68.860 | 69 | 0.02 |
| 26 | 68.918 | 69 | 0.01 |
| 27 | 68.936 | 69 | 0.01 |

[a] $N = 369$.

various times after release. These results are only marginally different from those reported in Table 8.2 for all program participants. It appears that program completion has the effect of slightly extending the improvement in postrelease behavior. Specifically, significantly fewer (10% level, two-tailed test) individuals who completed the Sandhills program returned to prison in North Carolina than predicted by our models during the first seven months after release. One cannot, of course, unambiguously attribute this marginal improvement to program effects, because individuals who complete the program may differ from all program participants in some way not captured by our models, thus causing a problem of sample selection bias in these results.

## 8.6. Summary and Conclusions

In this chapter we have illustrated a method of evaluating correctional programs, using models of criminal recidivism. This method uses the models to predict a measure of recidivism for a group that participates in a program and compares this prediction with the actual recidivism experienced by the group. *If the models are accurate*, any significant difference between predicted and actual recidivism may be attributed to program participation. The emphasized phrase is important, because this evaluative technique is only as good as the models on which it is based. We believe that we have presented (in Chapters 5 and 7) convincing evidence for the adequacy of the models used here, based on the accuracy of their predictions for random samples of individuals not used in the estimation of the models.

This technique of evaluation is most appropriate for evaluating programs that are in operation throughout a system. For unit or group-specific programs, it is impossible to unambiguously attribute favorable performance to program participation, because other unit or group differences not reflected in our models may cause the observed effect. However, even in this instance, the results of using the evaluation technique described in this paper are useful because they will indicate potentially effective programs for which the expense of a true experimental design may be justified.

Our evaluation of the Sandhills vocational evaluation program gave mixed results. The evaluation based on our models of time sentenced gave weak evidence that the program was successful. However, the variance in time sentenced is so large that even fairly large percentage differences between actual and predicted outcomes failed to be very significant. On the other hand, our evaluation based on models of length of time until recidivism indicated positive program effects for the first six months after release, and no significant effects thereafter. Thus, there is some believable evidence that the program works and may merit a full-scale experimental evaluation.

## Notes to Chapter 8

1. See Campbell and Stanley (1966) or Cook and Campbell (1976) for descriptions of a number of quasi-experimental techniques. Grizzle and Witte (1980) provide a survey of the use of these and other techniques in criminal justice research, and Klein and Teilmann (1980) provide a list of articles on criminal justice evaluation techniques.

2. With just a dummy variable as explanatory variable, the intercept term may vary across subsample, but the coefficients of the other explanatory variables must be the same for the two subsamples. With separate models, all parameters may vary across subsamples.

# PART II

## Testing the Economic Model of Crime

In this part of the book, we discuss economic models of criminal behavior and provide empirical tests of these models. Our empirical work differs from most previous empirical work that tests the economic model of crime in that we use data on individuals rather than data that has been aggregated over jurisdictions (cities or states). Our work provides weak but fairly consistent support for economic models of criminal behavior.

In Chapter 9 we provide a survey of economic models of criminal behavior. A common and central feature of these models is that they assume that the decision whether or not to commit a crime is made rationally. Simply put, an individual commits a crime if he or she expects to be better off by committing the crime than by not committing it. This decision is influenced by anything that affects the relative returns to criminal activity and legal activity. Thus, according to such models, we should expect that the number of crimes committed could be reduced by improving opportunities for potential criminals to conduct legitimate activities or by increasing the probability of detection or the severity of punishment. However, to prove mathematically that this should be so is difficult, or even impossible, in all except the simplest of models. In Chapter 9 we explain in detail why this is so, and we stress the assumptions that are necessary to obtain unambiguous conclusions (e.g., that increasing punishment deters crime). These assumptions are stringent, perhaps unreasonably so. Nevertheless, the conclusions of such models are for the most part reasonable and should not be dismissed casually. For example, the real question is not, in our opinion, whether deterrence exists but rather whether it is strong enough to be relevant for purposes of policy. The latter question is inherently empirical and cannot be addressed by theoretical models.

In Chapter 10 we test some of the implications of a simple economic model of crime by estimating empirical models using data on the postrelease behavior of North Carolina prison releasees. The models seek to explain the arrest and conviction rates of these individuals on the basis of individual characteristics and measures of the variables suggested by the economic model of crime. Analyses are done for all crimes of all members of the sample and also separately for individuals specializing in four different types of crimes.

Our results are generally consistent with our simple economic model of crime. Somewhat surprisingly, they are also similar to results that others have obtained using aggregate data for jurisdictions.

In Chapter 11 we investigate the labor market for prison releasees. Perhaps surprisingly, the individuals in our sample had little or no difficulty in finding jobs after their release from prison. However, they had considerable difficulty in finding *good* jobs. The wage rates at which these individuals worked were very low. Furthermore, they exhibited considerable job instability, with short periods of work interrupted by periods of leisure or job search.

In Chapter 11 we estimate models for two measures of postrelease labor market success: wages received (on the first job after release) and a measure of job stability. We find that wages affect job stability but not vice versa. Another interesting finding is that neither education nor age significantly affects either measure of labor market success. This is surprising, because, for random samples of the general population, age and education are very important determinants of labor market outcomes. Our results suggest that neither traditional educational programs nor job placement programs are likely to be very effective in improving a prisoner's labor market success upon release.

Finally, in Chapter 12 we estimate a more complex economic model of crime, in which criminal activity (measured by the arrest rate) and labor market success (measured by wages at release) are jointly determined. In essence, we jointly redo one of the analyses of Chapter 10 (arrest rate) and one of the analyses of Chapter 11 (wage). In doing so we can test whether criminal activity and labor market activity are determined jointly or independently.

For individuals specializing in income-generating offenses (e.g., theft), our results generally support the economic model of crime and indicate that criminal and labor market decisions are made jointly. However, the results for other types of offenders are much less supportive of the economic model of crime. Particularly for individuals specializing in "consumption" offenses (e.g., assault), it may be necessary to build different models of crime commission.

# Chapter 9

## Economic Models of Criminal Behavior

### 9.1. Introduction

In recent years economists have developed a number of models seeking to explain criminal behavior. The basic premise of these models is that people, including potential criminals, behave "rationally," in the sense that they act in a way calculated to maximize their economic welfare. Thus economists believe that people commit crimes because they expect to be better off committing crimes than not committing crimes. Becker (1968, p. 176) has succinctly stated this position as "a person commits an offense if the expected utility to him exceeds the utility he could get by using his time and other resources at other activities."

An important implication of this view is that criminals react to incentives just as "the rest of us" do. Thus economic models of crime generally support the concept of "deterrence"; that is, that crime can be reduced by increasing its expected cost to the potential criminal (e.g., by punishing convicted criminals more severely). From an economist's standpoint, an individual's decision to commit a crime is not qualitatively different from his or her decision to buy an orange. Just as an increase in the price of oranges should decrease consumption of oranges so should an increase in the ex-

expected cost of committing a crime decrease the number of crimes committed.[1]

Of course, it is questionable whether individuals really decide whether or not to commit crimes in such a rational and calculated way. A casual glance at the daily newspaper often reveals examples of crimes so ill planned and obviously doomed to failure that no reasonable calculation could have led to the conclusion that they were likely to be in the criminal's best interests. One possible reconciliation is to view economic models of crime as relevant mainly to crimes where rational premeditation is possible and the gains are primarily monetary, such as income tax evasion or professional auto theft. However, most economists believe that most individuals consider potential gains and losses even when committing such offenses as murder and assault. Economists feel that true "crimes of passion" are relatively rare. Even drunken husbands contemplating beating their wives will be less likely to do so if they believe that they are relatively certain to be punished severely or if the wife has relatively attractive alternatives to the marriage (e.g., good job prospects) and so may choose to leave it.

In this chapter we provide a survey of economic models of crime, with careful attention given to the assumptions necessary to imply that deterrence occurs. The organization of the chapter is as follows. Section 9.2 summarizes the standard economic theory of consumer demand and labor supply; at least some familiarity with this material is essential to understand the advantages and limitations of economic models of crime. Section 9.3 summarizes the economic theory of behavior toward risk and uncertainty, which is relevant to economic models of crime because the results of criminal activity are assumed to be uncertain. Sections 9.4–9.7 discuss four different economic models of crime and illustrate the way in which the strength of one's conclusions decreases as the generality (and plausibility) of the model increases. Section 9.8 provides an exhaustive survey of economic models of crime, again focusing on the ways in which their assumptions and conclusions differ. Finally, Section 9.9 gives our conclusions.

## 9.2. The Theory of Consumer Demand and Labor Supply

In this section we provide a brief summary of the economic theory of consumer demand and labor supply. These are standard topics in intermediate microeconomic theory, and more details can be found in a standard text such as Hirshleifer (1980). A more advanced treatment is given by Deaton and Muellbauer (1980).

We begin with the problem of consumer demand, putting the question of labor supply aside for the moment. The question that is addressed in the consumer demand problem is a simple one: given that the consumer is not rich enough to buy everything that he or she wants, how does the individual decide what to buy?

To analyze this problem, we put some structure into it as follows. We assume that we are concerned with a specific individual in a specific period of time. This person has a fixed amount of *income*, say $I$, to be spent in this time period. (How $I$ is determined is not addressed here.) The person may spend this income on a number of *goods* (such as apples, oranges, hats, or gasoline). There are $n$ such goods, where $n$ is a given integer (which may be very large and which the economist need not specify). Good $i$ (for $i = 1, 2, \ldots, n$) has a price (per unit purchased) of $p_i$, which is given to the consumer and which he or she cannot influence. Finally, we shall denote the quantity of good $i$ that the consumer decides to purchase (or consume) by $x_i$. Note that the consumer is given a fixed income $I$ and fixed prices $p_1, \ldots, p_n$ but decides the quantities $x_1, \ldots, x_n$ of the goods to consume.

The consumer is not allowed to spend more than his or her income. To purchase $x_i$ units of good $i$ at price $p_i$ per unit requires an expenditure of $p_i x_i$ on good $i$. Adding over all goods (all $i$) gives total expenditure, which must not exceed income. Thus the consumer must obey the equation

$$\sum_{i=1}^{n} p_i x_i \leq I, \qquad (9.2.1)$$

which is called the *budget constraint*. But this is the only restriction that the consumer faces (apart from the obvious fact that $x_i \geq 0$ for all $i$); the consumer may pick any set (or *bundle*) of goods $\{x_1, x_2, \ldots, x_n\}$ that satisfies the budget constraint (9.2.1).

In general there are many possible bundles of goods that satisfy the budget constraint and that the consumer could purchase. We must therefore specify how he or she decides which particular bundle of goods to consume. This is done by assuming that the consumer has a *utility function* of the form

$$U = U(x_1, x_2, \ldots, x_n), \qquad (9.2.2)$$

which says that the level of "utility" depends on the individual's levels of consumption of the $n$ goods. Thus every possible bundle of goods gives rise to a level of utility, and we assume that the consumer picks the bundle of goods that yields the highest possible level of utility. Thus we have a mathematically and logically well-defined problem: the consumer acts to maximize (9.2.2) by choosing $x_1, x_2, \ldots, x_n$, subject to the budget constraint (9.2.1).

The utility function (9.2.2) is intrinsically unobservable, and the assumption that the consumer acts to maximize such an unobserved construct may seem to be without content. However, this is not so. The assumption that the consumer acts to maximize utility has testable implications for his or her observable behavior. Indeed, there is a considerable literature on the testing of the hypothesis of utility maximization, a good survey of which is Varian (1982).

It is clear that the consumer's decisions, that is, the levels of $x_i$ chosen, will depend on the prices $p_i$ the individual faces and the individual's level of income $I$. We can express this dependence formally by the *demand functions*

$$x_i = g^i(p_1, p_2, \ldots, p_n, I), \qquad i = 1, 2, \ldots, n, \tag{9.2.3}$$

which summarize the way in which the level of good $i$ consumed (or "demanded") would change if any price changed or if income changed.

Among economists it is a fundamental act of faith that the demand for a good is inversely related to its price; for example, if the price of oranges rises, fewer oranges will be demanded. In terms of the demand functions in (9.2.3), this is the statement that the partial derivative of the demand function $g^i$ with respect to $p_i$ should be negative:

$$\partial x_i/\partial p_i = \partial g^i(p_1, \ldots, p_n, I)/\partial p_i < 0. \tag{9.2.4}$$

In other words, if other prices ($p_j$ for $j \neq i$) are held constant and if the consumer's income is held constant, then an increase in $p_i$ should lead to a decrease in $x_i$, and conversely.

The question then arises as to whether one can prove that (9.2.4) holds. The answer is no, and thus the demand for a good cannot be shown to be inversely related to its price. But we can prove a relationship, given next, that leads to the conclusion that (9.2.4) should hold under all but the most exceptional circumstances.

The relationship that can be proven is

$$\partial x_i/\partial p_i = \text{substitution effect} + \text{income effect}, \tag{9.2.5}$$

where "substitution effect" and "income effect" have precise mathematical definitions (which we shall give shortly), so that (9.2.5) is a legitimate mathematical result.

First consider the substitution effect. It is calculated as $dx_i/dp_i$, holding constant all prices other than $p_i$ but changing income according to the rule $dI = x_i dp_i$ (i.e., $dI/dp_i = x_i$). This is exactly the change in income it takes so that the consumer could purchase precisely what he or she did before. As an example, suppose an orange costs \$1, and a consumer currently eats 4 oranges per week. If the price of an orange rises to \$2, it requires an extra income of \$4 per week to maintain exactly the present consumption pattern. Thus in defining the substitution effect, we are considering a price change with a compensating change in income so that exactly the old bundle of goods could still be chosen. However, the important point is that the old bundle of goods will in fact *not* be chosen. It can be proven that the substitution effect *must* be negative. In the preceding example, the consumer will reduce consumption of oranges and increase consumption of substitutes for oranges (e.g., apples, lemons), because the price of oranges has risen relative to the prices of substitutes for oranges.

We now consider the income effect in (9.2.5). If we increase the price of oranges, holding constant all other prices and income, the consumer cannot buy the bundle that he or she previously bought because its cost now exceeds the individual's income. Therefore, the consumer must reduce his or her consumption levels of at least some goods, possibly including oranges, to make his or her expenditures again satisfy the budget constraint. This reduction in consumption is entirely analogous to the reduction that would be forced by a decrease in income. Indeed, the income effect is calculated as $-x_i(\partial x_i/\partial I)$, where $\partial x_i/\partial I$ is the partial derivative of (9.2.3) with respect to $I$, and shows how consumption of good $i$ would change if $I$ changed (holding constant all prices).

We shall call good $i$ a *normal good* if $\partial x_i/\partial I > 0$; that is, if it is a good for which consumption would increase with increasing income. As the name indicates, normal goods should be the rule rather than the exception. For a normal good, the income effect of a price increase is necessarily negative. Because the substitution effect is always negative, it is clear from (9.2.5) that for a normal good $\partial x_i/\partial p_i$ is negative; quantity demanded is inversely related to price. Oranges are probably a normal good for most people. Thus an increase in the price of oranges should reduce the quantity of oranges demanded, for two reasons. First, people will switch to other similar products because oranges are relatively more expensive (substitution effect). Second, because an increase in the price of oranges reduces people's incomes in real terms, they will have to cut back their consumption of most goods, including oranges (income effect).

We shall call good $i$ an *inferior good* if $\partial x_i/\partial I < 0$; that is, if it is a good for which consumption would decrease with increasing income. An example might be cuts of meat such as fatty hamburger, which is eaten by most people only if nothing better is affordable. For an inferior good the income effect of a price increase is positive, whereas the substitution effect is negative. Thus the relationship of quantity demanded to price $\partial x_i/\partial p_i$ is ambiguous. However, note that the income effect will be small unless the good in question is consumed in large quantity, because the level of consumption $x_i$ appears in the expression $-x_i \partial x_i/\partial I$. Thus for the income effect to outweigh the substitution effect would require that the good be both inferior and heavily consumed. This is typically argued to be unlikely, a widely noted exception being potatoes in Ireland during the last two centuries.

To summarize, we cannot prove on a priori grounds that the quantity consumed of a particular good by a particular individual is inversely related to the price of the good. However, we can prove a result that identifies the conditions necessary for the opposite to occur (i.e., a strong and perverse income effect), and we can argue that these conditions are not very likely to be widely encountered in practice.

We now modify the model just presented to allow consideration of the problem of labor supply. Basically, we now relax the assumption that the individual's income $I$ is fixed. Instead we assume that an individual can work (supply labor services to someone else) to earn income and that he or she does so at a fixed wage rate $w$. Let $H$ represent the number of hours that the individual decides to work, so that the individual's earnings are $wH$; note that $w$ is taken as given but $H$ is decided upon by the individual. If the individual has income in amount $A$ from other sources (e.g., interest, rent, transfer payments), his or her total income is $A + wH$, and the budget constraint (9.2.1) is modified to become

$$\sum_{i=1}^{n} p_i x_i \leq A + wH. \tag{9.2.6}$$

If we did not modify the utility function (9.2.2), the individual would decide to work 24 hours/day; income would be $A + 24w$, and the theory previously discussed would apply without further change. To avoid this nonsensical result, we change the utility function to include not only quantities of goods consumed but also time not spent working (i.e., leisure). Thus the utility function becomes

$$U = U(x_1, x_2, \ldots, x_n, 24 - H), \tag{9.2.7}$$

and the problem the consumer faces is to maximize (9.2.7) with respect to $(x_1, x_2, \ldots, x_n, H)$, subject to the budget constraint (9.2.6).

Now, if we define leisure $L$ by $L = 24 - H$, we can rewrite the budget constraint (9.2.6) as

$$\sum_{i=1}^{n} p_i x_i + wL \leq A + 24w. \tag{9.2.8}$$

Thus we can interpret the problem as follows. The consumer has a potential income of $A + 24w$, which he or she can spend on any or all of the $n$ goods or "spend" on leisure. An hour of leisure "costs" $w$, the amount that could have been earned by working during that hour. That is, the individual's wage is his or her *opportunity cost* for leisure.

In this model, the interesting question is the effect of a change in $w$. An economist's normal reaction would be that an increase in the wage should lead to an increased supply of labor, that is, more hours worked. In other words, an increase in the price of leisure should reduce consumption of leisure. However, as for a change in any of the prices $p_i$ of the goods, this need not be so, and the reason is the income effect of such a change. It can be shown that the derivative $\partial H/\partial w$, which shows how hours worked change when $w$ changes, can be broken into a substitution effect and an income effect. The substitution effect is unambiguously positive. If we increase $w$ but decrease nonlabor income $A$ so that the individual's income (at the old number of hours worked) is unchanged, he will necessarily respond by working more hours. However, the income effect arises because, in the absence of such a compensating change in nonlabor income, an increase in wages makes one richer and thus capable of affording more of all goods, including leisure.

The important point here is that, if leisure is a normal good (as one would suppose), then the income effect is of opposite sign from the substitution effect, so that the effect of a change in wages on hours worked is ambiguous. (This is in contrast to the case previously considered, a change in $p_i$, where normally the substitution and income effects are of the same sign and reinforce each other.) If wages increase, the substitution effect makes the consumer work more hours, but the income effect makes him or her work fewer hours. Leisure is more expensive, but on the other hand, the consumer is better able to afford it.

This is relevant to the economics of crime because the models we shall consider all contain an expected "return to crime," which is analogous to the wage rate in the labor supply model. Thus, for example, an increase in the severity of punishment of convicted criminals reduces the net return to criminal activity, and this is analogous to a decrease in wages. We can therefore expect that the results of a change in the severity of punishment may have an ambiguous effect on the time spent on criminal activity; the substitution effect would support deterrence but the income effect would not.

## 9.3. Behavior toward Risk

In this section we give a brief summary of some aspects of the economic theory of behavior toward risk. The essential question addressed by this theory is how people choose among uncertain alternatives.[2] This is relevant to our discussion of economic models of crime because in such models criminal activity is risky in the sense that its outcome is uncertain; the potential criminal does not know in advance whether he or she will be apprehended and punished.

We begin by assuming that an individual wishes to choose among various possible alternatives and that each alternative is characterized by a number of possible amounts of money (or income), with associated probabilities. (In other words, each alternative is really a probability distribution of income.) This may be made clearer by an example. Suppose an individual has an income of \$100. One alternative is to receive this \$100 with probability one. Another possibility is to keep \$99 and to buy a \$1 ticket in a state lottery, which returns \$500 with probability .001 and returns \$0 with probability .999. Thus the second alternative is characterized as yielding \$599 with probability .001 and \$99 with probability .999. A third possibility might be to bet the \$100 with someone on the flip of a coin; this alternative yields \$0 with probability .5 and \$200 with probability .5.

How would the individual choose among these alternatives? One possible answer, of some intuitive appeal, is that the individual seeks to maximize the expected value of income. Thus the second alternative might be rejected because its expected value is (.001)(\$599) + (.999)(\$99) = \$99.50, which is less than \$100. This rejection amounts to not buying the lottery ticket because it is an unfair gamble (to the ticket buyer). This is not an unreasonable conclusion, because most people do not buy lottery tickets, at least not very often. However, the first and the third alternatives both have an expected value of \$100, and a maximizer of expected income would be indifferent between the two. This is probably not a reasonable conclusion, because most individuals would pick alternative one over alternative three. Alternative three is riskier than alternative one, and most individuals dislike risk or, in economic jargon, are "risk averse," a term that we shall shortly make precise. To capture this notion requires a model slightly more complicated than the expected income maximization model.

We therefore assume that the individual has a utility function giving his or her level of utility as a function of the level of income:

$$U = U(I). \tag{9.3.1}$$

We can think of this as arising from the maximization of a utility function like (9.2.2) subject to a budget constraint like (9.2.1). Given a set of prices, which we ignore by assuming them constant, (9.3.1) gives the maximal utility attainable for a given level of income. Clearly, higher income should lead to higher utility, and thus we assume $U' > 0$, where $U' = dU/dI$ is the derivative of the utility function with respect to $I$ and is called the *marginal utility of income*.

If income is random (uncertain), then so is utility. We assume that the individual chooses among uncertain alternatives by choosing the one that yields the largest expected value of utility; that is, he or she seeks to maximize $E[U(I)]$. The way in which this differs from the maximization of $E(I)$ depends critically on the second derivative of the utility function, $U'' = d^2U/dI^2$, which is of vital importance in determining the individual's preferences toward risk.

We first consider the case of $U'' = 0$. This is equivalent to $U'$ being constant, so that the marginal utility of income is constant. Thus $U$ is a linear function of $I$. In this case we shall say that the individual is *risk neutral*, because maximization of $U(I)$ is equivalent to maximization of $I$ itself. In other words, for a risk-neutral individual the maximization of expected utility is the same as the maximization of expected income. For example, if $U = 10 + 5I$, a function with $U'' = 0$, then $E(U) = 10 + 5E(I)$, and in our preceding example the first and last alternatives each have expected utility of 510, so that the risk-neutral individual is indifferent between them.

Next we consider the important case in which $U'' < 0$. This is equivalent to assuming that $U'$ decreases as $I$ increases, so that the marginal utility of income falls with income. (This seems reasonable; an extra dollar means more to a penurious professor than to a wealthy oil baron.) Thus the utility function increases with income, but at a decreasing rate. It is concave from below, which has the important implication that $E[U(I)] \leq U[E(I)]$; among all alternatives with the same $E(I)$, the "sure thing" that equals $E(I)$ with probability one yields the highest utility and is therefore preferred. As a result, if $U'' < 0$ we shall say that the individual is *risk averse*, that is, among outcomes with equal expected income, the individual prefers the outcome that is least risky (e.g., certain).

As an example, consider the utility function $U(I) = \sqrt{I}$. This exhibits risk aversion because $U'' = -1/(4I\sqrt{I}) < 0$. In our previous example, the first alternative had $I = 100$ with certainty, so $E[U(I)] = U(I) = \sqrt{100} = 10$. The third alternative had $I = 200$ with probability .5 and $I = 0$ with probability .5, so $E[U(I)] = (.5)(\sqrt{200}) + (.5)(\sqrt{0}) = 7.07$. Thus the sure thing is preferred over the risky asset, despite their both having the same expected value for income.

Indeed, the third alternative yields the same expected utility (namely 7.07) as a "sure thing" with $I = 50$. Thus an individual confronted with the third alternative would be willing to pay a *risk premium* of \$100 – \$50 = \$50 to obtain a sure thing. This is a rather large risk premium (perhaps unreasonably so; we suspect most people would prefer a one-half chance of \$200 to a sure thing of \$50), because the utility function $U = \sqrt{I}$ exhibits rather strong risk aversion. A common measure of the degree of risk aversion is

$$R(I) = -U''(I)/U'(I), \tag{9.3.2}$$

*the Arrow–Pratt measure of absolute risk aversion.* It can be shown to be approximately proportional to the risk premium that the individual will pay; see Pratt (1964). There is also a similar measure of so-called relative risk aversion, which equals the Arrow–Pratt measure multiplied by $I$, but we do not need to discuss it here.

It is commonly believed that most individuals are risk averse. It is also commonly believed that risk aversion decreases with income (i.e., $R' < 0$), though this belief is probably not quite as strong as the previous one. Of course, that the general population appears to be risk averse does not necessarily mean that this is also true of the population of potential criminals, some of whom appear to have a penchant for risky activities. We shall return to this point later.

Finally, we consider the case in which $U'' > 0$. This implies that the marginal utility of income rises with income, that the utility function is convex from below, and that the individual is *risk-loving* in the sense that he or she prefers a risky alternative to a sure thing with the same expected value of income. For example, with the utility function $U(I) = I^2$, a sure thing of \$100 yields $U = E(U) = 10{,}000$, whereas a one-half chance of \$200 and a one-half chance of \$0 yields $E(U) = 20{,}000$. Thus the risky alternative is preferred.

Risk-loving behavior is commonly assumed not to exist. We do sometimes observe individuals taking actions that increase risk without increasing expected income. For example, people buy lottery tickets even though they know (or at least we think they know) that the odds are against them; a risk-averse or a risk-neutral person should not do so. However, the standard explanation is that such people obtain utility not just from income but also directly from some aspect of participating in the lottery, such as excitement. In other words, they buy lottery tickets to buy excitement, not to alter the probability distribution of income.[3] Similarly, we sometimes observe criminals engaging in very risky activities, such as armed robberies of gasoline stations or convenience stores, which have expected incomes that appear to be dominated by sure (and legal) alternatives. One explanation is that such individuals are risk lovers, but a more convincing explanation is that they think it is fun to rob gas stations or stores. They are not doing it for the money; or, more precisely, they are not doing it for the variance in their income distribution that it induces.

## 9.4. A Simple Economic Model of Crime

In this section we present an extremely simple model of criminal behavior. The model we present is identical to Model I of Heineke (1978a) and is in turn similar to a number of models of tax evasion, such as that of Allingham and Sandmo (1972). The model is really too simple to be very realistic, but we present it as an example of how simple an economic model of crime must be to yield unambiguous conclusions.

We assume that an individual has a given amount of wealth (or income) $A$. The individual must decide a proportion $\chi$ (satisfying $0 \leq \chi \leq 1$) of $A$ to devote to illegal activities. For example, the model could apply to the decision whether to underreport one's income for tax purposes, in which case $\chi$ would be the fraction of income not reported.

Let us suppose that there is a gain to the illegal activity, which we shall represent by the function $G(\chi,\alpha)$. Here $\alpha$ is a parameter that we insert so that later we can talk about the effects of a change in the gains function; it is a "shift parameter." We assume that $G(\chi,\alpha) \geq 0$, $G(0,\alpha) = 0$, and $G_\chi \equiv \partial G/\partial\chi > 0$; that is gains increase with the level of illegal activity. Also note that we treat $G(\chi,\alpha)$ as a monetary gain; if there are nonmonetary (psychic) gains to crime, these are monetarized and included in $G$.

Similarly, we assume that there is a loss if the individual is apprehended. We represent this by the function $F(\chi,\beta)$, where $\beta$ is another shift parameter. We assume $F(\chi,\beta) \geq 0$, $F(0,\beta) = 0$, and $F_\chi \equiv \partial F/\partial\chi > 0$. The function $F$ represents monetary loss plus the monetary equivalent of any other losses (e.g., lost reputation).

There are two possible states of the world. If the criminal activity is successful (not detected), income to the individual is

$$I_s = A + G(\chi,\alpha). \tag{9.4.1}$$

On the other hand, if the criminal activity is unsuccessful (detected and punished), income to the individual is

$$I_u = A + G(\chi,\alpha) - F(\chi,\beta). \tag{9.4.2}$$

Let us assume that the probability of detection is $p$ and note that we treat this as a constant (independent of $\chi$). If the individual has a utility function $U(I)$, as discussed in Section 9.3, then the individual's expected utility is

$$E[U(I)] = (1 - p)U(I_s) + pU(I_u). \tag{9.4.3}$$

This depends on $\chi$ because $I_s$ and $I_u$ depend on $\chi$, as is evident from (9.4.1) and (9.4.2). The individual picks the value of $\chi$ that maximizes (9.4.3). (For convenience, Table 9.1 contains definitions of all symbols used in developing models.)

The value of $\chi$ that the individual picks so as to maximize his or her expected utility will depend on certain variables beyond the individual's control (i.e., exogenous to the model), notably $A$, $p$, $\alpha$, and $\beta$. The point of the model is to say how $\chi$ will change if any of these parameters change. As in Section 9.2, we examine the effects of such changes by evaluating derivatives of the form $d\chi/dp$, for example, showing how the level of $\chi$

**TABLE 9.1.** Basic Symbols Used in the Models

| Symbol | Definition |
|---|---|
| $t_L$ | Time spent in labor market activity |
| $t_I$ | Time spent in illegal activity |
| $T$ | Total time available |
| $I_i$ | Total income or wealth in state $i$ |
| $A$ | Nonlabor income or wealth |
| $U(I)$ | Function that converts income to a level of utility |
| $E[U(I)]$ | Expected value of the utility function |
| $F^j(t_I, \beta)$ | Penalty for $t_I$ hours of illegal activity if the $j$th criminal justice outcome occurs (including the monetary equivalent of psychic costs) |
| $G(t_I, \alpha)$ | Gains from $t_I$ hours of illegal activity (net of the monetary equivalent of psychic costs) |
| $L(t_L, \delta)$ | Value of $t_L$ hours spent in labor market activities (net of the monetary equivalent of psychic costs) |
| $\beta$ | Exogenous shift parameter in the penalty functions |
| $\alpha$ | Exogenous shift parameter in the illegal-gains function |
| $\delta$ | Exogenous shift parameter in the returns to labor market activity function |
| $p_i$ | Probability that the $i$th state occurs |
| $p_a$ | Expected probability of arrest |
| $p_{c/a}$ | Expected probability of conviction, given arrest |
| $p_{J/c}$ | Expected probability of restrictions on freedom, given conviction |
| $e$ | Expected unemployment rate |

changes if $p$ is changed. We expect $d\chi/dp < 0$ if we believe in deterrence, and the question is whether the model implies this. Incidentally, economists call results like $d\chi/dp < 0$ *comparative static* results. A virtue of the current model is that it leads to relatively unambiguous comparative static results.

We begin with the effect of a change in $p$, the probability of apprehension (and punishment). This result is unambiguous: $d\chi/dp < 0$.[4] Thus deterrence is supported, in the sense that an increase in the probability of apprehension reduces the level of criminal activity.

Next we consider the effect of a change in $A$, the exogenously given level of income. This does not affect the rate of return to crime, and it affects the level of criminal activity only to the extent that the willingness to bear risk differs at different levels of income. If the individual is risk neutral, $d\chi/dA = 0$ and there is no effect on the level of criminal activity. If the individual is risk-averse, the effect of a change in $A$ depends on how risk aversion varies with income. Under the standard assumption that risk aversion decreases with increasing income (i.e., $R' < 0$, where $R$ is the Arrow–Pratt measure discussed in Section 9.3), $d\chi/dA > 0$. The wealthier individual devotes more of his income to illegal activities.

The effect of a change in the gains to crime is represented by a change in the shift parameter $\alpha$ in the function $G(\chi,\alpha)$. We adopt the convention $G_\alpha \equiv \partial G/\partial\alpha > 0$ and that $G_{\chi\alpha} \equiv \partial^2 G/\partial\chi\partial\alpha > 0$, so that an increase in $\alpha$ represents an increase in the total and marginal gains to criminal activity. Intuitively, we expect $d\chi/d\alpha > 0$; an increase in the gains to crime should lead to more crime, that is, a substitution effect. However, this is not unambiguously so, because a change in $\alpha$ also has an income as well as a substitution effect. (At a given level of $\chi$, an increase in $\alpha$ raises income.) As we have just seen in considering a change in exogenous income $A$, an income effect in this model is ambiguous unless we make assumptions about behavior toward risk. Thus to ensure that $d\chi/d\alpha > 0$ requires the same assumptions that ensure that $d\chi/dA \geq 0$, namely, either risk neutrality or else risk aversion that decreases with income.

The effect of a change in sanctions is represented by a change in the shift parameter $\beta$ in the function $F(\chi,\beta)$. We assume $F_\beta > 0$ and $F_{\chi\beta} > 0$ so that an increase in $\beta$ represents an increase in total and marginal sanctions. The concept of deterrence suggests that $d\chi/d\beta < 0$; increased sanctions should decrease crime. Indeed, this turns out to be the case. We have $d\chi/d\beta < 0$, assuming either risk neutrality or risk aversion. (In contrast to the previous case, there is no need to assume that risk aversion decreases with income.)

This concludes our listing of the comparative static results of this model. The conclusions are in line with what one would expect from an economic model of crime. Crime is reduced by reducing the monetary gains to crime or by increasing the probability or severity of punishment. However, to obtain these conclusions, even in so simple a model as this one, required some assumptions about attitudes toward risk.

## 9.5. A Simple Model of the Allocation of Time to Crime

This model is similar to the model of Section 9.4, but it treats time (rather than income) as that to be allocated between legal and illegal activities. An individual can spend his or her time on legal activities (e.g., working at a legal job or searching for work) or on illegal activities. Let the amounts of time so spent be $t_L$ and $t_I$, respectively. We let the net gains to time spent on illegal activities be represented by the function $G(t_I,\alpha)$, and we let the penalty if the crime is detected be given by the function $F(t_I,\beta)$. (These functions are the counterparts of the functions $G$ and $F$ of the previous model.) We let the net gains to time spent on legal activities be represented by the function $L(t_L,\delta)$ where $\delta$ is a shift parameter. We make assumptions similar to those of the last section about these functions:

$$G(t_I,\alpha) \geq 0, \qquad G(0,\alpha) = 0, \qquad G_t \equiv \partial G/\partial t_I > 0,$$
$$G_\alpha = \partial G/\partial \alpha > 0, \qquad G_{t\alpha} = \partial^2 G/\partial t \partial \alpha > 0,$$

and similarly make assumptions for the functions $F$ and $L$. We let $A$ represent nonlabor income; that is, income not resulting from either use of time. Finally, we let $U(I)$ be the individual's utility function, as before. Table 9.1 contains definitions of the basic symbols used in developing the model.

If the criminal activity is undetected, income is

$$I_s = A + L(t_L,\delta) + G(t_I,\alpha). \tag{9.5.1}$$

If the criminal activity is detected, on the other hand, income is

$$I_u = A + L(t_L,\delta) + G(t_I,\alpha) - F(t_I,\beta). \tag{9.5.2}$$

We again assume a fixed probability $p$ that the criminal activity is detected. Thus the individual's expected utility is given by

$$E[U(I)] = (1 - p)U(I_s) + pU(I_u). \tag{9.5.3}$$

The individual chooses $t_I$ and $t_L$ to maximize expected utility (9.5.3).

We now distinguish two versions of this model, depending on the relationship between $t_L$ and $t_I$. The version that we shall discuss first, which is identical to Model II of Heinecke (1978a), arises from the unconstrained maximization of (9.5.3) with respect to $t_I$ and $t_L$. This model seems odd to us because it assumes that the value of leisure is zero. On the other hand, the version that we shall discuss later, which is essentially the model of Ehrlich (1973), is based on the maximization of (9.5.3) subject to the constraint that $t_I + t_L$ equals some specified quantity. This amounts to assuming leisure time to be fixed, so that $t_I + t_L$ adds to the total time (24 hours/day) minus fixed leisure. In our opinion neither model adequately handles the question of time allocation, and we shall return to this point in Section 9.7.

In the unconstrained (Heineke) version of the model, an extremely important result is that $t_L$ and $t_I$ are determined recursively. This is so mathematically because the derivative of (9.5.3) with respect to $t_L$ is zero (a necessary condition for an internal maximum) if and only if

$$L_t \equiv \partial L/\partial t_L = 0, \tag{9.5.4}$$

and thus the maximizing value of $t_L$ is determined by (9.5.4) independently of $t_I$. The individual allocates his or her time to legal activities until the net (marginal) returns there are zero, and this decision is independent of (and logically prior to) the decision of the allocation of time to illegal activities. On the other hand, the choice of $t_I$ depends on the level of $t_L$.

The maximizing values of $t_I$ and $t_L$ depend on the level of the exogenous factors $p$, $A$, $\alpha$, $\beta$, and $\delta$. However, because of the recursive nature of the model, the value of $t_L$ if unaffected by $p$, $A$, $\alpha$, or $\beta$. In other words, the time devoted to legal activities is unaffected by nonlabor income, the probability of apprehension, the gains to criminal activity, and the sanctions if apprehended. This does not strike us as reasonable, but it is implied by the model when $t_L$ and $t_I$ are unconstrained. On the other hand, $t_L$ is affected by a change in $\delta$, representing a change in the return to legal activity, and it is the case that $dt_L/d\delta > 0$, unambiguously. Thus increasing the return to legal activity increases the amount of legal activity, which seems reasonable.

We now consider the effects of changes in exogenous factors on $t_I$, time devoted to criminal activities. The results are similar to those obtained from the model of Section 9.4. First, $dt_I/dp < 0$. An increase in the probability of apprehension decreases the time devoted to criminal activity. This supports the notion of deterrence. Second, the sign of $dt_I/dA$ depends on preferences toward risk. Nonlabor income has no effect on time devoted to criminal activity ($dt_I/dA = 0$) if the individual is risk neutral. However, under the standard assumption that the individual is risk averse and that his or her rate of risk aversion decreases with income, the time devoted to criminal activity rises with income ($dt_I/dA > 0$). Third, although we expect $dt_I/d\alpha > 0$, its sign is ambiguous except when the income effect can be signed. Thus we can conclude that an increase in the return to crime leads to more time allocated to criminal activity, but only by assuming either risk neutrality or decreasing absolute risk aversion. Fourth, it is the case that $dt_I/d\beta < 0$ as long as the individual is risk neutral or risk averse. Thus, given risk neutrality or risk aversion, an increase in sanctions will lead to a decrease in the time devoted to criminal activity. Finally, it is interesting that $dt_I/d\delta$ is proportional to $dt_I/dA$ and is therefore positive under the standard assumptions of decreasing absolute risk aversion; this means that an increase in the return to legal activity increases the time devoted to criminal activity. (It also increases the time spent on legal activity; the two uses of time are complements rather than substitutes.) This last result is purely an income effect and is dependent on the fact that there was no restriction placed on $t_L$ and $t_I$ in maximizing expected utility.

We now turn to the (Ehrlich) version of the model, in which leisure is fixed and hence $t_L + t_I$ is restricted to some predetermined level. Clearly, then, $t_L$ and $t_I$ must be substitutes, because any change in $t_I$ must be matched by an equal but opposite change in $t_L$. This version of the model is not very different from the version described before as far as effects of parameters on $t_I$ are concerned. In particular, the statements about the effects on $t_I$ of changes in $p$, $A$, $\alpha$, and $\beta$ are still correct. However, changes in these parameters now affect $t_L$ (in the opposite way that they affect $t_I$), whereas in the previous version of the model, changes in these parameters did not affect $t_L$.

We conclude this section with two general comments. First, this model is a fairly direct generalization of the model of Section 9.4, the only real difference being that it is time that is allocated here rather than income. Therefore, it should not be surprising that the conclusions of this model about the effects of the various parameters ($p$, $A$, $\alpha$, $\beta$) on the level of criminal activity are essentially identical to those of the model of Section 9.4. Second, in our opinion it is not possible to model the allocation of time adequately without having at least the level of leisure in the utility function. The unconstrained version of this section's model seems unreasonable to us because there is no guarantee that the net marginal returns to legal activity will be exhausted at a level of $t_L$ less than 24 hours/day. Presumably the main reason why such returns should ever be exhausted is that leisure becomes more valuable as it becomes more scarce. But the amount of leisure must depend on the level of $t_I$ as well as the level of $t_L$, and thus the (unreasonable) recursive nature of the model will be lost if leisure is a source of utility. The constrained version of the model is also somewhat unreasonable because changes in parameters certainly should affect the optimal amount of leisure. As we shall see in Section 9.7, however, one price of modeling the time allocation process more reasonably is the loss of the unambiguous results that this model yields.

## 9.6. Another Time Allocation Model

In this section we present an enriched version of the time allocation model of the previous section. We have two purposes in presenting it. First, it is interesting to see the extent to which rather modest changes in the previous model alter the conclusions that can be drawn. Second, it is this version of the model that guides our empirical work in Chapters 10 and 11.

Whereas the model of the last section had only two possible states (apprehended or not), the present model has eight possible states. First, an individual may be employed or unemployed. The probability of unemployment is denoted by $e$. Second, we have four possible criminal justice states: (1) not apprehended, (2) arrested but not convicted, (3) convicted and fined, and (4) convicted and freedom restricted (e.g., incarcerated or placed on probation). The probabilities of these states are determined by the probability of arrest $p_a$, the probability of conviction given arrest $p_{c/a}$, and the probability of restricted freedom given conviction $p_{J/c}$. We assume that the employment and criminal justice outcomes are independent. The eight possible states for the individual and the respective probabilities of these states are given in Table 9.2.

**TABLE 9.2.** States with Associated Probabilities and Income Levels

| State of the world | Probability of occurrence[a] | Income level |
|---|---|---|
| Employed and not apprehended for offenses | $p_1 \equiv (1 - e)(1 - p_a)$ | $I_1 \equiv A + L(t_L, \delta) + G(t_I, \alpha)$ |
| Unemployed and not apprehended for offenses | $p_2 \equiv e(1 - p_a)$ | $I_2 \equiv A + G(t_I, \alpha)$ |
| Employed and arrested but not convicted | $p_3 \equiv (1 - e)p_a(1 - p_{c/a})$ | $I_3 \equiv A + L(t_L, \delta) + G(t_I, \alpha) - F^1(t_I, \beta)$ |
| Unemployed and arrested but not convicted | $p_4 \equiv (e)p_a(1 - p_{c/a})$ | $I_4 \equiv A + G(t_I, \alpha) - F^1(t_I, \beta)$ |
| Employed, arrested, convicted, and fined | $p_5 \equiv (1 - e)p_a p_{c/a}(1 - p_{J/c})$ | $I_5 \equiv A + L(t_L, \delta) + G(t_I, \alpha) - F^2(t_I, \beta)$ |
| Unemployed, arrested, convicted, and fined | $p_6 \equiv (e)p_a p_{c/a}(1 - p_{J/c})$ | $I_6 \equiv A + G(t_I, \alpha) - F^2(t_I, \beta)$ |
| Employed, arrested, convicted, and freedom restricted | $p_7 \equiv (1 - e)p_a p_{c/a} p_{J/c}$ | $I_7 \equiv A + L(t_L, \delta) + G(t_I, \alpha) - F^3(t_I, \beta)$ |
| Unemployed, arrested, convicted, and freedom restricted | $p_8 \equiv (e)p_a p_{c/a} p_{J/c}$ | $I_8 \equiv A + G(t_I, \alpha) - F^3(t_I, \beta)$ |

[a] These probabilities assume that labor market and criminal justice outcomes are independently distributed.

The income levels for the various states are also given in Table 9.2. They are specified by functions giving the gains to legal and illegal uses of time and the sanctions corresponding to the criminal justice outcomes. The gains and sanctions are in monetary terms so that any nonmonetary (psychic) component has been monetized and included.

We represent the gains to time spent in legal activities by the gains function $L(t_L,\delta)$, as in the previous section, where $t_L$ is time spent in illegal activities and $\delta$ a shift parameter. Similarly, the gains to time spent in illegal activity are represented by the function $G(t_I,\alpha)$, where $t_I$ is time spent in illegal activities. The sanctions of the criminal justice system are represented as $F^j(t_I, \beta)$, for $j = 1$ (arrest), 2 (fine), 3 (*j*ail). In all cases we assume that the functions increase with the relevant measure of time and with the shift parameter. Thus we assume $L_t \equiv \partial L/\partial t_L > 0$, $L_\delta \equiv \partial L/\partial \delta > 0$, $L_{t\delta} \equiv \partial^2 L/\partial t_L \, \partial \delta > 0$, and similarly for $G$ and for the $F^j$.

An individual's income in any state is the sum of three components: (1) nonlabor income or wealth $A$, (2) labor income if the individual is employed, and (3) the net gains from illegal activity. This last component is composed of the gross gains to illegal activity $G$ minus the cost of any criminal justice sanction $F^j$ imposed. Note that we assume labor income to be zero if the individual is unemployed.

Given the individual's utility function $U(I)$, the individual's expected utility is given by

$$E[U(I)] = \sum_{i=1}^{8} p_i U(I_i), \tag{9.6.1}$$

where $i = 1, 2, \ldots, 8$ refers to the eight states listed in Table 9.2. The individual is assumed to choose $t_L$ and $t_I$ to maximize (9.6.1). In Section 9.5 we distinguished between Heineke's model (our first version) and an Ehrlich–Sjoquist-type model (our second version) on the basis of whether the time allocated to leisure is allowed to vary. We shall assume, as does Heineke, that the time devoted to leisure may vary. Thus we are left with only the constraints that $t_L$ and $t_I$ be nonnegative and that their sum should not exceed $T$, the total time available (e.g., 24 hours/day):

$$t_L \geq 0, \qquad t_I \geq 0, \qquad t_I + t_L \leq T. \tag{9.6.2}$$

However, like Heineke, we shall do our analysis by assuming an interior maximum; in other words, we shall assume that these constraints are not binding. This amounts to assuming that the individual finds it optimal to allocate some time to all three activities (crime, work, and leisure). Mathematically, it means that we simply consider the unconstrained maximization of (9.6.1).

The first-order conditions for such a maximum are derived in Appendix 9.1. They imply that the individual first allocates time to the labor market[5] until the expected net marginal returns there are pushed to zero. Thus the determination of time devoted to the labor market is logically prior to the determination of criminal activity, in this model as in Heineke's model. Next, the individual chooses how much of his or her remaining time to allocate to illegal activity. The individual will allocate time to illegal activity until the expected increase in utility from additional illegal activity is equal to the expected decrease in utility from the penalty. For this condition to hold, the gains from an additional hour of illegal activity must be less than the value of the penalty for this extra activity for at least some criminal justice outcomes.

We wish to determine how the individual will alter his or her time allocation if factors beyond the individual's control change. In our model these factors are: (1) the subjective probabilities of apprehension, conviction, and imprisonment ($p_a$, $p_{c/a}$, $p_{J/c}$); (2) the level of nonlabor income or wealth $A$; (3) the shift parameter in the function reflecting returns from allocating time to the labor market $\delta$; (4) the shift parameter in the function reflecting the gains from illegal activity $\alpha$; (5) the shift parameter in the penalty functions $\beta$; and (6) the expected unemployment rate $e$. In Appendix 9.1 we give details of the way we determine the effect of changes in each of these parameters.

As in the Heineke version of the model of Section 9.4, the recursive nature of the present model implies that the time spent on legal activities is unaffected by changes in most parameters. In particular, $t_L$ is unaffected by changes in nonlabor income, the probabilities or levels of criminal justice sanctions, the gains to crime, or the unemployment rate.[6] However, $dt_L/d\delta > 0$, so that an increase in the returns to labor market activity does increase the level of such activity.

On the other hand, the time devoted to illegal activity depends on all of the preceding parameters. We now consider how $t_I$ changes with changes in these parameters.

We find that an increase in the expected probability of apprehension $p_a$ decreases the time allocated to illegal activity. As detailed in Appendix 9.1, we require only very common assumptions to obtain this result. This model predicts that increases in police arrests (or increased awareness of the likelihood of such arrests) that change potential criminals' expectations will lead to decreases in the amount of time these potential criminals allocate to criminal activities. Policies that lead to increases in the expected probability of arrest will deter criminal activity, according to this model.

We cannot unambiguously determine the effect of increases in the expected probabilities of conviction or imprisonment on time allocated to illegal activities. The reason for the ambiguity of these effects is that they depend on the marginal gains to illegal activity net of the marginal costs of criminal justice sanctions for all criminal justice outcomes [e.g., the sign of $(G_t - F_t^1)$]. We have no a priori evidence on these net gains.[7] However, reasonable assumptions would lead increases in the expected probability of arrest, conviction, or imprisonment to cause decreases in the time allocated to illegal activities. For example, risk neutrality is sufficient to yield these conclusions, as is risk aversion plus some restrictions on the net returns $(G_t - F_t^j)$. Details can be found in Appendix 9.1.

The effect of a change in nonlabor income $A$ is essentially the same as it was in the Heineke model of Section 9.5. In particular, the effect of $A$ on $t_I$ depends entirely on the individual's behavior toward risk. If the individual is risk neutral, $dt_I/dA = 0$, and there is no effect. Under more standard assumptions (the individual is risk averse, with risk aversion decreasing with increasing income), we find that increasing levels of nonlabor income will lead to increased time allocation to illegal activities ($dt_I/dA > 0$). Individuals allocate more time to riskier, illegal activity when they are richer. If instead we assume that individuals dislike risk more when they are wealthier, they will spend more time in illegal activity when they are poor. Although this is not the normal assumption in economics, it may not be unreasonable for individuals moving from very low levels of wealth to, say, the middle class. If we assume that increasing wealth at first increases and then decreases individual's dislike of risk, we might expect the very poor and the very wealthy to be those who allocate the most time to illegal activity. The type of illegal activities for the two groups might, of course, be quite different, with the wealthy participating in such activities as tax evasion and organizational crime (e.g., price fixing) and the poor in such activities as assault, robbery, and larceny.

We next consider the effect on $t_I$ of a change in the gains to illegal activity, represented by a change in the shift parameter $\alpha$. (For example, the gains to illegal activity could increase as a result of decreased levels of self-protection or increased property holdings.) Our result is identical to the result of the earlier models we have considered, in that it is ambiguous to the extent that the effect of a change in nonlabor income is ambiguous. We expect that an increase in the gains to crime will increase the time allocated to crime ($dt_I/d\alpha > 0$), but we can prove this unambiguously only when the income effect is nonnegative ($dt_I/dA \geq 0$). Thus to prove that $dt_I/d\alpha > 0$ requires assuming either risk neutrality or decreasing absolute risk aversion.

A change in the penalties for illegal activity (e.g., because of stiffening police, prosecutorial, or judicial policies) is represented by a change in the shift parameter $\beta$. The effect of such a change on time spent in illegal activity is slightly more ambiguous than in the earlier models. There we had $dt_I/d\beta < 0$ if the individual is risk neutral or risk averse. In the present model, to prove $dt_I/d\beta < 0$ requires risk neutrality, or risk aversion plus some restrictions on the net marginal returns to crime under different sanctions, or decreasing absolute risk aversion. However, given these fairly mild assumptions, deterrence is still supported.

We have already indicated that a change in the returns to labor market activity (represented by a change in the shift parameter $\delta$) affects time spent in the labor market and that $dt_L/d\delta > 0$ as expected. In the Heineke version of the model of Section 9.5, $dt_I/d\delta > 0$ under reasonable assumptions, so that the times spent in legal and illegal activities were gross complements. In the present model, the sign of $dt_I/d\delta$ is more ambiguous. We can show that $dt_I/d\delta = 0$ if the individual is risk neutral. If the individual is risk averse and displays decreasing absolute risk aversion, we expect that $dt_I/d\delta > 0$; this is an income effect. That the time spent on illegal activities increases with returns to time spent in the labor market is odd because we would normally expect improved legitimate income prospects to decrease crime. We therefore remind the reader that the source of this result in our model (and in Heineke's model of Section 9.5) is the failure to fix time allocated to leisure. When returns to legal activity increase, the individual allocates less time to leisure and more time to both legal and illegal activities. If we fix the time allocated to leisure as do Ehrlich (1970, 1973, 1974) and Sjoquist (1973), legal and illegal activity would be substitutes. The time allocated to illegal activity would decrease with an increase in the wage rate.

Finally, in the present model we can also consider the effect of a change in the expected unemployment rate $e$ on the time devoted to criminal activity. Intuitively, it seems reasonable that an increase in the unemployment rate should increase crime, so that $dt_I/de$ should be positive. However, this does not follow except in unreasonable circumstances. Given risk neutrality, $dt_I/de = 0$, so a change in the unemployment rate has no effect on the time allocated to crime. Under the standard assumption that the individual is risk averse and that his or her risk aversion decreases with increasing income, we obtain (subject to the qualifications noted in Appendix 9.1) the result that $dt_I/de < 0$. Thus an increase in the unemployment rate decreases time devoted to crime under standard assumptions. This is an unexpected result and indicates that further work is needed on modeling unemployment in economic models of crime. It arises in this model because a change in the unemployment rate leads to an income effect, and decreasing income decreases crime (given decreasing absolute risk aversion) in this model as well as in the models of the previous two sections.

The model we developed in this section has a number of implications for our empirical models of Chapters 10 and 11. First, it suggests what variables should be in our empirical model. For example, it suggests the following model for time allocated to illegal activities:

$$t_I = f(p_a, p_{c/a}, p_{J/c}, e, L, G, F^j, A, \text{tastes}). \tag{9.6.3}$$

Second, it suggests that, although the time allocated to illegal activity is affected by work time, the opposite is not true. A model of $t_I$ and $t_L$ should be recursive rather than simultaneous. In essence, the model suggests that we can analyze the level of criminal activity separately from labor market activity although we should control for labor market conditions. We do this in Chapter 10. It also suggests that labor market activity is determined first and independently of current criminal decision. Thus we can analyze the determinants of labor market performance independently of current criminal activity. We do this in Chapter 11.

Finally, the model developed in this section gives us expectations as to the signs of the coefficients on a number of variables in our model of criminality. Specifically, it suggests that we should find positive coefficients for the level of illegal gains, the wage rate, and the level of nonlabor income or wealth. These expectations require assumptions about individual attitudes toward risk, as discussed previously. Thus the sign of the coefficient on nonlabor income or wealth may give us an indirect indication of the attitude toward risk of those who participate in illegal activities. The sign of the coefficient on the wage rate will give us further insights on this matter, although a negative sign for the coefficient of this variable could indicate either that those who participate in illegal activity display increasing risk aversion or that a model that assumes that a fixed amount of time is allocated to leisure is appropriate.

The model in this section also suggests that we should find negative coefficients on variables reflecting the expected probability of apprehension and the expected cost of the various possible criminal justice penalties. Finally, examination of the signs and relative magnitudes of the coefficients on various criminal justice probabilities (i.e., $p_a$, $p_{c/a}$, $p_{J/c}$) may allow us to infer indirectly the signs of the marginal net gains to illegal activity.

## 9.7. A More Complex Model of the Allocation of Time

In this section, we develop a more complex model of criminal behavior, which allows the individual's level of utility to depend directly on the time allocation chosen as well as wealth or income. In this model, in contrast to the model of the previous section, an individual may have a very different level of utility if he or she allocates, say, all time to illegal activities than if he or she allocates all time to legal activities, even though the two time allocations may produce exactly the same levels of income. For example, an individual who greatly values adherence to the law would find the level of utility associated with the second time allocation much higher than that associated with the first. Introduction of the time allocation into the utility function allows individuals to have different attitudes toward both work and crime. It also allows us to address the question of the determination of leisure. Increasing time spent in either legal or illegal activities (holding the other constant) decreases leisure, and this should indeed affect utility.

We begin by presenting a modified version of our model of Section 9.6, which allows time as an argument in the utility function. We still assume eight possible states, with probabilities and income levels as given in Table 9.2. The only difference is that we now assume the utility function to depend on time spent in legal and illegal activities as well as on income:

$$U = U(I, t_{\mathrm{L}}, t_{\mathrm{I}}). \tag{9.7.1}$$

We also change slightly our interpretation of the functions giving the gains to time spent in legal and illegal activities [$L(t_{\mathrm{L}},\delta)$ and $G(t_{\mathrm{I}},\alpha)$]. These now measure monetary gains only. Nonmonetary (psychic) gains or losses to the individual, which depend on $t_{\mathrm{L}}$ and $t_{\mathrm{I}}$, are already taken into account in the utility function. Indeed, we no longer assume that such psychic gains or losses can necessarily be expressed in monetary terms. However, we still assume that the sanctions $F^j(t_{\mathrm{I}},\beta)$ are expressed in monetary terms, so that their psychic component is monetized. We could avoid this by adding the levels of sanctions to the utility function. Heineke (1978a) does so in his Model III, which is an extension of his Model II (presented in our Section 9.5) in the same way that our model here is an extension of our model of Section 9.6. However, adding three sanctions variables to the utility function makes the model very complicated, and we shall not do so here.

Unfortunately, the added realism of this model is purchased at the expense of ambiguity in the comparative static results. It is impossible to obtain unambiguous results for the effects of changes in parameters on $t_{\mathrm{L}}$ and $t_{\mathrm{I}}$ without making four kinds of exceedingly strong assumptions concerning (1) attitudes toward risk (e.g., the individual is risk averse); (2) the net returns to crime (e.g., the net gain to crime is negative if the individual is convicted); (3) the way in which the marginal utility of one activity (e.g., labor time) changes when the amount of time allocated to another (e.g., illegal) activity changes; and (4) the way in which the marginal utility of an activity (e.g., time spent in the labor market) changes when income changes. The first two types of assumptions were also required in our previous models, but the last two types were not. They are especially troublesome because economic theory does not provide a way of determining the signs of the relevant cross-partials of the utility function, and thus we are unable to sign comparative static results involving them.

The nature of the mathematical problems we have described is discussed by Heineke (1978a, pp. 23–26). We shall not provide details for our own model, which is even more complicated than Heineke's Model III. However, we do provide mathematical details in Appendix 9.2 for a model that is simpler than either our model or Heineke's Model III. The model of Appendix 9.2 is essentially identical to our model of Section 9.5 (Heineke's Model II) except that utility depends on income $I$ and on leisure $N$:

$$U = U(I,N), \tag{9.7.2}$$

where $N = 24 - t_L - t_I$. This is a special case of the utility function (9.7.1) in that here utility depends only on $t_L + t_I$, not on each separately. In Appendix 9.2 we show that even the simplest of comparative static results is ambiguous without unreasonably strong assumptions. For example, to show $dt_I/dp < 0$ (which is unambiguously true in Section 9.5) requires $\partial^2 U/\partial I\, \partial N = 0$ plus either risk neutrality or constant or increasing absolute risk aversion. The fact that results are so ambiguous in a very simple model with leisure in the utility function is not encouraging for the prospects of obtaining results in more complicated models.

Although our current model produces no comparative static results and, thus, no expected signs for estimated coefficients, it still provides some guidance for our later empirical work. It suggests the following two-equation model for legal and illegal activity:

$$t_I = f(t_L, p_a, p_{c/a}, p_{J/c}, e, L, G, F^1, F^2, F^3, \text{tastes}),$$
$$t_L = g(t_I, p_a, p_{c/a} p_{J/c}, e, L, G, F^1, F^2, F^3, \text{tastes}).$$

An important implication is that this model, unlike the model of Section 9.6, is not recursive; we must estimate models of criminal activity simultaneously with models of labor market activity. We do this in Chapter 12.

## 9.8. A Survey of Economic Models of Crime

In Sections 9.4–9.7 we provided a rather detailed treatment of certain economic models of crime. In this section, on the other hand, we provide a more general survey of the literature on economic models of crime. In doing so we note the extent to which models do or do not share the features of the models that we have discussed, and we make some comments on the strengths and weaknesses of such models.

Table 9.3 summarizes some major features of a selection of economic models that we believe are representative of the genre. Persuing the first and second columns of this table, one notes that economists have developed models for a wide variety of offenses. Early work tended to develop models of crime commission in general, whereas more recent models have devoted attention to various specific types of offenses (e.g., property offenses). In virtually all models, the individual criminal decides how much of some resource (time or wealth) to allocate to criminal activity so as to maximize his or her expected utility. Models in which utility depends on more than one argument (usually income) are rare because they lead to too many ambiguous results. Attitudes toward risk are important in almost every model, because crime is inherently risky in the sense that the criminal does not know whether he or she will be punished. A variety of different assumptions about aversion to risk have been made, as is clear from the next to last column of

**TABLE 9.3.**

| Study | Type(s) of offense(s) considered | Primary analytic concepts | Objective | Allocation to achieve the objective | Functional form |
|---|---|---|---|---|---|
| Becker (1968) | All offenses | Expected utility function | To maximize expected utility which is a direct function only of wealth | Implicitly time and other resources | Unspecified |
| Ehrlich (1970, 1973, 1974) | Property offenses | Expected utility function | To maximize expected utility, which is a direct function only of wealth | Only time explicitly | Unspecified in theoretical work; log linear in empirical work |
| Sjoquist (1973) | Property offenses | Expected utility function | To maximize expected utility, which is a direct function only of wealth | Time | Unspecified in the theoretical work; log linear in empirical work |
| Allingham and Sandmo (1972), Kolm (1973), Singh (1973) | Income tax evasion[b] | Expected utility function | To maximize expected utility, which is a direct function only of wealth | Wealth | Unspecified |

Major Features of Selected Economic Models of Criminal Behavior

| Taste factors controlled | Nature of interpersonal interaction | Relationship of decisions | Assumed attitudes toward risk | Distribution assumed for criminal justice outcomes |
|---|---|---|---|---|
| A portmanteau vector for tastes is included; suggests such things as law abidingness are in this vector | None | Number of offenses is affected by legal alternatives, but not determined simultaneously with them | Risk aversion[a] | Probability of conviction has a Bernoulli distribution |
| None in theoretical model; race, age, education, geographic location and sex in the empirical work | None | Crime function and labor supply function are inversely related | Risk aversion; constant risk preference[a] | Probability of arrest has a Bernoulli distribution |
| None in theoretical model; race, population density education, city size in the empirical work | None | Crime function and labor supply function are inversely related | Risk aversion | Probability of conviction has a Bernoulli distribution |
| Unspecified shift parameters in illegal-gain and penalty function | None | Crime function is inversely related to the amount of wealth devoted to other activities | Risk aversion and decreasing absolute risk aversion | The probability that the evasion attempt is unsuccessful has a Bernoulli distribution |

(*Table continues*)

**TABLE 9.3.**

| Study | Type(s) of offense(s) considered | Primary analytic concepts | Objective | Allocation to achieve the objective | Functional form |
|---|---|---|---|---|---|
| Block and Heineke (1975) | Property offenses | Expected utility function | To maximize expected utility, which depends on wealth and time allocation | Time | Unspecified |
| Ehrlich (1975) | Murder | Expected utility function | To maximize expected utility, which depends on the level of consumption of murderer and victim | Nothing explicitly | Unspecified theoretically; log linear empirically |
| Heineke (1978a) Model II | Crimes in general | Expected utility function | To maximize expected utility, which is a direct function only of wealth | Time | Unspecified |
| Heineke (1978b) | Larceny, burglary and robbery | Expected utility function | To maximize expected utility, which depends on time allocation and level of consumption | Time and wealth | Unspecified theoretically; translog empirically |
| Lachman (1978) | Crimes involving interpersonal conflict | Compensated demand function | To attain a target level of utility at minimum cost | Not explicitly indicated, but appears to be time | Unspecified |

(*Continued*)

| Taste factors controlled | Nature of interpersonal interaction | Relationship of decisions | Assumed attitudes toward risk | Distribution assumed for criminal justice outcomes |
|---|---|---|---|---|
| Tastes for labor and theft | None | Time in theft and working are determined simultaneously | Risk aversion and decreasing absolute risk aversion | Probability of arrest has an unspecified, but general distribution |
| Dislike of others theoretically; age, historic period, race and population empirically | Murder occurs because the murderer's utility increases when victim's consumption is reduced to zero | Only consumption levels explicitly in theoretical model; discussion indicates interdependence with legal labor market | None explicitly made | Arrests, conviction and execution are subject to Bernoulli processes |
| Unspecified shift parameters in legal and illegal gains and penalty functions | None | Time allocated to legal and illegal activity are determined recursively | Risk aversion and decreasing absolute risk aversion | Probability of failure at illegal activity is a Bernoulli process |
| Tastes for alternative time allocations | None | All time allocations and level of consumption determined simultaneously | None explicitly made | All criminal justice probabilities are Bernoulli processes |
| Responses to aggression, social sanctions, internal sanctions | Unspecified reaction function with positive and then negative derivatives | Harm function and other activity levels are determined simultaneously | None explicitly made | All criminal justice probabilities are Bernoulli processes |

(*Table continues*)

**TABLE 9.3.**

| Study | Type(s) of offense(s) considered | Primary analytic concepts | Objective | Allocation to achieve the objective | Functional form |
|---|---|---|---|---|---|
| Witte (1980) | Production and consumption offenses | Utility function | To maximize utility, which depends on time allocation and expected wealth | Time | Unspecified theoretically; linear empirically |
| Long, Witte, and Karr (1983) | Family violence | Expected utility function | To maximize expect utility, which depends on time allocation and level of income | Time | Unspecified |

[a] These articles also considered other assumptions concerning risk.
[b] Our presentation and description of these models is derived directly from Heineke (1978a).

(*Continued*)

| Taste factors controlled | Nature of interpersonal interaction | Relationship of decisions | Assumed attitudes toward risk | Distribution assumed for criminal justice outcomes |
|---|---|---|---|---|
| Tastes for alternative time allocations theoretically; age, previous record, race, addiction, supervision, marital status, and previous behavior empirically | None | All time allocations are determined simultaneously | None explicitly made | All criminal justice probabilities are Bernoulli processes |
| Tastes for family violence and work | Assaulter's decisions are constrained by necessity of maintaining a level of utility for victim superior to best alternative | | Risk aversion and decreasing absolute risk aversion | All criminal justice probabilities are Bernoulli processes |

Table 9.3. Finally, in virtually every model there are fixed probabilities for criminal justice outcomes such as arrest and imprisonment. This is a manifestly unreasonable state of affairs, because (at least for most crimes) the probability of arrest or conviction must rise with the number of offenses. A more reasonable treatment can be found in Block and Heineke (1975).

In virtually all models, there are functions representing the gains to legal activity, the gains to illegal activity, and the penalty if the crime is detected. Table 9.4 summarizes the major features relating to the legal-gain function for selected economic models. As can be seen in this table, economists modelling criminal behavior have most frequently assumed that the net return to labor market activity is simply the wage rate multiplied by the number of hours spent working. The wage rate is assumed to be exogenously determined by all models of which we are aware. Most economic models assume that returns for time allocated to the labor market are certain. This is a bit odd and has been assumed largely to simplify the required mathematics. Ehrlich (1970, 1974) and Witte (1980) explicitly introduce and analyze the effect of unemployment on participation in illegal activities. They find that, although an increase in unemployment increases the incentives to participate in illegal activities, it may not increase actual participation if individuals dislike risk sufficiently (i.e., are sufficiently risk averse), and the returns to legal activity are either larger or more certain than the gains to illegal activity. Most economic models assume that the gains to legal activities are either simply monetary or at least can be monetized by an appropriately specified function. As we saw in Section 9.7, a more reasonable alternative is to allow the time allocation to affect utility directly. However, this results in a model with few (if any) unambiguous comparative static results.

Table 9.5 summarizes the major features of the illegal-gain function for selected economic models. As can be seen in this table, most economists developing models have assumed that gross illegal gains (illegal gains disregarding any penalty), like legal gains, are certain and, indeed, are fully retained even if one is punished for the offense. Gains may be offset or incorporated in the penalty, but the level of gross illegal gains is not seen as subject to uncertainty. Most models assume that illegal gains are either solely monetary or at least may be monetized. Models concerned with assaultive offenses generally see gains as mainly psychic and represent these gains by entering the time allocation, level of harm, or level of consumption of the victim directly into the utility function. In some models (Block and Heineke, 1975; Witte, 1980) the psychic costs of property offenses are represented by entering the time spent in theft directly into the utility function, but this is not generally the case, again because it introduces too much ambiguity into the results.

The final argument of the income function is the penalty if caught. Table 9.6 summarizes the major features of sanctions, including the penalty function, for selected models. As can be seen in this table, a relatively narrow range of sanction alternatives are generally considered in these models, with a single "probability of apprehension" and a single penalty being most common. Most models consider the expected sanction to be simply the probability of apprehension times the penalty, although Lachman (1978) has introduced discontinuities in sanction functions. In general, models assume either that penalties are monetary (i.e., a fiine) or that they can be monetized. Attempts to introduce nonmonetary aspects of the penalty, say, by entering the sanction directly into the utility function, have generally produced models that yield no comparative static results. Oddly, most models have assumed that probabilities associated with criminal justice sanctions are exogenous and constant. It would seem to be more realistic to assume that those probabilities depend on the time spent in illegal activity or the number of offenses committed. (Indeed, this is the assumption usually made regarding the level of penalty.)

Having outlined the major features of selected economic models of criminal activity, we are now ready to indicate what these models predict will happen to the level of criminal activity as exogenous factors change. These comparative static results are summarized in Table 9.7. This table also indicates the major advance represented by each research effort. As can be seen in the last column of this table, Becker's (1968) article provided the major stimulus for this type of research. Ehrlich (1970, 1973, 1974) and Sjoquist (1973) formalized and extended Becker's suggestions concerning the "criminal supply of offense function" for traditional property offenses. Allingham and Sandmo (1972), Kolm (1973), and Singh (1973) extended this line of research to tax evasion and introduced insights from the portfolio theory of finance. In major advances, Block and Heineke (1975) and Heineke (1978a) explored the assumptions that were central to the comparative static results obtained for the above models. Block and Heineke (1975) found that it was necessary to assume that all costs and gains could be monetized and were independent of wealth and that criminal justice sanctions follow a Bernoulli process to obtain comparative static results under normal preference restrictions. Somewhat later, Heineke (1978a) showed that Ehrlich's and Sjoquist's models indicated that labor market activities and theft were substitutes only because they assume that the time spent in leisure is fixed. When one relaxes this assumption these two time allocations become complements, not substitutes. Other work has embellished the basic model (for example, by introducing unemployment or enriched criminal justice sanctions) or developed models for particular types of persons offenses. For example, Ehrlich (1975) developed a model

**TABLE 9.4.** Major Features of the Legal-Gain Function for Selected Models

| Study | Type(s) of offense(s) considered | Arguments in the legal-gain function | Certainty or uncertainty of legal gains | Functional form | Assumptions about nature of legal gains |
|---|---|---|---|---|---|
| Becker (1968) | All offenses | None explicitly specified | Certain | Unspecified | Unspecified |
| Ehrlich (1970, 1973, 1974) | Property offenses | The wage rate and the time spent working[a] | Certain in main model; uncertain in extended model | Multiplicative | Monetary |
| Sjoquist (1973) | Property offenses | The wage rate and the time spent working | Certain | Multiplicative | Monetary (psychic costs are assumed to be reflected in wage rate) |
| Allingham and Sandmo (1972), Kolm (1973), Singh (1973) | Income tax evasion | None specified | N.A.[b] | N.A. | N.A. |
| Block and Heineke (1975) | Property offenses | Rate of return to legal activity and time spent in that activity | Certain | Multiplicative | Monetary and psychic costs related to time allocated to labor market activity |

| | | | | | |
|---|---|---|---|---|---|
| Ehrlich (1975) | Murder | None specified | N.A. | N.A. | N.A. |
| Heineke (1978a) Model II | Crimes in general | Time allocated to legal activity and exogenous shift factor | Certain | Unspecified, but gains increase with time allocation and shift parameter | Either monetary or can be monetized |
| Heineke (1978b) | Larceny, burglary and robbery | Rate of return to legal activity and time spent in that activity | Certain | Multiplicative | Monetary |
| Lachman (1978) | Crimes involving interpersonal conflict | None explicitly specified | N.A. | N.A. | N.A. |
| Witte (1980) | Production and consumption offenses | The expected unemployment rate, the expected wage rate and the number of hours in labor market activities | Uncertain | Multiplicative | Monetary and psychic costs related to time allocated to labor market activity |
| Long, Witte, and Karr (1983) | Family violence | The wage rate and time spent in legal activity | Certain | Multiplicative | Monetary and psychic related to labor market activity |

[a] Ehrlich also develops a model where returns to legal activities are stochastic because of the possibility of being unemployed.
[b] Not applicable.

**TABLE 9.5.** Major Features of the Illegal-Gain Function for Selected Models

| Study | Type(s) of offense(s) considered | Arguments in illegal-gain function | Functional form | Assumption about nature of illegal gains | Effect on illegal gains if caught |
|---|---|---|---|---|---|
| Becker (1968) | All offenses | Number of offenses | Unspecified | Unspecified | Unspecified |
| Ehrlich (1970, 1973, 1974) | Property offenses | Net gains to illegal activity and time in that activity | Multiplicative | Monetary or at least may be monetized | A portion of gains may be lost and this amount is included in the penalty function |
| Sjoquist (1973) | Property offenses | Gains to illegal activity and time in that activity | Multiplicative | Monetary or at least may be monetized | Implicitly all illegal gains are retained although penalty may effectively confiscate them |
| Allingham and Sandmo (1972), Kolm (1973), Singh (1973) | Income tax evasion | Proportion of income allocated to illegal activity and an exogenous shift factor | Multiplicative | Monetary or at least may be monetized | Implicitly all illegal gains are retained although penalty may effectively confiscate them |
| Block and Heineke (1975) | Property offenses | Rate of return to illegal activity and number of offenses, which depends on time allocated to illegal activity; psychic costs through time allocation | Multiplicative for monetary gains with number of offenses increasing in an unspecified way with time allocation; unspecified for psychic costs | Monetary and psychic | Gains are retained but may be offset by penalty |

| | | | | | |
|---|---|---|---|---|---|
| Ehrlich (1975) | Murder | Decrease in level of consumption of victim | Unspecified | Decrease in utility of victim may be converted to utility increase for murderer by utility function | Illegal gains are retained, although they may be offset by penalty |
| Heineke (1978a) Model II | Crimes in general | Time allocated to illegal activities and an exogenous shift parameter | Unspecified; but gains increase with time allocation and shift parameter | May be monetized | Gains are retained but penalty may offset them |
| Heineke (1978b) | Larceny, burglary, robbery | Unit returns and time allocated to illegal activity | Multiplicative | Monetary or at least may be monetized | Gains are retained but may be offset by penalty |
| Lachman (1978) | Crimes involving interpersonal conflict | Harm enters the utility function directly | Unspecified | Harm decrease stress | Not explicitly specified |
| Witte (1980) | Production and consumption offenses | Rate of return to illegal activity and number of offenses which depends on time allocation; psychic costs and benefits through time allocation | Multiplicative for monetary gains with number of offenses increasing in an unspecified way with time; unspecified for psychic costs and benefits | Monetary and psychic for productive offense, psychic only for consumption offenses | Retained although they may be offset by penalty |
| Long, Witte, and Karr (1983) | Family violence | Harm enters utility function directly | Unspecified | Psychic | Retained |

**TABLE 9.6.** Major Features of the Criminal Justice Sanctions for Selected Models

| Study | Type(s) of offense(s) considered | Sanctions considered | Functional form | Assumptions about nature of penalty | Factor(s) affecting probabilities | Factor(s) affecting penalties |
|---|---|---|---|---|---|---|
| Becker (1968) | All offenses | Probability of conviction and punishment | Multiplicative | May be monetized | Depends on number of offenses | Constant per convicted offense |
| Ehrlich (1970, 1973, 1974) | Property offenses | Probability of apprehension and penalty if apprehended | Multiplicative | May be monetized | Exogenously determined and constant[a] | Time allocated to illegal activities |
| Sjoquist (1973) | Property offenses | Single probability of arrest, conviction and punishment; cost of penalty | Multiplicative | Monetary | Exogenously determined and constant | Assumed constant |
| Allingham and Sandmo (1972), Kolm (1973), Singh (1973) | Income tax evasion | Probability of failure and monetary penalty | Multiplicative | Monetary | Exogenously determined and constant | Proportion of income allocated to illegal activity and an exogenous shift parameter |
| Block and Heineke (1975) | Property offenses | Stochastic failure, capture or arrest rate; and the fine per offense | Multiplicative | Monetary | Exogenously determined and constant | Exogenous and constant per offense |
| Ehrlich (1975) | Murder | Probability of apprehension; probability of conviction given apprehension; probability of execution given conviction | Multiplicative | Execution or an alternative | Exogenously determined and constant | Exogenous and constant per offense |

| | | | | | | |
|---|---|---|---|---|---|---|
| Heineke (1978a) Model II | Crimes in general | Probability of apprehension and penalty | Multiplicative | May be monetized | Exogenously determined and constant | Time allocated to illegal activity and an exogenous shift parameter |
| Heineke (1978b) | Larceny, burglary and robbery | Subjective probability of arrest; probability of conviction given arrest; penalty | Multiplicative | May be monetized | Exogenously determined and constant | Time allocated to illegal activity and level of wealth |
| Lachman (1978) | Crimes involving inter-personal conflict | Probability of imposition of legal penalty; legal penalty which is discontinuous if victim dies | Multiplicative with discontinuity if victim dies | Measured in common unspecified terms | Depends on level of harm | Depends on level of harm |
| Witte (1980) | Production and consumption offenses | Expected probabilities of arrest, conviction given arrest, restrictions on freedom given conviction; and expected fine | Multiplicative | Monetary | Exogenously determined and constant | Time allocated to illegal activities |
| Long, Witte, and Karr (1983) | Family violence | Probability of criminal justice sanctions being imposed and penalty | Multiplicative | May be monetized | Exogenously determined and constant | Time in violence and an exogenous shift parameter |

[a] In an appendix Ehrlich (1974) allows the probability of apprehension to depend on law enforcement expenditures and the criminal's expenditures on self protection.

**TABLE 9.7.** Results and Advances of Selected Models

| Study | Type(s) of offense(s) considered | Results | Major advance over previous work |
|---|---|---|---|
| Becker (1968) | All offenses | Increases in penalty or fine decrease the number of offenses; increased fines are relatively more effective than increased probabilities for the risk averse | Resurrection of Becaria's and Bentham's insights and their statement in terms of modern economics |
| Ehrlich (1970, 1973, 1974) | Property offenses | Time allocated to illegal activity decreases with increases in probability of apprehension, penalty, and wage rate; increases with increased wealth and illegal gains; fines are relatively more effective for risk averse | Elaboration of Becker's insights; explicitly introduces both gains and losses in illegal activity and gains in legal activity. |
| Sjoquist (1973) | Property offenses | Time allocated to illegal activity decreases with increases in probability of sanctions, wage rate, and level of sanctions; increases with returns to illegal activity | Elaboration of Becker's insights; explicitly introduces both gains and losses in illegal activity and gains in legal activity. |
| Allingham and Sandmo (1972), Kolm (1973), Singh (1973) | Income tax evasion | Proportion of wealth allocated to illegal activities decreases with increases in penalty or the probability of its imposition; increases with increases in wealth and illegal gains; increased fines are more effective than increased probabilities for the risk averse | Marriage of Becker's model and portfolio theory to model tax evasion |
| Block and Heineke (1975) | Property offenses | No comparative static results forthcoming under normal preference restrictions | Introduces time allocation directly into the utility function; allows the probability of arrest to have a general, rather than Bernoulli, distribution; shows restrictions needed to get comparative static results |

**TABLE 9.7.** *(Continued)*

| Study | Type(s) of offense(s) considered | Results | Major advance over previous work |
|---|---|---|---|
| Ehrlich (1975) | Murder | Expected utility from crime decreases with all probabilities associated with criminal justice sanction; the probability of arrest is relatively more effective than the probability of conviction, which is relatively more effective than the probability of execution | Introduction of interdependent utilities and enrichment of criminal justice outcomes |
| Heineke (1978a) Model II | Crimes in general | Time allocated to illegal activity decreases with increases in the penalty and the probability of imposition; increases with increases in wealth, illegal gains, and legal gains; increased fines are relatively more effective than increased probabilities for the risk averse | Shows that when amount of leisure is allowed to vary, legal and illegal activities are gross complements; points up the nature of restrictive assumptions in Ehrlich's and Sjoquist's models |
| Heineke (1978b) | Larceny, burglary and robbery | No comparative static results are forthcoming | Models joint labor supply decision for larceny, burglary, robbery, and the labor market. This explicitly allows considerations of substitution among property offenses |
| Lachman (1978) | Crimes involving inter-personal conflict | Comparative static results assumed rather than derived; harm increases with increase in price of alternative activity (e.g., job search); decreases with increases in formal sanctions, the probability of their imposition, and internal or societal informal sanctions. | Allows for informal social and individual sanctions and individual interaction; introduces response functions from oligopoly theory |

(*Table continues*)

TABLE 9.7. *(Continued)*

| Study | Type(s) of offense(s) considered | Results | Major advance over previous work |
|---|---|---|---|
| Witte (1980) | Production and consumption offenses | No comparative static results forthcoming | Combines insights from Block/Heineke and Ehrlich by explicitly introducing an unemployment rate, enriched criminal justice sanctions, and time allocation into the utility function |
| Long, Witte, and Karr (1983) | Family violence | If crime is a normal good increases in time costs of sanction will deter; increases in size of sanction will lead to an income and substitution effect | Combines insights from the economics of marriage and economics of crime literature to model family violence |

of murder, and Lachman (1978) a model of interpersonal conflict. Generally, these models yield only restricted [e.g., Long, Witte, and Karr (1983)] comparative static results, or none at all.

As is noted in column three of Table 9.7, only early models, the restrictiveness of which have already been noted, yield large numbers of unambiguous comparative static results under normal preference restrictions. If there are costs or gains from either legal or illegal activities that cannot be monetized, the economic model of crime will not unambiguously support the deterrence hypothesis. Even if all costs and gains can be monetized, the deterrence hypothesis will only be supported if these costs and gains are independent of the individual's level of income or wealth. Only if one assumes that the amount of time spent in leisure activities is fixed will increases in legal gains necessarily cause decreases in illegal activity.

## 9.9. Summary and Conclusions

In this chapter, we surveyed a selected group of economic models of criminal behavior and developed two models of our own. Our survey and modeling effort highlighted a number of aspects of formal economic modeling, some of which are unique to models of criminal behavior and some of which are more general. For example, our work indicated the centrality of the assumption of rational maximizing behavior. Further, economic models of criminal behavior assume that all items affecting individuals' well being may be converted to common units of measurement via a utility function. Economic models of criminal behavior generally assume that it is only the individual's level of income or wealth that enters the utility function directly. This implies that individuals are indifferent among different time allocations as long as they produce equal levels of income or wealth. According to this type of model, an individual would be indifferent between earning $25,000/yr as a professional thief or as a lawyer. The reason economists have made this rather unappealing assumption is that it often allows them to determine unambiguously the effect of changes in such things as the level of unemployment or of criminal sanctions on the level of criminal activity.

Economic models that allow either the level of sanctions or the time allocation to enter the utility function directly are more appealing intuitively. They allow individuals to have different attitudes toward sanctions, work, and illegal activity, and they answer the question of how leisure is determined. However, this increased realism is not without its price. These models do not allow us to determine unambiguously how changes in criminal justice practices or opportunities to conduct legal activities will affect participation in illegal activities. The ultimate effect of stiffened penalties, increased probabilities of apprehension, or improved legal opportunities becomes an empirical question. This type of model merely provides guidance to empirical work.

Given the limited results obtained for realistic models, have economists' efforts to model illegal behavior been worthwhile? We believe that they have for a number of reasons, although we can hardly be considered unbiased. First, we believe that economists' analyses of criminal behavior have provided a useful challenge to those in disciplines more commonly analyzing this type of behavior. Although not all criminals may be rational, more may be than was previously assumed by many psychologists and sociologists. Many criminals are affected by opportunities, even though small differences in opportunities cannot be expected to affect radically their behavior. Second, the rigor and formality with which economists develop their models has proved a useful counterbalance to a tradition of prosaic models with many unmeasurable concepts. Economists' efforts will have been worthwhile if models developed by sociologists and psychologists are more often stated formally and in terms of measurable variables. Finally, economic models, even when they cannot indicate the way in which criminal justice policies and legal opportunities affect criminality, provide a badly needed formal guide to empirical work.

## Appendix 9.1. Derivation of Comparative Static Results for the Model of Section 9.5

The individual is assumed to maximize expected utility, as given by Eq. (9.6.1), with respect to $t_L$ and $t_I$. The symbols used in (9.6.1) are defined in Table 9.1, and the probabilities and income levels used are defined in Table 9.2. As noted in the text, the constraints $t_L \geq 0$, $t_I \geq 0$, $t_L + t_I < T$ exist but are ignored by assuming that they are not binding.

The first-order conditions for a local maximum, obtained by setting the partial derivatives of (9.6.1) with respect to $t_L$ and $t_I$ to zero, are the following:

$$H_1 = \sum_{i=1,3,5,7} p_i U_i' L_t = 0, \tag{A9.1.1}$$

$$H_2 = \sum_{i=1}^{2} p_i U_i' G_t + \sum_{i=3}^{4} p_i U_i'(G_t - F_t^1) + \sum_{i=5}^{6} p_i U_i'(G_t - F_t^2) + \sum_{i=7}^{8} p_i U_i'(G_t - F_t^3) = 0. \tag{A9.1.2}$$

Here, as a matter of notation, $U_i' \equiv U'(I_i)$, $L_t \equiv \partial L(t_L, \delta)/\partial t_L$, $G_t \equiv \partial G(t_I, \alpha)/\partial t_I$, $F_t^j \equiv \partial F^j(t_I, \beta)/\partial t_I$, $j = 1, 2, 3$.

It is important to note that (A9.1.1) requires $L_t = 0$ and that this determines the level of $t_L$. Thus the individual's time allocation to the labor market is independent of income and of all attributes of illegal gains and penalties. In this model, labor market decisions are made first and criminal activity decisions determined afterward; that is, the model is analogous to a recursive model in econometrics. For the second condition to hold, it is necessary that the net marginal returns to criminal activity be negative for at least some levels of criminal justice sanctions. Indeed, it is necessary for some combination of the last six terms to be negative and equal to the sum of all positive terms in this equation. We assume that $F_t^3 > F_t^2 > F_t^1 > 0$ and $G_t > 0$. This plus (A9.1.2) implies that

$$G_t - F_t^3 < 0, \qquad G_t - F_t^3 < G_t - F_t^2 < G_t - F_t^1. \tag{A9.1.3}$$

However, the signs of $G_t - F_t^2$ and $G_t - F_t^1$ are ambiguous.

We now wish to determine the effects of the various exogenous factors ($p_a$, $p_{c/a}$, $p_{J/c}$, $\alpha$, $\beta$, $\delta$, $e$, $A$) on $t_I$. We omit a discussion of the effects of the parameters on $t_L$ because $t_L$ is affected only by one of them, namely $\delta$, and because the argument showing that $dt_L/d\delta$ is positive is identical to that of Heineke (1978a).

Let $\theta$ be any parameter, and let $H_{11} = \partial H_1/\partial t_L$, $H_{22} = \partial H_2/\partial t_I$, $H_{12} = H_{21} = \partial H_1/\partial t_I = \partial H_2/\partial t_L$. If we differentiate (A9.1.1) and (A9.1.2) with respect to $\theta$, we obtain

$$\frac{\partial H_1}{d\theta} + H_{11}\frac{dt_L}{d\theta} + H_{12}\frac{dt_I}{d\theta} = 0,$$
$$\frac{\partial H_2}{\partial\theta} + H_{12}\frac{dt_L}{d\theta} + H_{22}\frac{dt_I}{d\theta} = 0, \quad \text{(A9.1.4)}$$

which we wish to solve for $dt_L/d\theta$ and $dt_I/d\theta$. This is simplified considerably by the observation that, at the optimum, $H_{12} = 0$ because

$$H_{12} = p_1 U_1'' L_t G_t + p_3 U_3'' L_t(G_t - F_t^1) + p_5 U_5'' L_t(G_t - F_t^2) + p_7 U_7'' L_t(G_t - F_t^3)$$

and $L_t = 0$ at the optimum. [Here $U_i'' \equiv U''(I_i)$.] Thus for $dt_I/d\theta$, we have simply

$$\frac{dt_I}{d\theta} = -\frac{1}{H_{22}}\frac{\partial H_2}{\partial\theta}. \quad \text{(A9.1.5)}$$

Now $H_{22} < 0$ by the second-order conditions for a local maximum, which we assume to hold. Therefore we arrive at the important conclusion: *The sign of $dt_I/d\theta$ is the same as the sign of $\partial H_2/\partial\theta$.* Thus we need only to try to find the sign of $\partial H_2/\partial\theta$ for the various possible $\theta$'s.

We first choose $\theta = p_a$ and show that $\partial H_2/\partial p_a < 0$. To do so we evaluate $\partial H_2/\partial p_a$ as

$$\frac{\partial H_2}{\partial p_a} = -\frac{1}{1-p_a}\sum_{i=1}^{2} p_i U_i' \frac{\partial I_i}{\partial t_I} + \frac{1}{p_a}\sum_{i=3}^{8} p_i U_i' \frac{\partial I_i}{\partial t_I}. \quad \text{(A9.1.6)}$$

Now the first term on the right-hand side is negative because

$$\sum_{i=1}^{2} p_i U_i' \,\partial I_i/\partial t_I = p_1 U_1' G_t + p_2 U_2' G_t > 0.$$

The second-order term on the right-hand side of (A9.1.6) is also negative because

$$\sum_{i=3}^{8} p_i U_i' \,\partial I_i/\partial t_I = H_2 - \sum_{i=1}^{2} p_i U_i' G_t$$

and $H_2 = 0$ whereas $\sum_{i=1}^{2} p_i U_i' G_t > 0$. Thus we conclude that (A9.1.6) is negative, and $dt_I/dp_a < 0$. This conclusion requires nothing beyond the existence of a local maximum.

We next consider the effect of a change in $p_{J/c}$. We have

$$\partial H_2/\partial p_{J/c} = -(1-e)p_a p_{c/a} U_5'(G_t - F_t^2) - e p_a p_{c/a} U_6'(G_t - F_t^2)$$
$$+ (1-e)p_a p_{c/a} U_7'(G_t - F_t^3) + e p_a p_{c/a} U_8'(G_t - F_t^3). \quad \text{(A9.1.7)}$$

We cannot unambiguously determine the sign of this expression. However, $\partial H_2/\partial p_{J/c} < 0$ (so $dt_I/dp_{J/c} < 0$) under three alternative sets of sufficient conditions. First, $\partial H_2/\partial p_{J/c} < 0$ if $G_t - F_t^2 > 0$. This is so because we know $G_t - F_t^3 < 0$ from (A9.1.3). The assumption that $G_t - F_t^2 > 0$ is that crime pays even if it is known that it will result in conviction and a fine (but not imprisonment), which is questionable. Second, $\partial H_2/\partial p_{J/c} < 0$ if the individual is risk neutral. In this case $U_5' = U_6' = U_7' = U_8'$ and the result follows because $F_t^2 - F_t^3 < 0$. Third, $\partial H_2/\partial p_{J/c} < 0$ if the individual is risk averse. Because $I_7 < I_5$, risk aversion implies $U_7' > U_5'$. Also $|G_t - F_t^3| > |G_t - F_t^2|$ (when $G_t - F_t^2 < 0$) from (A9.1.3). Thus $|U_7'(G_t - F_t^3)| > |U_5'(G_t - F_t^2)|$, and similarly for terms involving $U_8'$ and $U_6'$. So the last two terms in (A9.1.7), which must be negative, outweigh the first two terms. We conclude that $dt_I/dp_{J/c} < 0$ under conditions that are not very restrictive.

The effect of a change in $p_{c/a}$ is also somewhat ambiguous, though $dt_I/dp_{c/a} < 0$ under reasonable conditions. We have

$$\begin{aligned}\partial H_2/\partial p_{c/a} = {} & [-(1-e)p_a U_3' - e p_a U_4'](G_t - F_t^1) \\ & + [(1-e)p_a(1-p_{J/c})U_5' + e p_a(1-p_{J/c})U_6'](G_t - F_t^2) \\ & + [(1-e)p_a p_{J/c} U_7' + e p_a p_{J/c} U_8'](G_t - F_t^3).\end{aligned}$$

This can be shown to be negative under three alternative sets of conditions, by arguments more or less identical to those employed in the discussion of $p_{J/c}$. First, it is negative if the individual is risk neutral. Second, it is negative if $G_t - F_t^3 < 0$ and $G_t - F_t^2 < 0$ but $G_t - F_t^1 > 0$, which is so if the net marginal return to crime is positive if arrested but not convicted but negative if convicted. Third, it is negative if $G_t - F_t^j < 0$ for $j = 1, 2, 3$ and if the individual is risk averse. However, unless the individual is risk neutral, the result is ambiguous if $G_t - F_t^2 > 0$. This makes some intuitive sense because, in this case, conviction need not yield negative marginal net returns to crime.

The effect of a change in nonlabor income depends entirely on the individual's preferences toward risk. We have

$$\partial H_2/\partial A = \sum_{i=1}^{8} p_i U_i'' \, \partial I_i/\partial t_I.$$

Clearly this is zero if the individual is risk neutral ($U'' = 0$). If the individual is risk averse, substitute $U_i'' = -U_i' R(I_i)$ (where $R$ is the Arrow–Pratt measure) to obtain

$$\partial H_2/\partial A = -\sum_{i=1}^{8} p_i R(I_i) U_i' \, \partial I_i/\partial t_I. \tag{A9.1.8}$$

This is equal to zero if $R(I_i)$ is constant for all $I_i$ (constant absolute risk aversion), because it then equals $-R$ multiplied by (A9.1.2). If we make the standard assumption of decreasing absolute risk aversion, $R(I_i)$ is larger when $I_i$ is smaller, so $R(I_8) > R(I_6) > R(I_4) > R(I_2)$ and similarly for 7, 5, 3, and 1. Thus the sum in (A9.1.8) weights the negative (higher-indexed) terms more heavily than does (A9.1.2) and is negative, so (A.9.1.8) is positive, which implies $dt_\text{I}/dA > 0$. The opposite would occur if we assumed increasing absolute risk aversion.

Next we consider a change in the gains to criminal activity, represented by a change in the shift parameter $\alpha$. We have

$$\partial H_2/\partial\alpha = \sum_{i=1}^{8} p_i U_i'' G_\alpha\, \partial I_i/\partial t_\text{I} + \sum_{i=1}^{8} p_i U_i' G_{\text{t}\alpha},$$

where $G_\alpha \equiv \partial G(t_\text{I}, \alpha)/\partial\alpha > 0$ and $G_{\text{t}\alpha} \equiv \partial^2 G(t_\text{I}, \alpha)/\partial t_\text{I}\,\partial\alpha > 0$. This can be rewritten as

$$\frac{\partial H_2}{\partial\alpha} = G_\alpha \frac{dt_\text{I}}{dA} + G_{\text{t}\alpha} \frac{\partial E[U(I)]}{\partial A}. \tag{A9.1.9}$$

The second term on the right-hand side of (A9.1.9) is unambiguously positive. For $dt_\text{I}/d\alpha$ to be unambiguously positive the first term must be zero or positive. As we have just seen, this requires either risk neutrality or else decreasing absolute risk aversion.

The effect of a change in criminal penalties is represented by a change in the shift parameter $\beta$. Note that $\beta$ shifts all three penalty functions ($F^1$, $F^2$, and $F^3$); we could of course have introduced three separate shift parameters. We find

$$\frac{\partial H_2}{\partial\beta} = \sum_{i=1}^{8} p_i U_i'' \frac{\partial I_i}{\partial t_\text{I}} \frac{\partial I_i}{\partial\beta} + \sum_{i=1}^{8} p_i U_i' \frac{\partial^2 I_i}{\partial t_\text{I}\partial\beta}. \tag{A9.1.10}$$

The second term on the right-hand side of (A9.1.10) is negative because

$$\partial^2 I_i/\partial t_\text{I}\partial\beta = \begin{cases} 0 & \text{for } i = 1, 2 \\ -F^1_{\text{t}\beta} & \text{for } i = 3, 4 \\ -F^2_{\text{t}\beta} & \text{for } i = 5, 6 \\ -F^3_{\text{t}\beta} & \text{for } i = 7, 8 \end{cases}$$

and we assume $F^j_{\text{t}\beta} > 0$ for $j = 1, 2, 3$. The first term on the right-hand side of (A9.1.10), on the other hand, is

$$\sum_{i=1}^{8} p_i U_i'' \frac{\partial I_i}{\partial t_\text{I}} \frac{\partial I_i}{\partial\beta} = \sum_{i=3}^{4} p_i U_i''(G_\text{t} - F^1_\text{t})(-F^1_\beta) + \sum_{i=5}^{6} p_i U_i''(G_\text{t} - F^2_\text{t})(-F^2_\beta)$$
$$+ \sum_{i=7}^{8} p_i U_i''(G_\text{t} - F^3_\text{t})(-F^3_\beta). \tag{A9.1.11}$$

We require (A9.1.11) to be zero or negative to conclude that $dt_I/d\beta < 0$, and this is so under several possible sets of conditions. First, if the individual is risk neutral, (A9.1.11) equals zero. Second, (A9.1.11) is negative if the individual is risk averse and if $G_t - F_t^j \leq 0$ for $j = 1, 2, 3$. Third, (A9.1.11) is negative if the individual is risk averse and displays decreasing absolute risk aversion and if we impose some restrictions on $F_\beta^1, F_\beta^2, F_\beta^3$. To see this, rewrite (A9.1.11) as

$$\sum_{i=1}^{8} p_i U_i'' \frac{\partial I_i}{\partial t_I} \frac{\partial I_i}{\partial \beta} = \sum_{i=3}^{4} p_i U_i'(G_t - F_t^1)[R(I_i)F_\beta^1]$$

$$+ \sum_{i=5}^{6} p_i U_i'(G_t - F_t^2)[R(I_i)F_\beta^2]$$

$$+ \sum_{i=7}^{8} p_i U_i'(G_t - F_t^3)[R(I_i)F_\beta^3]. \qquad \text{(A9.1.12)}$$

Without the terms in brackets, (A9.1.12) would be negative by the first-order conditions (A9.1.2). It will remain negative if the "weights" in brackets are heavier for the negative (higher-indexed) terms, for example, if $R(I_8)F_\beta^3 > R(I_6)F_\beta^2 > R(I_4)F_\beta^1$ and $R(I_7)F_\beta^3 > R(I_5)F_\beta^2 > R(I_3)F^1$. Decreasing absolute risk aversion implies $R(I_8) > R(I_6) > R(I_4)$ and $R(I_7) > R(I_5) > R(I_3)$, so we obtain our result if $F_\beta^3 \geq F_\beta^2 \geq F_\beta^1$, or indeed even if this is not so, as long as the differences in changes in the penalties do not outweigh the differences in the levels of risk aversion.

We next consider the effect of a change in the return to legal labor market activity, represented by a change in the shift parameter $\delta$. We have

$$\partial H_2/\partial\delta = L_\delta[p_1 U_1'' G_t + p_3 U_3''(G_t - F_t^1) + p_5 U_5''(G_t - F_t^2) + p_7 U_7''(G_t - F_t^3)]. \qquad \text{(A9.1.13)}$$

Clearly this is zero under risk neutrality. If the individual is risk averse, things are less clear. We can note that the term in brackets in (A9.1.13) contains exactly half of the terms in $\partial H_2/\partial A$ as given earlier; specifically, it contains the terms corresponding to the employed states but not those corresponding to the unemployed states. We expect that $\partial H_2/\partial\delta$ behaves like $\partial H_2/\partial A$ and thus is positive if risk aversion decreases with increasing income. This is a reasonable conclusion because the effect of increasing $\delta$ is to increase the individual's income from the labor market, and the resulting income effect should not differ from the effect of a change in nonlabor income.

Finally, we consider a change in the unemployment rate $e$. It is easily calculated that

$$\partial H_2/\partial e = (p_1 + p_2)(U_2' - U_1')G_t + (p_3 + p_4)(U_4' - U_3')(G_t - F_t^1) + (p_5 + p_6)(U_6' - U_5')(G_t - F_t^2) + (p_7 + p_8)(U_8' - U_7')(G_t - F_t^3). \quad \text{(A9.1.14)}$$

Clearly this is zero under risk neutrality. Given risk aversion, its sign depends on how risk aversion varies with income. If we make the standard assumption of decreasing absolute risk aversion, then we argue (but do not prove rigorously) the unexpected result that $\partial H_2/\partial e < 0$ (and hence $dt_I/de < 0$). Our argument runs as follows. Note that $I_2 - I_1 = I_4 - I_3 = I_6 - I_5 = I_8 - I_7 = L(t_L, \delta)$ is the same for each such pair of indices (e.g., 1 and 2). Now, by the mean value theorem, we can write

$$U_2' - U_1' = (I_2 - I_1)U_{1,2}'' = L(t_L, \delta)U_{1,2}'',$$

where $U_{1,2}''$ is $U''$ evaluated at some income between $I_1$ and $I_2$. Doing the same for the other similar terms and inserting into (A9.1.14), we obtain

$$\partial H_2/\partial e = L(t_L, \delta)[(p_1 + p_2)U_{1,2}''G_t + (p_3 + p_4)U_{3,4}''(G_t - F_t^1) + (p_5 + p_6)U_{5,6}''(G_t - F_t^2) + (p_7 + p_8)U_{7,8}''(G_t - F_t^3)]. \quad \text{(A9.1.15)}$$

Comparing (A9.1.15) with (A9.1.2), the difference is that in (A9.1.2) we weight the terms of the sum by $U'$, whereas in (A9.1.15) we weight the terms by $U''$. As we move to higher-numbered states (e.g., 2 to 4 to 6 to 8), income falls. Given decreasing risk aversion, both U′ and $U''$ rise, but $U''$ rises faster than $U'$. Thus in (A9.1.15) we weigh the negative terms more heavily than in (A9.1.2), and thus we conclude that $\partial H_2/\partial e < 0$.

This argument is fairly convincing (tc us), but it is not really a proof because we do not know, for example, at what income (between $I_1$ and $I_2$) $U_{1,2}''$ is evaluated. If, in (A9.1.15), $p_1 G_t$ were multiplied by $U_1''$, $p_2 G_t$ were multiplied by $U_2''$, and so forth, we could prove that the expression was negative by comparison with (A9.1.2).

## Appendix 9.2. Analysis of a Model in Which Time Enters the Utility Function

In this appendix we consider a model that is almost identical to our first model of Section 9.5 (i.e., Heineke's Model II). The individual chooses time spent in the labor market $t_L$ and time spent on illegal activities $t_I$. There are two possible states, with income levels

$$I_s = A + L(t_L, \delta) + G(t_I, \alpha),$$

$$I_u = A + L(t_L, \delta) + G(t_I, \alpha) - F(t_I, \beta).$$

The individual achieves income $I_s$ with probability $1 - p$ and income $I_u$ with probability $p$.

The way in which this model differs from the model of Section 9.5 is that utility depends not only on income but also on leisure $N$, defined by

$$N = 24 - t_L - t_I. \tag{A9.2.1}$$

Thus the utility function is

$$U = U(I, N). \tag{A9.2.2}$$

This is a less general function than the utility function used by Heineke in his Model III, which included $t_L$ and $t_I$ separately [whereas (A9.2.2) depends only on $t_L + t_I$] as well as including a nonmonetized sanctions variable. If comparative statics results are not forthcoming from this model, they will surely not be forthcoming from more complicated models such as Heineke's Model III or our model of Section 9.7.

The consumer chooses $t_L$ and $t_I$ to maximize expected utility

$$E[U(I, N)] = (1 - p)U(I_s, N) + pU(I_u, N). \tag{A9.2.3}$$

The first-order conditions for a local maximum (assuming positive values for all three of $t_L$, $t_I$, and $N$) are

$$\begin{aligned} H_1 &= (1 - p)[U_I(I_s, N)L_t - U_N(I_s, N)] \\ &\quad + p[U_I(I_u, N)L_t - U_N(I_u, N)] = 0, \end{aligned} \tag{A9.2.4}$$

$$\begin{aligned} H_2 &= (1 - p)[U_I(I_s, N)G_t - U_N(I_s, N)] \\ &\quad + p[U_I(I_u, N)(G_t - F_t) - U_N(I_u, N)] = 0. \end{aligned} \tag{A9.2.5}$$

Here as a matter of notation $U_I \equiv \partial U/\partial I$ and $U_N \equiv \partial U/\partial N$; we use $U_I$ rather than $U'$ for the marginal utility of income because utility now has more than one argument.

One immediate implication is that the model is not "recursive" in the sense that our first model of Section 9.5 and our model of Section 9.6 were. Time spent in legal activities in this model is determined jointly with time spent in illegal activities and will be affected by a change in any of the parameters of the model. The reason for this is simple. The individual chooses $t_L$ so that the net marginal return to time spent in legal activities is zero. This net marginal return includes the marginal disutility of decreasing leisure, which in this model depends (as it should) on $t_I$ as well as $t_L$.

To consider the effects of changes in the parameters on $t_L$ and $t_I$, we define the notation

$$\begin{aligned} H_{11} &= \partial H_1/\partial t_L, \\ H_{12} &= H_{21} = \partial H_1/\partial t_I = \partial H_2/\partial t_L, \\ H_{22} &= \partial H_2/\partial t_I, \\ |H| &= H_{11}H_{22} - H_{12}^2. \end{aligned} \tag{A9.2.6}$$

Then for an arbitrary parameter $\theta$ (which could be $p$, $A$, $\alpha$, $\beta$, or $\delta$), differentiating (A9.2.4) and (A9.2.5) with respect to $\theta$ and solving for $dt_L/d\theta$ and $dt_I/d\theta$ yields

$$\frac{dt_L}{d\theta} = \frac{1}{|H|}\left[H_{12}\frac{\partial H_2}{\partial \theta} - H_{22}\frac{\partial H_1}{\partial \theta}\right], \tag{A9.2.7}$$

$$\frac{dt_I}{d\theta} = \frac{1}{|H|}\left[H_{12}\frac{\partial H_1}{\partial \theta} - H_{11}\frac{\partial H_2}{\partial \theta}\right]. \tag{A9.2.8}$$

The second-order conditions for a local maximum imply that $|H| > 0$, $H_{11} < 0$, and $H_{22} < 0$. However, to determine the signs of (A9.2.7) or (A9.2.8) will require determining the signs of $H_{12}$, $\partial H_1/\partial\theta$, and $\partial H_2/\partial\theta$.

We shall now look carefully at $H_{12}$ because it appears in the expressions for the effects on $t_L$ and $t_I$ of a change in any of the parameters. Direct calculation yields

$$\begin{aligned} H_{12} = {} & (1 - p)[U_{II}(I_s, N)L_tG_t + U_{NN}(I_s, N) - U_{IN}(I_s, N)(G_t + L_t)] \\ & + p[U_{II}(I_u, N)L_t(G_t - F_t) + U_{NN}(I_u, N) \\ & - U_{IN}(I_u, N)(G_t + L_t - F_t)], \end{aligned} \tag{A9.2.9}$$

where $U_{II} \equiv \partial^2 U/\partial I^2$, $U_{NN} \equiv \partial^2 U/\partial N^2$, and $U_{IN} \equiv \partial^2 U/\partial I\,\partial N$.

Now for some of the terms in (A9.2.9) we can make reasonable assumptions. For example, it is clear that $L_t > 0$, $G_t > 0$, $F_t > 0$, and $G_t - F_t < 0$. Also, $U_{II}$ is interpretable in terms of risk aversion: $U_{II} = 0$ under risk neutrality and $U_{II} < 0$ under risk aversion. We would not feel uncomfortable with the assumption that $U_{NN} < 0$, which is simply the assumption of decreasing marginal utility of leisure. However, there is little guidance for assumptions about $U_{IN}$. Mathematically, we can assume concavity of $U$, which implies $U_{IN}^2 < U_{II}U_{NN}$, but this is not much help. Alternatively, the conditions that $H_{11} < 0$ and $H_{22} < 0$ contain information about $U_{IN}$, but, again, not enough information. Economically, we can recognize that $U_{IN}$ tells us the rate at which the marginal utility of leisure changes as income changes. For example,

$U_{IN} > 0$ if rich people value leisure more than poor people. But there is no good basis for such an assumption (or for the opposite one).

If we are willing to make assumptions about $U_{IN}$, the most powerful is $U_{IN} = 0$, which amounts to an assumption of "separability." Then we have

$$H_{12} = (1 - p)[U_{II}(I_s, N)L_t G_t + U_{NN}(I_s, N)] + p[U_{II}(I_u, N)L_t(G_t - F_t) + U_{NN}(I_u, N)]. \quad \text{(A9.2.10)}$$

Clearly this is negative if we assume risk neutrality ($U_{II} = 0$) plus decreasing marginal utility of leisure ($U_{NN}$) in addition to separability. But if we assume risk aversion, it is still ambiguous; three terms are negative but the term $U_{II}(I_u, N)L_t(G_t - F_t)$ is positive. Defining the Arrow–Pratt measure $R = -U_{II}/U_I$, we can rewrite (A9.2.10) as

$$H_{12} = [(1 - p)U_{NN}(I_s, N) + pU_{NN}(I_u, N)] - L_t[(1 - p)R(I_s, N)U_I(I_s, N)G_t + pR(I_u, N)U_I(I_u, N)(G_t - F_t)]. \quad \text{(A9.2.11)}$$

The first term in brackets and $-L_t$ are clearly negative, so we try to show that the last term in brackets is positive. Now the first-order conditions (A9.2.5) imply that

$$(1 - p)U_I(I_s, N)G_t + pU_I(I_u, N)(G_t - F_t) > 0,$$

and thus that

$$|(1 - p)U_I(I_s, N)G_t| > |pU_I(I_u, N)(G_t - F_t)|. \quad \text{(A9.2.12)}$$

Thus if $|R(I_s, N)| \geq |R(I_u, N)|$, we could conclude that the last term in brackets in (A9.2.11) is positive and therefore that $H_{12} < 0$. However, because $I_s > I_u$, $R(I_s) \geq R(I_u)$ requires constant or increasing absolute risk aversion, the opposite of the usual assumption. Under the usual assumption of decreasing risk aversion, $H_{12}$ is still ambiguous.

This means that any comparative static results are likely to be ambiguous unless we assume both $U_{IN} = 0$ and risk neutrality ($U_{II} = 0$). For example, if we consider the effect of a change in $p$, we have

$$\partial H_1/\partial p = L_t[U_I(I_u, N) - U_I(I_s, N)] + [U_N(I_s, N) - U_N(I_u, N)], \quad \text{(A9.2.13)}$$

$$\partial H_2/\partial p = (G_t - F_t)U_I(I_u, N) - G_t U_I(I_s, N) + [U_N(I_s, N) - U_N(I_u, N)]. \quad \text{(A9.2.14)}$$

The sign of the last term in brackets in each expression depends on the sign of $U_{IN}$ and is ambiguous without some assumption about $U_{IN}$. If we make the strong assumption that $U_{IN} = 0$ as before, then these last terms equal zero and $\partial H_1/\partial p$ is zero under risk neutrality and positive under risk aversion, whereas $\partial H_2/\partial p$ is unambiguously negative. By (A9.2.8),

$$\frac{dt_{\mathrm{I}}}{dp} = \frac{1}{|H|}\left[H_{12}\frac{\partial H_1}{\partial p} - H_{11}\frac{\partial H_2}{\partial p}\right].$$

Given risk neutrality plus $U_{\mathrm{IN}} = 0$, we have shown that $|H| > 0$, $H_{11} < 0$, $H_{12} < 0$, $\partial H_1/\partial p = 0$, and $\partial H_2/\partial p < 0$, which implies $dt_{\mathrm{I}}/dp < 0$. However, given risk aversion instead of risk neutrality (but still given $U_{\mathrm{IN}} = 0$), we have $|H| > 0$, $H_{11} < 0$, $\partial H_1/\partial p > 0$, $\partial H_2/\partial p < 0$, and $H_{12}$ ambiguous. We can rescue the conclusion $dt_{\mathrm{I}}/dp < 0$ only by assuming constant or increasing absolute risk aversion, which suffices to make $H_{12} < 0$.

Without leisure in the utility function, $dt_{\mathrm{I}}/dp < 0$ was the most certain of the comparative static results, requiring no assumptions beyond existence of a local maximum. As we have just seen, with leisure in the utility function, we cannot show $dt_{\mathrm{I}}/dp < 0$ except under unreasonably strong assumptions. This is so despite the fact that this model is simpler than both Heineke's Model III and our model of Section 9.7.

## Notes to Chapter 9

1. Of course, one difference is that the price of oranges is readily defined and observed, whereas the "expected cost of committing a crime" is less tangible.

2. There is a distinction, dating back to Knight (1921) and sometimes still made, between "risk" and "uncertainty." According to Knight, "risk" simply refers to the random nature of a relevant outcome; one may know the probabilities of the possible outcomes but not know which will occur. On the other hand, according to Knight, "uncertainty" refers to imperfect knowledge of the probabilities. However, the influential work of Savage (1952) argued that this distinction is irrelevant, because what matters are the individual's subjective probabilities of the various outcomes, and accordingly, the distinction is seldom made any more. We shall use the terms "risk" and "uncertainty" interchangeably, to denote what Knight called "risk."

3. Admittedly, such an argument can explain away any behavior. For example, that people buy insurance is often argued to be evidence of risk aversion, but maybe people just like to deal with insurance agents. On the other hand, few can argue that buying insurance is exciting.

4. This result depends on only one assumption not explicitly mentioned, namely, that $G_\chi - F_\chi < 0$. This is simply the assumption that increasing $\chi$ would not pay if apprehension were certain.

5. Throughout this study, when we refer to "the labor market" and "wages" we mean only the market for, and wages earned from, activities regarded as legal. See Simon and Witte (1982) for a discussion of illegal labor markets, such as those for prostitutes and thieves.

6. That $t_{\mathrm{L}}$ is unaffected by a change in the unemployment rate is rather strange. It arises because in this model there is no utility derived from leisure.

7. It should be noted that the ambiguity in the results is because there is more than one possible sanction. It is not related to the introduction of possible unemployment into the model.

# Chapter 10

## Estimating a Simple Economic Model of Criminal Behavior

### 10.1. Introduction

In Section 9.6 we developed a simple economic model that explored the factors determining the amount of time that an individual will allocate to illegal activity. Individual expectations concerning criminal justice sanctions and the relative gains to time devoted to legal and illegal activities were central to this model. Recall that the model indicated that time devoted to criminal activity is independent of time devoted to labor market activity. Thus for this model it is permissible to analyze, as we do in this chapter, the determinants of criminal activity separately from the determinants of activity in the labor market.

The organization of the chapter is as follows. In the next section, we develop the empirical model that we shall estimate. We discuss the type of data that would be best suited to estimate this model and the data that we have available. We also discuss measures in this data set that we use to represent the variables in our theoretical model and the statistical methodology that we employ. Sections 10.3–10.4 report and discuss the results we obtain when we estimate our model. Section 10.3 contains our discussion of the supply function for all types of offenses, and Section 10.4 contains our discussion of similar functions for four types of offenses. The final section of the chapter contains our summary and conclusions.

## 10.2. An Empirical Model of Criminal Activity

In Section 9.6 our theoretical model indicated that the amount of time that an individual would spend in illegal activity, denoted $t_I$, depends on the following factors: the probability of arrest $p_a$, of conviction given arrest $p_{c/a}$, of jail given conviction $p_{J/c}$, and of being unemployed $e$; the returns to time spent in the labor market (if employed) $L$, and to time spent on illegal activities $G$; the sanctions imposed if arrested $F^1$, convicted $F^2$, and/or jailed $F^3$; nonlabor income $A$; and tastes. In this section we convert this theoretical model to an empirical model to be estimated. This conversion requires three basic things: (1) a data set, (2) choice of empirical measures for the factors just listed, and (3) a specification of the mathematical form of the function relating these measures. We discuss each of these in turn.

It is important to recognize that, whereas the theoretical model of crime deals with behavior at the individual level, the existing empirical literature by and large does not estimate an individual supply of offenses function but rather estimates an equation to determine the crime rate in a jurisdiction (e.g., city, state, nation). This literature has been the subject of extensive criticism,[1] some of which is relevant in the present context. Thus, although these efforts have sought to test a model of individual behavior, they have used data for jurisdictions (i.e., aggregate data), not data for individuals. We believe this choice of data was made for two basic reasons: (1) this type of data was readily available and (2) it gave the appearance of allowing broad generalizations. Unfortunately, it is not easy to infer things about individual behavior from empirical work using aggregate data. Such inferences require strong assumptions concerning the nature and/or diversity of individual behavior. For example, to determine the nature of the supply-of-offense function for a community (e.g., a city) from his model of individual behavior, Ehrlich (1973) assumes that all individuals are identical. Sjoquist assumes that the parameters of the individual crime function (i.e., tastes) "are the same for all individuals in a given community and that the density function between individual values and the community mean of the variable are homogenous of degree one with respect to changes in the individual values and community means" (Sjoquist, 1973, p. 441). Needless to say, these assumptions are quite strong and are not likely to reflect reality adequately.

Most individuals who have estimated the economic model with aggregate data have used the FBI's Uniform Crime Report as their primary source. The quality and reliability of those data have been criticized widely. We shall not repeat these criticisms but rather affirm our support for the conclusions of two applied statisticians that little will come from attempts to test the economic model of crime with this type of data [see Brier and Fienberg (1980, p. 188)].

Given our decision to use data on individuals, we are left with the problem of finding an adequate individual data base. The ideal data base would contain information on the allocation of time for a random sample of the population. Such a sample would be large in order to contain enough individuals allocating time to illegal activities to make the analysis meaningful. For this large sample, one would elicit a complete time budget. The most difficult information to obtain would be information on the amount of time allocated to illegal activities. Most illegal activity is not observed and much that is observed is not recorded or reported to criminal justice agencies. Thus, official records are likely to provide only a poor reflection of the time allocated to illegal activities for general population groups. Criminologists and sociologists have attempted to obtain accurate "self-reports" of criminal activity for some time. [See Farrington (1973), Reiss (1973), and Petersilia (1977) for surveys of this work.] Techniques for eliciting this information have improved markedly,[2] but the reliability and validity of data obtained in this manner are open to serious question. In one instance, when the sophisticated randomized response model of interviewing was used, self-reports understated drunk driving charges by 35% (Locander, Sudman, and Bradburn, 1976, p. 271).

The current data set falls short of the ideal just described in two major ways. First, it is not a random sample from the population but rather a random sample of men imprisoned in one state. Second, it contains information only on officially reported criminal activity. Specifically, the data used in this chapter consist of information on the postrelease activities of two samples, taken in 1969 and 1971, of 641 men who were in prison in North Carolina in either or both of those years. The activities of these men were followed for an average period of 37 months after their release from incarceration.[3] Although the sample was drawn from a single prison administrative area, the population from which it was drawn is quite representative of the population in medium- and minimum-custody prison units throughout North Carolina.[4] Indeed, men were released in 39 of the 100 counties of North Carolina.

The nature of this sample restricts the generality of the results that we report but should provide a stringent test of the economic model of crime, because men who have been imprisoned generally have allocated substantial portions of their time to illegal activity in the past. Such men are of further interest because of the large contribution they make to the overall level of crime in the United States. According to a report of the Subcommittee on Courts, Civil Liberty, and Administration of Justice of the House Judiciary Committee, probably two-thirds of all serious crimes are committed by persons who have been in jail.[5] The restriction of the sample to North Carolina, although more difficult to justify, was dictated by the original purpose for which the data were collected, an evaluation of the North Carolina prisoner work release program.

Only information on officially reported criminal activity was considered, because we felt that the possible usefulness of self-reports was more than outweighed by the difficulty of obtaining them.[6] We took great care, however, to collect unusually complete criminal records[7] and details of legal activities through personal interviews. In regard to self-reports, it is interesting that men in our sample tended to grossly understate even their reported criminal activity.

Given a data set, we next need to determine empirical measures for each of the variables in our theoretical model. We begin with the dependent variable, the time allocated to illegal activity. In our data set, we do not observe the time allocated to illegal activity but rather observe a certain number of arrests, convictions, and imprisonments. We can justify using one of these measures as a proxy for the time spent in illegal activity if we assume that the measure selected is monotonically related to the time allocated to illegal activity. We make this assumption and are left with the decision whether to use arrests, convictions, or imprisonments as our proxy. Given the way in which our criminal justice system operates, using imprisonments seems clearly unacceptable. Reasonable cases can be made, however, for using either convictions or arrests as our proxy. Arrests seem an attractive proxy because they are the first point of formal contact with the criminal justice system and thus information has passed through fewer selective filters than have records for later stages of criminal processing. However, the prior records of the men in our sample and the police practice of multiple charging seem likely to make the number of arrests received an overestimate of the actual number of offenses committed.[8] In contrast, due process requirements, nonreporting of offenses, and low clearance rates seem likely to make the number of convictions received an underestimate of the number of offenses committed, perhaps even approximating a lower bound.[9] In our empirical work, we shall analyze both arrests and convictions. This seems preferable to choosing one or the other in an arbitrary fashion.

One final adjustment to the dependent variable is necessary owing to the nature of the data used. This adjustment is to divide the number of arrests and convictions received by the length of time spent outside of prison during the follow-up period. Because the activities of men in our sample were followed for varying lengths of time and because men in our sample were out of prison for varying portions of the follow-up period, time at risk (time out of prison) for various individuals differed substantially (from less than 1 month to 69 months). Ten arrests (or convictions) in 1 year indicates a greater level of criminal activity than 10 arrests (or convictions) in 3 years; hence, the dependent variables analyzed are the number of arrests per month outside of prison, denoted *ARRAT*, and the number of convictions per month outside of prison, denoted *CVRAT*.

Having selected dependent variables to analyze, we next select an empirical measure for each of the explanatory variables in our model. We were unable to obtain any direct measure of the returns to time spent in illegal activity. However, opportunities to conduct illegal activities are likely to be related to various factors (to be discussed later) that we shall use to measure tastes. Thus, we hope to control at least partially for illegal gains when we introduce our taste measures into the specification. Nonlabor income or wealth is generally very low for prison releasees[10] and in many cases consists only of "gate money."[11] However, approximately half of the men in our sample participated in the prisoner work release program, and shortly after release they received the funds that they had accumulated while on the program. These funds were often substantial and averaged more than $400. The total amount of these funds received is used as a measure of initial wealth and is denoted *TPOWR*. The number of months until an individual obtains his first job and the hourly wage on that job, denoted *MFJAR* and *WAGEAR*, respectively, will be used as measures of the expected unemployment rate and expected rate of return to time spent in labor market activity. These measures assume that an individual forms his expectation about the labor market in the period immediately after release. These measures are not ideal and indeed may be endogenous to the system[12] but they were the best measures available.

The variables related to the expected probabilities of various criminal justice outcomes are particularly difficult to measure. The present data set provides no way of estimating the probability of arrest, because we do not observe an individual's actual criminal activity. Given that 80% of the men in the sample were rearrested during the period their activities were followed, it would seem fair to assume that the subjective probability of arrest is very high for most former prison inmates. Hence, the probability of arrest may be of fairly minor importance in their time-allocation decision. Given the data at hand, there are two possible ways of estimating expected probabilities of conviction (given arrest) and of prison (given conviction). First, we can estimate them from the past records of the individual.[13] This assumes that individuals leaving prison form their expectations by evaluating their own past experience. This approach is intuitively appealing, allowing as it does for individual differences in ability and type of crime. Second, we can estimate these probabilities from the immediate postrelease experience of individuals who specialize in the same type of illegal activity. This assumes that individuals leaving prison form their expectations by evaluating the postrelease experience of men who specialize in the same type of criminal activity as they do. The geographic concentration of the sample makes this assumption less tenuous than it might appear at the first reading. Although both of these measures of expected probabilities were used, only the results using probabilities calculated in the first way are reported. Results when probabilities are calculated in the second way are similar, although weaker.

The final criminal justice variables entering the model are the expected costs of the various outcomes (sanctions) of the criminal justice process. We have no direct information on the cost of arrest, but this should be related to an individual's wealth, wage rate, and socioeconomic group. The data set also lacks information on the average amount of fines imposed. However, for this particular group, consisting of former inmates, it seems reasonable to assume that by far the most relevant sanction is further imprisonment. Although we cannot measure the costs of such imprisonment, we assume that these costs are directly related to the average prison sentence one expects to receive, denoted *EXLOS*. As in the case of the probabilities discussed previously, two alternative estimates of these expectations are possible: one based on an individual's historic experience and the other based on the postrelease experience of individuals specializing in a similar type of crime. As in the case of probabilities, both of these alternatives were used, although only the results with historic measures are reported, because postrelease measures gave similar, although weaker, results.

The final variable entering the empirical model is tastes. We assume that tastes are shaped by the socioeconomic group to which one belongs and are revealed by one's past activity. Thus, we attempt to control for differences in tastes with a fairly long list of variables that represent characteristics of the individual and of his past behavior. Table 10.1 lists all of the variables in our theoretical model, the empirical measures we use to represent them, and the signs that we expect to obtain for their estimated coefficients.

We now turn to the last of the three basic decisions needed to prepare our theoretical model for estimation, namely, the form of the function relating the explanatory variables to the dependent variable. In other words, we need to pick a statistical model to use. In the present analysis, the salient features of the dependent variables (*ARRAT* and *CVRAT*) are that they are nonnegative and that zero is a common value. In 20% of the sample

**TABLE 10.1.** Summary of Variables and Expected Signs for Coefficients

| Theoretical variable | Empirical measure: Acronym | Empirical measure: Definition of variable | Expected sign of coefficient(s) |
|---|---|---|---|
| Dependent | | | |
| Time spent on illegal activity $t_I$. | ARRAT | Number of arrests per month free | |
| | CVRAT | Number of convictions per month free | |
| Independent | | | |
| Non labor income $A$ | TPOWR | Accumulated work release funds (in $100) received after release | Positive |
| Probability of unemployment $e$ | *MFJAR* | Number of months until first job after release | Positive |
| Gains to legal activity $L$ | *WAGEAR* | Hourly wage rate after release | Negative |
| Gains to illegal activity $G$ | | No measure | |
| Probability of arrest $p_a$ | | No measure | |
| Probability of conviction given arrest $p_{c/a}$ | *P(C/A)* | Number of convictions divided by number of arrests prior to release from 1969/71 imprisonment | Negative |
| Probability of jail given conviction $p_{J/C}$ | *P(J/C)* | Number of convictions resulting in imprisonment divided by total number of convictions prior to release from 1969/71 imprisonment | Negative |
| Cost of arrest $F^1$ | | Directly related to taste variables, wealth, and wage | |
| Cost of conviction $F^2$ | | No measure | |
| Cost of jail $F^3$ | *EXLOS* | Individual historical average sentence length received (in months) prior to release in 1969/71 | Negative |
| Tastes[a] | *AAR* | Age (in years) at release | Positive |
| | *AAR*$^2$ | Squared value of *AAR* | Negative |
| | *AFA* | Age (in years) at first arrest | Negative |
| | *ARRBS* | Number of arrests before incarceration in 1969 or 1971 | Positive |
| | *CONVBS* | Number of convictions before incarceration in 1969 or 1971 | Positive |

**TABLE 10.1.** *(Continued)*

| Theoretical variable | Empirical measure: Acronym | Empirical measure: Definition of variable | Expected sign of coefficient(s) |
|---|---|---|---|
| | *RACE* | A dummy variable equal to 1 for nonwhites and 0 for whites | Conflicting |
| | *ALCHY* | A dummy variable equal to 1 if an individual's history indicates a serious alcohol problem and 0 otherwise | Positive |
| | *JUNKY* | Dummy variable equal to 1 if an individual's history indicates drug use and 0 otherwise | Positive |
| | *SUPER* | Dummy variable equal to 1 if an individual was supervised (e.g., on parole) when released and 0 otherwise | Negative |
| | *MS* | A dummy variable equal to 1 if an individual was married and 0 otherwise | Negative |
| | *RULE* | The number of rule violations during 1969 or 1971 prison term | Positive |

[a] For reviews of the literature from which these expected signs are derived, see Monahan (1981), Pritchard (1977), or Service (1972).

*ARRAT* = 0 (no arrests), and in 26% *CVRAT* = 0 (no convictions). For dependent variables with these features, an obvious model to consider is the Tobit model. This model is discussed in detail in Chapter 4 (Section 4.3 in particular), and it was used in Chapter 5 in our analysis of time sentenced; we shall use it again here. The chief advantages of the Tobit model are that it takes into account the censored nature of the dependent variable and that it allows us to use both the observations for which the dependent variable is positive and those for which it equals zero.

## 10.3. Estimates of a Model for All Criminal Behavior

Table 10.2 presents the empirical results obtained when estimating a model for all types of criminal behavior. (We shall later consider various types of criminal behavior separately.) Regressions 1 (dependent variable *ARRAT*) and 2 (dependent variable *CVRAT*) use only measures of initial wealth, probabilities, costs, and noncriminal alternatives as independent variables. In Regressions 3 (dependent variable *ARRAT*) and 4 (dependent variable *CVRAT*), measures of tastes as explanatory variables have been added. We believe that the tastes variables are important. However, Regressions 3 and 4 suffer from a considerable degree of multicollinearity, and we therefore present Regressions 1 and 2 without the taste variables to see how much difference it makes whether or not they are included. A dummy variable equal to one if an individual remains on his work release job and zero otherwise, denoted *MSTAY*, has also been added to the specification to adjust for the unusually low wage rate of work release jobs.[14] The results of all regressions except Regression 2 are significant at any normal level of statistical significance. Regression 2 is only significant at the 10% level.[15]

**TABLE 10.2.** Empirical Results when Dependent Variables are Total Arrests and Convictions per Month Free[a]

| | Regressions | | | |
|---|---|---|---|---|
| Variables | 1 | 2 | 3 | 4 |
| Dependent | *ARRAT* | *CVRAT* | *ARRAT* | *CVRAT* |
| Independent | | | | |
| *CNST* | .5177*** | .2991*** | .5739*** | .4711*** |
| | (4.379) | (3.005) | (3.301) | (3.192) |
| *P(C/A)* | −.1760*** | −.0442 | −.0643 | −.0319 |
| | (−2.650) | (−.794) | (−.998) | (−.588) |
| *P(J/C)* | −.1376* | −.0988 | −.0858 | −.0784 |
| | (−1.422) | (−1.207) | (−.927) | (−.995) |
| *EXLOS* | −.0010*** | −.0008*** | −.0006** | −.0004* |
| | (−3.222) | (−2.843) | (−1.663) | (−1.338) |
| *WAGEAR* | −.0196 | −.0155 | −.0251* | −.0189 |
| | (−.991) | (−.930) | (−1.337) | (−1.197) |
| *MSTAY* | −.0577* | −.0353 | −.0254 | −.0119 |
| | (−1.380) | (−1.009) | (−.648) | (−.361) |
| *TPOWR* | −.0024 | −.0023 | −.0004 | −.0000 |
| | (−.513) | (−.580) | (−.093) | (−.384) |
| *MFJAR* | −.0086 | −.0076 | −.0088 | −.0075 |
| | (−1.093) | (−1.148) | (−1.208) | (−1.224) |
| *AAR* | — | — | −.0104 | −.0118* |
| | | | (−1.116) | (−1.496) |
| $AAR^2$ | — | — | .0000 | .0000 |
| | | | (.459) | (.784) |
| *AFA* | — | — | .0024 | .0024 |
| | | | (.679) | (1.131) |
| *ARRBS* | — | — | .0160*** | — |
| | | | (5.093) | |

**TABLE 10.2.** *(Continued)*

| | Regressions | | | |
|---|---|---|---|---|
| Variables | 1 | 2 | 3 | 4 |
| *CONVBS* | — | — | — | .0164*** |
| | | | | (4.311) |
| *RACE* | — | — | −.0771*** | −.0802*** |
| | | | (−2.656) | (−3.281) |
| *MS* | — | — | −.0155 | −.0267 |
| | | | (−.496) | (−1.014) |
| *ALCHY* | — | — | .0292 | .0435** |
| | | | (.982) | (1.731) |
| *JUNKY* | — | — | .1182** | .1101** |
| | | | (1.991) | (2.216) |
| *SUPER* | — | — | −.0801*** | −.0572** |
| | | | (−2.469) | (−2.09) |
| *RULE* | — | — | .0164** | .0153** |
| | | | (1.851) | (2.063) |
| $\hat{\sigma}^2$ | .0650 | .0371 | .0490 | .0310 |
| Likelihood ratio test[b] | 23.948*** | 13.987* | 88.361*** | 76.466*** |

[a] Asterisk indicates level of significance, one-tailed test: *** = .01 level, ** = .05 level, * = .10 level. Values in parentheses under coefficients are "$t$-ratios," which are asymptotically $N(0, 1)$ under the null hypothesis that the coefficient is zero.

[b] This is $-2\log(\lambda)$, where $\log(\lambda)$ is the difference between the log of the maximized value of the likelihood function with only a constant term as an independent variable and the log of the maximized value of the likelihood function with the independent variables in the regression under consideration. This statistic is distributed $x_k^2$, where $k$ is the number of explanatory variables (excluding the constant) in the regression under consideration. The statistic tests the joint significance of the independent variables and is equivalent to the $F$ test in least squares regression.

The results presented in Table 10.2 seem reasonable and are generally consistent with earlier results that were obtained using aggregate data. Of the measures that emerge directly from the theoretical model (measures of initial wealth, probabilities, costs, and legitimate alternatives), only the measure of initial wealth $A$ has a coefficient with a sign that contradicts the results of the theoretical model of Chapter 9. We shall discuss this finding later. Another (to us) surprising finding is that our measure of the expected unemployment rate *MFJAR* has a negative rather than a positive coefficient. Although our simple economic model yields an expectation of a negative coefficient (see Appendix 9.1) both intuition and previous empirical work lead us to believe that a higher unemployment rate will be associated with a higher crime rate. If *MFJAR* is the information on which an individual forms expectations about the unemployment rate, the larger the number of months until an individual finds a job, the larger should be his expected unemployment rate. Hence, one would expect a positive coefficient for *MFJAR*, but instead a negative coefficient (though an insignificant[16] one) is found for this variable in every case. A possible interpretation of this result is that individuals who take longer to find a job do so either because they are allocating substantial amounts of time to criminal activity or because they are searching for satisfying legitimate employment. If this interpretation is correct, then *MFJAR* does not measure the expected unemployment rate but rather reflects the time allocation decision.

The measure of the expected probability of conviction given arrest $P(C/A)$ has a coefficient with the expected sign in every case, but the coefficient is statistically significant only when the dependent variable is *ARRAT* and measures of tastes are excluded, that is, in Regression 1. Similarly, the measure of the expected probability of imprisonment given conviction, $P(J/C)$, has a coefficient with the expected sign in every case, but the coefficient is not even marginally significant except in the case of Regression 1. Recall from Chapter 9 that to prove that increases in the probability of conviction (given arrest) or of jail (given conviction) would deter crime, we had to make rather strong assumptions. With only traditional (weak) assumptions about individual preferences, our results were ambiguous. From this perspective our empirical results are not surprising. They certainly do not contradict the hypothesis that increases in the probabilities of conviction and imprisonment will deter crime, but neither do they support it very strongly.

The coefficient on the measure of the costs of incarceration *EXLOS* has the traditional sign and is at least marginally significant in all four regressions. However, the significance of this coefficient drops markedly when measures of tastes are included in the regression.[17] Note that our findings indicate a more consistently significant effect for increases in penalties than for increases in the probabilities of conviction or imprisonment. This is consistent with the theoretical results obtained in the previous chapter.

If one considers the elasticity of conviction or arrest rates[18] with respect to $P(C/A)$, $P(J/C)$, and *EXLOS* implied by the four regressions of Table 10.2, one finds that the elasticities with respect to the probabilities are higher than the elasticity with respect to *EXLOS* in all four cases. However, in all but the case of Regression 1, the elasticity with respect to $P(J/C)$ is higher than that with respect to $P(C/A)$. Whereas the former finding is consistent with most previous work on deterrence, the latter is inconsistent with Ehrlich's (1975) findings and seems unlikely to be forthcoming from our own theoretical results. Given the low level of significance of many of the coefficients on which the preceding is based, however, these findings should be viewed as suggestive only.

The coefficient of the measure of returns to labor market activity *WAGEAR* has a negative sign in all cases but is even marginally significant only in Regression 3. Recall from Chapter 9 that the coefficient one would expect for this variable depended critically on whether one assumes leisure time to be fixed and how attitudes toward risk vary with income levels. Thus, again, our result is consistent with our theoretical model but offers only very weak support for the contention that improved opportunities to conduct legal activities will deter crime.

The coefficient on our measure of initial wealth *TPOWR* does not have the expected sign in any of the regressions but is never even marginally significant. Recall from the previous chapter that the comparative static result we obtained for initial wealth depended critically on how the individual's attitude toward risk changed with income or wealth. Our result may indicate that prison releasees have unusual preferences toward risk, which is not so farfetched, or it may just indicate that *TPOWR* is a poor proxy for nonlabor income.

The coefficients on the measures of tastes all have the expected signs except for the age variables *AAR*, $AAR^2$, and *AFA*. Previous studies have found that crime first increases with age, peaks in the late teens to mid-twenties, and then declines with age thereafter. The results of Table 10.2 seem to indicate a continuous decline in the number of offenses with age. To check on this, Regressions 3 and 4 were rerun with $AAR^2$ dropped from the specification. As expected, *AAR* maintains its negative sign and becomes statistically significant. This continuous decline of crime with age is probably due to the high average age of our sample members ($\overline{AAR} = 32$ years). Apparently most members of our sample are in the declining sector of the age/crime profile. The sign of *AFA* is unexpectedly positive although not significantly different from zero at normal confidence levels. This is contrary to most previous findings where a negative coefficient for this variable has been interpreted as indicating that an early age for first arrest shows a strong taste for illegal activities.

Of the remaining taste variables, the coefficients of previous record (*ARRBS* and *CONVBS*), drug use (*JUNKY*), release supervision (*SUPER*), and behavior while incarcerated (*RULE*) are all significant and have the traditional signs. Thus, individuals who have had fewer prior arrests or convictions, do not use drugs, are supervised when released, and behaved well when last incarcerated will tend to be arrested and convicted less often when free, other things being equal. *ALCHY* is significant only when the dependent variable is *CVRAT* (Regression 4), indicating that alcoholic problems significantly affect the number of convictions but not the number of arrests. Considering this and the relative significance of the coefficients of other variables, it appears that being married, free of drug or alcohol problems, and well behaved in prison have a more significant effect on whether one is convicted than on whether one is arrested. This seems reasonable, because these variables are likely to affect, consciously or unconsciously, the decisions of judges and juries. The greater significance of the coefficients of previous record and release supervision for arrests than convictions also seems reasonable. Indeed, the former is at least somewhat supportive of the argument made before that people with criminal records are more likely to be arrested than those without, other things being equal.

Two other differences between the *CVRAT* and *ARRAT* regressions are of interest. First, the stochastic element in the determination of *CVRAT* is larger than in the determination of *ARRAT*. This is probably a reflection of the stochastic element in court decisions. Second, taste variables play a relatively more significant role for *CVRAT* than *ARRAT*. As before, this probably reflects the fact that the factors we have used to measure tastes are the ones that judges and juries use in making decisions. It also shows that there are a number of alternative plausible interpretations for the variables we have identified as taste variables. For example, age (*AAR*), race (*RACE*), measures of addiction (*ALCHY* and *JUNKY*), and the postrelease supervision indicator (*SUPER*) might be interpreted as measuring opportunity cost rather than tastes and preferences.

The existing literature provides no systematic evidence on the effect of race on criminality. Whereas studies that use aggregate data [e.g., Ehrlich (1973)] have shown the percentage of nonwhites in an area to be positively and significantly related to crime rates, studies that use individual data [e.g., the work in Part I and Palmer and Carlson (1976)] have shown weak effects of conflicting signs for race variables. In both Regressions 3 and 4 the coefficient of *RACE* is negative and highly significant, indicating that nonwhites have fewer arrests and convictions than whites, other things being equal. This is consistent with our earlier analyses of this data set in Chapter 3 and Section 5.2.

Comparing Regressions 3 and 4 to Regressions 1 and 2, one notes substantial changes in the size of the estimated coefficients of the theoretical variables, although the signs of the coefficients remain unchanged. As noted previously, we believe these changes to be largely the result of collinearity between the theoretical variables and our measures of tastes.

## 10.4. Results for Specific Types of Offenses

The results just reported assume that the parameters of the regressions estimated do not vary with the type of illegal activity an individual undertakes. This section will explore the appropriateness of this assumption. Specifically, this section will estimate separate Tobit models for each of four general crime groups and test the equality of the coefficients across these four crime groups. Results are reported only when the dependent variable is the conviction rate (*CVRAT*), because results for the arrest rate are similar.

Members of the sample were assigned to crime groups on the basis of the general nature of the criminal activity they had participated in prior to release. We defined the groups to distinguish individuals who primarily commit predatory offenses that usually do not generate income (termed consumption crimes) from individuals who primarily commit offenses that result in economic gain (termed income crimes). There is also a residual group, which contains individuals who primarily commit violations of rules and regulations (e.g., nonsupport) and victimless offenses (e.g., drug use, gambling). Specifically, the crime groups are

(1) serious consumption crimes (e.g., murder, assault with a deadly weapon) and nonserious consumption crimes (e.g., simple assault and public drunkenness);
(2) serious income offenses (e.g., robbery and sale of narcotics);
(3) nonserious income offenses (e.g., larceny and violations in the sale of liquor); and
(4) the residual category (e.g., nonsupport and obstructing justice).

It was necessary to group serious and nonserious consumption crimes together to have an adequate sample size for the analysis. The seriousness distinction is essentially the distinction between offenses classified as felonies and those classified as misdemeanors.

Table 10.3 reports the results of the analysis when the independent variables are measures only of initial wealth, probabilities, costs, and noncriminal alternatives, and Table 10.4 reports results when the independent variables include measures of tastes as well. The most striking aspect of these results is the marked difference in the results obtained for the different crime types. Tests for equality of the coefficients confirm this impression. Significant differences in the coefficients exist between all crime groups, with the largest difference existing between crime groups 3 and 4 and the least between groups 1 and 3. The differences in coefficients tend to be largest and most persistent for $P(C/A)$, $P(J/C)$, *WAGEAR*, *MS*, and *JUNKY*.

The coefficients of the variables that emerge directly from the theoretical model reveal a much more complex pattern when one disaggregates by crime type, as would be expected. The coefficient of $P(C/A)$ has the expected negative sign in most of the regressions; however, its coefficient is significant only for the residual crime group. $P(J/C)$ has the expected negative and significant coefficient for individuals who primarily committed

**TABLE 10.3.** Empirical Results of *CVRAT* Regressed on Variables Emanating Directly from the Theoretical Model[a]

| Independent variables | Crime group: Serious and nonserious consumption | Serious income | Nonserious income | Residual |
|---|---|---|---|---|
| *CNST* | .2608** | −.0466 | .7548** | .0445 |
| | (1.900) | (−.280) | (2.425) | (.199) |
| *P(C/A)* | .0557 | .0582 | −.0633 | −.2596*** |
| | (.568) | (.793) | (−.359) | (−2.484) |
| *P(J/C)* | −.0967 | −.0549 | −.3580* | .2082 |
| | (−.851) | (−.357) | (−1.639) | (.995) |
| *EXLOS* | −.0011*** | .0000 | −.0013 | −.0005 |
| | (−2.662) | (.078) | (−1.180) | (−.311) |
| *WAGEAR* | −.0242 | .0524** | −.0958* | .0373 |
| | (−1.063) | (1.886) | (−1.476) | (.997) |
| *MSTAY* | −.0984** | .0242 | −.1411* | −.0612 |
| | (−1.876) | (.452) | (−1.306) | (−.976) |
| *TPOWR* | −.0010 | .0042 | −.0979** | −.0012 |
| | (−.144) | (.723) | (−1.708) | (−.08) |
| *MFJAR* | .0009 | −.0013 | −.0008 | −.0025 |
| | (.218) | (−.298) | (−.071) | (−.203) |
| $\hat{\sigma}^2$ | .03556 | .02158 | .06274 | .02178 |
| Likelihood test ratio[b] | 14.652* | 5.054 | 10.023 | 10.67 |
| *N* | 130 | 125 | 77 | 77 |

[a] Asterisk indicates level of significance, one-tailed test: *** = .01 level, ** = .05 level, * = .10 level. Values in parentheses under coefficients are "$t$-ratios," which are asymptotically $N(0, 1)$ under the null hypothesis that the coefficient is zero.

[b] This is $-2\log(\lambda)$, where $\log(\lambda)$ is the difference between the log of the maximized value of the likelihood function with only a constant term as an independent variable and the log of the maximized value of the likelihood function with the independent variables in the regression under consideration. This statistic is distributed $x_k^2$, where $k$ is the number of explanatory variables (excluding the constant) in the regression under consideration. The statistic tests the joint significance of the independent variables and is equivalent to the $F$ test in least squares regression.

**TABLE 10.4.** Results of *CVRAT* Regressed on all Variables by Crime Type[a]

| Independent variables | Crime group: Serious and nonserious consumption | Serious income | Nonserious income | Residual |
|---|---|---|---|---|
| *CNST* | .4122** | .2952* | 1.0731** | .0459 |
| | (1.789) | (1.326) | (2.207) | (.167) |
| *P(C/A)* | .0372 | −.0196 | −.2218 | −.2837*** |
| | (.435) | (−.297) | (−1.174) | (−2.403) |
| *P(J/C)* | .0109 | .0341 | −.5801*** | .4405** |
| | (.110) | (.247) | (−2.530) | (2.167) |

TABLE 10.4. *(Continued)*

| Independent variables | Crime group: Serious and nonserious consumption | Serious income | Nonserious income | Residual |
|---|---|---|---|---|
| *EXLOS* | −.0004 | .0000 | −.0003 | .0019 |
| | (−.789) | (.126) | (−.196) | (1.052) |
| *WAGEAR* | −.0261* | .0497** | −.1408** | .0417 |
| | (−1.350) | (2.013) | (−1.859) | (1.195) |
| *MSTAY* | −.0715* | .0428 | −.100 | −.0871 |
| | (−1.624) | (.856) | (−.975) | (−1.195) |
| *TPOWR* | .0009 | −.0039 | −.0031 | −.0017 |
| | (.252) | (−.925) | (−.227) | (−.148) |
| *MFJAR* | −.0062 | .0048 | −.1162** | −.0048 |
| | (−1.087) | (.965) | (−2.024) | (−.383) |
| *AAR* | −.0011 | −.0280** | −.0068 | −.0161 |
| | (−.992) | (−1.969) | (−.271) | (−1.258) |
| $AAR^2$ | .0000 | .0000** | −.0000 | .0000 |
| | (.616) | (1.748) | (−.372) | (.336) |
| *AFA* | .0003 | .0050 | .0192** | .0075* |
| | (.089) | (1.099) | (1.667) | (1.334) |
| *MS* | .0138 | −.0153 | −.2118** | −.0231 |
| | (.377) | (−.402) | (−2.182) | (−.531) |
| *RACE* | −.0985*** | −.0623** | .0326 | −.0824** |
| | (−2.519) | (−1.827) | (.448) | (−2.024) |
| *ALCHY* | .0457 | .0158 | .0625 | .0476 |
| | (1.120) | (.479) | (.687) | (1.172) |
| *JUNKY* | −.067 | .2193*** | −.1962 | .2596*** |
| | (−.513) | (4.089) | (−1.106) | (2.839) |
| *SUPER* | −.0883*** | −.0513* | .0049 | −.1128** |
| | (−2.199) | (−1.452) | (.056) | (−1.751) |
| *RULE* | .026* | .0312*** | .0167 | −.0002 |
| | (1.599) | (3.607) | (.522) | (−.012) |
| *CONVBS* | .0171*** | .0136** | .0164 | .0456** |
| | (4.221) | (2.131) | (1.120) | (2.193) |
| *Serious/ nonserious*[b] | −.0121 | — | — | — |
| | (−.144) | | | |
| $\hat{\sigma}^2$ | .0219 | .01547 | .05337 | .01482 |
| Likelihood ratio test[c] | 66.28*** | 46.682*** | 23.665 | 40.982*** |

[a] Asterisk indicates level of significance, one-tailed test: *** = .01 level, ** = .05 level, * = .10 level. Values in parentheses under coefficients are "*t*-ratios," which are asymptotically $N(0, 1)$ under the null hypothesis that the coefficient is zero.

[b] A dummy variable equal to one if the individual's general crime type was serious consumption and zero if nonserious consumption. This variable was added to the consumption regression to allow for differences between serious and nonserious consumption offenses.

[c] This is $-2\log(\lambda)$, where $\log(\lambda)$ is the difference between the log of the maximized value of the likelihood function with only a constant term as an independent variable and the log of the maximized value of the likelihood function with the independent variables in the regression under consideration. This statistic is distributed $x_k^2$, where $k$ is the number of explanatory variables (excluding the constant) in the regression under consideration. The statistic tests the joint significance of the independent variables and is equivalent to the $F$ test in least squares regression.

nonserious income crimes, group 3, but when taste variables are included it has a significantly positive coefficient for the residual group 4. *EXLOS* has the expected negative coefficient in most of the regressions, but its coefficient is significant only for group 1 when taste variables are excluded. *WAGEAR* has a negative coefficient for groups 1 and 3 and a positive coefficient for groups 2 and 4. *TPOWR* generally has an insignificant coefficient, though its coefficient is significantly negative for group 3 when variables measuring tastes are omitted. *MFJAR* has a positive coefficient for group 2, but it is insignificantly different from zero. For all other groups this variable has a negative coefficient, and for group 3 this coefficient is significantly different from zero.

Comparing the regressions of Table 10.3 with those of Table 10.4, one notes that (in contrast to our previous work) when variables measuring tastes are added a number of theoretical variables change either signs or significance levels. For offenders in group 1, the addition of variables measuring tastes lessens the significance of deterrence variables. This seems supportive of our interpretation of those variables as measures of taste, because one expects tastes to play a large role in consumption decisions. Indeed, one would not be too surprised if rational calculations played a small part relative to tastes in aberrant consumption decisions (e.g., assault, rape) of the sort considered here. For individuals who primarily commit nonserious income offenses, the addition of variables measuring tastes generally increases the significance of both the deterrence variables and the wage variable. A possible interpretation is that, when we control for the tastes of this type of offender, rational calculation of benefits and costs becomes more apparent. For individuals who primarily commit serious income offenses and those in the "residual" category, the addition of variables measuring tastes causes the coefficient of a variable with a nontraditional sign to become more significant. This is hard to explain.

These results are interesting and may tentatively be interpreted to indicate that deterrence works through different variables for individuals who specialize in different types of crime. For individuals who specialize in consumption offenses, longer expected sentences appear to provide the most effective deterrent, whereas for individuals who primarily commit nonserious income offenses a higher probability of imprisonment seems most effective, and for individuals who specialize in crimes other than consumption or income offenses, the probability of conviction seems most effective. Unfortunately, deterrence does not seem to work for offenders in group 2; this will be discussed later. The preceding findings might be interpreted as indicating that individuals concentrate attention on, and hence are deterred most by, the most likely outcome of the criminal justice process for their specific crime specialty. Better legitimate opportunities appear to have a significant deterrent effect only for individuals who specialize in nonserious income offenses and may even have a perverse effect for individuals who specialize in serious income offenses.

As with the variables discussed before, the coefficients of the variables measuring tastes show wide and significant variations across crime groups. Age (significant when "age squared" is deleted) has a negative coefficient, as found in the aggregate runs, for all crime groups except the "serious income offenses" group. It appears that for this group a curvilinear relationship with "conviction rate" is more appropriate; however, the nature of this relationship indicates that conviction rates first decrease and then increase with age. This may indicate the increasing financial need of older men specializing in this type of offense. This possibility is reinforced when one notes the highly significant coefficient for the drug-use variable for this group. The significance of the coefficient for the drug-use variable may also help to explain the lack of significance of deterrence and legal alternatives for individuals who specialize in serious income offenses. If drugs are essential and even relatively good wages do not provide the finances necessary for drug purchases, good noncriminal alternatives or more certain and/or severe penalties will have little or no effect.[19]

Of the remaining taste variables, *RACE*, *SUPER*, and *CONVBS* have significant coefficients of the same sign as found in the aggregate runs for all crime groups except the "nonserious income offenses" group. They indicate that, other things being equal, an individual who specializes in consumption offenses, serious income offenses, or offenses falling into the residual category will have fewer convictions if he is nonwhite, is supervised when released, and has fewer previous convictions. The coefficient on *RULE* is significant and positive for the serious income group and marginally significant and positive for the consumption group. Being married appears to decrease significantly the conviction rate for individuals who specialize in nonserious income offenses.

## 10.5. Summary and Conclusions

In this chapter, we have estimated a simple economic model of criminal behavior using data reflecting the postrelease behavior of a sample of North Carolina prison releasees. In our empirical model, the dependent variables were the number of arrests per month out of prison (*ARRAT*) and the number of convictions per month out of prison (*CVRAT*). We investigated the determinants of these variables using Tobit analysis.

Our results are generally consistent with the simple economic model developed in the previous chapter and are, somewhat surprisingly, similar to previous empirical results obtained using aggregate data. They support the contention that deterrence works and, indeed, that a percentage increase in the probability of being punished has a relatively larger effect on the number of arrests or convictions than does an equal percentage increase in the expected sentence. (That is, certainty deters more than severity.) It should be noted that the support we provide is relatively weak. Only 5 (out of 24) of the coefficients on the probabilities of being punished are more than twice their estimated standard errors, and one of these has a nontraditional sign. Support for the deterrent effect of longer prison sentences is only somewhat stronger. (Three out of twelve coefficients are more than twice their standard errors.) Still, it is quite unlikely that this support could have been generated by a purely random process. The empirical analysis also suggests that the manner in which deterrence works varies markedly with the type of crime in which an individual specializes. For individuals who specialize in consumption offenses (e.g., assaultive or drug-use offenses), the expected sentence has the most significant effect, whereas for individuals who specialize in nonserious income offenses (e.g., larceny and liquor sales), the probability of imprisonment is most significant, and for individuals who specialize in a residual category of neither consumption nor income offenses (e.g., nonsupport or obstructing justice), the probability of conviction is most significant. For individuals who specialize in serious income offenses (e.g., robbery and drug sales), none of the deterrence variables has a coefficient that is even marginally significant. This is unexpected because it seems to suggest that deterrence fails to work for this group. A priori, one would have expected income offenders to behave more rationally than other types of offenders.

When one turns to the effect of legitimate opportunities on illegal activity, one finds that higher wages tend to decrease the expected number of arrests or convictions, but this effect is statistically significant (one-tailed test, 5% level) in only one case, for the "nonserious income offenses" group. The lack of significance of the coefficients for the wage rate may be the result of our inability to include an explicit measure of the payoff to illegal activity. However, an advantage gained from the use of individual data is that the legal wage rate can be unambiguously identified, which has not been possible in tests of economic models that use aggregate data.

When one examines the relative effect of higher wages on individuals who specialize in various crime types, one finds that higher wages seem most effective in deterring crime for specialists in nonserious income offenses and appear to increase crime for specialists in serious income offenses. This perverse wage effect, coupled with the earlier finding that criminal justice sanctions have no deterrent effect for this group, is unexpected, because one would certainly feel that an economic model would be most relevant for those who commit crime primarily for economic gain. Examination of the other variables in the model reveals a possible explanation of this seeming paradox. The most significant variable determining the number of arrests or convictions for people who specialize in serious income offenses is whether or not they are drug users. The high correlation between drug use and serious income offenses is well known to criminal justice authorities but makes testing of the economic model of crime for this group extremely difficult. Possibly the need for money for drugs largely eliminates the rational decision process that the economic model of crime assumes.

The variable thought to be measuring the expected unemployment rate, *MFJAR*, has an unexpected negative coefficient for all groups except the "serious income offense" one, indicating that a longer period out of the labor force or in job search after release leads to less crime. It may be that this variable is not measuring the expected unemployment rate but rather is measuring legitimate job search time, which results in discovery of more satisfying legitimate employment. In this casc the negative sign for this variable would be more reasonable. Cook (1975, p. 22) has suggested that low-quality jobs are readily available to former offenders but that higher-quality jobs are more difficult to find. However, if this line of reasoning is correct, *MFJAR* becomes a variable endogenous to the system, and simultaneous equations methods should be used to estimate the model. We use such techniques in Chapter 12.

Greater initial wealth was found in almost all cases to lead to less criminal activity, but the coefficient of this variable was insignificantly different from zero in all cases. If standard assumptions about attitudes toward risk are made, the economic model of crime implies the opposite finding: greater initial wealth should lead to more criminal activity. A possible reconciliation is that prison releasees exhibit increasing (with income), rather than decreasing, risk aversion. Another possible explanation is that initial wealth cannot be measured satisfactorily by accumulated work release payments.

What can one conclude about the economic model of crime based on the preceding results? First, one must realize that results obtained with individual data are likely to lead to findings that can be generalizable to only a limited degree. The current sample well illustrates this point. Our sample consists of men from a single state during a given time period. Moreover, our sample consists only of individuals who had been caught and convicted —the losers of the criminal world. Thus, our results can be generalized to only a very small portion of the population to whom the economic model is thought to pertain. The broadest conclusion we can make based on the evidence presented in this chapter is that releasees from North Carolina's prison system during the early 1970s behaved in a manner that was weakly supportive of the simple economic model of crime. Broader generalizations would require additional tests using different samples. It would be desirable if these samples could be drawn so that they contain individuals who do not participate in criminal activities as well as those who do. We hope that a contribution of this chapter will be to stimulate additional tests using individual data.

How do the results obtained here compare with similar work using aggregate data? There have been three recent surveys of the work that attempts to estimate the deterrent effect of criminal justice sanctions (Brier and Fienberg, 1980; Cook, 1977; Nagin, 1978). Cook well summarizes the conclusion that emerges from these surveys:

> there is strong evidence from some of these studies that an increase in the threat of punishment can reduce the amount of some crimes in some circumstances, but very little evidence about the long-term effects, the typical magnitudes involved, the relevance of process, the responsiveness of juveniles to threats, or the extent to which some important crime categories (such as murder) are responsive to changes in the threat level (Cook, 1977, p. 173).

Further, these surveys find that the strength and consistency of the evidence supporting the deterrent effect of high probabilities of apprehension and punishment are much greater than that supporting the deterrent effect of longer prison sentences. These conclusions from surveys of aggregate studies of deterrence are generally similar to those of this chapter. We too find that the deterrent effect of criminal justice sanctions varies markedly across crime types, that deterrence seems to reduce some types of offenses in a particular circumstance, and that estimates of the size of the deterrent effect are very sensitive to model specification. We find, as does the aggregate literature, that the elasticities associated with the probabilities of conviction and imprisonment are generally larger than those associated with expected sentence length, but in contrast to work using aggregate data, our results are slightly more significant for the expected sentence length than for the probabilities for sanctions. Given the obvious differences between our data and the aggregate data sets that others have used, the extent to which the results agree is rather remarkable and provides further relatively unique evidence in support of the deterrence hypothesis.

There have been relatively few previous tests of the effect of legitimate opportunity on the level of criminal activity. As noted previously, aggregate studies have difficulty identifying appropriate variables to reflect legitimate opportunities; however, there has been some work at the individual level on this question. Long and Witte (1981) have recently surveyed both the aggregate and individual studies that seek to determine if there is a relationship between criminal activity and legitimate opportunity. Their survey concludes that the evidence only very weakly supports the simple economic model (i.e., that higher incomes and lower unemployment rates are associated with lower levels of criminal activity). This conclusion is consistent with the results just reported.

Of the variables measuring tastes, those representing age, previous record, race, drug use, release supervision, and behavior in prison significantly affect arrest and conviction rates in the traditional manner. These results indicate that an old, nonwhite individual who had little or no criminal record, did not use drugs, was supervised on release, and behaved well in prison will have fewer arrests and convictions after release, other things being equal.

As a whole, our results point out the need for additional tests of the economic model of crime using data on individuals. Such tests would be most beneficial if they dealt with groups less committed to criminal activity than former prison inmates generally are. A random sample of the entire population may be too much to hope for. Perhaps the most realistic sampling frame would be individuals arrested in a given area. In addition, exploration of the way in which individuals form expectations about the criminal justice system and income-generating activities would be extremely useful.

Creators of new data sets should also make every possible effort to obtain explicit estimates of the expected payoff from illegal activity. For income offenses, information obtained from fences (i.e., dealers in stolen property) could prove invaluable. For consumption offenses, prior criminal records may act as a stand-in for expected payoff, because they may provide at least a weak measure for psychological problems. When analyzing individuals who specialize in serious income offenses, our results seem to indicate that it is essential to separate individuals who use drugs from those who do not. Perhaps the economic model of crime will prove stronger for non-drug-using offenders in this group. Finally, our results indicate that the way in which individuals react differs markedly depending on the type of crime in which they specialize. Future studies should be careful to control adequately for an individual's crime specialty when testing the economic model.

## Notes to Chapter 10

1. See Cook (1977), Blumstein, Cohen, and Nagin (1978), or Brier and Fienberg (1980) for reviews and critiques of the literature dealing with the deterrence hypothesis. Long and Witte (1981) provided a summary and critique of the literature related to effects of legal opportunities on criminal activity.

2. Researchers are currently using such advanced interviewing techniques as randomized response [e.g., see Locander *et al.* (1976) or Westat (1980)] and are more carefully structuring their interview instruments [see Elliott and Ageton (1980)].

3. A follow-up period of three years is commonly recommended for studies of former offenders [see U. S. President's Commission on Law Enforcement and the Administration of Justice Task Force (1967, p. 68) and Mulvilhill and Tumin (1969, p. 549)].

4. See Witte (1975) for a detailed discussion of sampling and data collection methods, and Appendix A for a briefer description. Owing to the original purpose for which the sample was selected, an evaluation of the North Carolina prisoner work release program, the population

from which it was drawn excludes men convicted of sex offenses, serious drug offenses, or public drunkenness. The current sample, therefore, is not representative of these groups.

5. See *The New York Times* (1974). Other information paints a similar if less dramatic picture. See Cook (1975, pp. 11–12) and U. S. Department of Justice, Federal Bureau of Prisons (1975, p. 43).

6. Men in our sample often became quite upset even in discussing their officially reported activity.

7. We obtained records from all jurisdictions where North Carolina Department of Correction's records, self-reports, or FBI records indicated that an individual had had contact with the criminal justice system.

8. These factors are offset somewhat by nonreporting. See Skogan (1974) and Tittle and Rowe (1974) for a discussion of various measures of crime in another context.

9. Although innocent men are occasionally convicted even with due process, this seems likely to be more than outweighed by other factors discussed in the text.

10. Glaser (1964, p. 319) found that 85% of his sample of federal releasees had no external savings and the median savings of the remaining 15% was $433. Pownall (1969, p. 182) found the median amount of cash possessed by men in his postrelease survey was only $50.

11. "Gate money" is money provided by the state to inmates on release. In North Carolina during the 1970s gate money ranged from $0 (if an individual had served less than 2 years) to $25 (if an individual served more than 15 years).

12. We estimate a simultaneous equations model in Chapter 12.

13. The criminal records of sample members were in general quite extensive (mean number of arrests = 3, $\sigma = 6$; mean number of convictions = 2, $\sigma = 4$) because the average age for the group was 32 and all had at least one prison conviction.

14. For a discussion of this problem, see Witte (1976).

15. Significance of a regression refers to significance of the test statistic used to test the null hypothesis that all of the coefficients (except the constant) equal zero.

16. A variable (or its coefficient) is judged to be statistically significant if a one-tailed hypothesis test at the 5% level ($\alpha = .05$) would lead to a rejection of the null hypothesis that the coefficient of the variable is equal to zero. A variable (or its coefficient) is judged to be marginally significant if a one-tailed hypothesis test at the 10% level ($\alpha = .10$) would lead to a rejection of the hypothesis that the coefficient is equal to zero.

17. The changing significance of coefficients reported for most variables when measures of tastes are added to the specification is largely the result of extensive multicollinearity between measures of tastes and the other variables.

18. These elasticities were evaluated at the mean values of the dependent and independent variables.

19. This hypothesis is supported by the findings of Leveson (1972) on drug addiction. See also Bachman and Witte (1980).

# Chapter 11

## Labor Markets for Prison Releasees

### 11.1. Introduction

In this chapter, we explore the determinants of labor market performance for prison releasees. Recall that the simple economic model of crime that we developed in Section 9.6 indicated that it is possible to analyze labor market performance separately from the level of criminal activity because the amount of time allocated to the labor market is determined independently of the amount of time allocated to criminal activity.

Researchers have studied a number of measures of postrelease labor market performance, ranging from hourly wages and income to hours and work stability. In Section 11.2 we develop a reduced-form model of postrelease labor market performance based on both supply and demand considerations. This model incorporates variables that reflect the prison experience of releasees and some of their unusual attributes. In Sections 11.3 and 11.4 we present and discuss our estimates of models for the hourly wage received on the first job obtained after release from prison and for the stability of employment during a follow-up period, respectively. In Section 11.5 we survey previous studies of postrelease labor market performance and compare our results with them. Section 11.6 contains our summary and conclusions.

## 11.2. An Empirical Model of Postrelease Labor Market Performance

Recall that the simple model that we developed in Section 9.6 indicated that the amount of time devoted to the labor market and to criminal activity were determined in a recursive fashion. According to this model, an individual first allocates time to the labor market until the net marginal returns there are exhausted. The individual next makes a decision concerning the time to allocate to illegal endeavors. This model implies that we can analyze postrelease labor market performance as we do in this chapter, that is, without regard to decisions concerning participation in illegal activities. Specifically, we explore the factors determining two measures of postrelease labor market performance. The first measure is the wages (in dollars per hour) on the first job obtained after release, denoted *WAGAR*. The second measure is the stability (jobs per free employed year) of work, denoted *WKSTABAR*.[1]

We chose to model these two aspects of labor market performance for a number of reasons. First, they measure aspects of labor market performance that are possibly quite distinct: pay and job satisfaction. Second, neoclassical and institutionalist labor market theories suggest different models for these two measures; thus, the results of our modeling effort should shed some light on the relative importance of these two theoretic bases in explaining labor market performance for prison releasees. Finally, use of these two measures allows us to compare our results easily with previous work.

The factors determining these two variables are complex because they result from the joint decision of the individual releasee and employers. We do not attempt to analyze these separate decisions. Rather, we seek to develop reduced-form equations for these two variables that will reflect the exogenous factors affecting both the releasees' and employers' decisions. In developing these reduced-form models, we consider both neoclassical (e.g., human capitalist) and institutional approaches to the labor market [see Cain (1976) for a review]. Institutional approaches seem particularly relevant because they focus attention on the nature of labor markets for low-skilled workers. Prison releasees have few skills and concentrate dramatically in low-skill occupations.

Neoclassical labor market theory suggests that labor market performance will depend on the marginal productivity of a worker in a particular job and on the individual's tastes for labor and leisure. An individual's productivity on a particular job will be affected by his or her ability and efforts, the quality of management, and the quality and quantity of other inputs available. The individual's stability of employment will be affected by the employer's assessment of performance and by the individual's satisfaction with the job. Job satisfaction will, of course, be affected by the quantity and quality of alternative employment opportunities. As noted later, most studies of prison releasees indicate that job termination was generally the releasee's rather than the employer's choice.[2] Thus we shall interpret our measure of work stability as primarily a reflection of the releasee's job satisfaction. It would obviously be preferable to separate job changes by reason and analyze voluntary and involuntary stability separately. Unfortunately, our data do not allow us to do this.

We shall estimate our models of postrelease labor market performance using the same data set as in the last chapter. This data set was discussed briefly in Section 10.2 and is discussed in more detail in Appendix A. Table 11.1 contains a listing of variables that neoclassical and institutionalist labor market theory suggest would affect postrelease labor market performance. It has been necessary to adapt this theory somewhat to account for the unusual life styles and characteristics of prison releasees. We shall discuss our reasons for including all variables next. In addition, this table lists the empirical measures of the theoretical variables used in the current study, and the expected sign of each variable's coefficient.

Neoclassical human capital theory suggests that the first two theoretical variables of Table 11.1, education (measured by *SG* and *HS*) and experience (*AAR* and $AAR^2$), would be important determinants of the wage an individual receives. In addition, this theory suggests that, owing to discrimination or difference in tastes, personal characteristics such as race (*RACE*) and marital status (*MS*) may be important wage determinants. Both institutionalist and neoclassical models would suggest that the previous work record (*WKSTABS*) would affect wages, although these models suggest different reasons for the effect. Neoclassical labor theorists would suggest that work stability affects wages mainly through the demand side of the labor market. That is, employers set wages at least partially based on the prior work record. Segmented labor market theorists, however, suggest that there is a simultaneous relationship between wages and work stability. They see low-wage, low-quality jobs as causing work instability.

Institutional theories of the labor market see wages as determined primarily by the nature of one's job. Thus, they see as important such things as the industrial and occupational group in which one's job falls. In addition, they feel that the permanence of one's job (*REGJAR*) may be quite important. Geographic location (*SMSA*) is also thought to affect wages, both for institutional reasons and because of cost-of-living differentials.

Prison releasees often have unusual life styles and personal habits that potential employers may find distasteful. The most obvious example is the criminal record, which all releasees necessarily have. We represent the extent of one's criminal record by the individual's number of previous convictions, denoted *CONVBS*, and by the age at which the individual was

**TABLE 11.1.** Listing of Explanatory Variables

| Theoretical variable | Empirical measure: Acronym[a] | Empirical measure: Definition | Expected sign in *WAGAR* equation |
|---|---|---|---|
| Education | *SG* | Number of years of schooling completed | Positive |
| | *HS** | Equals 1 if an individual has graduated from high school and 0 if not[b] | Positive |
| Experience | *AAR* | Age at release (in years) | Positive |
| | $AAR^2$ | Squared value of *AAR* | Negative |
| Discrimination or unobservable personal characteristics | *RACE** | Equals 1 for nonwhites and 0 otherwise | Negative |
| | *MS** | Equals 1 if an individual was married and 0 if he was not | Positive |
| Previous work record | *WKSTABS* | Number of jobs per year prior to sample incarceration | Negative |
| Type of employment | *REGJAR** | Equals 1 if an individual's first job after release was permanent and 0 if not | Positive |
| Industry of employment | *IAGMIN–IPSERV* | Set of 13 dummy variables representing the industries of employment for members of our sample,[c] with the textile industry (SIC 22) serving as reference group[d] | Varies depending on industry |
| Occupation | *OFARM–OSALE* | Set of 5 dummy variables representing the occupations of members of our sample, with service workers serving as reference category[e] | Varies depending on occupation |
| Geographic location | *SMSA** | Equals 1 if an individual's first residence after release was in an SMSA and 0 if not[f] | Positive |
| Addiction | *ALCHY** | Equals 1 if an individual has a serious problem with alcohol and 0 if not | Negative |
| | *JUNKY** | Equals 1 if an individual has a history of drug use and 0 if not | Negative |
| Offense type | *PERSON** | Equals 1 if an individual's incarceration was for a crime against a person and 0 if not | Negative |
| | *PROPTY** | Equals 1 if an individual's incarceration was for a crime against property and 0 if not | Negative |
| Previous record | *CONVBS* | Number of convictions prior to last incarceration | Negative |
| | *AFA* | Age in years at first arrest | Positive |

**TABLE 11.1.** *(Continued)*

| Theoretical variable | Empirical measure: Acronym[a] | Empirical measure: Definition | Expected sign in *WAGAR* equation |
|---|---|---|---|
| Type of release | *SUPER** | Equals 1 if an individual's release was supervised and 0 if not | Negative |
| Period of incarceration | *TSERVD* | Number of months an individual was incarcerated prior to release | Negative |
| Program effects | *STAY** | Equals 1 if an individual retains his work release[g] job after release and 0 if not | Negative |
| | *NSTAY** | Equals 1 if an individual participated in the work release program but did not retain his work release job after release | Positive |
| | *TPOWR* | The funds accumulated (in 100s of $) while on work release and received after release | Positive |
| Labor market and general economic conditions[h] | *Y69, Y70, Y71** | Set of 3 dummy variables representing the year an individual was released[h] with 1972–1973 serving as a reference category[i] | All negative |

[a] Asterisk indicates a dummy variable.
[b] No individual in our sample had a college degree.
[c] For a complete listing of these binary variables, see Table 11.2. The Standard Industrial Classifications in each variable are available from A. Witte on request.
[d] The textile industry is the major low wage employer in North Carolina.
[e] For a complete listing of these binary variables, see Table 11.2. The census occupational categories in each variable are available on request from A. Witte.
[f] A dummy variable equal to 1 if an individual's first residence after release was in the South and 0 if not was also tried and had an estimated coefficient that was negative and highly significant. However, because we had very few individuals whose first residence was in the North, we dropped this variable and the individuals released in the North.
[g] The current data set was originally developed to evaluate North Carolina's prisoner work release program (a program that allows inmates to work during the day and return to prison at night). The work release program is the major rehabilitative program in the North Carolina prison system.
[h] Individuals in our sample were released between January 1969 and June 1973.
[i] This variable is virtually identical to "year of first job," because 93% of the individuals in our sample obtained their first job within one month of release.

first arrested, denoted *AFA*. It seems likely that potential employers would be repelled more by certain types of criminal records than others. For example, some employers might feel that employing individuals convicted of offenses such as assault would be quite risky. Others might feel that former property offenders represent a serious threat to raw material and/or inventory. We attempt to control for these factors by including two variables in our specification. The first, denoted *PERSON*, indicates whether the incarceration from which the individual was just released was for an offense against a person. The second, denoted *PROPTY*, indicates whether this incarceration was for an offense against property.

Approximately 50% of our sample either used drugs or had relatively serious problems with alcohol use. One might expect lower wages for such individuals owing to lower productivity or employer discrimination. It would also seem likely that such individuals would have lower work stability than individuals without addictive habits. We attempt to control for these factors by including a variable that indicates whether an individual had a serious problem with alcohol usage, denoted *ALCHY*, and a variable that indicates whether the individual had a history of drug use, denoted *JUNKY*. In addition to these factors, prison releasees are unique because they are coming from a unique environment—a prison. The prison experience may affect postrelease labor market performance in a number of ways. First, in the absence of work or training, the time in prison will allow work skills and the work habit to atrophy. We attempt to capture such effects by including a variable measuring the time spent in prison, denoted *TSERVD*, in our specification. In North Carolina, as in other states, most prison inmates are provided with work opportunities and other rehabilitative programs while they are in prison. The major program of this type for members of our sample was the prisoner work release program. We represent participation in this program by three variables. The first two, indicating whether an individual participated in the program, differ in that the first, denoted *STAY*, indicates that the individual participated and retained his work release job after release and the second, denoted *NSTAY*, indicates participation but no job retention. Recall that in the last chapter we indicated that wages on work release jobs tended to be very low. The use of two binary variables rather than one is designed to capture this effect. The third variable indicates the total amount of funds the individual accumulated while on the work release program, denoted *TPOWR*. We would expect the sign of the coefficient on this variable to be positive for two reasons. First, a greater amount of accumulated funds generally indicates that the individual participated in the work release program for a longer period and at a higher wage rate. Both the longer participation and the higher wage are an indication of labor market skills that should result in better postrelease labor market performance. Second, for those who do not stay on their work release jobs, accumulated work release funds allow a longer period of job search, which should also be reflected in improved labor market performance.

Approximately one-third of the members of our sample were supervised (e.g., on parole) in some way after release from prison. One would expect such supervision to affect postrelease labor market performance. We would expect it to increase work stability, because maintaining a steady job is generally a condition for continued freedom, but to decrease wages because the type of job taken is constrained. We attempt to control for these effects by including a binary variable, denoted *SUPER*, that reflects whether or not an individual was supervised when released, in our specification.

Finally, labor market performance will be affected by general economic conditions. We include a dummy variable to reflect year of release because general economic conditions varied relatively widely during 1969–1973, when individuals in our sample were released.

## 11.3. Empirical Results for Wages after Release

In Table 11.2 are reported the results of regressing *WAGAR* on all of the variables listed in Table 11.1. Considering the nature of our data (individual, cross-sectional), we "explain" a surprisingly high proportion of the variance in *WAGAR* with our model, 31% ($\bar{R}^2 = .22$). Based on the results reported in Table 11.2, it appears that variables suggested by the demand side of the neoclassical model and/or institutionalist labor market theories are more important in explaining postrelease wages for former prison inmates than are either human capital variables or variables reflecting unique attributes and experiences of prison releasees. A large number of both the industry and occupational variables are highly significant. Specifically, other things being equal, prison releasees who are employed in automobile services or construction industries and/or whose occupation is professional or in sales, clerical, craft, or operative will have significantly higher wages than those employed in other industries or occupations. On the other hand, none of the variables related to human capital accumulation turns out to be even marginally significant. Neither education (*SG*, *HS*) nor age (*AAR*, $AAR^2$) had any effects that approached statistical significance.

**TABLE 11.2.** Results of Regression of *WAGAR* on All Variables[a]

| Variable | Coefficient estimate | *t* Ratio[e] |
|---|---|---|
| Constant | 1.987 | 3.86*** |
| *SG* | 0.012 | 0.63 |
| *HS* | −0.011 | −0.09 |
| *AAR* | −0.002 | −0.06 |
| $AAR^2$ | 0.000[d] | 0.05 |
| *RACE* | −0.254 | −3.10*** |

(*Table continues*)

TABLE 11.2. (Continued)

| Variable | Coefficient estimate | *t* Ratio[e] |
|---|---|---|
| *MS* | 0.188 | 2.39*** |
| *WKSTABS* | −0.151 | −2.21** |
| *REGJAR* | 0.407 | 2.97*** |
| *IAGMIN*[b] | 0.017 | 0.07 |
| *ICONS* | 0.451 | 4.20*** |
| *IFOOD* | 0.107 | 0.60 |
| *IFURN* | 0.171 | 0.93 |
| *INMET* | 0.003 | 0.01 |
| *IMACH* | 0.119 | 0.64 |
| *IMANUO* | 0.080 | 0.38 |
| *ITRAN* | 0.197 | 1.06 |
| *IWHOL* | −0.014 | −0.07 |
| *IAUTO* | 0.529 | 2.13** |
| *IRETL* | −0.185 | −1.04 |
| *ISERV* | 0.130 | 0.83 |
| *IPSERV* | 0.197 | 0.91 |
| OFARM[c] | −0.456 | −1.28* |
| *OOPER* | 0.204 | 1.35* |
| *OCRAFT* | 0.374 | 2.16** |
| *OCLRK* | 0.409 | 1.28* |
| *OSALE* | 1.041 | 2.81*** |
| *SMSA* | 0.087 | 1.05 |
| *ALCHY* | −0.014 | −0.13 |
| *JUNKY* | −0.129 | −0.63 |
| *PERSON* | 0.125 | 1.18 |
| *PROPTY* | 0.016 | 0.17 |
| *CONVBS* | −0.001 | −0.07 |
| *AFA* | −0.003 | −0.41 |
| *SUPER* | −0.119 | −1.41* |
| *TSERVD* | −0.002 | −0.81 |
| *STAY* | −0.151 | −1.34* |
| *NSTAY* | −0.001 | −0.01 |
| *TPOWR* | 0.013 | 1.30* |
| *Y69* | −0.269 | −2.33** |
| *Y70* | −0.137 | −1.19 |
| *Y71* | −0.138 | −1.40* |

[a] $N = 343$, $R^2 = .31$, $\bar{R}^2 = .22$, $F_{41,301} = 3.35$***.

[b] *IAGMIN–IPSERV* are binaries that indicate employment in a particular industry according to SIC codes. The exact specification for the binaries is available from A. D. Witte on request.

[c] *OFARM–OSALE* are binaries that indicate employment in a particular occupation according to DOT codes. The exact specification for these binaries is available from A. D. Witte on request.

[d] Coefficient very small owing to large size of squared value.

[e] Number of asterisks indicates level of significance, one-tailed test: *** = .01 level, ** = .05 level, * = .10 level.

Both *RACE* and *MS* have highly significant coefficients of the expected sign. Whether this result occurs because of discrimination or other unobservable characteristics associated with these variables is impossible to determine in the current context. Furthermore, a previous record of job stability and occupancy of a permanent (rather than part-time, seasonal, etc.) job contribute to higher postrelease wages. Of the variables reflecting unique attributes and experiences of prison releasees, only *SUPER*, *STAY*, and *TPOWR* are even marginally significant. The coefficients of these variables indicate that, other things equal, being supervised when released or remaining on one's work release job lowers one's postrelease wages, whereas having greater funds available raises them. These findings are interesting because they point out a potentially detrimental effect of postrelease supervision and the low-wage, low-skill nature of work release jobs [see Witte (1975, ch. IV)]. The wage-depressing effect of parole is particularly interesting in light of recent evidence that higher wages are associated with lower levels of criminal activity [see Sickles, Schmidt, and Witte (1979) and Witte (1980)]. Considering this evidence, any salutory effect of supervision may be dissipated because of its wage-depressing effects. Being on parole might lower wages owing to an "ex-con" stigma, the need to maintain a steady job, or the limited mobility possible on parole. This last explanation gains some support from the fact that former offenders tend to earn highest wages in occupations requiring mobility, such as construction.

There are at least three potential interpretations of the positive coefficient obtained for *TPOWR*. First, *TPOWR* may be serving as a proxy for unobservable characteristics of the individual that lead to favorable labor market outcomes. Individuals with high values of *TPOWR* tend to have relatively high-wage work release jobs and to hold them for a relatively long time, and have thus demonstrated themselves to be capable of securing and holding a relatively good job. Second, the positive coefficient may be the result of some direct benefit of participation in the work release program (e.g., skill maintenance or enhancement, development of a stable work history). Third, it may reflect the benefit of the funds accumulated, that is, a pure wealth effect. Based on our discussions with former inmates and other evidence developed by Cook (1973, 1975), we believe the last is at least a partial explanation. Cook believes and develops evidence that parolees have no trouble obtaining jobs but have significant difficulties obtaining good jobs. A likely benefit of accumulated work release funds is that they allow a releasee to search for a "good" job rather than taking the first job offered.

Finally, two of the variables measuring labor market and general economic conditions are significant. Other things being equal, these results indicate that individuals released in 1969 or 1971 will have significantly lower wages on their first jobs than those released in 1972 or 1973. The result for 1969 is probably a reflection of wage inflation, because this was a period of high employment. The slightly more significant negative effects of release in 1971 than 1970 may be partially because of the high rates of unemployment in 1971.

Because many of the explanatory variables in the regression reported in Table 11.2 had coefficients that were insignificantly different from zero at usual confidence levels, we redid the analysis without these variables.[3] The results of the regression of *WAGAR* on this reduced specification are given in Table 11.3. These results are similar to those of Table 11.2 and do not merit further discussion. However, fearing that some of the variables dropped might be jointly if not individually significant, we tested for the joint significance of all variables dropped using a joint *F*-test. The value of this statistic, which is distributed as $F_{21,301}$ under the null hypothesis

**TABLE 11.3.** Results of Regression of *WAGAR* on Reduced Specification[a]

| Variable | Coefficient estimate | *t* Ratio[b] |
|---|---|---|
| Constant | 2.01 | 9.11*** |
| *RACE* | −0.228 | −3.10*** |
| *MS* | 0.187 | 2.69*** |
| *WKSTABS* | −0.133 | −2.19** |
| *REGJAR* | 0.414 | 3.15*** |
| *ICONS* | 0.382 | 4.45*** |
| *IAUTO* | 0.485 | 2.11** |
| *IRETL* | −0.217 | −1.35* |
| *OFARM* | −0.473 | −1.55* |
| *OOPER* | 0.171 | 1.30* |
| *OCRAFT* | 0.364 | 2.34*** |
| *OCLRK* | 0.328 | 1.11 |
| *OSALE* | 0.993 | 2.86*** |
| *SMSA* | 0.095 | 1.27 |
| *PERSON* | 0.100 | 1.15 |
| *SUPER* | −0.132 | −1.83** |
| *STAY* | −0.159 | −1.68** |
| *TPOWR* | 0.013 | 1.53* |
| *Y69* | −0.237 | −2.19** |
| *Y70* | −0.111 | −1.02 |
| *Y71* | −0.110 | −1.22 |

[a] $N = 343$, $R^2 = .30$, $\bar{R}^2 = .26$, $F_{20,322} = 6.97$***.
[b] Number of asterisks indicates level of significance, one-tailed test: *** = .01 level, ** = .05 level, * = .10 level.

that the coefficients of all deleted variables equal zero, was .24, which is far from significant.[4]

Perhaps the most important result emanating from estimates of the wage equation is the failure to find significant coefficients for major human capital variables *SG*, *HS*, *AAR*, and $AAR^2$. There are at least two possible interpretations of this result. First, human capital variables, at least as measured here, do not significantly affect the wages of prison releasees. Second, the effects of human capital variables are being masked by collinearity with other variables. One might reasonably expect collinearity between the human capital variables and previous work performance *WKSTABS*, or the industrial and occupational dummy variables. That is, one might reasonably expect better education and more experience to encourage work stability and to allow one to find employment in higher paying occupations and industries, but not to have additional effects once work stability, industry, and occupation are given. However, even dropping these other variables from the specification did not result in significant coefficients for the human capital variables. The best we could do was a *t*-statistic of 1.21 for *SG* when the occupational variables were dropped.

On the basis of the preceding and our original results, we conclude that the human capital variables have no significant effect on the wage rate after release from prison for members of our sample. This result has two important implications. First, it indicates one possible explanation for the failure of traditional educational programs to affect recidivism. These programs were expected to affect recidivism by improving labor market prospects. If they do not even affect labor market performance, it is not surprising that they do not reduce recidivism. Second, it gives support to segmented labor market theories, because these human capital variables are generally significant for other population groups.

## 11.4. Empirical Results for Work Stability

In this section we analyze the determinants of work stability for prison releasees. Our measure of work stability *WKSTABAR* is the number of jobs per employed year outside of prison, so a higher value indicates less work stability.

As in our analysis of the wage rate, we wish to analyze work stability independently of the level of criminal activity, as suggested by the simple model of Chapter 9. However, whereas *WAGAR* is measured (essentially) at the time of release, *WKSTABAR* is measured over the entire follow-up period and seems likely to be influenced by criminal activity. Because the reverse is also true, one solution would be to model *WKSTABAR* and criminal activity jointly. This would be complicated and expensive, however; see Chapter 12 for a similar analysis. We therefore chose instead to ignore the level of criminal activity and to analyze *WKSTABAR* only for those individuals who were not incarcerated during the follow-up period. In doing so we hoped to avoid the problem of simultaneity, but we introduced a potential problem of sample selection bias, as discussed in Section 4.5. It is not clear whether our results, based on a sample of nonrecidivists, will generalize to samples of all releasees.

Another potential problem of simultaneity arises because our equation for *WKSTABAR* includes *WAGAR* as an explanatory variable. The rationale is that higher pay increases the incentive to keep one's job. On the other hand, our equation for *WAGAR* in Chapter 10 did not include *WKSTABAR* as an explanatory variable. Under these circumstances, the correlation (or lack of correlation) between the disturbance terms of these two equations is crucial. If the disturbances are uncorrelated, *WKSTABAR* has no effect whatsoever on *WAGAR*, and the model explaining *WAGAR* and *WKSTABAR* is *recursive* (i.e., *WAGAR* affects *WKSTABAR* but not vice versa). This has the important implication that the *WKSTABAR* equation can be estimated consistently by ordinary least squares; there is no problem of simultaneous equations bias (see Section 4.6). On the other hand, if the disturbances in the two equations are correlated, then *WKSTABAR* affects *WAGAR* indirectly through this correlation. This would have the important implication that the *WKSTABAR* equation could not be estimated consistently by ordinary least squares. Rather, a more complicated procedure, such as two- or three-stage least squares, would be necessary. We assume this correlation to be zero, thus justifying ordinary least-squares estimation. A justification for this assumption is that when three-stage least squares was applied, the estimated correlation was $-1.3 \times 10^{-15}$, or essentially zero.[5]

Table 11.4 contains the results of regressing *WKSTABAR* on all variables. Overall, the results are similar to those we reported for *WAGAR*. We explain 33% of the variance in *WKSTABAR*, a surprisingly large proportion. Variables suggested by the demand side of the neoclassical model and/or segmented labor market theories have coefficients that are more significant than those of human capital variables or variables reflecting unique attributes and experiences of prison releasees. One industry variable and three occupational variables significantly affect work stability. Our coefficient estimates indicate that, other things being equal, individuals employed in machine manufacturing and/or employed as farmers, operatives, or craftspersons are more stable than those employed in other industries or occupations. None of the coefficients of the variables related to human capital accumulation are even marginally significant. The significant coef-

**TABLE 11.4.** Results of Regression of *WKSTABAR* on All Variables[a]

| Variable | Coefficient estimate | *t* Ratio[b] |
|---|---|---|
| Constant | 7.265 | 3.66*** |
| *WAGAR* | −0.314 | −1.54* |
| *SG* | −0.078 | −1.13 |
| *HS* | 0.140 | 0.29 |
| *AAR* | −0.095 | −0.97 |
| $AAR^2$ | 0.001 | 0.49 |
| *RACE* | −0.631 | −2.12** |
| *MS* | 0.102 | 0.37 |
| *WKSTABS* | −0.000 | −0.00 |
| *REGJAR* | 0.016 | 0.03 |
| *IAGMIN* | −0.060 | −0.08 |
| *ICONS* | −0.265 | −0.67 |
| *IFOOD* | 0.072 | 0.12 |
| *IFURN* | −0.468 | −0.80 |
| *INMET* | −0.772 | −0.84 |
| *IMACH* | −0.934 | −1.48* |
| *IMANUO* | −0.861 | −1.12 |
| *ITRAN* | 0.636 | 1.05 |
| *IWHOL* | −0.930 | −1.25 |
| *IAUTO* | −0.421 | −0.28 |
| *IRETL* | −0.010 | −0.16 |
| *ISERV* | −0.584 | −1.10 |
| *IPERSV* | −0.210 | −0.30 |
| *OFARM* | −2.792 | −1.86** |
| *OOPER* | −1.071 | −2.17** |
| *OCRAFT* | −1.382 | −2.35*** |
| *OCLRK* | −0.083 | −0.06 |
| *OSALE* | 0.746 | 0.48 |
| *SMSA* | 0.536 | 1.80** |
| *ALCHY* | 0.630 | 1.43* |
| *JUNKY* | −0.530 | −0.67 |
| *PERSON* | −0.378 | −0.92 |
| *PROPTY* | −0.020 | −0.06 |
| *CONVBS* | 0.017 | 0.34 |
| *AFA* | 0.001 | 0.03 |
| *SUPER* | 0.147 | 0.48 |
| *TSERVD* | −0.001 | −0.14 |
| *STAY* | 0.132 | 0.32 |
| *NSTAY* | 0.289 | 0.86 |
| *TPOWR* | −0.027 | −0.73 |
| *Y69* | −1.026 | −2.48*** |
| *Y70* | −1.424 | −3.54*** |
| *Y71* | −0.753 | −2.30*** |

[a] $N = 206$, $R^2 = .33$, $\bar{R}^2 = .16$, $F_{42,163} = 1.94$***.

[b] Number of asterisks indicates level of significance, one-tailed test: *** = .01 level, ** = .05 level, * = .10 level.

ficient of *RACE* indicates that, other things being equal, nonwhite releasees will have more stable work records than white releasees. The greater work stability of nonwhite releasees may be because of fewer job opportunities or differences in tastes. Only one of the variables reflecting releasee attributes, *ALCHY*, is even marginally significant. Unsurprisingly, the coefficient of this variable indicates that, other things being equal, releasees with alcohol problems have less stable work records than releasees without such problems. All three of the variables measuring labor market and general economic conditions are significant. The significantly negative coefficients obtained for the year-of-release variables seem likely to be the result of two factors. First, there is the purely algebraic fact that an earlier release date gives an individual the possibility of occupying a job for a longer period. The first year or so after release is a period of considerable job instability. Individuals who were released earlier had longer follow-ups and therefore were more likely to have had a chance for their job stability to increase, whereas later releasees had shorter follow-ups, and their first-year job instability carried more weight. Second, there were considerable changes in the general economic climate from 1969 to 1973. This might explain why, for example, those released in 1970 have more stable work records than those released in 1969, other things being equal. This is probably a reflection of the increased job stability associated with the onset of a recessionary period.

The coefficients of two variables that were insignificant in the *WAGAR* regressions are significant in the *WKSTABAR* regression. The first, *WAGAR*, of course did not appear in the *WAGAR* regressions. The coefficient of this variable is negative and marginally significant in the *WKSTABAR* regression. This result indicates that, other things being equal, higher wages lead to more stable work records. Unlike the similar finding of Doeringer and Piore (1971) and Cook (1973), it appears possible to support this interpretation (given a significant negative coefficient on the wage variable) because previous work records were controlled for. The coefficient of this variable supports segmented labor market theories. The second significant coefficient is that for Standard Metropolitan Statistical Areas (SMSAs), that is, cities and their surrounding densely populated areas. The coefficient for this variable indicates that, other things being equal, releasees living in SMSAs will have less stable work records than those who live elsewhere. This is probably the result of the greater variety and number of jobs available in large metropolitan areas.

Because many of the variables of the *WKSTABAR* equation of Table 11.4 had coefficients that were insignificantly different from zero at usual confidence levels, we redid the analysis without these variables. (See Note 3 for the exact criterion used.) The results of the regression of *WKSTABAR* on

**TABLE 11.5.** Results of Regression of *WKSTABAR* on Reduced Specification[a]

| Variable | Coefficient estimate | *t* Ratio[b] |
|---|---|---|
| Constant | 4.876 | 8.05*** |
| *WAGAR* | −0.376 | −2.33*** |
| *RACE* | −0.738 | −2.93*** |
| *IMACH* | −0.758 | −1.31* |
| *IMANUO* | −0.807 | −1.18 |
| *ITRAN* | 0.830 | 1.58* |
| *IWHOL* | −0.694 | −1.08 |
| *ISERV* | −0.502 | −1.12 |
| *OFARM* | −2.606 | −2.18** |
| *OOPER* | −1.086 | −2.72*** |
| *OCRAFT* | −1.649 | −3.57*** |
| *SMSA* | 0.535 | 2.06** |
| *Y69* | −1.352 | −3.82*** |
| *Y70* | −1.623 | −4.39*** |
| *Y71* | −1.076 | −3.94*** |

[a] $N = 206$, $R^2 = .24$, $\bar{R}^2 = .18$, $F_{14,191} = 4.41$***.

[b] Number of asterisks indicates level of significance, one-tailed test: *** = .01 level, ** = .05 level, * = .10 level.

this reduced specification are given in Table 11.5. The results are similar to those of Table 11.4 for the signs of the coefficients, but the significance level of a number of coefficients changes. Most interestingly, the negative coefficient for *WAGAR* is much more significant than in the full specification. We tested for the joint significance of the variables dropped and found them to be jointly as well as individually insignificant. The value of the test statistic, which is distributed as $F_{28,163}$ under the null hypothesis that the coefficients of all deleted variables equal zero, was .78, which is far from significant.

## 11.5. An Assessment of the Evidence on Postrelease Labor Market Performance

Realizing the uniqueness of our sample and thus the limited degree to which our results can be generalized, in this section we survey the results of other studies of postrelease labor market performance and compare them with our own. Most of the previous work on the labor market performance of correctional releasees has been descriptive and has focused on prison releasees, usually parolees. See Glaser (1964), Evans (1966, 1968),

Pownall (1969), Feyerherm (1976), Waller (1974), and Witte (1976) for examples of this descriptive work. See Euler and Franks (1976, pp. 161–170) for a bibliography on employment of former offenders. This work provides a general picture of the labor market experience of prison releasees, which will serve as background for understanding empirical work on the determinants of labor market performance for these groups.

The situation of a correctional releasee immediately after release depends on the nature of his or her correctional experience, the type of release (supervised or unsupervised), and the availability of family and community services. Probationers and releasees from community correctional facilities generally have already established labor market ties (if they ever will) and are relatively well adjusted to coping with freedom because their activities have generally not been greatly constrained by their correctional experience. Parolees generally have a job prior to release, as having a job is often a prior condition to parole. Generally, the jobs obtained by parolees are of a low-wage, low-skill nature, and parolees often experience substantial job instability as they seek to improve their labor market position. The labor market position of unconditional releasees from prison and jails is perhaps most difficult, although the establishment of work release programs, prison industries that pay wages, and prerelease programs has eased their plight in some areas. As noted in Chapter 10, such individuals have few resources other than gate money and are thus usually forced to accept the first job that is offered.

Existing evidence indicates that employment for correctional releasees depends on the conditions in local labor markets. Evidence surveyed by Cook (1973) and Witte (1975) indicates that prison releasees have little trouble finding jobs, although the jobs found are usually rather dismal. However, Feyerherm's (1976, pp. 147–148) study of a cohort of Wisconsin releasees during the 1974 recession found that only half of the releasees studied were able to find full-time employment within a month of release.

Most studies find unemployment rates for prison releasees to greatly exceed those of comparable population groups. However, these studies generally find, in contrast to Feyerherm (1976), that unemployment does not usually result from an inability to find a job but rather from short periods of leisure and/or job search during frequent job changes.

Jobs obtained by prison releasees are generally low-skilled and often transient in nature. Witte found the jobs on release of 54% of the North Carolina releasees studied to be classified in the three lowest skill categories of the U.S. Department of Labor's occupational classifications.[6] Even an average of 3 years after release, 39% of these prison releasees still occupied jobs that were so classified. Employment tends to be concentrated in large manufacturing industries employing mainly unskilled or semiskilled labor (e.g., textiles in North Carolina, metal working in Wisconsin), in service industries, and in construction. When the jobs of prison releasees require skills, they usually require skills in relationship to things (objects) rather than skills related to data or people. Common occupations are manufacturing operative, craftsperson (e.g., painters, cement finishers), and nonfarm laborer.

Earnings on release tend to be low relative to comparable population groups. Pownall (1969) found his federal releasees to earn approximately half the median income of the population as a whole and Feyerherm's (1976) releasees earned approximately 65% of the average weekly wage of production workers in Wisconsin. Witte (1976) found that approximately 3 years after release, the North Carolina releasees she studied earned a mean annual income of only 70% of that earned by all adult males in a similar geographic area. Interestingly, the only two studies that include unconditional releasees as well as parolees [Waller (1974) and the work of Witte and Reid (1980), reported in this chapter], find that parolees have significantly lower wages than do unconditional releasees.

As noted previously, all studies find marked instability of employment among prison releasees. Cook (1973) found the Massachusetts releasees in his sample to have a new job every 3 months on average. Pownall (1969) found that his federal releasees remained on their first job a median period of only 4.1 months and on their last job only slightly longer, 5.2 months. Using a longer follow-up period (averaging 37 months), Witte (1976) found a median job tenure of 10 months. In general the available evidence (Cook, 1973; Glaser, 1964; Pownall, 1969; Witte, 1976) seems to indicate that this labor market instability is chosen, as most job terminations are voluntary.

Considering the previous descriptive work as a whole, one might paint the following picture of the labor market performance of the typical prison releasee. On or shortly after release (within 2 to 3 weeks), the releasee generally obtains a low-skill, low-paying job as a manufacturing operative or nonfarm laborer, which he or she maintains for only a short period (3–4 months). Through time, the jobs of releasees improve only moderately in terms of pay and skill level. The releasee's employment pattern is generally that of frequent job changes with short periods of unemployment between jobs. For many releasees (approximately one-third), labor market activity is also frequently interrupted by periods of imprisonment. The low skills and unstable work patterns of prison releasees mean that they generally earn substantially less than comparable general population groups.

With the preceding background, we now turn to empirical attempts to analyze wage rates for correctional releasees. As far as we are aware, there have been only three published attempts (Borus, Hardin, and Terry, 1976; Hardin, 1975; and the work of Witte and Reid (1980), reported in this chapter) to systematically analyze the factors affecting wage rate or other income measures for correctional releasees. As was the case with the descriptive work cited before, this work deals solely with prison releasees, usually parolees.

The Appendix to this chapter summarizes in some detail the results of these three studies. As can be seen in this Table A11.2 of this appendix, previous empirical work has been able to explain relatively little of the variation in income for prison releasees. The low explanatory power of the models results mainly from the nature of the data (individual, cross-sectional), but the explanatory power of these models is still generally lower than similar models for other population groups. [Estimated wage determination models using individual, cross-sectional data for other groups generally explain approximately one-third of the variation in wage rates. See Griliches (1976), for example.] A possible explanation for this is that wage or income determination for prison releasees simply has a larger stochastic element than does wage or income determination for other population groups.

The most surprising result of the work reported in Table A11.2 is the failure to find significant coefficients on any variables related to either education or age. Previous work on other population groups [see Fleisher and Kniesner (1980) or Fearn (1981) for reviews] has generally found increased education to significantly increase wage and/or income and that wage (and/or income) significantly increases with age until approximately the mid-fifties and decreases thereafter. The empirical results available so far seem to indicate that neither education nor age significantly affects the income of prison releasees. This first finding, as noted earlier, offers little hope that educational programs aimed at prison inmates will be effective in raising their wages.

Sex, race, family characteristics, and physical characteristics generally have been found to significantly affect the wage (and/or income) of prison releasees. These results indicate that, other things being equal, a white, able-bodied, married man with many dependents will receive higher wages (or income) than other types of releasees. Because three of the variables (sex, race, and able-bodiedness) are beyond social control, and the fourth (family characteristics) is largely so, these results do not seem to have major policy implications, although they do point out the need to control for these factors when studying wages for prison releasees.

In contrast, the significantly positive effect on releasees' income of release through a correctional center or halfway house (and, to a lesser extent, wage rate) is potentially of considerable policy importance. These results might be interpreted as indicating that gradual, supported transition from prison to the community improves the labor market performance of prison releasees. The results also suggest two useful research projects. First, it would be useful to try to replicate the result obtained in a different geographic area and/or time period. Second, it would be useful to conduct a careful study (a process analysis) of Michigan correctional centers and halfway houses to determine the precise nature of the program that caused the observed beneficial effects.

The results of wage or income studies reported in Table A11.2 also indicate that job characteristics significantly affect wages, in particular, that permanent employment in construction, automotive services, crafts, or sales leads to higher wages, other things being equal. These results point out the potential usefulness of programs that seek to obtain such desirable jobs for work releasees. In another context, Cook (1975) has made a similar point.

As was the case for wage determination, there have been few attempts to estimate equations determining the hours of work for correctional releasees. Indeed, we are aware of only two published studies, Hardin (1975) and Borus, Hardin, and Terry (1976), that do so. Both these studies are based on a single data set for Michigan parolees released during the first quarter of 1974.

The results of these studies are presented in Table A11.3. As was the case for wages, empirical efforts to date have been able to explain relatively little of the variance in the average hours of work of prison releasees. A likely cause of this low explanatory power is the ad hoc nature of the empirical specifications used to date. Note that all cases are based on a single-equation model, which omits many variables that theory leads one to believe are important in determining hours of work.

As was the case for wages, neither education nor age appear to significantly affect hours of work. On the other hand, sex, race, and family characteristics significantly affect hours, with white married men working longer hours than others, when other factors to be equal. Release through a correctional center or halfway house significantly increases the average time worked per week. Graduated release from imprisonment appears to lead to significantly higher hours and wages, thus having a marked effect on total income.

As far as we are aware, there have been only two attempts to model variables related to employment stability for correctional releases (Cook, 1973; and the work of Witte and Reid (1980), reported previously in this chapter). Cook's study uses a sample of Massachusetts male parolees released from felony-level institutions in 1959, whereas data of Witte and Reid reflects the behavior of a sample of male releasees between 1969 and 1973 from one administrative area of the North Carolina Department of Correction.

The results of these studies are compared in Table A11.4. Previous work has been able to explain relatively little of the variation in employment stability. It would seem likely that this low explanatory power stems, at least in part, from mixing voluntary and nonvoluntary movement. Models that separate these two types of movement are likely to be more successful.

Both Cook's (1973) and Witte and Reid's (1980) work indicate that an individual's wage significantly affects work stability. This result indicates that, other things being equal, higher wages will lead to greater employment stability (longer job tenure). As noted earlier, this finding supports segmented labor market theorists' contention that wage and employment stability are intimately related. Cook's results indicate that nonproperty offenders with low IQ will have less stable job records than other individuals, other things being equal. This finding is not confirmed by Witte and Reid's work.

### 11.6. Summary and Conclusions

In this chapter, we have developed a model of postrelease labor market performance for prison releasees. This model combines insights from neoclassical and institutionalist labor market theories. In addition, the model recognizes that prison releasees have unique attributes (e.g., a criminal record) and experiences (e.g., prison experiences) that will be likely to affect labor market performance. We estimate models for the hourly wage received on the first job obtained after release and for the stability of employment during a follow-up period. These models are estimated using data for a combined sample, taken in 1973, of men imprisoned in North Carolina during 1969 or 1971. Recognizing the uniqueness of this sample, we compare and contrast our results with those from previous analyses of postrelease labor and market performance. This comparison leads to a number of conclusions and research suggestions. We shall discuss our conclusions first.

All studies conducted to date seem to indicate that neither education nor age significantly affects the postrelease labor market performance of prison releasees. This is surprising, because studies of other population groups seem to indicate that these factors are major determinants of labor market performance. The finding that the level of education does not affect postrelease labor market performance provides one possible explanation for the consistent finding that formal educational programs in prisons do not affect recidivism. These programs have commonly been believed to affect recidivism by improving labor market performance. The type of job a prison releasee obtains appears to be a major factor affecting postrelease labor market performance. In addition, sex, race, family characteristics, and physical characteristics seem to have major effects on postrelease performance. Higher wages appear to encourage work stability. Although the relationship between wages and work stability is intimate, it appears to be recursive rather than simultaneous. Finally, graduated release through community treatment centers or halfway houses appears to improve performance, whereas being on parole appears to make labor market performance worse than it otherwise would be.

Our conclusions have obvious implications for policy. One point that is surprisingly often missed is that programs designed to reduce recidivism by improving labor market performance must be designed so that they really do improve labor market performance. Results obtained to date seem to indicate that programs aimed at general improvements in either basic skills or vocational skills have not been effective in improving the labor market performance of prison releasees. Job placement efforts, even when extensive, have generally been found to be similarly ineffective.[7] Our results, the other results we survey here, and the results of two recently completed national experiments[8] seem to indicate that two different types of programs may be effective in improving the labor market performance of releasees. The first type of program provides money to releasees during the transition period after release from prison. It appears that the provision of such funds (whether from accumulated earnings while in prison or from unemployment payments) improves the labor market performance of those who work. We do not know why this is the case but believe it to be related to the possibility of longer job search when immediate financial need is less dire. The second type of program provides supportive environments rather than financial aid. Whether these environments are halfway houses or supportive working environments, they seem to improve labor market performance for certain types of individuals (e.g., former heavy drug users) in some circumstances.

Our survey of work on factors affecting the labor market performance of releasees also suggests some potentially beneficial areas for future research. Many rehabilitative programs, innovative as well as traditional, have rested on an implicit theoretical model that has yet to be fully tested. This model assumes two effects. First, it assumes that the rehabilitative program (e.g., formal or vocational education, work release, transitional aid, supported work) will affect the labor market performance of prison releasees. Second, it assumes that this improved labor market performance will lower releasees' levels of criminal activity. Existing evidence indicates that the strength of the first assumed effect will depend on the nature of the program (weak or nonexistent effects from formal education, perhaps stronger effects from work release and transitional aid). Evidence on the second assumed effect indicates that both higher wages and more satisfying jobs tend to reduce the level of criminal activity of at least some individuals. To design effective rehabilitative programs, full specification and careful estimation of this complete model would be useful. The potential benefits of doing so are well illustrated in a recent evaluation of transitional aid payments [see Rossi, Berk, and Lenihan (1980)].

## Appendix 11.1. Comparison of Studies of Labor Market Performance of Prison Releases

This appendix summarizes the results of studies analyzing the factors affecting wage rate or other income measures, working hours, and employment stability for correctional releasees. Table A11.1 describes the samples and variables used in each of the studies, and Tables A11.2, A11.3, and A11.4 present the empirical results of these studies.

Hardin (1975) discusses results for a large number of regressions but gives parameter estimates only for selected ones. To capture the full flavor of his results, we give parameter estimates when they are available, and, when parameter estimates are not available, we note that the discussion indicates that the parameter estimate was insignificantly different from zero by "Insig" and that the parameter estimate was significantly different from zero by "Sig".

**TABLE A11.1.** Dependent Variables and Description of Samples of Selected Studies

| Study | Dependent variable | Independent variables | Description of sample and follow-up |
|---|---|---|---|
| Hardin (1975) | Natural logarithm of starting hourly rate of pay after release | (1) Correctional experience regression: Race, previous criminal record, type of current offense, correctional experience<br>(2) Eclectic regression: as for (1), but with previous work experience added and the squared value of previous record and the binary for property offenses deleted<br>(3) Other results: Education and native ability | Selected male parolees from Michigan Department of Corrections, 1st quarter, 1974; 73–181-day follow-up |
| | Average weekly hours of work | Same as (2) | Same as preceding |
| | Days from parole to first job | Same as (1) | Same as preceding |

**TABLE A11.1.** *(Continued)*

| Study | Dependent variable | Independent variables | Description of sample and follow-up |
|---|---|---|---|
| Borus, Hardin, and Terry (1976) | Total gross earnings per week | As in Hardin (1975) regression (2), but with education, age, sex, years in, years of work experience, job placement program, family characteristics, drug, and geographic-area binaries added. | As in Hardin (1975), but with the addition of female and a few other male parolees |
| | Weekly take-home pay | Same as preceding | Same as preceding |
| | Number of working hours per week after parole | Same as preceding | Same as preceding |
| | Number of calendar days employed per week after parole | Same as preceding | Same as preceding |
| Witte and Reid (1980) (presented in Chapter 11) | Starting hourly wage rate after release | As in Borus, Hardin, and Terry, with *HS*, *WKSTABS*, *AFA*, *TPOWR*, *SUPER*, *MS*, *ALCHY*, *SMSA*, *REGJAR*, *PROPTY*, industrial and occupational binaries, and years of release binaries added; and $SG^2$, years of working experience, sex, halfway house and job placement binaries, number of dependents, physical disabilities binary, and locational binaries deleted | Selected releasees from N. C. Department of Correction, 1969–1973; 3–71-month follow-up |
| | Number of jobs per employed year outside of prison during the follow-up period | As just defined, with starting hourly wage rate *WAGAR* added | Selected releasees not reincarcerated during a follow-up of 3 to 71 months |
| Cook (1973) | Tenure (in months) of longest job during first 12 months of parole | Education, age, type of work experience, family characteristics, race, previous criminal record, type of current offense, correctional experience, native ability, length of time until first job, wage | Selected parolees from Massachusetts felony-level institutions released in 1959; 18 month follow-up |

In Tables A11.2 and A11.3, we present what we believe to be the most informative of Hardin's regression results. Specifically, in Table 11.2 we give full results for two regressions. The first explores the effect on the hourly wage of the correctional experience and the previous criminal record of the individual. The second regression in Table 11.2 contains "variables that had been found significant or nearly significant" in preliminary regression analyses of the hourly wage rate (Hardin, 1975, p. 332). We also give a general indication of the nature of Hardin's other analyses of wage rates in Table 11.2.

In Table 11.3, we present Hardin's regression analysis of the average weekly number of hours worked and the number of days from parole until the first job, which we felt most informative. The independent variables of Hardin's (1975) work are defined as follows:

1. Education—years of formal schooling completed (denoted in the tables by the acronym *SG*) and its squared value;

2. Previous work experience—a binary variable equal to 1 if the individual had "occupational attachment prior to parole" (Hardin, p. 331) and 0 otherwise;

3. Race—a binary variable equal to 1 if the parolee was white and 0 otherwise;

4. Previous criminal record—equal to the total number of jail and prison terms prior to the last incarceration (denoted in the tables by the acronym *CONVBS*); in the "correctional experience" regression the squared value of this variable is included as well;

5. Type of current offense—three binary variables, the first indicating that the offense was violent, analogous to, and reported in the same row as the Witte and Reid variable *PERSON*; the second, that the offense was against morals; and the third, that the offense was against property (denoted in the tables as *PROPTY*); a fourth offense category, which served as reference category, contained such things as motor vehicle offenses and weapons possession;

6. Correctional experience—a binary variable equal to 1 if the individual was paroled from a corrections center or other kind of halfway house and 0 otherwise;

7. Native ability—an indicator of mental ability ranging from a low of 1 to a high of 7.

The independent variables in the Borus, Hardin, and Terry (1976) study were the same as for the Hardin study, with their coefficients indicated on the tables in the same rows as those of Hardin, except for the following variables:

1. Age at release—age (in years) at release (denoted in the tables as *AAR*) and its squared value;

**TABLE A11.2.** Empirical Results of Previous Studies of Wage or Income[a]

| Independent variables[e] | Dependent variables: Natural logarithm of starting hourly rate of pay after release[b] (1) | (2) | (3) | Total gross earnings per week[c] | Weekly take-home pay[c] | Starting hourly wage rate after release[d] |
|---|---|---|---|---|---|---|
| Education: | | | | | | |
| *SG* | | | Insig. | 3.37 (0.45) | 6.13 (1.04) | 0.012 (0.63) |
| $SG^2$ | | | Insig. | 7.20 (0.86) | 5.83 (0.87) | |
| *HS* | | | | | | −0.011 (−0.09) |
| Age at release: | | | | | | |
| *AAR* | | | | 1.69 (0.41) | 2.72 (0.84) | −0.002 (−0.06) |
| $AAR^2$ | | | | −0.013 (−0.35) | −0.19 (−0.63) | 0.000 (0.05) |
| Previous work experience: | | | | | | |
| Years experience | | | | −0.25 (−0.23) | 0.12 (0.14) | |
| Occupational attachment | | 0.245* (1.92) | | | | |
| *WKSTABS* | | | | | | −0.151 (−2.21) |
| Sex | | | | 53.44** (2.28) | 42.82** (2.29) | |
| Race | 0.0876 (1.57) | 0.0833 (1.50) | | −36.63*** (−3.99) | −29.44*** (−4.02) | −0.254*** (−3.10) |
| Previous criminal record: | | | | | | |
| *CONVBS* | −0.0508 (−1.63) | −0.0223** (−1.99) | | −0.92 (−0.54) | −0.22 (−0.16) | −0.001 (−0.07) |
| $CONVBS^2$ | 0.00326 (0.92) | | | | | |
| *AFA* | | | | | | −0.003 (−0.41) |
| Type of current offense: | | | | | | |
| *PERSON* | −0.00114 (−0.01) | 0.0916 (1.40) | | −8.72 (−0.45) | −8.89 (−1.21) | 0.125 (1.18) |
| Morals | −0.0869 (−0.70) | 0.0618 (0.61) | | | | |
| *PROPTY* | 0.0989 (1.07) | | | | | 0.016 (0.17) |

(*Table continues*)

**TABLE A11.2.** *(Continued)*

| Independent variables | Dependent variables: Natural logarithm of starting hourly rate of pay after release[b] (1) | (2) | (3) | Total gross earnings per week[c] | Weekly take-home pay[c] | Starting hourly wage rate after release[d] |
|---|---|---|---|---|---|---|
| Correctional experience: | | | | | | |
| *TSERVD* | | | | −2.36 | −1.46 | −0.002 |
| | | | | (−1.15) | (−0.90) | (−0.81) |
| Halfway house | 0.117* | 0.0964 | | 30.80*** | 26.76*** | |
| | (1.75) | (1.45) | | (2.99) | (3.26) | |
| Job placement | | | | −0.92 | 1.63 | |
| | | | | (−0.10) | (0.21) | |
| *TPOWR* | | | | | | 0.013 |
| | | | | | | (1.30) |
| *SUPER* | | | | | | −0.119 |
| | | | | | | (−1.41) |
| Family characteristics: | | | | | | |
| No. dependents | | | | 7.78*** | 6.23*** | |
| | | | | (2.78) | (2.79) | |
| *MS* | | | | | | 0.188*** |
| | | | | | | (2.39) |
| Native ability | | | Insig. | | | |
| Physical characteristics | | | | −28.42* | −20.85* | |
| | | | | (−1.90) | (−1.75) | |
| Addictions: | | | | | | |
| *JUNKY* | | | | −13.25 | −13.18* | −0.129 |
| | | | | (−1.55) | (−1.94) | (−0.63) |
| *ALCHY* | | | | | | −0.014 |
| | | | | | | (−0.13) |
| Geographical area: | | | | | | |
| Locational binaries | | | | Bsig. | | |
| *SMSA* | | | | | | 0.087 |
| | | | | | | (1.05) |
| Job characteristics: | | | | | | |
| *REGJAR* | | | | | | 0.407*** |
| | | | | | | (2.97) |
| Occup. and Ind. binaries | | | | | | Bsig. |
| General economic conditions: | | | | | | |
| Year-of-release binaries | | | | | | Bsig. |
| $\bar{R}^2$ | .036 | .049 | | .16 | .18 | .22 |
| *N* | 172 | 172 | | 266 | 266 | 343 |

[a] Values in parentheses following regression coefficients are *t*-ratios. Asterisks indicate level of significance, two-tailed test: *** = .01 level, ** = .05 level, * = .10 level. "Insig." indicates that the discussion reported that a variable was insignificant although no *t*-statistic was reported. "Bsig." indicates that a series of binaries was used to represent this factor and that at least some of these binaries were significant.

[b] From Hardin (1975). (1), (2), and (3) indicate separate regressions.

[c] From Borus, Hardin, and Terry (1976).

[d] From Witte and Reid (1980); also reported in Chapter 11.

[e] All acronyms are as defined in Table 11.1.

**TABLE A11.3.** Empirical Results of Previous Studies of Hours of Work and Related Variables[a]

| | Dependent variables | | | | |
|---|---|---|---|---|---|
| Independent variables[d] | Average weekly hours of work[b] | Days from parole to first job[b] | Other[b] | Number of hours per week after parole[c] | Number of calendar days employed per week after parole[c] |
| Education: | | | | | |
| *SG* | | | Insig. | 2.38 | 0.51* |
| | | | | (1.20) | (1.70) |
| $SG^2$ | | | Insig. | 2.00 | 0.12 |
| | | | | (0.89) | (0.35) |
| Age: | | | | | |
| *AAR* | | | | 1.08 | 0.19 |
| | | | | (0.99) | (1.19) |
| $AAR^2$ | | | | −0.01 | −0.002 |
| | | | | (−1.00) | (−1.13) |
| Previous work experience: | | | | | |
| Years experience | | | | 0.27 | 0.06 |
| | | | | (0.93) | (1.37) |
| Occupational attachment | 4.67 | | | | |
| | (1.05) | | | | |
| Sex | | | | 13.88** | 2.25*** |
| | | | | (2.21) | (2.39) |
| Race | 4.13** | −17.1*** | | −9.19*** | −1.17*** |
| | (2.13) | (−3.06) | | (−3.74) | (−3.16) |
| Previous criminal record: | | | | | |
| *CONVBS* | −0.432 | 3.12 | | 0.05 | 0.009 |
| | (−1.11) | (1.00) | | (1.13) | (0.13) |
| $CONVBS^2$ | | −0.386 | | | |
| | | (−1.08) | | | |
| Type of current offense: | | | | | |
| *PERSON* | −0.715 | 14.3 | | −4.34* | −0.59 |
| | (−0.31) | (1.39) | | (−1.76) | (−1.59) |
| Morals | 1.35 | −11.7 | | | |
| | (0.38) | (−0.94) | | | |
| *PROPTY* | | −5.66 | | | |
| | | (−0.61) | | | |
| Correctional experience: | | | | | |
| *TSERVD* | | | | −0.02 | 0.025 |
| | | | | (−0.44) | (0.30) |
| Halfway house | 1.67 | −25.8*** | | 7.58*** | 1.14*** |
| | (0.72) | (−3.85) | | (2.75) | (2.71) |
| Job placement | | | | 1.15 | 0.34 |
| | | | | (0.44) | (0.87) |

(*Table continues*)

**TABLE A11.3.** *(Continued)*

| Independent variables | Dependent variables: Average weekly hours of work[b] | Days from parole to first job[b] | Other[b] | Number of hours per week after parole[c] | Number of calendar days employed per week after parole[c] |
|---|---|---|---|---|---|
| Family characteristics: | | | | | |
| No. dependents | | | | 1.99** | 0.37*** |
| | | | | (2.65) | (3.36) |
| Native ability | | | Insig. | | |
| Physical characteristics | | | | −5.92 | −0.62 |
| | | | | (−1.48) | (−1.03) |
| Addiction: | | | | | |
| *JUNKY* | | | | −2.51 | −0.53 |
| | | | | (−1.10) | (−1.56) |
| Geographic area: | | | | | |
| Locational binaries | | | | Binsig. | Generally Binsig. |
| $\bar{R}^2$ | .01 | .18 | | .18 | .19 |
| $N$ | 172 | 172 | | 266 | 266 |

[a] Values in parentheses following regression coefficients are $t$-ratios. Asterisks indicate level of significance, two-tailed test: *** = .01 level, ** = .05 level, * = .10 level. "Insig." indicates that the discussion reported that a variable was insignificant although no $t$-statistic was reported. "Binsig." indicates that a series of binaries was used to represent this factor and that at least some of these binaries were insignificant.
[b] From Hardin (1975).
[c] From Borus, Hardin, and Terry (1976).
[d] All acronyms are as defined in Table 11.1.

2. Previous work experience—total years of work experience at time of interview;
3. Sex—1 if parolee was male and 0 if otherwise;
4. Years in—the number of years since sentencing (analogous to, and reported in the same row as, the Witte and Reid variable *TSERVD*);
5. Job placement—a binary variable equal to 1 if the individual participated in a job placement program and 0 otherwise;
6. Family characteristics—the number of dependents at time of interview;
7. Physical characteristics—a binary variable equal to 1 if the parolee was disabled and 0 otherwise;
8. Drug use—a binary variable equal to 1 if the parolee was known to have used drugs and 0 otherwise (denoted in the tables by the acronym *JUNKY*);

9. Geographic area—a series of binaries was used to represent this factor (e.g., a binary equal to 1 if the individual was released in Lansing and 0 otherwise); "Bsig." indicates that at least some of the coefficients on the binaries were significant, and "Binsig." indicates that the coefficients on those binaries were insignificant.

Many of the independent variables used in the work of Witte and Reid reported in Table A11.2 and A11.3 are analogous to those used in the Borus, Hardin and Terry study, and in the tables their coefficients are reported in the same rows as that study. Those variables that are different from the Borus, Hardin, and Terry study are listed next. All acronyms used here have been defined in Table 11.1, page 220–221.

1. Education—the binary variable *HS*,
2. Previous work experience—*WKSTABS*,
3. Previous criminal record—*AFA*,
4. Correctional experience—*TPOWR* and the binary variable *SUPER*,
5. Family characteristics—the binary variable *MS*,
6. Addictions—the binary variable *ALCHY*,
7. Geographic area—the binary variable *SMSA*,
8. Job characteristics—the binary variable *REGJAR* and the binary series *IAGMIN–IPSERV* and *OFARM–OSALE*,
9. General economic conditions—the three binary variables *Y69*, *Y70*, and *Y71*.

The work of Witte and Reid reported in Table A11.4 includes all of the independent variables defined previously, with the addition of the binary variable *STAY* and the hourly wage received on the first job after release.

Cook's (1973) independent variables include only two nonbinary variables:

1. Number of months imprisoned, and
2. Weekly wage;

and the following binary variables:

3. Education—two variables, equal to 1 if the parolee had less than 8 years of schooling and 0 otherwise (denoted as "Elementary ed"); and 1 if the parolee had 12 or more years of schooling and 0 otherwise (analogous to, and reported in the same row as, *HS*);
4. Age on release—two variables, equal to 1 for parolees aged 16–25 on release and 0 otherwise; and equal to 1 for parolees aged 25–35 on release and 0 otherwise;
5. Profession—1 if the parolee had a skilled or professional occupation prior to incarceration and 0 otherwise;
6. Marriage—1 if parolee was married and 0 otherwise;
7. Race—1 if parolee was black and 0 otherwise;
8. Prior sentences—1 if the number of prior sentences was one or more and 0 otherwise;

**TABLE A11.4.** Empirical Results of Previous Work Related to Employment Stability[a]

| | Dependent variables | |
|---|---|---|
| Independent variables[d] | Tenure (in months) of longest job during first 12 months of parole[b] | Number of jobs per free employed year during the follow-up period[c] |
| Education | | |
| *SG* | | −0.078<br>(−1.13) |
| Elementary ed. binary | −1.6<br>(−1.3) | |
| *HS* | 3.3<br>(1.1) | 0.140<br>(0.29) |
| Age at release: | | |
| 16–25 | −1.3<br>(−0.69) | |
| 25–35 | −1.2<br>(−0.66) | |
| *AAR* | | −0.095<br>(−0.97) |
| $AAR^2$ | | 0.001<br>(0.49) |
| Previous work experience | | |
| Skill occup. before | 0.69<br>(0.33) | |
| *WKSTABS* | | −0.000<br>(−0.00) |
| Family characteristics: | | |
| *MS* | −1.4<br>(−1.1) | 0.102<br>(0.37) |
| Race | 0.38<br>(0.25) | −0.631**<br>(−2.12) |
| Previous criminal record: | | |
| Prior sentence | −1.4<br>(−1.1) | |
| *CONVBS* | | 0.017<br>(0.34) |
| *AFA* | | 0.001<br>(0.03) |
| Job characteristics: | | |
| *REGJAR* | | 0.016<br>(0.03) |
| Occup. and ind. binaries | | Bsig. |
| Geographical location: | | |
| *SMSA* | | 0.536*<br>(1.80) |
| Type of current offense | | |
| *PERSON* | | −0.378<br>(−0.92) |

TABLE A11.4. (Continued)

| Independent variables | Dependent variables: Tenure (in months) of longest job during first 12 months of parole[b] | Dependent variables: Number of jobs per free employed year during the follow-up period[c] |
|---|---|---|
| *PROPTY* | −2.3* (−1.8) | −0.020 (−0.06) |
| Correctional experience: | | |
| *TSERVD* | 0.064 (1.6) | −0.001 (−0.14) |
| *STAY* | | 0.132 (0.32) |
| *TPOWR* | | −0.027 (−0.73) |
| *SUPER* | | 0.147 (0.48) |
| Native ability: | | |
| IQ < 80 | 3.2*** (2.6) | |
| IQ > 110 | −0.68 (−0.31) | |
| Length of job search: | | |
| ≤3 months | 1.4 (1.0) | |
| >3 months but ≤6 months | −0.34 (−0.21) | |
| Wage: | | |
| Weekly | 0.09*** (2.4) | |
| Hourly | | −0.314 (−1.54) |
| Addiction: | | |
| *JUNKY* | | −0.530 (−0.67) |
| *ALCHY* | | 0.630 (1.43) |
| General economic conditions: | | |
| Year-of-release binaries | | Bsig. |
| $\bar{R}^2$ | .09 | .16 |
| *N* | 323 | 206 |

[a] Values in parentheses following regression coefficients are *t*-ratios. Asterisks indicate level of significance, two-tailed test: *** = .01 level, ** = .05 level, * = .10 level. "Insig." indicates that the discussion reported that a variable was insignificant although no *t*-statistic was reported. "Bsig." indicates that a series of binaries was used to represent this factor and that at least some of these binaries were significant.
[b] From Cook (1973, p. 62).
[c] From Witte and Reid (1980); also reported in Chapter 11.
[d] All acronyms are as defined in Table 11.1.

9. Property offense—1 if the parolee was convicted of a property offense and 0 otherwise;

10. IQ—two variables, equal to 1 if IQ was less than 80 and 0 otherwise, and 1 if IQ was greater than 110 and 0 otherwise;

11. Length of job search—two variables, equal to 1 if parolee's job was obtained in first three months after release and 0 otherwise, and 1 if job was obtained in second three months after release and 0 otherwise.

## Notes to Chapter 11

1. Specifically, this variable is the number of jobs per employed year outside of prison during the follow-up period.

2. For example, in our sample, only 4% said that they left their work release job after release because they were fired or laid off. Of those who were unemployed at the time they were interviewed, only 7% said they were fired and 3% said they were laid off.

3. Specifically, we used the "maximum $\bar{R}^2$" method of model selection suggested by Theil (1960, pp. 210–215). This is equivalent to minimizing the estimated standard error of the disturbance and will, on the average, choose the correct model. Variables are excluded from the final specification if, when added individually, their $t$ ratios would be less than one in absolute value.

4. A plot of residuals for the reduced specification of Table 11.3 revealed no systematic patterns. Specifically, this plot did not indicate the presence of heteroscedasticity or nonnormality.

5. Note that the system was identified by the exclusion from the wage equation of the variables found to be insignificantly related to wages. That is, in running a three-stage least squares analysis, the specification of the wage equation was that of Table 11.3, whereas the specification of the work stability equation was that of Table 11.4.

6. These are Classifications 885, 886, and 887.

7. This is the conclusion of Borus, Hardin, and Terry's (1976) work. See also Lenihan (1977).

8. See Rossi, Berk, and Lenihan (1980) and Board of Directors, Manpower Demonstration Research Corporation (1980), for reports of the results of these two national experiments.

# Chapter 12

## An Estimate of a Simultaneous Model of Criminal Behavior and Labor Market Success

### 12.1. Introduction

In this chapter we estimate a complex economic model of criminal behavior and labor market success using a simultaneous equation estimating technique that allows one of the dependent variables to be censored. Recall from Chapter 9 that our more complex model of criminal behavior, developed in Section 9.7, yielded a two-equation model for the determination of the time allocated to legal and illegal activities. If this model is accurate, one should not estimate a model for criminal activity independently of a model for performance in the labor market, because performances in legal and illegal activity are interrelated. Recall also from Chapter 10 that our measure of the level of criminal activity was the number of arrests (convictions) per month out of prison. As we noted in that chapter, this variable calls for some care in statistical analysis, because it is censored at zero and we observe a number of individuals who are at this censoring point. In Chapter 10, we used the Tobit technique to estimate our single-equation model for arrest and conviction rates. In Chapter 11, we analyzed two aspects of postrelease labor market performance: the wage on the first job after release and the stability of employment during a follow-up period. We found these two variables to be related in a recursive fashion. Drawing on results from all three previous chapters, in this chapter we estimate a model for the arrest rate and the wage on the first job after release, using a simultaneous Tobit technique developed by Sickles and Schmidt (1978).

The organization of this chapter is as follows. In the next section, we develop the empirical model that we shall estimate using the same data as used in the two previous chapters. Section 12.3 contains our empirical results and a discussion of their interpretation. The final section contains our summary and conclusions.

## 12.2. The Empirical Model

Recall from Section 9.7 that the more complex model of criminal behavior that we developed implied a two-equation model in which the respective amounts of time allocated to legal and to illegal activities were determined by a set of variables reflecting outcomes of these activities. These variables are listed in the first paragraph of Section 10.2.

An important feature of this model is that the amount of time allocated to legal activities will be influenced by the amount of time allocated to illegal activities, and vice versa. In our empirical model we allow for such influences directly by including our measure of labor market success in the illegal-activity equation and our measure of illegal activity in the labor-market-success equation. We also allow the error terms in the two equations to be correlated, thus allowing for indirect effects of one dependent variable on the other through the correlation of their random (unexplained) components.

Recall from Chapter 10 that we do not observe the amount of time allocated to illegal activity directly but rather observe a certain number of arrests, convictions, and imprisonments during a follow-up period. In Chapter 10 we analyzed both the number of arrests and the number of convictions per month out of prison. We found conviction rates to be influenced markedly by variables that seemed to reflect the criminal justice decision-making process. Because we wish to analyze the variable that we believe provides the clearest reflection of the individual's level of criminal activity, in this chapter we analyze only arrest rates. Estimation of models for both arrest and conviction rates was precluded by the high cost of estimating the model we use.

The empirical measures of the theoretical variables in our equation for the arrest rate are almost identical to those utilized to analyze this variable in Chapter 10. See Table 10.1 for a complete listing and description of these variables. We change our specification only by adding four variables and changing our measure of one of the variables in our original specification. The first variable added is a measure of the expected returns to illegal activity, denoted *EROR*. This variable is the actual monetary gain reported by local law enforcement agencies to the FBI for the type of crime for which the individual was most commonly arrested before his most recent imprisonment. For each individual, we determined the monetary gain in the county and year of actual release. The second and third variables were added to determine if the relative leniency of juvenile statutes in North Carolina had been adequately captured by our model. The second variable, denoted *JUVEN*, is a dummy variable equal to one if the individual was less than 21 years old when released from prison and zero otherwise. The third variable, denoted *JEXLOS*, interacts *JUVEN* with our measure of the expected sentence length. The final variable added is the number of school years completed, denoted *SG*. We changed our measure of the expected unemployment rate because of questions raised concerning our original measure and its poor performance. Our new measure of the expected unemployment rate, denoted *UNEMPAR*, is the unemployment rate in the county of release at the time the individual was released from prison.[1]

Note that our model for the arrest rate contains quite a large number of variables (21, to be exact). Further, recall from Chapter 10 that our results indicated that it was not possible to estimate a single "supply-of-offense" function, but rather that it is necessary to estimate separate offense functions for individuals specializing in different types of crimes. Although our total data set is quite large, there are not always large numbers of observations available on individuals specializing in specific crime types that contain complete information on all variables in our model. For example, our data set contains complete information on only 138 individuals generally arrested for income (i.e., property) offenses. The number of degrees of freedom available when estimating our models is important, because the maximum likelihood estimation technique that we utilize has desirable statistical properties only asymptotically. Also, the number of parameters is important because the cost of estimating the simultaneous Tobit model rises rapidly with the number of parameters. Therefore we do not attempt to estimate our completely specified model for the wage received on the first job after release. Rather, for individuals specializing in each of three offense types (i.e., income, consumption, and all other offenses), we develop a reduced specification for the wage equation.[2] It is this reduced specification and the expanded specification for the arrest rate that we estimate for groups of individuals specializing in income, consumption, and other types of offenses.

We utilize a simultaneous Tobit technique developed by Sickles and Schmidt (1978) to estimate our model. This technique is described in some detail in Section 4.6. The empirical model we developed in the last section consists of two equations, one for the arrest rate and one for the wage received on the first job after release. Formally,

$$ARRAT_i^* = \gamma_1 WAGAR_i + \delta_1' X_{i1} + \varepsilon_{i1},$$

$$WAGAR_i = \gamma_2 ARRAT_i + \delta_2' X_{i2} + \varepsilon_{i2},$$

where

$$ARRAT_i = \begin{cases} ARRAT_i & \text{when} \quad ARRAT_i^* > 0 \\ 0 & \text{otherwise} \end{cases}$$

and where $X_{i1}$ and $X_{i2}$ are vectors of exogenous variables affecting the arrest rate and the wage rate, respectively, $\delta_1$ and $\delta_2$ vectors of parameters to be estimated, and $\gamma_1$ and $\gamma_2$ parameters to be estimated. We observe *ARRAT* and *WAGAR* but not *ARRAT**. Note that it is the actual arrest rate that affects the wage after release, not the unobserved *ARRAT**.[3]

We assume that the error terms $\varepsilon_{i1}$ and $\varepsilon_{i2}$ are independently and identically distributed as $N(0, \Sigma)$, where $\Sigma$ is of the form

$$\Sigma = \begin{bmatrix} \sigma_{11} & \sigma_{12} \\ \sigma_{21} & \sigma_{22} \end{bmatrix}.$$

We estimate our model by maximum likelihood. The likelihood function is given by Eq. (4.6.4). We maximize this likelihood function using a numerical optimization program to obtain estimates for the parameters of our model.[4] We obtain asymptotic standard errors from the information matrix that is obtained by numerical differentiation, owing to the complexity of the expressions for the first and second derivatives. The maximum likelihood estimates we obtain are consistent and asymptotically efficient. However, they are very expensive to obtain.[5] An alternative estimation technique that yields consistent but inefficient estimates is provided by Sickles and Schmidt (1978, p. 13). Given normal computational budgets, it may be necessary to use this technique in some applications.

## 12.3. The Empirical Results

Table 12.1 contains the empirical results we obtain when we estimate our model for the arrest rate *ARRAT* using the simultaneous Tobit technique and data for individuals who specialize in income (i.e., property) offenses, consumption offenses, and other types of offenses. As can be seen in this table, variables coming explicitly from our theoretical model significantly affect the arrest rate of individuals who specialize in income and miscellaneous offenses but seem to have little, if any, effect on individuals who specialize in consumption offenses. The endogenous wage variable has the traditional negative coefficient for all three types of offenders, but the

**TABLE 12.1.** Results of Estimating the Arrest Rate Equation for Three Crime Groups[a]

| | Crime group | | |
|---|---|---|---|
| Variable | Income | Consumption | Other |
| *CONSTANT* | 0.9058*<br>(1.58) | 0.5020**<br>(1.80) | 0.9151**<br>(1.81) |
| Endogenous | | | |
| *WAGAR* | −0.0687<br>(−0.81) | −0.0199<br>(−0.55) | −0.0056<br>(−0.08) |
| Exogenous | | | |
| *P(C/A)* | −0.1445*<br>(−1.39) | −0.0140<br>(−0.17) | −0.2379**<br>(−2.09) |
| *P(J/C)* | −0.3945***<br>(−2.65) | −0.0335<br>(−0.33) | 0.1111<br>(0.53) |
| *EXLOS* | −0.0021<br>(−1.21) | 0.0001<br>(0.09) | −0.0140**<br>(−1.91) |
| *JUVEN* | 0.0659<br>(0.66) | 0.0768<br>(0.98) | −0.0422<br>(−1.41) |
| *JEXLOS* | 0.0016<br>(0.92) | −0.0005<br>(−0.37) | 0.0096*<br>(1.36) |
| *UNEMP* | −0.0683**<br>(−1.93) | −0.0124<br>(−0.69) | −0.0310<br>(−1.18) |
| *TPOWR* | −0.0017**<br>(−1.96) | −0.0003<br>(−0.51) | −0.0012<br>(−0.94) |
| *EROR* | 0.2E−04<br>(0.34) | Measured by *ARRBS* | Measured by *ARRBS* |
| *AAR* | −0.0066<br>(−0.20) | −0.0137*<br>(−1.36) | −0.0400**<br>(−2.28) |
| *AAR*$^2$ | 0.0001<br>(0.20) | 0.0001<br>(0.81) | 0.0004*<br>(1.59) |
| *AFA* | 0.0147**<br>(2.08) | 0.0018<br>(0.62) | 0.0070*<br>(1.35) |
| *MS* | −0.0322<br>(−0.57) | 0.0705**<br>(2.01) | −0.0193<br>(−0.39) |
| *RACE* | −0.1116**<br>(−2.02) | −0.0904***<br>(−2.48) | −0.1159**<br>(−2.18) |
| *ALCHY* | −0.0900<br>(−1.05) | 0.0668<br>(1.28) | 0.0467<br>(0.78) |
| *JUNKY* | 0.0422<br>(0.43) | −0.1546<br>(−0.71) | N/A[b] |
| *SUPER* | −0.0537<br>(−0.92) | −0.0876**<br>(−1.94) | 0.0423<br>(0.59) |
| *RULE* | 0.0202<br>(1.17) | −0.0137<br>(−0.68) | 0.0203<br>(0.84) |

(*Table continues*)

**TABLE 12.1.** *(Continued)*

| Variable | Crime group | | |
|---|---|---|---|
| | Income | Consumption | Other |
| *ARRBS* | 0.0036 | 0.0121*** | 0.0353** |
| | (0.50) | (3.65) | (1.89) |
| *SG* | −0.0187* | −0.0040 | 0.0068 |
| | (−1.54) | (−0.54) | (0.66) |
| $\hat{\sigma}_{11}$ | 0.079*** | 0.0747*** | 0.1960 |
| | (7.38) | (5.93) | (4.93) |
| $\hat{\sigma}_{12}$ | 0.0610** | −0.2742*** | −0.0114 |
| | (1.80) | (−4.74) | (−0.57) |
| $\hat{\sigma}_1 \div \overline{ARRAT}$[c] | 1.50 | 1.45 | 1.15 |
| *N* | 138 | 112 | 65 |

[a] Asterisk indicates level of significance, one-tailed test: *** = .01 level, ** = .05 level, * = .10 level. Values in parentheses under coefficients are "*t*-ratios" that are distributed $N(0, 1)$ asymptotically.
[b] There were no individuals in this crime group with a history of drug use.
[c] $\hat{\sigma}_1$ is the estimated standard error.

coefficient on this variable is never even close to being significant at normal confidence levels. Thus it appears, at least for our sample, that wages do not directly affect arrest rates. However, the estimated covariance of the error terms in the wage-rate and arrest-rate equations indicates that for income and consumption offenders there are indirect effects between wages and arrest rates. These indirect effects are large and significant for consumption offenders, of moderate size and marginally significant for property offenders, and small and insignificant for miscellaneous offenders.[6]

For those whose crimes lead mainly to monetary gain (i.e., income offenders), we find higher probabilities of both conviction and imprisonment to be associated with lower rates of arrest. It appears that these probabilities deter income offenders in our sample. The expected sentence has the traditional negative coefficient, but this coefficient is not significantly different from zero at ordinary levels of statistical significance. Our results indicate that higher levels of initial wealth are associated with lower arrest rates for income offenders. Property crime appears to be an inferior way to make a living. This finding is consistent with Heineke's (1978b) finding, which he obtains using aggregate data. It is interesting that our measure of initial wealth appears to significantly affect criminality only when the simultaneity of criminal and labor market decisions is explicitly modeled. Our new measure of the expected unemployment rate, denoted *UNEMP*, has an unexpectedly negative (as did our former measure) and significant coefficient. Our results are consistent with the hypothesis that poorer employment prospects are associated with decreased arrest rates for income offenders. This is odd and may indicate that we still have not developed an adequate measure for the expected unemployment rate. The new variables that we added to our specification, *JUVEN*, *JEXLOS*, and *EROR*, do not significantly affect the arrest rate of the income offenders in our sample. Few taste variables are significantly related to the arrest rate for income offenders. Only age at first arrest, race, and education have coefficients that are even marginally significant at normal confidence levels. The coefficients on these variables indicate that an income offender in our sample will, other things being equal, have a higher arrest rate if he was older when first arrested, is white, and has completed little formal education.

Variables emanating directly from our theoretical model explain little, if any, of the variation in arrest rates for individuals convicted of consumption offenses. Indeed, the coefficients on all such variables except prior criminal record have "*t*-statistics" less than one in absolute value. Worse previous records are associated with higher arrest rates. This variable may (as we have hypothesized) reflect the perceived gains to criminal activity. Alternatively, it may reflect ability, police practices, or unmeasured tastes. Of the variables we used to measure tastes, only age, marital status, race, and postrelease supervision are found to significantly affect the arrest rates of consumption offenders in our sample. The coefficients on these variables indicate that, other things being equal, consumption offenders in our sample will have higher arrest rates if they are younger, white, married, and unsupervised after release from prison. It is interesting to note that the results for consumption offenders that we obtained by using the simultaneous-equation model are markedly different from those we obtained by using a single-equation estimation technique (see Table 10.4). This is quite understandable when one notes that there is a relatively large correlation between the error terms of the wage-rate and arrest-rate equations for this type of offender. Our results for consumption offenders seem to indicate that the economic model of crime as currently developed is poorly adapted to explaining arrest rates for consumption offenders. Recall from Chapter 9 that there have been a number of models developed in recent years that are more directly designed to explain violent offenses. It is possible that such models would prove more successful in explaining arrest rates for consumption offenders in our sample. One interesting aspect of our results is that arrest rates for offenders in the "consumption offenses" category are higher if they are married. This fact, coupled with the fact that arrest for assault on a female is a fairly common charge, may indicate that models of family violence are appropriate for at least a subset of offenders in this category.

Generally, for offenders convicted of crimes other than those against property and persons, both higher probabilities of conviction and longer sentences appear to be deterrents. Further, our results suggest that longer sentences are likely to be more effective for adults than for juveniles committing these types of offenses. Our results for criminal justice variables for this type of offender are much more reasonable in the current model than they were in the simpler model of Chapter 10. Note also that worse previous records are associated with higher arrest rates during the follow-up period. As in the case of those committing offenses against persons, we hypothesize that this variable reflects the level of expected return from this type of illegal activity. As in the case of consumption offenders, a large number of variables that we have used to measure tastes affect the arrest rate for this residual group of offenders. Specifically, our results indicate that offenders in the "other-types-of-offenses" category will have higher arrest rates if they are young or old, if they are white, and if they were older when first arrested. Only two of the results regarding age are unexpected. We would generally expect that arrest rates would decrease with age monotically for the group of offenders analyzed here because the mean age (32 years) is quite high, and that arrest rates would be highest for offenders who are arrested at younger ages. On the contrary, we find that those who are old and those first arrested when older have higher arrest rates; however, the coefficients on which these results are based are only marginally significant.

Turning now to results obtained for the wage-rate equation (see Table 12.2), we note first that the arrest rate significantly affects wages received on the first job after release for offenders specializing in all three types of offenses. For income offenders, the coefficient on this endogenous variable has the expected negative sign, but for consumption offenders and those specializing in other types of offenses, this variable has an unexpected positive coefficient. Further, this unexpected coefficient is highly significant for consumption offenders. We believe that this result, like the other unexpected results just reported for consumption offenders, indicates that traditional economic models do not adequately reflect the behavior of this type of individual. It is interesting that we find higher arrest rates to be significantly associated with lower wage levels for income offenders. In terms of our model this provides some support for the proposition that property crime and work may be seen as alternative methods of "making a living" for this type of offender. Overall, our wage model explains the level of postrelease wages for income offenders and those committing neither income nor consumption offenses much better than it explains variation in this variable for those committing consumption offenses.

For income offenders, we find that arrest rates during the follow-up period, work history, race, a high school diploma, employment in certain industries, and earlier release without supervision significantly affect the wages an individual receives on his first job after release. Specifically, our

**TABLE 12.2.** Results of Estimating the Wage Rate Equation for Three Crime Groups[a]

| Variable | Crime group: Income | Consumption | Other |
|---|---|---|---|
| *CONSTANT* | 2.6467*** (15.43) | 0.4399 (1.13) | 2.1653*** (11.27) |
| Endogenous | | | |
| *ARRAT* | −0.7527** (−1.93) | 2.8534*** (4.68) | 0.9049* (1.48) |
| Exogenous | | | |
| *WKSTABS* | −0.1774*** (−2.36) | — | −0.2435** (−1.89) |
| *TSERVD* | — | −0.0033 (−0.68) | 0.0165** (2.09) |
| *PERSON* | — | — | −0.2810 (−1.14) |
| *SUPER* | −0.1518* (−1.62) | — | — |
| *ALCHY* | — | — | 0.2296* (1.39) |
| *JUNKY* | — | −0.1482 (−0.17) | — |
| *NSTAY* | — | 0.3936*** (2.54) | — |
| *TPOWR* | — | 0.0061*** (2.41) | −0.0051* (−1.30) |
| *RACE* | −0.2010* (−2.23) | — | — |
| *HS* | 0.2407** (1.90) | — | — |
| *REGAR* | — | 1.1831*** (4.06) | — |
| *ICONS* | 0.4744*** (4.90) | 0.8663*** (5.12) | 0.3155*** (1.78) |
| *IMACH* | — | — | 0.4566* (1.42) |
| *IWHOL* | 0.5887*** (2.84) | — | — |
| *IAGMIN* | −0.5002** (−1.85) | — | — |
| *OCRFT* | — | — | 0.6437*** (3.45) |
| *OSALE* | — | 5.8084*** (6.13) | — |

(*Table continues*)

**TABLE 12.2.** *(Continued)*

| Variable | Crime group: Income | Consumption | Other |
|---|---|---|---|
| *SMSA* | — | 0.0184 | — |
| | | (0.12) | |
| *Y69* | −0.4211*** | — | — |
| | (−3.66) | | |
| *Y71* | −0.1611** | — | — |
| | (−1.89) | | |
| $\hat{\sigma}_{22}$ | 0.2283*** | 1.345*** | 0.2873*** |
| | (5.77) | (4.10) | (5.51) |
| $\hat{\sigma}_2 \div \overline{WAGAR}$[b] | 0.21 | 0.74 | 0.22 |
| *N* | 138 | 112 | 65 |

[a] Asterisk indicates level of significance, one-tailed test: *** = .01 level, ** = .05 level, * = .10 level. Values in parentheses under coefficients are "*t*-ratios" that are distributed $N(0, 1)$ asymptotically.
[b] $\hat{\sigma}_2$ is the estimated standard error.

results indicate that an individual will receive higher wages on release if he is a white high school graduate employed in construction, wholesaling, or primary industry; if his arrest rate is lower during the follow-up period; if he has a stable work record; if he is unsupervised when released; and if he was released in 1970, 1972, or 1973. These results are similar to those we obtained for all offenders (see Chapter 11) for most variables; however, the results for income offenders using the present model indicate that one human capital variable (high school graduation) and two additional industrial dummy variables (one for wholesale trade and one for employment in a primary industry) affect postrelease wages for this type of offender.

As noted earlier, our results for offenders in the "consumption" category are quite disappointing. Only postrelease arrest rates, failure to remain on the work release job after release, our measure of initial wealth *TPOWR*, and job characteristics are found to significantly affect wages. Our results indicate that, other things being equal, postrelease wages will be higher if the postrelease arrest rate is higher, if the individual left his work release job immediately after release, if he had more accumulated funds, and if he obtained a permanent job in construction or sales. For the variables in the model, these results are similar to the results we obtain for all offenders (see Chapter 11).

Our model appears to explain a great deal of the variation in wage rates for our residual group of offenders, but the coefficients on a number of variables are different than expected. Our results indicate that this group of offenders will have higher postrelease wages if they are arrested *more* frequently during the follow-up period, have more stable work histories, served *more* time in prison, *had* a serious alcohol problem, had *fewer* funds available when released, and were employed in construction, machine manufacturing, or crafts. The italicized words indicate unexpected results.

## 12.4. Summary and Conclusions

In this chapter, we developed an empirical model for the arrest rate during a follow-up period and for wages on the first job after release from incarceration. Our model sees the postrelease arrest rate and wages as being determined simultaneously. We estimate our model using a simultaneous Tobit technique that allows one dependent variable (the arrest rate) to be censored and the other (wages) to be continuous.

Our results for income offenders are quite supportive of our simultaneous model of criminal activity. Specifically, our results indicate that there are interrelationships between level of criminal activity and labor market performance for this type of offender. Higher arrest rates significantly decrease postrelease wages. Although the wage rate at release has no significant direct effect on the arrest rate, it does have indirect effects, which operate through the correlation between the error terms of the wage and arrest rate equations. We find higher probabilities of both conviction and imprisonment to deter significantly those who specialize in income offenses. Higher initial wealth is associated with lower levels of arrest. This finding is consistent with the hypothesis that prison releasees become more risk averse as they become wealthier. If this hypothesis were true, it would provide a potential explanation for recent finding that postrelease income supplements significantly decrease criminality. We find our measure of the expected unemployment rate to lead to lower arrest rates, an unexpected result. This finding is similar to our previous finding (see Chapter 10) for an alternative measure of the expected unemployment rate. It appears either that increased levels of unemployment are associated with lowered levels of criminal activity, at least for prison releasees who specialize in property offenses, or that we have yet to find an adequate proxy for this variable.

Of the taste variables, we find only age at first arrest, race, and education to affect the arrest rate significantly. The coefficients on these variables indicate that those who are older when first arrested, white, and better educated will be arrested with greater frequency, other things being equal. Our results for the wage-rate equation are broadly similar to the results reported in Chapter11, with one important exception: a human capital variable is now significant. Specifically, our results indicate that receipt of a high school diploma significantly increases the postrelease wage rate of income offenders.

Our results for offenders in the consumption and residual categories are less supportive of the traditional economic model of crime. It appears that, particularly for consumption offenders, it may be necessary to build special models of crime commission. Our results give some potentially useful insights for such models. First, they suggest that there is substantial interaction between criminal and labor market activity for consumption offenders. Higher arrest rates are associated with higher wages, perhaps indicating some sort of complementarity between the two types of activities. Further, it appears that variables reflecting actions of the criminal justice system only weakly affect the behavior of specialists in consumption offenses. Taste variables are more important determinants of arrest rates: being married, young, white, and unsupervised, and having a considerable previous criminal record, were associated with increased frequencies of arrest. Our results for supervision and marital status are particularly interesting. Of the three groups studied, postrelease supervision appears to have a beneficial effect on postrelease behavior only for offenders in the consumption category and appears to have a detrimental affect on the postrelease behavior of offenders in the income category. Perhaps it would be wise to devote more parole resources to those who commit assaultive crimes. Our result for marital status is intriguing and seems to reflect at least in part the prevalence of family violence.

The more complex simultaneous model of labor market and criminal activity appears to be needed least for our residual group of offenders. For this type of offender, labor market and criminal activity decisions appear to be made relatively independently.

## Notes to Chapter 12

1. Unemployment rates for the counties of North Carolina were estimated by the North Carolina Bureau of Employment Security Research. Quarterly estimates were available from 1968 to 1971 and monthly estimates for 1972 and 1973.

2. Specifically, we estimated our full model for the wage equation using an instrument for the arrest rate obtained from a Tobit analysis. From this model, we dropped all variables that were not significant at the 10% level (two-tailed test when no a priori sign for the coefficient and one-tailed otherwise). We next checked to see that all dropped variables were jointly as well as individually insignificant using an *F*-test.

3. This distinction is important. If it is the unobserved *ARRAT** that affects *WAGAR*, then the model developed by Amemiya (1979) and Nelson and Olson (1978) would be appropriate.

4. The program utilized was *GQOPT*.

5. The results reported in this chapter resulted in computer charges of almost $10,000.

6. The test of significance for these effects is the test of significance for $\sigma_{12}$.

# PART III

## The Use of Production and Cost Theory In Criminal Justice Research

In this part of the book, we discuss and estimate cost functions for large-scale prisons. We begin in Chapter 13 by reviewing the economic theory of production and cost. A standard definition of a cost function is that it gives the minimum possible level of cost as a function of the level of output and of the prices of the inputs into the productive process. We discuss various properties of total and average costs in the short run, in which the capital stock is assumed to be fixed, and in the long run, in which the capital stock is assumed to be variable. We present commonly used functional forms for cost functions and discuss some statistical considerations in fitting these to data. We also discuss the implications of the failure of firms to minimize cost; this is especially relevant when dealing with organizations such as prisons, for which profit is not an objective.

In Chapter 14 we develop operational models of the short-run and long-run costs of large-scale prisons. We choose the individual prison as our unit of analysis, and we choose our measure of the direct output of a prison as the number of person-days of incarceration. This is a measure of confinement, which can in turn be viewed as an input to other socially desirable goals such as punishment, incapacitation, deterrence, and rehabilitation. We therefore introduce into the model measures of the quality of output (e.g., provision of rehabilitative services) as well as measures of the quality of the inputs (e.g., the amount of living space per inmate). We choose a particular functional form for the cost function and a set of prisons and period of time for which the cost function will be fit.

In Chapter 15, we estimate a short-run cost function for each of 22 federal prisons and 8 California prisons. These cost functions are estimated from a time series of observations for each prison and are interpreted as short-run cost functions because there is little or no variation in the capital stock of a given prison over the sample time period. Our most important finding is that for most prisons, short-run average costs decrease as prison size increases, at least over reasonable levels of output. We also present some interesting and useful results about the effects of other variables on costs; for example, that older inmates are cheaper to incarcerate than younger inmates and that drug addicts are more expensive to incarcerate than nonaddicts.

In Chapter 16 we estimate a long-run cost function for a group of six Federal Correctional Institutions that appear to have identical technologies. This cost function is interpreted as a long-run cost function because there is considerable variation in the capital stock across institutions. The long-run cost function is U-shaped, with a minimum point at an inmate population of 1075. Thus the prison with the minimum possible level of average costs is large, but not huge. Deviations from this economically optimal size are costly. A prison with a population of 600 inmates will have an average cost that is about 50% higher than the optimal size prison; so will a prison with a population of 1800 inmates.

Overall, we feel that our attempt to apply the economic theory of cost to large-scale prisons is fairly successful. For the most part, our results are plausible. The result that larger prisons are cheaper to operate is very robust to changes in the specification and data and is supported very strongly by the data, and it has obvious policy implications. Some of our other results are less strongly supported by the data, and further work will be necessary to see how much faith they warrant. However, we hope that, at the least, we have established the feasibility and usefulness of this type of analysis.

# Chapter 13

## Modern Production and Cost Theory and Its Use in the Study of Production in Public Organizations

### 13.1. Introduction

Economists have spent much time and energy in recent years analyzing the way in which production takes place and the costs associated with such production. Although much of this work is mathematical and theoretical, there have also been numerous practical applications of production and cost theory to study the nature of production in many different settings [see Fuss, McFadden, and Mundlak (1978, pp. 267–268) for a brief survey]. These applications were made possible by the increasing availability of data for productive units and the development of modern econometric techniques. Also, although production and cost theory was originally developed for profit-seeking private-sector firms, it has by now been adapted to analyze production in public nonprofit organizations.[1]

To set the stage for our use of production and cost theory in analyzing the nature of production in large-scale prisons, in this chapter we introduce the reader to the basic concepts utilized in production and cost theory. In addition, we suggest practical applications for various concepts developed in production and cost theory. This chapter serves as background for the chapters that follow and may be skipped by those familiar with modern production and cost theory.

The organization of this chapter is as follows. In the next section we describe the standard, intermediate textbook version of the neoclassical theory of cost and production. This section serves as background for those readers who have either not been exposed to this theory or whose exposure did not "take" or has worn off. In Section 13.3 we extend this model by discussing more advanced concepts (i.e., elasticity of substitution and homotheticity), and the way in which the theory developed has been represented mathematically (i.e., functional forms) and estimated empirically. Section 13.4 describes the way in which production and cost theory has been adapted to analyze the nature of production in public organizations. The final section summarizes the chapter and briefly outlines the way in which we use the theory and methods described to analyze the nature of production in large-scale prisons in the chapters that follow.

## 13.2. The Basic Theory of Cost and Production[2]

Consider a profit-maximizing firm that employs homogeneous inputs to produce a single homogeneous output. Classical economic theory develops a model of cost and production for such a firm, assuming that the firm has no effect on either the price of the product it produces or the inputs it purchases. That is, in originally developing their production and cost models for a simple firm, economists assumed perfect competition in both output and input markets. Under these circumstances, the firm maximizes profits by selecting a level of output in the short run and a firm size and level of output in the long run.

Economists define the *short run* as that period in which at least one input is not subject to variation by the firm; the "fixed" input is usually thought to be the firm's physical capital stock. On the other hand, the *long run* is that period in which the firm may vary its use of all inputs. Note that these two time periods are operationally rather than temporally defined. In the long run the firm just described, because of its competitive environment, must be both technically efficient (i.e., able to produce its output with the fewest resources possible) and allocatively efficient (i.e., able to produce its output with the least cost combination of inputs). Otherwise it will lose money and be forced out of business by its more efficient competitors.

Economists characterize the technical conditions governing the firm's production activities by use of a production function. A production function summarizes mathematically the nature of technically efficient production. It indicates the maximum output attainable for any specified level of inputs, given the existing technology or state of the art.

The nature of a firm's production function depends on the time period under consideration. For simplicity, we shall assume that there are only two inputs—capital and labor—to the production process under consideration. Capital inputs include all buildings and machinery used in the productive process, and labor inputs consist of the work of all employees. In the short run, economists usually assume that the firm can vary its labor inputs (by changing the hours of its employees or by hiring more employees) but cannot vary its capital inputs. For example, the firm cannot double its floor space instantaneously. Economists represent the firm's short-run productive relationship, its production function, as

$$Q = f_1(L, \bar{K}), \tag{13.2.1}$$

where $Q$ is a measure of output (e.g., the number of units produced), $f_1$ a general (unspecified) function, $L$ a measure of the amount of labor utilized in production (e.g., person-hours), and $K$ a measure of the amount of capital utilized in production (e.g., machine hours). The bar over $\bar{K}$ indicates that in the period under consideration the amount of capital utilized is fixed—beyond the control of the firm. In words, Eq. (13.2.1) simply indicates that the quantity $Q$ of output produced by the firm is some function $f_1$ of the amount of inputs $L$ and $\bar{K}$ the firm employs when its technology is given.

As noted previously, the firm maximizes profit by choosing a level of output. In the short run the firm can change output only by changing the amount of labor it employs, because all other factors are beyond its control. A measure of the responsiveness of output to a change in labor is the *marginal product* of labor, defined as the partial derivative of $Q$ with respect to $L$:

$$\text{marginal product of } L = \partial Q/\partial L = \partial f_1/\partial L, \tag{13.2.2}$$

where $f_1$ is the function defined in (13.2.1). Roughly speaking, it measures the change in output resulting from a one-unit change in $L$: for example, the additional output that would result from using one more person-hour of labor. It is important to note that the quantity of all other inputs (in this case, $\bar{K}$) is held constant in computing this marginal product.

The marginal product that results from the employment of one more laborer will depend on the total number of employees and the amount of capital available to the firm. At first the additional product resulting from one more employee will increase as the number of employees increases. That is, the extra product for the last worker will be greater than that for the previous workers hired. This is because of increased specialization of labor and improved utilization of machines. However, as increasing amounts of labor crowd around a given number of machines in a building of given size, a point will be reached beyond which the additional output attributable to the last worker hired will be below that of previous workers. This relationship is known as the *law of diminishing returns* and has been observed to hold for numerous productive processes. Mathematically, it means that the second partial derivative of $Q$ with respect to $L$, $(\partial^2 Q/\partial L^2)$, is negative for large enough $L$.

In the long run, the firm has considerably more flexibility because it can now decide on the amount of capital and type of technology to employ as well as the amount of labor to hire. Economists represent the firm's long-run production function in its most general form as

$$Q = f_2(L, K), \tag{13.2.3}$$

where $L$ and $K$ are as defined before and $f_2$ is an unspecified function. Note that $K$ no longer has a bar over it because the amount of capital is now free to vary. The firm may select the best-available technology and a plant size designed to produce its preferred level of output most efficiently. The long run is often referred to as the planning horizon, and the questions facing the firm are those associated with charting the evolution of the firm over time: for example, what is the least-cost size for the physical plant and the least-cost technology, given input prices?

An alternative way of looking at the productive relations of the firm is through the firm's cost function. The cost function indicates the minimum cost of producing any specified level of output, given input prices and the prevailing technology. In the short run (when the amount of capital a firm may use is fixed) the firm's total cost of production may be represented as

$$SRTC = P_K\bar{K} + f_3(Q, \bar{K}, P_L), \tag{13.2.4}$$

where $SRTC$ is short-run total cost, $P_K$ and $P_L$ the prices of a unit of capital and labor, respectively, $f_3$ an unspecified function, and all other symbols are as defined previously. Often, for convenience and ease of exposition economists will work with the average-cost rather than the total-cost function. This average-cost function is obtained by dividing Eq. (13.2.4) by the level of output to obtain the cost per unit of output:

$$\frac{SRTC}{Q} = SRAC = \frac{P_K\bar{K}}{Q} + \frac{f_3(Q, \bar{K}, P_L)}{Q}, \tag{13.2.5}$$

where $SRAC$ is short-run average cost and all other symbols are as defined previously. Note that in the short run, costs are made up of two distinct elements. The first term on the right-hand side of Eq. (13.2.5) is the cost per unit of output of the fixed amount of capital that the firm employs and is referred to as average fixed costs. The second term is the cost per unit of output of the variable amount of labor that the firm chooses to employ and is referred to as average variable costs. Note that in the short run the fixed costs of production must be paid regardless of how much the firm produces or whether it produces at all, whereas the amount of variable costs incurred by the firm is determined by the firm when it decides on a level of output.

The precise way in which short-run average costs change with output will depend on the technology employed by the firm. However, economists have often found short-run average cost curves to assume a U shape. Consider why this might be so. Note that average fixed cost declines continually as output increases, although at a decreasing rate. This is so because the numerator of average fixed cost is a constant, whereas the denominator (output) is continually increasing. The general nature of the relationship between average fixed costs and output is illustrated in Fig. 13.1.

The way in which average variable cost changes with changes in output is more complex. Recall that, according to the law of diminishing returns, the amount of additional output forthcoming as a result of hiring an additional laborer (marginal product) depends on the total number of laborers employed. When there are few employees, the additional output increases with each additional laborer hired. However, as more and more laborers are hired, a level of employment is reached beyond which the amount of extra output decreases with each additional laborer hired. This implies that, beyond this point, the additional cost of producing an additional unit of output will increase; beyond the point of diminishing returns, an additional unit of output requires more additional labor, and therefore adds more to cost.

We define *marginal cost* as the derivative of total cost with respect to output:

$$SRMC = d(SRTC)/dQ = \partial f_3/\partial Q. \tag{13.2.6}$$

Roughly speaking, it measures the change in cost resulting from a one-unit change in output. As argued in the previous paragraph, the law of diminishing returns implies that marginal cost eventually (i.e., beyond some level of output) increases as output increases. The expected relationship between marginal costs and output is depicted in Fig. 13.1.

The shape of the average variable cost curve is determined by the shape and level of the marginal cost curve. As long as marginal cost is below average variable cost, average variable cost will be decreasing, because the extra cost of producing the last unit of output is below the average cost of producing all units. (For example, if 4 units of output are produced at an average variable cost of \$10 and a fifth unit is produced at a marginal cost of

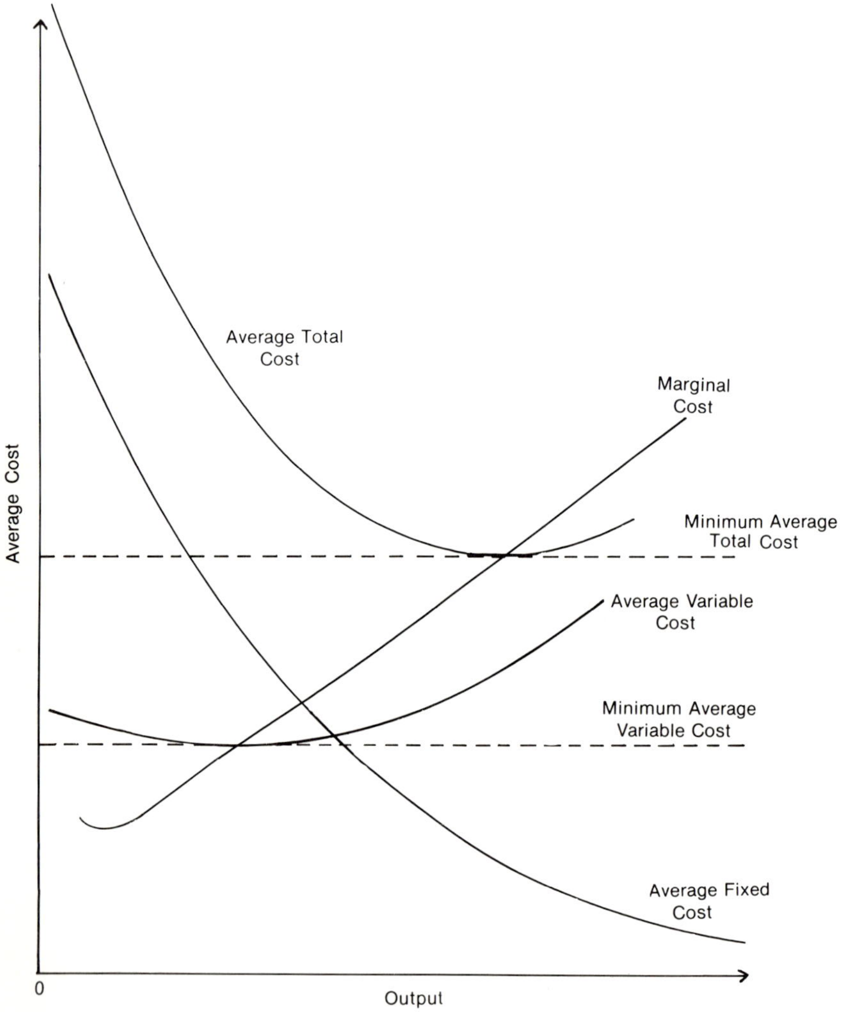


**Fig. 13.1** Relationship between various costs and output in the short run.

\$5, average variable cost falls to \$45/5 = \$9.) Conversely, average variable cost must be increasing whenever marginal cost exceeds average variable costs. The average variable cost curve is depicted in Fig. 13.1; note that its relationship to the marginal cost curve is as just described.

Because short-run average total cost is simply the sum of average fixed and average variable cost, it will also usually be U-shaped, but the point at which it is a minimum will be to the right of the minimum point of average variable costs, because average fixed costs are continually declining. The way in which economists expect short-run average total costs to change with changes in output is also illustrated in Fig. 13.1.

Note that one would have to observe the firm producing a wide range of outputs in a relatively short period to observe the entire short-run average total cost curve. If a firm produces a relatively narrow range of outputs, one may observe short-run average costs only decreasing with output, more or less unchanged as output changes, or only increasing with output.

Short-run cost functions can provide managers with information that will aid them in planning their operations. For example, a profit-maximizing firm in a competitive industry should set its output at the level at which marginal cost equals the price it receives for a unit of output. This may not be very relevant to nonprofit entities such as prisons. As a more relevant example, knowledge of the short-run cost function allows one to determine what level of output will give a minimum unit cost of production, given that the size of the plant cannot be altered. In the correctional context, if one were to obtain estimates of short-run cost curves for each correctional institution, one could determine for each institution the level of population that would be associated with minimum costs per confined day. Further, for an existing prison system, short-run cost functions can indicate the way in which inmates should be assigned to prisons to minimize costs. To minimize total system costs, one should assign inmates to prisons in such a way that the extra (marginal) cost of holding the last inmate at each institution in the system is equal. Although such least-cost assignment may not be possible because it implies either unacceptable population mixes (e.g., men housed with women or short-term, youthful offenders housed with long-term, adult felons) or unacceptable security levels for some inmates, the short-run cost function can still indicate the least-cost assignment of inmates given these and other constraints.[3]

Short-run cost functions may also be used for projecting likely costs associated with different levels of output and different input costs. In a correctional setting, short-run cost curves could be combined with population projections to obtain systemwide and individual-institution cost projections for use in budget preparation and executive and legislative review. In addition, the likely budgetary effects of input cost inflation could be calculated.

In the long run, the firm may vary its employment of capital as well as labor. This means that, in the long run, the manager of the firm will select a plant that will produce the firm's output at minimum cost. The long-run cost function indicates the minimum cost of producing all possible levels of output when the manager is free to vary the size of the plant as well as the quantity of labor utilized. That is, each point on a long-run cost curve is associated with a plant of whatever size is necessary to minimize the cost of producing that output. This situation contrasts markedly with the situation in the short run, where we considered the costs of producing various output in a plant of given size.

In the long run, costs are a function of the level of output and the prices of capital and labor, given that the best productive technology is utilized. Formally,

$$LRTC = f_4(Q, P_K, P_L), \tag{13.2.7}$$

where $LRTC$ is long-run total costs, $f_4$ an unspecified function, and all other symbols are as defined previously. Dividing Eq. (13.2.7) by output, one may obtain an equation for long-run average costs $LRAC$:

$$LRTC/Q = LRAC = f_4(Q, P_K, P_L)/Q. \tag{13.2.8}$$

The relationship between long-run average costs and output will depend on the way in which average costs change when the entire scale of operation of the firm is altered. Economists refer to the way in which long-run average costs change when output changes as returns to scale. "Increasing returns to scale" are said to exist when larger output is associated with lower long-run average costs; "decreasing returns to scale," when a larger output entails higher long-run average costs. Finally, "constant returns to scale" are said to exist if a larger output is associated with no change in long-run average costs.

The exact shape of the long-run average cost curve will depend on the nature of returns to scale facing the firm. Economists often assume that long-run average costs curves are U-shaped. This implies that increasing returns to scale prevail as one moves from very small plants to larger ones, that constant returns to scale prevail for plants of middle size, and that decreasing returns to scale prevail for very large plants. This situation is illustrated in Fig. 13.2. The actual shape of the long-run average cost curve for any given output, however, is an empirical question with flat (constant returns to scale at all outputs), continuously decreasing (increasing returns to scale at all outputs), and continuously increasing (decreasing returns to scale at all outputs) long-run average cost functions as well as U-shaped functions possible.

Returns to scale in cost functions have a counterpart in *homogeneity* in production functions. Homogeneity tells by its degree what happens to output when all inputs change proportionately. Again, consider what happens to output if all inputs double. If the production function is homogenous of degree less than one, output will less than double and decreasing returns will prevail. If the production function is homogenous of degree equal to one, output will exactly double and returns to scale will be constant.

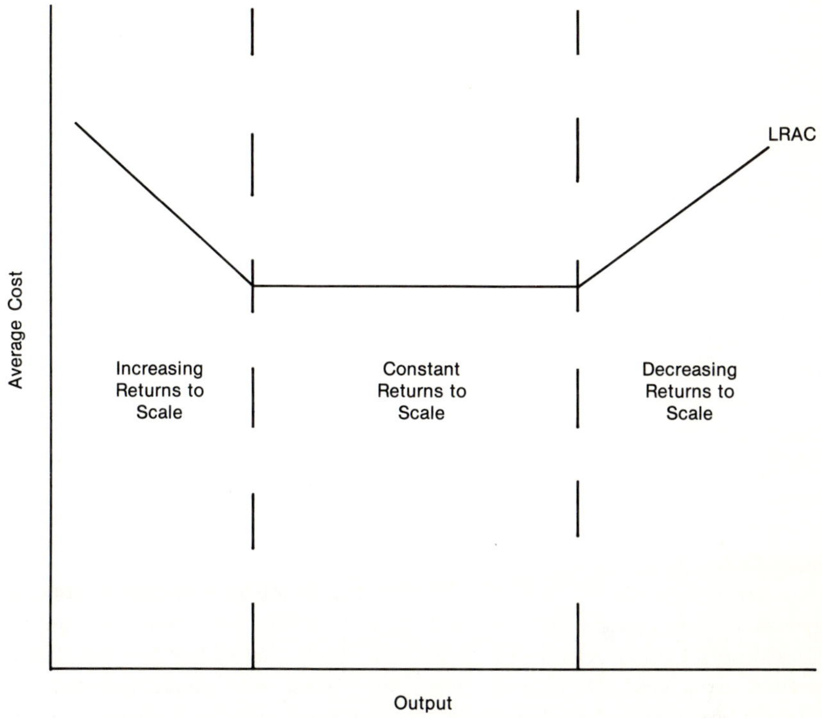


**Fig. 13.2** Relationship between long-run average cost and output.

If the production function is homogenous of degree greater than one, production will more than double and increasing returns will prevail.

Estimates of long-run cost functions allow one to determine what size plant will produce desired output with minimum average costs. For example, in the correctional context, one could determine the size of prison to build to have the lowest-possible prison system costs. Another use of the long-run cost function is to allow managers to estimate the likely long-run budgetary effects of changes in input costs.

This discussion of cost and production relationships makes it clear that there is an intimate connection between the production function (which represents the technology available to the firm) and the cost function (which gives the cost of producing any level of output, given that technology). The exact nature of this relationship was first rigorously developed by Shepard (1953, 1970), who demonstrates that there exists a unique and reversible one-to-one relationship between "well-behaved"[4] production and cost functions. At least in principle, one can learn exactly the same facts about a given productive unit by studying either the production or cost function for the unit. For example, one can determine the nature of returns to scale for a firm equally well by examining its production or cost function.

## 13.3. Some Extensions of Production and Cost Theory

Although the simple model just developed illustrates basic features of economic cost and production theory, a number of extensions are necessary before this theory can be applied. The most important extensions that we discuss in this section are the specification of functional forms for the cost and production functions and the specification of likely random elements in the observed production and cost data. We shall discuss each of these extensions in turn.

Before economists can estimate either a cost or production function, it is necessary for them to specify mathematically the nature of the relationship between output and inputs or among costs, input prices, and output—that is, the functional form of the production or cost function. Knowledge of the nature of technological relations restricts the functional forms that economists will accept as reasonable for both production and cost relationships. For example, most economists insist that the functional form used for a production or cost relationship reflect the law of diminishing returns.

In addition to placing technological restrictions on functional forms, economists generally make a number of other assumptions that restrict the nature of the technological relationship that may be observed. For example, restrictions on the nature of returns to scale are commonly imposed.

Many commonly used production and cost functions also place restrictions on the *elasticity of substitution*, a measure of the ease with which one type of input can be substituted for another. Consider a change in the ratio $P_K/P_L$ of input prices. This will cause a change in the ratio $K/L$ of the input levels. The elasticity of substitution is then defined as the percentage change in $K/L$ divided by the percentage change in $P_K/P_L$. For example, an elasticity of substitution equal to one implies that a 10% increase in the price of labor relative to the price of capital will lead to a 10% increase in the use of capital relative to labor. An elasticity of substitution equal to zero indicates that it is impossible to substitute one factor for another. For example, when there are only capital and labor inputs and the elasticity of substitution is zero, the product can be produced with only one combination of capital and labor. As the elasticity of substitution becomes larger, the manager has more and more flexibility in substituting one factor for another in the productive process.

The earliest functional form used and one that is still much utilized today is the Cobb–Douglas form. The simplest Cobb–Douglas form implies the production function

$$Q = AL^{\alpha}K^{1-\alpha}, \tag{13.3.1}$$

where $A$ and $\alpha$ are parameters to be estimated and the other symbols are as defined in Section 13.2.

The Cobb–Douglas form is restrictive in two important ways. First, it assumes constant returns to scale, and hence yields average total costs that are invariant with respect to output. Second, its elasticity of substitution equals one for all levels of output.

Under the assumption that producers minimize costs, one may obtain the long-run cost function associated with the preceding functional form. Specifically, if the firm minimizes total production costs and is constrained by a simple Cobb–Douglas technology, the firm's long-run average cost function will be

$$LRAC = A^{-1}\alpha^{-\alpha}(1 - \alpha)^{\alpha-1}P_L^{\alpha}P_K^{1-\alpha}. \tag{13.3.2}$$

Note that because the simple Cobb–Douglas form assumes constant returns to scale, long-run average costs depend only on the level of input prices, not on the level of output. Note also that all the parameters that appear in the production function also appear in the long-run average cost function, and thus these two functions can provide exactly the same information about the nature of production.

If we assume that the amount of capital employed by the firm is constant, one may obtain the short-run average cost function

$$SRAC = (P_K K/Q) + P_L(A^{-1/\alpha}K^{(\alpha-1)/\alpha}Q^{(1-\alpha)/\alpha}). \tag{13.3.3}$$

Note that short-run average costs depend on the level of input prices $P_K$ and $P_L$, the amount of capital employed by the firm, and the level of output. The amount of capital and the level of output affect average costs in the short run, although not in the long run, because the law of diminishing returns holds in the short run even if returns to scale are constant in the long run.

In recent years, economists have used a number of forms that make less restrictive assumptions about the nature of returns to scale and the elasticity of substitution. We shall discuss three such forms—the generalized Cobb–Doublas, the constant elasticity of substitution, and the homothetic constant elasticity of substitution—and present the mathematical form of the production functions implied. Associated with each of these production functions is a short- and long-run cost function; however, we shall not present the mathematical form of these associated functions at this time.

The simple Cobb–Douglas form generalizes easily to allow returns to scale to be increasing or decreasing for all levels of output, but it cannot allow returns to scale to vary with output or the elasticity of substitution to be other than one. The mathematical form of this generalized Cobb–Douglas production function is

$$Q = AL^{\alpha}K^{\beta}, \tag{13.3.4}$$

where $\beta$ is now an additional parameter to be estimated and $\alpha + \beta$ gives the value of returns to scale: increasing if $\alpha + \beta > 1$, decreasing if $\alpha + \beta < 1$, and constant [as in Eq. (13.3.1)] if $\alpha + \beta = 1$. In any case, the level of returns to scale does not vary with output.

To allow the elasticity of substitution to vary from one, economists were forced to use more complex functional forms. A popular form of this type is the *constant elasticity of substitution* production function. The mathematical form of this function is

$$Q = \gamma[\delta L^{-\rho} + (1 - \delta)K^{-\rho}]^{-m/\rho}, \tag{13.3.5}$$

where the elasticity of substitution $\sigma = 1/(1 + \rho)$; $\gamma, \delta, \rho$ and $m$ are parameters to be estimated; and other symbols are as defined previously. This functional form assumes that the elasticity of substitution is a constant, but it may be either greater than or less than one. Returns to scale for this functional form need not equal one but they may not vary with output.[5]

Most recently economists have sought functional forms that allow either the elasticity of substitution or returns to scale (or both) to vary with output. One class of functions that allows returns to scale to vary with output is the class of *homothetic* functions. All homothetic functions assume that the elasticity of substitution is independent of output. That is, the elasticity of substitution does not depend on the level of output of the firm but rather is the same for all output levels. One popular type of homothetic form merely transforms the output variable of a production function to allow returns to scale to vary. Thus we can develop a homothetic Cobb–Douglas production function by an appropriate transformation of output. This function is

$$Qe^{\theta Q} = AL^{\alpha}K^{\beta}, \tag{13.3.6}$$

where $e$ is the base of natural logarithms, $\theta$ a parameter to be estimated, and all other symbols are as defined previously. The elasticity of substitution is still one, but returns to scale are $(\alpha + \beta)/(1 + \theta Q)$.

Similarly, if one wishes to allow the elasticity of substitution to be other than one and returns to scale to vary with output, one could use a homothetic constant elasticity of substitution production function

$$Qe^{\theta Q} = \gamma[\delta K^{-\rho} + (1 - \delta)L^{-\rho}]^{-m/\rho}, \tag{13.3.7}$$

where all symbols are as defined previously. These rather complex forms allow returns to scale to vary widely with changes in output and will allow one to observe the classical U-shaped average cost curves hypothesized by neoclassical theory if such cost curves are indeed appropriate for the technology being studied. This was not the case for any of the functional forms discussed previously.[6]

Finally, there are a variety of so-called flexible forms, which place few or no restrictions on the technology. Examples include the generalized Leontief (Diewert, 1971), generalized quadratic (Denny, 1974), and translog (Christensen, Jorgensen, and Lau, 1973) functional forms. These functional forms place virtually no restrictions on returns to scale or on the elasticity of substitution. Because of their flexibility, they are thought to be able to provide a good approximation to any well-behaved technology.

The most popular of the flexible forms is the translog, which is of the following mathematical form:

$$\ln Q = \beta_0 + \beta_1 \ln L + \beta_2 \ln K + \beta_3 (\ln K)^2 + \beta_4 (\ln L)^2 + \beta_5 (\ln K)(\ln L), \tag{13.3.8}$$

where $\beta_0, \ldots, \beta_5$ are parameters to be estimated. Its main problem, which it shares with the other flexible forms, is that it contains a lot of parameters to be estimated (which is indeed exactly why it is so flexible). Thus it may be difficult or impossible to obtain precise estimates of these parameters from a data set of reasonable size. In the translog case, the presence of squared $[(\ln K)^2, (\ln L)^2]$ and interactive $[(\ln K)(\ln L)]$ terms in the inputs makes multicollinearity a likely problem. The levels of the inputs, their squared values, and their values interacted are likely to be highly correlated. This high degree of correlation means that it will be difficult to separate out the individual effects of these variables on costs; that is, parameter estimates will be imprecise.

The preceding discussion of functional forms has been presented in terms of production functions. However, the same functional forms can be (and commonly are) used to represent cost functions. For example, with two inputs the translog cost function would be

$$\begin{aligned}\ln C = {} & \alpha_0 + \alpha_1 \ln Q + \alpha_2 \ln P_K + \alpha_3 \ln P_L \\ & + \alpha_4 (\ln Q)^2 + \alpha_5 (\ln P_K)^2 + \alpha_6 (\ln P_L)^2 \\ & + \alpha_7 (\ln Q)(\ln P_K) + \alpha_8 (\ln Q)(\ln P_L) + \alpha_9 (\ln P_K)(\ln P_L),\end{aligned} \tag{13.3.9}$$

the obvious adaptation of (13.3.8). However, it should be stressed that (13.3.9) is not the cost function that is dual to the production function (13.3.8), nor conversely. One makes a different assumption by assuming a translog cost function than by assuming a translog production function, and the same is true for all of the functional forms we have so far discussed, except the Cobb–Douglas form.

Which functional form will be appropriate for studying a particular productive process will depend on the nature of the technological process used and on the ease with which parameters of interest can be estimated. One should always choose the simplest functional form that is consistent with prior knowledge about the production process. For example, if we are quite certain that the elasticity of substitution does not vary with output but feel that returns to scale might, we might choose a homothetic constant elasticity of substitution form. However, if we know very little and are willing to assume very little about the production process studied, we may prefer one of the flexible forms, such as the translog. Of course, this must also depend on the size and quality of the data set. If the number of observations is small, for example, we cannot expect to estimate more than a few parameters successfully, and a fairly restrictive functional form will probably have to be used. Conversely, with more observations we can contemplate estimating more parameters and choose a form with more flexibility.

The functional forms just discussed all assumed an exact relationship between the level of output and the level of inputs or between the level of costs and the level of input prices and output. This is normally not the case for a number of reasons, including incomplete knowledge of product prices and technology, random events, behavior inconsistent with cost minimization, and measurement error. Given these factors, it is necessary to introduce random error terms, which will mirror these random effects, into our model. The exact way in which we introduce these random effects will depend on our knowledge of the nature of these effects and the assumptions we are willing to make.

An important first step is to determine which variables are within firm control (endogenous to the model) and which are largely beyond it (exogenous). In a correctional setting, the level of output (i.e., number of inmates confined) is largely beyond the warden's (or other prison administrators') control, because the prison system is required to accept all inmates sentenced to prison, and the warden's control over the timing of release (e.g., termination of sentence, parole, and pardon) is limited. On the other hand, costs are much more within the control of prison administrators, in the sense that their decisions affect costs. The costs of running a prison will depend on the type of labor and capital utilized (the technology) and the efficiency with which these inputs are combined. Prison wardens have considerable flexibility in their input-purchasing decisions, as long as they stay within budget. Indeed, the prisons of a number of correctional systems have been characterized as "feudal fiefs." In addition, through direct management, prison wardens can, to at least some extent, control the efficiency with which inputs are utilized.

Given that output is largely beyond prison administrators' control and that costs are within it, it will be more appropriate to estimate a cost function than a production function. The reason is simple. In estimating a regression equation, the desirable statistical properties of the estimates depend on the assumption that the error term is uncorrelated with the explanatory variables. In a cost function, the explanatory variables are the level of output and the input prices, and the error term reflects (at least in part) the decisions of the management (prison administrators). Thus it is plausible to assume the error to be uncorrelated with the explanatory variables, as long as output and the prices of the inputs are indeed not under management's control. Such an assumption would be less plausible in a production function, because the explanatory variables there are the levels of the inputs, some of which are presumably subject to the decisions of the firm. (For example, the prison administration can change the size of its labor force.)

A second important step is to decide exactly how to enter the random error term into the equation to be estimated. In general, this is done in such a way as to make the error term enter linearly into the equation, so that the equation can be estimated by some version of least squares. For example, to estimate the average cost curve (13.3.2), the error term $\varepsilon$ could be entered by multiplying the right-hand side by $e^{\varepsilon}$. Upon taking logarithms, (13.3.2) then becomes linear in $P_L$, $P_K$, and $\varepsilon$ and can be estimated by ordinary least squares.

## 13.4. Adaptations of Simple Production and Cost Theory

In addition to specifying a functional form and the type of random effects, economists have sometimes found it necessary to drop a number of the simplifying assumptions used in developing the simple model of Section 13.2. First, firms rarely produce a single homogeneous output. Many firms produce multiple outputs, and the outputs produced by either a single- or multiproduct firm are often of varying quality. A number of authors [see Hall (1973) and Hasenkamp (1976)] have explored both theoretically and empirically the nature of production in a multiproduct firm. However, work in this area is in its infancy, and as one might expect, the nature of the production process in the multiproduct firm rapidly becomes complex.

Even if a firm produces a single output, the output is rarely homogeneous. For example, although some automobile plants produce a single output (e.g., only one model of automobile), this output is of highly variable quality (e.g., the model can have all accessories or none). Researchers have adjusted for differences in product quality by introducing a number of quality indicators into the production or cost functions. For example, the general long-run average cost function [Eq. (13.2.8)] when output is of varying quality becomes

$$LRAC = f_5(Q, P_K, P_L, A)/Q, \tag{13.4.1}$$

where $A$ is a vector containing variables reflecting differences in product quality and all other symbols are defined as before. In applied research many researchers have succeeded in avoiding the difficulties associated with analyzing the multiproduct firm by considering relatively similar products to be a single product of varying quality.

Economists also often find it necessary to drop the assumption that firms seek to maximize profits. In the perfectly competitive system described in Section 13.2, firms are forced to attempt to maximize profit to survive. As noted there, competition from other firms forces each firm to produce efficiently. However, when competition is not present, firms are free to choose a course of action other than profit maximization. If the manager is also the owner of the firm, he or she is still likely to pursue the goal of profit maximization to maximize personal income. However, when management and ownership are separated, as they are in the modern corporation, profit maximization requires that corporate owners either closely supervise production or that a carefully constructed set of managerial guidelines be developed. If profit motivation is not enforced on managers by stockholders, they may choose to maximize market share, sales, or even managerial perquisites. Managers of firms with market power may choose to lead the quiet life, foregoing aggressive, profit-maximizing tactics for satisficing behavior. Such behavior does not usually lead to efficiency in production.

When one moves from the profit-making sector of the economy to the non-profit-making and public sectors, the plausibility of profit making as a goal disappears by definition. Consider the situation in a public productive unit, such as a police department or prison unit. The public provides such bodies with funds to produce certain goods and services. Most public services are not sold but rather are supplied to all who are eligible according to some set of guidelines. For example, police services are provided to all residents of a city, and correctional services are provided to all criminals with certain types of sentences. This means that, to some degree, public managers often do not control the type of product they produce or the conditions under which it is produced. Researchers [e.g., see Hirsch (1973)] studying production in public bodies suggest that the conditions of production and type of product imposed on public manager by those providing funds be controlled when estimating cost and production functions. Making these modifications, one might specify a general long-run average cost function for a public productive unit as

$$LRAC = f_6(Q, P_K, P_L, A, S)/Q, \tag{13.4.2}$$

where all symbols are defined as before, except that public managers may not control all aspects of product quality (all variables in the vector $A$), and $S$

is a vector of variables measuring the service conditions under which production takes place.

Because public bodies that do not sell their output do not receive revenue, they cannot maximize profits even if they wish to. Rather, the public often judges such bodies by its satisfaction with the services provided for its tax dollars. Although some public bodies seek to produce their services at minimum costs, many others do not; rather, they resort to various alternative types of bureaucratic decision making, such as maximizing their budget or the size of their organizations [Orzechowski (1977) provides a review of this literature]. In situations like this, efficiency cannot be assumed, and observed productive relationships do not well reflect the production and cost functions developed by economists. That is, actual production results probably do not indicate the maximum output attainable with the given inputs, and costs observed are not the minimum attainable. In such cases, the estimated production and cost functions are best viewed as representations of the actual behavior found in the sample and not as representations of efficient behavior.[7] For many policy purposes, representations of actual behavior are very useful—for example, in deciding how to allocate prisoners to prisons in the least costly way.

## 13.5. Summary and Conclusions

In this chapter, we surveyed relevant aspects of the economic theory of cost and production and discussed possible uses of this type of analysis for public managers, particularly correctional decision makers. In Section 13.2 we considered the productive relations of a simple, profit-maximizing firm operating under classical economic assumptions. We discussed the nature of both short- and long-run production and cost functions for such a firm, and we introduced the concept of duality.

In Section 13.3, we discussed two extensions of cost and production theory that are necessary to apply the theory: (1) the specification of a mathematical form for the production or cost function and (2) the specification of likely random elements in the production or cost data. We introduced a measure of the ease with which inputs can be substituted in a production process (the elasticity of substitution) and the concept of homotheticity. We discussed a number of mathematical forms of production and cost functions with which economists have worked. Specifically, we discussed and presented the mathematical formula for five functional forms (Cobb–Douglas, constant elasticity of substitution, homothetic versions of these two functions, and translog). We considered the relative merits of these different functional forms and criteria for choosing among them in particular applications. Using the simple Cobb–Douglas form, we illustrated how duality theory allows one to obtain the cost function associated with a production function. Finally, we discussed and illustrated the way in which random elements can be introduced when obtaining a form to estimate production or cost functions.

In Section 13.4, we discussed the way in which economists have adapted their cost and production models when there is not a single homogeneous output, when profit maximization is not an appropriate behavioral assumption, and when (as is usually the case in public organizations) certain external conditions are imposed on the way in which the productive unit produces its output. In doing so we set the stage for our empirical work to be presented in the following chapters in which we estimate short-run and long-run cost functions for large-scale prisons.

## Notes to Chapter 13

1. See Alesch and Dougharty (1971), Hirsch (1973), or Vernez (1976) for surveys of early work and Witte (1983) for a discussion of more recent work in six areas (education, fire protection, hospitals, libraries, police protection, and large-scale prisons).

2. More detailed examination of the concepts treated in this section can be had in any intermediate microeconomic theory text. See, for example, Leftwich (1979, chs. 8 and 9).

3. John Witters, Information Systems Officer, Federal Bureau of Prisons, pointed out the importance of these constraints to us.

4. The conditions necessary for the function to be well behaved are not very restrictive. See Varian (1978) for a discussion of these conditions.

5. See Varian (1978) for a more detailed discussion of both the Cobb–Douglas and constant elasticity of substitution forms.

6. See Shephard (1953) for a general discussion of homothetic functions and Lovell (1973) for a development of the implications of the homothetic form for the long-run cost function.

7. This distinction has given rise to the study of so-called "frontier" production functions, which attempt to represent efficient behavior. A survey of this literature can be found in Førsund, Lovell, and Schmidt (1980).

# Chapter 14

## A Model of Costs for Large-Scale Prisons

### 14.1. Introduction

In this chapter we develop a model of costs for large-scale prisons based on the material presented in the previous chapter, our knowledge of the California, North Carolina, and federal prison systems, and the extensive and diverse literature on prisons. The development of a theoretical model of costs requires that a number of assumptions and decisions be made: for example, what the productive unit is, what it is seeking to achieve, and what it is producing. Once the general nature of production is decided, the researcher faces a number of more specific decisions relating to the way in which the theoretical model will be operationalized so that it can be estimated using data that can realistically be expected to be available. For example, one has to decide on a mathematical form for the production or cost function and to select empirical measures for the variables in the theoretical model. This chapter details the assumptions and decisions we made in developing our theoretical model for large-scale prisons and discusses the way we operationalized our model so that we could estimate it using Federal Bureau of Prisons data. In addition, the chapter provides a general discussion of the role of prisons in the criminal justice system and the goals that prison systems seek to achieve.

The organization of the chapter is as follows. In the next section, we discuss the role of prisons in the criminal justice system and the way in which the operation of prison systems is affected by other executive, legislative, and judicial agencies. This section serves to place the prison system in perspective and to make clear the limitations of the model we develop. Having described the milieu in which a prison system operates, in Section 14.3 we discuss the goals that society and administrators have set for prison systems. Because most of the goals set for prison systems are only partially under the control of correctional administrators, in Section 14.4 we discuss the extent of prison administrator authority and the nature of the direct output of prisons. We also describe the reasons why we believe the prison to be an appropriate unit of analysis. In Section 14.5, we considerably narrow our focus to develop an explicit long-run model of the nature of production in large-scale prisons. Specifically, we discuss the mathematical form for our long-run cost function, our method of introducing random elements, and the empirical measures of the theoretical variables of our model. This section also explains why we estimate long-run cost curves using federal data and why we estimate these functions using only data for Federal Correctional Institutions. In Section 14.6, we similarly develop an explicit short-run model, which we estimate using data for both federal and California prisons. The final section of this chapter contains our summary and outlines our further work.

## 14.2. The Relationship of the Prison System to Other Organizations

Like any organization, the prison system does not function in isolation but rather interacts with a large number of other organizations and individuals in the course of providing correctional services. Indeed, a prison system is only one portion of the complex criminal justice system that society funds to administer justice. The criminal justice system is composed of three separate sets of agencies: the police, the courts, and the correctional organizations (e.g., probation offices and prisons). These agencies are charged with preventing crime and punishing criminals, both services being performed within legally defined constraints regarding due process and humane treatment. Although society sees the criminal justice system as an interlocking organization with definite goals, most people familar with the system know it to be composed of distinct agencies with only limited interaction and coordination. Indeed, ultimate decision-making authority for many of the agencies rests with different levels (e.g., local for police versus state for prisons) and branches (e.g., judicial for courts versus executive for police) of government. Although the actions of the agencies in each segment of the criminal justice system

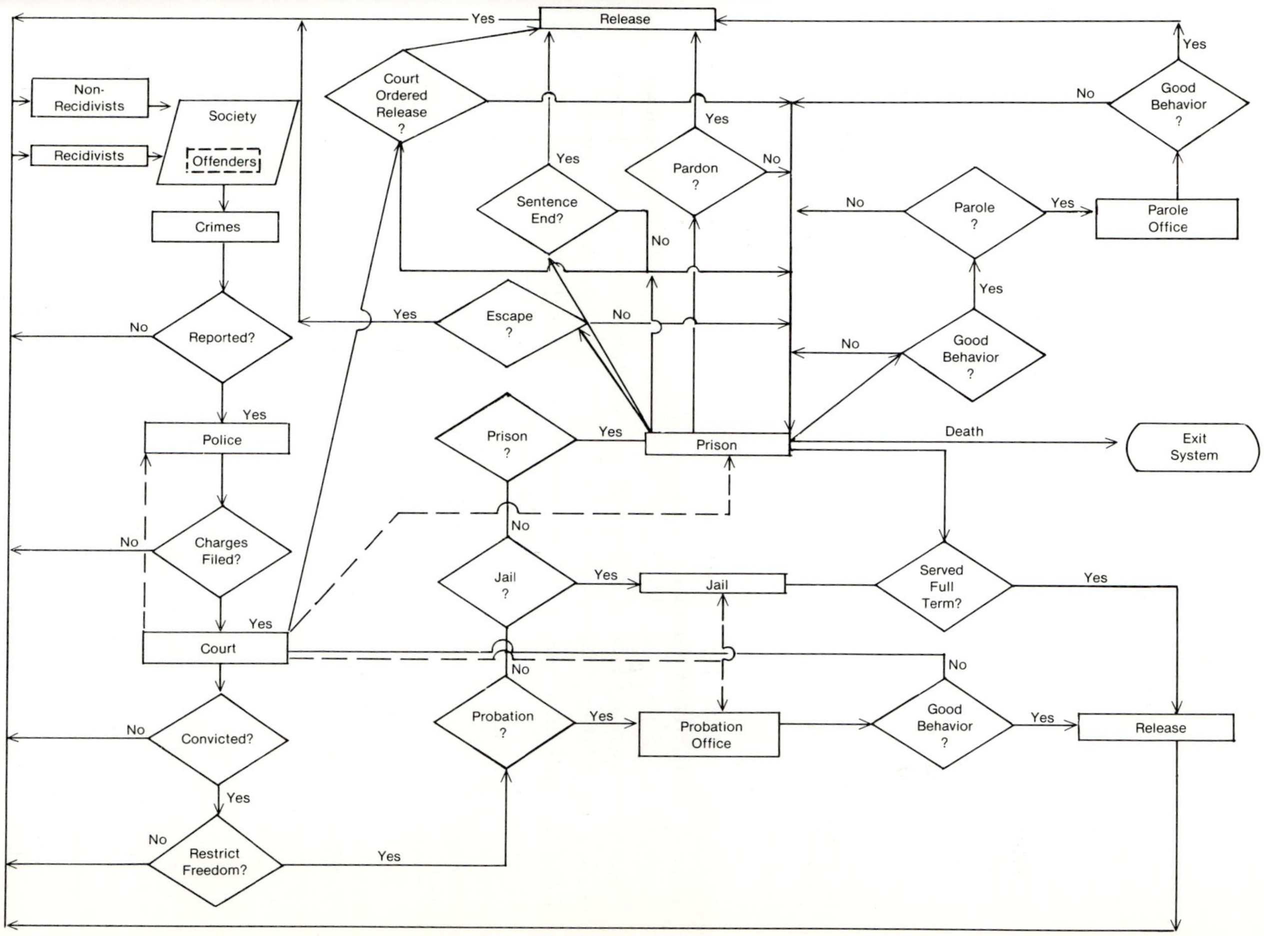


**Fig. 14.1.** Flow of offenders and organization interactions. The left side of this diagram was adapted from Blumstein and Larson (1976, p. 473).

affect the agencies in the other segments, these effects are rarely carefully thought out or considered when the administrators of a particular agency make decisions. There is no single administrator responsible for the efficient operation of the entire system; thus, it is not possible to think of the system as a productive unit seeking to effectively produce "justice." From an economist's perspective, we would not seek to model the nature of production and cost relations for the system as a whole, at least as the system is currently structured in the United States. However, in seeking to model the nature of these relationships for the individual segments of the system, it is important to understand the effect of segments other than that analyzed.

A number of researchers, mainly from operations research backgrounds, have described the way in which police, courts, and correctional agencies interact.[1] Figure 14.1 depicts these interactions, emphasizing the role of correctional agencies. The relationships among the components of the criminal justice system consist of a flow of individuals through the system and court surveillance of police and correctional activities.[2] As can be seen in Fig. 14.1, interactions between agencies are many and complex, and the number of alternative paths open to offenders is large. Managers in most agencies of the criminal justice system are relatively free (barring court intervention) to make day-to-day decisions about the way in which their organization will operate. For example, the administrators of a state prison system are relatively free to decide on the housing and care of inmates. Long-run decisions concerning the purchase of new capital equipment and buildings and major changes in methods of operation (technology) are subject to both legislative and judicial review but are largely made by agency managers or other executive branch personnel. Again, to use an example from corrections, correctional managers usually propose capital improvement plans to executive budget offices. These offices in turn decide which improvements to recommend to the legislature. The legislature finally decides whether funds will be provided for the proposed improvements.

## 14.3. The Goals of Prison Systems

The goals of prison systems (like those of other public organizations) are many and varied. Formal goals set a general tone but are often seen more as constraints than as things to be optimized. Prison systems are generally expected to hold convicted offenders securely under acceptable conditions. They are to provide for the offenders' basic needs (e.g., food, clothing, and medical care) and, in most prison systems, to provide programs and work to fill prisoners' time. We, as a society, fund prisons because we believe that for certain types of crimes they provide appropriate punishment and retribution.

In addition, we believe that prisons prevent some crime by separating those incarcerated from those who are free (i.e., prisons incapacitate inmates) and by deterring both those incarcerated (specific deferrence) and others (general deterrence) from committing future offenses.

We provide programs and work to fill prisoners' time for a number of reasons, the first of which is that the provision of some programs and work serves to lower the costs of the prison system. Second, we believe that some programs and some types of work may serve to rehabilitate convicted offenders. Finally, we provide programs and work because many members of our society believe that the provision of such activities is morally right because deprivation of liberty provides sufficient punishment and retribution for crime.

To summarize, we as a society expect our prison system to punish, incapacitate, and deter by securely holding convicted offenders. In addition, we hope that it will rehabilitate some offenders by providing programs and work opportunities. Finally, we would like all of this done as cheaply as possible and under conditions we deem acceptable. Given this list of often conflicting goals, it is not surprising that our prison systems seem at times to lack direction or to change directions at fairly frequent intervals.

Which correctional goals are emphasized has changed through time and varies from prison system to prison system [see Martin, Sechrest, and Redner (1981) for a brief survey]. Prior to the second half of the last century, prisons were funded mainly to provide punishment, to incapacitate, and to deter. The prison reform movement after the Civil War stressed the importance of rehabilitation and sought to change the way in which prisons were run. However, it was only after World War II that this goal became a central one for most prison systems.

A general hardening of public attitudes as crime rates rose in the 1960s and the appearance of research that seemed to indicate that rehabilitative programs did not rehabilitate[3] have caused the pendulum to again swing in the direction of increased emphasis on punishment, incapacitation, and deterrence. As early as 1975, Norman Carlson, director of the Federal Bureau of Prisons (FBOP), declared that the FBOP was giving up the notion that crime could be "cured"—that prisons can rehabilitate prisoners (*Behavior Today*, 1975, p. 1). In an introduction to a recent description of all federal prison facilities, Norman Carlson stated:

> More importantly, there has been a shift in philosophy. For many years, the major goal of incarceration was the rehabilitation of offenders. Within the Federal Prison System, we are trying to strike a new balance which recognizes that retribution, deterrence, and incapacitation are also valid reasons for incarceration. Medical terms such as "treatment" have been dropped because they imply that offenders are sick, that we know the causes of their crimes and we know how to affect cures, none of which is true.

> The goal of the Federal Prison System today is to make institutions more humane, to expand programs such as education and vocational training, but to make participation in these programs voluntary.
>
> Correctional institutions cannot coerce change in offenders. Offenders can and do change their behavior, but only when they themselves are motivated to do so. (U. S. Department of Justice, Federal Prison System, 1977, p. 3.)

Philosophical changes in the Califormia prison system also began to occur during this period. Changes in the California system were, if anything, more dramatic than changes in the federal system owing to the rise of large-scale prison violence in that state and the emergence of racially based prison gangs. Between 1970 and 1972, 11 California prison employees were killed. The 1977 California determinate sentence law states that "the purpose of imprisonment for crime is punishment" (California Department of Corrections, 1978, vol. II, p. 8). According to the recently published program planning report of the California Department of Corrections, the department exists to serve three primary functions:

> (1) as punishment for individuals adjudged guilty of serious crimes; (2) to protect society for a period of time by removing dangerous offenders from the community and providing close supervision following their return to the community; (3) as a deterrent to the individual from committing additional crimes and to others from committing any crimes. . . . In addition, since the majority of inmates will ultimately be returned to society, the department will direct its resources to providing a broad variety of programs, opportunities and experiences to enable individuals to develop in less destructive, more socially acceptable ways (California Department of Corrections, 1978, vol. II, p. 8).

As the philosophic switch from emphasizing rehabilitation to emphasizing punishment, incapacitation and deterrence began to change correctional practices, recessions, combined with taxpayer revolts, served to reemphasize the importance of cost containment. Finally, a number of judicial cases indicated that the federal courts would not tolerate severe overcrowding in prison systems or correctional conditions that were "shocking to the conscience of reasonably civilized people."[4]

As noted in the previous chapter, most economic models of cost and production assume that costs are minimized. The preceding discussion should make it clear that cost minimization is, at best, one of many goals pursued by correctional administrators. Pressures on correctional administrators to minimize costs generally come from outside the correctional system. For the Federal Bureau of Prisons, the pressures come primarily, in the executive branch, from the Office of Management and Budget, and, in the legislative branch, from congressional committees and the General Accounting Office [see Comptroller General of the United States (1976)]. For the California Department of Corrections, pressures to minimize costs come from the

Department of Finance, which speaks for the governor, and the Legislative Analyst's Office, which speaks for the legislature. A number of people feel that these pressures are becoming increasingly effective [e.g., see Cohn (1979, p. 14)].

Researchers studying public organizations [e.g., see Niskanen (1971) or Witte (1980a)] suggest that these external pressures for cost minimization are most likely to be successful if (1) they are strong, (2) the productive process is relatively well known, (3) output can be relatively well projected, (4) public interest and desire for the service are not excessive, (5) professional rather than political managers are in charge, and (6) work forces are not unionized. The situations in many prison systems are such that many of these conditions hold.

First, external pressures to minimize costs are currently quite strong owing to taxpayer revolts and difficult economic times. Such pressures tend to fall heavily on prison systems because spending money on convicted offenders is far down the list of social priorities. Increases in prison-system budgets often come only as a result of crises (e.g., a riot) or public or court outcry over prison conditions. In inflationary times, constant nominal budgets quickly lead to cutbacks and attempts to economize.

The second and third conditions relate to the ease with which executive and legislative branch oversight agencies can accurately project costs. In this regard, prison-system budgets can be broken down into two relatively distinct segments. The first segment consists of expenditures for basic living and security requirements and is directly related to the size of the prison population and the level of security in the system. This segment of the budget can be relatively accurately estimated by legislative and executive agencies if dramatic changes in population or security level do not occur. The second segment consists of expenditures for prison programs (e.g., community outreach, rehabilitative programs) and depends on the current correctional philosophy. This segment of the budget is difficult to estimate because the level of correctional programming may vary dramatically, both in terms of type of program and number of inmates involved. In addition, the effects of such programming on behavior, either while in prison or after release, are poorly understood [see Sechrest and Brown (1979)]. Legislative and executive oversight agencies will be hard-pressed to determine what level and type of correctional programming are appropriate, and thus this portion of prison budgets is hard to project.

The degree to which prison administrators are political varies markedly from state to state. However, with strong civil services and a long history of professional administration, both the federal and California systems tend to be influenced less by politics than are many state prison system. Finally, unionization of prison system employees has been spreading, although until recently the unions have not been particularly strong or militant. Both California and the federal prison system have employee unions.

As a whole, it appears that prison systems are generally under more pressure to minimize costs than are public bodies that produce more highly valued goods and services (e.g., education). However, the effectiveness of these pressures appears far from perfect. Extensive study of the incentives for administrators in the federal and California prison systems [see Witte *et al.* (1979)] reveals that the successful prison administrator runs a quiet prison within budget. As a long-time administrator in the California system, J. W. L. Park expressed it: "Prison administrators are judged as much, if not more, by the bad things as by the good things that happen at their prison units." Cost-saving innovations are risky, and it does not appear that the rewards for such risk are high in either the federal or California prison systems.

We conclude that the assumption that administrators in either the federal or California prison system minimize costs is tenuous, at best. Thus, the cost functions that we ultimately estimate are best interpreted as behavioral equations rather than the (minimum) cost functions of microeconomic theory. Inferences about the nature of the production function from these results in the absence of cost-minimizing behavior require the strong assumption that the inefficient behavior present merely neutrally transforms the cost curve (i.e., shifts the cost curve up equally everywhere). However, we feel that the "behavioral" cost curves we have estimated are in many cases as important as the cost curves of economic theory. They provide insight concerning the actual behavior of prison systems and thus may be more useful than economic cost curves in understanding the current nature of production in prisons and in projecting likely future behavior.

## 14.4. What Is the Productive Unit and What Does It Produce?

The structure of prison systems varies widely from state to state, but major prisons in all states are administered by a state government department or state administrative board [see American Correctional Association (1979) or Grizzle *et al.* (1982)]. Some state correctional organizations administer only prisons whereas others administer a number of other agencies. For example, the Federal Bureau of Prisons administers all federal prisons and many halfway-house-type community facilities. Figure 14.2 depicts the present administrative structure of the Federal Bureau of Prisons. California's prisons are administered by a director of corrections who is in the state health and welfare agency. The director of corrections not only administers all state prisons for adults but is also responsible for parole services and civilly committed narcotics addicts. Figure 14.3 shows the administrative structure of the California Department of Corrections.

Given the diversity of services provided and their often loose organizational structure, it is difficult—and we believe at this stage fruitless—to think of state-level "corrections departments" as the units that provide for the housing and care of prison inmates. Rather, we believe that it is the individual prison unit that is the entity that most closely resembles the "firm" of microeconomic theory. The degree to which a prison unit approximates the firm and appears to be the appropriate unit of analysis for studies of cost and production depends critically on the breadth of authority prison administrators are allowed.

Many people who have worked in prisons describe them as the "closest thing to fiefs in the modern world." This statement is true to varying degrees for various systems. The major factor forcing administrators to delegate authority in large prison systems is the difficulty of managing many geographically dispersed and often volatile prisons. In the federal prison system, there were 27 major prisons (U.S. Penitentiaries and Federal Correctional Institutions) in 1978, scattered from McNeil Island, Washington, to Miami, Florida. Although state systems are generally smaller and less complex, North Carolina, with its road-camp tradition, has even more prison facilities than does the federal system. The 10 California prisons range from isolated facilities that were formerly forest camps to the more centrally located Bastille-like Folsom and San Quentin facilities. Our own experience, working in many of the facilities of the North Carolina prison system and most recently working at the Federal Correctional Institution at Butner, North Carolina, leads us to believe that most prison wardens have substantial autonomy and that we can indeed use prisons as our unit of analysis. Somewhat surprisingly, our observations and conversations lead us to believe that the autonomy allowed prison administrators is greater in the California than in the federal system.

Having decided that the individual prison is the proper unit of analysis, we must next decide what this unit is producing. As noted in Section 14.3, we expect prisons to hold convicted offenders securely while providing for their basic needs, allowing them to participate in programs, and requiring them to work. Given these expectations, we see the basic *direct* output of a prison to be a certain number of prisoners confined for a specified period of time (e.g., a day, a month). That is, we see the basic output of a prison as incarceration. Although prisons also provide programs for those incarcerated, we see these programs as affecting the quality of incarceration and the prison environment rather than being a direct correctional output. As is illustrated in Fig. 14.4, we see the direct output of prisons—incarceration—as an input

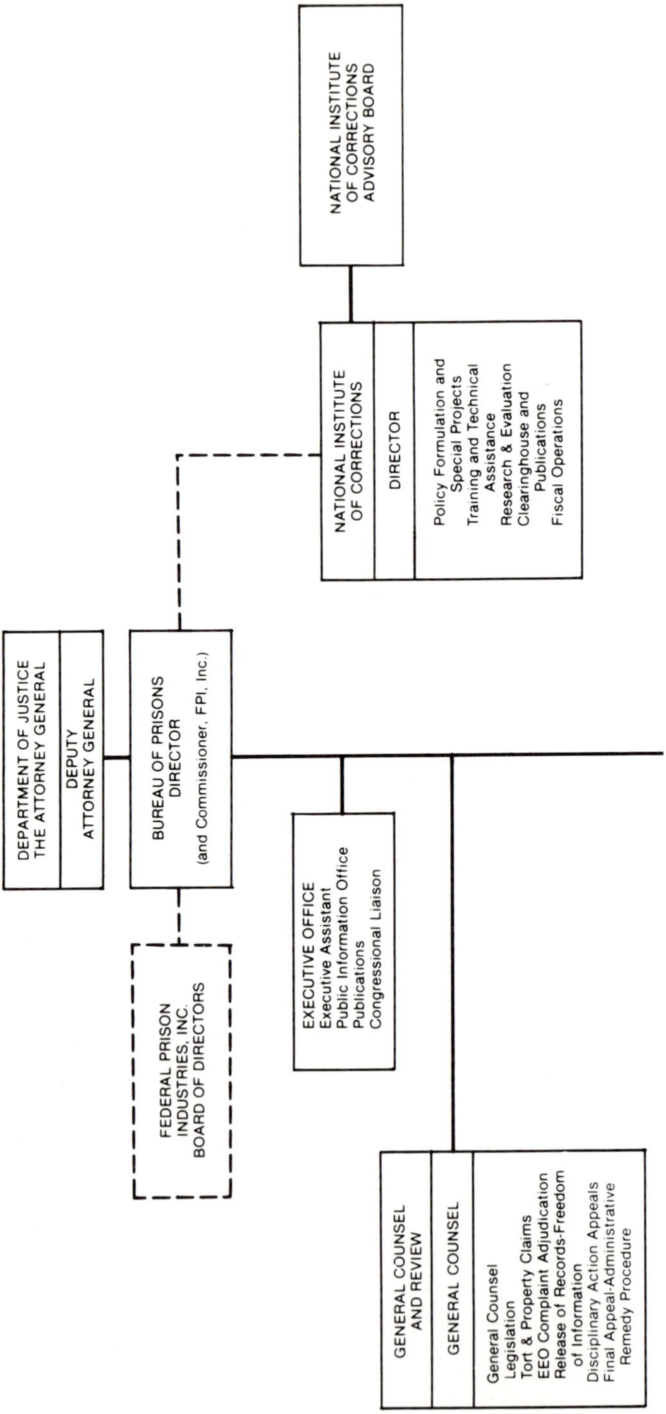
DEPARTMENT OF JUSTICE
THE ATTORNEY GENERAL
DEPUTY
ATTORNEY GENERAL
BUREAU OF PRISONS
DIRECTOR
(and Commissioner, FPI, Inc.)
FEDERAL PRISON
INDUSTRIES, INC.
BOARD OF DIRECTORS
NATIONAL INSTITUTE
OF CORRECTIONS
ADVISORY BOARD
NATIONAL INSTITUTE
OF CORRECTIONS
DIRECTOR
Policy Formulation and
Special Projects
Training and Technical
Assistance
Research & Evaluation
Clearinghouse and
Publications
Fiscal Operations
EXECUTIVE OFFICE
Executive Assistant
Public Information Office
Publications
Congressional Liaison
GENERAL COUNSEL
AND REVIEW
GENERAL COUNSEL
General Counsel
Legislation
Tort & Property Claims
EEO Complaint Adjudication
Release of Records-Freedom
of Information
Disciplinary Action Appeals
Final Appeal-Administrative
Remedy Procedure

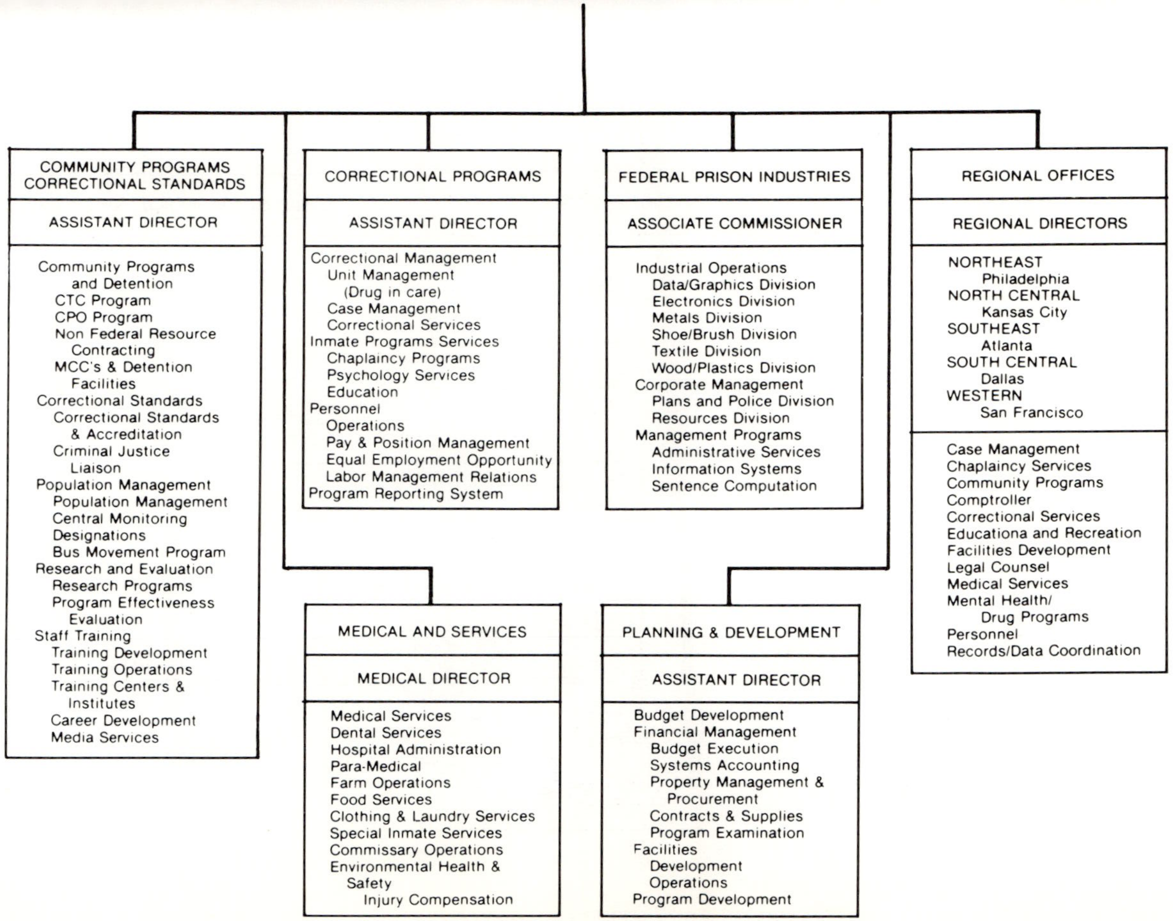


**Fig. 14.2.** Organizational chart for the Federal Prison System. From U.S. Department of Justice, Federal Prison System (1977, p. 102).

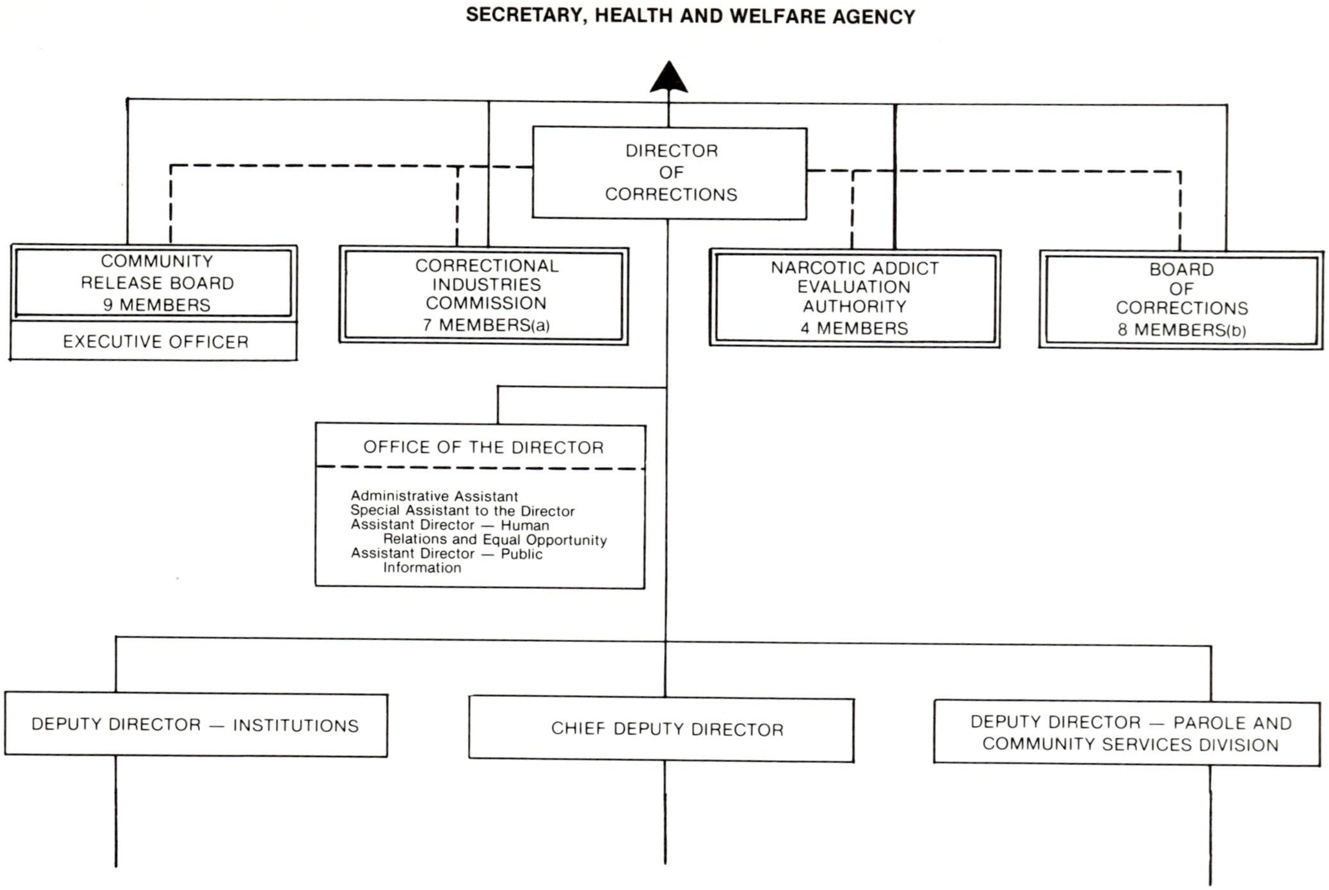
SECRETARY, HEALTH AND WELFARE AGENCY
DIRECTOR OF CORRECTIONS
COMMUNITY RELEASE BOARD 9 MEMBERS
EXECUTIVE OFFICER
CORRECTIONAL INDUSTRIES COMMISSION 7 MEMBERS(a)
NARCOTIC ADDICT EVALUATION AUTHORITY 4 MEMBERS
BOARD OF CORRECTIONS 8 MEMBERS(b)
OFFICE OF THE DIRECTOR
Administrative Assistant
Special Assistant to the Director
Assistant Director — Human Relations and Equal Opportunity
Assistant Director — Public Information
DEPUTY DIRECTOR — INSTITUTIONS
CHIEF DEPUTY DIRECTOR
DEPUTY DIRECTOR — PAROLE AND COMMUNITY SERVICES DIVISION

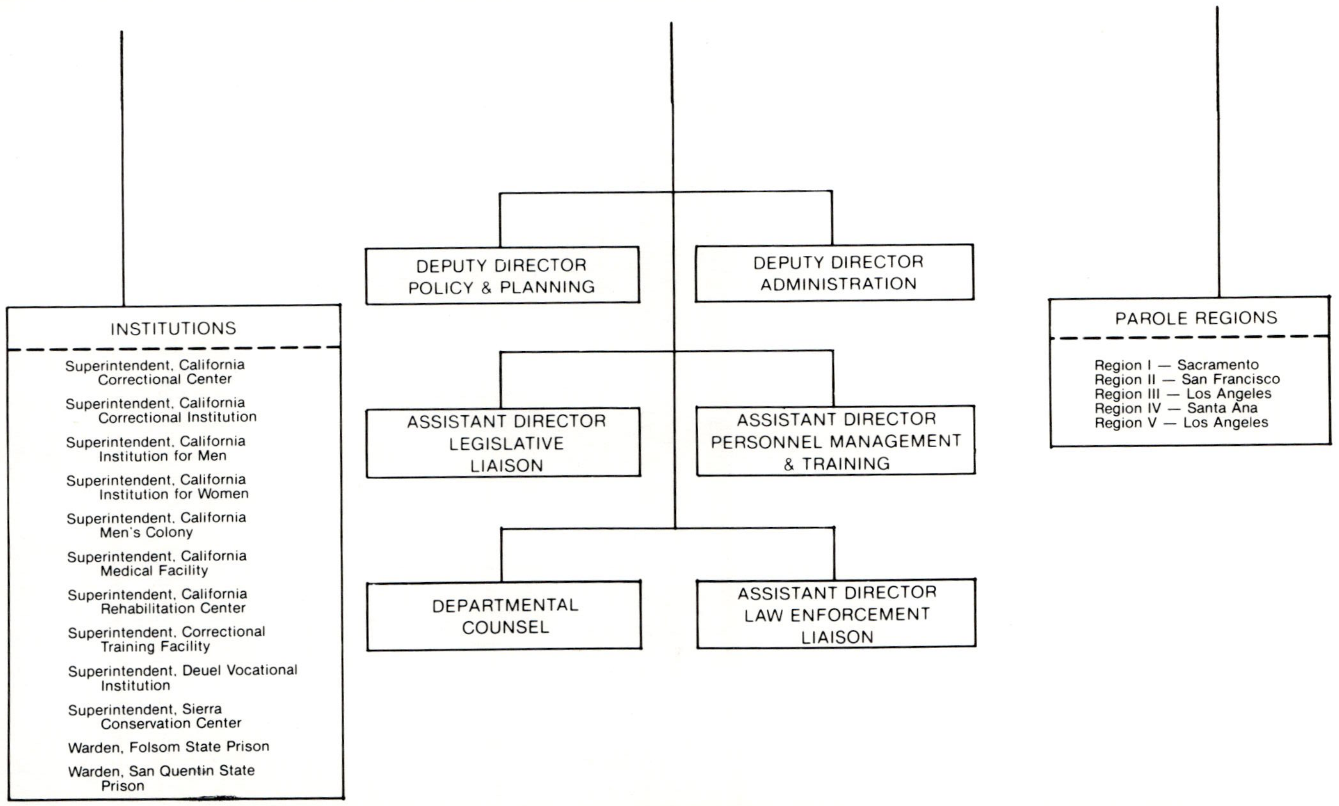


**Fig. 14.3.** Organizational chart for the California prison system. Director of Corrections is chairman of (a); secretary of Health and Welfare Agency is chairman, and the director of corrections is a member, of (b). Solid line indicates line of authority, dashed line indicates an advisory relationship, and double-lined boxes indicate an appointive board or commission. From California Department of Corrections (1978, vol. II, p. 10).

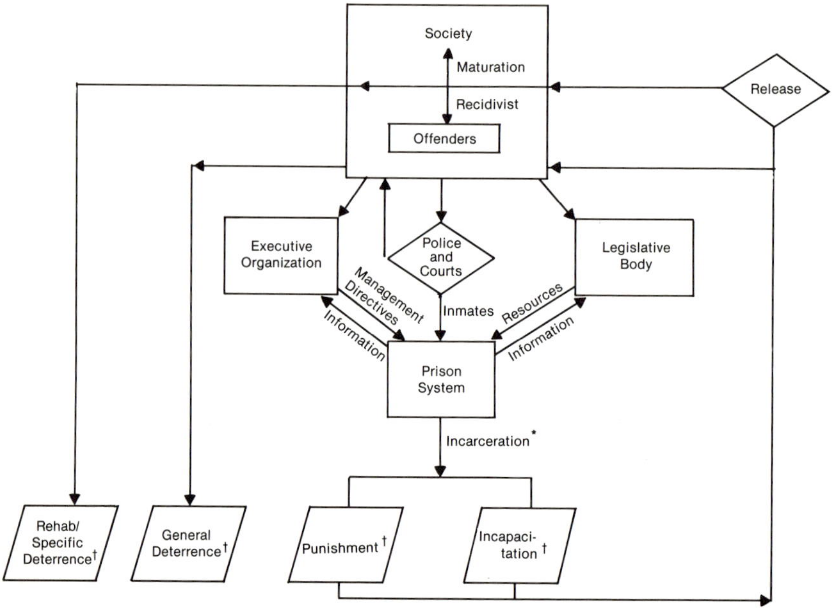


**Fig. 14.4.** A model of correctional production. Asterisk indicates direct output of prisons. Dagger indicates a social outcome that depends, at least in part, on the level of direct prison outputs.

into socially desired outcomes: (1) punishment, (2) incapacitation, (3) general deterrence, and (4) specific deterrence/rehabilitation. We shall directly model prisons' production of incarceration; however, in modeling the nature of this production, we shall be careful to control for the level of social outcomes likely to be associated with given levels and types of incarceration. For example, we shall control for the criminal proclivities of the incarcerated population, because the level of incapacitation ultimately provided is likely to be directly related to these proclivities. We shall control for the level of rehabilitative programming, because the level of rehabilitation should be related to programming effort.

## 14.5. A Long-Run Cost Model for Large-Scale Prisons

Recall that in the previous chapter we suggested that costs were under greater control of prison administrators than was output and that it was therefore more appropriate to estimate cost functions than production functions for prisons. In that chapter, we also indicated that estimation of a cost function requires that we specify the mathematical form of the function and the nature of random effects on costs. Further, we suggested that the appropriate mathematical form for modeling costs depends on what we know or are willing to assume about the nature of the productive process studied.

Unfortunately, we currently know little about the nature of production in prisons. Models of prisons have traditionally assumed that imprisonment is produced at constant average cost; that is, they implicitly assume that the production of incarceration is subject to constant returns to scale [e.g., see Leyval *et al.* (1969) or Tabasz (1975)]. However, two recent analyses of prison costs (McGuire, 1978; Block and Ulen, 1979) indicate that it is likely that both short- and long-run average costs for prisons are not constant but rather vary with the level of incarceration. Unfortunately, these studies provide no insights concerning the degree to which inputs can be substituted (i.e., the elasticity of substitution). The finding that cost varies with output suggests that we select a mathematical form for the cost function that allows costs to vary flexibly with the level of incarceration. Of the forms we discussed in the previous chapter, both the homothetic and the flexible functional forms allow the nature of returns to scale to vary with output and thus are good candidates for selection. The flexible forms may fail to be consistent with generally accepted restrictions on the nature of technologies (e.g., diminishing marginal physical product) if the range of observations in the data is wide. This is the case in our data sets. For example, in the federal prison system the smallest institution (Pleasanton) had an average rated capacity during the study period of only 122 inmates and used an average of only approximately 550,000 kilowatt-hours a month (kwh/month) of electricity, whereas the largest institution (Leavenworth) had an average rated capacity of 1627 and used an average of approximately 3,000,000 kwh/month. Variability in labor usage was comparably large, with Pleasanton using an average of 69,000 person-hours per month and Leavenworth 240,000. This wide variation gives us a preference for a more restrictive form. Specifically, we begin by assuming that long-run production in large-scale prisons may be characterized by a homothetic constant elasticity of substitution production function. Recall from the previous chapter that this production function has the mathematical form

$$Qe^{\theta Q} = \gamma[\delta K^{-\rho} + (1 - \delta)L^{-\rho}]^{-m/\rho}, \tag{14.5.1}$$

where $Q$ is the quantity of output produced (in our case the level of incarceration); $K$ and $L$ the quantities of capital and labor respectively, used in production; $\theta$, $\gamma$, $\delta$, $\rho$, and $m$ parameters to be estimated; and $e$ the base of natural logarithms.

Because costs are under greater control of prison administrators than output, we shall estimate the cost function associated with this production function rather than the production function directly. This long-run cost function has the form

$$LRTC = \gamma^{-1/m}[\delta^{1/(1+\rho)}P_K^{\rho/(1+\rho)} + (1-\delta)^{1/(1+\rho)}P_L^{\rho/(1+\rho)}]^{(1+\rho)/\rho}(Qe^{\theta Q})^{1/m}, \qquad (14.5.2)$$

where $LRTC$ is long-run total cost, $P_K$ and $P_L$ the unit prices of capital and labor, respectively, and all other symbols are as defined previously.

This functional form is quite flexible in the nature of returns to scale it allows. For example, using this functional form, one may find that returns to scale are constant, increasing, or decreasing as output changes. Further, the nature of returns to scale may vary with the level of output. Thus, this functional form allows, but does not require, us to find the U-shaped cost curves so extensively depicted in books on microeconomic theory. This form does not require that cost curves be symmetric; therefore, one may find that average cost decreases more rapidly with output as one moves from low to moderate levels of output than it increases when one moves from moderate to high levels of output.

The functional form selected allows less flexibility regarding the elasticity of substitution that one may find. Specifically, by choosing this functional form, we assume that the elasticity of substitution does not vary with output. However, this functional form allows the elasticity of substitution to assume a wide range of values, that is, from zero to very large numbers. This means that this form allows us to characterize both technologies where no substitution between capital and labor is possible (zero elasticity of substitution) and those where substitution between capital and labor is very easy (the elasticity of substitution is equal to a large number, say, 10 or more).[5]

Having specified a functional form, we now need to specify the nature of random effects on costs. We assume that random effects $\varepsilon$ enter multiplicatively in the average cost function. Specifically, we assume

$$LRTC = \gamma^{1/m}[\delta^{1/(1+\rho)}P_K^{\rho/(1+\rho)} + (1-\delta)^{1/(1+\rho)}P_L^{\rho/(1+\rho)}]^{(1+\rho)/\rho}(Qe^{\theta Q})^{1/m}e^{\varepsilon}. \qquad (14.5.3)$$

To make this equation linear, we take the natural logarithm and obtain a linear approximation to the term in brackets by a Taylor series expansion about the point $\rho = 0$, which corresponds to an elasticity of substitution equal to one.[6] We obtain

$$\ln(LRTC) = \beta_0 + \delta \ln P_K + (1-\delta)\ln P_L + \tfrac{1}{2}[\rho/(1+\rho)]\delta(1-\delta) \times [\ln(P_K/P_L)]^2 + [(1-m)/m]\ln Q + (\theta/m)Q + \varepsilon, \qquad (14.5.4)$$

where $\beta_0$ is a constant term and all other symbols are as defined previously.

This equation may be easily estimated by ordinary or generalized least squares as appropriate. One may obtain estimates of all parameters from the coefficient estimates obtained. For example, one may obtain an estimate of returns to scale $RTS$. The exact formula is

$$RTS = m/(1 + \theta Q). \tag{14.5.5}$$

Note that, as we mentioned previously, returns to scale will vary with output and are determined by the value of the parameters $m$ and $\theta$. One may also obtain an estimate of the elasticity of substitution $\sigma$:

$$\sigma = 1/(1 + \rho). \tag{14.5.6}$$

In our preliminary work using the cost function associated with the homothetic constant elasticity of substitution production function, we found that our estimates of $\sigma$ did not differ significantly from one. Thus, in the work reported in the next two chapters, we use a form for the cost function dual to the homothetic generalized Cobb–Douglas production function. Specifically, we assume

$$LRTC = \beta_0 + \delta \ln P_K + (1 - \delta) \ln P_L + (1/m) \ln Q + (\theta/m)Q + \varepsilon. \tag{14.5.7}$$

Note that this simplifies our work and does not appear to constrain the nature of the technology unrealistically.

To believe that estimation of the long-run cost curve provides estimation of production function parameters (e.g., $\theta$, $m$, $\rho$), we must be willing to assume either that prison administrators minimize costs (duality theory is directly applicable) or that any deviation from cost minimization is neutral in the sense that it merely shifts cost curves up equally everywhere. If we are not willing to assume either of these things, the cost curve still provides valuable behavioral information. It tells us how average costs actually do change with changes in output and input prices. Given that prisons do not minimize costs and are not likely to do so, these behavioral equations are of at least as much (if not more) use than the minimum cost curves of economic theory.

Note that the long-run cost curve specified so far is a cost curve appropriate for a private firm producing a single homogeneous output. More specifically, we have not introduced our vectors of product quality measures **A** and service conditions **S**. We enter these in a linear additive fashion here for simplicity, although the exact functional forms used for various members of these vectors vary as discussed later. Our expanded model is

$$\begin{aligned} \ln LRTC = \beta_0 &+ \delta \ln P_K + (1 - \delta) \ln P_L \\ &+ (1/m) \ln Q + (\theta/m)Q + A'\eta + S'\mu + \varepsilon. \end{aligned} \tag{14.5.8}$$

where $A'$ and $S'$ are, respectively, the transposes of vectors of measures of product quality and service conditions, $\eta$ and $\mu$ vectors of parameters to be estimated, and all other variables are as defined previously.

Having specified our model of long-run costs for large-scale prisons, it is next necessary to obtain data with which to estimate this model. When estimating long-run cost functions one wishes as much variation in firm size as possible so that it is possible to estimate a substantial portion of the long-run cost curve. For example, if one observes only a narrow range of firm sizes, one may find constant returns to scale although returns to scale may be other than constant for levels of output not observed in the data. It is true both in general and in our California and federal data sets that the range of firm (prison) size observed is much larger when one considers all prisons operating at a given time (the cross section) than when one observes a single firm operating through time (the time series). As a result economists generally use cross-sectional data to estimate long-run cost curves. When using cross-sectional data to estimate these curves, it is necessary to observe enough firms (prisons) to provide sufficient degrees of freedom to estimate all parameters of the model. However, in expanding the number of firms (prisons) observed, it is necessary to include only those firms that can reasonably be assumed to be using the same basic production methods (i.e., technology).

The federal prison system operated 27 large-scale prisons during the period for which we obtained data (October 1975 through June 1978), whereas the California system operated only 10 large-scale prisons during the period for which we obtained data on it (July 1968 through June 1978). In addition, we were in general able to obtain much more theoretically acceptable measures of economic variables (e.g., costs) and much more complete data for the federal than for the California prison system. (See Appendix C for a detailed discussion of both the federal and California data sets.) Because of both the larger sample size and the better data quality, we shall estimate our long-run cost curve using data for federal prisons.

Recall that there are two basic classes of large-scale federal prisons—U.S. Penitentiaries and Federal Correctional Institutions (FCIs). Our reading of FBOP publications led us to believe that U.S. penitentiaries and FCIs might not be using the same productive technologies. Consider the following recent description of FBOP's three oldest penitentiaries: "Bastille-like penitentiaries that incarcerate up to 2,000 inmates each in cages of concrete and steel" (U. S. Department of Justice, Federal Prison System, 1978, p. 20). The FBOP is committed to replacing these old penitentiaries with modern FCIs. These institutions are described as "designed to house no more than 500 inmates" (U. S. Department of Justice, Federal Prison System, 1978, p. 8), and they differ from penitentiaries in design as well as size. According to the

FBOP, these institutions "though ringed by fences, resemble a campus environment with housing units separate from administration, programmatic, and recreational areas" (U. S. Department of Justice, Federal Prison System, 1978, p. 8). To test formally for the appropriateness of combining FCIs and Federal Penitentiaries to estimate cost curves, we conducted the appropriate statistical test,[7] which indeed indicated that FCIs and Federal Penitentiaries were not using the same methods of productions. Thus, it was necessary to estimate different cost curves for the two types of prisons. We began by estimating short-run cost curves for each of 22 FCIs and U.S. penitentiaries that had complete monthly data for the period October 1975–June 1978. When estimating long-run cost curves we consider only FCIs, because there are more of these institutions and because they will become of increasing importance in the future. The Federal Bureau of Prisons is committed to closing U.S. penitentiaries and expanding the number of FCIs.[8] Further, because the federal system is considered a model for state systems, the FCI design is likely to be much utilized in these systems as well.

Given a specification for the long-run cost model and a set of prisons for which to estimate it, we are left with the need to specify empirical measures of the theoretical variables in the cost model. Table 14.1 summarizes our choices. We shall discuss each of our choices in some detail next.

Our measure of total cost for the federal prison system was obtained from the FBOP's accounting system. It includes the sum of actual disbursements, increments in accounts payable and nonfunded costs, changes in applied costs, and normal depreciation, computed according to FBOP guidelines.[9] This measure of total costs was selected in consultation with the staff of the FBOP's Financial Management System, who believed that it provided the most accurate measure of the resources consumed in production. Recall from Section 14.4 that we defined the direct output $Q$ of a prison to be the number of prisoners incarcerated during a specified time period (e.g., day, month). More specifically, for the federal system in the long run, we define direct output as the total number of confined days provided (denoted *CD-ALL*), where a confined day is one inmate held for one day.

Next we need to specify measures of input prices, that is, a measure of the unit price of capital $P_K$ and of labor $P_L$ facing federal prisons. Our empirical measure of labor costs, *LNCOST-L*, is the total remuneration to labor (straight wages or salary, overtime and premium pay, and fringe benefits), obtained from computerized payroll tapes, divided by the total number of hours worked at an institution; i.e., our measure of labor cost is the actual total labor costs per hour for the given prison.

Obtaining a measure $P_K$ of unit capital costs is much more difficult, because capital consists of heterogeneous mixtures of buildings and equipment. The theoretically correct way of obtaining a price for capital is to

**TABLE 14.1.** Variable Definitions and Expected Signs of Coefficients

| Theoretical variable | Empirical measure: Acronym | Empirical measure: Explanation | Expected sign of coefficient |
|---|---|---|---|
| Dependent variable | | | |
| Total cost *LRTC* | *LRTC* | Sum of actual disbursements, increments in accounts payable and nonfunded costs, changes in applied costs, and normal depreciation during the period | N.A. |
| Independent variable | | | |
| Output $Q$ | *CD-ALL* | Number of days of physical confinement produced during the period | Uncertain |
| | *LNCD-ALL* | Logarithm of *CD-ALL* | |
| Input prices $P_K$ and $P_L$ | *LNCOST-K* | Logarithm of the cost of capital, measured by the price of electricity | Positive |
| | *LNCOST-L* | Logarithm of the cost of labor, measured by average hourly renumeration to institutional staff | Positive |
| Product quality (members of the vector **A**) | | | |
| Security level | *SECURE* | Ratio of correctional officers to average confined population | Positive |
| Product quality and service conditions (members of the vectors **A** and **S**) | | | |
| Age | *AGE-I* | Average age of the inmate population, in months | Positive |
| | *AGE-I2* | Squared value of *AGE-I* | Negative |
| Racial composition | *RACE-I* | Percentage of the inmate population whose race is nonwhite | Uncertain |
| Sexual composition | *FEMALE* | Percentage of the inmate population whose sex is female | Uncertain |
| Occupation | *WCOLLAR* | Percentage of the inmate population whose longest job prior to incarceration was professional, technical, managerial, or in accounting | Uncertain |
| IQ | *BETAIQ* | Average beta IQ of the inmate population | Uncertain |
| Sentence | *LENGTH* | Average length, in years, of the sentences of the confined population | Uncertain |
| Crime type of offender | *O-PERS* | Percentage of the confined population sentenced for a crime against a person | Positive |
| | *O-PROP* | Percentage of the confined population sentenced for property offenses | Uncertain |

TABLE 14.1. (Continued)

| Theoretical variable | Empirical measure: Acronym | Empirical measure: Explanation | Expected sign of coefficient |
|---|---|---|---|
| Addiction | *ALCOL* | Percentage of inmates with a history of significant alcohol use | Positive |
| | *DRUGS* | Percentage of inmates with a history of significant drug use | Positive |
| Previous record | *RECORD* | Number of previous convictions that resulted in periods of incarceration of six months or more | Uncertain |
| Marital status | *MARRIED* | Percentage of inmates who are married | Negative |
| Rehabilitative activities | *IPRS* | Number of rehabilitative activities provided during the period | Uncertain |
| | *IPRS*2 | Squared value of *IPRS* | Uncertain |
| | *CD-ALL*IPRS* | Value of *IPRS* multiplied by *CD-ALL* | Uncertain |
| Incidents | *INCDNT* | Sum of institutional escapes, inmate assaults, and violent inmate deaths | Positive |
| Crowding: short-run deviations from planned output | *CROWD* | Ratio of average confined population to institutional physical capacity | Negative |
| | *CROWD*2 | Squared value of *CROWD* | Positive |
| Service conditions (members of the vector **S**) | | | |
| Racial balance | *R-BAL* | Ratio of the percentage of nonwhite in the correctional staff to the percentage of nonwhite in the inmate population | Negative |
| | *R-BAL*2 | Squared value of *R-BAL* | Positive |
| Auxiliary facilities | *PC-OTH* | Percentage of confined days output produced in an associated camp, female facility, or detention center | Uncertain |

obtain total capital costs by summing inflation-adjusted depreciation, repair and maintenance costs, operating costs, and the opportunity cost (e.g., interest charges) of funds tied up and to divide by the number of units of capital. [See Johnston (1960), Silberston (1972), and Nickell (1978).]

In practice economists have been forced to make do with much less comprehensive measures of the price of capital. Applied microeconomic theorists generally use a price index that reflects the prices of the widest spectrum of capital utilized possible. A measure of the opportunity cost for capital (i.e., an appropriate interest rate) will often be among the components of this index. When price indices for capital goods are not available, economists have relied on a number of different variables to measure the price of capital.

Lacking an appropriate price index that reflects the price of capital goods facing prisons, we use a measure for the price of capital $P_K$ suggested by the work of Foss (1963), Christensen and Jorgenson (1970), and Moody (1974). These researchers suggest that a good measure for the flow of capital services is the usage of electricity, because much equipment and buildings require electric usage when they are operating. We therefore use the price of electricity as our measure of the price of capital.

The next requirement before we estimate our model is that we specify our measures of output quality (the members of the vector $A$) and service conditions (the members of the vector $S$).

We view a given level of incarceration (i.e., a given number of confined days) to be of different quality if it produces different amounts of retribution and punishment (e.g., incarcerates more heinous criminals) and if it prevents more crime (incapacitates more active criminals and deters more crimes). In addition, many members of our society value incarceration more highly if inmates are housed under humane conditions and if they are provided with "productive" uses for their time. In addition, some of us still believe that rehabilitative programming and meaningful work experience can rehabilitate at least some offenders and, thus, prevent some crime.

Given that the perceived quality of incarceration will vary with the level of retribution and punishment, the amount of crime prevented, and the conditions under which it is provided, it is necessary to control for the level of these factors when examining the relationship between costs and the number of inmates incarcerated. As noted previously, the level of retribution and punishment perceived will depend on the nature of the offense committed. Recent research on the perceived seriousness of various offenses [e.g., see Center for Studies in Criminology and Criminal Law (1978)] indicates that there is general agreement on the relative seriousness of many offenses and that the perceived seriousness of different kinds of offenses varies widely. For example, this research indicates that we generally view offenses against persons (e.g., murder, assault) to be much more serious than most property offenses (e.g., auto theft). To control for the perceived level of retribution and punishment produced by a given number of confined days, we include variables designed to measure the seriousness of the offenses committed by the incarcerated population. Specifically, for federal prisons we include the average sentence length of the incarcerated persons, denoted *LENGTH*.[10] In addition, we include two variables that are designed to capture the greater perceived seriousness of persons offenses. The first of these variables (denoted *O*-PERS) is the percentage of inmates sentenced for a crime against a person.

The second (denoted *O*-PROP) is the percentage of inmates sentenced for property offenses.[11]

As noted in Section 14.3, prisons prevent crime by incapacitating those incarcerated, by deterring both those incarcerated and others, and perhaps by rehabilitating some inmates. The level of incapacitation associated with a given number of confined days will depend on the criminal proclivities of the confined population.[12] More specifically, it will depend on the number and type of crimes those incarcerated would have committed if free. We obviously cannot know this number, but research on incapacitation and recidivism[13] indicates that this number should be closely related to the personal characteristics (e.g., age), levels of addiction, types of current offense, and previous records of the incarcerated population. Recall that we have already controlled for the type of current offense to hold the level of punishment and retribution constant, so we need not control for this factor again here. To control further for the level of incapacitation associated with a given number of confined days, we include the following variables that reflect the personal characteristics of the inmate population in our empirical specification of the long-run cost curve: (1) the average age of the inmate population, denoted *AGE*-I; (2) the percentage of the inmate population that was nonwhite, denoted *RACE*-I;[14] (3) the percentage of the inmate population that was female, denoted *FEMALE*;[15] (4) the percentage of the inmate population whose longest job prior to incarceration was professional, technical, or in accounting, denoted *WCOLLAR*;[16] (5) the average beta IQ of the inmate population, denoted *BETAIQ*, and (6) the percentage of the confined population that was married, denoted *MARRIED*.[17]

The existing literature leads us to believe that criminal activity first increases with age, peaks in the late teens to mid-twenties, and finally declines with age thereafter [e.g., see Wolfgang, Figlio, and Sellin (1972)]. Thus we would expect the level of incapacitation to behave similarly, and we include a quadratic term (*AGE-I2*) as well as a linear term in age to allow for this type of relationship. The literature also suggests that white-collar workers, females, and married individuals are less likely to return to crime and thus that incarceration of such individuals is likely to lead to lower levels of incapacitation than confinement of other types of individuals. The literature contains conflicting conclusions regarding the way in which race and ability affect criminality. Much (but by no means all) of the literature indicates that members of minority groups are more likely to continue in *reported* criminal activity than are members of the white majority.[18] Only somewhat less equivocal results have been obtained by those studying the relationship between ability and continued criminality.

Most research indicates that individuals who are addicted to either drugs or alcohol are more likely to continue committing criminal acts than are those who are not. The finding for drugs is usually stronger than that for alcohol. To control for higher levels of incapacitation associated with incarcerating a more addicted population, we include two variables: (1) the percentage of the inmate population with a history of significant alcohol use, denoted *ALCOL*,[19] and (2) the percentage of the inmate population with a history of significant drug use, denoted *DRUGS*.[20]

When age is controlled for, the existing literature indicates that individuals with worse previous criminal records are more likely to continue criminal activity than are those with less severe records. Thus we would expect the level of incapacitation to be higher the worse the previous record of the inmate population. Specifically, when analyzing the costs of federal prisons, we control for the average number of previous incarcerations of 6 months or more of the inmate population, denoted *RECORD*.

In addition to the criminal proclivities of the population, the level of incapacitation will depend on the security with which the confined population is held. We include two measures of security in our model. The first measure is the ratio of correctional officers to confined population, denoted *SECURE*. The second is the actual number of escapes, which is included in our measure of the tension level in the institution, denoted *INCDNT*.

Theoretical reasoning (discussed in Chapter 9) and some empirical evidence[21] lead us to believe that the level of both general and specific deterrence associated with a given number of confined days will vary with the type of individuals incarcerated, the sentences they serve, the conditions under which they are incarcerated, and the public knowledge of both the fact and nature of incarceration. We have already controlled for the type of individual incarcerated and the sentences they are serving, so we need not control for these factors again. We have not previously controlled for the conditions under which inmates are incarcerated but shall now explain how we attempt to do so. First, we include the number of incidents of violence (contained in our empirical measure *INCDNT*) to reflect the level of tension in the prison and the threat of physical harm. Next, we control for the level of crowding at the institution by including the ratio of average confined population to institutional capacity, denoted *CROWD*. In addition to indicating the conditions under which inmates are held, our measure of crowding controls for the fact that prisons may not always be producing their planned level of output. Economic theory requires that deviations from planned levels of output be controlled if the long-run cost curve is to be estimated. This theory also leads us to believe that average costs are related to short-run deviations from planned output in a nonlinear way; thus we include a quadratic as well as a linear term in our measure of crowding (i.e., *CROWD*2 as well as *CROWD*).

Statements of leaders of both the federal and California prison systems indicate that they see participation in rehabilitative programs as an opportunity rather than as a direct input into crime prevention. Thus we include our measures of the level of rehabilitative programming in our product quality vector rather than as an additional output of the prison system. Specifically, our measure of the level of rehabilitative programming is the total number of inmates enrolled in educational programs (vocational and academic), psychological counseling, prison industries,[22] and certain miscellaneous activities (including prison maintenance in some cases), as documented by the FBOP Inmate Program Reporting System. This variable is denoted *IPRS*. To allow for changes in the nature of the relationship between rehabilitative activity and average costs per confined day, we enter our measure of rehabilitative activities in both linear and quadratic form (*IPRS* and *IPRS*2). In addition, we allow our measure of the level of rehabilitative activities to interact with our measure of output (*IPRS*CD-ALL*). This interaction was suggested to us by FBOP personnel. Their experience indicates that the way in which confined days are produced is quite different when inmates are involved in rehabilitative activities. In general, fewer guards are required when rehabilitative activities are underway.

The existing literature would also lead one to expect such an interaction between costs, rehabilitative inputs, and the size of a correctional institution. On the one hand, Morris (1974) alleges that rehabilitative inputs are less effectively provided in larger institutions. This would lead one to expect a positive coefficient on the term linking confined days with the level of rehabilitative activities. On the other hand, because many rehabilitative activities are educational in nature, one might expect increased provision levels to be associated with lower costs, at least up to a point, owing to economies of scale in the provision of educational services.

Recall that we wish to control for the service conditions that society imposes on prisons as well as product quality. Society imposes service conditions on prisons when it sentences a certain number and type of individual to prison. Prisons have no choice but to deal with those who are sent to them. Society also imposes service conditions when it provides resources and defines the conditions under which it wishes inmates held. For example, if society sentences individuals to prison in excess of existing prison capacity, society dictates that confined days will be provided under crowded conditions. Society provides resources for rehabilitative programs and thus suggests that it would like confined days produced in conjunction with programs. Because we have already controlled for the type of inmate, the level of rehabilitative programming, and the level of crowding, it will not be necessary to do so again. However, because we have not yet controlled for the type of staff and capital facilities provided, we shall now discuss how we do so. Specifically, we add two variables to our specification: (1) the ratio of the percentage of nonwhites in the correctional staff to the percentage of nonwhites in the inmate population, denoted *R-BAL*; and (2) the percentage of confined days produced in facilities associated with the main institution (e.g., camps, female facilities, and detention centers), denoted *PC-OTH*. We would expect costs to be lowest when the racial balance of the correctional staff approximated that of the inmate population and to increase as the ratio diverged from equality in either direction. Thus we include a quadratic as well as a linear term in the racial balance variable (*R-BAL* and *R-BAL2*).

As noted earlier, Table 14.1 summarizes our choices of empirical measures for the variable in our long-run cost model. This table also gives the acronym used for each variable and indicates the way in which we expect the value of each variable to affect average costs (i.e., the expected sign for the coefficient on each variable).

## 14.6. A Short-Run Cost Model for Large-Scale Prisons

The distinction between the short run and the long run is that in the short run a firm's capital stock is fixed, whereas in the long run it is variable. In the previous section, we described a model for long-run costs, to be estimated using a cross section of firms; capital stock is variable across firms. In this section we shall describe a model for short-run costs, to be estimated using a time series of observations for a given prison. (In other words, we shall estimate a separate short-run cost function for each prison.) For a given prison, the capital stock shows little or no variation over a reasonable length of time, so we are justified in interpreting our cost functions for individual prisons as short-run functions.

We shall estimate a short-run cost curve for each of 22 federal prisons and 8 California prisons. Not surprisingly, the data available for federal and California prisons differed in a number of respects. We describe the federal and California data sets used to estimate the short-run cost functions briefly here and in greater detail in Appendix C.

The federal data set used to estimate short-run cost functions differs from that used to estimate long-run functions in a number of ways. First, it contains data for U.S. penitentiaries as well as FCIs. Second, it contains monthly rather than quarterly observations for the period October 1975 through June 1978. It was necessary to use monthly rather than quarterly data to have enough degrees of freedom to estimate a cost curve for each institution. However, information on inmate enrollment in rehabilitative activities, electric cost and usage, and staff variables was available only quarterly. To obtain estimates of monthly values for these variables, we use an interpolation technique developed by Chow and Lin (1976). This technique, which is described in detail in Appendix C, produces estimates of the missing monthly data that are unbiased and have the least variance of all possible linear estimators.

Our measure of labor usage for federal prisons is the total hours of work performed by all employees at a given institution during a given period. This variable was obtained from the payroll tapes of the U.S. Department of Justice and thus should be quite accurate.

Discussions with accounting personnel at the Federal Bureau of Prisons indicated that there was a definite pattern to spending by prisons during a quarter. Specifically, they indicated that the wardens at most prisons spent most of their quarterly allocation early in the quarter. To capture such an intraquarterly fluctuation in spending, we add two binary variables to our short-run cost specification for federal prisons. The first of these variables, denoted *MONTH*-1, is equal to one during the first month of a quarter and zero otherwise. The second, denoted *MONTH*-2, is equal to one in the second month of a quarter and zero otherwise.

Knowing that the federal prison system was unique in a number of regards[23] and that it might thus produce cost curves that would not reflect state prison system operating conditions, we explored the possibility of obtaining data with which to estimate cost curves in eight states.[24] We obtained sufficient response from five of these states to evaluate our ability to estimate cost curves for those states. Unsurprisingly, we found that the data available for state prisons tended to be both less accessible and less extensive than those available for federal prisons. However, California had the best data available on state prisons, and their data were adequate to make estimation of cost curves feasible, if not always satisfying.[25] It should be noted, however, that even the California data set contains less complete data than the FBOP data set. For example, costs do not include depreciation on either buildings or equipment and are available only quarterly, measures of rehabilitative activities are only partial, and only part of the desirable set of inmate characteristics is available (e.g., no information on alcohol addiction was available). See Appendix C for additional details.

We use quarterly data for the period from July 1968 to June 1977 to estimate our short-run cost models for California. The beginning and ending periods for our data were suggested to us by officials of the California Department of Corrections. They felt that the nature of the prison facilities in the California system had stabilized by mid-1968. We ended our data with the quarter ending in June 1977 because this was the last quarter before California's determinate-sentencing law went into effect.[26] The implementation of this law was very disruptive to the California prison system, and the period immediately after its implementation cannot be considered at all typical for prisons in the system. Owing to gaps in the California data and to the fact that some portions were available only for certain time periods, we had to estimate some of the data. Small data gaps were filled in by linear interpolation. Annual and semiannual data were converted to a quarterly basis using the same Chow–Lin procedure that we used to obtain monthly data for some federal data. Appendix C contains the details of all procedures used.

Having described the data to be used to estimate our short-run cost functions, we now turn to the questions of the functional form to be used and the way in which random error is to be introduced. As in the long-run analysis, we assume that the technology of prison operation is characterized by a homothetic Cobb–Douglas production function of the form

$$Qe^{\theta Q} = AL^{\alpha}\bar{K}^{\beta}. \tag{14.6.1}$$

The capital stock $\bar{K}$ is assumed fixed. Output $Q$ varies over time but is outside the control of the firm (prison management). Given these facts and the technological constraint (14.6.1), we assume that the prison manager attempts to choose the amount of labor $L$ that will minimize the cost of producing the required level of output. However, under the present circumstances ($Q$ and $\bar{K}$ both outside the control of the firm), there is only one level of $L$ that can be chosen, and this is obtained by solving (14.6.1) as

$$L = [Qe^{\theta Q}/A\bar{K}^{\beta}]^{1/\alpha}. \tag{14.6.2}$$

We shall refer to (14.6.2) as the labor demand equation. It is the form of the production function that we shall estimate, because its dependent variable ($L$) is the variable that the prison management can influence. To estimate it, we assume that the random error $\varepsilon$ enters multiplicatively:

$$L = CQ^{1/\alpha}e^{(\theta/\alpha)Q}e^{\varepsilon}, \tag{14.6.3}$$

where $C = (A\bar{K}^{\beta})^{1/\alpha}$. Taking logarithms yields

$$\ln L = \ln C + (1/\alpha)\ln Q + (\theta/\alpha)Q + \varepsilon, \tag{14.6.4}$$

which is linear in parameters and thus may be estimated by traditional estimation techniques (e.g., generalized or ordinary least squares).

Recall that our measure of correctional output is a measure of the size of the prison population (*CD-ALL* for the federal system) and that our model of correctional costs requires that we adjust for product quality and service conditions. Adjusting our labor demand equation to reflect these aspects of our model and substituting $\beta_0$, $\beta_1$, and $\beta_2$ for $\ln C$, $1/\alpha$, and $\theta/\alpha$, respectively, we obtain the following labor demand equation for large-scale prisons:

$$\ln L = \beta_0 + \beta_1 \ln Q + \beta_2 Q + \mathbf{A}'\psi + \mathbf{S}'\gamma + \varepsilon, \tag{14.6.5}$$

where **A**′ and **S**′ are the transposes of vectors of product quality and service condition measures.

For our analyses of prisons in the federal system, the measures of product quality and service conditions are essentially as given in Table 14.1. However, because we are now modeling the short rather than the long run, the measures of crowding *CROWD* and *CROWD*2 are dropped from these vectors. Also, we add a time trend to our short-run service-condition vector to control for secular changes, such as general price inflation. This variable is denoted *TREND*1 and is equal to one for the first period when data are available and increases by one for each subsequent period. To further ensure the constancy of the capital stock, we enter the capacity[27] of the institution in our empirical model of the short-run cost function.

For our analysis of California prisons, the specification and some of the measures of the explanatory variables are slightly different, owing to differences between the California and federal data. Table 14.2 gives a detailed listing of the theoretical variables and empirical measures for our model of short-run costs for California prisons.

**TABLE 14.2.** Variable Definitions and Expected Sign of Coefficients

| Theoretical variable | Empirical measure: Acronym | Empirical measure: Explanation | Expected sign of coefficient |
|---|---|---|---|
| Dependent variable | | | |
| Quantity of labor | *LNSTFTOT* | Logarithm of the average daily number of staff | N/A |
| Independent variables | | | |
| Output | *ADPOP* | Average daily inmate population | Uncertain |
| | *LNADPOP* | Logarithm of *ADPOP* | Uncertain |
| Product quality | | | |
| Security level | *SECURE* | Ratio of correctional officers to average daily confined population | Positive |
| Product quality and service conditions | | | |
| Rehabilitative activities | *IPRS* | Average number of inmates assigned to prison industries or work furloughs daily | Uncertain |
| | *IPRS*2 | Squared value of *IPRS* | Uncertain |
| | *POP-IPRS* | Value of *IPRS* interacting with *ADPOP* | Uncertain |
| Age | *INAGE* | Average age of inmate population in years | Positive |
| | *INAGE* 2 | Squared value of *INAGE* | Negative |

(*Table continues*)

**TABLE 14.2.** *(Continued)*

| Theoretical variable | Empirical measure: Acronym | Empirical measure: Explanation | Expected sign of coefficient |
|---|---|---|---|
| Racial composition | *RACE-I* | Percentage of the inmate population whose race is nonwhite | Uncertain |
| Addiction | *INADD* | Average number of inmate addicts | Uncertain |
| Education | *INELEM* | Average grade placement of inmates as tested upon entering institution | Uncertain |
| Length of sentence | *LENGTH* | Average time served for inmates released during the period studied | Uncertain |
| Crime type of offender | *O-PERS* | Percentage of inmates sentenced for a crime against a person | Positive |
| | *O-PROP* | Percentage of inmates sentenced for property offenses | Uncertain |
| Previous record | *RECORD* | Percentage of inmates serving second prison sentence | Uncertain |
| | *REPEATS* | Percentage of inmates serving third or greater prison sentence | Uncertain |
| Sentence | *LIFE* | Percentage of inmates sentenced to death or lifetime imprisonment | Uncertain |
| Incidents | *INCDNT* | Sum of incidents, attempted escapes, and escapes during the period | Positive |
| | *JUMP* | Percentage of inmate population attempting or succeeding at an escape | Positive |
| Systemwide incident | *D*1 | Binary variable equal to one for 1973 and zero otherwise | Positive |
| Service conditions: | | | |
| Racial balance | *R-BAL* | Ratio of nonwhite to white staff divided by the ratio of nonwhite to white inmates | Uncertain |
| Adjustments: | | | |
| Capacity | *BEDCAP* | Planned institutional capacity in number of beds | Uncertain |
| Quarterly institutional expenditure adjustment | *QTR*-1 | Binary variable equal to one if first quarter of fiscal year and zero otherwise | Positive |
| | *QTR*-2 | Binary variable equal to one if second quarter of fiscal year and zero otherwise | Positive |
| | *QTR*-3 | Binary variable equal to one if third quarter of fiscal year and zero otherwise | Positive |
| Time trend | *TREND*1 | Variable equal to one for the first period and increasing by one with each successive period | Uncertain |

Although the equation that we actually estimate is the short-run labor demand equation, we can easily use it to solve for the short-run cost function. The details of this solution procedure will be given in Chapter 15.

## 14.7. Summary and Conclusions

In this chapter we developed a model of production in large-scale prisons. We began by describing the role of the correctional organizations in the criminal justice system and the way in which prison system operation is affected by executive and judicial agencies outside the criminal justice system. Although each component of the criminal justice system (police, courts, corrections) has substantial effects on the others, we found only limited interaction and coordination among agencies. As often noted, the criminal justice "system" is not really a system.

We next discussed the goals that society and administrators have set for the prison system. We found that currently, at least in the systems with which we worked, society wishes prison systems to punish, incapacitate, and deter criminals by incarcerating convicted offenders. Although prison systems provide extensive rehabilitative programming, neither correctional administrators nor others are sure whether these programs actually rehabilitate inmates. We found further that society wishes prisons to incarcerate inmates as cheaply as possible and that the judiciary, if not society as a whole, wishes inmates to be incarcerated under conditions that are not "shocking to the conscience of reasonably civilized people." We found pressures to minimize costs to be mainly imposed on prisons externally, by executive budget offices and legislative oversight organizations. Although prisons are under substantially more pressure to minimize costs than are organizations that produce more highly valued public services (e.g., police protection, defense, education), we do not believe that we can realistically assume that prisons are currently minimizing costs. This means either that we interpret the short- and long-run cost curves that we estimate using traditional techniques (e.g., ordinary or generalized least squares) as "behavioral" rather than economic cost functions or that we assume that the failure to minimize costs merely shifts costs curves upward neutrally. If the latter does not hold, it will not be possible to estimate production function parameters from cost function coefficients, or vice versa, because duality theory will not hold.

In Section 14.4, we discussed why we believe the individual prison most closely approximates the "firm" of economic theory and thus is the most appropriate unit of analysis when estimating cost functions. Although prison administrators do not have complete autonomy in making short- and long-run decisions concerning the way in which prisons will operate, they do have substantial control over many of the most basic factors (e.g., housing arrangements, staffing, budget requests) affecting the operation of the prison under their control. We explained why we see the basic *direct* output of prisons to be incarceration, that is, a certain number of inmates held for a certain time period. We see this direct prison output as an input into socially desired outcomes: (1) punishment, (2) incapacitation, (3) general deterrence, and (4) specific deterrence/rehabilitation. We see prison programs as affecting the quality of incarceration and the prison environment rather than being a direct correctional output. (See Fig. 14.4 for an illustration of these relationships.)

In Section 14.5 we operationalized our long-run cost model for large-scale prisons by selecting a mathematical form for the cost function, specifying random effects, selecting a data set with which to estimate the model, and specifying empirical measures of the theoretical variables of the model. Specifically, we selected the long-run cost function dual to a homothetic Cobb–Douglas production function. We introduced a random error term multiplicatively. We decided to estimate our long-run cost model using data for Federal Correctional Institutions. We did this because high-quality data are available and because we believe that this particular type of federal prison can reasonably be assumed to be using the same technology to produce incarceration. Finally, we selected empirical measures for long-run average costs, output, factor prices, product quality, and service conditions. Table 14.1 summarizes our choices. The model will be estimated in Chapter 16.

In Section 14.6, we similarly operationalized our short-run cost model for large-scale prisons. In this case, we chose to estimate the labor demand equation corresponding to a homothetic Cobb–Douglas production function, with a multiplicative error term. We shall estimate (separate) short-run cost functions for each of 22 federal prisons and 8 state prisons in Chapter 15.

## Notes to Chapter 14

1. For examples of this work see Blumstein and Larson (1970) and Blumstein (1975). Chaiken *et al.* (1976) provide an extensive survey of criminal justice models.

2. See Ducote (1977), Feldberg (1977), Johnson (1976), and Prigmore and Crow (1976) for discussion of recent court actions on prison conditions.

3. See Bailey (1966), Martinson (1974), Lipton, Martinson, and Wilks (1975), Brody (1976), and Greenberg (1977) for surveys of research that leads to this conclusion. See Palmer (1975), Halleck and Witte (1977), and Sechrest, White and Brown (1979) for dissenting views.

4. 309 F. Supp. 362 (E.D. Ark 1970), aff'd. 442 F. 2d 304 (8th Cir. 1971, 372–373).

5. This discussion of the cost curve dual to a homothetic constant elasticity of substitution production function rests heavily on the work of Lovell (1973).

6. We consider this a good expansion point, because elasticities of substitutions are usually

found to be approximately equal to one. Indeed, we find the elasticity of substitution between capital and labor in prisons to be close to one.

7. Specifically, we used an $F$-statistic to test the hypothesis that Federal Correctional Institutions and U.S. Penitentiaries were using the same technology. See Maddala (1977, pp. 200–201) for a discussion. For our data, the value of the $F$-statistic, which is distributed $F_{30,86}$ under the null hypothesis that the two classes of prisons use the same technology, was 3.49, which indicates that we should reject the null hypothesis at normal levels of statistical significance (e.g., $\alpha = .05, .01$). We conclude that U.S. Penitentiaries and Federal Correctional Institutions use different technologies and thus long-run cost curves must be estimated separately for the two types of prisons.

8. Since July 1, 1978, the FBOP has closed one U.S. penitentiary (McNeil Island) and is in the process of closing another (Atlanta). During our study period FBOP opened three new FCIs (Miami, Memphis, and Butner).

9. These guidelines use straight-line depreciation and assume a 40-year life for buildings, a 20-year life for major heating and cooling equipment (e.g., furnaces) and a 10-year life for smaller equipment (e.g., food service equipment). FBOP guidelines conform to Government Accounting Office (GAO) conventions.

10. There is a good deal of controversy concerning what is an appropriate measure of seriousness. [See Rossi, Waite, Bose and Berk (1974) for a review.] However, we feel that length-of-sentence is a useful measure for a number of reasons. First, it correlates highly with more sophisticated measures of seriousness [for evidence, see Sellin and Wolfgang (1964) and Shaw (1976)]. Second, it has the advantage of reflecting the judge's perception of seriousness. This perception may be influenced by extenuating circumstances, the results of presentencing investigations, and knowledge of the presence or absence of plea bargaining. Finally, it is generally available and thus less costly to use than more specialized indices.

11. For federal prisons, personal offenses are defined as FBOP offense codes 011, 120, 121, 161, 530, 880, 621, 622, 654, 661, 702, 721, 722, 902, 912, 922, and 982. (See listing of FBOP offense codes for definitions.) Property offenses are defined as FBOP offense codes 021–029, 031, 050, 051, 070, 071, 081–084, 100–102, 140–142, 150–153, 181, 191–196, 230, 241, 251, 261, 271, 281, 300, 301, 334, 541, 550–552, 801, 831, 832, 840, 841, 851, 852, 864, 865, 870–873, 601, 603, 605, 609, 613, 614, 641, 643, 644, 694, 701, 703, 705, 709, 713, 714, 741, 743, 744, 794, 901, 903, 905, 906, 909, 913, 914, 941, 942, 943, and 944.

12. Ultimately the level of incapacitation (number of crimes prevented) also depends on the elasticity of supply of the criminal population. However, this elasticity is outside the control of prison administrators. Research indicates that supply elasticities vary markedly with crime type (lower for person offenses, higher for property offenses), but that they are in no case infinitely elastic. See Cook (1977) for a survey.

13. See Cohen (1978) for a recent review of the literature on incapacitation; see Monahan (1980) or Witte (1980a) for recent surveys of the literature on recidivism.

14. Note that FBOP computer conventions required that we treat all Hispanics as white.

15. During the period studied a number of federal facilities were co-correctional. In addition, we estimate a cost curve for the federal facility for women at Alderson and for the federal prison at Pleasanton, which became an all-female facility at the end of 1977.

16. Specifically, an occupation was classified as white-collar if the first three digits of Department of Labor's occupational title were less than 200 or between 210 and 220. See U. S. Department of Labor, Bureau of Employment Security (1965).

17. Marital status classifications are: (1) single, (2) married, (3) widow(er), (4) divorced, (5) separated, (6) common law. An inmate is considered married if classified as either (2) or (6).

18. For examples of work that finds members of minority groups more likely to continue in criminal activity, see Cook (1975) or Palmer and Carlson (1976). Our own work using North

Carolina data consistently finds blacks less likely than whites to continue in reported criminal activity.

19. Individuals were designated as having a history of significant alcohol use if they were classified as (1) a former excessive user, (2) a significant user, (3) a habitual excessive user, and (4) other.

20. Individuals were designated as having a history of significant drug use if they were classified as (1) a former user, (2) a recent user, (3) a user (immediate past) and (4) a user (not withdrawn).

21. Witte (1980b) provides some evidence for specific deterrence. Although there has been much more research on general deterrence, this research is, in general, quite flawed. See Cook (1977), Nagin (1978), or Brier and Fienberg (1980) for reviews of the general deterrence literature.

22. Note that, although work in prison industries is included as a rehabilitative activity, the accounting system for federal prison industries (UNICOR) is entirely separated from the accounting system used to define average costs.

23. The federal prison system receives its prisoners from the federal court system, thus, most of the offenders it houses have been convicted of a federal offense. These offenders have typically committed offenses against federally owned or chartered facilities (e.g., post offices or banks), been involved in interstate transmission of forbidden or stolen property (e.g., narcotics or autos), counterfeited or forged federal documents, violated other specifically federal statutes (e.g., immigration, tax, securities, selective service), or committed a crime that would normally be punished by the state (e.g., murder, rape) in a federally administered area (e.g., a government reservation). Offenders convicted of these types of offenses are on the average better-educated and less violent than state prison populations.

Compared with state systems the federal prison system has been well financed. Indeed, by presidential mandate the system is to serve as a model for state prison systems (Comptroller General of the United States, 1976). Although the federal system still maintains a number of Bastille-like penitentiaries, most of its facilities are modern, with atmospheres not unlike a secure college campus. A number of new federal facilities have been opened in recent years (e.g., Butner, Memphis), and four new facilities are currently under construction. Being under federal civil service regulations, FBOP personnel are well paid and receive extensive benefits. In short, although money has not been lavished on the federal prison system, the quality of its facilities and pay levels of its personnel are markedly better than most state prison systems.

24. The states where officials were contacted were California, Illinois, Massachusetts, Michigan, Minnesota, New York, North Carolina, and Texas. These states were suggested to us by personnel of the National Institute of Justice as being likely to have substantial, high-quality data.

25. The five states considered were California, Michigan, Minnesota, New York, and North Carolina. We evaluated the possibility of estimating cost curves for these five states on the following criteria: (1) data availability, (2) sample size, (3) cost, (4) representativeness, (5) probability of use, and (6) cooperation. See Witte *et al.* (1979, App. 6.1, pp. 113–118) for details.

26. For discussion of the effect of this law, see California Department of Corrections (1976) or Howard (1978).

27. Capacity in prisons is a somewhat unusual concept in that it is affected both by the physical facilities available and by the needs and politics surrounding the particular prison system. Capacity varied somewhat for most institutions. However, our measure of capital and electricity usage, showed no systematic pattern of variation, and thus we believe that we are justified in estimating short- rather than long-run cost functions when using time series data.

# Chapter 15

## Short-Run Cost Functions for Large-Scale Prisons*

### 15.1. Introduction

In his chapter we estimate and discuss models of short-run average costs for prisons in the federal and California prison systems. Our model of short-run prison costs is as presented in Section 14.6. Specifically, we assume that prison operations can be characterized by a homothetic Cobb–Douglas production function [see Eq. (14.6.5)] and that labor inputs are variable and capital inputs fixed in the short run. We estimate our model of short-run costs for 22 federal and 8 California prisons.[1]

The organization of the chapter is as follows. In Section 15.2 we present our empirical results for the estimation of short-run cost functions for each of 22 federal prisons. In Section 15.3 we present our results for a similar analysis of 8 California prisons. In Section 15.4 we discuss some policy implications of our results. Finally, Section 15.5 presents our summary and conclusions.

* Coauthored with Pamela Reid.

## 15.2. Empirical Results for Federal Prisons

For each institution, we begin by estimating the labor demand function

$$\ln L = \beta_0 + \beta_1 \ln CD\text{-}ALL + \beta_2 CD\text{-}ALL + A'\psi + S'\gamma + \delta K + \mu MONTH\text{-}1 + \eta MONTH\text{-}2 + \varepsilon \quad (15.2.1)$$

using ordinary least squares (OLS).[2] $K$ is the planned capacity of the institution. Because we are using monthly time-series data to estimate this labor demand equation, it is quite likely that the error terms in our estimated models will not be independent. Specifically, we might expect autocorrection in our data owing to time trends not captured by *TREND*-1 or to accounting conventions not captured by *MONTH*-1 and *MONTH*-2. We check the residuals from our OLS regression for autocorrelation using a Durbin–Watson statistic. If this statistic indicates that there is no autocorrelation in the model, we continue to use ordinary least squares to estimate the labor demand function for that institution. If this statistic indicates that autocorrelation is present, we determine the pattern of association between error terms and correct for it using generalized least squares (GLS).[3] Of the 22 institutions for which we present results here, the residuals we obtain from estimating Eq. (15.2.1) using OLS indicate that autocorrelation was present for all but 4 institutions. Specifically, OLS residuals indicate that the error terms for 13 institutions are characterized by a first-order autoregressive process, the error terms for 4 institutions are characterized by a second-order autoregressive process, and the error terms for 1 institution are characterized by a third-order autoregressive process.

In general, our labor demand model, whether estimated by OLS or GLS, explains a large proportion of the variation in labor demand (usually more than half) for prisons in the federal system.

Although our overall models explain a significant portion of the variation in labor demand, many of the individual coefficients are statistically insignificant because of multicollinearity in the explanatory variables. To lessen the effects of multicollinearity and to attempt to rid our specification of variables unrelated to costs, we follow a somewhat complicated method of model reduction. A flowchart describing this model-reduction method is given in Fig. 15.1.

We begin with our test for autocorrelation. If the model is found to have autocorrelated errors, we determine and use the appropriate generalized least-squares estimator. Models with autocorrelated errors are then reduced in the same way as the models with uncorrelated errors.

We drop or retain variables according to two criteria. First, we retain the independent variables suggested by the production function we have selected (the homothetic Cobb–Douglas production function) regardless of statistical significance, owing to the theoretical support for their inclusion in our cost-curve specification. Second, we use Theil's residual-variance criterion (Theil, 1960, pp. 210–215) to determine which variables in the product-quality, service-condition, and adjustment vectors to retain. In the present context, the application of these rules means that we retain *CD-ALL* and *LNCD-ALL* in our specification regardless of their $t$-statistics, owing to theoretical support for the inclusion of these variables. We delete all other variables with an absolute value of the $t$-statistic less than one. For models without autocorrelation, we then use a joint-$F$-test (Neter and Wasserman, 1974, pp. 84–89) to assure that the dropped variables were jointly insignificant. For autocorrelated models, we use an analogous likelihood ratio test (Kendall and Stuart, 1976, 279–287). If the appropriate test indicates that the deleted variables were jointly significant, we reenter the independent variables with the highest $t$-statistics one at a time until the delected variables are jointly insignificant. Next, for models without autocorrelation in the full specification, we calculate a Durbin–Watson statistic for the reduced model. If this statistic indicates that the residuals of the estimated model are autocorrelated, we reenter the independent variables with the highest $t$-statistics one at a time until the residuals of the model no longer show autocorrelation. We feel that this approach is appropriate because the emergence of autocorrelation in a reduced model is generally the result of model misspecification. Finally, we reapply Theil's criterion. If this criterion is satisfied, we have our final reduced model; otherwise, we begin the reduction process again.

Tables containing the results of the original and the reduced specifications for 22 prisons in the federal system are contained in Witte *et al.* (1979, ch. 9). The number of intermediate runs needed to reduce the model varied across institutions, ranging from 0 to 12. Tables 15.1a–c summarize the results of the final specifications for these 22 federal prisons.

We next wish to use the results in Tables 15.1a–c to obtain short-run average total cost curves for each prison. We generate the short-run average cost curve for essentially the range of outputs observed at each institution during the time period studied.[4] When generating the cost curve, we assume that all variables other than output are equal to the mean value observed in the data for that institution. The process of generating the average cost curve is simple. For a given output $Q$ (and with other variables equal to the sample mean value), Eq. (15.2.1) yields the necessary quantity of labor $\hat{L}$. Average variable cost then equals $P_L\hat{L}/Q$, where $P_L$ is the per-unit price of labor. To this we need to add average fixed cost, which is calculated as fixed cost divided by $Q$, where fixed cost in turn is calculated as $TC$ (total cost) minus $P_L L$ (payments to labor), with both $TC$ and $L$ evaluated at the sample mean for the particular prison. Thus we have the short-run average total cost for

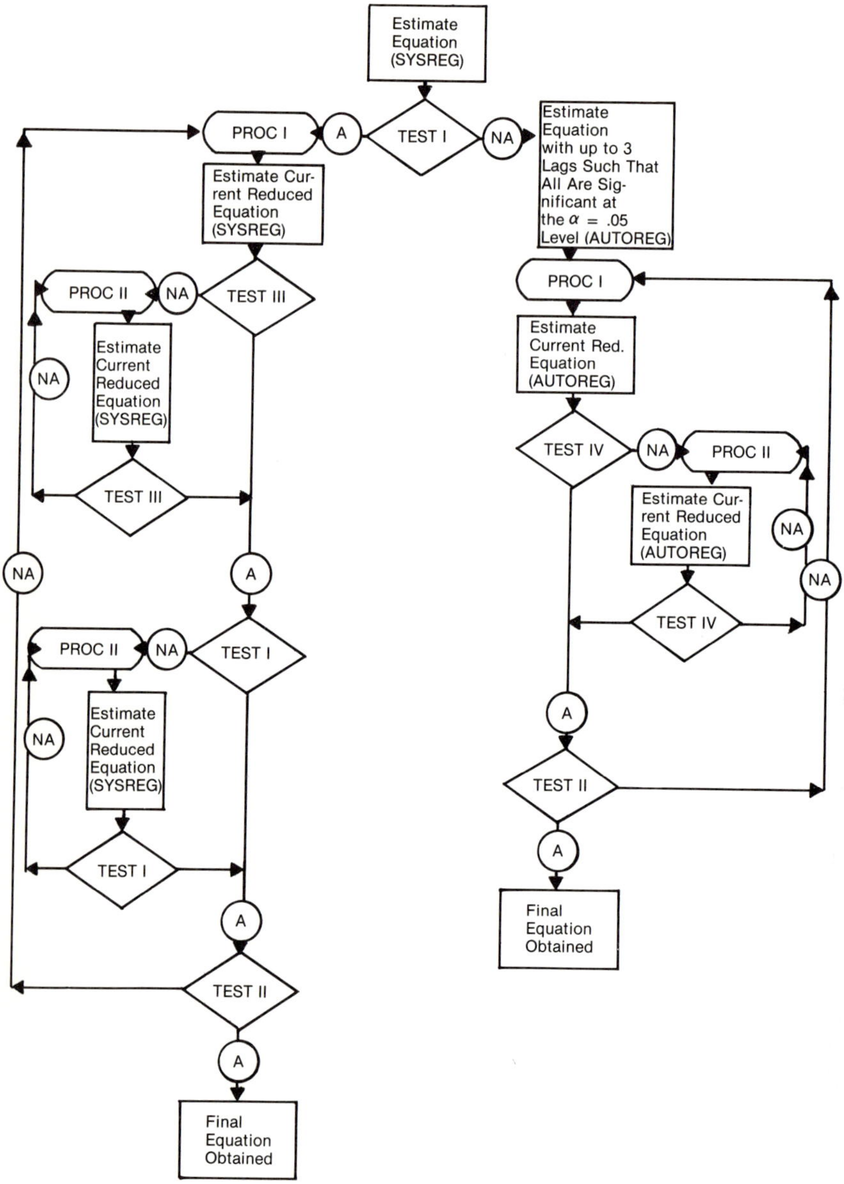


**Fig. 15.1.** Flowchart of model reduction method.

Key to Fig. 15.1

| Symbol | Explanation |
|---|---|
| TEST I | Durbin–Watson test. $H_0: \rho = 0$; $H_A$: not $H_0$. |
| TEST II | Theil criterion. $H_0$: For each variable in specification, $\|t\| > 1$; $H_A$: not $H_0$. |
| TEST III | Joint $F$-test for significance of dropped variables at $\alpha = .05$ level. $H_0$: $\beta$'s of all dropped variables $= 0$; $H_A$: not $H_0$. |
| TEST IV | Likelihood-ratio test for joint significance of dropped variables at $\alpha = .05$ level. $H_0$: $\beta$'s of all dropped variables $= 0$; $H_A$: not $H_0$. |
| A | Accept $H_0$. |
| NA | Do *not* accept $H_0$. |
| PROC I | Drop all variables (other than *CD-ALL* and *LNCD-ALL*) with $\|t\| < 1$ from specification of equation. |
| PROC II | Add previously dropped variable with highest $\|t\|$ to specification of equation. |
| SYSREG | SAS procedure using an ordinary least-squares estimation technique. |
| AUTOREG | SAS procedure using a generalized least-squares procedure that estimates a set of autoregressive parameters and then transforms the data by a linear combination of these parameters. |

**TABLE 15.1a.**

| Independent variables | No autocorrelation | | | |
|---|---|---|---|---|
| | Atlanta | Danbury | Lewisburg | Petersburg |
| Output | | | | |
| *LNCD-ALL* | −11.633268(−.921) | 6.311010(1.067) | 2.921351 (.385) | 26.035336(1.467) |
| *CD-ALL* | .000187(.949) | −.000290(−1.0522) | −.000036(−.234) | −.001385*(−1.720) |
| Production quality | | | | |
| *CD-IPRS* | | .000000(1.091) | | |
| *IPRS* | | | .000106(1.636) | .003264**(2.066) |
| *IPRS2* | | | | −.000001*(−1.772) |
| *SECURE* | 15.422119(1.538) | 1.907836(1.866) | −4.925459***(−3.274) | −4.941866**(−2.07) |
| Product quality and service conditions | | | | |
| *AGE-I* | −.465884***(−2.993) | | 24.037659***(2.176) | 44.251057***(2.775) |
| *AGE-I2* | | | −.336177**(−2.147) | −.901524***(−2.789) |
| *RACE-I* | | −.030559(−1.349) | | |
| *BETAIQ* | | −.054050(−1.104) | | |
| *WCOLLAR* | | | .099249**(2.430) | .072431(1.045) |
| *DRUGS* | .050984**(2.522) | −.035102***(−2.964) | | |
| *ALCOL* | | | .176735***(3.720) | |
| *LENGTH* | | .131986(1.115) | .322235(1.619) | |
| *O-PERS* | −.086881(−1.383) | .201041***(3.119) | .158109*(1.762) | |
| *O-PROP* | | | −.138495***(−3.001) | |
| *RECORD* | | | | |
| *MARRIED* | | | −.047752**(−2.059) | |
| Service conditions | | | | |
| *INCIDENT* | | | −.0113046(−1.287) | |
| *R-BALN* | | −3.108592***(−4.642) | 19.843046***(5.457) | |
| *R-BALN2* | | | | |
| *PC-OTH* | | | .014239(1.138) | |
| *FEMALE* | | | | |
| Adjustments | | | | |
| *SIZE-K* | | | .000483*(1.784) | .001950*(1.812) |
| *MONTH-1* | | | | .136920***(2.915) |
| *MONTH-2* | | | | |
| *TREND* 1 | | −.011596*(−1.744) | −.068959***(−4.524) | |
| *INTERCEPT* | 143.958563(1.134) | −38.480426(−.748) | −446.569708*(−1.937) | −764.234023***(−3.077) |
| Statistics and tests | | | | |
| *N* | 33 | 33 | 33 | 33 |
| $\bar{R}^2$[b] (*F*-ratio) | .2132(2.445) | .5773(4.974) | .7557(6.826) | .6573(7.139) |
| Durbin–Watson | 1.839 | 1.8417 | 1.9809 | 1.9123 |
| Jt. F[c] | .8833 | .2845 | .2972 | 1.913 |
| Chi-square[d] | N/A | N/A | N/A | N/A |
| No. intermediate runs[e] | 2 | 10 | 11 | 6 |
| Estimated autoregressive parameters | | | | |
| $\rho^1$ | N/A | N/A | N/A | N/A |
| $\rho^2$ | N/A | N/A | N/A | N/A |
| $\rho^3$ | N/A | N/A | N/A | N/A |

[a] Values in parentheses are *t*-ratios. Asterisks indicate level of significance of coefficient, two-tailed test: * = .10 level, ** = .05 level, *** = .01 level.

[b] Indicates the percentage of variation explained by the independent variables in the model, correcting for degrees of freedom.

[c] This is the calculated value of the *F*-statistic, which tests for the joint significance of all dropped variables. [See Kmenta (1971, p. 370).]

[d] This is the calculated value of the $\chi^2$-statistic, which tests for the joint significance of all dropped variables using a likelihood ratio test. [See Kendall and Stuart (1976, pp. 276–284).]

[e] This is the number of regressions estimated in moving from the initial to the reduced specification, which are not presented here.

Summary of Results of Estimating Short-Run Labor Demand Equations[a]

| | First-order autoregression | | | |
|---|---|---|---|---|
| | Ashland | Englewood | Fort Worth | La Tuna |
| | 1.510311(.293) | −.368233(−.270) | 9.203048**(2.154) | −3.288569(−.433) |
| | .000166(.678) | .000018(.162) | −.000687**(−2.266) | −.000062(−.163) |
| | −1.453E-7**(−2.575) | | 6.4701E-8(1.497) | .000000(1.405) |
| | .003182***(2.712) | | −.000995(−1.272) | −.003178(−1.268) |
| | −1.284322(−1.155) | | | |
| | −2.794622***(−3.480) | 4.653543***(3.429) | | |
| | .055538***(3.195) | −.098624***(−3.514) | | |
| | | | | .057880**(2.192) |
| | −.230678***(−3.028) | | | |
| | | | −.037177*(−1.754) | |
| | .054496***(4.763) | | | |
| | | −.065052**(−2.457) | | |
| | .027415**(2.123) | | .193196**(1.995) | |
| | | | | −.009416(−1.239) |
| | | −.066595***(−4.568) | | |
| | .119680***(4.174) | .051621***(4.019) | | |
| | | | | .321631*(1.941) |
| | | | | −.000706**(−2.505) |
| | −.050849***(−2.598) | −.018660**(−2.201) | | |
| | 45.115401(1.009) | −37.617929*(−1.885) | −66.923804*(−1.825) | 44.557527(.658) |
| | 33 | 33 | 33 | 33 |
| | .6131(5.23) | .5104(5.17) | .111(1.62) | .5661(6.22) |
| | N/A | N/A | N/A | N/A |
| | N/A | N/A | N/A | N/A |
| | 1.485 | 3.728 | 4.317 | 3.006 |
| | 1 | 1 | 9 | 3 |
| | .086778(.5004) | −.022782(−.131) | −.473615**(−2.610) | −.260340(−1.549) |
| | — | — | — | — |
| | — | — | — | — |

**TABLE 15.1b.**

| | First-order | | |
|---|---|---|---|
| Independent variables | Leavenworth | Lompoc | McNeil Island |
| Output | | | |
| *LNCD-ALL* | −9.936638(−1.286) | 29.668558**(2.101) | −6.539670(−1.382) |
| *CD-ALL* | .000167(1.313) | −.000680*(−1.910) | .000146(1.293) |
| Production quality | | | |
| *CD-IPRS* | | 4.0112E-8**(2.020) | |
| *IPRS* | | −.002013**(−2.259) | |
| *IPRS2* | 7.1737E-8***(8.316) | | |
| *SECURE* | | | −7.263463***(−5.971) |
| Product quality and service conditions | | | |
| *AGE-I* | 16.060751**(2.121) | | |
| *AGE-I2* | −.203684**(−2.081) | | |
| *RACE-I* | −.072145***(−2.942) | | .196347***(9.670) |
| *BETAIQ* | −.629600***(−6.945) | | |
| *WCOLLAR* | | −.060881**(−2.201) | |
| *DRUGS* | | | |
| *ALCOL* | .072302***(3.197) | | −.019660(1.674) |
| *LENGTH* | −.428944*(−4.935) | −.214786*(−1.835) | −.352305***(−3.694) |
| *O-PERS* | .154836***(3.426) | .068442(1.375) | |
| *O-PROP* | | .075867**(2.430) | .053910***(6.952) |
| *RECORD* | −.690457**(−2.439) | | |
| *MARRIED* | −.092561***(−3.228) | −.029894**(−1.977) | |
| Service conditions | | | |
| *INCIDENT* | | | |
| *R-BALN* | −1.789100***(−2.848) | | 4.443892***(6.952) |
| *R-BALN2* | | | |
| *PC-OTH* | | | .083624***(3.989) |
| *FEMALE* | | | |
| Adjustments | | | |
| *SIZE*-K | | | |
| *MONTH*-1 | −.028075*(−1.728) | | |
| *MONTH*-2 | −.024626 (−1.510) | | −.075369***(−3.303) |
| *TREND* 1 | | −.025992**(−2.360) | |
| *INTERCEPT* | −125.45986(−.646) | −275.6383**(−2.035) | 67.990347(1.442) |
| Statistics and tests | | | |
| *N* | 33 | 33 | 33 |
| $\bar{R}^{2}$[b] (*F*-ratio) | .8947(19.15) | .7740(11.96) | .8374(17.48) |
| Durbin–Watson | N/A | N/A | N/A |
| Jt.F[c] | N/A | N/A | N/A |
| Chi-square[d] | 3.6741 | 2.64 | 1.918 |
| No. intermediate runs[e] | 2 | 5 | 1 |
| Estimated autoregressive parameters | | | |
| $\rho^1$ | .277245(1.658) | .097313(−.562) | .452101***(2.9117) |
| $\rho^2$ | — | — | — |
| $\rho^3$ | — | — | — |

[a] Values in parentheses are *t*-values. Asterisks indicate level of significance of coefficient, two-tailed test: * = .10 level, ** = .05 level, *** = .01 level.

[b] Indicates the percentage of variation explained by the independent variables in the model, correcting for degrees of freedom.

[c] This is the calculated value of the *F*-statistic, which tests for the joint significance of all dropped variables. [See Kmenta (1971, p. 370).]

[d] This is the calculated value of the $\chi^2$-statistic, which tests for the joint significance of all dropped variables using a likelihood ratio test. [See Kendall and Stuart (1976, pp. 276–284).]

[e] This is the number of regressions estimated in moving from the initial to the reduced specification, which are not presented here.

Summary of Results of Estimating Short-Run Labor Demand Equations[a]

autoregression

| Marion | Oxford | Sandstone | Seagoville | Terre Haute |
|---|---|---|---|---|
| 5.562119(.783) | −5.454714***(−2.618) | .660734(.637) | −7.269954**(−2.030) | −5.575279(−.880) |
| −.000294(−.748) | .000355***(3.010) | −.000017(−.285) | .000425*(1.733) | .000068(.471) |
| | | −2.5807E-8***(−2.899) | | |
| .000387***(5.483) | .000248***(7.906) | | | |
| −7.1131E-8**(−2.006) | | .000000**(2.350) | | |
| | | | −4.868228***(−2.876) | |
| | −.487159***(−6.826) | | .302913***(3.568) | 37.113310***(4.527) |
| | | | | −.561614***(−4.547) |
| −.022772(−1.183) | | .024465**(2.575) | | |
| | −.063420**(−1.980) | | | −.192751***(−4.802) |
| −.021993(−1.187) | .078595***(8.169) | −.024591**(−2.169) | | |
| | −.011968**(−1.991) | | .087716***(6.610) | |
| −.061727(−1.191) | | | | .044015*(1.843) |
| | −.331964***(−6.469) | | | −.259379***(−4.959) |
| −.110406***(−4.210) | .130908***(7.515) | | | .329593***(5.495) |
| −.088677***(−2.838) | .088868***(7.202) | | | |
| | 1.007568***(4.328) | | −1.064400***(−3.262) | |
| | −.052362***(−3.456) | | .093420***(4.475) | |
| 1.153946(1.330) | −4.689476***(−5.001) | −5.182198***(−7.839) | .837399***(4.293) | 7.050767***(6.203) |
| .012621(1.263) | | | | |
| −.007823(−1.518) | .005332*(1.835) | | | −.000775**(−2.360) |
| −.044720(−1.664) | | | | |
| −.026465(−1.106) | −.027388**(−2.127) | | −.069707**(−2.260) | |
| −.015356***(−2.817) | .036126***(6.170) | | −.021294**(−2.118) | |
| 24.516304(−.400) | 68.549693***(3.738) | 4.359911(.484) | 61.475629**(2.001) | −524.84477***(−3.224) |
| 33 | 33 | 33 | 33 | 33 |
| .8724(15.57) | .957(45.55) | .7656(15.93) | .6321(6.50) | .8525(19.50) |
| N/A | N/A | N/A | N/A | N/A |
| N/A | N/A | N/A | N/A | N/A |
| 1.72 | .6669 | 1.616 | 3.3157 | 3.324 |
| 3 | 1 | 1 | 4 | 1 |
| .061350(.353) | .605092***(4.366) | −.192353(−1.126) | .070246(.405) | .2694(1.607) |
| — | — | — | — | — |
| — | — | — | — | — |

**TABLE 15.1c.**

| | First-order autoregression | |
|---|---|---|
| Independent variables | Terminal Island | Texarkana |
| Output | | |
| *LNCD-ALL* | 48.805828***(3.426) | −16.727072(−1.280) |
| *CD-ALL* | −.001481***(−3.180) | .000811(1.310) |
| Production quality | | |
| *CD-IPRS* | | |
| *IPRS* | | |
| *IPRS2* | | |
| *SECURE* | 8.797594***(2.819) | |
| Product quality and service conditions | | |
| *AGE-I* | 1.206183***(3.441) | |
| *AGE-I2* | | |
| *RACE-I* | −.098513***(−2.273) | |
| *BETAIQ* | −.398154***(−2.850) | |
| *WCOLLAR* | | |
| *DRUGS* | | .025332(1.352) |
| *ALCOL* | | |
| *LENGTH* | .803978***(2.854) | |
| *O-PERS* | −.379204***(−2.753) | |
| *O-PROP* | | |
| *RECORD* | −1.413551***(−3.238) | |
| *MARRIED* | | |
| Service conditions | | |
| *INCIDENT* | | .022560*(1.727) |
| *R-BALN* | −1.356875**(−2.137) | |
| *R-BALN2* | | |
| *PC-OTH* | .062349**(2.599) | |
| *FEMALE* | | |
| Adjustments | | |
| *SIZE*-K | −.000957(−1.070) | |
| *MONTH*-1 | | |
| *MONTH*-2 | .168500***(3.044) | |
| *TREND* 1 | −.016765(−1.520) | |
| *INTERCEPT* | −447.43429***(−3.316) | 159.525901 (1.363) |
| Statistics and tests | | |
| *N* | 33 | 33 |
| $\bar{R}^{2}$[b] (*F*-ratio) | .4341(2.75) | .0768(1.67) |
| Durbin–Watson | N/A | N/A |
| Jt.F[c] | N/A | N/A |
| Chi-square[d] | | 3.3294 |
| No. intermediate runs[e] | 3 | 4 |
| Estimated autoregressive parameters | | |
| $\rho^1$ | .116952(.676) | .096446 (.5566) |
| $\rho^2$ | — | — |
| $\rho^3$ | — | — |

[a] Values in parentheses are *t*-values. Asterisks indicate level of significance of coefficient, two-tailed test: * = .10 level, ** = .05 level, *** = .01 level.

[b] Indicates the percentage of variation explained by the independent variables in the model, correcting for degrees of freedom.

[c] This is the calculated value of the *F*-statistic, which tests for the joint significance of all dropped variables. [See Kmenta (1971, p. 370).]

[d] This is the calculated value of the $\chi^2$-statistic, which tests for the joint significance of all dropped variables using a likelihood ratio test. [See Kendall and Stuart (1976, pp. 276–284).]

[e] This is the number of regressions estimated in moving from the initial to the reduced specification, which are not presented here.

Summary of Results of Estimating Short-Run Labor Demand Equations[a]

| Second-order autoregression | | | Third-order autoregression |
|---|---|---|---|
| Alderson | El Reno | Milan | Lexington |
| −.269078(−.053) | 11.008310***(5.361) | −5.128536**(−2.008) | −5.484390***(−4.620) |
| .000377(1.017) | −.000325***(−5.639) | .000248*(1.959) | .000374***(6.545) |
| −2.2283E-7***(−2.762) | | | −5.6400E-8***(−6.545) |
| .004281***(3.101) | .000629***(9.110) | .000378***(8.633) | .001993***(7.211) |
| | −5.6256E-8***(−3.055) | | |
| | 2.569511***(2.817) | | |
| 8.022390***(2.385) | | | −.681462***(−6.601) |
| −.129280***(2.475) | −.002298(−2.513) | | |
| −.074800***(−5.767) | −.119197(−8.705) | | |
| −.076660*(−1.810) | | | |
| .060463***(4.644) | | | .100038***(5.326) |
| | | | −.125926***(−6.185) |
| −.056453*(−1.836) | .043180***(5.327) | | −.194537***(−7.752) |
| .705255***(7.591) | .204454***(4.675) | | −1.350723***(−6.468) |
| .140928***(4.449) | | −.128716**(−2.111) | |
| .071057***(4.314) | .122793***(8.257) | | |
| −.083325***(−4.836) | | | |
| −.036097***(−4.231) | | | .049547***(6.129) |
| −1.953595***(−3.197) | −2.335830***(−7.428) | | .988467(1.499) |
| | | | .256784***(7.709) |
| | | | .264109***(8.360) |
| −.006221***(−4.208) | −.007799***(−4.349) | | |
| −.024235(−1.180) | .044019***(3.696) | | −.065220***(−4.433) |
| .057337***(2.481) | .071252***(5.633) | | |
| .012740**(2.005) | .015199(1.641) | −.012687***(−5.475) | .055406***(4.994) |
| −112.94848*(−1.768) | −89.5448848***(−4.689) | 56.493125**(2.477) | 61.367199(5.470) |
| 33 | 33 | 33 | 33 |
| .9661(46.51) | .995(435.35) | .7442(19.62) | .8528(13.36) |
| N/A | N/A | N/A | N/A |
| N/A | N/A | N/A | N/A |
| .8212 | .909 | 2.996 | 4.01 |
| 0 | 2 | 5 | 2 |
| .471789***(2.988) | .192394(1.345) | −.780698***(−5.600) | .274458(1.626) |
| .421304***(2.669) | .570095***(3.986) | .598893***(4.296) | .025296(.144) |
| — | — | — | .244242(1.447) |

output $Q$ calculated as

$$SRATC(Q) = (TC - P_L L + P_L \hat{L})/Q. \qquad (15.2.2)$$

In investigating the shape of the short-run average cost curve, we shall distinguish two cases. In the first such case, the interaction between output *CD-ALL* and the level of rehabilitative activities *IPRS* does not appear in the final specification. This is so for 14 of our 22 federal prisons, as listed in Table 15.2. In this case the estimated cost function (14.6.5) corresponds to a homothetic Cobb–Douglas production function of the form of (14.6.1), and we can solve for the (estimated) production function parameters in terms of the (estimated) cost function parameters: $\theta = \beta_2/\beta_1$, $\alpha = 1/\beta_1$. The shape of the average cost function is determined by the values of $\alpha$ and $\theta$. Table 15.3 lists seven possible combinations of ranges for $\alpha$ and $\theta$ and the shapes that they imply. The Appendix to this chapter demonstrates the mathematics that leads to Table 15.3.

Although we have been able to determine the shape of the short-run average cost curve for all possible values of $\alpha$ and $\theta$, not all of the shapes for

**TABLE 15.2.** Institutions with Cost Curves Dual to a Homothetic Cobb–Douglas Production Function

| Institution | Minimum-cost inmate population[a] | Observed inmate population | | Observed shape of average cost curve[d] |
|---|---|---|---|---|
| | | Minimum[b] | Maximum[c] | |
| Atlanta | 2894 | 1947 | 2347 | Decreasing |
| El Reno | N/A | 984 | 1331 | Decreasing |
| Englewood | 2851 | 282 | 530 | Decreasing |
| Leavenworth | 2165 | 1866 | 2240 | ∪-shaped |
| Lewisburg | N/A | 1443 | 1771 | ∩-shaped |
| Marion | N/A | 539 | 662 | Decreasing |
| McNeil Island | 1731 | 1108 | 1556 | Decreasing |
| Milan | 821 | 538 | 812 | Decreasing |
| Oxford | 614 | 445 | 650 | ∪-shaped |
| Petersburg | N/A | 647 | 801 | Decreasing |
| Seagoville | 665 | 411 | 567 | Decreasing |
| Terminal Island | N/A | 868 | 1095 | ∩-shaped |
| Terre Haute | 3276 | 1305 | 1651 | Decreasing |
| Texarkana | 726 | 630 | 770 | ∪-shaped |

[a] This is the average daily inmate population that minimizes average cost. It equals the cost-minimizing value of *CD-ALL* divided by 30.5 and is not applicable for prisons with an average cost curve that is ∩-shaped or decreasing over all possible outputs.
[b] Defined as the sample mean minus two standard deviations.
[c] Defined as the sample mean plus two standard deviations.
[d] Shape of the average cost curve between the minimum and maximum observed inmate populations.

**TABLE 15.3.** Shape of the Average Cost Function for Specific Parametric Values

| Case | Values of $\alpha$ and $\theta$ | Shape of average cost curve |
|---|---|---|
| 1 | $\alpha > 1;\ \theta > 0$ | ∪-shaped |
| 2 | $0 < \alpha < 1;\ \theta > 0$ | Positively sloped |
| 3 | $\alpha < 0;\ \theta > 0$ | Negatively sloped |
| 4 | $\alpha > 1;\ \theta < 0$ | Negatively sloped |
| 5 | $0 < \alpha < 1;\ \theta < 0$ | ∩-shaped |
| 6 | $\alpha < 0;\ \theta < 0$ | ∪-shaped |
| 7 | $\alpha = 1;\ \theta = 0$ | Horizontal |

all values of $\alpha$ and $\theta$ accord with economic theory. For example, the parametric values for case 5 of Table 15.3 imply an inverted ∪ shape for the short-run average cost curve. The other shapes appear to be in accord with economic theory, but some actually are not. This is the case for all levels of output for case 3 and for some levels of output for cases 4 and 6.[5] For these output and parameter combinations, the marginal product of labor is less than zero. This clearly is at odds with economic theory and good management practices, because it indicates that either hiring additional workers or increasing the hours of existing workers will actually *decrease* output.

There are two possible ways of handling these aberrant cases. First, we could restrict the possible value of our coefficient estimates so that aberrant results would not be obtained. For example, we could restrict the possible values for $\beta_1$ and $\beta_2$ so that $\theta$ could never be negative when $\alpha$ was between 0 and 1 (i.e., case 5 would never occur). Second, we could refrain from imposing such restrictions and see whether the results are in accord with our theoretical expectations. We choose the second course because we are interested in determining the degree to which prison operations accord with the tenets of economic theory.

In the second possible case, the interaction between *CD-ALL* and *IPRS* appears in the final specification. This is so for 8 of our 22 federal prisons, as listed in Table 15.4. In this case the cost function corresponds to a production function of more complex form; it is no longer dual to a simple homothetic Cobb–Douglas production function. We now need to explore the shape of the cost function with this specification.

Note first that the level and shape of the cost function for these institutions will depend on the level of rehabilitative activities provided; that is, there is no unique cost curve but rather a different cost curve for each level of rehabilitative activities. One may separately determine the least-cost inmate population for any given level of rehabilitative activities and the least-cost number of rehabilitative activities for any given prison population, or one can jointly determine the combination of population size and level of rehabilitative activities that will minimize costs globally. We shall give (in Table 15.4), for each institution, the population and level of rehabilitative activities that would jointly minimize short-run average costs, and we shall indicate the shape of the short-run average cost curve over the observed range of output. [See Witte *et al.* (1979) for a detailed discussion.]

Consider first the estimated short-run average cost curves for the 14 institutions whose cost functions correspond to a homothetic Cobb–Douglas production function if costs are minimized. For these institutions, Table 15.2 indicates the population for which short-run average costs would be a minimum (in some cases there is no such output as indicated), the sample range of the inmate population (as defined in Note 4), and the shape of the short-run average cost curve over this range. An inspection of the last column of this table indicates that the cost curves for these institutions assume three different shapes over the range of observed output: (1) average cost decreases continuously as output increases, (2) average cost at first decreases and then increases (i.e., a ∪-shaped average cost curve), and (3) average cost at first increases and then decreases (i.e., a ∩-shaped cost curve). Recall from our previous discussion that the first two shapes for the average cost curve accord with economic theory, whereas the last does not.

The short-run average total cost curve for the U.S. Penitentiary at Marion, Illinois, depicted in Fig. 15.2, well illustrates the first type of cost curve, which is the most common type encountered. (Nine of the 14 prisons in Table 15.2 exhibit this type of cost curve.) Note that for small populations (around 500 inmates) costs are quite high (about $33 per inmate-day), whereas for larger populations (around 700 inmates) they are much smaller (about $27 per inmate-day). For this type of institution it appears that larger populations are associated with lower short-run operating costs, at least within the population range observed. Marion is a relatively unusual prison in the federal system. It is the "back-up" facility and the only maximum-security prison in the system. As a whole, our results seem to indicate that older, more secure facilities are likely to be characterized by this type of short-run average cost curves. Indeed, four of the six U.S. Penitentiaries have this type of cost curve.[6] It is interesting to note that the coefficient on the interaction term between population and the level of rehabilitative activities *CD-IPRS* is insignificantly different from zero for all six U.S. Penitentiaries. This seems to indicate that for these large, old, highly secure institutions, the size of the inmate population and the level of rehabilitative activities may have independent effects on costs, but they do not affect costs jointly. Indeed, the level of rehabilitative activities appears in general to have little effect on costs for these types of institutions.

**TABLE 15.4.** Institutions with Cost Curves with More Complex Duals

| Institutions | Minimum-cost inmate population[a] | Observed inmate population | | Minimum-cost IPRS | Observed IPRS | | Observed shape of average cost curve[d] |
|---|---|---|---|---|---|---|---|
| | | Minimum[b] | Maximum[c] | | Minimum[b] | Maximum[c] | |
| Alderson | 473[e] | 473 | 650 | 964[e] | 964 | 1432 | Increasing |
| Ashland | 565[e] | 565 | 767 | 1011[e] | 1011 | 1785 | Increasing |
| Danbury | N/A | 629 | 822 | 2180 | 140 | 2180 | ∩-shaped |
| Fort Worth | 703[e] | 427 | 703 | 726[e] | 726 | 2307 | Decreasing |
| La Tuna | 861[e] | 713 | 861 | 797[e] | 797 | 1415 | Decreasing |
| Lexington | 617[e] | 617 | 1327 | 1503[e] | 1503 | 2950 | ∪-shaped |
| Lompoc | 1265[e] | 1265 | 1583 | 3054[e] | 1000 | 3054 | Increasing |
| Sandstone | N/A | 359 | 690 | 1153 | 0 | 1265 | Decreasing |

[a] This is the average daily inmate population that minimizes average cost. It equals the cost-minimizing value of *CD-ALL* divided by 30.5, and is not applicable for prisons with an average cost curve that is ∩-shaped or that decreases over all possible outputs.
[b] Defined as the sample mean minus two standard deviations.
[c] Defined as the sample mean plus two standard deviations.
[d] Shape of the average cost curve between the minimum and maximum observed inmate populations.
[e] These values are boundary solutions from Witte *et al.* (1979, app. 9.3, case II).

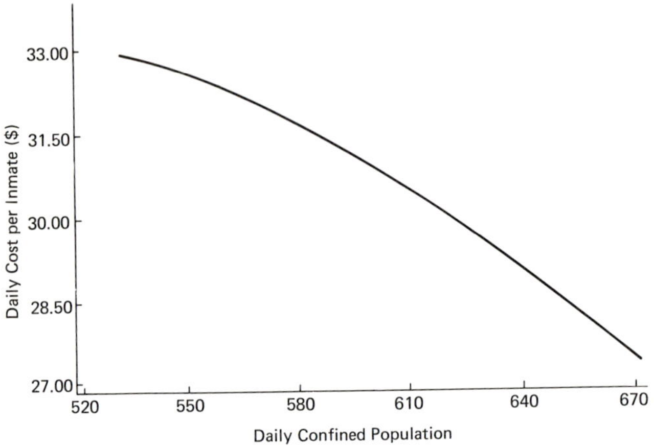


**Fig. 15.2.** Average cost curve, Federal Penitentiary, Marion, Illinois.

The second type of cost curve, ∪-shaped, is well illustrated by the short-run average total cost curve for the Federal Correction Institution (FCI) at Texarkana, Texas, depicted in Fig. 15.3. Note that costs for relatively small populations (around 600 inmates) are quite high ($20.50 per inmate-day) but that these costs fall quite rapidly, reaching a minimum of approximately $17.75 per inmate-day for a population of 726 inmates. Costs rise slowly for populations above this size and are approximately $18.25 per day for a population of 770 inmates. Note that, for prisons characterized by this type of short-run cost curve, there is a unique population size that will minimize

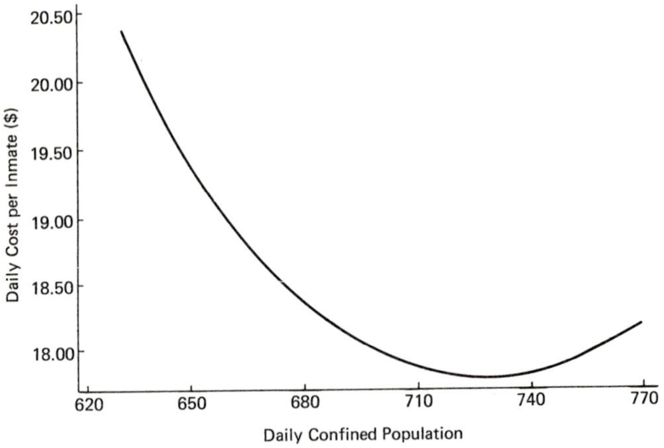


**Fig. 15.3.** Average cost curve, Federal Correctional Institution, Texarkana, Texas.

short-run operating costs. The FCI at Texarkana is a medium-security, adult-male institution with a physical capacity of 430. The institution has a prison industry that makes office furniture and employs 90–95 inmates. As can be seen by inspecting the horizontal axis in Fig. 15.3, this institution was continually operating above its rated physical capacity during the period studied. Two other federal prisons have this type of short-run average total cost curve. One is the large (capacity 1625), close-security U.S. Penitentiary at Leavenworth, Kansas, and the other is a relatively small (capacity 480), medium-security FCI at Oxford, Wisconsin. The three prisons with this type of cost curve seem to have two things in common: (1) they were usually operating above capacity during the period studied and (2) they had relatively large numbers of inmates working in prison industries.

Two prisons, the FCI at Terminal Island, California and the U.S. Penitentiary at Lewisburg, Pennsylvania) have the third type of cost curve, ∩-shaped, which, as noted previously, does not conform to the shape predicted by economic theory. This type of short-run average total cost curve is well illustrated by the cost curve for the FCI at Terminal Island, California, depicted in Fig. 15.4. Note that costs for this institution are low (about \$10.80) for relatively small populations (around 850 inmates), rise to a maximum of approximately \$24 per day for an inmate population of around 1050, and decline slightly for populations above this level. Note that for prisons characterized by this type of curve, it appears that short-run operating costs can probably be minimized by having a relatively small population. However, further investigation of the nature of operations of these two prisons during the period studied leads us to believe that there were

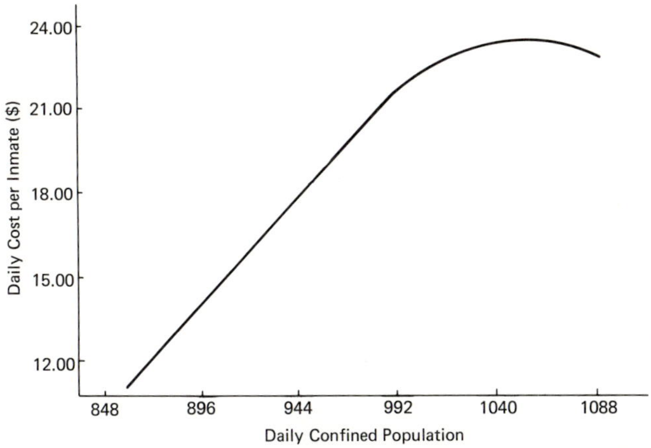


**Fig. 15.4.** Average cost curve, Federal Correctional Institution, Terminal Island, California.

sufficiently major shifts in the nature of prison operations to make estimating a single cost curve for the period inappropriate. Specifically, the FCI at Terminal Island began the period studied as a co-correctional institution. In November 1977, it changed to an all-male facility. Beginning in April 1978, this FCI operated a detention center for individuals awaiting trial in the Federal District Court of Los Angeles. Thus it would appear necessary to estimate three different cost curves for this facility during the period studied, rather than one.[7]

The unexpected results obtained for the FCI at Terminal Island and the U.S. Penitentiary at Lewisburg, Pennsylvania, allow two important observations. First, it is probably better to estimate cost curves without constraining parameter estimates to conform to economic theory. Aberrant results may well, as in the present instance, point up important factors that had been excluded from consideration in the original modeling effort. Second, estimation of cost curves or production functions is best done with detailed knowledge of the institutions being studied.

Consider next the eight institutions for which the interaction between *CD-ALL* and *IPRS* was included in the final specification of the cost function. The cost function for these institutions is dual to a production function that is more complex than a homothetic Cobb–Douglas function. Table 15.4 contains summary information related to the cost curves for these institutions. Specifically, this table contains (where relevant) the level of population and the level of rehabilitative activities for which short-run average total costs are minimized, the smallest and largest observed population and level of rehabilitative activities, and the shape of the average cost curve (over the observed sample range) for each institution.

The average cost curves take on four different shapes in the observed range of output for this group of institutions: increasing, decreasing, ∪-shaped, or ∩-shaped. As noted previously, a ∩-shaped cost curve is not consistent with economic theory. Only one institution in this group, Danbury, has this humpbacked shape. As was the case for the previous institutions with cost curves of this shape, investigation of the nature of operation at Danbury during the period studied indicated that major changes occurred.[8] Thus our estimates of a single cost function for this institution during the period studied is inappropriate, and our results for this institution should not be considered valid.

Three institutions in this group, Forth Worth, La Tuna, and Sandstone, have short-run cost curves that continously decrease as the size of the inmate population increases. The cost curve for the FCI at Sandstone, Minnesota, depicted in Fig. 15.5, illustrates this type of cost curve well. Note that for small populations (around 300 inmates) costs are quite high (about $33 per inmate-day) but that costs decline relative rapidly and are only approximately

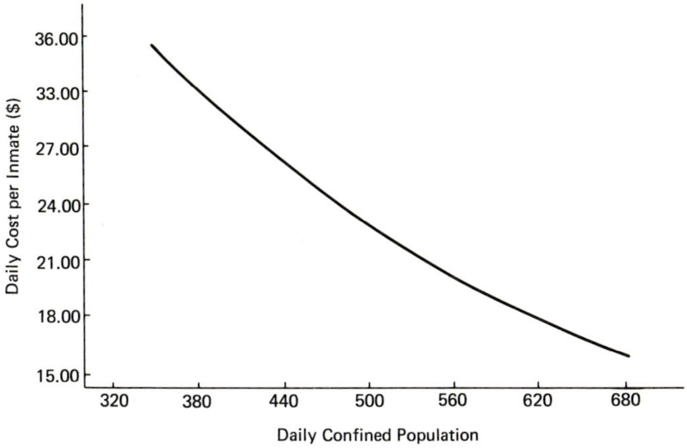


**Fig. 15.5.** Average cost curve with optimal level of rehabilitative activities, Federal Correctional Institution, Sandstone, Minnesota.

$15 per inmate-day for a population of approximately 700 inmates. Thus it appears that for institutions with this type of cost curve, correctional managers may lower costs by increasing the population, at least within the range of populations observed in our sample. Sandstone is a relatively small FCI (physical capacity 315 inmates) that was reopened in 1959. It houses older males (27 and over) with relatively short sentences (5 years or less) in a medium-security environment with extensive rehabilitative activities available. The other two institutions with this type of cost curve are similar to Sandstone in a number of respects. They are relatively small institutions that house inmates with relatively little time left to serve, and they provide relatively large amounts of rehabilitative activities.

Three institutions in this group, Alderson, Ashland, and Lompoc, have short-run cost curves that continuously increase as the inmate population increases. The cost curve for the FCI at Alderson, West Virginia, depicted in Fig. 15.6, illustrates the type of cost curves obtained for these institutions. In contrast to all reasonable cost curves seen to this point, costs at this institution are lowest for a small population (about $12 per inmate-day for a population of 470 inmates) and increase as population rises (reaching approximately $36 per inmate-day for a population of 650 inmates). Thus it appears that costs can be lowered for institutions of this type by keeping the inmate population small. It is interesting to note that all three institutions with this type of cost curve house "special" populations; Alderson houses only females, and Ashland and Lompoc house young males.

One institution in this group, Lexington, has a ∪-shaped cost curve, depicted in Fig. 15.7. Costs for this institution are lowest when populations

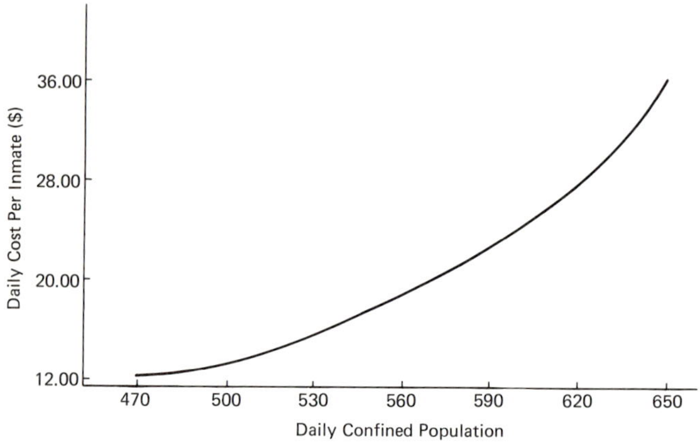


**Fig. 15.6.** Average cost curve with optimal level of rehabilitative activities, Federal Correctional Institution, Alderson, West Virginia.

are relatively small, being a minimum (about $16 per day) for a population of approximately 800 inmates. Costs rise relatively rapidly for populations above 800, reaching approximately $44 per inmate-day for a population of 1300 inmates. Lexington is a relatively unusual FCI because it specializes in the short-term care (averaging 15 months) of inmates with drug-abuse, alcohol, or chronic medical problems. The institution is a relatively new (opened in 1974), co-correctional, minimum-security facility.

Proceeding with our analysis, we now consider the effects on cost of the independent variables other than the level of output *CD-ALL*. We do not

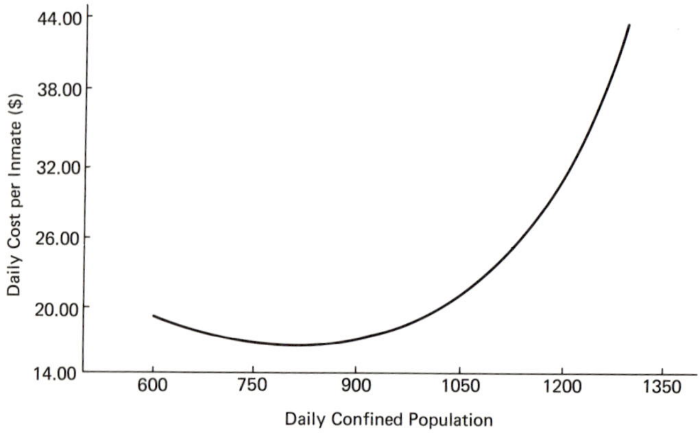


**Fig. 15.7.** Average cost curve with optimal level of rehabilitative activities, Federal Correctional Institution, Lexington, Kentucky.

include Danbury, Lewisburg, and Terminal Island in this examination because, as previously discussed, we do not feel that we have modeled the production process at these three institutions appropriately.

There are two variables that indicate the level of rehabilitative activities but do not involve output, *IPRS* and its squared value, *IPRS*2. We had no a priori expectation of the signs of the coefficients on these variables because there are two possibly conflicting effects on costs: providing rehabilitation is more expensive owing to extra staffing and materials but may reduce costs by promoting a calmer atmosphere at the prison. For 6 of the 19 institutions for which we obtained meaningful results, no variable involving *IPRS* is found to significantly affect cost. As mentioned previously, we found that the level of population and the level of rehabilitative activities affected cost jointly with output rather than independently for a number of institutions (7 of the 19 for which we obtained meaningful results.) For these institutions, we determined the level of rehabilitative activities that would be associated with minimum cost. This level is reported in Table 15.4. As can be seen in this table, the least-cost level of rehabilitative activities occurs between the upper and lower values observed for only one institution, Sandstone. For this institution it appears that providing relatively large numbers of rehabilitative activities will result in the lowest costs. For all other institutions of this type, the least-cost level of rehabilitative activities to provide is either the lowest or highest observed. For six institutions, it appears that costs will be lowest if the level of provision of rehabilitative activities is very low, and, for one institution (Lompoc), if the level of provision is very high. For the remaining six institutions, the coefficient of *IPRS* is generally positive; more rehabilitative activities implies a greater cost, at least for relatively low levels of provision. This positive relationship between *IPRS* and cost always holds when *IPRS*2 is also in the specification, which it is for three of these institutions. In this case, the coefficient of *IPRS*2 is always negative. Thus the cost of providing rehabilitative activities first increases and then decreases as more activities are provided. For one institution (Leavenworth), *IPRS* does not enter the final specification of the cost curve, but *IPRS*2 does, and the coefficient on this variable is positive. This result implies that costs increase at an increasing rate as more rehabilitative activities are provided at this institution. As a whole, our results indicating the effect of the provision of rehabilitative activities on short-run prison costs are diverse and suggest that the effect may depend critically on the nature of the particular institution being studied. Certainly, additional work studying both how and why the level of rehabilitative activities affects prison system costs would be useful.

Two variables, *AGE-I* and *AGE-I*2, indicate the effect of inmate age on costs. The existing literature suggests that inmates in their late teens and early twenties should be most costly to incarcerate. The coefficient on *AGE-I* is generally positive. For every institution with *AGE-I* positive, *AGE-I2* is negative. This result implies that costs increase with age until a certain point and then decrease. When *AGE-I2* does not appear in the final specification, *AGE-I* is always negative. Thus, as age increases, costs decrease continuously for these institutions.

*BETAIQ* is a measure of the average IQ of the inmate population. Though we had no a priori expectation as to the sign of the coefficient for this variable, it was negative in all cases. Thus our results indicate that short-run costs will be lower when the average IQ of the inmates is higher.

Two variables, *ALCOL* and *DRUGS*, indicate the extent of drug and alcohol problems among the inmates at each institution. A priori, we expect costs to increase as the extent of these problems increases. In general, costs rise as *DRUGS* increases but decline slightly as *ALCOL* increases. The relationship between the extent of alcohol problems and costs is not what we expected, but it may be because of the currently prevalent method of treating inmates with alcohol problems by housing them in special units with programs designed especially for them. Often these programs are more psychological than medical in their approach, and the counseling and group therapy that are applied may boost the morale of these inmates. This improved outlook may have a positive effect on inmate behavior, thereby reducing the level of tension and violence at the institution, which reduces costs. Alternatively, it may be that the effects of alcohol on the inmates with such problems are sufficiently debilitating to make them less difficult and thus cheaper to incarcerate.

Though we had no prior expectation as to the relationship between average length of sentence and costs, the sign of the coefficient of *LENGTH* is almost always negative. There are at least two possible explanations for this finding. First, inmates with longer sentences may adjust to prison life and thus may become more manageable prisoners. Second, there may be fixed costs associated with the incarceration of inmates.

We expected institutions with a higher percentage of inmates incarcerated for crimes against persons to have higher costs. This expectation is supported by our results. The sign of the coefficient on *O*-PERS is generally positive.

The variable *R-BAL* measures the ratio of the percentage of minority staff to the percentage of minorities in the inmate population. Generally, *R-BAL* takes on values between zero and one. As its value approaches one, the racial composition of the staff more closely approximates the racial composition of the inmate population. This racial similarity should improve staff–inmate relations. We expected the sign of this variable to be negative because better staff–inmate relations should lower the cost of incarceration. The signs of the coefficients on this variable have an interesting pattern. The estimated coefficient for *R-BAL* is generally negative, as expected, for Federal Correctional Institutions. This supports our hypothesis that racial similarity between staff and inmates lowers costs. However, for Federal Penitentiaries, the coefficient on *R-BAL* is, contrary to our expectations, generally positive. This unexpected finding may be due to the limited staff–inmate interaction at penitentiaries.

The percentage of confined days produced at an associated camp, female facility, or detention center is indicated by the variable *PC-OTH*. We had no a priori expectation as to the sign of the coefficient on this variable; however, it was positive in all cases. Thus, as the percentage of output produced at an associated facility increases, costs also increase.

The variable *FEMALE* is in the final specification of the cost curve for one institution, Lexington. The sign of the coefficient on this variable is positive, which indicates that costs increase as the percentage of females in the inmate population increases. As noted earlier, Lexington is a relatively unusual co-correctional institution, treating individuals with drug, alcohol, and serious medical problems.

The variable *SIZE-K*, which adjusts for changes in planned capacity, has an estimated coefficient that is generally negative, indicating that costs decrease as capacity increases, other things being constant. A possible explanation is that increases in planned capacity reduce overcrowding or perhaps increase the space and/or facilities available per inmate, which tends to lower costs.

Our model contains two variables, *MONTH*-1 and *MONTH*-2, to adjust for the quarterly spending patterns of prison officials. Whereas we expected the coefficients of these variables to be positive to indicate higher spending in the first two months of a quarter, the coefficients were generally negative. Our expectations of the spending patterns came from conversations with FBOP accounting personnel; however, it appears that the spending patterns discussed apply mainly to costs other than labor.

The variable *TREND*1 accounts for long-term time trends. We had no particular expectation as to the probable sign of the coefficient for this variable; it is usually negative. Because we are actually estimating labor demand, this result indicates a decrease in the use of labor over time. The negative sign could result from increased pressure on prison officials to reduce operating costs.

Coefficients on other variables, regardless of our a priori expectations, showed no consistent sign across institutions. These variables are *SECURE*, *RACE-I*, *WCOLLAR*, *O*-PROP, *RECORD*, *MARRIED*, and *INCIDENT*.

## 15.3. Empirical Results for California Prisons

We estimated short-run average cost curves for eight California prisons using the data described in Section 14.6 and the same methods used to obtain short-run average cost curves for federal prisons, as just described. Table

15.5 summarizes the results for the final specification of the labor demand function for these prisons. Note that we explain a surprisingly large amount of the variation in labor demand at these institutions. As is discussed in Appendix C, we believe that this results largely from the fact that we were forced to interpolate to obtain some observations on both the dependent and independent variables. Given this problem and the generally less satisfying data available for California prisons, we believe that results for these prisons should be considered only in relation to our results for federal prisons, in which we have far more confidence.

Encouragingly, results for California prisons are broadly similar to those for federal prisons, thus reinforcing some of our previous discussion. Table 15.6 contains a summary of our results indicating the way in which short-run operating costs vary with output in the California prisons studied. As we found for the federal system, we find for California prisons that there are independent but not joint effects for the level of rehabilitative activities and the population for most institutions. We obtain reasonable shapes for the cost curve for seven of the eight prisons studied. As was the case for similar institutions in the federal system, the one institution with a cost curve shaped contrary to economic theory had experienced significant operational shifts during the period studied.[9] We feel our results for this institution are meaningless because we have not adequately modeled the nature of its operations.

Results for all institutions with reasonable cost curves indicate that short-run operating costs for California prisons decrease as populations increase. In the short run, California prisons will be cheaper to run if they are large. Note that this was also the result obtained for the majority (12 of 19 prisons) of the federal prisons studied.

Results indicating the effect of the level of rehabilitative activities on short-run costs for California prisons are diverse and similar to results obtained for federal prisons, with one exception. When the squared term *IPRS*2 in rehabilitative activities is the only measure of the level of rehabilitative activities entering the final specification of the labor demand equation, it enters with a coefficient that is negative, rather than with the positive coefficient that was obtained for similar prisons in the federal system. Indicating as it seems that short-run operating costs decrease (and at an increasing rate) as the level of rehabilitating activities increases, this is an intriguing result. We obtain this result for two California prisons, the California Institution for Men at Chino and California's Men's Colony at San Luis Obispo. Both of these institutions are large (design capacity 2400 and 2681 inmates, respectively) but are broken up into small "program" units.

Results indicating the effect of inmate age on costs are also generally like those for federal prisons. Costs at first rise as average inmate age rises and then decline. However, when only one measure of average age, *INAGE*2, enters the final specification, the coefficient on this variable is positive, indicating that costs increase continuously and at an increasing rate as average inmate age rises. We obtain this result for one California prison, the California Training Facility at Soledad. This huge (design capacity 3041 inmates) facility contains three distinct institutions, two with medium security and one with minimum security.

As we had no measure of IQ for inmates in the California system, we entered a variable measuring the average tested grade placement of the inmate population on entering prison, denoted *INELEM*. We had no prior expectation about the sign of the coefficient on *INELEM*. However, in every case the sign of *INELEM* is positive. Costs increase as average tested educational level of the inmate population increases. In contrast, we found that inmates with higher IQs were cheaper to incarcerate in federal prisons.

Contrary to our finding for the federal system, it appears that in California prisons individuals convicted of persons offenses are relatively cheaper to incarcerate. Given the much larger proportion of this kind of offenders in the California system, it may be that the system is better equipped to deal with them. It is interesting to note that the coefficient on the variable measuring the proportion of the inmate population convicted of property offenses is also generally negative. Thus it appears that in California prisons it is individuals convicted of neither property or persons offenses who are most expensive to house. In the California system a large number of these individuals have been convicted of drug-related offenses.

In contrast to the generally insignificant and sometimes conflicting findings for the federal system, we find that higher levels of security lead to markedly higher costs in the California system.

Coefficients on other variables, regardless of expectations, showed no consistent sign across prisons in the California system.

This comparison of results for federal and California prisons seems to indicate that results obtained using data for federal prisons may at least be generally applicable to large state systems despite their different types of inmates and facilities. To further explore similarities and differences in the operation of federal and California systems, we shall choose a prison from each system with similar roles and compare their short-run cost curves. Specifically, we compare the short-run results for the U.S. Penitentiary at Marion, Illinois, and for Folsom State Prison in California. Each of these institutions is the back-up maximum-security prison for its prison system. Marion is the only maximum-security prison in the federal system. It has a design capacity of 500 inmates and was opened in 1963 to replace Alcatraz. Housing is in single cells, and the population tends to include the most difficult inmates to manage in the federal system. Folsom is much older (opened in 1880) and larger (single-cell capacity 1778) but serves, for the

**TABLE 15.5.**

| Independent variables | No autocorrelation | First-order | | |
|---|---|---|---|---|
| | Tehachapi | Chino | Soledad | Tracy |
| Output | | | | |
| *LNADPOP* | 2.439336***(8.531) | −2.192424(−1.279) | 1.689893***(14.227) | 1.369628***(13.798) |
| *ADPOP* | −0.001827***(−7.144) | 0.001221(1.517) | −0.000133***(−2.891) | −0.000435***(−7.571) |
| Product Quality | | | | |
| *POP–IPRS* | 0.000001***(14.654) | | −5.4774E-7***(−8.518) | −2.535E-7*(−1.906) |
| *IPRS* | | | 0.003391***(16.345) | 0.001158***(8.064) |
| *IPRS*2 | | −0.000004***(−4.661) | −0.000003***(−8.326) | −0.000002***(−4.293) |
| *SECURE* | 2.925921***(19.344) | 5.317437***(11.203) | 5.591111***(33.582) | 3.444294***(37.703) |
| Product quality and service conditions | | | | |
| *INAGE* | | | | 2.422452(2.458) |
| *INAGE*2 | | | 0.000349***(3.212) | |
| *RACE-I* | 0.596113***(10.925) | | 0.536970***(4.785) | −0.052478**(−2.458) |
| *INADD* | | | | |
| *INELEM* | | | | |
| LENGTH | 0.161740***(10.654) | | | |
| *O*-PERS | | | −0.676469***(−4.290) | |
| *O*-PROP | −0.236757***(−5.420) | | | 0.290732***(5.727) |
| *RECORD* | | | | |
| *REPEATS* | | | | 0.613681***(5.068) |
| *LIFE* | | | 0.000123(1.126) | −0.136339***(−2.449) |
| Service conditions | | | | |
| *INCIDENT* | | | | 0.000332***(3.710) |
| *JUMP* | 0.980697***(10.801) | −5.066058*(−1.867) | | |
| *R-BAL* | | | | −0.333492***(−5.359) |
| Adjustments | | | | |
| *INTERCEPT* | −11.692424***(−6.644) | 20.160590*(1.774) | −8.099628***(−8.942) | −32.317397***(−2.940) |
| *BEDCAP* | 0.000107*(1.927) | | | |
| *QTR*-1 | 0.014152***(4.660) | | | −0.004184***(−3.129) |
| *QTR*-2 | 0.013761***(5.167) | | | −0.003017**(−2.427) |
| *QTR*-3 | | | | |
| *D*1 | | | | |
| *TREND*1 | | | | 0.001298***(4.431) |
| Statistics and tests | | | | |
| *N* | 36 | 36 | 36 | 36 |
| $\bar{R}^{2\,b}$ (*F*-ratio) | .9969(1050.619) | .9554(151.07) | .9989(2739.71) | .9987(1763.62) |
| Durbin–Watson | 1.941 | N/A | N/A | N/A |
| Joint-F[c] | .5203 | N/A | N/A | N/A |
| Chi-square[d] | N/A | 6.063 | 2.965 | 1.70 |
| No. intermediate runs[e] | 3 | 7 | 4 | 0 |
| Estimated autoregressive parameters | | | | |
| $\rho^1$ | N/A | .046611(0.280) | 0.096066(0.579) | 0.240270(1.485) |
| $\rho^2$ | N/A | N/A | N/A | N/A |

[a] Values in parentheses are *t*-ratios. Asterisks indicate level of significance of coefficient, two-tailed test: * = .10 level, ** = .05 level, *** = .01 level.

[b] Indicates the percentage of variation explained by the independent variables in the model, correcting for degrees of freedom.

[c] This is the calculated value of the *F*-statistic, which tests for the joint significance of all dropped variables. [See Kmenta (1971, p. 370).]

[d] This is the calculated value of the $\chi^2$-statistic, which tests for the joint significance of all dropped variables, using a likelihood tatio test. [See Kendall and Stuart (1976, pp. 276–284).]

[e] This is the number of regressions estimated in moving from the original to the reduced specification, which are not presented here.

Summary of Results of Estimating Short-Run Labor Demand Equations[a]

| Autoregression | | Second-order autoregression | |
|---|---|---|---|
| San Quentin | Jamestown | San Luis Obispo | Folsom |
| | | | |
| 2.420579***(15.211) | 0.867596***(1.647) | 1.964215***(10.127) | 1.815082***(20.867) |
| −0.000525***(−15.495) | −0.000578*(−1.878) | −0.000716***(−10.729) | −0.00578***(−24.021) |
| −0.001046***(−5.485) | 0.030655***(12.703) | | 0.000246***(4.207) |
| 0.000001***(4.540) | −0.000489***(−11.514) | −3.4476E-7***(−11.773) | −5.3454E-7***(−12.646) |
| 5.838236***(11.837) | | | 4.255908***(13.134) |
| 2.669412***(5.087) | | 0.140599***(10.199) | 0.708266***(6.034) |
| −0.042448***(−5.053) | | −0.000769***(−4.329) | −0.008556***(−5.742) |
| 0.330244***(2.627) | | −0.372435*(−1.906) | 1.330096***(5.104) |
| | | | 0.000185***(5.885) |
| −0.020609(−1.188) | 0.072111(1.291) | 0.423080***(18.076) | 0.196355***(14.571) |
| 1.524550***(6.185) | | −0.345049***(−2.943) | −1.277477***(−8.116) |
| −2.394167***(−6.050) | | −1.745372***(−10.696) | −0.709176***(−3.624) |
| 2.227979***(6.084) | | 0.936575***(5.000) | −1.422016***(−12.477) |
| 1.973206***(4.714) | | −4.140336***(−16.739) | −0.701617***(−6.618) |
| −4.095913***(−11.923) | | | 1.216572***(3.482) |
| | | | −0.002959***(−6.202) |
| | 2.387714**(2.496) | 2.199886***(6.827) | |
| 0.222099*(1.914) | | 0.203630**(2.022) | 0.731066***(2.816) |
| −53.694018***(−5.979) | 1.356429(0.392) | −12.803676**(−10.527) | −22.350027***(−8.640) |
| 0.000027***(7.412) | −0.018282*(−1.869) | −0.000008**(−2.039) | |
| | | | −0.007770***(−2.096) |
| | | | −0.007437***(−2.897) |
| 0.006935***(2.774) | | 0.003198(1.483) | −0.002905*(−1.799) |
| 0.054957***(4.608) | −0.085614***(−3.519) | 0.58540***(15.913) | −0.004884*(−1.943) |
| | −0.006192***(−3.466) | −0.001157(−1.453) | −0.002025*(−1.949) |
| 36 | 36 | 36 | 36 |
| .9991(2389.50) | .9816(209.13) | .9974(787.48) | 1.000(16730.75) |
| N/A | N/A | N/A | N/A |
| N/A | N/A | N/A | N/A |
| .5026 | 3.754 | 3.21 | .0238 |
| 1 | 1 | 1 | 0 |
| 0.501827***(3.481) | 0.192897(1.180) | 0.219977(1.022) | .427028***(2.739) |
| N/A | N/A | 0.202526(1.24) | .353430***(2.67) |

**TABLE 15.6.** Characteristics of Short-Run Average Cost Curves

| Prison | Type of production function | $ADPOP^{\min a}$ | $ADPOP^{\max b}$ | Observed[c] shape of average cost curve |
|---|---|---|---|---|
| Chino | Cobb–Douglas[d] | 1476 | 2808 | Decreasing |
| Folsom | Cobb–Douglas | 1255 | 2711 | Decreasing |
| Jamestown | Cobb–Douglas | 1204 | 2214 | Decreasing |
| San Luis Obispo | Cobb–Douglas | 1753 | 3907 | Decreasing |
| San Quentin | Cobb–Douglas | 1365 | 4114 | ∩-shaped |
| Soledad | Complex[e] | 1696 | 3514 | Decreasing |
| Tehachapi | Complex | 937 | 1342 | Decreasing |
| Tracy | Complex | 1010 | 2028 | Decreasing |

[a] This is the minimum observed output, where "minimum" is defined as the sample mean minus two standard deviations.
[b] This is the maximum observed output, where "maximum" is defined as the sample mean plus two standard deviations.
[c] This is the shape of average cost curve for relevant range of output, i.e., from $ADPOP^{\min}$ to $ADPOP^{\max}$.
[d] The estimated cost function is dual to a homothetic Cobb–Douglas production function.
[e] The estimated cost function is dual to a production function which is more complex than a homothetic Cobb–Douglas production function.

California system, a function similar to Marion's in the federal system. Folsom is California's only maximum-security institution and houses primarily persons serving long sentences, habitual criminals, and hard-to-manage individuals. Marion and Folsom have similarly designed physical facilities and management systems. Both house inmates in cell blocks of two to five tiers and both are the only units in their respective system that do not break down the institution into separate functional units for management purposes. Both prisons provide on-site vocational training and have large prison industries. Inmates in these two prisons tend to be much older (averaging 9 years older for Folsom and 7 years older for Marion) than the average inmate in their respective systems.

Figure 15.8 depicts the long-run average total cost curve we estimate for Folsom. As can be seen in this figure, costs are quite high for a relatively small population ($16 per day for a population of 1250 inmates) and decline continually as population increases, going down to approximately $11.50 per day for a population of 2600. If one compares the cost curve for Folsom with that for Marion, one notes that they have similar shapes (costs decreasing continually as population rises). Cost per inmate-day appears consistently higher at Marion than at Folsom. This is the result primarily of the different measures of costs utilized in the two systems (costs for the federal system include depreciation and other expenditures that are missing

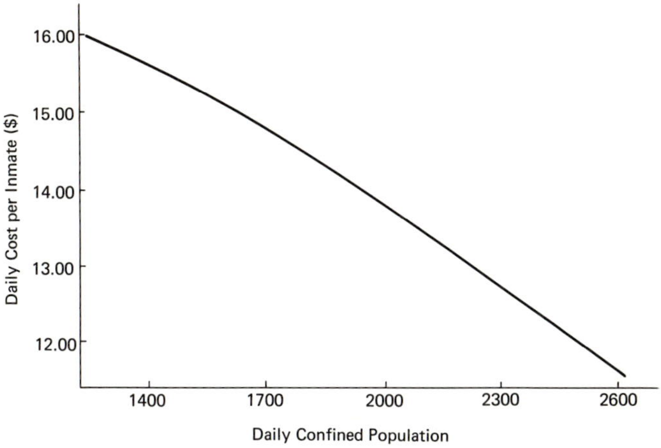


**Fig. 15.8.** Average cost curve, Folsom State Prison, Folsom, California.

from our measure of costs in the California system). However, it may result in part from the larger size and generally fewer amenities available at Folsom.

Comparison of the factors influencing short-run operating costs for these two institutions (compare the relevant columns in Tables 15.2b and 15.5) indicate that most factors in our initial specification significantly affect costs at Folsom, whereas far fewer of these initial variables affect costs at Marion. However, significant coefficients on all variables affecting costs at both institutions have the same sign. For example, the provision of rehabilitative activities at both institutions at first increases and then decreases costs, and increases in capacity tend to lower costs. The relatively similar results obtained for these two institutions provide some indication that the results we obtain using federal data will apply in general to large state correctional systems.

## 15.4. Policy Implications and Possible Uses of the Short-Run Results

As noted in Chapter 13, short-run cost curves can provide correctional administrators with insights that can be quite valuable when making decisions concerning existing prisons. These insights are of two basic types. First, the relationships found between the average costs of incarceration and the size of the inmate population can allow correctional administrators to estimate the probable cost consequences of alternative assignments of inmates to institutions. Second, the relationship found between average costs and certain other variables suggests that there are certain types of alterations that at certain institutions will serve to lower operating costs. In addition, the short-run cost curve can be used to predict the likely short-run cost effects of various changes in service conditions or inmate type (e.g., lengthened sentences and aging of the inmate population). We shall discuss a few possible implications of our short-run federal results next.

The large-scale federal prisons that we have studied in this chapter have a wide range (406–2147) of average daily inmate population. Thus we have observed widely varying levels of output. As noted previously, costs can vary markedly with the size of the inmate population (generally decreasing as populations increase). However, even similar-sized populations can result in quite different costs at different institutions, owing to unique aspects of the short-run cost curve for particular institutions. Estimated daily costs per inmate at the least-cost ($CD\text{-}ALL^*$) and mean observed ($\overline{CD\text{-}ALL}$) inmate population are given for 15 federal prisons in Table 15.7. As can be seen in this table, estimated daily costs per inmate at the mean observed population range from a low of $14.07 at the U.S. Penitentiary at Atlanta, Georgia, to $36.20 at the U.S. Penitentiary at Leavenworth, Kansas. The range of daily inmate costs at the minimum cost level of output covers a wider range, from $4.05 for the U.S. Penitentiary at Terre Haute, Indiana, to $27.64 for the similar institution at Leavenworth. The difference between estimated average daily costs at these 2 population levels for the 15 institutions provides an indication of the range of cost savings that might be possible if these federal

**TABLE 15.7.** Daily Costs and Cost Savings per Inmate

| Institution | Daily cost per inmate at $CD\text{-}ALL^*$ | Daily cost per inmate at $\overline{CD\text{-}ALL}$ | Average daily cost savings per inmate |
|---|---|---|---|
| Alderson | 12.26 | 19.41 | 7.15 |
| Ashland | 18.37 | 21.48 | 3.11 |
| Atlanta | 13.13 | 14.07 | 0.94 |
| Englewood | 7.95 | 32.44 | 24.48 |
| Fort Worth | 14.01 | 30.40 | 16.39 |
| La Tuna | 15.07 | 19.81 | 4.74 |
| Leavenworth | 27.64 | 36.20 | 8.56 |
| Lexington | 19.78 | 22.94 | 3.16 |
| Lompoc | 7.87 | 17.50 | 9.63 |
| McNeil Island | 14.83 | 18.28 | 3.46 |
| Milan | 12.20 | 21.64 | 9.45 |
| Oxford | 20.38 | 26.76 | 6.38 |
| Seagoville | 19.49 | 25.63 | 6.14 |
| Terre Haute | 4.05 | 15.79 | 11.75 |
| Texarkana | 17.81 | 17.99 | 0.18 |

prisons had operated with the minimum-cost population size rather than the average-size populations that they actually had during the period we studied them. Several institutions are operating very close to their minimum-cost output and thus would experience little savings by moving to the minimum-cost population size. For example, we estimate that the U.S. Penitentiary at Atlanta and the FCI at Texarkana would have costs savings of less than a dollar per inmate-day for such a population change. However, other institutions would experience large cost decreases for the same type of population change. For example, we estimate that the FCIs at Fort Worth and Englewood would have decreases in average daily inmate costs of over $15 if their inmate populations were to increase to the least-cost level.[10] Given a choice, correctional administrators might be well advised to increase populations at the institutions where large cost savings might result.

A comparison of the marginal daily cost of similar types of institutions can allow correctional administrators to consider the cost implications of alternative inmate assignments. For example, we estimate that it costs much more to house an extra inmate in the U.S. Penitentiary at Leavenworth than at the broadly similar institution at Atlanta. Specifically, for a prison of the least-cost size, it costs approximately $15 more per inmate-day to incarcerate an additional prisoner at Leavenworth than at Atlanta. FBOP policy is to assign close-security adult male inmates to these two institutions on the basis of state of origin. This type of inmate is usually assigned to Atlanta if from the Eastern United States and to Leavenworth if from the Midwest or West. This method of assignment has obvious advantages because it allows more contact between inmates and their families. However, rather large differences in estimated marginal daily costs could be considered when making assignments for inmates without families or with families located in the eastern portion of the Midwest. Obviously, costs cannot be the only consideration when assigning inmates to institutions. However, it is at least one of the many factors to be considered.

Four factors in our analysis, all of which can be affected by prison officials, indicate potential ways of lowering prison costs. These factors are the level of rehabilitative activities at the institution, the racial similarity of staff and inmates, the percentage of output produced at an associated facility, and the planned capacity of the institution. We discuss the policy implications of our findings related to each of these factors in turn.

The level of rehabilitative activities can affect costs in several ways. In our sample, however, our results indicate that costs generally increase until a certain level of rehabilitative activities is provided and then decline thereafter. This result would imply that the initial cost of rehabilitation programs may be high, but as more inmates become involved in the programs, the cost decreases. Thus correctional adminstrators may find rehabilitation programs to be a good investment, particularly if inmate populations continue to rise.

Our results indicate that racial similarity between staff and inmates at FCIs tends to lower costs. Thus correctional administrators may be able to lower costs at such institutions by continuing their efforts to employ staff members similar in race to the inmate population.[11] It is interesting that the effort to increase minority employment, which has been quite vigorous in both the California and federal systems, should have the beneficial side effect of lowering costs.

Costs rise as the percentage of output produced at an associated facility increases, according to our results. This result may indicate that costs could be lowered if these facilities were administered separately. Correctional officials could restructure the administration of these institutions and note cost effects to explore this potential cost saving.

Our results indicate that as the planned capacity of an institution increases, costs usually decrease. Prison officials may use these results when deciding whether to expand a current institution or build a new one. The short-run cost curve for the facility being considered for expansion could be used to estimate the operating costs of the expanded facilities, and the long-run cost curve, to be developed in Chapter 16, could be used to estimate operating costs for the new facility.

As noted previously, our short-run results can be used to estimate the short-run cost effects of changes in the type of inmate incarcerated. During the period studied, the average inmate became younger in both the California and the federal system. Our results would lead us to believe that this change led to higher prison operating costs. The aging of the baby-boom population since the period studied, however, should be reflected in an older inmate population. This "greying" of the inmate population should, according to our results, lower prison operating costs.

Current sentencing trends appear to be resulting in an inmate population with longer average sentences. Our results seem to indicate that this trend may be less expensive than would first appear. Longer sentences will raise prison costs, because it will be necessary to incarcerate individuals for longer periods of time. However, the increase in prison system costs may be at least somewhat less than expected, because our results indicate that inmates with longer sentences are cheaper to incarcerate.

## 15.5. Summary and Conclusions

In this chapter, we developed a model of short-run average costs for large-scale prisons and presented and discussed the results of estimating this model for 22 federal and 8 California prisons. In general, we found that short-run average total costs decrease as the size of prisons increases; that is, we found that larger prisons generally have lower short-run operating costs. This appears to be particularly true for old, large, high-security facilities like Folsom State Prison in the California system and the U.S. Penitentiary at Atlanta. For some federal prisons we found that costs at first decrease and then increase (i.e., have ∪-shaped short-run average cost curves), and for a few prisons housing special types of inmates (females and young males) we found that costs continually rise as populations increase.

We found that the provision of rehabilitative activities at first increases and then decreases short-run operating costs. Thus it appears that short-run prison operating costs at most prisons will be lowest if relatively few or a greater number of such activities are provided.

Our results indicated that short-run prison operating costs will also at first rise and then decline as the average age of the inmate population increases. Thus prisons with older populations will be, in general, cheaper to operate than will prisons with very young populations. We found that inmates with higher IQs are generally cheaper to incarcerate in the federal system but that inmates with higher-tested educational achievement are more expensive to incarcerate in the California system. In general, we found that the incarceration of individuals with drug problems is more expensive than the incarceration of individuals without such problems. However, at least in the federal system, we found that individuals with alcohol problems are no more expensive to incarcerate than other individuals. We found that, at least for Federal Correctional Institutions (generally smaller, newer, lower-security prisons), short-run costs will be less if the racial composition of the staff approximates that of the inmate population. Equal employment opportunity appears, at least in this instance, to be good business. In the federal system, we found that expansions of capacity generally reduce costs and that, in the California system, higher levels of security are associated with higher costs.

Comparison of our results for California and federal prisons seemed to indicate that results obtained for federal prisons will hold, at least in general, for prisons in large state systems. This finding is important because, at least at present, much less satisfying data to estimate cost curves are likely to be available for state than federal prisons.

We illustrated three potential uses of our results. First, we indicated that at least for some prisons studied, substantial decreases in average cost could result from increased prison populations. Next, we indicated that, in the assignment of given types of inmates (e.g., close-security adult males), it may be useful to at least consider the differences in marginal costs among prisons designed for the type of population under consideration. Finally, we suggested that our short-run results may be used to project the likely cost effects of changes in inmate and facility types.

The results we obtained when estimating short-run cost curves suggest a number of conclusions. First, we believe that our results indicate the feasibility and potential usefulness of this type of research. Second, our results indicate that the study of the nature of operations at prisons is best done on a prison-by-prison basis. Detailed knowledge of the nature of prison operations at particular institutions appears to be essential when attempting to understand short-run operational costs. Finally, it appears better to estimate short-run cost functions without restricting coefficients to conform to the tenets of economic theory. In our experience, seemingly aberrant results pointed to major changes in prison operations that we had failed to model.

## Appendix 15.1. Determination of the Shape of the Average Cost Function for Two Specific Parametric Combinations

The two combinations of values for $\alpha$ and $\theta$ examined here are cases 1 and 4 of Table 15.4. To determine the shape of the short-run average cost curve for these cases, we need to calculate the first and second derivatives of average variable cost $AVC$ with respect to output. The first derivative is

$$\partial AVC/\partial Q = (AVC/\alpha)[\theta + (1 - \alpha)/Q], \tag{A15.1}$$

and the second is

$$\partial^2 AVC/\partial Q^2 = (AVC/\alpha^2)[\theta + (1 - \alpha)/Q]^2 - (AVC/Q^2)[(1 - \alpha)/\alpha]. \tag{A15.2}$$

First, we shall determine the output for which the first derivative of $AVC$ will equal zero. This output will be associated with minimum or maximum average costs or will be an inflection point. The output is

$$Q^*_{AVC} = (\alpha - 1)/\theta. \tag{A15.3}$$

Note that for case 1 this will be a positive level of output, whereas for case 4 this will be a negative level of output. Because we are only interested in positive levels of output, we shall define a variable $\beta > -1$ and evaluate the first and second derivatives of $AVC$ at $Q = Q^*_{AVC} + \beta Q^*_{AVC}$. Substituting Eq. (A15.3) into this expression one obtains

$$Q = (\alpha - 1)(\beta + 1)/\theta. \tag{A15.4}$$

Substituting this expression in turn into the expressions for the first and second derivatives of $AVC$, one obtains

$$f'(Q) = (AVC/\alpha)[\theta\beta/(\beta + 1)] \tag{A15.5}$$

and

$$f''(Q) = (\theta AVC/\alpha)[\beta/(\beta + 1)]^2 - (\theta^2 AVC)/[\alpha(\alpha - 1)(\beta + 1)^2], \quad \text{(A15.6)}$$

where $f'(Q)$ and $f''(Q)$ indicate that the first and second derivatives of $AVC$ with respect to output are being evaluated at various positive levels of output.

We are now ready to determine the shape of the average cost function for positive levels of output for cases 1 and 4. First consider case 1 ($\alpha > 1; \theta > 0$). There are three subcases for specific values of $\beta$:

a. $-1 < \beta < 0 \Rightarrow 0 < Q < Q^*_{AVC} \Rightarrow f'(Q) < 0$ and $f''(Q) > 0$. That is, $AVC$ is decreasing but at a decreasing rate.
b. $\beta = 0 \Rightarrow Q = Q^*_{AVC} \Rightarrow f'(Q) = 0$ and $f''(Q) > 0$. That is, we are at the minimum point on the $AVC$ curve.
c. $\beta > 0 \Rightarrow Q > Q^*_{AVC} \Rightarrow f'(Q) > 0$ and $f''(Q) > 0$. That is, $AVC$ is increasing at an increasing rate.

Based on these three cases, we conclude that if $\alpha > 1$ and $\theta > 0$, the $AVC$ is ∪-shaped. Incidently, the $SRATC$ curve will also be ∪-shaped, although its minimum point $Q^*_{ATC}$ will be to the right of $Q^*_{AVC}$. Specifically,

$$Q^*_{ATC} = (\alpha - 1)/\theta + (\alpha/\theta)(AFC/AVC). \quad \text{(A15.7)}$$

Next consider case 4 ($\alpha > 1$; $\theta < 1$). Note that $Q^*_{AVC}$ is negative for this case. Thus we are interested in evaluating $f'(Q)$ and $f''(Q)$ only for values of $\beta < -1$. For such values, $f'(Q) < 0$ and $f''(Q)$ is ambiguous. This implies a negatively sloped $AVC$ curve for all possible outputs.

The shape of the $AVC$ curve for the five other cases can be determined in a similar manner.

## Notes to Chapter 15

1. Actually, we estimated short-run cost curves for all but 3 of the 27 large-scale prisons operating in the federal system during the October 1975–July 1978 time period. We did not feel that there were adequate observations available to make estimation of a short-run cost curve for Memphis meaningful because it only opened in July 1977. We could not estimate a cost curve for Pleasanton, owing to missing data, or for Talahassee, owing to large accounting adjustments in the cost data for that institution. We estimated cost curves but do not present the results here for two FCIs that opened during our study period (Butner and Miami). Results for these two institutions may be found in Witte *et al.* (1979, ch. 15). We estimated short-run cost curves for 8 of the 12 prisons operated by the California Department of Correction during the July 1968–July 1978 period. We did not collect data for the California Medical Facility (Solano County) or the California Rehabilitation Center (for civilly committed addicts, San Bernardino County) because we felt these facilities represented unique production processes unlike the other large-scale prisons studied. The California Correctional Center (Susanville) and the California Institute for Women (Frontera) were not analyzed, owing to incomplete data.

2. This is the specification developed in Section 14.6.

3. See Barr, Goodnight, Sall, and Helwig (1976) for details of the technique utilized. The approach to autocorrelation utilized is implicitly suggested in an article by Fomby and Guilkey (1978).

4. The range of output that we chose is the sample mean of $CD\text{-}ALL \pm 2(\hat{\sigma}_{CD\text{-}ALL})$, where $\hat{\sigma}_{CD\text{-}ALL}$ is the estimated standard deviation of $CD\text{-}ALL$ for the particular institution. The time period is from October 1975 to June 1978.

5. Mathematically, the marginal product of labor for our model is

$$\partial Q/\partial L = \alpha Q/L(\theta Q + 1),$$

or, in terms of elasticities,

$$\partial \ln Q/\partial \ln L = \alpha/(\theta Q + 1).$$

Note that when $\alpha$ and $\theta$ are both positive (cases 1, 2, and 7) the marginal product of labor is always positive. When $\alpha$ is negative and $\theta$ is positive (case 3), the marginal product of labor is always negative. When $\alpha$ is positive and $\theta$ is negative (cases 4 and 5) or when both $\alpha$ and $\theta$ are negative, the sign of the marginal product of labor depends on the level of output. The marginal product of labor will take on unacceptable (i.e., negative) values in cases 4 and 5 when $1/Q < |\theta|$, and in case 6 when $1/Q > |\theta|$.

6. The three other penitentiaries with this type of average cost curve are located at Atlanta, Georgia; McNeil Island, Washington; and Terre Haute, Indiana. The other prisons having this type of cost curve are FCIs. Their only common characteristic appears to be their age; all were opened prior to 1945. Incidentally, it is possible to distinguish cases in which our model implies that average costs would decline over all possible levels of output (Marion, El Reno, and Petersburg) from cases in which our model implies a U-shaped average cost curve, but with its minimum point greater than our maximum observed output (Atlanta, Englewood, McNeil Island, Milan, Seagoville, and Terre Haute).

7. Similarly dramatic, if different, changes in operation occurred at the U.S. Penitentiary at Lewisburg, Pennsylvania. See Witte *et al.* (1979, p. 213) for details. Conversations with personnel at the other prisons listed in Table 15.2 indicated that no such dramatic changes in operation occurred at these institutions.

8. Until 1976, Danbury was the psychiatric facility for the northeast region. The psychiatric facility at Butner (an FCI) replaced the Danbury facility when it opened in 1977. Since 1976 Danbury severely reduced its medical staff, and the hospital at the institution is no longer accredited. Though the change at Danbury was gradual, it was nevertheless marked. The production process at the end of our sample period was radically different from the process at the beginning.

9. San Quentin operated under three management schemes during our time period. From before July 1968 until approximately 1971, San Quentin was converting to a system of functional unit management. In 1971 this process was halted owing to lack of funds; however, functional unit management became active again in 1976. San Quentin operated under functional unit management from 1976 until the end of our time period. Thus we observe three different production processes.

10. The potential saving of Englewood may well be overstated because the minimum cost population is substantially (over four times) greater than the largest observed output.

11. This actually only refers to blacks because, owing to the limited inmate racial data, we were unable to include Hispanics as minorities.

# Chapter 16

## Long-Run Cost Functions for Federal Correctional Institutions*

### 16.1. Introduction

In this chapter we estimate long-run cost curves for Federal Correctional Institutions. The original specification for the cost curve is based on the model developed in Chapter 14. We estimate the model using traditional estimation techniques (ordinary and generalized least squares) and Federal Bureau of Prisons (FBOP) data. Our results for variables other than input prices appear reasonable, but our results for input prices lead us to question our original model. We revise our original model and estimate an expanded model that contains measures of input quality as well as other variables. Our revised model gives results that appear quite reasonable and allow us to estimate the likely cost effects of some recently advocated correctional standards.

The organization of this chapter is as follows. In the next section, we briefly describe the data used to estimate the long-run cost curve. (Appendix C contains a more detailed description of the data set utilized.) In Section 16.3,

* Coauthored with William Trumbull and Diane Woodbury.

we present and interpret the results of estimating our expanded model of long-run prison costs. We also discuss the implications of our model for the likely cost of imposing correctional standards. The final section of the chapter contains our summary and conclusions.

## 16.2. The Data

There were 21 FCIs operating during the period for which we collected data (October 1975 through June 1978).[1] In Chapter 15 we estimated short-run cost functions using monthly data for most of these institutions. We chose to use quarterly rather than monthly data to estimate our long-run functions, for two major reasons. First, this allows us to work with data that have not been interpolated. This was not possible when estimating the short-run functions because there were insufficient quarters of data to allow estimation of separate cost functions for each prison. Second, our discussions with the FBOP's accounting personnel indicated that quarterly cost figures obtained from the FBOP's accounting system would be much less subject to lump-sum accounting adjustments than monthly data would be.

We would like to estimate our long-run cost curves using data for as many of the 21 institutions as possible. However, it is only possible to pool data for institutions to estimate a cost curve if all institutions are using the same methods of operation (technology). The short-run cost functions that we estimated in Chapter 15 seem to indicate wide variation in methods of operation. We conducted $F$-tests to see if methods of operation for FCIs in the short run were indeed different. Results indicated that there were highly significant differences in methods of operation. We proceeded to search among the FCIs for a subgroup for which we could accept the hypothesis of identical technologies in the short run. We found six such FCIs.[2]

Having identified six FCIs with similar methods of operation in the short run, it was next necessary to test whether these six institutions also had similar methods of operation in the long run, when the size of the institution is variable. We began by examining the characteristics of these six institutions and noted that they varied rather markedly in the level of security (from an average of .43 guards per inmate at the FCI at Oxford, Wisconsin, to an average of .25 guards per inmate at the FCI at Lompoc, California). We proceeded to split the six institutions into two subgroups: a high-security subgroup consisting of the FCIs at Alderson, West Virginia, and Oxford, Wisconsin, and a low-security group consisting of the other four FCIs. We next estimated a long-run cost curve[3] for the larger of these two subgroups and used an $F$-test to determine whether the cost curves for this subgroup were insignificantly different from the cost curve for all six institutions. Our results indicated that we could accept the null hypothesis that methods of operation in the long run were insignificantly different.[4] Thus we conclude that we have identified six institutions with similar methods of operation and that we may pool them to estimate a long-run cost curve.

The long-run cost model developed in Chapter 14 requires that we estimate 29 parameters. Because we were only able to identify six FCIs that used similar methods of operation during the period for which we collected data, it was necessary to pool data for a number of quarters to obtain sufficient degrees of freedom to estimate our model. We tested for the appropriateness of pooling quarterly beginning with quarters arranged symmetrically around the third quarter of 1977, when detailed descriptions of the capital stock were available. An *F*-test indicated that we were justified in pooling data for the ten quarters beginning with the first quarter of 1976 and ending with the second quarter of 1978.[5]

In summary, we begin by estimating the original long-run cost model of Chapter 14 for six FCIs using data for ten quarters, 1976.I–1978.II. That is, we pooled our cross-sectional data (observations on six FCIs at a given point in time) and a selected subset of our time-series data (observations on FCIs over time). In addition to increasing our sample size and thus allowing us to estimate the completely specified long-run cost curve, this pooling increases the degree to which our results reflect FBOP experience in the late 1970s.

## 16.3. Empirical Results

Results for our original model were quite reasonable except that the coefficients on factor prices that we obtained did not conform to our expectations. The coefficient on labor costs, although positive, was substantially greater than one, which should not be possible according to our model or, indeed, according to any standard economic theory of costs. The coefficient on capital costs was negative rather than positive but was only significant at the .10 level of statistical significance. We considered why this might have occurred and decided that a likely explanation was that correctional managers were not hiring factor inputs in such a way as to equate each inputs input's cost to its value in production. To test for this possibility, we added a vector of input-quality measures to the specification of our long-run cost curve and reestimated our long-run model. Table 16.1 contains a list of the variables we added to the specification. Our results indicated that a number of input-quality measures (*AGE-S*, *SQFPER*, *SINGLE*, and *SANPER*) were significantly related to costs. Thus we conclude that our revised specification provides a superior model of long-run costs in large-scale prisons.[6]

Using the residuals from our revised model, we next tested to see if there was autocorrelation in the time series and if the error terms for the various

**TABLE 16.1.** Measures of Input Quality Entered into the Revised Specification

| Variable | Empirical measure | |
|---|---|---|
| | Acronym | Explanation |
| Labor quality | | |
| Staff type | *RATIO*-S | Ratio of guards to other staff |
| Education | *ED*-S | Average years of education |
| Race | *RACE*-S | Percentage of staff that is nonwhite |
| Age | *AGE*-S | Average age of staff |
| Sex | *SEX*-S | Percentage of staff that is male |
| Capital quality | | |
| Living area | *SQFPER* | Square feet of living area per bed |
| Single beds | *SINGLE* | Proportion of design capacity housed in single bed cells or rooms |
| Sanitary facilities | *SANPER* | Number of toilets and urinals divided by design capacity |

FCIs were independent. We were able to accept the hypothesis of no autocorrelation but rejected the hypothesis of independence of the error terms across FCIs.[7]

On the basis of the preceding tests, we reestimated our model using a generalized least-squares procedure that allowed for the correlation of the error terms across institutions. Our results are reported in Table 16.2. Significant coefficients do not have unreasonable signs, but many variables have coefficients that are insignificant.

Desiring to rid our average cost-curve specification of variables unrelated to costs, we selected two basic rules for reducing our specification. First, we retained the independent variables suggested by economic theory, regardless of significance, owing to the theoretical support for their inclusion in our cost-curve specification. Second, we used Theil's (1960, pp 210–215) residual-variance criterion to determine which variables in the product quality and service condition vectors to retain.

In the present context, the application of these rules means that we retain *CD-ALL*, *LNCD-ALL*, *LN-COST-E*, and *LNCOST-L* in our specification, regardless of significance, owing to theoretical support for their inclusion. We delete all other variables with an absolute value of the "$t$-statistic" less than one, subject to the condition that the $\chi^2$-statistic testing for the joint insignificance of all dropped variables be insignificant. We added this last restriction to ensure that we did not drop sets of variables that were insignificant only because of the presence of multicollinearity.

After one additional regression run we arrived at a specification in which all of the preceding criteria were satisfied.[8] Results for this reduced specification are reported in Table 16.2. The average cost curve implied by our estimate is illustrated in Fig. 16.1.

Examining first the coefficients on the variables suggested by economic theory, we note that the coefficients on both output variables are significant. They indicate that the average cost of confining inmates declines until the inmate population contains approximately 1075 individuals and increases for populations above that size. Note that the average cost curve is not symmetric; the cost penalty for prisons housing 600 inmates fewer than the minimum-cost number is much larger than that for prisons housing 600 inmates more than that amount. Note also that costs do not vary markedly as prison size goes from 900 to 1300 inmates. Costs per inmate-day decrease from \$39.31 when the inmate population is 500 to a minimum of \$22.83 when it is 1075 and increase again to \$30.49 when 1700 inmates are confined. The implications of our results are fairly obvious: prisons are cheapest to run when they are quite large but not behemoth.

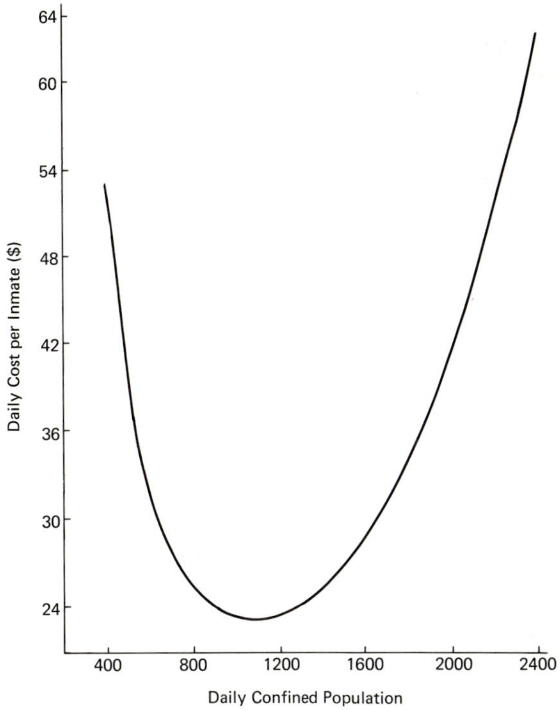


**Fig. 16.1.** Estimated average cost curve for Federal Correctional Institutions.

**TABLE 16.2.** Results of Estimating the Long-Run Cost Function Using GLS[a]

| Variable | Initial specification | | Final specification | |
|---|---|---|---|---|
| | Coefficient | "*t*-Ratio" | Coefficient | "*t*-Ratio" |
| Intercept | 54.1855* | 2.02 | 40.4118*** | 6.17 |
| Output | | | | |
| *CD-ALL* | $3.300 \times 10^{-5}$ | 1.23 | $2.394 \times 10^{-5}$*** | 3.70 |
| *LNCD-ALL* | −2.6612 | −1.20 | −1.3554** | −2.46 |
| Factor prices | | | | |
| *LNCOST-L* | −.8024 | −1.21 | −.2690 | −.60 |
| *LNCOST-E* | −.4712 | −1.70 | −.0835 | −.69 |
| Product quality | | | | |
| *SECURE* | 2.1707 | 0.75 | | |
| Product quality and service conditions | | | | |
| *CD-IPRS* | $8.711 \times 10^{-5}$ | .67 | | |
| *IPRS* | $-5.529 \times 10^{-5}$ | −.72 | | |
| *IPRS2* | −.0025 | −.20 | | |
| *AGE-I* | −.0877 | −.17 | | |
| *AGE-I2* | .0006 | .08 | | |
| *RACE-I* | −.0752** | −2.14 | −.0327*** | −3.41 |
| *BETAIQ* | .0054 | .06 | | |
| *WCOLLAR* | .0207 | .78 | | |
| *DRUG* | .0074 | .49 | | |
| *ALCOHOL* | .0549 | 1.37 | .0391*** | 2.97 |
| *LENGTH* | .0857 | .56 | | |
| *O*-PERS | −.0223 | −.37 | | |
| *O*-PROP | .0367** | 2.13 | .0205** | 2.42 |
| *RECORD* | .0658 | .26 | | |
| *MARRIED* | .0224 | 1.15 | | |
| *FEMALE* | .0580*** | 3.86 | .0319*** | 5.56 |
| *INCDNT* | .0145 | .91 | | |
| *CROWD* | 3.1791 | .95 | | |
| *CROWD2* | −.9266 | −.72 | | |
| Service conditions | | | | |
| *R-BAL* | −2.7795 | −.87 | | |
| *R-BAL2* | −.3640 | −.14 | | |
| *PC-OTH* | −.0311 | −1.03 | −.0144** | −2.58 |
| Labor quality | | | | |
| *RATIO*-S | .1544 | .17 | | |
| *AGE*-S | −.3266*** | −3.44 | −.2370*** | −6.14 |
| *ED*-S | .0722 | .73 | | |
| *RACE*-S | .0598 | 1.24 | −.0267** | −2.23 |
| *SEX*-S | .0151 | .85 | | |
| Capital quality | | | | |
| *SQFPER* | −.0792 | −1.03 | −.0431** | −2.50 |
| *SINGLE* | −3.5076** | −2.45 | −2.0580*** | −5.72 |
| *SANPER* | 3.4247 | 1.57 | 1.8929** | 2.68 |
| *N* | 60 | | 60 | |

[a] Number of asterisks indicates level of significance, two-tailed test: * = .10, ** = .05 level, *** = .01 level.

Neither the coefficient on labor costs nor that on capital costs is significantly different from zero at ordinary levels of statistical significance; indeed, the "*t*-ratios" for both of these variables are less than one in absolute value. For both input prices, but particularly for *LNCOST-L*, the insignificant coefficients obtained appear to stem mainly from the extremely low variance observed in these variables.[9] Although this fact can be bemoaned, it cannot be attributed to a weakness of our model, but rather reflects a weakness in our data. Such data weaknesses are not uncommon. Many previous economic studies have had difficulty obtaining observations with sufficient variation in input prices to generate significant coefficients.

Five product quality and service condition variables remain in the final specification for our cost model. The coefficients on these variables indicate that, if other factors are equal, the costs of operating an FCI will be lower if the inmate population contains a larger proportion of male, nonwhite inmates who have no alcohol problems and were not convicted of property offenses. Further, the higher is the proportion of confined days produced in an associated camp, female facility, or detention center, the lower the costs.

Two measures of labor quality, *AGE-S* and *RACE-S*, remain in the final specification of the cost function. The coefficients on these variables indicate that, if other things are equal, the costs of operating a FCI will be lower if the staff is older and contains a larger proportion of nonwhite individuals.

All measures of capital quality remain in the final specification. The coefficients on these variables indicate that costs will be lower if inmates have relatively ample living space, are housed in single cells, and have fewer sanitary facilities available. The significance and signs of the coefficients on these variables are intriguing, given the current controversy surrounding attempts to implement correctional standards. A number of these standards relate to variables we have used to measure capital quality. Some groups have also espoused standards related to prison size. Our results can also give some indication of the likely cost increases associated with the small prisons advocated. Table 16.3 contains a summary of relevant standards advocated in *James v. Wallace*[10] by the National Advisory Commission on Criminal Justice Standards and Goals (1973) and by the Commission on Accreditation for Corrections (1977). Table 16.4 contains some related descriptive statistics for the six FCIs used to estimate our long-run cost model. As can be seen by comparing these two tables, most FCIs in our sample fail to meet the relatively generous standards espoused by the Commission on Accreditation and the National Advisory Commission. However, some FCIs even fail to meet the much lower standards advocated for the Alabama prison system in *James* v. *Wallace*. As the facilities in the federal system tend to be better than those available in most state systems, this comparison points out the large-scale changes in state systems likely to be necessary if such standards are implemented.

**TABLE 16.3.** Summary of Standards

| Standard | *James* v. *Wallace* | Commission on Accreditation | National Advisory Commission |
|---|---|---|---|
| Prison size | None specified | Maximum of 500 inmates | Small enough to allow superintendent to develop a personal relationship with each inmate |
| Cell size or living area | 60 $ft^2$ per inmate | 60 $ft^2$ for inmates locked up 10 hr or less per day, 80 $ft^2$ otherwise | 80 $ft^2$ |
| Cell type | None specified | Single-bed cell or room | Single-bed cell or room |
| Sanitary facilities | One toilet per 15 inmates<br>One urinal per 15 inmates | One toilet per cell or room | One toilet per cell or room implied but not specified |

Somewhat surprisingly, the coefficients on capital quality measures in our final specification seem to indicate that the change in operating costs associated with the adoption of such standards may not be nearly as large as currently feared. Our results indicate that increases in living area and the proportion of single cells may actually *decrease* the average costs of operating a prison. However, increases in the availability of sanitary facilities will increase such costs, according to our results. The elasticities associated with the coefficients on these variables indicate that a 1% increase in living area or a similar increase in the proportion of single cells will reduce operating costs by 2.7 and 1.2%, respectively. The elasticity associated with the variable measuring the availability of sanitary facilities indicates that a 1% increase in the availability of such facilities increases operating costs by .8%. Taken

**TABLE 16.4.** Summary of Corresponding Variables of Sample Prisons

| Variable | Mean | Maximum | Minimum |
|---|---|---|---|
| Prison size (number of inmates housed during sample period) | 822 | 1542 | 495 |
| Cell size or living area per bed ($ft^2$) | 63.8 | 76.2 | 49.5 |
| Cell type (percentage of total beds that are in single-bed cells) | 58 | 100 | 0 |
| Sanitary facilities (sum of toilets and urinals per bed) | .42 | .63 | .20 |

as a whole, our results indicate that adopting standards that increase living space, at least within the range observed (50–76 $ft^2$/bed), may actually lower the operating costs of prisons. Such decreases in operating costs would be likely to require fairly large initial capital outlays. However, our results indicate that these initial outlays would be recouped in the long run. Our results are more equivocal concerning the likely cost effects of requiring that inmates be provided with individual cells equipped with sanitary facilities, as advocated by the Commission on Accreditation and the National Advisory Commission. Although the provision of single cells appears to reduce costs, the provision of sanitary facilities appears to increase costs in an approximately offsetting manner. Thus our results would be consistent with finding no effect on operating costs if standards requiring single cells with sanitary facilities were required. However, this result should be viewed with some caution, as the variable *SANPER* actually measures the size and availability of common bathrooms rather than bathrooms in single cells, because most sanitary facilities in the FCIs studied were communal.

Further investigation is necessary to determine why single cells and increased living area reduce average cost. However, the National Advisory Commission on Criminal Justice Standards and Goals (1973, p. 355) provides the possible explanation that "without privacy and personal space, inmates become tense and many begin to react with hostility. As tension and hostility grow, security requirements increase; and a negative cycle is put into play."

As noted in Table 16.3, the Commission on Accreditation for Corrections advocates that prisons house a maximum of 500 inmates. Our results indicate that operation of such small prisons would result in costs per inmate-day that are almost double ($39.31 vs. $22.83 per inmate per day) those associated with operating a facility that houses the minimum-cost number of 1075 inmates. Comparing the costs of a 500-bed prison and the minimum-cost-sized prison, we obtain an upper bound estimate of the cost of imposing standards that advocate small-sized prison. While altering no other factor, confining 1075 inmates in prisons housing 500 rather than the minimum-cost number of inmates would result in increased prison system costs of $6,466,340 per year, assuming that both sizes of prisons had the same value of other variables affecting cost. Given the FBOP's population in 1978, 29,803 inmates [see U.S. Department of Justice (1980)], we estimate that it would have cost the system $179,271,010 more per year to house these inmates in facilities of size 500 rather than in facilities of the minimum-cost size. This cost differential is substantial and should be carefully considered when imposing standards that require prisons of small size. Although small prisons may well have substantial benefits (e.g., personal contact and more humane conditions) that we have failed to reflect in our modeling effort, these

**TABLE 16.5.** Average Costs for Prisons of Various Capital Configurations

| Characteristics and cost | Prison type | | | | | | |
|---|---|---|---|---|---|---|---|
| | Average | Minimum-cost size | Large living space | All single cells | Large living space, single cells | Minimum-cost size, large living space, single cells | "Up to standards" |
| Number of inmates (*CD-ALL*) | 822 | 1075 | 822 | 822 | 822 | 1075 | 500 |
| Living area in square feet (*SQFPER*) | 63.8 | 63.8 | 70 | 63.8 | 70 | 70 | 70 |
| Proportion of single cells (*SINGLE*) | .58 | .58 | .58 | 1.0 | 1.0 | 1.0 | 1.0 |
| Average cost ($) | 24.68 | 22.83 | 18.87 | 10.50 | 8.03 | 7.43 | 12.79 |
| Savings over "average" prison per confined day ($) | — | 1.85 | 5.81 | 14.18 | 16.65 | 17.25 | 11.89 |

benefits should be carefully weighed against the markedly increased costs associated with the operation of such prisons.

The mean inmate population of prisons in our sample was 822 inmates, approximately three-quarters the size of the minimum-cost prison. We estimate that housing all inmates in the federal prison system in 1978 in this rather than in the minimum-cost-sized prison would result in increased system operating costs of $20,124,476 per year. Again, this figure is only illustrative, but it does point out the potential significance of considering costs when constructing prisons.

Table 16.5 further illustrates the cost implications of some of our findings. The first column under the heading "Prison Type" shows the estimated average cost of an average-sized prison with the mean number of inmates for prisons in our sample (822), mean living area (63.8), and mean proportion of single cells (.58). The second column under "Prison Type" shows the estimated average cost of a prison that is similar except that it houses 1075 inmates, the minimum-cost number. Our results indicate that prisons like the average prison observed in our sample will have costs per inmate-day that are $1.85 higher than the minimum-cost-sized prison. The third column gives the cost implications of increasing the living area to 70 $ft^2$/inmate while holding other characteristics constant. As can be seen in this column, such an increase results in cost savings of larger magnitude than increasing prison size from the average to the minimum cost size. The last four columns present cost figures for other types of prisons. Note that the cheapest prison to operate ($7.43 per inmate-day) would be relatively large (housing an average of 1075 inmates), provide 70 $ft^2$ of living space per inmate, and have an individual cell for each inmate. Although this type of prison may seem unattractive owing to its size, the other amenities associated with it may make it acceptable to both correctional staff and inmates. The cost of the type of prison described in the last column may be of particular interest, because this type of prison is most likely[11] to meet the standards of the Commission on Accreditation. Note that this type of prison is less expensive to operate than a prison with characteristics equal to the average in our sample. This is somewhat surprising and suggests that imposition of standards of the type analyzed in Table 16.5 may have much less severe long-run cost consequences than are currently anticipated. However, note the cost penalty associated with the small prison advocated by these standards.

## 16.4. Summary and Conclusions

In this chapter, we estimated a model of long-run correctional costs using traditional estimation techniques (generalized least squares) and Federal Bureau of Prisons (FBOP) data for the 1976–1978 time period. Our results generally seem reasonable. They indicate that prisons are cheaper to run if they are quite large but not behemoth, and house relatively large numbers of inmates in associated camps or female facilities. Further, prisons that house larger proportions of male, nonwhite inmates who have no alcohol problems and were not convicted of a property offense will have lower costs if other factors are equal.

The estimated coefficients for factor prices are insignificantly different from zero, owing to the limited variability of these variables in our sample. However, the coefficients on a number of variables measuring input quality are significant. The coefficients on these variables indicate that the cost of prison operation will be lower if a larger proportion of nonwhite and older staff are used and if inmates have ample living space, are housed in single cells, and have relatively few sanitary facilities.

Our results regarding prison size and capital quality allow us to explore possible cost implications associated with the imposition of some recently advocated correctional standards. Specifically, our results indicate that providing single cells for inmates and rather substantial amounts of living space may actually decrease the cost of operating prisons. However, providing increased sanitary facilities and smaller prisons appears likely to increase prison costs. These results are best illustrated by considering the costs per inmate-day in a minimum-cost prison, defined as a prison that houses 1075 inmates in single cells with an average of 70 $ft^2$ of living space, and a prison that would be likely to meet the standards espoused by the Commission on Accreditation for Corrections—an "up-to-standards" prison, defined as a prison that houses 500 inmates in single cells with 70 $ft^2$ of living space. We estimated that the cost per inmate-day in the minimum-cost-sized prison would be \$7.43, whereas the up-to-standards prison would cost \$12.79 per inmate-day. In contrast, a prison with the average characteristics observed in our sample, housing 822 inmates with 58% in single cells and an average of 64 $ft^2$ of living space, would cost \$24.68 per inmate-day to run. Our results seem to indicate that the FBOP could lower its operating costs if it constructed larger prisons with more living space and single cells.

Our work leads us to suggest a number of directions for future research. First, we would suggest that additional work be done to develop better measures of the cost of capital to which correctional decision makers respond when making their capital construction decisions. We believe that this can probably be done most effectively if the capital decision-making process in one or more correctional systems is carefully studied. Second, we suggest that a number of our findings with policy implications be carefully explored to determine their robustness and the reason for their existence. We have explored the robustness of our finding relating to prison size and have found that quite diverse specifications and data indicate that the minimum-cost-sized prison will probably house between 700 and 1500 inmates. Our findings regarding the effect on costs of the provision of ample living space and single cells could usefully be explored as well. Third, future research could beneficially study and model the way in which operating decisions are made at a number of different prisons. Our results indicate that the usual behavioral assumption of economics, cost-minimizing behavior, may be inappropriate in a prison environment. It would be useful to model the nature of prison operation using more realistic behavioral assumptions. As it currently stands, we suggest that cost functions estimated using traditional estimation techniques (e.g., those in this chapter and Chapter 15) be interpreted as behavioral relationships rather than the minimum-cost relationships postulated by economic theory.

## Notes to Chapter 16

1. October 1975 was the first month in which FBOP accounting personnel felt cost data to be reliable. Because we collected data in July 1978, June 1978 was the last month for which we could obtain data.

2. These institutions are Ashland, Lompoc, Lexington, Oxford, Texarkana, and Alderson. The value of the test statistic for the appropriateness of this cross-sectional pooling, which is distributed as $F_{125,48}$ under the null hypothesis that pooling is appropriate, was 1.979.

3. The specification for the long-run cost curve was identical to the final specification of Table 16.2.

4. We used this $F$-test rather than the customary Chow test (Chow, 1960) because it was not possible to estimate the long-run cost curve for the subgroup containing only two institutions. (The data matrix for the two high-security institutions was singular.) The value of the $F$-test, which is distributed $F_{20,24}$ under the null hypothesis, was 1.73.

5. The test statistic for the appropriateness of this time series pooling, which is distributed $F_{45,10}$ under the null hypothesis, was 0.794.

6. At first glance this appears to cast doubt on the short-run results that we reported in Chapter 15. However, this is not the case, because there is no variation in capital quality in the short run, and variation in labor quality is very limited at any given institution.

7. For each cross-sectional unit, we tested for autocorrelation using $\hat{\rho}_i/\sqrt{(1-\hat{\rho}_i)/T}$ as a test statistic, where $\hat{\rho}_i$ is the estimated first-order autoregressive parameter and $T$ the number of time-series observations for each cross-sectional unit (in our case, 10). This test statistic is distributed normally asymptotically. Values of the test statistic, which ranged from $-2.06$ for Oxford to .43 for Ashland, allowed us to accept the null hypothesis of no autocorrelation at the .01 level.

We used a Lagrangian multiplier test recently developed by Breusch and Pagan (1980) to test for independence across units. The value of the test statistic, which is distributed $\chi^2_{15}$ under the null hypothesis, was 42.945, which is significant at normal levels of statistical significance (e.g., $\alpha = .01$).

8. Specifically, we dropped all 20 service conditions and input and output quality variables with $|$"$t$-ratios"$| < 1$ and tested for the joint significance of these 20 deleted variables. The test statistic, which is distributed $\chi^2_{20}$ under the null hypothesis, was 19.814, which is insignificant at normal levels (e.g., $\alpha = .01$ or .05). Estimation of the reduced specification, which contained

16 independent variables, resulted in a coefficient on one variable, *MARRIED*, with |“*t*-ratio”| < 1. We deleted this variable and arrived at the final specification reported in Table 16.2.

9. *LNCOST-L* had a mean of 2.31 and a standard deviation of 0.06.

10. 406 F. Supp. 318 (M. D. Ala., 1976).

11. The prison listed in the last column would satisfy the standards of the Commission on Accreditation if the ratio of cells for inmates locked up over 10 hours per day to those locked up 10 or fewer hours per day is one or less.

# Chapter 17

## Summary and Conclusions

### 17.1. Introduction

In this book we illustrated the use of a number of advanced statistical techniques and developed models of criminal behavior and criminal justice system operation using modern economic theory. We believe that the use of these methods and techniques to study crime and the administration of justice is important for at least two reasons. First, the substantive conclusions we reach are in many cases unique, and they provide valuable guidance to criminal justice researchers, administrators, and policy makers. Second, we hope that our use of these techniques will stimulate further use and development of both advanced statistical techniques and mathematical modeling in areas related to law enforcement and the administration of justice. In this chapter we summarize the book and draw conclusions about both the substance of our research and our research methods themselves.

### 17.2. Summary of Part I

In the first part of this book we used various statistical techniques designed to model dependent variables that are either qualitative or limited in some manner to analyze the postrelease criminal behavior of prison releasees. In each instance we first discussed in some detail the type of statistical technique to be utilized and then illustrated its use.

In Chapter 2 we discussed and compared four methods that have been used to analyze qualitative dependent variables: (1) logit analysis, (2) probit analysis, (3) discriminant analysis, and (4) special logit techniques used when all explanatory variables are qualitative. In Chapter 3, we illustrated the use of these techniques by analyzing two separate qualitative measures of postrelease criminal behavior: (1) whether an individual was not convicted, convicted of a misdemeanor, or convicted of a felony during a follow-up period and (2) the type of crime for which an individual was convicted (a persons offense, a property offense, or another type of offense). The data used contain detailed information on a data set of two samples, taken in 1973, of 641 individuals incarcerated in North Carolina prisons in either 1969 or 1971.

A number of important results were found in both analyses. An individual is more likely to be convicted of a crime during his follow-up period the larger the number of his previous convictions, the lower his age at release, the longer his follow-up period, and if he is an alcoholic or user of hard drugs. However, none of these variables was useful in predicting the nature of the offense, either as to seriousness (misdemeanor versus felony) or type (person versus property versus other offense). Conversely, the nature of the last previous offense did not affect the overall probability of a conviction but did affect the nature of the recidivist offense (if one was committed). Basically, individuals were found to commit the same type of crimes that they had previously committed, although there is some evidence of property offenders switching to crimes against persons.

In Chapter 4 we discussed methods of statistical analysis that have been developed for variables that are censored or truncated. We concentrated on a particular censored normal model, the Tobit model, although we discussed a more complex two-part Tobit model and a sample selection model. In Chapter 5, we illustrated the use of the Tobit model by analyzing the total length of time sentenced during a follow-up period for two distinct samples of releasees. The first sample is the same as was used when modeling the qualitative measures of criminal justice outcome. For this sample total length of time sentenced includes jail as well as prison sentences. The second sample analyzed consists of all individuals released from prison in North Carolina in the first half of 1975. Because all information on members of this sample was obtained from the computerized records of the N.C. Department of Correction, length of time sentenced reflects only prison, and not jail, sentences. We believe that analysis of the first sample is of interest because of the unusually complete criminal records and other data available.

Thus this sample provides valuable insights into the causes of crime and criminal justice outcomes. Analysis of the second sample is useful for at least two reasons. First, the sample is much more representative of all prison releasees. Second, the use of data generally available in a corrections department ensures wider potential use of the models developed. Indeed, the N.C. Department of Corrections has computerized the models developed for this release cohort and is using them to predict recidivism and evaluate correctional programs.

Our analysis of the first sample indicated that the type of individual likely to accumulate a long total length of time sentenced is a young, white, unmarried alcoholic or hard drug user, who was first arrested at an early age, was young at the time of release, was not on the North Carolina work release program, and had many previous prison convictions. These results are similar to previous analyses of postrelease criminality, which generally use a simpler, binary (reconviction or rearrest versus no such action) definition of postrelease criminal activity, with two exceptions. The first is the finding that whites are more likely to accumulate more and/or longer sentences. The second is that work release, a correctional program, seems to affect post-release behavior beneficially.

We began our analysis of the second sample by estimating a model for total North Carolina prison sentences, using Tobit analysis. The sample used to estimate this "overall" model consists of a random sample of 1616 individuals for which all data that we believed necessary to model recidivism were available. It should be noted that extensive missing data on addiction causes this sample to be not entirely representative of all North Carolina prison releasees during this period. Our results indicate that the type of individual who is most likely to accumulate a long total length of time sentenced is a young, black, male alcoholic with a lot of previous convictions, whose release was unsupervised, and whose sample crime was against property. These results are generally similar to those obtained for the previous sample, except for race. Results for these two analyses of length of time sentenced and the two analyses of the length of time until reconviction (reported in Chapter 7) led us to believe that differences between our two samples and data were the cause of these conflicting results for race. It seems that it is the appearance of large numbers of habitual, white, misdemeanant offenders (e.g., public drunks or those who do not support their families) who accumulate numerous short jail sentences that led to our original finding that whites accumulated more time sentenced than blacks. When many of these offenders were no longer in the sample studied (as in 1975, owing to legal changes) and jail sentences are no longer counted, it is blacks rather than whites who accumulated more time sentenced. We have no way of knowing whether this is because of larger amounts of serious criminal activity among blacks, bias in the criminal justice system, or the nonrepresentativeness of the 1975 sample.

Our original purpose in developing models for the 1975 release cohort was to provide the N.C. Department of Correction with models that would predict postrelease criminal activity, which would impact on the department, as accurately as possible. The department wished to use those models to predict postrelease criminal activity, to evaluate correctional programs using the "predicted versus actual" method described in Chapter 8, and to aid in prediction of future prison populations. To improve our predictions of total length of time sentenced for groups not used in the estimation of our models, we estimated separate models of total length of time sentenced for various race–sex–age groupings. We found differences in the significance of factors affecting recidivism for most groups; however, it was only for females that differences in the way various factors affected recidivism were important. In terms of predicting postrelease criminality for those not included in the sample, a group-specific model predicted better than an overall model for nonblack male adults, nonblack male youths, and black male youths. Thus it appears that there is a complex interaction between age and race and total length of time sentenced. Using the best model for each group, we predicted the average length of time sentenced during a follow-up period for 600 individuals released from prison in 1975 with complete data, not used in estimating the model. The predicted value of 6.090 months compares well with the actual average length of time sentenced of 5.503, and indeed, the predicted value is insignificantly different from the actual. We also used our models to predict total length of time sentenced for those with incomplete data and, somewhat surprisingly, found that our models predicted very well for this group as well. Thus, at least for purposes of prediction, the nonrepresentativeness of our estimation sample does not appear to be too damaging.

In Chapters 6 and 7 we again altered our dependent variable of interest and considered the analysis of "survival time" (length of time until recidivism, in the current instance). In Chapter 6, we discussed statistical techniques designed to analyze survival time and argued that analysis of survival time is statistically more efficient than is analysis of whether or not return to criminal activity occurs during a follow-up period. We also argued that analyses of survival time should at least explore the possibility that personal characteristics and previous activities affect individual survival times. This has not been common for most analyses of survival time to date. We discussed the use of four different types of distributions to analyze survival time (i.e., exponential, Weibull, lognormal, and truncated normal), as well as a split population technique. In Chapter 7, we analyzed our 1969 and 1971 sample and 1975 release cohort, using what we believed to be a particularly promising technique—a censored lognormal distribution for which the mean survival time depends on individual characteristics and past activity. As noted earlier, this type of analysis is more efficient statistically than simple analyses (for example, analyses of whether or not one returns to crime). In addition, estimation of the distribution of length of time until return to criminal activity allows one to predict the rate of recidivism for any time within the follow-up period.

For the 1969 and 1971 data set, we analyzed the length of time from release until the first arrest that results in a conviction. Note that this is a very general definition of recidivism, because the reconviction may result in such things as a suspended sentence or fine as well as a jail or prison sentence. Our results indicate that an individual is significantly more likely to remain without a conviction longer if he is black, had fewer prior convictions and fewer rule violations while in prison, was older at release, and is not an alcoholic or a user of hard drugs. Note that again for this sample we find that blacks are significantly less likely to return to crime than whites. Note also that a number of personal characteristics and indicators of previous activity significantly affect survival time. We believe that this provides strong evidence that mean survival time should be analyzed carefully rather than assumed to be the same for all individuals or to depend on only a few factors. We present evidence that our model fits the actual data utilized quite well and, indeed, that the censored lognormal distribution fits the data better than the normal, censored normal, or censored exponential distributions.

As before, for the 1975 release cohort we analyzed a less general measure of recidivism (the length of time from release from imprisonment until reimprisonment in North Carolina). Analysis of this dependent variable provides less general information on the causes of return to the criminal justice system but is much more readily available for analysis and practical use. We began our analysis of this release cohort by fitting a censored lognormal model for the same 1616 individuals as used to estimate the overall model of total length of time sentenced discussed earlier. Our results indicated that the type of individual likely to return to prison in North Carolina soonest is a young, black male with a lot of previous convictions and rule violations, with little formal education, whose sample crime was a felony that was not a crime against property, whose release was unsupervised, and who participated in the work release program. These results are similar to our results for the 1969 and 1971 data set with two important exceptions. The first is that the effect of race is precisely the opposite that we found in the 1969 and 1971 data set. Because we have discussed possible reasons for this previously, we shall not repeat ourselves here. The second exception is that addiction to alcohol or drugs does not appear to affect the length of time until reimprisonment in North Carolina, although it did affect the length of time until any reconviction. We do not know the precise reason for this change in results. However, the change can possibly be explained as (1) an artifact of the particular samples used, (2) a reflection of changes from the early to mid 1970s, or (3) a result of the difference in definition of the dependent variable analyzed. As in the case of race, we lean toward the third possible explanation, although we can provide no convincing evidence for it. On a priori grounds it seems likely that alcohol and drug addiction would lead to minor sentences (e.g., fines, short jail terms) that are reflected in the dependent variable analyzed for the 1969 and 1971 data set but not in the dependent variable analyzed for the 1975 release cohort.

Because variables reflecting alcohol and drug addiction did not significantly affect survival time for the 1975 cohort, we were able to greatly expand the proportion of the release cohort (from 45 to almost 80%) that we were able to utilize for our analyses. (Data on addictive problems was missing for approximately a third of the members of the cohort.) The resulting expanded data set is quite representative of the entire release cohort, tending to exclude only short-term misdemeanant offenders, who are increasingly being diverted from the prison system. We randomly split this expanded data set into an estimation sample of 2848 individuals and a validation sample of 1000 individuals. We first fit a censored lognormal model to a randomly selected sample of 1000 individuals in the estimation sample. Our results indicate that an individual will return to prison sooner if he or she is poorly educated, is older, has had many previous convictions and rule violations, is married, and was last convicted of a crime against a person. Note that results for the first four variables are similar to those for the previous estimation sample but that the last two variables were not significantly related to survival time in the previous analysis. The direction of the effect for previous conviction of a persons offense is similar but that for marital status is reversed. Note also that race, sex, postrelease supervision, participation in work release, and whether the previous conviction was for a felony or for a property offense no longer significantly affect survival time for the expanded sample as they did for the previously analyzed sample. This points up the desirability of samples that are as representative of the population of interest as possible. Indeed, it provides some support for our racial findings being an artifact of the particular sample analyzed.

As we did previously for total time sentenced, we next estimated separate models of survival time for various race–sex–age groupings to improve the predictions of our model for the validation sample. We found that a group-specific model predicts best for females and nonblack (white and Native American) male adults (21 years old or older).

Using the best model for each subgroup, we were able to predict survival time for members of the validation sample surprisingly accurately. We overpredicted recidivism by only 2.5%, and this overprediction is statistically insignificant. This is a marked improvement over most previous attempts to predict recidivism. Furthermore, we predicted the number of individuals returning to prison month by month for follow-up periods of 2 to 25 months. Even with this stringent test our predictions proved quite accurate, and indeed, the predicted number of recidivists for each month is insignificantly different from the actual. We slightly overpredicted recidivism for short and long follow-up times and slightly underpredicted for follow-up periods of 7 to 21 months. We believe that this ability to predict recidivism by month is convincing evidence of the usefulness of analyzing representative release cohorts using advanced statistical techniques.

In the final chapter of Part I, we illustrated one potential use of our models of recidivism—to simply and quickly provide an evaluation of correctional programs. Specifically, we used our best models of total length of time sentenced and survival time to predict the recidivism of youthful offenders who participated in an innovative vocational evaluation and job development program. We compared the recidivism predicted by our models with that actually experienced by those who participated in the program to determine if there is any evidence for the effectiveness of the program. We find weak statistical evidence that the program reduces length of time sentenced and stronger evidence that the program slightly lengthens time until recidivism. We used this chapter to comment on the relative strengths and weaknesses of this method of evaluation, which we call the "predicted versus actual" technique. This method of evaluation is, of course, only as strong as the models used to make the predictions. We believe that our models are quite good, and thus that evaluations using them are also reasonably reliable. However, the technique has obvious weaknesses. For example, if program selection criteria are related to outcomes in ways not reflected in the model, then estimates of program effects will be biased. For these and other reasons, this technique is best used in conjunction with a carefully designed quasi-experiment. However, even if such an experiment is not possible, we believe that this technique provides an easy and simple method for obtaining preliminary indications of program effects.

## 17.3. Conclusions from Part I

Our analyses of Part I provide convincing evidence that previous record, age, and type of most recent crime are significantly related to the timing, type, and extent of recidivist criminal activity. Specifically, our results indicate that individuals who are younger at release, who have had many previous convictions, and who were most recently convicted of a property offense are more likely to return to crime sooner, showing greater persistence and committing more serious offenses. Further, our analysis of the type of offense indicates that persons offenders tend to be unique and are rarely convicted of other types of offenses, whereas property offenders are likely to be convicted of persons offenses later in their careers. Results for other variables are less clear. For example, individuals who misbehave while in prison are significantly more likely to return to prison sooner but do not commit significantly more or more serious offenses. Individuals with more education are significantly less likely to return to prison, but education has no significant effect on the extent or seriousness of postrelease criminal activity. There is weak evidence that this is also the case for individuals who are married. In contrast, there is evidence that females and those without addictive problems commit significantly less serious and extensive offenses when released, although their timing of recidivism is similar to that for other groups. We obtain our most equivocal results for race, finding with one data set that blacks are significantly more likely to return to criminal activity and with another that this is the case for whites. We can give no definitive reason for these conflicting results, but we believe that they point out the need to investigate both racial differences in criminality and the effect of race on criminal justice outcomes. There has been some interesting recent work on the latter topic.

Our conclusions about our research methods are, we believe, equally important. Perhaps the first and most surprising conclusion is that it is possible by use of reasonably good data and advanced statistical techniques to predict recidivism accurately for individuals not in the sample used to estimate the models on which the predictions are based. This is important and should provide a basis for much more accurate projections of the workloads of the courts and correctional agencies. Our second conclusion is that effective analysis of measures of recidivism requires considerable statistical sophistication, care in analysis, and data sets that are as representative and extensive as possible. For example, our analysis of survival time, which we believe to be one of the most informative single measures of recidivism, indicates that it is very important to consider the appropriate distribution carefully and to allow at least some parameters of the distribution to depend on the personal characteristics and previous activity of the individuals being analyzed. Our third conclusion is that, although for some explanatory variables (i.e., age, previous record and type of offense) analyses of most measures of postrelease criminal activity give similar conclusions, for many other variables conclusions depend critically on the precise measure of recidivism analyzed. For this reason, we suggest that whenever possible, measures of the timing, extent, and seriousness of postrelease activity should all be analyzed. Our final research conclusion is that it would be extremely useful to sort out the respective effects of factors affecting criminality and factors affecting the criminal justice process. For example, it seems quite possible that the relatively strong effect of addictive problems and sex on total time sentenced may be reflecting, at least in part, the way in which the police and courts operate.

## 17.4. Summary of Part II

In the second part of this book, we illustrated the way in which economists have developed formal mathematical models of criminal activity and estimated these models using the 1969–1971 data set analyzed in Part I. Our main focus in this and the next part of the book is to illustrate the way in which economic theory can be used to analyze criminality and the administration of justice.

In Chapter 9, we surveyed a selected group of economic models of crime that we believe represent the richness and diversity of this type of modeling effort. We also developed two models of criminal activity that serve to guide our empirical work in the remaining chapters of this part. Our survey and modeling effort highlights a number of aspects of formal economic modeling, some of which are unique to models of criminal behavior and some of which are more general. For example, this work indicates the centrality of the assumption of rational maximizing behavior. Further, economic models of criminal behavior assume that all items affecting individuals' well being may be converted to common units of measurement via a utility function. This utility function is generally assumed to be continuous and differentiable. Further, economic models of criminal behavior generally assume that only the individual's level of income or wealth enters the utility function directly. This implies either that individuals are indifferent to allocations of their time as long as they produce equal levels of income or wealth or that differences in tastes for different types of activities are fully reflected in income levels. According to this type of model, an individual would be indifferent between earning $25,000 per year as a professional thief or a lawyer. The reason economists have made this rather unappealing assumption is that it often allows them to determine unambiguously the effect of changes in such things as the level of unemployment or the level of criminal sanctions on the level of criminal activity. For example, the first model we develop unambiguously predicts that individuals will allocate less time to criminal activity the higher is the probability of apprehension or the more costly are criminal justice sanctions.

Economic models that allow either the level of sanctions or the allocation of time to enter the utility function directly are more appealing intuitively. They allow individuals to have different attitudes toward sanctions, work, and illegal activity. However, this increased realism is not without price. These models do not allow us to determine unambiguously how changes in criminal justice practices or legal opportunities will affect participation in illegal activities. In these models, individual responses will differ, and thus no unambiguous total response can be predicted. The ultimate effects of stiffened penalties, increased probabilities of apprehension or improved legal opportunities become an empirical question. This type of general model merely provides guidance to empirical work.

We reported the results of our efforts to estimate economic models of crime using individual data in Chapters 10, 11, and 12. In Chapter 10, we estimated single-equation models for conviction and arrest rates during a follow-up period, which contain measures of criminal justice system operation (i.e., deterrence variables), legal opportunity, and individual tastes. Our results were generally consistent with the simpler economic models of crime, and, indeed, with previous results obtained using aggregate data. Specifically, our results support the contention that deterrence works and that a percentage increase in the probability of being punished has a relatively larger effect on the number of arrests or convictions than does a percentage increase in the expected sentence. (That is, certainty deters more than severity.) It should be noted that the support we provide is relatively weak. Only 5 (out of 24) of the coefficients on the probabilities of being punished are more than twice their estimated standard errors, and one of these has a nontraditional sign. Support for the deterrent effect of longer prison sentences is only somewhat stronger. (Three out of 12 coefficients are more than twice their standard errors.) Still, it is quite unlikely that this support could have been generated by a purely random process. The empirical analysis also suggests that the manner in which deterrence works varies markedly with the type of crime in which an individual specializes. For individuals who specialize in consumption offenses (e.g., assaultive or drug use offenses), the expected sentence has the most significant effect, whereas for individuals who specialize in nonserious income offenses (e.g., larceny and illegal liquor sales), the probability of imprisonment is most significant, and for individuals who specialize in neither consumption nor income offenses (e.g., nonsupport or obstructing justice), the probability of conviction is most significant. For individuals who specialize in serious income offenses (e.g., robbery and illegal drug sales), none of the deterrence variables has a coefficient that is even marginally significant at normal levels of statistical significance. This is unexpected, suggesting as it seems to that deterrence fails to work for this group. A priori, one would have expected income offenders to behave more rationally than other types of offenders.

When one turns to the effect of legitimate opportunities on illegal activity, one finds that higher wages tend to decrease the expected number of arrests or convictions but only significantly (one-tailed test, 5% level) in one case (for nonserious income offenders). The low significance of the coefficients for the wage rate may be the result of our inability to include an explicit measure of the payoff to illegal activity. However, an advantage gained in the use of individual data is that the legal wage rate can be unambiguously identified, which has not been possible in tests of the economic model that use aggregate data.

When one examines the effect of higher wages on individuals who specialize in various crime types, one finds that higher wages seem most effective in deterring crime for nonserious income offenders and appear if anything to increase crime for serious income offenders. This perverse wage effect, coupled with the earlier finding that criminal justice sanctions have no deterrent effect for this group, is unexpected, because one would certainly feel that an economic model would be most relevant for income offenders. Examination of the other variables in the model reveals a possible explanation of this seeming paradox. The most significant variable determining the number of arrests or convictions for people who specialize in serious income offenses is whether or not they are drug users. The high correlation between drug use and serious income offenses is well known to criminal justice authorities but makes testing of the economic model of crime for this group extremely difficult. Possibly the need for money for drugs largely eliminates the rational decision process that the economic model of crime assumes.

The variable thought to be measuring the expected unemployment rate (the number of months after release until employment) has an unexpected negative coefficient for all groups except serious income offenders, indicating that a longer period out of the labor force or in job search after release leads to less crime. It may be that this variable is not measuring the expected unemployment rate but rather is measuring legitimate job search time, which results in discovery of more satisfying legitimate employment. In this case the negative sign for this variable may be reasonable. Cook (1975, p. 22) has hypothesized that low-quality jobs are readily available to former offenders but higher-quality jobs are more difficult to encounter. However, if this line of reasoning is correct, our measure of expected unemployment becomes a variable endogenous to the system, and simultaneous equations methods should be used to estimate the model. We used such techniques in Chapter 12.

Higher initial wealth was found in almost all cases to lead to less criminal activity, but the coefficient of this variable was insignificantly different from zero in all cases. Our comparative static results had led us to expect higher initial wealth to be associated with higher levels of illegal activity. However, to obtain this result we assume that individuals dislike risk more when they are poorer. If, instead, the low levels of wealth of members of our sample are such as to make them dislike risk more when they are richer, then our empirical and theoretical results support one another. Another possible reconciliation is that higher initial wealth is a reflection of favorable individual characteristics (e.g., willingness to work) that we have not completely captured in our model.

In Chapter 11, we estimated single-equation models for the hourly wage received on the first job obtained after release from prison and for the stability of employment during the follow-up period. We also surveyed other studies that investigated the determinants of labor market performance for prison releasees and compare them with our own. Both our results and the results of others lead to the following conclusions. First, neither education nor age appears to affect significantly the postrelease labor market performance of prison releasees. This is surprising, because studies of other population groups seem to indicate that these factors are major determinants of labor market performance. The finding that the level of education does not affect postrelease labor market performance provides one possible explanation for the rather consistent finding that formal educational programs in prisons do not affect recidivism. Second, sex, race, family, and physical characteristics seem to have major effects on postrelease labor market performance. Third, higher wages appear to encourage work stability, which in turn leads to higher wages. Finally, graduated release through community treatment centers or halfway houses appears to improve performance, whereas being on parole appears to make labor market performance worse than it otherwise would be.

In the final chapter of Part II, we estimated a two-equation model of post release criminal activity and labor market performance. Specifically, the dependent variables in our simultaneous equation models are the arrest rate during the follow-up period and the wage on the first job after release. We estimated this two-equation model using a simultaneous Tobit technique. Our results for income offenders are supportive of more complex models of criminal activity. Specifically, our results indicate that there are interrelationships between the level of criminal activity and labor market performance for this type of offender. The error terms in the equations for the arrest rate and the wage after release are correlated, and furthermore, higher arrest rates significantly decrease postrelease wages. However, the wage rate after release does not appear to directly affect the arrest rate for this or any other group of offenders. We found that higher probabilities of both conviction and imprisonment significantly deter income offenders. Higher initial wealth is associated with lower levels of arrest. This finding is consistent with the hypothesis that prison releasees become more risk averse as they become wealthier. If this hypothesis were true, it would provide a potential explanation for recent findings that postrelease income supplements significantly decrease criminality. Although we changed our measure for the expected unemployment rate to the actual unemployment rate of the time and place of release, we still found our measure to be associated with lower levels of criminal activity. Of the taste variables, we found that only age at first arrest, race, and education significantly affected the arrest rate. The coefficients on these variables indicate that those who are *older* when first arrested, white, and better educated will be arrested with greater frequency, other things being equal. Our results for the wage rate equation are broadly similar to the results of Chapter 11 with one important exception: a human capital variable is now significant. Specifically, our results indicate that receipt of a high school diploma significantly increases the postrelease wage rate of income offenders.

Our results for consumption offenders and the residual category of offenders are less supportive of the traditional economic model of crime. It appears that, particularly for consumption offenders, it may be necessary to build special models of crime commission. Our results give some potentially useful insights for such models. First, they suggest that there is substantial interaction between criminal and labor market activity for consumption offenders. Higher arrest rates are associated with higher wages, perhaps indicating some sort of complementarity between the two types of activities. Further, it appears that variables reflecting criminal justice system actions only weakly affect the behavior of consumption offenders. Taste variables are more important determinants of arrest rates, with unmarried, older, non-white individuals with a supervised release and little if any previous criminal record having lower frequencies of arrest. Our results for supervision and marital status are particularly interesting. Of the three groups studied, postrelease supervision appears to have a beneficial effect on postrelease behavior only for consumption offenders and appears to have a detrimental affect on the postrelease behavior of "other" offenders. Perhaps it would be wise to devote more parole resources to assaultive offenders. Our result for marital status is intriguing and seems to reflect at least in part the prevalence of family violence.

The more complex, simultaneous model of labor market and criminal activity appears to be needed least for our residual group of offenders. For this type of offender, labor market and criminal activity decisions appear to be made relatively independently. Higher probabilities of conviction and longer sentences are associated with lower arrest rates for the residual group.

## 17.5. Conclusions for Part II

Our results in Part II indicated that economic models of crime provide useful insights concerning crime causation, particularly for income offenders.

Economic models appear less insightful for consumption and other types of offenders. Our estimates of both single-equation and simultaneous-equation models of crime commission provide rather weak, but for certain types of property offenders consistent, support for the "deterrence hypothesis." We believe that this support is important because ours is one of the few attempts to test the deterrence hypothesis using individual data.

We found the effect of legitimate opportunity on criminality to be more complex than reflected in most current economic models of crime. Specifically, although we generally found higher wages to be associated with lower levels of criminal activity, it appears that the effect of wages on criminal activity is indirect rather than direct. We consistently found higher levels of wealth to be associated with lower levels of criminal activity, although the coefficient on this variable is only significant in one instance. This result contradicts the normal prediction of simple economic models of crime and may indicate that prison releasees become more risk averse as they become wealthier.

Our investigation of the determinants of labor market performance and the work of others lead us to conclude that labor markets for prison releasees are unique. Indeed, our results would be consistent with the conclusion that most prison releasees are employed in the secondary labor market described by dual labor market theorists.

In terms of research methods, our work in Part II allows us to make a number of suggestions. First, external factors (labor market conditions, criminal justice system operation) appear to affect criminality. Thus individuals developing models for crime commission should be careful to include measures of external factors in their models. Second, the effect of external factors (and indeed of internal ones such as personal characteristics) appears to be more complex than is reflected in current models. We need more complex models and believe that these models will best be constructed for particular, relatively homogeneous crime types (e.g., assaultive offenses, property crimes). Third, the role of addiction in criminality needs to be explored carefully. It may be necessary to exclude individuals with serious addictive problems when estimating models which assume rational maximizing behavior.

## 17.6. Summary of Part III

In the final part of this book, we turned our attention to the way in which a particular type of criminal justice organization, a large-scale prison, operates. In the first chapter of Part III, we briefly discussed the modern economic theory of the firm. The concepts of cost and production functions have been adapted by economists to study the way in which public organizations operate. In Chapter 14, using the concepts of production and cost functions as a base, we developed a model of the operation of large-scale prisons. This model sees the direct output of prisons as a certain number of individuals confined for a certain number of days—that is, incarceration. This direct output is in turn an input to socially desired outcomes—punishment, incapacitation, deterrence, and rehabilitation. We modeled the direct output of prisons but were careful to control for the level of social outcomes in this modeling effort. We also controled for output quality (i.e., the quality of incarceration) by controlling for such things as the availability of rehabilitative programming. Our final model viewed prison costs as determined by the number of inmates incarcerated (i.e., the level of direct output), the prices of the factors used to operate the prison (i.e., capital and labor), the quality of output, and the conditions under which prisons operate.

In Chapter 15, we estimated short-run average cost curves for 22 federal and 8 California prisons. For the majority of prisons studied, we found that short-run average costs decrease as the size of the prison increases. This appears to be particularly true for old, large, high-security facilities like Folsom State Prison in the California system and the U.S. Penitentiary at Atlanta. For some federal prisons we found that costs at first decrease and then increase (∪-shaped short-run average cost curves), and for a few prisons housing special types of inmates (females and young males) we found that costs continually rise as populations increase.

We found that the provision of rehabilitative activities at first increases and then decreases short-run operating costs. Thus it appears that short-run prison operating costs at most prisons will be least if either relatively few or a large number of such activities are provided.

Our results indicate that short-run prison operating costs will also rise initially and then decline as the average age of the inmate population increases. Thus prisons with older populations generally will be cheaper to operate than will prisons with very young populations. We found that inmates with higher IQs generally are cheaper to incarcerate in the federal system but that inmates with higher-tested educational achievement are more expensive to incarcerate in the California system. In general, we found that the incarceration of individuals with drug problems is more expensive than the incarceration of individuals without such problems. However, at least in the federal system, we found that individuals with alcohol problems are no more expensive to incarcerate than other individuals. We found that, for FCIs (generally smaller, newer, lower-security prisons), short-run costs will be less if the racial composition of the staff approximates that of the inmate population. Equal employment opportunity appears, at least in this instance, to be good business. In the federal system, we found that expansions of capacity generally lower costs, and that, in the California system, higher levels of security are associated with higher costs.

In Chapter 16, we estimated a long-run cost curve using data for FCIs for the 1976–1978 time period. Our results indicated that prisons will be cheapest if they are quite large (housing between 700 and 1500 inmates), house mainly nonwhite, nonalcoholic males who have not been convicted of a property offense, house a relatively large proportion of this population in associated camps, have older staff, provide relatively substantial amounts of space in single cells and provide few sanitary facilities. Our results in this chapter are not totally generalizable as we use data for only six FCIs to obtain them. The result that proves to be most robust is that costs per inmate generally decrease as prison size increases, until prisons become quite large. We believe that this result holds for most types of prisons.

## 17.7. Conclusions for Part III

Our results in Part III indicated that costs per inmate are generally lower in larger prisons. This result is robust, and we believe it has major policy implications, given current recommendations and prison construction plans that call for small prisons (e.g., 500 or so inmates). We, as a society, may still wish to build such prisons, but it appears that there will be substantial costs in doing so. Our results also indicated that adoption of standards that suggest that inmates be housed in single cells with somewhat more living space than is currently the case (i.e., 60–80 $ft^2$) may actually lower long-run prison operating costs.

In the short run, we found that average costs per inmate generally decrease as the number of inmates increases, at least until prisons are substantially overcrowded. This result suggests that the current policies that have led many prisons to be overcrowded may actually be cost effective. One may, of course, fault such overcrowding on other grounds. We found that older inmates are generally less expensive to incarcerate than younger inmates and that inmates with drug problems tend to be expensive to house. Thus, the "greying" of the prison population may serve to decrease short-run operating costs, whereas its increased rate of drug problems may increase them.

Our conclusions about research methods are also important. First, we believe that we have amply demonstrated the potential usefulness of analysis of the operating costs of criminal justice organizations. We do not believe that policy and administrative decisions in criminal justice should be based on cost considerations alone, but do believe that costs should be at least one of the factors considered in making many decisions. Cost analyses of the type carried out in Part III can provide valuable insights. Thus we suggested that more such analyses be conducted. Second, we believe that the economic theory of the firm provides only a beginning for understanding the way in which public organizations operate. Further, we are not convinced that the adaptations in this theory made to date are sufficient to adequately reflect the complexity of public operations. Our experience led us to believe that it will be necessary to develop specific theories for particular types of public organizations. Finally, we believe that our understanding of production and costs can be improved most readily by detailed analyses of the individual productive unit and its environment.

## 17.8. General Conclusions

We believe that our work in this book has illustrated the desirability and usefulness of using advanced statistical techniques to analyze criminality and the administration of justice. However, it has also indicated the costs and difficulties involved. By using advanced statistical techniques, we were able in Part I to develop models that accurately predicted the timing, extent, and seriousness of postrelease criminal activity. In Part II, the use of such techniques allowed us to increase our understanding of the way in which individuals combine legal and illegal activity. In Part III, somewhat different techniques allowed us to increase our understanding of the way in which large-scale prisons operate and the factors affecting their costs of operation.

The costs of conducting the type of analyses that we have presented in this book are high. For example, the analyses of Part I required two years of effort of three professionals, even after all data were collected, and cost between \$50,000 and \$100,000. Collection of the 1969 and 1971 data set and the data sets used to analyze prison costs cost between \$50,000 and \$100,000 each, even with the extensive free help of many individuals working in criminal justice organizations.

The difficulties involved in these types of analyses are also substantial. For example, many times in the work reported in Part I and in Chapter 12, substantial time and effort were required before we could even obtain estimates. The appendix to Chapter 15 and Appendix C amply attest to the difficulties involved in obtaining data and estimating short-run cost functions.

We believe that our use of economic modeling techniques in Parts II and III illustrates both the usefulness and weaknesses of these techniques. We believe that the results of these two sections provide unique insights concerning the causes of crime and the way in which prisons operate. However, we believe that the results of these two sections also point out the desirability of further development and widening of the models developed by economists. For example, to understand the causes of criminality, it would be very useful to marry models for the formation of expectations and criminal justice organization operation to the economists' models of individual maximizing behavior. Further, it appears that current economic models are far more relevant for property offenses than for other types of offenses. Economists are beginning to develop specific models for other types of offenses, although such development is still in its infancy.

We close with a call for more careful, systematic, and interdisciplinary work in the study of crime and the administration of justice. The research needed will require much effort and understanding on the part of disciplinarily bound researchers, but we believe that the results will be well worth the effort.

# Appendix A

## Description of the 1969 and 1971 North Carolina Department of Correction Data Set

This data set contains information on a sample of inmates incarcerated in prisons in 1969 or 1971 in the South Piedmont Administrative Area (Charlotte, North Carolina, and surrounding area). The data were taken from four sources: (1) North Carolina Department of Corrections' records; (2) an extensive postrelease interview; (3) local criminal records; and (4) the FBI. North Carolina Department of Corrections' records were used to obtain prior record, work history, addictive history, education, and facts related to the correctional experience (e.g. the number of rule violations, time served, funds accumulated while on work release, whether supervised when released). The postrelease interview was used mainly to obtain postrelease work history and as one source of information on postrelease criminal activity. Interview information on postrelease employment was only checked (with employers) if the information given appeared to be markedly out of line with the previous employment history obtained from North Carolina Department of Corrections' records. Information on criminal activity was checked carefully and thoroughly. The data on postrelease criminal activity is a synthesis of information obtained from the sources just listed. We began to collect information on postrelease criminal activity by asking each member of the sample who was located the date, location, and disposition of all arrests since his release from the sample sentence (the sentence he was serving in 1969 or 1971). Each individual was also, in a much later portion of the questionnaire, asked to indicate all areas in which he had lived since his release from the sample sentence. The criminal records in all areas where a man claimed to have lived or to have been arrested were searched to determine the validity and completeness of the criminal histories elicited. Unsurprisingly, many of the men in the samples claimed substantially fewer contacts with the criminal justice authorities than they had actually had.

If we could not locate a member of the sample after an extensive search, an FBI check was run to determine whether the man had any criminal record that had been reported to the FBI since his release from the sample sentence. If the FBI check indicated that a man had been involved in criminal activity, we requested a complete criminal record from the jurisdiction of this involvement. Requests for criminal records also were sent to all locations where the North Carolina Department of Correction's records indicated that a man might be living.

We believe that the criminal records we finally developed are as complete and consistent as it was possible to make them. Further, we believe that the care taken and double checks made make these criminal histories unusually reliable.

The original reason for developing this data set was to evaluate the prisoner work release program in North Carolina. Owing to this original purpose, the sample was drawn as follows. First, the population of prison inmates (all male) in the South Piedmont (Charlotte, North Carolina, and surrounding counties) in 1969 and 1971 was divided into three groups: (1) a group that participated in work release in one or both of these years; (2) a group that was in prison in one or both of these years but never participated in the work release program; and (3) a group that was in prison in one or both of these years but participated in work release at some other time. Group 3 was dropped from consideration, and groups 1 and 2 were considered for sampling. Before sampling the following adjustments were made. First, members of either group who could not be followed up were eliminated. This group consisted of men who had not been released by June 1973, men who died in prison, and men who were listed as escaped. Next all members of the non-work-release group, Group 2, who were in prison for crimes that prevented their placement on work release during 1969 and 1971 were eliminated. This group consisted of all men in prison for sex crimes and serious drug offenses. In addition, all members of the non-work-release population who were convicted of the public drunk offense were eliminated, because they were not in prison long enough to be processed for work release. From these adjusted groups, a random sample of 297 work releasees from group 1 and 344 nonwork releasees from group 2 was drawn. The size of the two samples was set so that an estimate of a proportion (e.g., rate of recidivism) would not differ by more than 5% from the population proportion 95% of the time.

Interviews of sample members took place between the beginning of July 1973 and the end of June 1974. We were able to locate and interview 71% of the total sample. A larger proportion (72%) of former work releasees than of men who had not been on the work release program (69%) were interviewed. The project staff was able to obtain partial information on 15% of the 188 men who were not interviewed. Of men not interviewed, 25% were located but managed to elude us, 9% were located but refused to be interviewed (sometimes rather violently), and 66% were never located. We took some consolation on our inability to locate this last group from the fact that 23% of them were wanted by some law enforcement agency.

If one compares the individuals the project staff was able to interview with those it was not, one finds that the old, habitual misdemeanant offender is underrepresented in the interviewed group. Hence, information obtained during the interview does not adequately weight this group of individuals.

A more complete description of this data set is contained in Witte (1975).

# Appendix B

## Description of the 1975 Data Set

The data set described in this appendix contains information on all individuals released from the North Carolina Department of Correction during the first 6 months of 1975 (January 1–July 1). Information on the personal characteristics of these individuals was taken from the computerized inmate histories of the department. The postrelease criminal activity of these individuals was determined by a search of North Carolina Department of Correction records in February 1977. The follow-up period therefore ranged from 20 to 25 months.

There were 4881 individuals released from the Department of Correction during the first 6 months of 1975, so the basic data set contains 4881 observations. However, some individuals' records lacked information on variables that were needed for our analyses, so two subsamples of the basic data set were ultimately used for our analyses.

Our models of length of time sentenced (reported in Sections 5.3–5.4) were based on a subsample of 2216 individuals, whose records contained information on all the major factors believed to be related to criminal activity. This sample of 2216 individuals constitutes approximately 45% of the original sample of 4881 individuals. The most frequently missing information was that on alcohol and drug use (*ALCHY* and *JUNKY*); 41% of the cases did not contain information on alcohol use, and 42% lacked information on drug use. The only other variables for which information was at times missing were previous convictions (20% missing), school grade (.04% missing), and marital status (2% missing).

The sample of 2216 releasees can not be considered representative of the entire group of 4881, because there are significant differences between the 2216 individuals with complete data and the 2665 individuals with incomplete data. Tables B1–B3 illustrate some of these differences. It is obvious from the lines corresponding to "Length of time served" and "Sample conviction for felony" in Table B.1 and from Table B.2 that individuals incarcerated for more serious offenses (hence receiving longer sentences) were more likely to have missing information. This is because social history information, from which information on drug and alcohol use is obtained, was not computerized until 1973 and was therefore not available for individuals who began their incarceration prior to that year. Thus individuals for whom information was missing had served an average of 20 months before release in the first six months of 1975, whereas individuals for whom information was available served an average of only 8 months prior to release in 1975.

**TABLE B.1.** Comparison of Mean Values for Selected Characteristics

| Variable[a] | Description[b] | Individuals with all information[c] | Individuals with missing information[d] |
|---|---|---|---|
| *LTFPC** | Months until reimprisonment | 10.4[e] | 9.7[f] |
| *TTSENT** | Length of time sentenced after release | 5.2 | 7.4 |
| *AAR*** | Age at release | 345 | 376 |
| *RULE*** | Number of rule violations | 0.4 | 1.0 |
| *CONVBS*** | Number of previous convictions | 1.8 | 2.1[g] |
| *TSERVD*** | Length of time served in months (sample sentence) | 8.2 | 20.3 |
| *SG*** | Education claimed | 9.2 | 8.9[h] |
| *SUPER*** | Supervised release (d.v.) | .55 | .45 |
| *WR*** | Work release (d.v.) | .21 | .29 |
| *MF*** | Sample conviction for felony (d.v.) | .42 | .61 |

[a] Number of asterisks indicates level of significance, for group differences two-tailed test: ** = .05 level, * = .10 level.
[b] Dummy variables are indicated by (d.v.).
[c] $N = 2216$ unless indicated otherwise.
[d] $N = 2665$ unless indicated otherwise.
[e] $N = 542$.
[f] $N = 381$.
[g] $N = 1679$.
[h] $N = 2663$.

**TABLE B.2.** Comparison of Nature of Sample Offense[a]

| Crime category | Individuals with all information[b] Number | Individuals with all information[b] Percentage | Individuals with missing information[c] Number | Individuals with missing information[c] Percentage |
|---|---|---|---|---|
| Assault | 114 | 5.1 | 163 | 6.1 |
| Breaking and entering | 369 | 16.6 | 471 | 17.7 |
| Drug offenses | 237 | 10.7 | 163 | 6.1 |
| Other "Person" offenses | 121 | 5.5 | 256 | 9.6 |
| Other "Property" offenses | 544 | 24.6 | 702 | 26.3 |
| All other offenses | 831 | 37.5 | 910 | 34.2 |

[a] The two groups are significantly different at the 5% level ($\chi_5^2 = 66$).
[b] $N = 2216$.
[c] $N = 2665$.

Individuals on work release were also more likely to have missing information than the individuals who were not on the program. This is probably owing to lack of time for normal processing (including the social history) when an individual begins his or her participation in the work release program immediately on conviction.

Other differences between the two groups are that individuals with complete information on average are younger and better educated, have fewer rule violations and previous convictions, and are more likely to have a supervised release. Furthermore, whites and females are more likely to have complete information than blacks and males, as can be seen in Table B.3.

**TABLE B.3.** Comparison of Race–Sex Mix[a]

| Race and sex | Individuals with all information[b] Number | Individuals with all information[b] Percentage | Individuals with missing information[c] Number | Individuals with missing information[c] Percentage |
|---|---|---|---|---|
| White male | 1179 | 53.2 | 1249 | 46.9 |
| Black male | 849 | 38.3 | 1274 | 47.8 |
| Native American male | 51 | 2.3 | 68 | 2.6 |
| Oriental male | 2 | 0.1 | 1 | 0.04 |
| Other male | 4 | 0.2 | 1 | 0.04 |
| White female | 64 | 2.9 | 26 | 1.0 |
| Black female | 63 | 2.8 | 45 | 1.7 |
| Native American female | 4 | 0.2 | 1 | 0.04 |

[a] The two groups are significantly different at the 5% level ($\chi_7^2 = 72$).
[b] $N = 2216$.
[c] $N = 2665$.

If one considers post-1975-release criminal activity, differences between those for whom all information was available and those for whom it was not were smaller. Although individuals for whom information was missing returned earlier (an average of 9.7 versus 10.4 months for those with all information) and received longer sentences (an average of 7.4 versus 5.2 months), the differences between the two groups were significant only at the 10% level (two-tailed test).

We now turn to the expanded subsample of 3848 individuals used in our analyses of length of time until recidivism (reported in Sections 7.3–7.4). This corresponds to the subsample of 2216 individuals with complete information plus the 1632 individuals for whom all information except alcohol and drug use (*ALCHY* and *JUNKY*) was available. This expanded subsample represents approximately 70% of the total of 4881 individuals in the entire sample. The 1033 individuals who are still not in the expanded subsample were excluded primarily because they lacked information on the number of previous convictions (*CONVBS*).

When one compares the characteristics of individuals included in this expanded sample with those excluded, one still finds significant differences. Tables B.4–B.5 illustrate some of these differences. Individuals excluded from this expanded sample tended to be mainly short term, misdemeanant

**TABLE B.4.** Comparison of Mean Values for Selected Characteristics

| Variable[a] | Description[b] | Individuals in expanded sample[c] | Individuals not in expanded sample[d] |
|---|---|---|---|
| *LTFPC*** | Months until reimprisonment | 10.7[e] | 8.4[f] |
| *TTSENT** | Time sentenced after release | 5.8 | 8.7 |
| *AAR*** | Age at release | 352 | 398 |
| *RULE*** | Number of rule violations | 0.8 | 0.2 |
| *TSERVD*** | Time served in months (sample sentence) | 17.5 | 5.1 |
| *SUPER*** | Supervised release (d.v.) | .58 | .19 |
| *WR*** | Work release (d.v.) | .30 | .08 |
| *MF*** | Sample conviction for felony (d.v.) | .54 | .48 |
| *RACE* | Nonblack (d.v.) | .55 | .52 |
| *SEX*** | Male (d.v.) | .95 | .98 |

[a] Number of asterisks indicates level of significance, for group differences two-tailed test: ** = .05 level, * = .10 level. No asterisk indicates that difference is not significant at the .10 level.
[b] Dummy variables are indicated by (d.v.).
[c] $N = 3848$ unless indicated otherwise.
[d] $N = 1033$ unless indicated otherwise.
[e] $N = 659$.
[f] $N = 264$.

**TABLE B.5.** Comparison of Nature of Sample Offense[a]

| | Individuals in expanded sample[b] | | Individuals excluded from expanded sample[c] | |
|---|---|---|---|---|
| Crime category | Number | Percentage | Number | Percentage |
| Assault | 230 | 6.0 | 47 | 4.6 |
| Breaking and entering | 765 | 19.9 | 75 | 7.3 |
| Drug offenses | 361 | 9.4 | 39 | 3.8 |
| Other "Persons" offenses | 314 | 8.2 | 63 | 6.1 |
| Other "Property" offenses | 1013 | 26.3 | 233 | 22.6 |
| All other offenses | 1165 | 30.3 | 576 | 55.8 |

[a] The two groups are significantly different at the 5% level ($\chi_5^2 = 267$).
[b] $N = 3848$.
[c] $N = 1033$.

offenders. This is reflected in the fact that individuals included in the expanded sample had mean values of time sentenced and time served (prior to release in the first 6 months of 1975) of 43 and 18 months, respectively, whereas those excluded had mean values for these variables of 12 and 5 months. Ninety-five percent of those excluded from this expanded sample served 1 year or less prior to release in the first 6 months of 1975. Such offenders are less likely to participate in rehabilitative programs. This exclusion from program participation is reflected in the fact that a significantly smaller proportion of those excluded from the expanded sample had a supervised release or participated in the work release program. One important implication is that the expanded sample of 3848 individuals may be representative of the type of individual who is likely to participate in a rehabilitative program. This strengthens one's faith, for example, in a program evaluation using models (such as our models of length of time until reimprisonment) based on this expanded sample.

# Appendix C

## Description of Data Used to Estimate Cost Functions

In this appendix we describe the two data sets (federal and California) that we used to estimate the cost functions discussed in Chapters 14–16. We begin by discussing the federal data set, proceed to the California data set, and end with an evaluation of the strengths and weaknesses of these two data bases.

### C.1. The Data Available for the Federal Prison System

The basic federal data set from which we derive the data that we actually analyzed contains information on 27 federal prisons on a monthly basis for the period from November 1975 through June 1978. The data set includes information on all six Federal Penitentiaries (USPs) and all 21 Federal Correctional Institutions (FCIs) (including associated camps and female facilities) operating during the study period. These prisons and their associated facilities housed approximately 80% of the inmate population of the federal prison system during the study period.[1]

Data contained in the federal data set were obtained from a number of different sources within the Federal Bureau of Prisons (FBOP) and from the Department of Justice's System Design and Development Group. Institution-level data were available for total costs (FBOP 100.71),[2] the number of inmates confined (FBOP 70.53A), the number of inmates enrolled in rehabilitative activities (FBOP 72.90), planned institutional capacity (FBOP 70.52), electricity usage and cost (FBOP worksheets and institutional electricity bills and receipts), and incidents (FBOP regional incident report coding worksheets). In addition, detailed information on the capital stock was available for selected institutions[3] during the third quarter of 1977 owing to an unusually complete physical plant inventory conducted during that period.

Data were available on the characteristics of all inmates incarcerated in the federal prison system through FBOP's automated Inmate Information System (IIS). To obtain information on the characteristics of the inmates incarcerated at USPs and FCIs, it was necessary to determine where each individual in the federal prison system was at all times during the study period. We obtained a tape containing information on the 78,473 inmates who were incarcerated in the federal prison system during the November 1975–June 1978 period. We conducted logical checks (over 900 logical statements) of this individual data to determine data quality and discarded cases for which the information on the tape was inconsistent. Next we checked the data available for each individual to determine whether he or she was incarcerated in a USP or FCI during the study period and, if so, noted the institution and dates that the individual was admitted and released from the institution. We were forced to limit to two the number of institutions an inmate could reside in, owing to computer time and budgetary limitations.[4] However, less than 5% of the inmates resided in more than two institutions during the study period. The logical checks and search for inmates in USPs and FCIs during the study period resulted in a tape containing information on 58,430 inmates. For each inmate on this tape, we next determined the institution resided in for each month of the study period and the proportion of the month spent in each institution. Two passes were made through the tape, once for the individual's first institution and once for his or her second (if any). On each pass, new inmate data records were created, each containing all the inmate characteristics data and 66 new variables: 33 variables indicating the institution resided in for each month of the study period, and 33 variables indicating the proportion of the month the inmate resided in that institution. This "two-pass" approach caused inmates who resided in two institutions to be treated as two inmates, which greatly simplified subsequent processing. Using this expanded data set, we next obtained average inmate characteristics[5] for each institution for each month of the study period by sorting inmates into institutions and averaging their characteristics. These institution-level inmate data were added to the previously obtained institution-level data on costs, population, etc.

To obtain information on the staff at each USP and FCI during the study period, we obtained quarterly data on all personnel at the 27 prisons studied from Department of Justice payroll and Juniper tapes.[6] We sorted these personnel data by institution and quarter to obtain information for the staff at each prison during each quarter of the study period. These sorted data were used to obtain average staff characteristics, hours worked, and wage levels for each institution for each quarter of the study period. We added these institution-level staff data to the previously obtained institution-level data on inmates, costs, and so on, to obtain an institution-based data set. Information on all variables in this data set other than the staff variables, the capital stock variables, inmate enrollment in rehabilitative activities, and electric cost and usage variables was available on a monthly basis. Information on staff, inmate enrollment in rehabilitative activities, and electric cost and usage was available on a quarterly basis. Because it was necessary to use a monthly data set to estimate short-run cost functions,[7] we interpolated these quarterly data to obtain monthly data.

Traditional linear interpolation procedures fill data gaps by using the unweighted average of the known values surrounding the gap. This procedure is inefficient statistically and results in data that is "smoother" (more linear) than actual data would be. Because missing data are often a problem in applied analysis, a number of statisticians and econometricians have developed interpolation methods that are more statistically efficient and result in interpolated data with more desirable statistical properties.[8] We used an interpolation technique developed by Chow and Lin (1976) to obtain monthly figures from our quarterly data. We chose this technique because it appears to be the most statistically efficient technique available and because it produces interpolated data that are best linear unbiased estimates (BLUE)[9] of the true data. In addition, the Chow–Lin procedure is relatively easy to explain and program.

The Chow–Lin procedure views the interpolation problem as a statistical estimation of the desired time series (e.g., a monthly series without gaps) to be obtained from existing data. Specifically, the Chow–Lin procedure uses two types of available information to estimate the unobserved (e.g., monthly) data: the available (e.g., quarterly) observations on the desired series and the observations on series that are related to the desired series and are available for the desired period (e.g., monthly). The procedure may be viewed as a four-step process. In the first step the researcher must choose a set of related series that are available for the desired time period (e.g., monthly) and that are available without gaps. The series chosen should be as closely related to the desired series as possible but should not be needed in subsequent analyses. In the second step, the researcher converts the related series selected to the same time period as the data to be interpolated (e.g., quarterly) by averaging over the relevant time period. In the third step, the researcher estimates a model that has the variable to be interpolated as the dependent variable and the newly created related series that are for the same time period as the data to be interpolated (e.g., quarterly) as explanatory variables. The model may be estimated by ordinary least squares (if no autocorrelation is present) or by generalized least squares (if autocorrelation is present). In either case the estimation will provide a set of parameter estimates and a set of residuals. In the final step of the procedure, the researcher multiplies the parameter estimates obtained in the third step by the observations for the related series for the desired time period (e.g., monthly) and adds, for quarterly to monthly interpolation, one third of the quarterly residual. The result is a BLUE estimate of the variable of interest for the desired time period.

To obtain estimated monthly observations for the variables on which we had only quarterly observations (staff variables, inmate enrollment in rehabilitative activities, and electric cost and usage) we used the Chow–Lin procedure just outlined and proceeded as follows. We selected eleven[10] series that we felt would be related to the variables to be interpolated and that (1) had monthly observations and (2) would not be used in further analysis. Using stepwise regression, we selected a subset of six of these series that was most closely related to the variables we wished to interpolate.[11] We used the coefficients and residuals obtained in an ordinary least-squares (OLS) regression of each of the variables we wished to interpolate on the six related series to estimate monthly data for these series.

Incorporating the estimated monthly data for staff variables, inmate enrollment in rehabilitative activities, and electric cost and usage data with our other monthly data, we obtained our basic federal data set. Witte *et al.* (1979, app. 7.1) contains a codebook for this data set, a list of the 27 prisons studied, and the time period for which data were available for each institution.

## C.2. The Data Available for the California Prison System

The basic California data set from which we derived all our analysis data sets consists of information on 10 California prisons[12] on a quarterly basis for the July 1968–June 1978 period. Data contained in the California data set were obtained from numerous sources. Institution-level data were available on a quarterly basis for total expenditure and total wages paid (from the Quarterly Budget Report, for the July 1974–June, 1978 period, with annual data available for earlier periods),[13] average daily inmate population and inmates on work furlough (Actual Average Daily Population by Institution), and total inmates assigned to prison industries (Correctional Industries Revolving Fund Inmate Assignment Report by Institution, Program and Enterprise). Institution-level data for most other inmate characteristics (offense, ethnic group, median age, prior record, escape record, life and death sentence, addiction, and grade placement) and for staff ethnic breakdown were available on a semiannual basis.[14] Institution-level data on the total number and types of employees (The Governor's Budget), institutional capacity (Memoranda on Design Capacity), escapes (Escapes from Department of Corrections), and incidents (Incidents in the Institutions) were available on an annual basis only. The median time served by the male felon population was available for the system as a whole on a quarterly basis (Median Time Served by Male *Felons* Released from Prison) and the median time served for the female population was available for the system as a whole on a semiannual basis (Median Time Served in Prison before Release: Women Felons). Finally, we obtained information on electricity costs on an annual basis by geographic area from the California Public Utilities Commission.

Taken together, the preceding represents a highly diverse data set with varying units and time periods of observation. We proceeded to create a quarterly institution data base from this raw data in the following way. First we created six data sets: (1) a quarterly by-institution data set, (2) a semiannual by-institution data set, (3) an annual fiscal year by-institution data set, (4) an annual calendar year by-institution data set, (5) a quarterly systemwide data set, and (6) a semiannual systemwide data set. Next, we expanded the by-institution semiannual and quarterly data sets by adding the data in data sets (5) and (6) to them 10 times, once for each institution. That is, we used the systemwide data on median length of time served as our best estimate of median length of time served at each institution. As there were small gaps in some series, we next filled these gaps by linear interpolation.[15] We were now ready to use Chow and Lin's (1976) interpolation technique to convert all data to a quarterly basis. We used the total system population and enrollment in prison industries as related series.[16] Owing to the great diversity of the data available it was necessary to run 19 different Chow–Lin interpolation procedures to complete creation of our quarterly by-institution California data base. Witte *et al.* (1979, app. 7.2) contains a codebook for this data set and a list of the 10 institutions represented in the data base.

## C.3. Evaluation of the Data Bases

The federal data set is extremely diverse and rich. Large amounts and varieties of data are frequently available for a large number of institutions; these data are of various quality and usefulness. Total cost is broadly defined and includes actual disbursements, increments in accounts payable and nonfunded costs, changes in applied costs and normal depreciation computed according to FBOP guidelines.[17] However, monthly cost data are occasionally subject to a (often large) lump sum accounting adjustment. Such adjustments caused reported total costs actually to be negative for three institutions (Atlanta, Lewisburg, and Danbury) for a total of six months. Conversations with FBOP accounting personnel indicated that quarterly and annual figures were more likely to reflect true costs than were monthly data. Inmate information in the federal data set is derived by aggregation from the large-scale Inmate Information System (IIS) data base. The IIS data base represents a tremendous data collection effort and contains extensive and detailed information on the inmates of the federal prison system. However, our logical checks and conversations with FBOP personnel and other researchers using this data base convinced us that the quality control of this data base is not always strict. Staff data in the federal data set were taken from payroll and other personnel records of the U.S. Department of Justice. These data appear to be of very high quality. Overall, we believe that the federal data set represents a unique and high-quality data base. However, we would caution researchers against using monthly total cost figures without careful checks.

The California data set is much smaller than the federal one but still contains unusually comprehensive data for such a large prison system. In addition, the data span a period of philosophical change and turmoil within the California Department of Correction. Because of this, the data set is extremely valuable as it allows one to study how a prison system adjusts to large internal and external shocks (e.g., murder of guards and indeterminate sentence legislation, respectively). Total costs are not available for the California prison system, and we are forced to use total expenditures as a measure. However, the expenditure data available is of high quality and does not appear to suffer from lump sum accounting adjustments as do the federal cost data. The California data set is weaker than desirable because various data are collected for different levels of aggregation with different frequencies of observation. We used a sophisticated interpolation procedure to try to convert observations for annual and semiannual periods to a quarterly basis. However, the extensive interpolations that we were forced to make means that some relationships that we observe in this created quarterly data set may be a result of the interpolation procedure and not of relationships between the actual series studied. That it was necessary to interpolate annual data on total expenditures for early years (generally 1968–1973) is particularly worrisome. This interpolation of the dependent variable in our analysis may result in a spuriously high ability to explain variation in expenditures. This would occur if total expenditures are related to interpolated explanatory variables not solely owing to causation but owing to the similar interpolation procedure utilized. Overall, we feel that the California data base represents a useful beginning and is capable of producing valuable insights if used carefully.

## Notes to Appendix C

1. The rest of the federal prison population was housed in camps not associated with penitentiaries or correctional institutes (e.g., the camp at Eglin Air Force Base, Florida), Community Treatment Centers, detention centers, medical facilities, or metropolitan correctional centers.

2. This number is an FBOP document number. We shall refer to all FBOP documents by their document numbers.

3. Complete physical capital descriptions were available for Lompoc, Milan, Petersburg, Seagoville, Oxford, Danbury, La Tuna, Sandstone, Texarkana, and Ft. Worth.

4. Obtaining average inmate characteristics for each institution studied for one month required approximately 30 minutes of computer time and cost approximately $80. It was necessary to make 33 such runs for each institution, one for each month in the study period.

5. Note that in all cases the characteristics of those incarcerated for a period less than a month were weighted by the proportion of the month they were at the institution. For example, in calculating the average age of inmates for an institution, the age of an individual who was in an institution for only 15 days would be weighted by 15 divided by the number of days in that month, for example, 15/30 or 1/2, whereas the age of an individual in an institution for a full month would be given a weight of 1.

6. There were approximately 6800 employees in the prisons studied during the November 1975–June 1978 time period.

7. A quarterly data set would have given us only 11 time series observations. These are too few observations to allow meaningful short-run cost functions to be estimated.

8. See Chow and Lin (1971) or Doran (1974) for examples of this work and a survey of previous work.

9. Formally, BLUE estimates are estimates obtained from a linear statistical model that produce the "tightest" (least variance) possible estimates around the true monthly series, without being biased in any systematic way from the true values of the desired monthly series.

10. The related series selected were: (1) accounting days, (2) the percentage of inmates who reside in the South, (3) the average number of months of the longest prior work experience of the inmate population, (4) a variable reflecting the average level of rehabilitative programming needs of the inmate population, (5) the average age at first commitment of the inmate population, (6) the average length of longest prior commitment of the inmate population, (7) the average time remaining to be served by the inmate population if the population were to be confined until the expiration of term, (8) the percentage of the inmate population transferring into the prison in the last 60 days, (9) the percentage of the prison population imprisoned during the last 60 days, (10) criminal career length (the average difference in the inmate population between present age and age at first commitment), and (11) the ratio of the time spent in prison to criminal career length.

11. This subset contained variables (1), (2), (3), (5), (6), and (8) of Note 10.

12. We did not obtain information for the California Medical Facility (Solano County) or California Rehabilitation Center (for civilly committed addicts, San Bernardino County) because we felt that these facilities represented unique production processes unlike the other large-scale prisons studied.

13. Titles reported in parentheses in this section are the names of memoranda and reports internal to the California Department of Corrections.

14. More recent data on staff ethnic breakdown were available on a quarterly basis.

15. Data were missing for 1968 and half of 1969 for most inmate characteristics and inmate participation in prison industries. A quarter or two of some data was missing for other time periods for eight institutions. Number and type of personnel data was missing for the California Correctional Center and Sierra Conservation Center for 1970. Total wages and total expenditures data were missing for the California Correctional Institution for 1975, for Deuel for 1970, and for Folsom for 1977. Six semiannual observations on the staff ethnic breakdown were missing. All of these missing values were estimated by simple linear interpolation. As institutional capacity figures were only reported when they changed, we filled in the series by moving each existing figure forward in time to the next existing figure.

16. Because some institutions did not have prison industries, this variable could not be used as a related series to interpolate data for these institutions. For these institutions, only systemwide population was used as a related series.

17. These guidelines use straight line depreciation and assume a 40-year life for buildings, a 20-year life for major heating and cooling equipment (e.g., furnaces) and a 10-year life for smaller equipment (e.g., food service equipment). FBOP guidelines conform to Government Accounting Office (GAO) conventions.

# References

Akin, J., Guilkey, D., and Sickles, R. (1979). A random coefficient probit model with an application to a study of migration. *Journal of Econometrics* **11**: 233–246.

Alesch, D. J., and Dougharty, L. A. (1971). Economies-of-Scale Analysis in State and Local Government, R-748-CIR. Santa Monica, California: The Rand Corporation.

Allingham, M. G., and Sandmo, A. (1972). Income tax evasion: a theoretical analysis. *Journal of Public Economics* **1**: 323–338.

Amemiya, T. (1973). Regression analysis when the dependent variable is truncated normal. *Econometrica* **41**: 997–1016.

Amemiya, T. (1975). Qualitative response models. *Annals of Economic and Social Measurement* **4**: 363–372.

Amemiya, T. (1979). The estimation of a simultaneous equation Tobit model. *International Economic Review* **20**: 169–182.

Amemiya, T., and Boskin, M. (1974). Regression analysis when the dependent variable is truncated lognormal, with an application to the duration of welfare dependency. *International Economic Review* **15**: 485–496.

American Correctional Association (1979). ACA Directory: Juvenile and Adult Correctional Departments, Institutions, Agencies and Paroling Authorities. College Park, Maryland: American Correctional Association.

Anscombe, F. J. (1961). Estimating a mixed-exponential response law. *Journal of the American Statistical Association* **56**: 493–502.

Arabmazar, A., and Schmidt, P. (1982). An investigation of the robustness of the Tobit estimator to non-normality. *Econometrica* **50**: 1055–1063.

Bachman, J., and Witte, A. D. (1980). The effectiveness of legal sanctions on individuals addicted to alcohol and drugs. In *Qualitative Explorations in Drug Abuse Policy* (Irving Leveson, ed.), pp. 111–127. New York: Spectrum.

Bailey, W. C. (1966). Correctional outcome: an evaluation of 100 reports. *Journal of Criminal Law, Criminology and Police Science* **57**: 153–160.

Barr, A. J., Goodnight, J. H., Sall, J. R., and Helwig, J. T. (1976). *A User's Guide to SAS 76*. Raleigh, North Carolina: Sparks Press.

Bartholomew, D. J. (1963). The sampling distribution of an estimate arising in life testing. *Technometrics* **5**: 361–374.

Becker, G. (1968). Crime and punishment: an economic approach. *Journal of Political Economy* **76**: 169–217.

*Behavior Today* (1975). Giving up the medical model? Behavior Today **10**: 1.

Bishop, Y., Fienberg, S., and Holland, P. (1975). *Discrete Multivariate Analysis*. Cambridge, Massachusetts: MIT Press.

Block, M. K., and Heineke, J. M. (1975). A labor theoretic analysis of the criminal choice. *American Economic Review* **65**: 314–325.

Block, M. K., and Ulen, T. S. (1979). Cost function for correctional institutions. In *The Costs of Crime* (C. M. Gray, ed.), pp. 187–210. Beverly Hills, California: Sage Publications.

Bloom, H. S. (1979). Evaluating human service and correctional programs by modeling the timing of recidivism. *Sociological Methods and Research* **8**: 179–208.

Blumenthal, S., and Marcus, R. (1975). Estimating population size with exponential failure. *Journal of the American Statistical Association* **70**: 913–922.

Blumstein, A., and Larson, R. (1970). *Models of a Total Criminal Justice System*. Washington, D. C.: Institute for Defense Analysis.

Blumstein, A. (1975). A model to aid in planning for the total criminal justice system. In *Quantitative Tools for Criminal Justice Planning* (L. Oberlander, ed.). Washington, D. C.: Law Enforcement Assistance Administration.

Blumstein, A., and Cohen, J. (1978). A theory of the stability of punishment. *Journal of Criminal Law and Criminology* **64**: 198–207.

Blumstein, A., and Larson, R. C. (1972). Analysis of total criminal justice system. In *Analysis of Public Systems* (A. W. Drake, R. L. Keeney, and P. M. Morse, eds.), pp. 317–355. Cambridge, Massachusetts: MIT Press.

Blumstein, A., and Larson, R. (1976). Models of a total criminal justice system. In *The Economics of Crime and Law Enforcement* (L. R. McPheters and W. B. Strong, eds.), pp. 471–508. Springfield, Illinois: Thomas.

Blumstein, A., Cohen, J., and Nagin, D., eds. (1978). *Deterrence and Incapacitation: Estimating the Effects of Criminal Sanctions on Crime Rates*. Washington, D. C.: Nat. Acad. Sci.

Board of Directors, Manpower Demonstration Research Corporation (1980). *Summary and Findings of the National Supported Work Demonstration*. Cambridge, Massachusetts: Ballinger.

Borus, M. E., Hardin, E., and Terry, P. A. (1976). Job-placement services for ex-offenders; Comprehensive Offender Manpower Program (COMP) job-placement efforts. *Journal of Human Resources* **11**: 391–401.

Breusch, T. S., and Pagan, A. R. (1980). The Lagrange multiplier test and its application to model specification in econometrics. *Review of Economic Studies* **47**: 239–253.

Brier, S. S., and Fienberg, S. E. (1980). Recent econometric modeling of crime and punishment: support for the deterrence hypothesis? *Evaluation Review* **4**: 147–191.

Brody, S. R. (1976). *The Effectiveness of Sentencing: A Review of the Literature*. London: Her Majesty's Stationery Office.

Cain, G. G. (1975). Regression and selection models to improve nonexperimental comparisons. In *Evaluation and Experiment*. (C. A. Bennett and A. A. Lumsdaine, eds.), 297–318. New York: Academic Press.

Cain, G. G. (1976). The challenge of segmented labor market theories to orthodox theory: a survey. *Journal of Economic Literature* **14**: 1215–1257.

California Department of Corrections (1976). Implementation of AB 476. Unpublished document, Sacramento, California.

California Department of Corrections (1978). Program Planning Report, 4 vols. Report Prepared at the Request of the Joint Legislative Budget Committee of the California State Legislature, Sacramento, California.

Campbell, D. T., and Stanley, J. C. (1966). *Experimental and Quasi-Experimental Designs for Research.* Chicago, Illinois: Rand-McNally.

Center for Studies in Criminology and Criminal Law (1980). National Survey of Crime Severity: Final National Level Geometric Means and Ratio Scores by Offense Stimuli Items. University of Pennsylvania, Working Paper, Philadelphia, Pennsylvania.

Chaiken, J., *et al.* (1976). *Criminal Justice Models: An Overview.* Washington, D. C.: U. S. Gov. Printing Office.

Chaiken, J., and Chaiken, M. (1981). Varieties of Criminal Behavior. Santa Monica, California: The Rand Corporation.

Chow, G. C. (1960). Tests of equality between sets of coefficients in two linear regressions. *Econometrica* **28**: 591–605.

Chow, G. C., and Lin, A. (1971). Best linear unbiased interpolation, distribution, and extrapolation of time series by related series. *Review of Economics and Statistics* **53**: 372–375.

Chow, G. C., and Lin, A. (1976). Best linear unbiased estimation of missing observations in an economic time series. *Journal of the American Statistical Association* **71**: 719–721.

Christensen, L. R., and Jorgenson, D. W. (1970). U. S. real product and real factor inputs, 1929–67. *Review of Income and Wealth* **16**: 19–50.

Christensen, L. R., Jorgenson, D. W., and Lau, L. J. (1973). Transcendental logarithmic production functions. *Review of Economics and Statistics* **55**: 28–45.

Clarke, S. H., and Koch, G. G. (1976). The effect of income and other factors on whether criminal defendents go to prison. *Law and Society Review* **2**: 57–92.

Clarke, S. H., Freeman, J., and Koch, G. G. (1976). Bail risk: a multivariate analysis. *Journal of Legal Studies* **5**: 341–385.

Clotfelter, C. T. (1981). Tax Rates and Tax Evasion: Analysis of Micro Data. Paper presented at the meetings of the Southern Economic Association, New Orleans, Louisiana.

Cohen, J. (1978). The incapacitative effect of imprisonment: a critical review of the literature. In *Deterrence and Incapacitation: Estimating the Effect of Criminal Sanctions on Crime Rates* (A. Blumstein, J. Cohen, and D. Nagin, eds.), pp. 187–243. Washington, D.C.: Nat. Acad. Sci.

Cohn, Alvin W. (1979). The failure of correctional management: revisited. *Federal Probation* **43**: 10–15.

Commission on Accreditation for Corrections (1977). Manual of Standards for Adult Correctional Institutions. Rockville, Maryland: American Correctional Association.

Comptroller General of the United States (1976). Federal Prison Construction Plans Should be Better Developed and Supported. Washington, D. C.: General Accounting Office.

Cook, P. J. (1973). The Effect of Legitimate Opportunities on the Probability of Parolee Recidivism. Institute of Policy Sciences and Public Affairs, Duke University, Working Paper, Durham, North Carolina.

Cook, P. J. (1975). The correctional carrot: better jobs for parolees. *Policy Analysis* **1**: 11–51.

Cook, P. J. (1977). Punishment and crime: a critique of current findings concerning the preventive effects of punishment. *Law and Contemporary Problems* **41**: 164–204.

Cook, T. C., and Campbell, D. T. (1976). The design and conduct of quasi-experiments and true experiments in field settings. In *Handbook of Industrial and Organization Psychology* (M. D. Dunnette, ed.), pp. 223–326. Chicago, Illinois: Rand-McNally.

Cox, D. R. (1972). Regression models and life tables. *Journal of the Royal Statistical Society Series B* **34**: 187–220.

Cox, D. R. (1975). Partial likelihood. *Biometrika* **62**: 276–296.

Cragg, J. G. (1971). Some statistical models for limited dependent variables with application to the demand for durable goods. *Econometrica* **39**: 829–844.

Dawson, R. O. (1969). *Sentencing: The Decision as to Type, Length and Condition of Sentence.* Boston, Massachusetts: Little, Brown.

Deaton, Angus, and Muellbauer, John (1980). *Economics and Consumer Behavior.* London: Cambridge Univ. Press.

Deemer, W. L., and Votaw, D. F. (1955). Estimation of parameters of truncated or censored exponential distributions. *Annals of Mathematical Statistics* **26**: 498–504.

Denny, M. (1974). The relationship between functional forms for the production system. *Canadian Journal of Economics* **VII**: 21–31.

Diamond, S., and Zeisel, H. (1976). Sentencing councils: a study of sentencing disparity and its reduction. *University of Chicago Law Review* **43**: 109–149.

Diewart, W. E. (1971). An application of the Shephard duality theorem: A generalized Leontiff production function. *Journal of Political Economy* **70**: 481–507.

Doeringer, D. B., and Piore, M. J. (1971). *Internal Labor Markets and Manpower Analysis.* Lexington, Massachusetts: Lexington Books.

Doran, H. E. (1974). Prediction of missing observations in the time series of an economic variable. *Journal of the American Statistical Association* **69**: 546–554.

DuCote, Daniel C. (1977). James vs. Wallace: minimum constitutional standards for living conditions in prisons. *Baylor Law Review* **29**: 180–186.

Efron, B. (1975). The efficiency of logistic regression compared to normal discriminant analysis. *Journal of the American Statistical Association* **70**: 892–898.

Ehrlich, I. (1970). Participation in Illegitimate Activities: An Economic Analysis. Unpublished Ph.D. Dissertation, Department of Economics, Columbia University, New York.

Ehrlich, I. (1973). Participation in illegitimate activities: a theoretical and empirical investigation. *Journal of Political Economy* **81**: 521–565.

Ehrlich, I. (1974). Participation in illegitimate activities: an economic analysis. In *Essays in the Economics of Crime and Punishment* (G. S. Becker and W. M. Landes, eds.), pp. 68–134. New York: Columbia Univ. Press for the National Bureau of Economic Research.

Ehrlich, I. (1975). The deterrent effect of capital punishment: a question of life and death. *American Economic Review* **65**: 397–417.

Einstadter, W. J. (1966). Armed Robbery: A Career Study in Perspective. Unpublished dissertation, Department of Criminology, University of California, Berkeley.

Elliott, D. S., and Ageton, S. S. (1980). Reconciling race and class differences in self-reported and official estimates of delinquency. *American Sociological Review* **45**: 95–110.

Euler, Lawrence R., and Franks, W. A., Jr. (1976). *Report: The Governor's Conference on Employment and the Prevention of Crime.* Madison, Wisconsin: State Manpower Council.

Evans, R., Jr. (1966). The released offender in a changing labor market. *Industrial Relations* **5**: 118–124.

Evans, R., Jr. (1968). The labor market and parole success. *Journal of Human Resources* **3**: 201–212.

Farrington, D. P. (1973). Self reports of delinquent behavior. *Journal of Criminal Law and Criminology* **64**: 99–110.

Fearn, R. M. (1981). *Labor Economics: The Emerging Synthesis.* Cambridge, Massachusetts: Winthrop.

Feldberg, Michael S. (1977). Confronting the conditions of confinement: an expanded role for courts in prison reform. *Harvard Civil Rights–Civil Liberties Law Review* **12**: 367–404.

Feyerherm, W. (1976). The employment history of prison releasees. In *Report: The Governor's Conference on Employment and the Prevention of Crime* (Lawrence R. Euler and William A. Franks, Jr., eds.), pp. 145–160. Madison, Wisconsin: State Manpower Council.

Fleisher, B. M., and Kniesner, T. J. (1980). *Labor Economics: Theory, Evidence and Policy*. Englewood Cliffs, New Jersey: Prentice-Hall.

Fomby, T. B., and Guilkey, D. K. (1978). On choosing the optimal level of significance for the Durbin–Watson test and the Bayesian alternative. *Journal of Econometrics* **8**: 203–213.

Førsund, Finn R., Lovell, C. A. Knox, and Schmidt, Peter (1980). A survey of frontier production functions and of their relationship to efficiency measurement. *Journal of Econometrics* **13**: 5–25.

Foss, M. F. (1963). The utilization of capital equipment: postwar compared with prewar. *Survey of Current Business* **43**: 8–16.

Fuss, Melvyn, McFadden, Daniel, and Mundlak, Yair (1978). A survey of functional forms in the economic analysis of production. In *Production Economics: A Dual Approach to Theory and Applications*, vol. 1 (Melvyn Fuss and Daniel McFadden, eds.), pp. 219–268. Amsterdam: North-Holland Publ.

Glaser, D. (1964). *The Effectiveness of a Prison and Parole System*. Indianapolis, Indiana: Bobbs-Merrill.

Gottfredson, D. M., Wilkins, L. T., and Hoffman, P. B. (1978). *Guidelines for Parole and Sentencing*. Lexington, Massachusetts: Lexington Books.

Greenberg, D. F. (1977). The correctional effects of corrections: a survey of evaluations. In *Corrections and Punishment* (D. F. Greenberg, ed.), pp. 111–148. Beverly Hills, California: Sage Publications.

Greenwood, Peter W. (1981). Selective incapacitation, WD-1334. Santa Monica, California: The Rand Corporation.

Griliches, Z. (1976). Wages of very young men. *Journal of Political Economy* **84**: 569–585.

Grizzle, G., *et al.* (1982). *Basic Issues in Corrections Performance*. Washington, D. C.: U. S. Department of Justice.

Grizzle, G., and Witte, A. D. (1980). Criminal justice evaluation techniques: methods other than random assignment. In *Handbook of Criminal Justice Evaluation* (M. W. Klein and K. S. Teilman, eds.), pp. 259–302. Beverly Hills, California: Sage Publications.

Guze, S. B. (1964). A study of recidivism based upon a follow-up of 217 consecutive criminals. *Journal of Nervous and Mental Disease* **138**: 575–580.

Hall, Robert E. (1973). The Specification of technology with several kinds of output. *Journal of Political Economy* **81**: 878–892.

Halleck, S. L., and Witte, A. D. (1977). Is rehabilitation dead? *Crime and Delinquency* **23**: 372–382.

Hardin, E. (1975). Human capital and the labor market success of new parolees. In *Proceedings of the American Statistical Association, 1975*, pp. 330–335. Washington, D.C.: American Statistical Association.

Harris, C. M., Kaylan, A. R., and Maltz, M. D. (1981). Refinements in the statistics of recidivism measurement. In *Mathematical Frontiers in Criminology* (J. E. Fox, ed.), pp. 61–79. New York: Academic Press.

Hasenkamp, Georg (1976). *Specification and Estimation of Multiple-Output Production Functions*. Berlin: Springer-Verlag.

Hausman, J. A., and Wise, D. A. (1977). Social experimentation, truncated distributions and efficient estimation. *Econometrica* **45**: 919–938.

Hausman, J. A., and Wise, D. A. (1978). A conditional probit model for qualitative choice: discrete decisions recognizing interdependence and heterogeneous preferences. *Econometrica* **46**: 403–426.

Heckman, J. J. (1978). Simple statistical models for discrete panel data developed and applied to test the hypothesis of true state dependence against the alternative of spurious state dependence. *Annales de l'Institut National de la Statistique et des Etudes Economiques* **30–31**: 227–270.

Heckman, J. J. (1979). Sample selection bias as a specification error. *Econometrica* **47**: 153–162.

Heineke, J. M. (1978a). Economic models of criminal behavior: an overview. In *Economic Models of Criminal Behavior* (J. M. Heineke, ed.), pp. 1–33. Amsterdam: North-Holland Publ.

Heineke, J. M. (1978b). Substitution among crimes and the question of deterrence: an indirect utility function approach to the supply of legal and illegal activity. In *Economic Models of Criminal Behavior* (J. M. Heineke, ed.), pp. 153–209. Amsterdam: North-Holland Publ.

Hepburn, J. R. (1978). Race and the decision to arrest: an analysis of warrants issued. *Journal of Research in Crime and Delinquency* **16**: 54–73.

Hey, John D. (1979). *Uncertainty in Microeconomics*. New York: New York Univ. Press.

Hirsch, Werner Z. (1973). *Urban Economic Analysis*. New York: McGraw-Hill.

Hirshleifer, J. (1980). *Price Theory and Applications*. Englewood Cliffs, New Jersey: Prentice-Hall.

Hoffman, P. B., and Stone-Meierhoefer, B. (1979). Post-release arrest experiences of federal prisoners: a six-year follow-up. *Journal of Criminal Justice* **7**: 193–216.

Hood, R., and Sparks, R. (1970). *Key Issues in Criminology*. New York: McGraw-Hill.

Howard, Dick. (1978). Determinate Sentencing in California. Lexington, Massachusetts: The Council on State Government.

Institute of Government (1970). *Punishment Chart for Crimes of General Interest in the Superior Courts of North Carolina*. Chapel Hill, North Carolina: Univ. of North Carolina.

Johnson, Frank M. (1976). Observation: the constitution and the federal district judge. *Texas Law Review* **54**: 903–916.

Johnson, N. L., and Kotz, S. (1970). *Continuous Univariate Distributions—1*. Boston Massachusetts: Houghton.

Johnson, N. L., and Kotz, S. (1970). *Continuous Univariate Distributions—2*. Boston, Massachusetts: Houghton.

Johnston, J. (1960). *Statistical Cost Analysis*. New York: McGraw-Hill.

Kalbfleisch, J. D., and Prentice, R. L. (1980). *The Statistical Analysis of Failure Time Data*. New York: Wiley.

Kendall, M. G., and Stuart, A. (1973). *The Advanced Theory of Statistics*, vol. 2. New York: Hafner.

Kendall, M. G., and Stuart, A. (1976). *The Advanced Theory of Statistics*, vol. 3 (3rd ed.). New York: Hafner.

Kitchener, H., Schmidt, A. K., and Glaser, D. (1977). How persistent is post-prison success? *Federal Probation* **41**: 9–15.

Klein, M. W., and Teilmann, K. S. (1980). *Handbook of Criminal Justice Evaluation*. Beverly Hills, California: Sage Publications.

Kmenta, J. (1971). *Elements of Econometrics* New York: Macmillan.

Knight, F. H. (1921). *Risk, Uncertainty and Profit*. Boston, Massachusetts: Houghton.

Kolm, S. C. (1973). A note on optimum tax evasion. *Journal of Public Economics* **2**: 265–270.

Lachman, Judith (1978). A Theory of Interpersonal Conflict with Applications to Industrial Disputes. School of Law, Yale University, Working Paper, New Haven, Connecticut.

Leftwich, R. H. (1979). *The Price System and Resource Allocation*. Hinsdale, Illinois: Dryden Press.

Lenihan, K. (1977). *Unlocking the Second Gate*. U. S. Department of Labor R & D Monograph 45. Washington, D. C.: U. S. Govt. Printing Office.

Leveson, Irving (1972). Drug addiction: some evidence on prevention and deterrence. *Urban Affairs Quarterly* **8**: 131–160.

Leyval, E., *et al.* (1969). Preliminary Report on the Costs and Effects of the California Criminal Justice System and Recommendations for Legislation to Increase Support of Local Police and Corrections Programs. Sacramento, California: Staff Report prepared for the Assembly Ways and Means Committee.

Lipton, D., Martinson, R., and Wilks, J. (1975). *The Effectiveness of Correctional Treatment: A Survey of Treatment Evaluation Studies*. New York: Praeger.

Locander, W., Sudman, S., and Bradburn, N. (1976). An investigation of interview method, threat and response distortion. *Journal of the American Statistical Association* **71**: 269–275.

Long, Sharon K., and Witte, A. D. (1981). Current economic trends: implications for crime and criminal justice. In *Crime and Criminal Justice in a Declining Economy* (Kevin Wright, ed.), pp. 69–143. Cambridge, Massachusetts: Oelgeschlager, Gunn, and Hain.

Long, S. K., Witte, A. D., and Karr, P. (1983). Family violence: A microeconomic approach. *Social Science Research*, forthcoming.

Lovell, C. A. K. (1973). Homotheticity and the average cost function. *Western Economic Journal* **11**: 507–513.

Maddala, G. S. (1977). *Econometrics*. New York: McGraw-Hill.

Mannering, J. W. (1958). Significant characteristics of recidivists. *Probation and Parole Association Journal* **4**: 211–227.

Maltz, M. D., and McCleary, R. (1977). The mathematics of behavioral change: recidivism and construct validity. *Evaluation Quarterly* **1**: 421–438.

Martin, S. E., Sechrest, L. B., and Redner, R. (1981). *The Rehabilitation of Criminal Offenders: New Directions for Research*. Washington, D. C.: Nat. Acad. Sci.

Martinson, R. (1974). What works?—questions and answers about prison reform. *The Public Interest* **35**: 22–54.

McCall, G. J. (1975). *Observing the Law: Applications of Field Methods to the Study of the Criminal Justice System*. Rockville, Maryland: National Institute of Mental Health.

McFadden, D. (1976). A comment on discriminant analysis versus logit analysis. *Annals of Economic and Social Measurement* **5**: 511–523.

McFadden, D. (1978). Cost, revenue and profit functions. In *Production Economics: A Dual Approach to Theory and Applications*, vol. 1 (Melvyn Fuss and Daniel McFadden, eds.), pp. 3–109. Amsterdam: North-Holland Publ.

McGuire, W. J. (1978). An Economic Model of Criminal Correctional Institutions: Empirical Cost Analysis and Cost Benefit Measures. Unpublished Ph.D. dissertation, University of North Carolina, Chapel Hill, North Carolina.

McKelvey, R. D., and Zavoina, W. (1975). A statistical model for the analysis of ordinal level dependent variables. *Journal of Mathematical Sociology* **4**: 103–120.

Mendenhall, W., and Hader, R. J. (1958). Estimation of parameters of mixed exponentially distributed failure time distributions from censored life data. *Biometrika* **45**: 504–520.

Monahan, J. (1980). *The Clinical Prediction of Violent Behavior*. Washington, D. C.: U. S. Govt. Printing Office.

Monahan, J. (1981). *Predicting Violent Behavior: An Assessment of Clinical Techniques*. Beverly Hills, California: Sage Publications.

Moody, C. E., Jr. (1974). The measurement of capital services by electrical energy. *Oxford Bulletin of Economics and Statistics* **36**: 45–52.

Morris, Norval (1974). *The Future of Imprisonment*. Chicago, Illinois: Univ. of Chicago Press.

Mulvilhill, D. J., and Tumin, M. J. (1969). *Crimes of Violence*, vol. 12. Washington, D. C.: U. S. Govt. Printing Office.

Myers, S. (1982). Labor Market Discrimination and Racial Differences in Participation in Crime. Federal Trade Commission, Working Paper, Washington, D. C.

Myers, S. (1983). Estimating the economic model of crime: employment versus punishment effects. *Quarterly Journal of Economics* **98**: 157–166.

Nagin, D. (1978). General deterrence: a review of the empirical evidence. In *Deterrence and Incapacitation: Estimating the Effects of Criminal Sanctions on Crime Rates* (A. Blumstein, J. Cohen, and D. Nagin, eds.), pp. 95–139. Washington, D. C.: Nat. Acad. Sci.

National Advisory Commission on Criminal Justice Standards and Goals (1973). *Corrections.* Washington, D. C.: U. S. Govt. Printing Office.

Nelson, F., and Olson, L. (1978). Specification and estimation of a simultaneous equation model with limited dependent variables. *International Economic Review* **19**: 695–710.

Nerlove, M., and Press, S. J. (1973). Univariate and Multivariate Log–Linear and Logistic Models, R-1306. Santa Monica, California: The Rand Corporation.

Neter, John, and Wasserman, William (1974). *Applied Linear Statistical Models.* Homewood, Illinois: Richard D. Irwin, Inc.

*The New York Times* (1974). Panel says an informed public could demand prison reform. March 7, p. 18-C.

Nickell, S. J. (1978). *The Investment Decisions of Firms.* London: Cambridge Univ. Press.

Niskanen, W. A. (1971). *Bureaucracy and Representative Government.* Chicago, Illinois: Aldine.

Olsen, R. J. (1978). Note on the uniqueness of the maximum likelihood estimator for the Tobit model. *Econometrica* **46**: 1211–1216.

Orzechowski, W. (1977). Economic models of bureaucracy: survey, extensions, and evidence. In *Budgets and Bureaucrats: The Sources of Government Growth* (T. E. Borcherding, ed.), pp. 229–259. Durham, North Carolina: Duke Univ. Press.

Palmer, J., and Carlson, P. (1976). Problems with the use of regression analysis in prediction studies. *Journal of Research in Crime and Delinquency* **13**: 64–81.

Palmer, Ted (1975). Martinson revisited. *Journal of Research in Crime and Delinquency* **12**: 113–152.

Panel on Sentencing Research (1982). *Research on Sentencing: The Search for Reform.* Washington, D. C.: Nat. Acad. Sci.

Petersilia, J. R. (1977). The Validity of Criminality Data Derived from Personal Interview, P-5890. Santa Monica, California: The Rand Corporation.

Petersilia, J. R. (1980). Criminal career research: a review of recent evidence. In *Crime and Justice: An Annual Review of Research*, vol. 2 (N. Morris and M. Tonry, eds.), pp. 321–379. Chicago, Illinois: Univ. of Chicago Press.

Petersilia, J. R., Greenwood, P. W., and Lavin, M. (1977). Criminal Careers of Habitual Felons, R-2144-DOJ. Santa Monica, California: The Rand Corporation.

Peterson, Mark A., and Braiker, Harriet B. (1980). Doing Crime: A Survey of California Prison Inmates, R-2200-DOJ. Santa Monica, California: The Rand Corporation.

Pownall, G. A. (1969). Employment Problems of Released Offenders. Report to the Manpower Administration, U. S. Department of Labor.

Pratt, J. (1964). Risk aversion in the small and the large. *Econometrica* **32**: 122–136.

Press, S. J., and Wilson, S. (1978). Choosing between logistic regression and discriminant analysis. *Journal of the American Statistical Association* **73**: 699–705.

Prigmore, C. S., and Crow, R. T. (1976). Is the court remaking the american prison system? *Federal Probation* **40**: 3–10.

Pritchard, D. A. (1977). *Stable Predictors of Recidivism.* Washington, D. C.: Amer. Phych. Assoc.

Proschan, F. (1963). Theoretical explanation of observed decreasing failure rate. *Technometrics* **5**: 375–383.

Reiss, A. J., Jr. (1973). Surveys of Self Reported Delicts. Paper prepared for the symposium on Studies of Public Experience, Knowledge, and Opinion of Crime and Justice, Washington, D. C., March 17 and 18, 1972 (revised, 1973).

Rossi, P. H., Berk, R. A., and Lenihan, K. (1980). *Money, Work and Crime*. New York: Academic Press.

Rossi, P. H., Waite, E., Bose, C. E., and Berk, R. E. (1974). The seriousness of crimes: normative structure and individual differences. *American Sociological Review* **39**: 224–237.

Savage, L. J. (1952). *Foundations of Statistics*. New York: Wiley.

Schmidt, P., and Witte, A. D. (1980). Evaluating correctional programs: models of criminal recidivism and an illustration of their use. *Evaluation Review* **4**: 585–600.

Schmidt, P., Sickles, R., and Witte, A. D. (1979). An analysis of time sentenced after release from prison. In *Proceedings of the Summer 1978 Conference of the Criminal Justice Statistics Association*, pp. 77–86. Concord, New Hampshire: Criminal Justice Statistics Association.

Schnur, A. C. (1949). Prison conduct and recidivism. *Journal of Criminal Law and Criminology* **40**: 36–42.

Sechrest, L., White, S., and Brown, E. (1979). *The Rehabilitation of Criminal Offenders: Problems and Prospects*. Washington, D. C.: Nat. Acad. Sci.

Sellin, T., and Wolfgang, M. E. (1964). *The Measurement of Delinquency*. New York: Wiley.

Service, Phillip (1972). The Recidivism of Persons Released From Facilities of the North Carolina Department of Correction During January–July, 1968. Raleigh, North Carolina: North Carolina Department of Correction.

Shaw, L. (1976). Severity of Crime and Length of Sentence. Report to the North Carolina Department of Correction, Raleigh, North Carolina.

Shephard, R. W. (1953). *Cost and Production Functions*. Princeton, New Jersey: Princeton Univ. Press.

Shephard, R. W. (1970). *The Theory of Cost and Production Functions*. Princeton, New Jersey: Princeton Univ. Press.

Sickles, R. C., and Schmidt, P. (1978). Simultaneous equations models with truncated dependent variables: a simultaneous Tobit model. *Journal of Economics and Business* **31**: 11–21.

Sickles, R. C., Schmidt, P., and Witte, A. D. (1979). An application of the simultaneous Tobit model: a study of the determinants of criminal recidivism. *Journal of Economics and Business* **32**: 166–171.

Silberston, Aubrey (1972). Economies of scale in theory and practice. *Economic Journal* **82**: 369–391.

Simon, C., and Witte, A. D. (1982). *Beating the System: The Underground Economy*. Boston, Massachusetts: Auburn House.

Singh, B. (1973). Making honesty the best policy. *Journal of Public Economics* **2**: 257–263.

Sjoquist, D. L. (1973). Property crime and economic behavior: some empirical results. *American Economic Review* **63**: 439–446.

Skogan, W. G. (1974). The validity of official crime statistics: an empirical investigation. *Social Science Quarterly* **55**: 25–39.

Solomon, H. (1976). Parole outcome: a multidimensional contingency table analysis. *Journal of Research in Crime and Delinquency* **13**: 107–126.

Stollmack, S., and Harris, C. M. (1974). Failure rate analysis applied to recidivism data. *Operations Research* **23**: 1192–1205.

Sutton, L. P. (1978). *Federal Sentencing Patterns: A Study of Geographical Variations*. Washington, D. C.: U. S. Govt. Printing Office.

Tabasz, Thomas F. (1975). *Toward an Economics of Prisons.* Lexington, Massachusetts: Lexington Books.

Theil, H. (1960). *Economic Forecasts and Policy.* Amsterdam: North-Holland Publ.

Theil, H. (1969). A multinomial extension of the linear logit model. *International Economic Review* **10**: 251–259.

Theil, H. (1970). On the estimation of relationships involving qualitative variables. *American Journal of Sociology* **76**: 103–154.

Tittle, C. R., and Rowe, A. R. (1974). Certainty of arrest and crime rates: a further test of the deterrence hypothesis. *Social Forces* **52**: 455–462.

U. S. Department of Justice (1980). *Prisoners in State and Federal Institutions on December 31, 1978.* Washington, D. C.: U. S. Government Printing Office.

U. S. Department of Justice, Federal Bureau of Prisons (1975). *Statistical Report, Fiscal Year 1974.* Washington, D. C.: U. S. Government Printing Office.

U. S. Department of Justice, Federal Prison System (1977). *Federal Prison System: Facilities 1977.* Marion, Illinois: UNICOR.

U. S. Department of Justice, Federal Prison System (1978). *Federal Prison System, 1978.* Marion, Illinois: UNICOR.

U. S. Department of Labor, Bureau of Economic Security (1965). *Dictionary of Occupational Titles*, 3rd ed. Washington, D. C.: U. S. Govt. Printing Office.

President's Commission on Law Enforcement and the Administration of Justice. (1967). *Task Force Report: Corrections.* Washington, D. C.: U. S. Govt. Printing Office.

Van Alstyne, D. J., and Gottfredson, M. R. (1978). A multidimensional contingency table analysis of parole outcome. *Journal of Research in Crime and Delinquency* **15**: 172–193.

Varian, H. R. (1978). *Microeconomic Analysis.* New York: W. W. Norton.

Varian, H. R. (1982). The nonparametric approach to demand analysis. *Econometrica* **50**: 945–974.

Vernez, George (1976). Delivery of Urban Public Services: Production, Cost and Demand Functions, and Determinants of Public Expenditures for Fire, Police and Sanitation Services, P-5659. Santa Monica, California: The Rand Corporation.

Waldo, G., and Griswold, D. (1979). Issues in the measurement of recidivism. In *The Rehabilitation of Criminal Offenders: Problems and Prospects* (L. Seechrest, S. White, and E. Brown, eds.), pp. 225–250. Washington, D. C.: Nat. Acad. Sci.

Waller, Irvin (1974). *Men Released from Prison.* Toronto: Univ. of Toronto Press.

Westat Inc. (1980). Self Reported Tax Compliance: A Pilot Survey Report. Unpublished report to the Internal Revenue Service on Contract No. TIR-78-50.

Wilkins, L. (1970). The borstal prediction study. In *The Sociology of Punishment and Correction*, 2nd ed. (N. Johnston, L. Savitz, and M. Wolfgang, eds.), pp. 777–780. New York: Wiley.

Williams, K. (1979). The Scope and Prediction of Recidivism. Washington, D. C.: Institute for Law and Social Research.

Wolfgang, M. E., Figlio, R. M., and Sellin, Thorsten (1972). *Delinquency in a Birth Cohort.* Chicago, Illinois: Univ. of Chicago Press.

Witte, A. D. (1975). *Work Release in North Carolina: An Evaluation of Its Post Release Effects.* Chapel Hill, North Carolina: Institute for Research in Social Science.

Witte, A. D. (1976). Earnings and jobs of ex-offenders: a case study. *Monthly Labor Review* **99**: 31–39.

Witte, A. D. (1980a). Economics of Public Service Delivery Systems. Paper presented at the Special National Workshop on Research Methodology and Criminal Justice Program Evaluation, Baltimore, Maryland.

Witte, A. D. (1980b). Estimating the economic model of crime with individual data. *Quarterly Journal of Economics* **94**: 57–84.

Witte, A. D. (1980c). Promising Statistical Methods for Estimating Models of Post Release Criminal Activity. The Osprey Company, Working Paper 80-1, Raleigh, North Carolina.

Witte, A. D. (1980d). Theoretical Models for Some Measures of Post-Release Criminal Activity. Prepared under grant 78-NI-AX-0130 from the National Institute of Law Enforcement and Criminal Justice. Washington, D. C.: U. S. Department of Justice.

Witte, A. D., and Reid, P. H. (1980). An exploration of the determinants of labor market performance for prison releasees. *Journal of Urban Economics* **8**: 313–326.

Witte, A. D., and Schmidt, P. (1977). An analysis of recidivism, using the truncated lognormal distribution. *Applied Statistics* **26**: 302–311.

Witte, A. D., and Schmidt, P. (1979). An analysis of the type of criminal activity using the logit model. *Journal of Research in Crime and Delinquency* **16**: 164–179.

Witte, A. D., *et al.* (1979). Empirical Estimation of Correctional Cost Functions. Report to the National Institute of Law Enforcement and Criminal Justice on LEAA Grant No. 78-NI-AX-0059, Washington, D. C.

# Index

**QUANTITATIVE STUDIES IN SOCIAL RELATIONS**
*(Continued from page ii)*

*Peter H. Rossi, James D. Wright, and Eleanor Weber-Burdin,* NATURAL HAZARDS AND PUBLIC CHOICE: *The Indifferent State and Local Politics of Hazard Mitigation*

*Neil Fligstein,* GOING NORTH: *Migration of Blacks and Whites from the South, 1900–1950*

*Howard Schuman and Stanley Presser,* QUESTIONS AND ANSWERS IN ATTITUDE SURVEYS: *Experiments on Question Form, Wording, and Context*

*Michael E. Sobel,* LIFESTYLE AND SOCIAL STRUCTURE: *Concepts, Definitions, Analyses*

*William Spangar Peirce,* BUREAUCRATIC FAILURE AND PUBLIC EXPENDITURE

*Bruce Jacobs,* THE POLITICAL ECONOMY OF ORGANIZATIONAL CHANGE: *Urban Institutional Response to the War on Poverty*

*Ronald C. Kessler and David F. Greenberg,* LINEAR PANEL ANALYSIS: *Models of Quantitative Change*

*Ivar Berg (Ed.),* SOCIOLOGICAL PERSPECTIVES ON LABOR MARKETS

*James Alan Fox (Ed.),* METHODS IN QUANTITATIVE CRIMINOLOGY

*James Alan Fox (Ed.),* MODELS IN QUANTITATIVE CRIMINOLOGY

*Philip K. Robins, Robert G. Spiegelman, Samuel Weiner, and Joseph G. Bell (Eds.),* A GUARANTEED ANNUAL INCOME: *Evidence from a Social Experiment*

*Zev Klein and Yohanan Eshel,* INTEGRATING JERUSALEM SCHOOLS

*Juan E. Mezzich and Herbert Solomon,* TAXONOMY AND BEHAVIORAL SCIENCE

*Walter Williams,* GOVERNMENT BY AGENCY: *Lessons from the Social Program Grants-in-Aid Experience*

*Peter H. Rossi, Richard A. Berk, and Kenneth J. Lenihan,* MONEY, WORK, AND CRIME: *Experimental Evidence*

*Robert M. Groves and Robert L. Kahn,* SURVEYS BY TELEPHONE: *A National Comparison with Personal Interviews*

*N. Krishnan Namboodiri (Ed.),* SURVEY SAMPLING AND MEASUREMENT

*Beverly Duncan and Otis Dudley Duncan,* SEX TYPING AND SOCIAL ROLES: *A Research Report*

*Donald J. Treiman,* OCCUPATIONAL PRESTIGE IN COMPARATIVE PERSPECTIVE

*Samuel Leinhardt (Ed.),* SOCIAL NETWORKS: *A Developing Paradigm*

*Richard A. Berk, Harold Brackman, and Selma Lesser,* A MEASURE OF JUSTICE: *An Empirical Study of Changes in the California Penal Code, 1955–1971*

QUANTITATIVE STUDIES IN SOCIAL RELATIONS

*Richard F. Curtis and Elton F. Jackson,* **INEQUALITY IN AMERICAN COMMUNITIES**

*Eric Hanushek and John Jackson,* **STATISTICAL METHODS FOR SOCIAL SCIENTISTS**

*Edward O. Laumann and Franz U. Pappi,* **NETWORKS OF COLLECTIVE ACTION: *A Perspective on Community Influence Systems***

*Walter Williams and Richard F. Elmore,* **SOCIAL PROGRAM IMPLEMENTATION**

*Roland J. Liebert,* **DISINTEGRATION AND POLITICAL ACTION: *The Changing Functions of City Governments in America***

*James D. Wright,* **THE DISSENT OF THE GOVERNED: *Alienation and Democracy in America***

*Seymour Sudman,* **APPLIED SAMPLING**

*Michael D. Ornstein,* **ENTRY INTO THE AMERICAN LABOR FORCE**

*Carl A. Bennett and Arthur A. Lumsdaine (Eds.),* **EVALUATION AND EXPERIMENT: *Some Critical Issues in Assessing Social Programs***

*H. M. Blalock, A. Aganbegian, F. M. Borodkin, Raymond Boudon, and Vittorio Capecchi (Eds.),* **QUANTITATIVE SOCIOLOGY: *International Perspectives on Mathematical and Statistical Modeling***

*N. J. Demerath, III, Otto Larsen, and Karl F. Schuessler (Eds.),* **SOCIAL POLICY AND SOCIOLOGY**

*Henry W. Riecken and Robert F. Boruch (Eds.),* **SOCIAL EXPERIMENTATION: *A Method for Planning and Evaluating Social Intervention***

*Arthur S. Goldberger and Otis Dudley Duncan (Eds.),* **STRUCTURAL EQUATION MODELS IN THE SOCIAL SCIENCES**

*Robert B. Tapp,* **RELIGION AMONG THE UNITARIAN UNIVERSALISTS: *Converts in the Stepfathers' House***

*Kent S. Miller and Ralph Mason Dreger (Eds.),* **COMPARATIVE STUDIES OF BLACKS AND WHITES IN THE UNITED STATES**

*Douglas T. Hall and Benjamin Schneider,* **ORGANIZATIONAL CLIMATES AND CAREERS: *The Work Lives of Priests***

*Robert L. Crain and Carol S. Weisman,* **DISCRIMINATION, PERSONALITY, AND ACHIEVEMENT: *A Survey of Northern Blacks***

*Roger N. Shepard, A. Kimball Romney, and Sara Beth Nerlove (Eds.),* **MULTIDIMENSIONAL SCALING: *Theory and Applications in the Behavioral Sciences,*** Volume I – Theory; Volume II – Applications

*Peter H. Rossi and Walter Williams (Eds.),* **EVALUATING SOCIAL PROGRAMS: *Theory, Practice, and Politics***